T0211747

Lecture Notes in Artificial Intelligence   11946

Subseries of Lecture Notes in Computer Science

Series Editors

Randy Goebel
University of Alberta, Edmonton, Canada
Yuzuru Tanaka
Hokkaido University, Sapporo, Japan
Wolfgang Wahlster
DFKI and Saarland University, Saarbrücken, Germany

Founding Editor

Jörg Siekmann
DFKI and Saarland University, Saarbrücken, Germany

More information about this series at http://www.springer.com/series/1244

Mario Alviano · Gianluigi Greco ·
Francesco Scarcello (Eds.)

AI*IA 2019 –
Advances in
Artificial Intelligence

XVIIIth International Conference
of the Italian Association for Artificial Intelligence
Rende, Italy, November 19–22, 2019
Proceedings

 Springer

Editors
Mario Alviano (iD)
University of Calabria
Rende, Italy

Gianluigi Greco (iD)
University of Calabria
Rende, Italy

Francesco Scarcello (iD)
University of Calabria
Rende, Italy

ISSN 0302-9743   ISSN 1611-3349 (electronic)
Lecture Notes in Artificial Intelligence
ISBN 978-3-030-35165-6   ISBN 978-3-030-35166-3 (eBook)
https://doi.org/10.1007/978-3-030-35166-3

LNCS Sublibrary: SL7 – Artificial Intelligence

This Springer imprint is published by the registered company Springer Nature Switzerland AG
The registered company address is: Gewerbestrasse 11, 6330 Cham, Switzerland

Preface

This volume contains the papers presented at the main track of AI*IA 2019, the 18th International Conference of the Italian Association for Artificial Intelligence held during November 19–22, 2019, in Rende, Italy. The conference is organized by the Italian Association for Artificial Intelligence (AI*IA – Associazione Italiana per l'Intelligenza Artificiale), which is a non-profit scientific society founded in 1988 devoted to the promotion of Artificial Intelligence. The association aims to increase the public awareness of AI, encourage the teaching of it, and promote research in the field.

The main track of the conference received 86 submissions, and 67 of them were selected for the technical review process. Each selected submission was reviewed by at least three Program Committee members. The committee decided to accept 41 papers for presentation at the conference and publication in this volume. The program also included four invited talks by Giuseppe De Giacomo, Sridhar Mahadevan, Michela Milano, and Philipp Slusallek. Moreover, as in previous editions of the conference, the program was enriched by several workshops on specific fields of AI. Finally, a novelty for this edition of the conference was the presentation of discussion papers about recently published research.

We acknowledge EasyChair (https://easychair.org/) for providing their conference management system that significantly simplified the whole process from receiving the submissions to producing the proceedings. Finally, we thank all the authors who contributed to the workshops, the Program Committee members and the additional reviewers for their effort to produce timely and wise reviews.

October 2019

Mario Alviano
Gianluigi Greco
Francesco Scarcello

Organization

Conference Chair

Nicola Leone — University of Calabria, Italy

Program Chairs

Mario Alviano — University of Calabria, Italy
Gianluigi Greco — University of Calabria, Italy
Francesco Scarcello — University of Calabria, Italy

Organization Chairs

Francesco Ricca — University of Calabria, Italy
Chiara Ghidini — FBK Trento, Italy

Publicity Chair

Luca Pulina — University of Sassari, Italy

Program Committee

Fabrizio Angiulli — University of Calabria, Italy
Davide Bacciu — University of Pisa, Italy
Farshad Badie — Aalborg University, Denmark
Matteo Baldoni — University of Turin, Italy
Stefania Bandini — CSAI - Complex Systems and Artificial Intelligence Research Center, Italy
Roberto Basili — University of Roma Tor Vergata, Italy
Nicola Basilico — University of Milan, Italy
Federico Bergenti — University of Parma, Italy
Tarek Richard Besold — Alpha Health AI Lab, Telefonica Innovation Alpha, Germany
Stefano Bistarelli — University of Perugia, Italy
Andrea Burattin — Technical University of Denmark, Denmark
Elena Cabrio — Université Côte d'Azur, CNRS, Inria, I3S, France
Stefano Cagnoni — University of Parma, Italy
Marco Calautti — University of Calabria, Italy
Diego Calvanese — Free University of Bozen-Bolzano, Italy
Luigia Carlucci Aiello — Sapienza University of Rome, Italy
Amedeo Cesta — CNR - National Research Council of Italy, Italy
Federico Chesani — University of Bologna, Italy

Francesco Corcoglioniti	Fondazione Bruno Kessler, Italy
Gabriella Cortellessa	CNR-ISTC, Italy
Stefania Costantini	University of l'Aquila, Italy
Dario Della Monica	University of Udine, Italy
Claudio Di Ciccio	Vienna University of Economics and Business, Austria
Tommaso Di Noia	Polytechnic University of Bari, Italy
Carmine Dodaro	University of Calabria, Italy
Michele Donini	Amazon, USA
Agostino Dovier	University of Udine, Italy
Aldo Franco Dragoni	Polytechnic University of Marche, Italy
Stefano Ferilli	University of Bari, Italy
Johannes Fichte	TU Dresden, Germany
Alberto Finzi	University of Naples Federico II, Italy
Giancarlo Fortino	University of Calabria, Italy
Salvatore Gaglio	University of Palermo, Italy
Marco Gavanelli	University of Ferrara, Italy
Chiara Ghidini	Fondazione Bruno Kessler, Italy
Massimiliano Giacomin	University of Brescia, Italy
Laura Giordano	Università del Piemonte Orientale, Italy
Giuseppe Jurman	Fondazione Bruno Kessler, Italy
Evelina Lamma	University of Ferrara, Italy
Domenico Lembo	Sapienza University of Rome, Italy
Antonio Lieto	University of Turin, Italy
Marco Lippi	University of Modena and Reggio Emilia, Italy
Francesca Alessandra Lisi	University of Bari, Italy
Fabrizio Maria Maggi	Institute of Computer Science - University of Tartu, Estonia
Bernardo Magnini	FBK-irst, Italy
Marco Manna	University of Calabria, Italy
Marco Maratea	University of Genoa, Italy
Simone Marinai	University of Florence, Italy
Andrea Marrella	Sapienza University of Rome, Italy
Viviana Mascardi	University of Genoa, Italy
Fulvio Mastrogiovanni	University of Genoa, Italy
Alessandro Mazzei	University of Turin, Italy
Stefano Melacci	University of Siena, Italy
Paola Mello	University of Bologna, Italy
Alessio Micheli	University of Pisa, Italy
Alfredo Milani	University of Perugia, Italy
Stefania Montani	University of Piemonte Orientale, Italy
Angelo Oddi	ISTC-CNR, Italy
Matteo Palmonari	University of Milano-Bicocca, Italy
Andrea Passerini	University of Trento, Italy
Viviana Patti	University of Turin, Italy
Ruggero G. Pensa	University of Turin, Italy
Roberto Pirrone	University of Palermo, Italy

Piero Poccianti	Consorzio Operativo Gruppo MPS, Italy
Daniele Porello	Free University of Bolzano-Bozen, Italy
Gian Luca Pozzato	University of Turin, Italy
Fabrizio Riguzzi	University of Ferrara, Italy
Andrea Roli	University of Bologna, Italy
Riccardo Rosati	Sapienza University of Rome, Italy
Silvia Rossi	University of Naples Federico II, Italy
Salvatore Ruggieri	University of Pisa, Italy
Emanuel Sallinger	University of Oxford, UK
Fabio Sartori	University of Milan-Bicocca, Italy
Marco Schaerf	Sapienza University Rome, Italy
Giovanni Semeraro	University of Bari, Italy
Luciano Serafini	Fondazione Bruno Kessler, Italy
Domenico Talia	University of Calabria, Italy
Stefano Teso	Katholieke Universiteit Leuven, Belgium
Mauro Vallati	University of Huddersfield, UK
Eloisa Vargiu	Eurecat Technology Center - eHealth Unit, Spain
Marco Villani	University of Modena and Reggio Emilia, Italy
Giuseppe Vizzari	University of Milano-Bicocca, Italy
Antonius Weinzierl	Vienna University of Technology, Austria

Additional Reviewers

Agramunt, Sebastia
Augello, Agnese
Bellodi, Elena
Bertagnon, Alessandro
Bianchi, Federico
Biondi, Giulio
Cerrato, Mattia
Crecchi, Francesco
Dal Palù, Alessandro
De Benedictis, Riccardo
De Paola, Alessandra
Ercolano, Giovanni
Fracasso, Francesca
La Rosa, Massimo

Lieto, Antonio
Malek, Salim
Narducci, Fedelucio
Philipp, Tobias
Polato, Mirko
Polignano, Marco
Rizzi, Williams
Romeo, Luca
Santini, Francesco
Schidler, André
Taticchi, Carlo
Tiezzi, Francesco
Vahdati, Sahar

Contents

Machine Learning for AI

AI and Humans

Knowledge Representation for AI

Tight Integration of Rule-Based Tools in Game Development

Denise Angilica, Giovambattista Ianni, and Francesco Pacenza[✉]

Department of Mathematics and Computer Science,
University of Calabria, Rende, Italy
{angilica,ianni,pacenza}@mat.unical.it
https://www.mat.unical.it

Abstract. In the wider perspective of narrowing down some of the gaps that prevent the adoption of declarative logic programming within highly dynamically changing environments, we focus in this paper on the context of integrating reasoning modules in real-time videogames. Integrating rule-based AI within the commercial game development life-cycle poses a number of unsolved challenges, each with non-obvious solution. For instance, it is necessary to cope with strict time performance requirements; the duality between procedural code and declarative specifications prevents easy integration; the concurrent execution of reasoning tasks and game updates requires proper information passing strategies between the two involved sides. In this work we illustrate our recent progress on how to embed rule-based reasoning modules into the well-known Unity game development engine. To this end, we report about *ThinkEngine*, a framework in which a tight integration of declarative formalisms within the typical game development workflow is made possible. We prove the viability of our approach by developing a proof-of-concept Unity game that makes use of ASP-based AI modules.

Keywords: *Answer Set Programming* · *Artificial Intelligence* · Game Programming · Knowledge Representation and Reasoning · Logic Programs · Rule-based Systems · Unity

1 Introduction

When comparing declarative, rule-based, formalisms with imperative languages, one can notice how it can be much easier to solve a problem using the first approach rather than the second one in a variety of settings. On the one hand, rule-based knowledge representation techniques feature solid theoretical bases, they do not need algorithm encoding and they are based on easily modifiable and maintainable knowledge bases; on the other hand, imperative languages enjoy a better efficiency, a much wider user base, easier interoperability and better handling of arbitrary data structures.

Combining these two radically different paradigms, so to achieve the benefits of both worlds, is therefore desirable. Consider for instance the context of

© Springer Nature Switzerland AG 2019
M. Alviano et al. (Eds.): AI*IA 2019, LNAI 11946, pp. 3–17, 2019.
https://doi.org/10.1007/978-3-030-35166-3_1

videogames, one of the real world applications based on imperative languages with strict real-time requirements. In general, AI techniques have (or could have) a role in numerous task applications in the game industry, ranging from programming the behavior of non-player characters to game level and content generation. Especially when considering real-time videogames, this particular context is really challenging for researchers since it means to work within an highly reactive environment, requiring really fast responses from a KR system.

Beside performance problems, a second fundamental issue concerns the technical integration of an external KR module in an Object Oriented environment, and specifically, a game development engine. It is important to clearly distinguish run-time settings from design-time settings. At run-time, a main module, that we will call the *procedural side*, takes care of updating the game world. Reasoning modules that control artificial players or other aspects of the game, will play the role of the *reasoning side*. Screen updates cannot be interrupted: thus computationally demanding reasoning tasks must be executed within multiple concurrent execution flows.

To make an embedded reasoning module aware of the state of the videogame world and to make the main update module able of applying decisions provided from the reasoning module, it is necessary to devise a proper information passing strategy. Devising such a strategy is not so trivial, mainly because of synchronization issues (the world can change while a reasoner is running), and because of the different data types and representations used respectively on the reasoning side and on the procedural side. This latter problem requires appropriate data reflection techniques, allowing to examine, introspect, and modify data structures and behavior of the procedural side at run-time, and to map logical propositions with object oriented data structures. It is thus clear that, the usage of KR systems along with imperative languages, can not be seen as a mere call to an external tool, rather as a tight integration of reasoning capabilities inside the main environment.

In this work we present our developments in the integration of AI declarative modules within applications developed in the known Unity game development engine; in particular we report about the *ThinkEngine* module that we developed, which extends our first prototypical system presented in [3] in several ways:

- we obtained a tight sharing of data structures between the procedural side and the declarative side; this has been obtained by introducing reflection techniques which work properly both at design-time and at run-time. Game designers are relieved from the burden of manually mapping data structures to and from the two worlds;
- an appropriate asynchronous execution model has been introduced in order to handle time-consuming reasoning tasks with no interferences with the game main thread. This required to devise a proper, concurrent, information passing strategy between reasoning threads and the canonical game thread;
- we introduced the possibility of attaching a reasoning task to a trigger condition or at scheduled times.

In the remainder of this paper, we first illustrate the Unity engine and the requirements that must be met when integrating rule-based reasoning techniques in the context of such a game development engine. We then describe the *ThinkEngine* module, which has been developed in the form of a Unity reusable asset, and we showcase a Unity-based game where the player is controlled by rule-based reasoning modules programmed in ASP.

2 Integrating Declarative Formalisms into Unity

Unity [4] is a cross-platform game engine primarily used to develop videogames or simulations for more than 25 different platforms like mobile, computers and consoles. It supports 2D and 3D graphics, has many visual development aids, and allows scripting the game logic using the C# language.

Rapid development speed, a very active community, cross-platform integration and the wide availability of *assets* such as 3D models, ready to use scripts, shaders and other extensions, make Unity a user-friendly game engine easy to learn and to use also for beginners; indeed, Unity is currently the leader of the global game development engine market, holding the 45% share, nearly three times the size of its nearest competitor.

Although the Unity community offers a wide range of re-usable assets, only few of them are aimed to provide *Artificial Intelligence* capabilities[1], and currently none of them enables developers to make use of a rule-based reasoning module.

As it can be seen from Fig. 1, the main run-time execution workflow for a Unity videogame is mostly single-threaded based. Game designers can customize the game behavior by implementing specific user callback functions, which are executed within the main thread. For instance, the game designer can provide her/his own code for the `FixedUpdate` block, or provide her/his own coroutine. *Coroutines* constitute a way for implementing asynchronous cooperative multitasking within a single thread.

The run-time game world consists of a collection of game objects (GOs in the following), which are subject to continuous updates depending on user input, on the physics simulation of the game world, and on the game logic enforced by the game designer. A game object consists of a recursive hierarchy of basic properties, such as numeric, string and boolean fields, and complex properties, such as matrices, collections, nested objects, etc.

At design-time, it is possible to work on game objects using the above property-based philosophy, while the game logic can be edited by attaching scripted code to specific game events.

3 The *ThinkEngine* Framework Architecture

The Unity execution model discourages multithreaded programming both for efficiency and ease of development reasons. Auxiliary threads are allowed in

---

[1] https://assetstore.unity.com/categories/tools/ai.

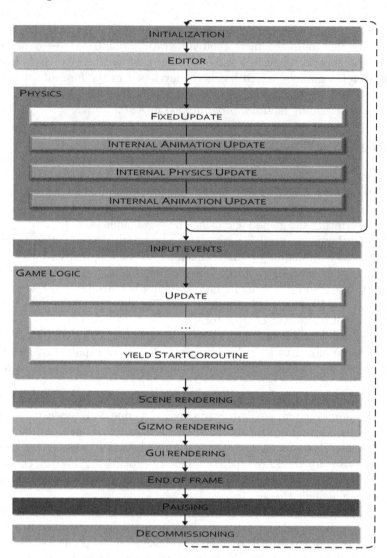

Fig. 1. Unity workflow

Unity; however, within these latter most of the Unity API and game object data structures are purposely made not accessible in that they are not thread-safe. On the other hand, reasoning tasks are time-consuming and cannot be easily accommodated in a single-thread execution flow, without slowing down the game workflow. We thus delegated reasoning tasks to auxiliary threads and introduced an information passing layer allowing the reasoning side to access and act on a representation of the game world. This representation is independent from the

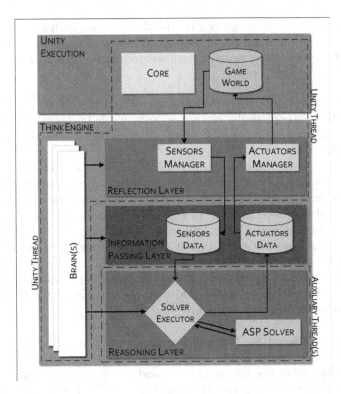

Fig. 2. General run-time architecture of the *ThinkEngine* framework

Unity API and can be accessed separately. The whole run-time *ThinkEngine* architecture is shown in Fig. 2.

In particular the *ThinkEngine* consists of:

1. A *reasoning layer*, in which the game world is accessible and encoded in terms of logical assertions. An answer set solver [5] can elaborate the current state of the game and produces decisions which are encoded in form of *answer sets*.
2. An *information passing layer* which allows to mediate between the reasoning layer and the actual game logic. In this layer, *sensors* store data originated from the upper layers. Sensors correspond to parts of the game world data structures which are visible from the reasoning layer. On the other hand, *actuators* collect decisions taken by the reasoning layer and are used to modify the game state.
3. A *reflection layer*, in which a *Sensors Manager* and an *Actuators Manager* keep the mapping between the game world data structures and the lower layers. On the one hand the *Sensors Manager* reads selected game world data which, this way, is made accessible from the reasoning layer. On the other hand the *Actuators Manager* updates selected parts of the game world, based on input coming from the reasoning layer.

4. One or more *brains* that can control the three layers. Each brain can access his own view of the world (i.e. a selected collection of sensors and actuators), and can be used for programming a separate reasoning activity, like a separate artificial player logic, etc.

A brain controls both the *Sensors Manager* and the *Solver Executor*. The former is activated periodically or after a configurable trigger condition is met. The *Sensors Manager* is responsible of updating all the sensors data mapped to the current brain.

The brain at hand can concurrently wake the *Solver Executor* up. This can happen either when a sensors update is completed or on a configurable trigger condition. When a *Solver Executor* is started, it will generate a representation W of the world expressed in terms of logical assertions (set of input facts) and it will invoke the ASP solver. The ASP solver is fed in input with W and with a logical knowledge base *KB* encoding the AI of the current brain. As soon as the solver provides *decisions* encoded in form of an answer set, the *Solver Executor* populates the actuators associated with the corresponding brain. The *Actuators Manager* monitors actuators values and updates accordingly the properties of the GO associated with each actuator.

Design-Time Configuration. When configuring a brain at design-time it is possible to explore the game objects used in the game and to visually select which sensors are exposed to the reasoning layer, and which actuators will be used to apply decisions derived from the AI to the game world. These bindings will be then used by brains at run-time.

Data Structures Reflection. We defined a proper mapping strategy between the game world data and ASP logic assertions. We introduced a mapping discipline for basic data types, such as numbers, strings and boolean values. As for complex data types we focused on matrices, since almost every game has a map represented as a matrix[2]. For each game data property p it can be chosen a particular aggregation filter function. For instance, when p is of numeric type, one can choose between *maximum, minimum, average, oldest or newest value.*

In general, if p is a property belonging to the game object o, the filtered value of p is translated to a logic assertion in the form:

```
sensor.name(gO.Name(property^i.name(nested_property^{i1}.name(
        ...(basic_type_property^i.name(VALUE))...)))).
```

where

- `sensor.name` is the name of the sensor;
- `gO.name` is the name of the GO o associated to the sensor;
- `property^i.name` is the name of the i-th property in the first layer of the properties hierarchy of o;

---

[2] For space reasons we will not describe how matrices are translated.

- nested_property^{ij}.name is the name of the j-th property of the object referred by the i-th property;
- basic_type_property^i.name is the textual name of p, i.e. the i-th *basic type* property selected in the properties hierarchy of o;
- the VALUE is the current value of the filter associated to p.

4 Rule-Based Reasoning Modules into Unity at Work

In order to give an idea of how AI declarative modules can be integrated within applications developed in Unity via the *ThinkEngine*, we developed a showcase application. We started from a public available open-source project[3], inspired from the original Tetris game, and we modified this project to obtain an automated player whose artificial intelligence is managed by an ASP program. Note that we are not proposing a state-of-the-art Tetris player, rather a demonstration of how an AI can be easily developed by means of logical rules and then deployed in Unity.

In the following we briefly describe how our framework has been set up and configured in order to cooperate with the Unity game scene. First, we will show how we configured the *sensors and actuators modules*, then how the *brain component* were set up. Finally we will describe our ASP *encoding*.

4.1 Sensors and Actuators Configuration

Developers can access to a list of the GOs used in the game scene via a custom Unity window editor[4] as in Fig. 3. It is possible to browse objects and select which properties are mapped on the reasoning side. We will use next some of the typical terminology used to describe our infrastructure and the Tetris game, as recalled here:

Arena: as shown in Fig. 3, the arena is a GO that contains all the properties relative to the playable game scene (i.e. a matrix of tiles, the properties *maxTileX*, *maxTileY* etc.);

_tiles: a matrix of GOs of type ArenaTile. This matrix can be expanded by the user in order to configure some extra properties;

Tetromino: a geometric shape composed of four squares;

currentTetromino: in the Tetris game it represents the tetromino that is currently dropping in the Arena;

Spawner: a GO that manages the generation of a new Tetromino when the previously created one can not drop further down in the Arena.

We bound to the reasoning side, as sensors, the *Arena*, the *currentTetromino* and the *Spawner*, and, in a similar way, we configured the actuators. By means of the

---

[3] https://github.com/MaciejKitowski/Tetris.

[4] I.e. a window similar to the Unity inspector. The inspector displays detailed information about the currently selected game object, including all attached components.

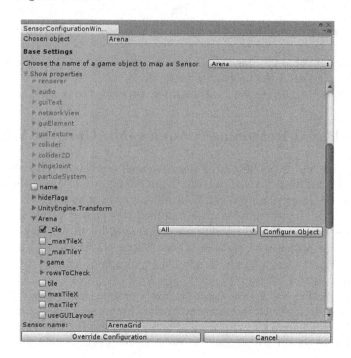

Fig. 3. Editor window for the sensor configuration

Actuator Configuration Window one can select the AI script that is needed to be mapped within the ASP module. The single selected actuator, called *player*, contains the properties: *nMove, nLatMove, nRot, typeLatMove*. The meaning of these properties will be explained in Subsect. 4.2 when we will discuss the AIPlayer script.

4.2 Brain Component

After configuring the sensors (*arenaGrid, tetromino* and *spawner*) and the actuator (*player*), we added to the GO hierarchy a new GO with an attached component of type brain. The brain consists in a standard script belonging to the *ThinkEngine* asset that will coordinate the sensors, the actuator and the solver executor.

The brain component can be configured via the inspector tab (Fig. 4). Sensors, actuators and some other additional features can be attached to a brain via the visual interface. In our example, we setup the conditions[5] to meet in order to *(a)* update the sensors and run the ASP Solver; *(b)* let the *Actuators Manager* apply the actuators actions.

When the game starts, thus at run-time, the brain will start updating sensors and will also run an external thread that will execute the ASP solver if sensors

---

[5] Conditions are selected from a set of boolean functions customized by the developer.

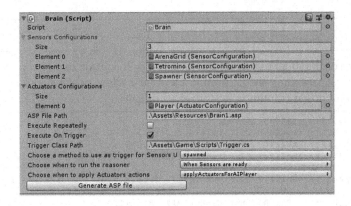

Fig. 4. Configuration of the brain.

have data to share and the solver is not already running. Every time that it is necessary to invoke the solver, the Sensor Mapper produces a representation, in the form of logical assertions, of the filtered sensors values attached to the brain. Then, the ASP solver is invoked by passing it this sensor representation and a knowledge base KB_T expressing the desired brain AI. After the ASP solver ends its execution, its answer sets (i.e. a set of output logical assertions), will be mapped to actuators by means of the actuators manager, thus influencing the game world.

In the setting of the Tetris game, the solver's output encodes the position and orientation in which the current tetromino should be dropped. This is then translated to the corresponding number of rotations and lateral moves of the tetromino. In turn, a corresponding number of simulated swipes is commanded via Unity procedural code and the tetromino is eventually dropped.

4.3   ASP Encoding

The ASP declarative specification KB_T driving the brain decision is based on the *Guess/Check/Optimize* paradigm [1]. The idea is to range in the search space of columns of the Tetris grid and of rotations of the tetromino; to exclude combinations of columns and rotations such that the piece cannot be geometrically placed; choose the optimal combination among the remaining candidates. For the sake of simplicity the optimality criterion looks for positions not leaving holes in the grid, and with lesser priority, lower dropping positions in the grid are preferred. The reader can refer to [5] for a detailed illustration of syntax and semantics of answer set programming.

The *guess* phase is expressed in the rule

```
bestSol(X,Y,C) | notBestSol(X,Y,C):-col(C), availableConfig(X,Y).
```

where the `availableConfig(X,Y)` predicate keeps track of all the possible rotations for the current tetromino. This assertion, combined with the strong constraints.

```
:- #count{Y,C: bestSol(X,Y,C)} > 1.
:- #count{Y,C: bestSol(X,Y,C)} = 0.
```

assures that each model produced by the solver will contain exactly one `bestSol`.

The lowest row that the tetromino can reach when positioned with a given rotation in a chosen column is described as follows.

```
1.  free(R,C,C1):- tile(R,C,true), C1=C+1.
2.  free(R,C,C2):- free(R,C,C1), tile(R,C1,true),C2=C1+1.
3.  firstEmpty(R):- nCol(C), #max{R1:free(R1,0,C)}=R.
4.  canPut(R):- bestSol(X,Y,C), free(R,C,C1), firstEmpty(R), confMaxW(X,Y,W),
                C1=C+W.
5.  canPut(R):- bestSol(X,Y,C), canPut(R1), free(R,C,C1), confMaxW(X,Y,W),
                C1=C+W, R=R1+1.
6.  freeUpTo(R):- canPut(R), not canPut(R1), R1=R+1.
7.  oneMore(R1):- bestSol(X,Y,C), botSpace(X,Y,I,J), freeUpTo(R), R1=R+1,
                  free(R1,C1,C2), C1=C+I, C2=C+J.
8.  twoMore(R1):-bestSol(X,Y,C), oneMore(R), extraRow(X,Y), botSpace(X,Y,I,J),
                 free(R1,C1,C2), R1=R+1, C1=C+I, C2=C+J.
9.  bestRow(R):- freeUpTo(R), not oneMore(R2), botSpace(X,Y,0,0), R2=R+1,
                 bestSol(X,Y,_).
10. bestRow(R1):- freeUpTo(R), not oneMore(R2), not extraRow(X,Y),
                  bestSol(X,Y,_), not botSpace(X,Y,0,0), R1=R-1, R2=R+1.
11. bestRow(R1):-bestSol(X,Y,_), not oneMore(R2), freeUpTo(R), extraRow(X,Y),
                 not botSpace(X,Y,0,0), R1=R-2, R2=R+1.
12. bestRow(R1):- oneMore(R), not twoMore(R1), bestSol(X,Y,_), R1=R+1,
                  not extraRow(X,Y).
13. bestRow(R):- twoMore(R).
14. :-#count{R:bestRow(R)}=0.
```

The `tile`[6] predicate is used to derive in which rows the tetromino can be placed. The space occupied by a tetromino is encoded by a number of assertions, like e.g. `confMaxW(x,y,w)` which expresses that the maximum horizontal amount of cells occupied by the tetromino x on which it has been applied the rotation y is w; other similar assertions are `botSpace(x,y,c,c1)`, `topSpace(x,y,h)`, `leftSpaceWrtSpawn(x,y,l)`, `extraRow(x,y)`.

Rules 1. and 2. describe, for each row of the arena, all the sequences of free slots of the matrix $(0-2, 0-3...0-10, 1-2, ..., 1-10...$, note that the second index is exclusive). Rule 3. derives the highest row in the arena completely empty, thus the first row in which the tetromino can be placed in whatever column. Starting from this row, rules from 4. to 8. describe in which row the tetromino, in the chosen rotation configuration, is allowed to be placed, according also with the current tetromino shape. Finally, rules from 9. to 13., describe the lowest line that the tetromino will drop to.

The next set of rules describe which row the tetromino will reach (in height) once it is placed (rule 15.) and how many holes will remain in the row immediately below (rules from 16. to 20.).

---

[6] This assertion maps facts derived from the *ArenaGrid* sensor mapped by the predicate `arenaGrid(arena(arena(tiles(X,Y,arenaTile(empty(T)))))).`

```
15. reach(R):- bestSol(X,Y,_), bestRow(R1), topSpace(X,Y,W), R=R1-W.
16. hole(R,C1):-bestSol(X,Y,C), bestRow(R1), tile(R,C1,true),confMaxW(X,Y,W),
            R=R1+1, C1>=C, C<W1, W1=C+W.
17. hole(R,C1):- bestSol(X,Y,C), botSpace(X,Y,I,J), tile(R,C1,true), L=I+J,
            L>0, C1>=C, C1<C2, C2=C+I, oneMore(R).
18. hole(R,C1):- bestSol(X,Y,C), botSpace(X,Y,I,J), tile(R,C1,true), L=I+J,
            L>0, C1>=C2, C2=C+J, C1<C3, C3=C+W, oneMore(R), confMaxW(X,Y,W).
19. hole(R,C1):- bestSol(X,Y,C), botSpace(X,Y,I,J), tile(R,C1,true), L=I+J,
            L>0, C1>=C, C1<C2, C2=C+I, twoMore(R).
20. hole(R,C1):- bestSol(X,Y,C), botSpace(X,Y,I,J), tile(R,C1,true), L=I+J,
            L>0, C1>=C2, C2=C+J, C1<C3, C3=C+W, twoMore(R), confMaxW(X,Y,W).
```

The last fragment of declarative code represent optimization criteria, which are expressed in terms of *weak constraints*. Roughly speaking, a weak constraint is a condition that, if met, increases the cost of a possible tetromino drop configuration.

```
21. :~ #count{R,C:hole(R,C)}=N, #int(N1),#int(N),N1=3*N. [N1:4]
22. :~ bestRow(R),numOfRows(N),D=N-R. [D:4]
23. :~ reach(R),numOfRows(N),D=N-R.  [D:3]
24. :~ bestSol(X,Y,C). [C:2]
25. :~ bestSol(X,Y,C). [Y:1]
```

Weak constraints 21. and 22. have been assigned to the same priority (4) since we want, at the same time, to minimize the number of holes and to maximize the lowest line that the tetromino will drop to. However, since we want to give a bit more importance to the holes, we decided to assign a triple weight with respect to the lowest row optimization criterion. At a lower priority level, we find the minimization of the row reached in height by the tetromino (23.). The last two constraints, 24. and 25., are used to assure that no more than one answer set is produced. Indeed, when having two answer sets with the same costs for respectively the number of holes criterion, for the lowest line criterion and for the top most row criterion, we will choose the solution occupying the leftmost column and requiring the lowest number of rotations.

Note that this artificial player, although not optimal, can be easily modified by changing the heuristic associated to the weight of constraint in 21.; introducing new weak constraints expressing other desiderata; changing the priority level of the constraints and so on. The above artificial player, including both the declarative code and all the procedural code, can be downloaded at https://github.com/DeMaCS-UNICAL/Tetris-AI4Unity.

5 Benchmark

One of the most common measuring indicators used for assessing the performance of a videogame is the framerate. i.e. the number of frames that can be displayed in a second.

The framerate appears to be a good measure even for the evaluation of the *ThinkEngine* impact on the game performance. Using the Tetris showcase, we compared the framerate of the game when played by a human agent and the framerate obtained using the *ThinkEngine* asset. The performance is expected to be higher when a human agent controls the game, since the thinking phase is absent and substituted by a quick keyboard reading; on the other hand if the game is controlled by *ThinkEngine*, some impact on performance is expected. Videogames are generally designed in order to keep a constant acceptable framerate, which, in the case of Unity games, is set by default to a target of 60 frames per second. Figure 5 shows how, for our setting, the framerate is not constant, but it can vary on each frame. The two curves represent, respectively, the framerate obtained when a human is playing (the blue one) and when the game is controlled by the *ThinkEngine* (the red one). The two curves generally keep the target framerate, although they present some occasional negative spikes. However, the *ThinkEngine* framerate has specific negative spikes that are caused by the overhead introduced by the sensors update phase (red crosses in the figure). These spikes do not have a visible impact on the graphical update as they are sufficiently isolated and the moving average (light green curve in Fig. 5) over 25 frames is almost constant. This analysis can be used as an indication for how often one should update the sensors: the game would stall if this is done too often. The actuators update step, instead, has no appreciable impact on the performance of the game (green diamonds in the figure). Obviously, the sensors update needs more time with respect to actuators since they have to track down an entire matrix of values on the game board.

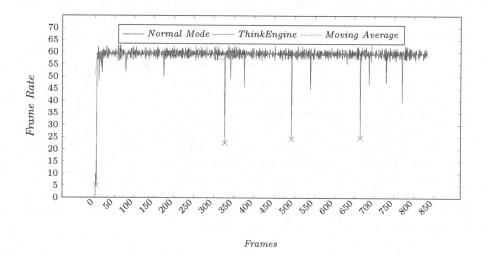

Fig. 5. Frame rate evaluation on Tetris game. (Color figure online)

Another aspect that is interesting to look at, is the time that the *ThinkEngine* needs to auto-generate the input facts for the ASP solver and how fast is this latter in producing a solution. These two measures cannot be tracked in the framerate analysis since the two operations are performed in a separate thread and the main one which is in charge of updating the graphics. However, an intuition of the amount of time elapsed between a sensors update and a solution generation can be spotted in the Fig. 5. Indeed, the number of frames between a sensors update and an actuators update is really low. The Table 1 shows the time needed on average on a single Tetris match for both facts and answer set generation: the last row is the overall average.

Table 1. Generation time

Run	Facts (ms)	AnswerSets (ms)
1	537.17	628.60
2	548.86	623.00
3	609.00	785.86
4	310.60	444.20
5	228.00	421.00
6	426.20	607.80
7	342.25	544.75
8	493.60	596.25
9	435.80	522.00
AVG	**436.83**	**574.83**

6   Related Work

Although several solutions aiming to the integration of Answer set programming in object-oriented environments have been proposed during the last decade, to the best of our knowledge *ThinkEngine* is one of the first attempt at integrating rule-based reasoning in videogame development environment.

In general integration solutions can be categorized in *(a) API-based approaches* and *(b) hybrid languages*. The first type of technique basically consists in creating a library that exposes APIs allowing to access an ASP solver, from a specific object-oriented language. The *DLV Java Wrapper* [11], is a first attempt in this direction: it consists in a Java library allowing to access and run answer set programs from Java code. With this solution, however, a programmer must take care of the integration of ASP in Java. A smoother integration level is reported in [6], where authors present a framework for the integration of ASP and Java. *JASP* is based on an hybrid language that allows ASP programs to access Java variables and, in the opposite direction, answer sets are stored in Java objects (even using Object-Relational Mapping tools like Hibernate).

The *Clingo5* system [8] is the last version of the *clingo* solver series, improving further integration facilities and accessibility from external applications. Scripting facilities (using *Lua* and *Python* languages) allow to control the execution of the clingo solver. The main objective of this solution is make ASP suitable also for dynamic environments and for problems that can take advantage of the incremental reasoning. The *EmbASP* architecture [2], also used in this work for calling external ASP solvers, is an abstract architecture allowing to integrate ASP in external tools for which authors presented a Java and a Python implementation. The *EmbASP* architecture can be easily implemented in any programming language, deployed for multiple platforms and can take advantage of different, non necessarily ASP, solvers.

Similar to EmbASP, with dual aspects, is *PY-ASPIO* presented in [10]. Even if this solution is annotations-based, these can be put in the ASP program instead that in the external application.

In [9], it has been proposed the *Videas* infrastructure as a different way of making ASP useful for object-oriented programmers. The authors proposed a visual tool based on the model-driven engineering in fact encouraging programmers to use ER diagram to describe a data model. In this way designers can automatically generate constraints in the ASP program obtained from a ER diagram. Finally, the ActHex system [7] allows to attach and execute action scripts to specific truth values appearing in answer sets, and to generate execution plans accordingly.

7   Conclusions and Future Work

In this paper we illustrated our recent progress on how to embed rule-based reasoning modules into a game development environment.

In future work we aim to tighten the integration of reasoning based modules even further in several respects: first, analyze the formal and technical issues arising when one aims to stop and restart a reasoning task, if needed; second, introduce sequences of actions (plans), and propose a model in which plans are executed transparently and can be aborted, restarted, or modified on-the-fly; last, but not least, add new data type mappings (collections, arrays and so on) for both sensors and actuators.

References

1. Buccafurri, F., Leone, N., Rullo, P.: Strong and weak constraints in disjunctive datalog. In: Dix, J., Furbach, U., Nerode, A. (eds.) LPNMR 1997. LNCS, vol. 1265, pp. 2–17. Springer, Heidelberg (1997). https://doi.org/10.1007/3-540-63255-7_2
2. Calimeri, F., Fuscà, D., Germano, S., Perri, S., Zangari, J.: Fostering the use of declarative formalisms for real-world applications: the EmbASP framework. New Gener. Comput. **37**(1), 29–65 (2019)
3. Calimeri, F., Germano, S., Ianni, G., Pacenza, F., Perri, S., Zangari, J.: Integrating rule-based AI tools into mainstream game development. In: Benzmüller, C., Ricca, F., Parent, X., Roman, D. (eds.) RuleML+RR 2018. LNCS, vol. 11092, pp. 310–317. Springer, Cham (2018). https://doi.org/10.1007/978-3-319-99906-7_23
4. Creighton, R.H.: Unity 3D game development by example: a seat-of-your-pants manual for building fun, groovy little games quickly. Packt Publishing Ltd (2010)

5. Eiter, T., Ianni, G., Krennwallner, T.: Answer set programming: a primer. In: Tessaris, S., et al. (eds.) Reasoning Web 2009. LNCS, vol. 5689, pp. 40–110. Springer, Heidelberg (2009). https://doi.org/10.1007/978-3-642-03754-2_2

6. Febbraro, O., Leone, N., Grasso, G., Ricca, F.: JASP: a framework for integrating answer set programming with Java. In: KR (2012)

7. Fink, M., Germano, S., Ianni, G., Redl, C., Schüller, P.: ActHEX: implementing HEX programs with action atoms. In: Cabalar, P., Son, T.C. (eds.) LPNMR 2013. LNCS (LNAI), vol. 8148, pp. 317–322. Springer, Heidelberg (2013). https://doi.org/10.1007/978-3-642-40564-8_31

8. Gebser, M., Kaminski, R., Kaufmann, B., Ostrowski, M., Schaub, T., Wanko, P.: Theory solving made easy with clingo 5. In: ICLP. Technical Communications (2016)

9. Oetsch, J., Pührer, J., Seidl, M., Tompits, H., Zwickl, P.: VIDEAS: a development tool for answer-set programs based on model-driven engineering technology. In: Delgrande, J.P., Faber, W. (eds.) LPNMR 2011. LNCS (LNAI), vol. 6645, pp. 382–387. Springer, Heidelberg (2011). https://doi.org/10.1007/978-3-642-20895-9_45

10. Rath, J., Redl, C.: Integrating answer set programming with object-oriented languages. In: Lierler, Y., Taha, W. (eds.) PADL 2017. LNCS, vol. 10137, pp. 50–67. Springer, Cham (2017). https://doi.org/10.1007/978-3-319-51676-9_4

11. Ricca, F.: The DLV Java wrapper. In: de Vos, M., Provetti, A. (eds.) ASP 2003, pp. 305–316 (2003)

A Comparison of MCMC Sampling for Probabilistic Logic Programming

Damiano Azzolini[1]([⊠]) [iD], Fabrizio Riguzzi[2] [iD], Franco Masotti[2] [iD],
and Evelina Lamma[1] [iD]

[1] Dipartimento di Ingegneria, University of Ferrara,
Via Saragat 1, 44122 Ferrara, Italy
{damiano.azzolini,evelina.lamma}@unife.it
[2] Dipartimento di Matematica e Informatica, University of Ferrara,
Via Saragat 1, 44122 Ferrara, Italy
fabrizio.riguzzi@unife.it, franco.masotti@student.unife.it

Abstract. Markov Chain Monte Carlo (MCMC) methods are a class of
algorithms used to perform approximate inference in probabilistic models. When direct sampling from a probability distribution is difficult,
MCMC algorithms provide accurate results by constructing a Markov
chain that gradually approximates the desired distribution. In this paper
we describe and compare the performances of two MCMC sampling algorithms, Gibbs sampling and Metropolis Hastings sampling, with rejection
sampling for probabilistic logic programs. In particular, we analyse the
relation between execution time and number of samples and how fast
each algorithm converges.

Keywords: Approximate inference · Markov Chain Monte Carlo ·
Probabilistic Logic Programming

1 Introduction

Probabilistic Logic Programming (PLP) is a useful paradigm for encoding models characterized by complex relations heavily depending on probability [10,13].
One of the main challenges of PLP is to find the probability distribution of query
random variables, a task called *inference*. Real world problems often require very
complex models. In this case, exact inference, which tries to compute the probability values in an exact way, is not feasible. Approximate inference overcomes
this issue providing approximate results whose accuracy increases as the simulation continues. Markov Chain Monte Carlo methods are a class of algorithms
used to perform approximate inference, especially when direct sampling from the
probability distribution is not practical. In this paper we propose the first Gibbs
sampling algorithm for PLP and we analyse how MCMC algorithms, Metropolis
Hastings sampling and Gibbs sampling in particular, behave in terms of execution time and accuracy of the computed probability.

© Springer Nature Switzerland AG 2019
M. Alviano et al. (Eds.): AI*IA 2019, LNAI 11946, pp. 18–29, 2019.
https://doi.org/10.1007/978-3-030-35166-3_2

The paper is structured as follows: in Sect. 2 we introduce Probabilistic Logic Programming. In Sect. 3 we offer an overview of Markov Chain Monte Carlo (MCMC) techniques and we analyse Metropolis Hastings sampling and Gibbs sampling. Section 4 shows the results of our experiments and Sect. 5 concludes the paper.

2 Probabilistic Logic Programming

Several approaches have been proposed for combining logic programming and probability theory. Here we consider languages based on the distribution semantics proposed by Sato in [15]. All the languages based on this semantics presented so far differ only in the way they encode choices for clauses but they all have the same expressive power [13].

A probabilistic logic program without function symbols defines a probability distribution over normal logic programs called *instances* or *worlds*. Logic Programs with Annotated Disjunctions (LPADs) [16] are a PLP language based on the distribution semantics. In these types of programs, the possible choices are encoded using annotated disjunctive heads of clause. An annotated disjunctive clause has the form $h_1 : \Pi_1; \ldots; h_m : \Pi_m :- b_1, \ldots, b_n$, where $h_1, \ldots, h_m$ are logical atoms, $b_1, \ldots, b_n$ are logical literals and $\Pi_1, \ldots, \Pi_m$ are real numbers in the interval $[0, 1]$ that sum to 1. $b_1, \ldots, b_n$ is called *body* while $h_1 : \Pi_1; \ldots; h_m : \Pi_m$ is called *head*. In case of $\sum_{k=1}^{m} \Pi_m < 1$, the head of the annotated disjunctive clause implicitly contains an extra atom *null* that does not appear in the body of any clause and whose annotation is $1 - \sum_{k=1}^{m} \Pi_m$.

Each world is obtained by selecting one atom from the head of each grounding (i.e. substitution of variables with terms in all possible ways) of each annotated disjunctive clause.

Consider the following LPAD:

$$mistake(X) : 0.6 :- drunk(X).$$
$$mistake(X) : 0.7 :- bad\_player(X).$$
$$drunk(iverson).$$
$$bad\_player(iverson).$$

This program can be read as: if X is drunk, then X makes a mistake with probability 0.6 and nothing happens with probability $1 - 0.6 = 0.4$. If X is a bad player, then X makes a mistake with probability 0.7 and nothing happens with probability 0.3. The last two clauses state that *iverson* certainly is a bad player and is drunk.

The probability of a query in a probabilistic logic program without function symbol is computed by extending the probability distribution over normal logic programs defined by the probabilistic logic program, to a joint distribution of the query and the worlds. Then, the probability is obtained by summing out the worlds. When a program contains also function symbols, the previous definition must be extended. This is because its grounding is infinite. So, the number of atomic choices in a selection that defines a world is infinite as well as the number of words. For a detailed definition see [12].

Performing inference, i.e. computing the probability distribution of the truth values of a query, can be done using exact or approximate methods. Exact inference can be performed in a reasonable time only when the size of the domain is relatively small, due to the #P-completeness of the task [7]. For larger domains, approximate inference is needed. Moreover, in programs with function symbols, goals may have an infinite number of possible infinite explanations and exact inference may not terminate [13]. Consider a one-dimensional random walk problem where a particle starts at position $X > 0$. At each time step, the particle can move one unit left (-1) or right $(+1)$ with equal probability. The walk stops as soon as the particle reaches 0. In this case, the walk terminates with probability one [5] but there is an infinite number of walks with nonzero probability [6]. In this example, exact inference, which tries to find the set of all explanations and then computing the probability of the query from it, will loop because the number of explanations is infinite.

Approximate algorithms using sampling are implemented in *cplint* [14] in the MCINTYRE [11] module. To be able to sample a query from a program, MCINTYRE applies a program transformation to the original program and then queries the modified program. Consider a disjunctive clause

$$C_i = h_{i1} : \Pi_{i1} \vee \ldots \vee h_{im_i} : \Pi_{im_i} :- b_{i1}, \ldots, b_{in_i},$$

where $\sum_{k=1}^{m_i} \Pi_{ik} = 1$. C_i is transformed into the set of clauses $MC(C_i) = \{MC(C_i, 1), \ldots, MC(C_i, m_i)\}$:
$MC(C_i, 1) = \quad h_{i1} :- b_{i1}, \ldots, b_{in_i},$
$$sample\_head(PL, i, VC, NH), NH = 1.$$

$\ldots$

$MC(C_i, m_i) = h_{im_i} :- b_{i1}, \ldots, b_{in_i},$
$$sample\_head(PL, i, VC, NH), NH = m_i.$$

where VC is a list containing each variable appearing in C_i and PL is a list containing $[\Pi_{i1}, \ldots, \Pi_{im_i}]$. If the parameters do not sum up to 1, the last clause (the one for *null*) is omitted. In other words, a new clause is constructed for each head. Then, using the predicate `sample_head/4`, a head index is sampled at the end of the body. If this index coincides with the head index, the derivation succeeds, otherwise it fails. The internal database of the SWI-Prolog engine [17] is used to record all samples (sampled random choices) taken with `sample_head/4` using the predicate `assertz/1`. Notice that `sample_head/4` is placed at the end of the body because at that point all the variables of the clause are ground (since we assume that the program is range restricted). The truth of a query in a sampled program can be tested by asking the query to the resulting normal program. This is equivalent to taking a sample of the query.

In general we are interested in computing approximate conditional probabilities: we want to compute the probability of an event $Y = y$ given that an event $E = e$ has been observed (i.e. $P(y \mid e)$) where Y and E are conjunctions of ground atoms and y and e are either true or false. In the rest of the paper we analyze three different algorithms available in *cplint* [14] for performing approximate inference with sampling: Gibbs sampling (Subsect. 3.1), Metropolis-Hastings (Subsect. 3.2) and rejection sampling.

Rejection sampling [7] is one of the simplest Monte Carlo algorithms. To take a sample of the query, it works in two steps: (1) it queries the evidence e. (2) If the query is successful, it queries the goal g in the same sample (that is, computing $P(g \mid e)$). Otherwise it discards the sample. The pseudocode for rejection sampling is shown in Algorithm 1.

Algorithm 1. Function Rejection: Rejection sampling algorithm.

```
 1: function REJECTION SAMPLING(P, query, evidence, Samples)
 2:     Input: Program P, query, evidence, number of samples Samples
 3:     Output: P(query|evidence)
 4:     Succ ← 0
 5:     n ← 1
 6:     while n ≤ Samples do
 7:         Call evidence
 8:         if evidence succeeds then
 9:             Call query
10:             if query succeeds then
11:                 Succ ← Succ + 1
12:             end if
13:             n ← n + 1
14:         end if
15:     end while
16:     return Succ/Samples
17: end function
```

However, rejection sampling has a disadvantage: if the evidence is very unlikely, many samples are discarded, making the algorithm very slow. For example, if the probability of the evidence ($P(e)$) is very low, say 10^{-4}, then even for $N = 10^5$ samples the expected number of unrejected samples is 10. So, to obtain at least *Samples* unrejected samples, we need to generate on average $N = Samples/P(e)$ samples from the distribution [7]. There are several alternatives to deal with low probability evidence, such as *likelihood weighting* [3] or Markov Chain Monte Carlo (MCMC) methods.

3   MCMC Sampling

Markov Chain Monte Carlo (MCMC) methods generate samples from the posterior distribution when directly sampling from the posterior is not feasible, due to the complexity of the distribution itself. The main idea of MCMC methods is to iteratively construct a Markov chain in which sampling can be done directly. As the number of samples increases, the approximation gets closer to the desired posterior distribution. In this way, MCMC methods are theoretically capable of getting arbitrarily close to the true posterior distribution. During the execution of MCMC algorithms, usually the first few samples are discarded because they may not represent the desired distribution. This phase is called *burnin* phase.

In this section we analyse two of the most famous MCMC sampling algorithms: Gibbs sampling and Metropolis Hastings sampling.

Algorithm 2. Function Gibbs: Gibbs MCMC algorithm

1: **function** Gibbs(*query, evidence, Mixing, Samples, block*)
2:     GibbsCycle(*query, evidence, Mixing, block*)
3:     **return** GibbsCycle(*query, evidence, Samples, block*)
4: **end function**
5: **function** GibbsCycle(*query, evidence, Samples, block*)
6:     $Succ \leftarrow 0$
7:     **for** $n \leftarrow 1 \rightarrow Samples$ **do**
8:         Save a copy of samples C
9:         SampleCycle(*evidence*)
10:         Delete the copy of samples C
11:         $ListOfRemovedSamples = $ RemoveSamples(*block*)
12:         Call *query*   ▷ new samples are asserted at the bottom of the list
13:         **if** *query* succeeds **then**
14:             $Succ \leftarrow Succ + 1$
15:         **end if**
16:         CheckSamples(*ListOfRemovedSamples*)
17:     **end for**
18:     **return** $\frac{Succ}{Samples}$
19: **end function**
20: **procedure** SampleCycle(*evidence*)
21:     **while** *true* **do**
22:         Call *evidence*
23:         **if** *evidence* succeeds **then**
24:             $TrueEv \leftarrow true$
25:             **return**
26:         **end if**
27:         Erase all samples
28:         Restore samples copy C
29:     **end while**
30: **end procedure**
31: **function** RemoveSamples(*block*)
32:     $SampleList \leftarrow []$
33:     **for** $b \leftarrow 1 \rightarrow block$ **do**
34:         retract sample $S = (Rule, Substitution, Value)$ ▷ samples are retracted from the top of
        the list
35:         Add $(Rule, Substitution)$ to $SampleList$
36:     **end for**
37:     **return** $SampleList$
38: **end function**
39: **procedure** CheckSamples(*ListOfRemovedSamples*)
40:     **for all** $(Rule, Substitution) \in ListOfRemovedSamples$ **do**
41:         **if** $(Rule, Substitution)$ was not sampled **then**
42:             Sample a value for $(Rule, Substitution)$ and record it with assert
43:         **end if**
44:     **end for**
45: **end procedure**

3.1   Gibbs Sampling

The idea behind Gibbs sampling is the following: when sampling from a joint distribution is not feasible, we can sample each variable independently considering the other variables as observed [4]. In details, suppose we have n variables $X_1, \ldots, X_n$. First we set these variables to an initial value $x_1^{(0)}, \ldots, x_n^{(0)}$, for instance by sampling from a prior distribution. At each iteration (or until convergence) we take a sample $x_m^{(t)} \sim P(x_m \mid x_1^{t-1}, x_2^{t-1}, \ldots, x_{m-1}^{t-1}, x_{m+1}^{t-1}, \ldots, x_n^{t-1})$. There is also the possibility to perform blocked Gibbs sampling, i.e, group together two or more variables and sampling from their joint distribution conditioned on all other variables, instead of sampling each one individually.

Gibbs sampling is available on *cplint*. The code is shown in Algorithm 2. A list of sampled random choices is stored in memory using Prolog asserts. Function GIBBSCYCLE performs the main loop. To take a sample, we query the evidence using function SAMPLECYCLE that performs a type of rejection sampling: it queries the evidence until the value true is obtained. When the evidence succeeds, we remove *block* random choices from the list of saved random choices using function REMOVESAMPLES. Then, we ask the query and, if the query is successful, the number of successes is incremented by 1. The last step consist in calling function CHECKSAMPLES. This function checks if there are some rules not sampled in the list of removed random choices. If so, a value is sampled and stored in memory. This is due to the necessity of assigning a value to x_m even if it was not involved in the new derivation of the query. The probability is returned as the ratio between the number of successes and the total number of samples.

3.2   Metropolis Hastings

In Metropolis Hastings sampling, a Markov chain is built by taking an initial sample and, starting from this sample, by generating successors samples. Here we consider the algorithm developed in [9] and implemented in cplint [14]. Algorithm 3 goes as follows: (1) it samples random choices so that the evidence is true to build an initial sample. (2) It removes a fixed number (defined as *lag*) of sampled probabilistic choices to build the successor sample. (3) It queries again the evidence by sampling starting from the undeleted samples. (4) If the evidence succeeds, the query is asked by sampling. It is accepted with probability $min\{1, N_0/N_1\}$ where N_0 is the number of choices sampled in the previous sample and N_1 is the number of choices sampled in the current sample. (5) If the query succeeds in the last accepted sample then the number of successes of the query is increased by 1. (6) The final probability is computed as the number of successes over the total number of samples.

In details, function MH returns the probability of the query given the evidence. Function RESAMPLE(*lag*) deletes *lag* choices from the sampled random choices. In [9] *lag* is always 1. Function INITIALSAMPLE builds the initial sample with a meta-interpreter that starts with the goal and randomizes the order in which clauses are used for resolution during the search to make the initial sample unbiased. This is achieved by collecting all the clauses that match a subgoal and trying them in random order. Then the goal is queried using regular sampling.

4   Experiments

We tested the performances of Gibbs sampling, Metropolis Hastings sampling, and rejection sampling using four different programs. For each program, we ran the queries mc_gibbs_sample/5, mc_mh_sample/5 and mc_rejection_sample/5 provided by the MCINTYRE module [11] implemented in cplint. All the algorithms are written in Prolog and tested in SWI-Prolog [17] version 8.1.7. For

---

Algorithm 3. Function MH: Metropolis-Hastings MCMC algorithm

1: **function** MH(*query, evidence, lag, Samples*)
2:      MHCYCLE(*query, evidence, lag*)
3:      **return** MHCYCLE(*query, evidence, Samples*)
4: **end function**
5: **function** MHCYCLE(*query, evidence, Samples*)
6:      *TrueSamples* ← 0
7:      *Ssample* ← INITIALSAMPLE(*evidence*)
8:      Call *query*
9:      **if** *query* succeeds **then**
10:          *querySample* ← *true*
11:      **else**
12:          *querySample* ← *false*
13:      **end if**
14:      Save a copy of the current samples *C*
15:      *n* ← 0
16:      **while** *n* < *Samples* **do**
17:          *n* ← *n* + 1
18:          *SamplesList* ← RESAMPLE(*lag*)
19:          Call *evidence*
20:          **if** *evidence* succeeds **then**
21:              Call *query*
22:              **if** *query* succeeds **then**
23:                  *querySample'* ← *true*
24:              **else**
25:                  *querySample'* ← *false*
26:              **end if**
27:              let *CurrentSampled* be the current number of choices sampled
28:              **if** $min(1, \frac{CurrentSampled}{PreviousSampled}) > RandomValue(0, 1)$ **then**
29:                  *PreviousSampled* ← *CurrentSampled*
30:                  Delete the copy of the previous samples *C*
31:                  Save a copy of the current samples *C*
32:                  *querySample* ← *querySample'*
33:              **else**
34:                  Erase all samples
35:                  Restore samples copy *C*
36:              **end if**
37:          **else**
38:              Erase all samples
39:              Restore samples copy *C*
40:          **end if**
41:      **end while**
42:      Erase all samples
43:      Delete the copy of the previous samples *C*
44:      **return** $\frac{TrueSamples}{Samples}$
45: **end function**
46: **function** RESAMPLE(*lag*)
47:      **for** *n* ← 1 → *lag* **do**
48:          Delete a sample *Sample*
49:          *NewSample* ← SAMPLE(*Ssample*)
50:          Assert *NewSample*
51:      **end for**
52:      **return** *SamplesList*
53: **end function**

---

each query we show how the number of samples affects the execution time and the computed probability. All the experiments were conducted on a cluster[1] with Intel® Xeon® E5-2630v3 running at 2.40 GHz. Execution times are computed using the SWI-Prolog built-in predicate `statistics/2` with the keyword

---

[1] http://www.fe.infn.it/coka/doku.php?id=start.

`walltime`. The results are averages of 10 runs. For both Gibbs and Metropolis Hastings sampling, we set the number of deleted samples (*burnin*) to 100.

For the first comparison, we consider a program that generatively defines a random arithmetic function[2]. The problem is to predict the value returned by the function given one or two couples of input-output, i.e., to compute a conditional probability. The peculiarity of this program is that it has an infinite number of explanations. As described in Sect. 2, approximate inference is needed, as exact inference may loop. In this example, the evidence has probability 0.05. Results are shown in Fig. 1. In this case, Metropolis Hastings sampling and Gibbs sampling have comparable execution time, but Gibbs sampling converges more slowly.

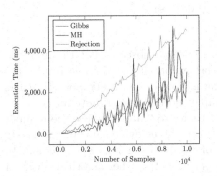 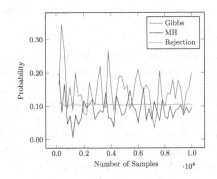

Fig. 1. Results for random arithmetic functions test.

The second program encodes a hidden Markov model (HMM) for modeling DNA sequences. The model has three states, `q1`, `q2` and `end`, and four output symbols, `a`, `c`, `g`, and `t`, corresponding to the four nucleotides (letters)[3] [2]. We compute the probability that the model emits the sequence `[a,c]` observing that from state `q1` the models emits the letter `a`. The evidence has probability 0.25. Results are shown in Fig. 2. In this case, all the three algorithms converge to the same probability value, but Metropolis Hastings is the slowest one with execution time several times larger than Gibbs and rejection sampling.

For the third test we consider a Latent Dirichlet Allocation (LDA) model[4] [1]. LDA is a generative probabilistic model especially useful in text analysis. In particular, it models the distribution of terms and topics in documents in order to predict the topic of the analysed text. This program, differently from the others, is hybrid, i.e., it contains also continuous random variables. For this test, we fix both the number of words considered in a document (10) and the number of topics (2) and we compute the relation between number of samples,

---

[2] http://cplint.eu/example/inference/arithm.pl.
[3] http://cplint.eu/example/inference/hmm.pl.
[4] http://cplint.eu/example/inference/lda.swinb.

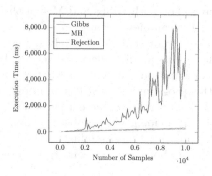
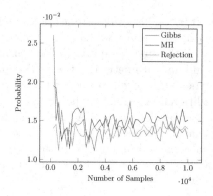

Fig. 2. Results for HMM test.

probability and execution time. In this example, we observe that the first two words of the document are equal, which has probability 0.01. The results are shown in Fig. 3: in this case Gibbs sampling is slower than Metropolis Hastings both in execution time and number of samples needed to compute an accurate probability. Then we also fix the number of topics to 2 and increase the number of consecutive equal words from 1 to 8. In this test, the evidence is progressively extended, i.e., we observe that n number of words (from 1 to 8) are equal. In this case Metropolis Hastings sampling outperforms the other algorithms (Fig. 4 left). For Gibbs sampling and rejection sampling, the number of words in the plot is at most 6 since, for a value bigger than that, each query requires more than one hour of computation.

The last program describes a university domain[5] [8] characterized by students, professors and courses. Each professor is related to a course and each student attends a course. We are interested in computing the probability that a

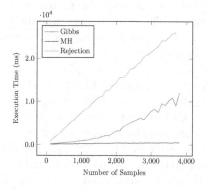
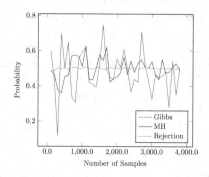

Fig. 3. Results for LDA model.

---

[5] http://cplint.eu/example/inference/uwcse.pl.

professor teaches a course given that the same professor is advisor of some students of the same course. We fixed the number of students to 10, and both the number of professors and courses to 1. In this case the evidence has probability 0.09. Results are shown in Fig. 5. As for the previous experiment, we also incremented the number of students up to 20 and plot how execution time changes (Fig. 4 right). In both cases, Gibbs sampling is still the slowest algorithm, but the performances are not so different from Metropolis Hastings and rejection sampling.

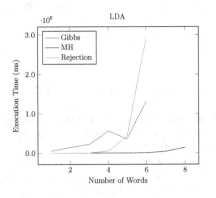
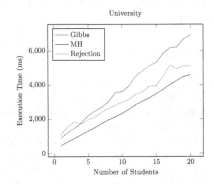

Fig. 4. Both graphs show how the number of facts affects the execution time. The left one is related to the LDA model while the right one to the university model. For both we fixed the number of samples to 10^4.

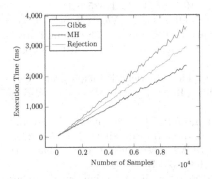
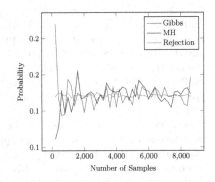

Fig. 5. Results for the university domain.

5 Conclusions

In this paper we proposed the first Gibbs sampling algorithm for PLP. We also compared it with Metropolis-Hastings and rejection sampling. The three algorithms are available in the cplint suite and online in the web application cplint.eu.

For each algorithm we conducted several experiments to compare execution time and convergence time. In three of the four experiments, Metropolis Hastings outperformed Gibbs sampling and rejection sampling in terms of accuracy and execution time. However, in the second experiment (HMM), Gibbs sampling has better performances than Metropolis Hastings and it is comparable to rejection sampling in terms of execution time. Also, in this test, Metropolis Hastings is the least accurate (it overestimates the probability) while Gibbs sampling and rejection sampling converge faster. Experimental analysis showed that Metropolis Hastings is the fastest among the three unless the evidence has a relatively high probability as in HMM where it has probability 0.25: in that case, Gibbs performs better.

References

1. Blei, D.M., Ng, A.Y., Jordan, M.I.: Latent Dirichlet allocation. J. Mach. Learn. Res. **3**, 993–1022 (2003)
2. Christiansen, H., Gallagher, J.P.: Non-discriminating arguments and their uses. In: Hill, P.M., Warren, D.S. (eds.) ICLP 2009. LNCS, vol. 5649, pp. 55–69. Springer, Heidelberg (2009). https://doi.org/10.1007/978-3-642-02846-5_10
3. Fung, R.M., Chang, K.C.: Weighing and integrating evidence for stochastic simulation in Bayesian networks. In: 5th Conference Conference on Uncertainty in Artificial Intelligence (UAI 1989), pp. 209–220. North-Holland Publishing Co. (1989)
4. Geman, S., Geman, D.: Stochastic relaxation, Gibbs distributions, and the Bayesian restoration of images. In: Readings in Computer Vision, pp. 564–584. Elsevier (1987)
5. Hurd, J.: A formal approach to probabilistic termination. In: Carreño, V.A., Muñoz, C.A., Tahar, S. (eds.) TPHOLs 2002. LNCS, vol. 2410, pp. 230–245. Springer, Heidelberg (2002). https://doi.org/10.1007/3-540-45685-6_16
6. Kaminski, B.L., Katoen, J.-P., Matheja, C., Olmedo, F.: Weakest precondition reasoning for expected run–times of probabilistic programs. In: Thiemann, P. (ed.) ESOP 2016. LNCS, vol. 9632, pp. 364–389. Springer, Heidelberg (2016). https://doi.org/10.1007/978-3-662-49498-1_15
7. Koller, D., Friedman, N.: Probabilistic Graphical Models: Principles and Techniques. Adaptive Computation and Machine Learning. MIT Press, Cambridge (2009)
8. Meert, W., Struyf, J., Blockeel, H.: Learning ground CP-Logic theories by leveraging Bayesian network learning techniques. Fundam. Inform. **89**(1), 131–160 (2008)
9. Nampally, A., Ramakrishnan, C.: Adaptive MCMC-based inference in probabilistic logic programs. arXiv preprint arXiv:1403.6036 (2014)
10. Fadja, A.N., Riguzzi, F.: Probabilistic logic programming in action. In: Holzinger, A., Goebel, R., Ferri, M., Palade, V. (eds.) Towards Integrative Machine Learning and Knowledge Extraction. LNCS (LNAI), vol. 10344, pp. 89–116. Springer, Cham (2017). https://doi.org/10.1007/978-3-319-69775-8_5
11. Riguzzi, F.: MCINTYRE: a Monte Carlo system for probabilistic logic programming. Fundam. Inform. **124**(4), 521–541 (2013)
12. Riguzzi, F.: The distribution semantics for normal programs with function symbols. Int. J. Approx. Reason. **77**, 1–19 (2016)
13. Riguzzi, F.: Foundations of Probabilistic Logic Programming. River Publishers, Gistrup (2018)

14. Riguzzi, F., Bellodi, E., Lamma, E., Zese, R., Cota, G.: Probabilistic logic programming on the web. Softw.-Pract. Exper. **46**(10), 1381–1396 (2016)
15. Sato, T.: A statistical learning method for logic programs with distribution semantics. In: Sterling, L. (ed.) ICLP 1995, pp. 715–729. MIT Press, Cambridge (1995)
16. Vennekens, J., Verbaeten, S., Bruynooghe, M.: Logic programs with annotated disjunctions. In: Demoen, B., Lifschitz, V. (eds.) ICLP 2004. LNCS, vol. 3132, pp. 431–445. Springer, Heidelberg (2004). https://doi.org/10.1007/978-3-540-27775-0_30
17. Wielemaker, J., Schrijvers, T., Triska, M., Lager, T.: SWI-Prolog. Theor. Pract. Log. Prog. **12**(1–2), 67–96 (2012)

Augmenting Datalog$^{\pm}$ with Customizable Metalogic Features for Powerful Ontological Reasoning

Stefania Costantini[1] and Andrea Formisano[2(✉)]

[1] Università di L'Aquila, via Vetoio, 67010 L'Aquila, Italy
stefania.costantini@univaq.it
[2] INdAM-GNCS and Università di Perugia, via Vanvitelli 1, 06123 Perugia, Italy
andrea.formisano@unipg.it

Abstract. In recent work by Gottlob et al., the usefulness and adequacy of Datalog, and precisely Datalog$^{\pm}$ augmented with rules with existential heads to implement ontological reasoning has been shown. Also, it has been shown how to express forms of reasoning that go beyond the expressive capabilities of Description Logics. In our recent work [25] we present a methodology for introducing customizable metalogic features in logic-based knowledge representation and reasoning languages. We made the specific case of Answer Set Programming (ASP), where such features may be part of software engineering toolkits for this programming paradigm. In this paper we show how such metalogic features can further enrich Datalog$^{\pm}$ with minor changes to its operational semantics (provided in terms of "chase") and no additional complexity burden.

Keywords: Ontologies · Meta-reasoning · Datalog$^{\pm}$

1 Introduction

In [16–18] a family of expressive extensions of Datalog is presented, called Datalog$^{\pm}$, and is proposed as a new paradigm for query answering over ontologies. Languages of the Datalog$^{\pm}$ family are enriched, with respect to standard Datalog, with existentially quantified variables in rule heads, where suitable restrictions are introduced to ensure highly efficient ontology querying, thus leading to "guarded Datalog$^{\pm}$". The authors show, in fact, that guarded Datalog$^{\pm}$ is PTIME-complete in data complexity. They also enrich the language with negative constraints and a general class of key constraints, where ontology querying remains tractable. Languages belonging to the Datalog$^{\pm}$ family are able to express widely-used tractable ontology languages, in particular, the DL-Lite family [3,19] of Description Logics, which are highly suitable for ontological modeling

Supported by INdAM GNCS-17 and GNCS-19 projects, by project B.I.M.–2018.0419.021, by Univ.of Perugia (projects "ricerca-di-base-2016", YASMIN, CLTP, and RACRA). Supported by Action COST CA17124 "DigForASP".

© Springer Nature Switzerland AG 2019
M. Alviano et al. (Eds.): AI*IA 2019, LNAI 11946, pp. 30–45, 2019.
https://doi.org/10.1007/978-3-030-35166-3_3

and reasoning. DL-Lite logics are able to define some relevant conceptual modeling formalisms, such as Entity-Relationship model and UML class diagrams. DL-Lite logics retain tractability of the most important reasoning tasks, such as ontology satisfiability and query answering of arbitrary (union of) conjunctive queries (ground and not ground). It has been shown that reasoning over ontologies of the DL-Lite family is LOGSPACE-hard in data complexity, and can be thus delegated to a standard DBMS technology. Datalog$^{\pm}$ is the core of Vadalog, which is empowered in view of implementing KGMS (Knowledge Graphs Management Systems) and so includes numeric computations, monotonic aggregation, probabilistic reasoning, and primitives for access to external data sources or computational resources of various kinds.

The OWL ontology language [1,37] provides a powerful data modeling language, and automated reasoning abilities based upon Description Logics [4]. There are, as it is well known, different versions of OWL depending upon the kind of reasoning one wishes to use and can computationally afford; in fact, such versions range from the expressiveness of DL-Lite (OWL 2 QL), with reasoning capabilities equivalent to SQL, to very complex reasoning capabilities even leading to undecidability. Relevant aspects concerning knowledge representation and reasoning that can be found in OWL are: (i) properties of relations: e.g., symmetry/asymmetry, transitivity, functionality, reflexivity/irreflexivity, domain/range; (ii) relations between relations (meta-properties): e.g., inverse-of, equivalence, disjointness, subclass; (iii) cardinality of relations.Such aspects are present even in OWL-Lite, one of the less expressive sub-languages of OWL, where however reasoning is still non-tractable in general.

The possibility to express properties of relations has widely demonstrated its usefulness in the definition and use of ontologies in the Semantic Web. We believe that they would find useful application in many knowledge engineering and automated reasoning languages. In fact, ontologies are pervading many areas of knowledge and data representation and management, and a lot of effort has been spent on the development of sufficiently expressive languages for the representation and querying of ontologies. In particular, as Datalog$^{\pm}$ has been since long advocated as capable to perform useful and significant ontological reasoning: in this paper, we present a methodology for introducing OWL-like features in Datalog$^{\pm}$. Our approach is based on concepts of introspection and reflection discussed, among others, in [7,26,34,38]. In order to implement an engine realizing properties and meta-properties of relations inspired by those expressible in OWL, we employ meta-level axiom schemata based upon a naming (reification) device. We propose a method for extending the Datalog$^{\pm}$ semantics accordingly. In practice, such schemata should be seemingly added by default to any program/knowledge base, and can be freely used by a programmer. We do not claim to reproduce all OWL features and maybe not even most of them. In fact we could not, as we stay within decidable frameworks based upon CWA (Closed-World Assumption). However, the features that we reproduce are widely used, and they are useful in many practical contexts. Moreover, we improve over OWL as customized and user-defined new properties are allowed in our proposal. So, the average programmer does not define and does not need to see the definition of properties of relations, but rather just uses predefined ones though the skilled programmer is enabled to define new properties.

The possibility of improving knowledge engineering capabilities by means of metaprogramming and metareasoning has been explored in the past [23]. In logic settings such as Prolog [40] the aim was to enlarge representation and reasoning possibilities while avoiding to resort to a higher-level setting, mainly by using meta-interpreters [14] and trying to equip them with a logical semantics [12,20], or by devising specialized language extensions [7,36]. Recently, the Rulelog language [32] features some seemingly higher-order characteristics inspired by the HiLog second-order language [21], though transposed into a simple (though limited under the point of view of reasoning capabilities) first-order representation. Our proposal, that in this paper we apply to Datalog$^\pm$, has the merit of being language-independent: it is in fact generally applicable within the realm of knowledge representation languages based upon computational logic and logic programming [40], syntactically based upon some first-order language. Among them are Prolog, Datalog$^\pm$, ASP, and many agent-oriented programming languages [13].

In this paper we discuss the extension with metalevel features for Datalog$^\pm$, which is a successful logic programming and knowledge representation paradigm, oriented to ontological reasoning, knowledge integration and many other practical problems. We will show in detail how the approach can be quite naturally applied to Datalog$^\pm$ with notable practical advantages.

The paper is organized as follows. We first shortly summarize the basic principles of the OWL language in Sect. 2, and we recall the concept of *reification* (naming) of first-order terms and atoms (Sect. 3). Then, we present our approach in Sects. 4 and 5. Later, after shortly recalling Datalog$^\pm$ (Sect. 6), is the core part of the paper. In Sect. 7 we show (by examples) how our approach can be usefully applied to Datalog$^\pm$. In Sect. 8 we extend Datalog$^\pm$ procedural semantics, called 'the chase' and based on a 'chase rule', with our constructs. Finally, in Sect. 9 we discuss some related work and draw conclusions. We assume basic knowledge about Prolog/Datalog; the reader may refer to [40].

2   Background: OWL

OWL is a language for the definition of *ontologies* (the reader may refer to www.w3.org/TR/2012/REC-owl2-primer for an introduction). The term ontology has a complex history in Philosophy, and recently in Computer Science. In Knowledge Representation, an ontology is a set of formal statements aimed to describe some part of the world (often referred to as the "domain of interest" or the "subject matter" of the ontology). Precise descriptions satisfy several purposes, among which: they prevent misunderstandings in human communication and they ensure a better software behavior, especially when different software modules interact.

In order to precisely describe a domain of interest, the OWL language is based upon a *vocabulary*. The meanings of terms is established by stating how each term is interrelated to the other terms (and similarly for classes, properties, and individuals). A terminology, providing a vocabulary together with such interrelation information constitutes an essential part of an OWL ontology. Besides this "terminological" knowledge, usually called TBOX, an ontology might also contain so called "assertional knowledge" (ABOX) that introduces concrete objects of the considered domain. The TBOX part is the analogous of the set of rules of a Prolog program, while the ABOX is the analogous of the set of facts.

OWL 2 is not a programming language, rather it provides a declarative way to describe knowledge in a logical way. For the decidable fragments of OWL, appropriate tools (so-called *reasoners*) can then be used to infer further information from a given TBOX+ABOX description. How these inferences are realized algorithmically depends on the specific implementations and on the fragments of OWL considered. Still, the correct answer to any of such question is predetermined by the OWL formal semantics.

In OWL it is possible to define classes of objects/individuals, membership to classes, class inclusion, equivalence and disjointness, class hierarchies. Concerning object properties, they correspond to binary predicates, i.e., to relations, and are expressed concerning specific objects which are related by each property. It is also possible to express negative assertions, concerning individuals *not* enjoying some property. It is possible to specify hierarchies of properties (e.g., to state that some properties are sub-properties of other ones) and to define domain and range of each property. Among the "Advanced Use of Properties", one can state that certain properties are reflexive or irreflexive, symmetric or asymmetric, transitive, equivalent to some other properties, or disjoint from them. It can be stated that a property is functional, or that its inverse is functional.

3   Background: Naming Mechanisms

A *reification mechanism*, also known as "naming relation", is a method for representing within a first-order language expressions of the language itself, without resorting to higher-order features. Naming relations can be introduced in several manners. For a discussion of different possibilities, with their advantages and disadvantages, see, e.g., [5,6,33,35]. However, all of them are based upon introducing distinguished constants, function symbols (if available) and predicates, devised to construct names. For instance, given an atom $p(a, b, c)$, a name might be $atom(pred(p'), args([a', b', c']))$ where p' and a', b', c' are new constants intended as names for the syntactic elements p and a, b, c. Notice that: p is a predicate symbol (which is not a first-class object in first-order settings), *atom* is a distinguished predicate symbol, *args* a distinguished function symbol and [...] is a list.

More formally, let us consider a standard first-order language $\mathcal{L}$ including sets of *predicate*, *constant* and (possibly) *function* symbols, and a (possibly denumerable) set of symbols of *variables*. As usual, well-formed formulas have *atoms* as their basic constituents, where an atom is built via the application of a predicate to a number n (according to the predicate arity) of *terms*. The latter can be variables, constants, or compound terms built by using function symbols (if available). We augment $\mathcal{L}$ with new symbols, namely a new constant (say of the form p') for each predicate symbol p, a new constant (say f') for each function symbol f, a new constant (say c') for each constant symbol c, and a denumerable set of metavariables, that we assume to have the form X' so as to distinguish them syntactically from "plain" object-level variables X. The new constants are intended to act as names, where we will say that, syntactically, p' denotes p, f' denotes f, and c' denotes c, respectively. The new variables can be instantiated to *meta-level formulas*, i.e., to terms involving names, where we assume that plain variables can be instantiated only to terms *not* involving names, so-called *object-level* terms. We assume an underlying mechanism managing the naming relation (however defined), so we can indicate the name of, e.g., atom $p(a, b, c)$ as $p'(a', b', c')$ and the name of a generic atom A as $\uparrow A$; vice versa the atom named by A' is denoted by $\downarrow A$. We will consider only names of *object-level* atoms, i.e., atoms not including meta-constants and meta-variables. We assume that $\uparrow A$ is constructed out of $p' = \uparrow p$ if p is the predicate occurring in A, and $k' = \uparrow k$ for each constant k occurring in A. Also, we consider only names of *ground* atoms, i.e., atoms not containing variables. Since this paper is concerned with Datalog, we do not need names of function symbols either. Notice however that, as discussed in the aforementioned references, it is possible to construct names of names (... of names) and names of every kind of atoms and formulas.

Notice that, as discussed in [22] naming relation can be a sort of "input parameter" for a meta-language. In fact a meta-language can be, if carefully designed, to a large extent independent of the syntactic form of names, and of which are the expressions that are named. In [6] and [7] a full theory of definable naming relations is developed.

4 Background: Metalogic for Properties of Relations

Our focus is on rule-based languages, where rules are typically represented in the form *Head* $\leftarrow$ *Body* or equivalently *Body* $\rightarrow$ *Head* where $\leftarrow$ and $\rightarrow$ indicate implication; other notations for this connective can alternatively be employed. In Prolog/Datalog-like practical systems, $\leftarrow$ is often indicated as :−, and *Body* is intended as a conjunction of literals (atoms or negated atoms) where conventionally a comma stands for $\wedge$.

We will represent properties of relations in OWL style by means of metalevel rules, building on past work [8,9,24,26]. To define such rules, we assume to augment the language $\mathcal{L}$ at hand not only with names, but with the introduction of two distinguished predicates, *solve* and *solve_not* (clearly, the specific name of these predicates is immaterial). An atom A is a *base atom* or *object-level* atom if it does not involve names and its predicate is neither *solve* nor *solve_not*. Distinguished predicates will allow us to respectively extend/restrict the meaning of the other predicates in a declarative way. In fact, *solve* and *solve_not* take as arguments (names of) atoms (involving any predicate excluding themselves), and thus they are able to express sentences about relations. Names of atoms, in particular, are allowed *only* as arguments of *solve* and *solve_not*. Also, *solve* and *solve_not* can occur in the body of a metarule *only if* the predicate of its head is in turn either *solve* or *solve_not*.

So, metalevel rules in general allow arguments of predicates to be names of predicates, function symbols, and constants. A particular kind of metarules, that we call *metaevaluation rules*, have distinguished predicates *solve* and *solve_not* in their head, and possibly also in their body, taking as argument names of atoms.

Below is a simple example of the use of *solve* to specify which properties a reflexive predicate p meets. Namely, that $p(a, a)$ can be derived for any element a belonging to the predicate domain; here, this is elicited from a occurring in the extensional definition of p. The first rule is a metaevaluation rule, featuring predicate *solve* in its head, taking as argument the name of an atom; the latter two rules are 'simple' metalevel rules taking as arguments metalevel constants.

$$solve(P'(X', X')) :- reflexive(P'), in\_domain(P', X').$$
$$in\_domain(P', X') :- solve(P'(X', Y')).$$
$$in\_domain(P', X') :- solve(P'(Y', X')).$$

Our objective is to make it automatic to derive $p(a, a)$ whenever a program includes this definition, a fact *reflexive*(p') occurs in the program, and a is in the domain of p. Vice versa, we can define:

$$solve\_not(P'(X', X')) : -irreflexive(P').$$

with the aim to prevent the derivation of $p(a, a)$ for any predicate p which have been declared to be irreflexive (i.e., for which a fact *irreflexive*(p') occurs in the program).

Following [27], in general terms we understand a semantics *SEM* for logic knowledge representation languages/formalisms as a function which associates a theory/program with a set of sets of atoms, which constitute the intended meaning. When saying that Π is a program, we mean that it is a program/theory in the (here unspecified) logic language/formalism that one wishes to consider.

We impose a restriction on sets of atoms that should be considered for the application of *SEM*. First, as customary, we only consider sets of atoms I composed of atoms occurring in the ground version of Π. The ground version of program Π is obtained by substituting in all possible ways variables occurring in Π by constants also occurring in Π. In our case, metavariables occurring in an atom must be substituted by metaconstants, with the following obvious restrictions: a metavariable occurring in the predicate position must be substituted by a metaconstant denoting a predicate; a metavariable occurring in the function position must be substituted by a metaconstant denoting a function; a metavariable occurring in the position corresponding to a constant must be substituted by a metaconstant denoting a constant. According to well-established terminology [40], we therefore require $I \subseteq B_\Pi$, where B_Π is the *Herbrand Base* of Π, given previously-stated limitations on variable substitution. Then, we pose some more substantial requirements. As said before, by $\uparrow A$ we intend a name of an object-level atom A.

Definition 1. *Let Π be a program. $I \subseteq B_\Pi$ is a* potentially acceptable set of atoms *iff for every object-level atom A belonging to I, solve($\uparrow A$) belongs to I.*

Definition 2. *Let Π be a program, and I be a potentially acceptable set of atoms for Π. I is an* acceptable set of atoms *iff I satisfies the following axiom schemata for every object-level atom A:*
    $A \leftarrow solve(\uparrow A)$
    $\neg A \leftarrow solve\_not(\uparrow A)$

We restrict *SEM* to determine acceptable sets of atoms only, modulo bijection: i.e., *SEM* can be allowed to produce sets of atoms which are in one-to-one correspondence with acceptable sets of atoms. In this way, we obtain the implementation of properties of relations that have been defined via *solve* and *solve_not* rules without modifications to *SEM* for any formalism at hand. For clarity however, it is convenient to filter away *solve* and *solve_not* atoms from acceptable sets. Thus, given a program Π and an acceptable set of atoms I for Π, the *Base version I^B* of I is obtained by omitting from I all atoms of the form $solve(\uparrow A)$ and $solve\_not(\uparrow A)$.

Procedural semantics and the specific naming relation that one intends to use remain to be defined. In fact, it is easy to see that the above-introduced semantics is independent of the naming mechanism. For approaches based upon (variants of) Resolution (like, e.g., Prolog) one can extend the procedure so as to be allowed to use rules with conclusion $solve(\uparrow A)$ to resolve a goal A and, vice versa, rules with conclusion A to resolve $solve(\uparrow A)$; if a goal G succeeds in this way with computed answer θ, then $solve\_not(\uparrow G\theta)$ should be attempted: if it succeeds, then G should be forced to fail; otherwise, success of G can be confirmed.

5   Background: Expressing OWL-Like Properties of Relations, and More

In the previous section we have shown the use of metalevel definitions involving *solve* and *solve_not* to define what it means of a predicate to be reflexive or, vice versa, irreflexive. These metalevel definitions are declarative yet executable, in that they suitably enlarge or restrict involved predicates' extension. In this section we show the metalevel representation of other properties of relations that can be expressed in OWL. We concentrate in particular on properties which are relevant and widely used. The objective is to convince the reader that most such properties can be represented in our approach without resorting to the powerful though complex Description Logics.

Symmetry can be simply defined as follows:

$solve(P'(X', Y')) :- symmetric(P'), solve(P'(Y', X'))$.
$symmetric(friend')$.

This rule specifies, in fact, the meaning of symmetry for any predicate, stating (via the predicate *solve* applied over a generic atom name) that $p(X, Y)$ can be derived if $p(Y, X)$ holds; notice that in this rule predicate *solve* occurs not only in the head but also in the body of the rule. The fact *symmetric(friend')* specifies that predicate *friend* is symmetric, via its name.

So, a programmer/knowledge-designer behaves very much like in OWL, save that properties of relations must be specified on the names of the predicates. Notice that different metaevaluation rules (with their auxiliary metalevel rules) can be defined and expressed in a modular way, and they naturally interact and compose with each other.

Below we consider *transitivity*, that can be expressed in the following way:

$$solve(P'(X', Y')) :- transitive(P'), solve(P'(X', Z')), solve(P'(Z', Y')).$$

This rule specifies the meaning of transitivity for any predicate, where a fact of the form *transitive(p')* declares that the predicate p' is transitive. The definition actually allows new facts to be derived. For example, if we have the following facts:

transitive(same_age').
same_age(ann, alice).
same_age(alice, chris).

via the previous rule we can derive *same_age(ann, chris)*. A possible variation is the transitive closure.

Another very useful feature, that increases flexibility to a great extent, is equivalence between properties, obtained by the following definition:

$$solve(P'(X', Y')) :- equivalent(P', R'), solve(R'(X', Y')).$$

This rule defines two relations as equivalent if they have the same extension. For example, stating that predicate *friend* is equivalent to predicate *amico* (the latter is the translation into Italian of the former):

equivalent(friend', amico').
friend(ann, alice).
symmetric(equivalent').

we can easily see that it becomes possible to derive *amico(ann, alice)*. The meta-meta statement *symmetric(equivalent')* allows the translation to be applied in both ways. The concept of equivalence can be customized via other meta-rules.

Focusing the attention on the concept of inheritance, we may have the following:

$$solve(P'(X', Y')) :- hereditary(P', R'), solve(R'(X', Z')), solve(P'(Z', Y')).$$

meaning that property P' is hereditary with respect to a relation R' if whenever an element of the domain of R' has property P' then also all the other elements have the same property.

It is important to notice that in the present setting new properties of relations can be defined upon need and immediately employed, in combination with already existing ones, and meta-meta properties can be also expressed.

So, overall, we have proposed an extended Datalog including names, predications over names, and *solve* and *solve_not* rules.

6   Background: Datalog$^{\pm}$

Below we report from the aforementioned papers by Cali, Gottlob et al. the basic notions about Datalog$^{\pm}$ and its procedural semantics.

The core of Datalog$^{\pm}$ languages consists of rules designated as "existential rules" (note that existential rules are also referred to as "Tuple Generating Dependencies", in short TGD's), which introduce existential quantifiers in rule heads. An example of existential rule is given below (where, in plain Datalog's style, we adopt lowercase for constants and predicates, and uppercase for variable, where $\bar{X}$ is to be intended as a tuple of variables and comma stands for conjunction); this rule encodes that a person is the child of some other person.

$$person(X) \rightarrow \exists Y \, hasChild(Y, X), person(Y)$$

More generally, existential rules take the following form, where ψ is called the rule *Head* and ϕ the rule *Body*, and they are conjunctions of atoms including constants and variables:

$$\forall \bar{X} \forall \bar{Y} \phi(\bar{X}, \bar{Y}) \rightarrow \exists \bar{Z} \psi(\bar{X}, \bar{Z})$$

The procedural semantics of a set of existential rules, (hereafter 'program') Π over a database D, denoted $\Pi(D)$ (composed of tuples, that we call 'facts' as in Prolog/Datalog), is defined via the so-called 'chase' procedure [16]. In essence, the chase incrementally adds new atoms to D, where null values (fresh constants used as placeholders) are used for satisfying the existentially quantified variables, until the final result $\Pi(D)$ satisfies all the existential rules of Π. The chase procedure can be extended to accommodate negative constraints ("it is false that...") and stratified negation.

In general, however, $\Pi(D)$ is infinite. In fact, considering the above example, from $D = \{person(mary)\}$ the chase derives $hasChild(v_1, X)$ and $person(v_1)$ where v_1 is a null value. However, the process can continue deriving $hasChild(v_2, v_1)$ and $person(v_2)$, and so on indefinitely. The notion of *Wardedness* and Warded Datalog$^{\pm}$, that hereafter we will take for granted, prevents such infinite derivations. Wardedness is satisfied in a program Π if for each composing rule (TGD) σ the following conditions hold: (i) all body-variables that can be unified with a null value when the chase algorithm is applied, where such null value is also propagated to the head of the rule (so-called "dangerous" variables) must coexist in a single body-atom α, called the 'ward', and (ii) the ward can share only "harmless" variables with the rest of the body, i.e., variables that are unified only with database constants during the construction of the chase.

We now provide a precise definition of chase, observing that by 'chase' the authors of the aforementioned paper refer both to the chase procedure and to its output $\Pi(D)$. The TGD chase rule defined in [16] is reported below, given the following preliminary assumptions: (i) an infinite universe of data constants Δ, (ii) an infinite set of (labeled) nulls ΔN (where different constants represent different values –unique name assumption–, while instead different nulls may represent the same value), and (iii) an infinite set of variables. A lexicographic order is assumed over $\Delta \cup \Delta N$ with symbols in ΔN occurring after all symbols in Δ. Notation $\bar{X}$ stands for sequences of variables $X_1, \ldots, X_k$ with $k > 0$.

CHASE RULE. Consider a database (set of facts) D and a (warded) TGD σ of the form $\forall \bar{X} \forall \bar{Y} \phi(\bar{X}, \bar{Y}) \rightarrow \exists \bar{Z} \Psi(\bar{X}, \bar{Z})$. Then, σ is applicable to D if there exists a homomorphism h that maps the atoms of $\phi(\bar{X}, \bar{Y})$ to atoms of D. Let σ be applicable, and h_1 be a homomorphism that extends h as follows: for each X_i in $\bar{X}$, $h_1(X_i) = h(X_i)$; for each Z_j in $\bar{Z}$, $h_1(Z_j) = z_j$, where z_j is a "fresh" null, i.e., constant z_j does not occur either in Π or in D, and z_j lexicographically follows all other nulls already introduced. The application of σ adds to D the atom $h_1(\Psi(\bar{X}, \bar{Z}))$ if not already in D.

We mention here Vadalog [10,11,29,31], a recent evolution of Datalog$^{\pm}$. In fact, Vadalog core corresponds Warded Datalog$^{\pm}$ (cf. [29]). The language is then enhanced by adding additional features that are useful in real-world applications such as: data types, expressions, Skolem functions, mapping functions to access external data sources or computational resources. So, our proposal is applicable to Datalog$^{\pm}$ but also to Vadalog.

7 Enhancing Properties of Relations in Datalog$^{\pm}$ via Metalogic

In the above-mentioned work, Georg Gottlob proved that Datalog$^{\pm}$ is under some respect more powerful that OWL, as for instance in Datalog$^{\pm}$ it is possible to express a form of symmetry more general that in OWL: to state that two people have been married from a date to another date, it is possible to express symmetry over spouse names, while leaving the from-to dates unaltered. This result is actually a combination of Markus Krötzsch et al. statement [39] that this example cannot be expressed in certain description logics, combined with Georg's formulation, shown below, of how to express it in Datalog$^{\pm}$:

$$\forall u, v, x, y.married(u, v, x, y) \rightarrow married(v, u, x, y)$$

Since such a form is suitable for other relations, such as, e.g., colleague, schoolmate, etc., a metalevel representation of such properties is in order, like:

$$solve(P'(V', U', X', Y')) :- symmetric2(P'), solve(P'(U', V', X', Y')).$$
$$symmetric2(married').$$
$$symmetric2(colleague').$$
$$symmetric2(schoolmate').$$
$$\ldots$$

In [30], it is extensively discussed how Datalog$^{\pm}$ can express part of the OWL 2 direct semantics entailment regime for OWL 2 QL. The following rules represent a significant fragment of this representation:

$$Type(x, y), Restriction(y, z) \rightarrow \exists w\, Triple(x, z, w)$$
$$Type(x, y), SubClass(y, z) \rightarrow Type(x, z)$$
$$Triple(x, y, z), Inverse(y, w) \rightarrow Triple(z, w, x)$$
$$Triple(x, y, z), Restriction(w, y) \rightarrow Type(x, w).$$

So, the above rules show that Datalog$^\pm$ is powerful enough for ontological reasoning and, as seen above for extended symmetry, even better than OWL at certain tasks. We may notice that these rules are in fact metarules, reasoning over data which are assumed to be represented by triples, in rdf style. Below we show how via a metalogic approach this kind of rules can be expressed on data represented in (or transposed into by some kind of import from external OWL ontologies) Datalog facts. Notice that, from now on we will consider rules in notation *Head :− Body* (traditional Datalog style) and *Body → Head* (Datalog$^\pm$ style) as interchangeable; whenever not mentioned, variables that are not existentially quantified are assumed to be universally quantified; we assume that each rule is terminated by a '.'.

Specifically, the above rules can be expressed, by exploiting the *solve* predicate, as follows.

$\exists W' solve(Pz'(X', W'))$:− $restriction(Py', Pz'), solve(Py'(X'))$.
$solve(Pz'(X'))$:− $subclass(Py', Pz'), solve(Py'(X'))$.
$solve(Pw'(Z', X'))$:− $inverse(Py', Pw'), solve(Py'(X', Z'))$.
$solve(Pw'(X'))$:− $restriction(Py', Pw'), solve(Py'(X', Z'))$.

We might add for instance facts:

$inverse(parent', child')$.
$symmetric(inverse')$.
$restriction(sociable', friend')$.
$subclass(female', person')$.
$subclass(male', person')$.

So, we might derive that a person who is friend of someone is sociable, derive who is a child form who is parent of whom (and vice versa, as we have declared 'inverse' is a symmetric property) and that both males and females are persons. Indeed there is an extension to our previous syntax, as we have introduced an existential in the head of a 'solve' rule.

One may notice that *solve* and *solve_not* rules are not, strictly-speaking, Datalog rules, because they may have compound terms as arguments. However, the distinguished predicates are used just as "containers' of seemingly higher-order expressions, that can thus be formulated within first-order via naming. In the following section we illustrate the practical treatment of such rules in the extended chase procedure, that should clarify this matter. Also, one may wonder whether the semantics of the OWL constructs on relations are fully captured in the proposed approach. About this point, notice that the metalevel definitions are user-defined, so this issue must be considered specifically for each set of metarules one wants to adopt. For the properties introduced in Sect. 5, there is a complete adherence to OWL semantics. The properties introduced in this section instead go beyond OWL.

8   Meta-chase

From previously-discussed examples, we can see that in our extended Datalog we have: (i) object-level atoms, where no metalevel constants and metavariables occur; (ii) metalevel atoms, where metalevel constants (names of object-level constants or of predicates) occur; (iii) metaevaluation atoms, where distinguished predicates *solve* or *solve_not* occur.

In order to extend the chase to such extended programs, we have to suitably extend the signature. We consider:

- a finite set of predicate symbols $\varXi$ and their names $\varXi'$, in the sense that for every predicate symbol $p \in \varXi$ there exists a metalevel constant $p' \in \varXi'$; we state the naming relation, i.e., $\uparrow p = p'$ and $\downarrow p' = p$;
- an infinite universe of data constants $\varDelta$ and their names $\varDelta'$, in the sense that for every (object-level) constant $c \in \varDelta$ there exists a metalevel constant $c' \in \varDelta'$; we state the naming relation, i.e., $\uparrow c = c'$ and $\downarrow c' = c$, different constants are assumed to represent different values (unique name assumption);
- an infinite set of (labeled) nulls $\varDelta N$ and their names $\varDelta N'$, in the sense that for every null value $v \in \varDelta N$ there exists a constant $v' \in \varDelta N'$; we state the naming relation, i.e., $\uparrow v = v'$ and $\downarrow v' = v$; different nulls may represent the same value; so, we now have object-level and metalevel nulls;
- an infinite set of (object-level) variables with name starting with an uppercase letter, say, e.g., X;
- an infinite set of metavariables with name starting with an uppercase letter and syntactic form distinct from object-level variables, say, e.g., X'.

A lexicographic order is assumed over $\varXi \cup \varXi' \cup \varDelta \cup \varDelta' \cup \varDelta N \cup \varDelta N'$; precisely, we have $\uparrow p$ (respectively, $\uparrow c$ and $\uparrow v$) for $p \in \varXi$ (respectively, $c \in \varDelta'$ and $v \in \varDelta N'$) occurring immediately after p (respectively, c and v). Notation $\bar{X}$ stands for sequences of variables and/or metavariables. Wardedness of existential rules is given for granted.

At first, we consider Datalog$^{\pm}$ programs enriched with metavariables and metaconstants, and with *solve* rules. We will discuss *solve_not* rules later. For the sake of simplicity we assume the head of rules to be an atom. In order to exploit *solve* rules, the given database (that, we assume, can involve metalevel facts but not *solve* facts) must be subjected to a pre-processing stage which ensures that the given database becomes a potentially acceptable set of atoms.

Definition 3 (Database Pre-Processing). *Let D be a database (set of facts). For every object-level fact A in D, the pre-processing stage adds to D the new fact $solve(\uparrow A)$.*

Definition 4 (Meta-CHASE RULE). *Consider a pre-processed database D, and a (warded) TGD σ of the form $\forall \bar{X} \forall \bar{Y} \phi(\bar{X}, \bar{Y}) \rightarrow \exists \bar{Z} \varPsi(\bar{X}, \bar{Z})$. Then, σ is applicable to D if there exists a homomorphism h that maps the atoms of the body $\phi(\bar{X}, \bar{Y})$ to atoms of D. Let σ be applicable, and h_1 be a homomorphism that extends h as follows:[1]*

- *for each X_i in $\bar{X}$, $h_1(X_i) = h(X_i)$;*

---

[1] Recall that, a "fresh" null is a constant that does not occur either in $\varPi$ or in D.

- *for each Z_j in $\bar{Z}$ which is an object-level variable, $h_1(Z_j) = z_j$, where z_j is a "fresh" null and z_j lexicographically follows all other object-level and metalevel nulls already introduced;*
- *for each Z_j in $\bar{Z}$ which is a metavariable, $h_1(Z_j) = z'_j$, where z'_j is a "fresh" null and z'_j lexicographically follows all other object-level and metalevel nulls already introduced.*

The application of σ adds to D the atom $A = h_1(\Psi(\bar{X}, \bar{Z}))$ if not already in D, and: (i) if A is an object-level atom, it adds also the atom $solve(\uparrow A)$; (ii) if $A = solve(\uparrow B)$, it adds also the atom B.

Let assume that the initial database has been preprocessed as in Definition 3, which produces a potentially acceptable set of atoms. Then we have:

Theorem 1. *At each stage of the chase, the database D is an acceptable set of atoms.*

This follows immediately from the definition of the Meta-Chase rule, which for every object-level atom adds the *solve* counterpart and for every metaevaluation atom adds the object-level counterpart of its argument.

Managing *solve_not* rules may seem trivial, as it would require to modify the Meta-chase rule so that an object-level atom A is added to D only if *solve_not*($\uparrow A$) does not belong to D. Only, since *solve_not*($\uparrow A$) must be derived, it might occur in D after A, and when A has been used in subsequent derivations already. To cope with this problem, one might limit the use of *solve_not* to *stratified* programs, extending to *solve_not* the concepts of stratification already developed for negation-as-failure [2]. This would guarantee that *solve_not*($\uparrow A$) would always be derived (if derivable) before A. For lack of space, we cannot discuss *solve_not* rules stratification here, so we defer this aspect to a future paper.

Another simpler but fairly effective way is to state that *solve_not* rules have in their bodies program facts only. Thus, a further pre-processing stage would compute all the *solve_not* conclusions before starting the chase. In this case, the last three lines of Definition 4 would become:

The application of σ adds to D the atom $A = h_1(\Psi(\bar{X}, \bar{Z}))$ if neither A itself not *solve_not*($\uparrow A$) are already in D, and: (i) if A is an object-level atom, it adds also the atom $solve(\uparrow A)$; (ii) if $A = solve(\uparrow B)$, it adds also the atom B.

9   Related Work and Conclusions

Related work exists about ontologies and Answer Set Programming (see [15] and the references therein). DLVHEX system [28] is a logic-programming reasoner for computing the models of so-called HEX-programs. In this approach ASP programs can import rdf triples from external ontologies and the basic ASP language is extended to define higher-order logic programs. Since, however, the semantics of higher-order rules is provided by eliminating the distinction between predicate and constant symbols, this rule may correspond to a number of weird instances (where, e.g., a constant symbol is in predicate position) and possibly, give rise to a combinatorial explosion of answer sets.

Our approach is not based upon higher-order rules, rather on names and metalevel rules. It has been introduced [25] for possible integration in every logic-based knowledge representation language, and as a proof of concept it has already been applied to ASP (see the mentioned reference). It adds a much higher practical expressive power, without impact on the complexity, as it is easy to believe given the minor modification to the chase rule that have been necessary. The fact however that such modifications were required demonstrates that the additions are not just syntactic sugar. A theoretical analysis of the extended language is deferred to future work. Issues to be considered are, e.g., whether the theoretical properties of Wardedness are impacted by the extensions, and whether or not they are applicable to other versions of the Datalog$^{\pm}$ languages.

References

1. Antoniou, G., Harmelen, F.: Web ontology language: OWL. In: Staab, S., Studer, R. (eds.) Handbook on Ontologies. IHIS, pp. 91–110. Springer, Heidelberg (2009). https://doi.org/10.1007/978-3-540-92673-3_4
2. Apt, K.R., Bol, R.N.: Logic programming and negation: a survey. J. Log. Program. **19**(20), 9–71 (1994)
3. Artale, A., Calvanese, D., Kontchakov, R., Zakharyaschev, M.: The DL-Lite family and relations. J. Artif. Intell. Res. **36**, 1–69 (2009)
4. Baader, F., Calvanese, D., McGuinness, D.L., Nardi, D., Patel-Schneider, P.F.: The Description Logic Handbook: Theory, Implementation, and Applications. Cambridge University Press, Cambridge (2003)
5. Barklund, J.: What is a meta-variable in Prolog? In: Meta-Programming in Logic Programming, pp. 383–98. The MIT Press (1989)
6. Barklund, J., Costantini, S., Dell'Acqua, P., Lanzarone, G.A.: Semantical properties of encodings in logic programming. In: Proceedings of 1995 International Symposium on Logic Programming, pp. 288–302. MIT Press (1995)
7. Barklund, J., Costantini, S., Dell'Acqua, P., Lanzarone, G.A.: Reflection principles in computational logic. J. Log. Comput. **10**(6), 743–786 (2000)
8. Barklund, J., Dell'Acqua, P., Costantini, S., Lanzarone, G.A.: SLD-resolution with reflection. In: Bruynooghe, M. (ed.) Proceedings of the 1994 International Symposium on Logic Programming. MIT Press (1994)
9. Barklund, J., Dell'Acqua, P., Costantini, S., Lanzarone, G.A.: Semantical properties of SLD-resolution with reflection. In: Sterling, L. (ed.) Proceedings of Logic Programming, ICLP 1995. MIT Press (1995)
10. Bellomarini, L., Gottlob, G., Pieris, A., Sallinger, E.: Swift logic for big data and knowledge graphs. In: Sierra, C. (ed.) Proc. of IJCAI 2017, pp. 2–10. ijcai.org (2017)
11. Bellomarini, L., Sallinger, E., Gottlob, G.: The Vadalog system: datalog-based reasoning for knowledge graphs. PVLDB **11**(9), 975–987 (2018)
12. Bonatti, P.A.: Model theoretic semantics for Demo. In: Pettorossi, A. (ed.) META 1992. LNCS, vol. 649, pp. 220–234. Springer, Heidelberg (1992). https://doi.org/10.1007/3-540-56282-6_15

13. Bordini, R.H., et al.: A survey of programming languages and platforms for multi-agent systems. Informatica (Slovenia) **30**(1), 33–44 (2006)
14. Bowen, K.A., Kowalski, R.A.: Amalgamating language and metalanguage in logic programming. In: Logic Programming, pp. 153–172. Academic Press (1982)
15. Brewka, G., Eiter, T., Truszczynski, M.: Answer set programming: an introduction to the special issue. AI Mag. **37**(3), 5–6 (2016)
16. Calì, A., Gottlob, G., Kifer, M.: Taming the infinite chase: query answering under expressive relational constraints. J. Artif. Intell. Res. **48**, 115–174 (2013)
17. Calì, A., Gottlob, G., Lukasiewicz, T.: A general Datalog-based framework for tractable query answering over ontologies. J. Web Semant. **14**, 57–83 (2012)
18. Calì, A., Gottlob, G., Lukasiewicz, T., Pieris, A.: Datalog+/-: a family of languages for ontology querying. In: de Moor, O., Gottlob, G., Furche, T., Sellers, A. (eds.) Datalog 2.0 2010. LNCS, vol. 6702, pp. 351–368. Springer, Heidelberg (2011). https://doi.org/10.1007/978-3-642-24206-9_20
19. Calvanese, D., De Giacomo, G., Lembo, D., Lenzerini, M., Rosati, R.: DL-Lite: tractable description logics for ontologies. In: Veloso, M.M., Kambhampati, S. (eds.) Proceedings of AAAI 2005, pp. 602–607. AAAI Press/The MIT Press (2005)
20. Carlucci Aiello, L., Levi, G.: The uses of metaknowledge in AI systems. In: Meta-Level Architectures and Reflection, pp. 243–254. North-Holland (1988)
21. Chen, W., Kifer, M., Warren, D.S.: HILOG: a foundation for higher-order logic programming. J. Log. Program. **15**(3), 187–230 (1993)
22. Costantini, S.: Semantics of a metalogic programming language. Int. J. Found. Comput. Sci. **1**, 233–247 (1990)
23. Costantini, S.: Meta-reasoning: a survey. In: Kakas, A.C., Sadri, F. (eds.) Computational Logic: Logic Programming and Beyond. LNCS, vol. 2408, pp. 253–288. Springer, Heidelberg (2002). https://doi.org/10.1007/3-540-45632-5_11
24. Costantini, S., Dell'Acqua, P., Lanzarone, G.A.: Extending Horn clause theories by reflection principles. In: MacNish, C., Pearce, D., Pereira, L.M. (eds.) JELIA 1994. LNCS, vol. 838, pp. 400–413. Springer, Heidelberg (1994). https://doi.org/10.1007/BFb0021987
25. Costantini, S., Formisano, A.: Augmenting knowledge representation and reasoning languages with customizable metalogic features. In: Proceedings of CILC 2019. CEUR Workshop Proceedings, vol. 2396, pp. 14–29. CEUR-WS.org (2019)
26. Costantini, S., Lanzarone, G.A.: A metalogic programming approach: language, semantics and applications. J. Exp. Theoret. Artif. Intell. **6**(3), 239–287 (1994)
27. Dix, J.: A classification theory of semantics of normal logic programs: I. Strong properties. Fundamenta Informaticae **22**(3), 227–255 (1995)
28. Eiter, T., et al.: The DLVHEX system. KI **32**(2–3), 187–189 (2018)
29. Gottlob, G., Manna, M., Pieris, A.: Polynomial rewritings for linear existential rules. In: Yang, Q., Wooldridge, M.J. (eds.) Proceedings of IJCAI 2015, pp. 2992–2998. AAAI Press (2015)
30. Gottlob, G., Pieris, A.: Beyond SPARQL under OWL 2 QL entailment regime: rules to the rescue. In: Yang, Q., Wooldridge, M.J. (eds.) Proceedings of IJCAI 2015, pp. 2999–3007. AAAI Press (2015)
31. Gottlob, G., Pieris, A., Sallinger, E.: Vadalog: recent advances and applications. In: Calimeri, F., Leone, N., Manna, M. (eds.) JELIA 2019. LNCS, vol. 11468, pp. 21–37. Springer, Cham (2019). https://doi.org/10.1007/978-3-030-19570-0_2
32. Grosof, B.N., Kifer, M., Fodor, P.: Rulelog: highly expressive semantic rules with scalable deep reasoning. In: Proceedings of the Doctoral Consortium, Challenge, Industry Track, Tutorials and Posters @ RuleML+RR 2017 hosted by RuleML+RR 2017. CEUR Workshop Proceedings, vol. 1875. CEUR-WS.org (2017)

33. Harmelen, F.: Definable naming relations in meta-level systems. In: Pettorossi, A. (ed.) META 1992. LNCS, vol. 649, pp. 89–104. Springer, Heidelberg (1992). https://doi.org/10.1007/3-540-56282-6_6

34. van Harmelen, F., et al.: Knowledge-level reflection. In: Enhancing the Knowledge Engineering Process - Contributions from ESPRIT, pp. 175–204. Elsevier Science (1992)

35. Hill, P.M., Lloyd, J.W.: Analysis of metaprograms. In: Meta-Programming in Logic Programming, pp. 23–51. The MIT Press (1988)

36. Hill, P.M., Lloyd, J.W.: The Gödel Programming Language. The MIT Press, Cambridge (1994)

37. Horrocks, I., Patel-Schneider, P.F., van Harmelen, F.: From SHIQ and RDF to OWL: the making of a web ontology language. J. Web Sem. 1(1), 7–26 (2003)

38. Konolige, K.: Reasoning by introspection. In: Meta-Level Architectures and Reflection, pp. 61–74. North-Holland (1988)

39. Krötzsch, M., Rudolph, S., Schmitt, P.H.: A closer look at the semantic relationship between datalog and description logics. Semant. Web 6(1), 63–79 (2015)

40. Lloyd, J.W.: Foundations of Logic Programming, 2nd edn. Springer, Berlin (1987). https://doi.org/10.1007/978-3-642-83189-8

Memory Management in Resource-Bounded Agents

Stefania Costantini and Valentina Pitoni[✉]

DISIM, University of L'Aquila, L'Aquila, Italy
stefania.costantini@univaq.it,
valentina.pitoni@graduate.univaq.it

Abstract. In intelligent agents, memory has a very important and decisive role for the choice of future behaviors, since it is progressively formed through the agent's interactions with the external environment. Previous work exists in the logic concerning the formalization of the reasoning on the formation of beliefs and the interaction with the background knowledge in non-omniscient agents. We extend this work by inserting the concept of time through a particular function that assigns a "timing" to beliefs and inferences.

1 Introduction

Memory in an agent system is a process of reasoning: in particular, it is the learning process of strengthening a concept. The interaction between the agent and the environment can play an important role in constructing its memory and may affect its future behaviour, the latter due to the proactive and deliberative capabilities of the agent themselves. In fact, through memory an agent is potentially able to recall and to learn from experiences so that its beliefs and its future course of action are grounded in these experiences. Most of the methods to design agent memorization mechanisms have been inspired by models of human memory [15,18] developed in cognitive science.

Atkinson and Shiffrin in [3] proposed a model of human memory which consists of three distinct memory stores, the sensory register where information are stored which are detected from senses, the short term memory (or working memory) where explicit beliefs are stored and the long term memory which stores the background knowledge; information passes from store to store in a linear way.

This model has been further enhanced by Gero and Liew in [14], and [10] for constructive memory. Memory construction occur whenever an agent uses past experience in the current environment in a situated manner. The exploitation of "memories" requires the interaction among this different memory components. Such correlation can be obtained in various ways, e.g., via neural networks, via mathematical models or via logical deduction.

In computational logic, [4] introduces DLEK (Dynamic Logic of Explicit beliefs and Knowledge) as a logical formalization of SOAR (State Operator And Result) Architecture [13], which is one of the most popular cognitive architecture.

© Springer Nature Switzerland AG 2019
M. Alviano et al. (Eds.): AI*IA 2019, LNAI 11946, pp. 46–58, 2019.
https://doi.org/10.1007/978-3-030-35166-3_4

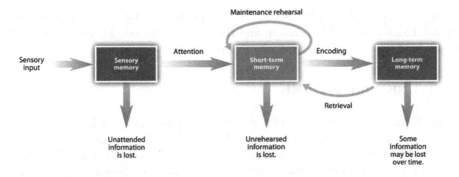

Fig. 1. Short-term memory and Long-term memory

The underlying idea is to represent reasoning about the formation of beliefs through perception and inference in non-omniscient resource-bounded agents. They consider perception, short-term memory (also called "working memory"), long-term memory (also called "background knowledge") and their interaction. DLEK is a logic that consists of a static part called LEK (Logic of Explicit beliefs and Knowledge), which is an epistemic logic, and a dynamic component, which extends the static one with "mental operations". Resource-boundedness in DLEK is modeled via the assumption that beliefs are kept in the short-term memory, while implications that allow reasoning to be performed are kept in the long-term memory. New beliefs can be formed in DLEK either from perception, or from previous beliefs in short-term memories and rules in the background knowledge. Inferences that add new beliefs are performed one step at a time via an interaction between short- and long-term memories in consequence of an explicit "mental operation" that will occur whenever an agent deems it necessary and can allot the needed time [1,11].

DLEK has however no notion of time, while agents' actual perceptions are inherently timed and so are many of the inferences drawn from such perceptions. So in [7] we have introduced explicit time instants and time intervals in formulas. This is relevant because agents' perceptions (that may become beliefs) are always inherently timed, and so are the conclusions that can be drawn from them. But to avoid problems with the management of the intervals and in order to not lose the logic of the formalization, in this paper we present an extension of LEK/DLEK to T-LEK/T-DLEK ("Timed LEK" and "Timed DLEK") obtained by introducing a special function which associates to each belief the arrival time and controls timed inferences. Through this function it is easier to keep the evolution of the surrounding world under control and the representation is more complete. The issue of time in agents has been coped with in several other works, (see, e.g., among many, [5,6,16,17]), where however the objective is that of dealing with time in communication and coordination among agents; thus, our attempt to deal with time in memory management is a novelty in the literature.

In the rest of the paper, Sects. 2 and 3 present syntax, semantics of the extended logic, the axiomatization, and the canonical model. In Sect. 4 we propose a brief discussion on complexity and conclude.

2   T-LEK and T-DLEK

As in [4], our logic consists of two different components: a static component, called T-LEK, which is mix between an Epistemic Logic and Metric Temporal Logic ([12]), and a dynamic component, called T-DLEK, which extend the static one with mental operation, which are vary important for "controlling" beliefs (adds new belief, update belief, etc).

2.1   Syntax

As it is customary in logic programming, we assume a signature specifying (countable) sets of *predicate, function,* and *constant* symbols. From constant and function symbols, compound terms are built as usual. The *Herbrand universe* is the collection of all such terms (which includes constant symbols). We assume that the integer numbers and the symbol ∞ are included among the constant symbols and that the arithmetic operators are included among the function symbols. Consequently, arithmetic expressions are terms of the signature. Atoms have the form $pred(\tau_1, \ldots, \tau_n)$ where *pred* is a predicate symbol, $n \geq 0$ is its arity and $\tau_1, \ldots, \tau_n$ are terms. We denote by *Atm* the countable set of atoms of the signature (i.e., the *Herbrand base*).

In our scenario we fix $Atm = \{p(t_1, t_2), q(t_3, t_4), \ldots, h(t_i, t_j)\}$ where $t_i \leqslant t_j$ and p, q, h are predicates, that can be equal or not. Moreover $p(t_1, t_2)$ stands for "*p is true from the time instant t_1 to t_2*" with $t_1, t_2 \in \mathbb{N}$ (*Temporal Representation* of the external world); as a special case we can have $p(t_1, t_1)$ which stands for "*p is true in the time instant t_1*". Obviously we can have predicates with more terms than only two but in that case we fix that the first two must be those that identify the time duration of the belief (i.e. $open(1, 3, door)$ which means "the agent knows that the door is open from time one to time 3"). Instead in the previous work [7] we considered atoms of the form p_I with $I = [t_1, t_2]$, which are the conjunction $p_{t_1} \wedge p_{t_1+1} \wedge \cdots \wedge p_{t_2}$ and also p_t stands for p_{I_t} with $I_t = [t, t]$; we have decided to change approach because p_I is too detached from propositional logic. Let also *Agt* be a finite set of agents.

Below is the definition of the formulas of the language $\mathcal{L}_{T\text{-}LEK}$, with a slight abuse, in this grammar we use I as terminal symbol standing for time intervals and $i \in Agt$:

$$\varphi, \psi \;\; := \;\; p(t_1, t_2) \mid \neg \varphi \mid \Box_I \varphi \mid B_i \varphi \mid K_i \varphi \mid \varphi \wedge \psi \mid \varphi \rightarrow \psi$$

Other Boolean connectives $\top, \bot, \leftrightarrow$ are defined from $\neg$ and $\wedge$ as usual. In the formula $\Box_I \varPhi$ the MTL Interval "always" operator is applied to a formula; I is a "time-interval" which is a closed finite interval $[t, l]$ or an infinite interval $[t, \infty)$

(considered open on the upper bound), for any expressions/values t, l such that $0 \leq t \leq l$ and $\square_{[0,\infty)}$ will sometimes be written simply as $\square$. The operator B_i identifies belief in the working memory and the operator K_i to denote knowledge and identifies what rules are present in the background knowledge.

Terms/atoms/formulas as defined so far are *ground*, namely there are no variables occurring therein. We introduce variables and use them in formulas in a restricted manner, as usual for example in answer set programming [9]. Variables can occur in formulas in any place constants can occur and are intended as place holders for elements of the Herbrand universe. More specifically, a ground *instance* of a term/atom/formula involving variables is obtained by uniformly substituting ground terms to all variables (*grounding* step), with the restriction that any variable occurring in an arithmetic expression (i.e., specifying a time instant) can be replaced by a (ground) arithmetic expressions only. Consequently, a non-ground term/atom/formula represents the possibly infinite set of its ground instances, namely, its *grounding*. Notice that the rational of considering ground formulas is that they represent perceptions (either new or already recorded in agent's memory) coming in general from the external world(we say "in general" as, in fact, in some of the aforementioned agent-oriented frameworks perceptions can also result from *internal events*, i.e., from an agent's observations of its own internal activities). As it is customary in logic programming, variable symbols are indicated with an initial uppercase letter whereas constants/functions/predicates symbols are indicated with an initial lowercase letter.

The language $\mathcal{L}_{T\text{-}DLEK}$ of Temporalized DLEK (T-DLEK) is obtained by augmenting $\mathcal{L}_{T\text{-}LEK}$ with the expression $[(G_I : \alpha)_{H_I}]\psi$, where α denotes a *mental operation*, ψ is a ground formula, G_I, H_I range over 2^{Agt} and $G_I \subseteq H_I$; the I is used to define that in a given interval we have a given set of agents and I depends on ψ. Moreover $[(G_I : \alpha)_{H_I}]\psi$ stands for "ψ holds after the mental operation α is performed by all the agent in G_I, and The mental operations that we consider are essentially the the agents in H_I have common knowledge abot this fact". Our mental operation are the following:

- $+\varphi$: learning perceived belief; where φ is a ground formula of the form $p(t_1, t_2)$ or $\neg p(t_1, t_2)$: the mental operation that serves to form a new belief from a perception φ. A perception may become a belief whenever an agent becomes "aware" of the perception and takes it into explicit consideration. Notice that φ may be a negated atom.
- $\cap(\varphi, \psi)$: beliefs conjunction; believing both φ and ψ, an agent starts believing their conjunction.
- $\vdash(\varphi, \psi)$: belief inference; where ψ is a ground atom, say $p(t_1, t_2)$: an agent, believing that φ is true and having in its long-term memory that φ implies ψ (in some suitable time interval including $[t_1, t_2]$), starts believing that $p(t_1, t_2)$ is true.
- $\dashv(\varphi, \psi)$: belief revision; where φ and ψ are ground atoms, say $p(t_1, t_2)$ and $q(t_3, t_4)$ respectively: an agent, believing $p(t_1, t_2)$ and having in the long-term memory that $p(t_1, t_2)$ implies $\neg q(t_3, t_4)$, removes the timed belief $q(t_3, t_4)$ if

the intervals match. Notice that, should q be believed in a wider interval I such that $[t_1, t_2] \subseteq I$, the belief $q(.,.)$ is removed concerning intervals $[t_1, t_2]$ and $[t_3, t_4]$, but it is left for the remaining sub-intervals (so, its is "restructured").

Example 1: We propose a small example to illustrate the form and the role of rules in the working memory and in the long-term memory. If at time $t = 2$ it is starting raining, in the working memory of agent i there will be the following belief: $B_i(raining(2, 2))$. And if we have in the background knowledge $K_i(rain(t_1, t_2) \rightarrow take(t_1, t_2, \text{umbrella}))$ and $2 \in [t_1, t_2]$ than agent i can infer $B_i(take(2, 2, \text{umbrella}))$, which is a new belief stored in the working memory.

And if we have also $K_i(rain(t_1, t_2) \land take(t_1, t_2, \text{umbrella}) \rightarrow go(t_1 + 1, \infty, \text{shops}))$ than the agent can infer $B_i(go(3, \infty, \text{shops}))$ which means that after getting the umbrella agent i can go around the shops.

Example 2: An example of a non-ground T-LEK formula is:

$$K_i(\square_{[t_1, t_2]}(enrollment(T, T)) \rightarrow \square_{[t_1, t_2]}\square_{[T, T+14]} send\_payment(T_1, T_1))$$

where we suppose that an agent knows that it is possible to enroll in the university in the period $[t_1, t_2]$ and that, after the enrollment, the payment must be sent within fourteen days (still staying within the interval $[t_1, t_2]$). Since, by the restrictions on formulas stated earlier, it must be the case that $T_1 \in [T, T + 14]$ and both $T, T + 14$ must be in $[t_1, t_2]$, only a finite set of ground instances of this formula can be formed by substituting natural numbers to the variables T, T_1 (specifically, the maximum number of ground instances is $t_2 - t_1 - 14 + 1$ assuming to pay on the last day t_2). In case one would consider the more general formula:

$$K_i(\square_{[t_1, t_2]}(enrollment(T, T, X)) \rightarrow \square_{[t_1, t_2]}\square_{[T, T+14]} send\_payment(T_1, T_1, X))$$

where X represents a student of that university, i.e., $student(.,., X)$ holds for some ground instance of X, then the set of ground instances would grow, as a different instance should be generated for each student (i.e., for each ground term replacing X). In practice, however, ground instances need not to be formed a priori, but rather they can be generated upon need when applying a rule; in the example, just one ground instance should be generated when some student intends to enroll in that university at a certain time $T = \hat{t}$.

2.2   Semantics

Semantics of DLEK and T-DLEK are both based on a set W of worlds. In both DLEK and T-DLEK we have the valuation function: $V : W \rightarrow 2^{Atm}$. Also we define the "time" function T that associates to each formula the time interval in which this formula is true and operates as follows:

- $T(p(t_1, t_2)) = [t_1, t_2]$, which stands for "$p$ is true in the time interval $[t_1, t_2]$" where $t_1, t_2 \in \mathbb{N}$; as a special case we have $T(p(t_1, t_1)) = t_1$, which stands for "p is true in the time instant t_1" where $t_1 \in \mathbb{N}$ (time instant);

- $T(\neg p(t_1, t_2)) = T(p(t_1, t_2))$, which stands for *"p is not true in the time inter-val $[t_1, t_2]$"* where $t_1, t_2 \in \mathbb{N}$;
- $T(\varphi \text{ op } \psi) = T(\varphi) \uplus T(\psi)$ with $op \in \{\vee, \wedge, \rightarrow\}$, which means the unique smallest interval including both $T(\varphi)$ and $T(\psi)$;
- $T(B_i \varphi) = T(\varphi)$;
- $T(K_i \varphi) = T(\varphi)$;
- $T(\square_I \varphi) = I$ where I is a time interval in $\mathbb{N}$;
- $T([(G_I : \alpha)_{H_I}]\varphi)$ there are different cases depends on which kind of mental operations we applied:
    1. $T((G_I : +\varphi)_{H_I}) = T(\varphi)$;
    2. $T((G_I : \cap(\varphi, \psi))_{H_I}) = T(\varphi) \uplus T(\psi)$;
    3. $T((G_I : \vdash(\varphi, \psi))_{H_I}) = T(\psi)$;
    4. $T((G_I : \dashv(\varphi, \psi)_{H_I}))$ returns the restored interval where ψ is true.

For a world w, let t_1 the minimum time instant of $T(p(t_1, t_1))$ where $p(t_1, t_1) \in V(w)$ and let t_2 be the supremum time instant (we can have $t_2 = \infty$) among the atoms in $V(w)$. Then, whenever useful, we denote w as w_I where $I = [t_1, t_2]$, which identifies the world in a given interval.

The notion of LEK/T-LEK model does not consider mental operations, discussed later, and is introduced by the following definition.

Definition 1. *A T-LEK model is a tuple $M = \langle W; N; \{R_i\}_{i \in Agt}; V; T \rangle$ where:*

- *W is the set of worlds;*
- *$V : W \rightarrow 2^{Atm}$ valuation function;*
- *T "time" function;*
- *$R_i \subseteq W \times W$ is the accessibility relation with $i \in Agt$, required to be an equivalence relation so as to model omniscience in the background knowledge s.t.*
  $R_i(w_I) = \{v_I \in W \mid w_I R v_I\}$ called epistemic state of the agent i in w_I, which indicates all the situations that the agent considers possible in the world w_I or, equivalently any situation the agent i can retrieve from long-term memory based on what it knows in world w_I;
- *$N : Agt \times W \rightarrow 2^{2^W}$ is a "neighbourhood" function, $\forall w \in W$, $N(i, w)$ defines, in terms of sets of worlds, what the agent i is allowed to explicitly believe in the world w_I; $\forall w_I, v_I \in W$, and $X \subseteq W$:*
    1. *if $X \in N(i, w_I)$, then $X \subseteq R_i(w_I)$: each element of the neighbourhood is a set composed of reachable worlds;*
    2. *if $w_I R_i v_I$, then $N(w_I) \subseteq N(v_I)$: if the world v_I is compliant with the epistemic state of world w_I, then the agent i in the world w_I should have a subset of beliefs of the world v_I.*

A preliminary definition before the Truth conditions:
let $M = \langle W; N; \{R_i\}_{i \in Agt}; V; T \rangle$ a T-LEK model. Given a formula φ, for every $w_I \in W$, we define

$$\| \varphi \|_{w_I}^M = \{v_I \in W \mid M, v_I \models \varphi\} \cap R_i(w_I).$$

Truth conditions for T-DLEK formulas are defined inductively as follows:

- $M, w_I \models p(t_1, t_2)$ iff $p(t_1, t_2) \in V(w_I)$ and $T(p(t_1, t_2)) \subseteq I$;
- $M, w_I \models \neg\varphi$ iff $M, w_I \not\models \varphi$ and $T(\neg\varphi) \subseteq I$;
- $M, w_I \models \varphi \land \psi$ iff $M, w_I \models \varphi$ and $M, w_I \models \psi$ with $T(\varphi), T(\psi) \subseteq I$;
- $M, w_I \models \varphi \lor \psi$ iff $M, w_I \models \varphi$ or $M, w_I \models \psi$ with $T(\varphi), T(\psi) \subseteq I$;
- $M, w_I \models \varphi \to \psi$ iff $M, w_I \not\models \varphi$ or $M, w_I \models \psi$ with $T(\varphi), T(\psi) \subseteq I$;
- $M, w_I \models B_i\varphi$ iff $\| \varphi \|_{w_I}^M \in N(w_I)$ and $T(\varphi) \subseteq I$;
- $M, w_I \models K_i\varphi$ iff for all $v_I \in R_i(w_I)$, it holds that $M, v_I \models \varphi$ and $T(\varphi) \subseteq I$;
- $M, w_I \models \Box_J\varphi$ iff $T(\varphi) \subseteq J \subseteq I$ and for all $v_I \in R_i(w_I)$, it holds that $M, v_I \models \varphi$;

In particular, considering formulas of the forms $B_i \varphi$ and $K_i \varphi$, we observe that $M, w_I \models B_i \varphi$ if the set $\| \varphi \|_{w_I}^M$ of worlds reachable from w_I which entail φ in the very same model M belongs to the *neighbourhood* $N(i, w_I)$ of w_I. Hence, knowledge pertains to formulas entailed in model M in every reachable world, while beliefs pertain to formulas entailed only in some set of them, where this set must however belong to the neighbourhood and so it must be composed of reachable worlds. Thus, an agent is seen as omniscient with respect to knowledge, but not with respect to beliefs.

Concerning a mental operation α performed by any agent i, we have: $M, w_I \models [(G_J : \alpha)_{H_J}]\varphi$ iff $M^{(G_J:\alpha)_{H_J}}, w_I \models \varphi$, $T((G_J : \alpha)_{H_J}) \subseteq I$, $J = T((G_J : \alpha)_{H_J})$ where $M^{(G_J:\alpha)_{H_J}} = \langle W; N^{(G_J:\alpha)_{H_J}}(i, w_I); \{R_i^{(G_J:\alpha)_{H_J}}\}_{i \in Agt};$ $V; T \rangle$. Here $R_i^{(G_J:\alpha)_{H_J}}(w_I) = \{v_I \in W \text{ s.t. } w_I R_i v_I \text{ and } J \subseteq I\}$ and α represents a mental operation affecting the sets of beliefs. In particular, such operation can add new beliefs by direct perception, by means of one inference step, or as a conjunction of previous beliefs. When introducing new beliefs, the neighbourhood must be extended accordingly, as seen below; in particular, the new neighbourhood:

- $N^{(G_J:\alpha)_{H_J}}(i, w_I) = \{X \in N^\alpha(i, w_I) \text{ if } i \in G_J \text{ and } J \subseteq I\}$: if agent i is in G_J then he has to change his neighbourhood accordingly to α;
- $N^{(G_J:\alpha)_{H_J}}(i, w_I) = \{X \in N(i, w_I) \text{ if } i \in H_J \backslash G_J \text{ and } J \subseteq I\}$: if agent i is in $H_J \backslash G_J$ then he does not have to change his neighbourhood because he does not perform the mental operation α but he knows that other agents in G_J have performed a operation;
- $N^{(G_J:\alpha)_{H_J}}(i, w_I) = \{X \in N(i, w_I) \text{ if } i \notin H \text{ and } J \subseteq I\}$: if agent i is not in H_J then he does not have to change his neighbourhood because he does not perform the mental operation α and also he do not know that other agents in G_J have performed a operation.

Where $N^\alpha(i, w_I)$ is defined for each of the mental operations as follows.

- Learning perceived belief:
  $N^{+\varphi}(i, w_I) = N(i, w_I) \cup \{ \| \varphi \|_{w_I}^M \}$ with $T(\varphi) \subseteq I$.
  The agent i adds to its beliefs perception φ (namely, an atom or the negation of an atom) perceived at a time in $T(\varphi)$; the neighbourhood is expanded to as to include the set composed of all the reachable worlds which entail φ in M.

- Beliefs conjunction:

$$N^{\cap(\psi,\chi)}(i,w_I) = \begin{cases} N(i,w_I) \cup \{ \, \| \, \psi \wedge \chi \, \|_{w_I}^M \, \} & \text{if } M,w_I \models B_i(\psi) \wedge B_i(\chi) \\ & \text{and } T(\cap(\psi,\chi)) \subseteq I \\ N(i,w_I) & \text{otherwise} \end{cases}$$

The agent i adds $\psi \wedge \chi$ as a belief if it has among its previous beliefs both ψ and χ, with I including all time instants referred to by them; otherwise the set of beliefs remain unchanged. The neighbourhood is expanded, if the operation succeeds, with those sets of reachable worlds where both formulas are entailed in M.

- Belief inference:

$$N^{\vdash(\psi,\chi)}(i,w_I) = \begin{cases} N(i,w_I) \cup \{ \, \| \, \chi \, \|_{w_I}^M \, \} & \text{if } M,w_I \models B_i(\psi) \wedge K_i(\psi \rightarrow \chi) \\ & \text{and } T(\vdash(\psi,\chi)) \subseteq I \\ N(w_I) & \text{otherwise} \end{cases}$$

The agent i adds the ground atom χ as a belief in its short-term memory if it has ψ among its previous beliefs and has in its background knowledge $K_i(\psi \rightarrow \chi)$, where all the time stamps occurring in ψ and in χ belong to I. Observe that, if I does not include all time instants involved in the formulas, the operation does not succeed and thus the set of beliefs remains unchanged. If the operation succeeds then the neighbourhood is modified by adding χ as a new belief.

- Beliefs revision (applied only on ground atoms).
  Given $Q = q(j,k)$ s.t. $T(q(j,k)) = T(q(t_1,t_2)) \cap T(q(t_3,t_4))$ with $j,k \in \mathbb{N}$ and $P = \{M,w_I \models B_i(p(t_1,t_2)) \wedge B_i(q(t_3,t_4)) \wedge K_i(p(t_1,t_2) \rightarrow \neg q(t_3,t_4))$ and $T(\dashv(p(t_1,t_2),q(t_3,t_4))) \subseteq I$ and there is no interval $J \supsetneq T(p(t_1,t_2))$ s.t. $B_i(q(t_5,t_6))$ where $T(q(t_5,t_6)) = J\}$:

$$N^{\dashv(p(t_1,t_2),q(t_3,t_4))}(i,w_I) = \begin{cases} N(i,w_I) \setminus \{ \, \| \, Q \, \|_{w_I}^M \, \} & \text{if P} \\ N(i,w_I) & \text{otherwise} \end{cases}$$

The agent i believes that $q(t_3,t_4)$ holds only in the interval $T(q(t_3,t_4))$ and has the perception of $p(t_1,t_2)$ where $T(p(t_1,t_2)) \subseteq T(q(t_3,t_4))$. Then, the agent replaces previous belief $q(t_3,t_4)$ in the short-term memory with $q(t_5,t_6)$ where $T(q(t_5,t_6)) = T(q(t_3,t_4)) \setminus T(q(t_1,t_2))$.
In general, the set $T(q(t_3,t_4)) \setminus T(q(t_1,t_2))$ is not necessarily an interval: being $T(p(t_1,t_2)) \subseteq T(q(t_3,t_4))$, with $T(p(t_1,t_2)) = [t_1,t_2]$, and $T(q(t_3,t_4)) = [t_3,t_4]$, we have that $T(q(t_3,t_4)) \setminus T(q(t_1,t_2)) = [t_3,t_1-1] \cup [t_2+1,t_4]$. Thus, $q(t_3,t_4)$ is replaced by $q(t_3,t_1-1)$ and $q(t_2+1,t_4)$ (and similarly if $t_4 = \infty$).

We write $\models_{T\text{-}DLEK}\varphi$ to denote that φ is true in all worlds w_I, of every TLEK model M.

Example 3: Let us consider the example of a person who is married or divorced, where only the perform can perform the *action* to be married or divorced. Let us assume that performed actions are recorded among an agent's perceptions, with the due time stamp. For reader's convenience, actions are denoted using a suffix "A". For simplicity, actions are supposed to always succeed and to produce an effect within one time instant. Let us consider the following rules (kept in long-term memory):

$$K_i(marry(T,T)A \rightarrow married(T+1,\infty))$$
$$K_i(divorce(T,T)A \rightarrow divorced(T+1,\infty)).$$

Let us now assume that a person married, e.g., at time 5; then, a belief will be formed of the person is married from time 6 on; however, if that person later divorced, e.g., at time 8, as a consequence result that s(he) is divorced from time 9. It can be seen that the application of previous rules in consequence of an agent's action of marring/divorcing determines some "belief restructuring" in the short-term memory of the agent. In absence of other rules concerning marriage, we intend that a person can not be simultaneously married and divorced. The related belief update is determined by the following rules:

$$K_i(married(T,\infty) \rightarrow \neg divorced(T,\infty))$$
$$K_i(divorced(T,\infty) \rightarrow \neg married(T,\infty))$$

With the above timing, the result of their application is that the belief formed at time 5, i.e., $married(6,\infty)$ will be replaced by $married(6,8)$ plus $divorced(9,\infty)$.

Property 1: *For the mental operations previously considered we have the following (where φ, ψ are as explained earlier):*

- $\models_{T\text{-}DLEK}[(G_J : +\varphi)_{H_J}]B_i\varphi$.
  Namely, as a consequence of the operation $+\varphi$ (thus after the perception of φ) the agent i adds φ to its beliefs.
- $\models_{T\text{-}DLEK}(B_i\varphi \wedge B_i\psi) \rightarrow [(G_J : \cap(\varphi,\psi))_{H_J}]B_i(\varphi \wedge \psi)$.
  Namely, if agent i has φ and ψ as beliefs, then as a consequence of the mental operation $\cap(\varphi,\psi)$ the agent starts believing $\varphi \wedge \psi$;
- $\models_{T\text{-}DLEK}(K_i(\varphi \rightarrow \psi) \wedge B_i\varphi) \rightarrow [(G_J : \vdash(\varphi,\psi))_{H_J}]B_i\psi$.
  Namely, if agent i has φ as one of its beliefs and has $K_i(\varphi \rightarrow \psi)$ in its background knowledge, then as a consequence of the mental operation $\vdash(\varphi,\psi)$ the agent starts believing ψ;
- $\models_{T\text{-}DLEK}(K(p(t_1,t_2) \rightarrow \neg q(t_3,t_4)) \wedge B_i(p(t_1,t_2)) \wedge B_i(q(t_3,t_4))) \rightarrow [(G_J : \dashv(p(t_1,t_2),q(t_3,t_4)))_{H_J}](B_i(q(t_5,t_6)))$
  where $T(q(t_5,t_6)) = T(q(t_3,t_4)) \setminus T(q(t_1,t_2))$.
  Namely, if agent i has $q(t_3,t_4)$ as one of its beliefs, q is not believed outside $T(q(t_3,t_4))$, the agent perceives $p(t_1,t_2)$ where $T(p(t_1,t_2)) \subseteq T(q(t_3,t_4))$, and has $K_i(p(t_1,t_2) \rightarrow \neg q(t_3,t_4))$ in its background knowledge.
  Then after the mental operation $\dashv(p(t_1,t_2),q(t_3,t_4))$ the agent starts believing $q(t_5,t_6)$ where $T(q(t_5,t_6)) = T(q(t_3,t_4)) \setminus T(q(t_1,t_2))$.

3   Axiomatization and Canonical Models

The logic T-DLEK can be axiomatized as an extension of the axiomatization of DLEK as follows. We implicitly assume modus ponens, standard axioms for classical propositional logic, and the necessitation rule. The T-LEK axioms are the following:

1. $K_i(\varphi) \wedge K_i(\varphi \rightarrow \psi) \rightarrow K_i(\psi)$;
2. $K_i(\varphi) \rightarrow \varphi$;
3. $K_i(\varphi) \rightarrow K_i K_i(\varphi)$;
4. $\neg K_I(\varphi) \rightarrow K_i \neg K_i(\varphi)$;
5. $B_i \varphi \wedge K_i(\varphi \leftrightarrow \psi) \rightarrow B_i \psi$;
6. $\Box_I \varphi \wedge \Box_I(\varphi \rightarrow \psi) \rightarrow \Box_I(\psi)$;
7. $\Box_I \varphi \rightarrow \Box_J \varphi$ with $J \subseteq I$;

The axiomatization of T-DLEK, involves these axioms:

1. $[(G_J : \alpha)_{H_J}]f \leftrightarrow f$ where $f = p$ or $f = p_t$ or $f = p_I$;
2. $[(G_J : \alpha)_{H_J}]\neg \varphi \leftrightarrow \neg[(G_J : \alpha)_{H_J}]\varphi$;
3. $[(G_J : \alpha)_{H_J}](\varphi \wedge \psi) \leftrightarrow [(G_J : \alpha)_{H_J}]\varphi \wedge [(G_J : \alpha)_{H_J}]\psi$;
4. $[(G_J : \alpha)_{H_J}]K_i(\varphi) \leftrightarrow K_i([(G_J : \alpha)_{H_J}](\varphi))$;
5. $[(G_J : +\varphi)_{H_J}]B_i \psi \leftrightarrow \left(B_i([(G_J : +\varphi)_{H_J}]\psi) \vee K_i([(G_J : +\varphi)_{H_J}]\psi \leftrightarrow \varphi)\right)$;
6. $[(G_J : \vdash(\varphi, \psi))_{H_J}]B_i \chi \leftrightarrow \left(B_i([(G_J : \vdash(\varphi, \psi))_{H_J}]\chi) \vee \left(B_i \varphi \wedge K_i(\varphi \rightarrow \psi) \wedge K_i([(G_J : \vdash(\varphi, \psi))_{H_J}]\chi \leftrightarrow \psi)\right)\right)$;
7. $[(G_J : \dashv(\varphi, \psi))_{H_J}]B_i \chi \leftrightarrow \left(B_i([(G_J : \dashv(\varphi, \psi))_{H_J}]\chi) \vee \left(B_i \varphi \wedge K_i(\varphi \rightarrow \neg\psi) \wedge K_i([(G_J : \dashv(\varphi, \psi))_{H_J}]\chi \leftrightarrow \neg\psi)\right)\right)$;
8. $[(G_J : \cap(\varphi, \psi))_{H_J}]B_i \chi \leftrightarrow \left(B_i([(G_J : \cap(\varphi, \psi))_{H_J}]\chi) \vee \left((B_i \varphi \wedge B_i \psi) \wedge K_i([(G_J : \cap(\varphi, \psi))_{H_J}]\chi \leftrightarrow (\varphi \wedge \psi))\right)\right)$;
9. $\dfrac{\psi \leftrightarrow \chi}{\varphi \leftrightarrow \varphi[\psi/\chi]}$ where $\varphi[\psi/\chi]$ denotes the formula obtained by replacing ψ with χ in φ.

We write T-DLEK $\vdash \varphi$ to indicate that φ is a theorem of TDLEK.

Both logics T-LEK and T-DLEK are sound for the class of T-LEK models. The proof that T-DLEK is strongly complete can be achieved by using a standard canonical model argument.

The *canonical T-LEK model* is a tuple $M_c = \langle W_c; N_c; \{R_{i,c}\}_{i \in Agt}; V_c; T_c \rangle$ where:

- W_c is the set of all maximal consistent subsets of $\mathcal{L}_{T\text{-}LEK}$; so, as in [4], canonical models are constructed from worlds which are sets of syntactically correct formulas of the underlying language and are in particular the largest consistent ones. As before, each $w \in W_c$ can be conveniently indicated as w_I.
- For every $w_I \in W$ and $w_I R_{i,c} v_I$ if and only if $K_i \varphi \in w_I$ iff $K_i \varphi \in v_I$; i.e., $R_{i,c}$ is an equivalence relation on knowledge; as before, we define $R_{i,c}(w_I) = \{v_I \in W \mid w_I R_{c_i} v_I\}$. Thus, we cope with our extension from knowledge of formulas to knowledge of formulas.

– Analogously to [4], for $w_I \in W$, $\Phi \in \mathcal{L}_{T\text{-}LEK}$ we define $A_\Phi(w_I) = \{v_I \in R_{i,c}(w_I) \mid \Phi \in v_I\}$. Then, we put $N_c(w_I) = \{A_\Phi(w_I) \mid B_i\Phi \in w_I\}$.
– V_c is a valuation function defined as before.
– T_c is a "time" function defined as before.

As stated in Lemma 2 of [4], there are the following immediate consequences of the above definition: if $w_I \in W_c$ and $i \in Agt$, then

– for $\Phi \in \mathcal{L}_{T\text{-}LEK}$, it holds that $K_i\Phi \in w_I$ if and only if $\forall v_I \in W$ such that $w_I R_{i,c} v_I$ we have $\Phi \in v_I$;
– for $\Phi \in \mathcal{L}_{T\text{-}LEK}$, if $B_i\Phi \in w_I$ and $w_I R_{i,c} v_I$ then $B_i\Phi \in v_I$.

Thus, while $R_{i,c}$-related worlds have the same knowledge and N_c-related worlds have the same beliefs, as stated in Lemma 3 of [4] there can be $R_{i,c}$-related worlds with different beliefs. The above properties can be used analogously to what is done in [4] to prove that, by construction, the following results hold:

Lemma 1. *For all $w_I \in W_c$ and $B_i\Phi, B_i\Psi \in \mathcal{L}_{T\text{-}LEK}$, if $B_i\Phi \in w_I$ but $B_i\Psi \notin w_I$, it follows that there exists $v_I \in R_{i,c}(w_I)$ such that $\Phi \in v_I \leftrightarrow \Psi \notin v_I$.*

Lemma 2. *For all $\Phi \in \mathcal{L}_{T\text{-}LEK}$ and $w_I \in W_c$ it holds that $\Phi \in w_I$ if and only if $M_c, w_I \vDash \Phi$.*

Lemma 3. *For all $\Phi \in \mathcal{L}_{T\text{-}DLEK}$ then there exists $\tilde{\Phi} \in \mathcal{L}_{T\text{-}LEK}$ such that $T\text{-}DLEK \vdash \Phi \leftrightarrow \tilde{\Phi}$.*

Under the assumption that the interval I is finite, the previous lemmas allow us to prove the following theorems.

Theorem 1. *T-LEK is strongly complete for the class of T-LEK models.*

Theorem 2. *T-DLEK is strongly complete for the class of T-LEK models.*

With the new formalization of time intervals proposed in this paper, the proof of the previous Theorem immediately follows from the proof proposed in [4].

4   Conclusion

In this work we extended an existing approach to the logical modeling of short-term and long-term memories in Intelligent Resource-Bounded Agents by introducing the T function, which manages the interval when an atom is true. Through this function we are also able to assign a "timing" to the epistemic operators B and K. Moreover we add the always operator $\square_I$ of the Metric Temporal Logic to increase the expressiveness of our logic. We considered not just adding new beliefs, rather we introduced a new mental operation not provided in DLEK, to allow for removing/restructuring existing beliefs. The resulting T-DLEK logic shares similarities in the underlying principles with hybrid logics (cf., e.g., [2]) and with temporal epistemic logic (cf., e.g., [8]); as concerns the differences, the former has time instants but no time intervals, and the latter has neither time instants nor time intervals.

With regard to complexity for the mono agent case for LEK it has been proved that the satisfiability problem is decidable and it has been proved to be in NP-complete, instead for DLEK it has been conjectured to be PSPACE. It is easy to believe that our extensions cannot spoil decidability because the T function do not interfere. Inference steps to derive new beliefs are analogous to D-LEK: just one modal rule at a time is used and a sharp separation is postulated between the working memory, where inference is performed, and the long-term memory.

Future developments could be the study of how to encode information from the working memory to the long term memory under certain conditions how it is illustrated in Fig. 1.

References

1. Alechina, N., Logan, B., Whitsey, M.: A complete and decidable logic for resource-bounded agents. In: 3rd International Joint Conference on Autonomous Agents and Multiagent Systems (AAMAS 2004), 19–23 August 2004, pp. 606–613. IEEE Computer Society, New York (2004)
2. Areces, C., Blackburn, P., Marx, M.: Hybrid logics: Characterization, interpolation and complexity. J. Symb. Log. **66**(3), 977–1010 (2001)
3. Atkinson, R.C., Shiffrin, R.M.: Human memory: a proposed system and its control processes. Psychol. Learn. Motiv. **2**, 89–195 (1968)
4. Balbiani, P., Duque, D.F., Lorini, E.: A logical theory of belief dynamics for resource-bounded agents. In: Proceedings of the 2016 International Conference on Autonomous Agents & Multiagent Systems, AAMAS 2016, pp. 644–652. ACM (2016)
5. Bansal, A.K., Ramohanarao, K., Rao, A.: Distributed storage of replicated beliefs to facilitate recovery of distributed intelligent agents. In: Singh, M.P., Rao, A., Wooldridge, M.J. (eds.) ATAL 1997. LNCS, vol. 1365, pp. 77–91. Springer, Heidelberg (1997). https://doi.org/10.1007/BFb0026751
6. Chesani, F., Mello, P., Montali, M., Torroni, P.: Monitoring time-aware commitments within agent-based simulation environments. Cybern. Syst. **42**(7), 546–566 (2011)
7. Costantini, S., Formisano, A., Pitoni, V.: Timed memory in resource-bounded agents. In: Ghidini, C., Magnini, B., Passerini, A., Traverso, P. (eds.) AI*IA 2018. LNCS (LNAI), vol. 11298, pp. 15–29. Springer, Cham (2018). https://doi.org/10.1007/978-3-030-03840-3_2
8. Engelfriet, J.: Minimal temporal epistemic logic. Notre Dame J. Formal Logic **37**(2), 233–259 (1996)
9. Gelfond, M., Kahl, Y.: Knowledge Representation, Reasoning, and The Design of Intelligent Agents: The Answer-Set Programming Approach. Cambridge University Press, Cambridge (2014)
10. Gero, J.S., Peng, W.: Understanding behaviors of a constructive memory agent: a Markov chain analysis. Knowl.-Based Syst. **22**(8), 610–621 (2009)

11. Grant, J., Kraus, S., Perlis, D.: A logic for characterizing multiple bounded agents. Auton. Agents Multi-Agent Syst. **3**(4), 351–387 (2000). https://doi.org/10.1023/A:1010050603219
12. Koymans, R.: Specifying real-time properties with metric temporal logic. Real-Time Syst. **2**(4), 255–299 (1990)
13. Laird, J.E., Lebiere, C., Rosenbloom, P.S.: A standard model of the mind: toward a common computational framework across artificial intelligence, cognitive science, neuroscience, and robotics. AI Mag. **38**(4), 13–26 (2017)
14. Liew, P.S., Gero, J.S.: An implementation model of constructive memory for situated design agent, pp. 257–276 (2002)
15. Logie, R.H.: Visuo-spatial working memory (1994)
16. Micucci, D., Oldani, M., Tisato, F.: Time-aware multi agent systems. In: Weyns, D., Holvoet, T. (eds.) Multiagent Systems and Software Architecture, Proceedings of the Special Track at Net. ObjectDays, pp. 71–78. Katholieke Universiteit Leuven, Belgium (2006)
17. Omicini, A., Ricci, A., Viroli, M.: Timed environment for web agents. Web Intell. Agent Syst. **5**(2), 161–175 (2007)
18. Pearson, D.G., Logie, R.H.: Effects of stimulus modality and working memory load on mental synthesis performance. Imagin. Cogn. Pers. **23**(2), 183–191 (2003)

A Rule-Based System for Hardware Configuration and Programming of IoT Devices

Salvatore Gaglio[ID], Leonardo Giuliana, Giuseppe Lo Re[ID],
Gloria Martorella[ID], Antonio Montalto, and Daniele Peri[✉][ID]

Department of Engineering, University of Palermo, Viale delle Scienze, Palermo, Italy
{salvatore.gaglio,giuseppe.lore,gloria.martorella,daniele.peri}@unipa.it
{leonardo.giuliana,antonio.montalto01}@community.unipa.it

Abstract. Simplifying programming, deployment, and configuration of heterogeneous networked IoT devices requires networking, hardware, representation of knowledge and concepts, design and programming skills. In fact, IoT applications are mostly built by adopting different existing paradigms and technologies on a case-by-case basis. As a result, programming tools hinder adaptability and interoperability of applications with their rigidity.

In this paper, we propose a rule-based system that configures and programs IoT devices automatically. The rule base holds formal specifications about hardware platforms, networking protocols, physical world concepts, and applications. Provided with a high-level application goal, the proposed system generates and delivers symbolic application code to the operating devices, which are then able to run it without any further translation. The tool also supports automatic configuration of IoT heterogeneous entities. Based on hardware specifications in the knowledge base, the system outputs the best configuration, i.e. the best way for connecting sensors and actuators to a specific board for a given purpose.

Keywords: Symbolic programming · Formal knowledge representation · FORTH · Code generation

1 Introduction

Emerging research trends and the growth of the Internet of Things (IoT) market, make application developers face several interrelated challenges. Among these, integrating knowledge and data representation on heterogeneous networks comprising both powerful and resource-constrained devices urges for novel standards and technologies to enable effective pervasive connectivity and to overcome the fragmentation caused by the multitude of existing infrastructures and frameworks [12].

Knowledge integration from different sources represents a fundamental shift towards effective interoperability since, regardless of their diversity, IoT objects

© Springer Nature Switzerland AG 2019
M. Alviano et al. (Eds.): AI*IA 2019, LNAI 11946, pp. 59–72, 2019.
https://doi.org/10.1007/978-3-030-35166-3_5

have to interpret, access, and exchange descriptions of both the physical world and of themselves, unambiguously [8].

For the purpose, ontologies are usually adopted for representing and managing high-level knowledge through the specification of concepts and their relationships. Besides the fact that many ontologies are domain specific, the updating process requires proper mechanisms to ensure that knowledge is correctly interpreted and synchronized among multiple devices.

In any case, formal description must be directly executable by the devices to enable effective semantic reasoning. This requires specific tools and frameworks. In this respect, description languages have also been proposed that provide generic metadata models to give semantics to data [6] and to specify structural and functional behaviors of systems.

A centralized approach, even based on the Cloud, is a common choice to overcome the issues arising from the growth of the description itself [14]. A central entity is often endowed with several frameworks to ease managing networks of IoT devices. However, such systems are quite fragmented as they result from linking together different paradigms, abstractions, and technologies. As a consequence, any change, update or upgrade becomes problematic.

An alternative approach adopts a formal representation relying on a knowledge base holding facts and logic rules. The knowledge base allows for a formal description of concepts, specification, and logic rules to represent the application domain with a high level of abstraction. Logic rules are exploited by an inference engine to manipulate the knowledge itself and to satisfy user goals. Several systems benefit of this approach, ranging from verification for ensuring security of controllers and actuators [1] to IoT service composition [2].

More generally, the complexity encountered in the lifecycle of IoT applications naturally suggests to encode the expertise needed for connecting, configuring, programming, deploying, and integrating different platforms successfully as well as to assist developers and designers in automatically prototyping and managing IoT applications, products, and services. Some solutions focus on easy configuration, access, and management of the available devices even by ordinary users [11]. Service management can also be built on rule-based systems so that each device can use inference to expose its services. In this case, each node can be queried by other clients to prove a set of theory axioms, while services are configured at runtime by a configurator [3].

In this paper, we present a rule-based system to support developers in implementing IoT applications. A knowledge base coalesces hardware and networking specifications as well as properties of the environment. To automate software development, an inference engine generates source code which is delivered to deployed devices "on the fly". Our tool acts as a configurator in the sense that the output source code automatically defines what it is required to execute an application on remote devices at bootstrap. Due to the adopted symbolic programming approach, the generated high-level application code conveys semantics still being directly executable by target devices without any translation step [5]. Hardware configuration is also supported to assist novice users and implementers. The best connections of hardware components to a specific board are inferred by the system, effectively. The remainder of the paper is organized as follows. Section 2 presents the related work. Section 3 defines the architecture of the rule-based system and highlights possible applications in real scenarios. The knowledge base organization is presented in Sect. 4. The used techniques and algorithms for hardware configuration and source code generation are detailed in Sects. 5 and 6, respectively. Section 7 describes the implementation of a prototype that interfaces with remote IoT devices to provide interoperability and customization. Section 8 describes the experimental setup and reports evaluations in terms of some metrics such as Lines of Code (LOC), number of rules, and size of source code. Section 9 includes our conclusions and possible future directions.

2 Related Work

IoT application development is an active research area. Several methodologies have in fact be proposed to speed up the development by automating the software generation process. Knowledge are abstracted by adopting models that are progressively refined until source code is generated. The process of transforming high-level abstraction models into lower-level models is made automatic in many proposed systems. Moreover, combining rule-based models and Domain Specific Languages has been proposed for application specification [9]. Other approaches aim at reducing the implementation effort by adopting a suite of tools. These usually include at least a domain-aware editor and a compiler, which automatically generates the implementation code after processing the high-level description. Deployment tools, which are responsible of sending the code, and run-time managers are also adopted [13]. In other cases, application development is undertaken using different languages that have to be integrated [10]. Other approaches are centered on rule-base systems. The use of a rule-based reasoner exploiting a knowledge base has been proposed for automatic IoT service composition [2] or to enable users to configure their own network and devices at home [11]. Exploiting powerful devices, such as network gateways, has been suggested to manage and access remote devices, and to automatically build high-level knowledge describing environmental properties [7]. A rule-based system implemented in Prolog has been also proposed to detect conflicts in sensors and controllers behaviors [1]. Similarly, a prototype implementation has been designed on the top of tuProlog engine for IoT service management. Each node exposes its services to multiple devices while applications can access or configure the services [3]. Agent-based computing paradigms have also been proposed to support IoT systems analysis, design, and implementation [4].

3 System Overview

The proposed rule-based system presents a modular architecture which can be logically decomposed into four main components:

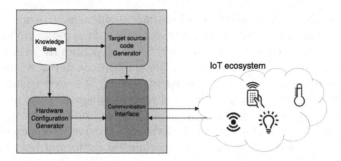

Fig. 1. Abstract view of the proposed system. The hardware configuration generator and the Target source code Generator extract information from the Knowledge Base and interact with the IoT ecosystem through the Communication Interface, which takes care of sending code and receiving responses.

- A *Knowledge Base* encodes heterogeneous information across multiple domains into a coherent whole. Facts and rules concerning the physical environment, hardware platforms, networking, and about the high-level application are included. For instance, symbolic code, classes of objects and their instances–e.g. IoT hardware platforms and products available in the market– and network protocols are formally specified from a structural and functional point of view.
- The *Target source code Generator* exploits a backward chaining inference engine and automatically generates symbolic code for run-time configuration, programming or updating of already deployed devices. Given a user-defined goal as input, this component outputs the related source code. Two distinct working modes are available: (i) generation of code for application configuration; (ii) generation of operational software. In the first case, the generator outputs the code to define procedures, routines, and symbols on remote devices, while in the second one the application code is generated automatically.
- The *Hardware Configuration Generator* exploits the inference engine and automatically generates and validates hardware configurations, that is, possible ways of connecting hardware components, such as sensors and actuators, to a specific microcontroller unit (MCU), correctly. This component takes also care of interfacing a given node with the system itself.
- The *Communication Interface* exposes rules for interfacing the system with the IoT ecosystem. In particular, it enables sending code from the system to remote IoT devices. Code transmission can adhere to different communication protocol, such as TCP, which has to be indicated by the user and specified in the knowledge base. Secure exchange of symbolic code is also enforced in this component.

The overall architecture is abstracted in Fig. 1.

4 Knowledge Base Structure

The knowledge base provides a formal representation of all of the aspects related to the IoT scenario, as a whole. The expertise needed to embrace different domains is encoded in a modular organization of distinct rule sets.

Physical world properties are modeled in the *Physical world* rule set. Concepts and rules are independent from a specific use context and can be used across multiple high-level application domains.

The *Application* rule set strictly relates to high-level applications. Aspects concerning objects, their states and locations, measurable physical parameters, and possible actions are formally defined. For instance, considering a IoT home scenario, the application domain includes the references to the involved objects as well as their placement in the house and possible states.

Hardware platforms are modeled in the *Hardware* rule set which encodes the expertise concerning structural low-level board components, and their operational modes. Facts and rules define MCUs in terms of their pins, peripherals, sensors, and actuators, as reported by technical documentation or data-sheets. As an example, in the knowledge base an instance of the ESP8266_12E board is defined with the code

```
mcu_name(myesp, esp8266_12e)
```

that associates the unique label myesp to the hardware platform ESP8266_12E.

The *Software* rule set holds useful facts and rules exploited by the Target source code Generator for constructing symbolic executable code for each of the possible operations.

The *Network* rule set provides a set of functionalities to transmit symbolic code to nodes and to manage the correct reception of feedbacks by nodes, when needed. Finally, network protocols are specified to control the remote connection between each device and the rule-base system for configuration and code transmission. Besides the inclusion of concepts as host name, IP address, and server port number, the system currently models the Transmission Control Protocol (TCP), which is the default protocol used for code exchange. For instance the IP address and TCP server port of the myesp device are specified as such:

```
mcu_net_address(myesp,
'myesp.local', 1983).
```

To enable secure interaction with nodes, this rule set also specifies the DES-CBC and AES128-CBC protocols.

4.1 Objects, States and Locations

In our formal description, objects, states, and locations belong to the Application rule set. While objects indicate real world devices, which are deployed in the environment and can be managed by the system, parameters and states refer to both environmental and object configurations. Objects such as lamps, LEDs,

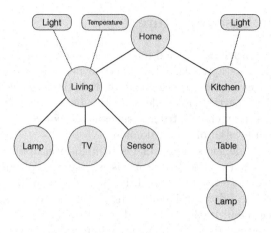

Fig. 2. Tree structure of a home environment. Circles represent locations, leaf nodes are objects, while rounded shapes are physical parameters.

HVACs, and TVs can be easily found at home. Their possible states are "ON" and "OFF", while the light level is a parameter of the home environment.

In our system, the term *location* indicates the effective placement of an object in the environment. Locations are structured in a hierarchy so that generic locations can be composed by other sub-locations, until a specific position is reached. Such a definition inherently suggests the use of a tree structure in which the root node represents a more general location, while internal nodes gradually identify specific positions. Finally, leaf nodes indicate object placements. As an example, the root location "Home" is composed of other sub-locations, e.g. "Kitchen" and "Living room". Real-world objects are thus leaf nodes, as shown in Fig. 2. This way, it is possible to find the object location by following the reverse path from the leaf, i.e. the object, to the root. The list of the objects in the same location can be also obtained. Locations not containing objects are also leaf nodes.

To operate on the system users can construct queries including:

- a reference to an object through its location;
- a reference to a category of objects in a given location; all the object belonging to the specified class and reachable by the indicated location are considered;
- a reference to all the objects in a given location, regardless of their category, and an action to be executed; for instance the command ON at the general location Home switches all the devices in the house on;
- a list of locations, a class of objects and an action; switching all the lamps that are not placed on a table on, prevents the lamps outside the house, or not placed on tables, from switching on.

In the end, the proposed tree structure, besides being easily implemented in Prolog, fosters interoperability with several IoT application protocols. For instance, the Message Queue Telemetry Transport (MQTT) protocol requires topics be structured in a hierarchy using the forward slash as a delimiter. For instance, `home/living/lamp` is a possible valid MQTT topic.

5   Automatic Generation of Hardware Configuration

The hardware configuration process consists in finding a possible connection of a given set of peripherals to the I/O pins available in the device MCU. The knowledge about pin usage and their functionalities, as found in the data-sheets, is encoded into the rule base. Structural description of sensors and actuators is also encoded in the knowledge base. Provided with all these specifications, consistent with the system in terms of both configuration and management of pins, as well as of all the sensors and actuators involved, the Hardware configuration Generator is given the task to find the best way of connecting an IoT device MCU to all the sensors and actuators involved in the application following the algorithm reported in Fig. 3.

As a first step, the Generator checks the existence of a node providing the function required by the user. If such a node is not available, the Generator looks for pins of the MCU that can be exploited to satisfy the user query. In case a possible connection is found, the knowledge base is updated with new facts and rules. It is also possible to specify multiple sensors or actuators to be connected to a specific MCU in order to find a valid configuration that includes them all. In this case, the generator proceeds through an incremental approach. It evaluates the availability of a valid connection for the first component, then for the second one, and so on. This way, each peripheral is connected taking into account just the assigned pins. In the event that a valid configuration does not exist, e.g. because there are no available pins, rollback procedures are triggered. The Hardware configuration Generator is implemented in Prolog in a few code lines as follows:

```
mcu_peripheral_make_connection(McuName, McuPin,
McuPinFunction, PeripheralName, PeripheralPin,
PeripheralPinFunction) :-
    mcu_peripheral_pin_connection(McuName, McuPin,
McuPinFunction, PeripheralName, PeripheralPin,
PeripheralPinFunction), ! ;
    mcu_peripheral_check_avaiability(McuName, McuPin,
McuPinFunction, PeripheralName, PeripheralPin,
PeripheralPinFunction),
    assert(mcu_peripheral_pin_connection(McuName, McuPin,
McuPinFunction, PeripheralName, PeripheralPin,
PeripheralPinFunction)).
```

The generation of hardware configurations is provided by the rule `mcu_peripheral_make_connection/6` which requires a list including: (i) an MCU instance, (ii) an MCU pin number, (iii) an MCU pin functionality (iv) an instance of a component, e.g. sensor or actuator, (v) a device pin number (vi) a device pin

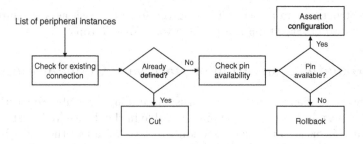

Fig. 3. Flow diagram representation of the hardware configuration generation process.

functionality. The indication of all of the required parameters leads to the verification of that specific connection, without considering any alternative. A partial specification of the parameters forces the generator to infer unassigned parameters, providing all the possible configurations. Finally, the rule mcu_init/1 accepts a list of configurations and exploits mcu_peripheral_make_connection to check configurations of peripherals and MCUs, as follows:

```
mcu_init([
    [myesp, 12, digital_output, relay1, 1, digital_input],
    [myesp, 14, digital_output, relay2, 1, digital_input],
    [myesp, _, _, lumsens, _, _]
]).
```

The code above connects two relay instances to the instance of ESP chip named myesp through the device pin number 1 and the MCU pin number 12 and 14, respectively. Such pins are defined in the knowledge base as digital output pins. An instance of a light sensor (lumsens) is also defined without specifying connection pins and their functionality. The system responds by assigning the light sensor to the ADC and provides the right pin numbers for the correct configuration.

6   Automatic Generation of Source Code

The Target source code Generator is intended to speed up the development of IoT applications through automation. Provided with a high-level task by the user, the system acts as an *Application Configurator* that outputs the executable code for device installation at bootstrap. Complementarily, the Source code Generator also infers the symbolic application code to match the user-defined goal. In both cases, the generated executable code adheres to a symbolic programming model, which raises the programming abstraction by enabling a tight coupling between semantics and implementation. Such a choice avoids the mandatory translation steps which are required by other systems to bind the description code to the executable code.

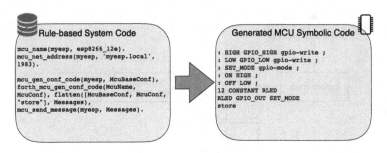

Fig. 4. Example of source code generation for the configuration of a simple application. In the leftmost box, the Prolog code to generate the configuration is reported. The rightmost box displays the generated symbolic code that defines a set of words, i.e. HIGH, LOW, SET_MODE and so on, as well as the constant RLED and the word store that records the configuration on the remote node.

The symbolic executable program produced by the system is a chain of words, each of which represents a computation and is defined using other, previously defined, words. On remote nodes, words are stored in a word dictionary which can be easily extended by users. Words are user-defined, in the sense that nothing prevents from choosing word that can be taken directly from natural language. The support to high-level knowledge is thus provided by the programming model itself, as implemented by the Forth language, which is both interpreted and compiled. Moreover, this paradigm can be adopted on either powerful devices or resource-costrained hardware, due to its low footprint [5].

For instance the following sentence:

```
LAMP ON
```

actuates on the environment switching the lamp on, while:

```
LAMP BLINK 3 TIMES
```

is an application that blinks a lamp three times.

Considering a "neutral" node, i.e. a device that does not run any code, the Source code Generator infers the code defining the necessary words for the application. An example of this operation is illustrated in Fig. 4. The mcu_gen_conf procedure provides the symbolic code for the MCU initialization as a list, while the forth_mcu_gen_conf procedure is used to build the symbolic code for all the allowed high-level actions.

Considering runtime code generation, the execution of:

$$exec(home, led, on)$$

generates the code to switch all the home LEDs on:

$$RLED ON$$

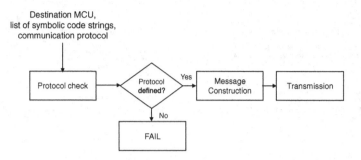

Fig. 5. Flow diagram of the required steps for symbolic code transmission to remote devices.

To read the only luminosity sensor in a house, the system is queried as such:

`execr(home, light, check, A).)`

In this case the variable A stands for 'answer' and holds the light sensor value. The generated symbolic code is:

`LUMSENS READ.`

The single-character word . (dot) displays the answer.

7   Symbolic Code Transmission

Symbolic code generated by the inference engine is sent to devices as simple textual strings. No other intermediate representation or translation is required. For transmission, after specifying the required communication protocol, the system exploits its definition in the knowledge base. In the event that the protocol is undefined, code is sent via TCP, the default protocol for communication. The system opens a TCP connection to the TCP-REPL listening port of the receiver device. After the connection has been established, the code is sent via TCP to the remote node and interpreted on receipt. The steps required for code transmission are illustrated in Fig. 5.

Through the mcu_send_message/2 procedure, which requires the destination node and the executable code in the form of a list of commands, the communication interface connects to the remote TCP-REPL server of myesp and sends it the symbolic code to make the RLED LED be switched on and then off after a 500 ms delay:

```
mcu_send_message(myesp,
['RLED ON 500 ms RLED OFF']).
```

A variant of this rule includes required feedbacks from the MCU. The response is a list of feedbacks, each of which refers to the list of commands sent by the system.

Secure interaction among the system and remote IoT devices is also supported, although this functionality can be also deactivated at any time. The user can choose to exchange symbolic code by using the DES-CBC or AES128-CBC encryption protocols. Before transmitting, strings are encoded using the Base64 algorithm. This step overcomes execution errors due to the presence of unprintable chars, such as CR, LF and NUL which are interpreted by the TCP-REPL server delimiters indicating the end of a line or of a string. Each MCU node holds a MasterKey, which is unique and has to be specified in the knowledge base. This key is adopted to exchange session keys between the system and a remote node, so to be used for effective encrypted communications.

8   Experimental Setup and Evaluation

A prototype implementation of the system that automatically configures and programs IoT node was implemented. The rule-base system is the central entity and runs on a Raspberry-Pi 1B, equipped with a 700 MHz single-core ARM1176JZF-S CPU. The board also includes a 512 MB RAM memory shared with the Broadcom VideoCore IV GPU. The operating system is Raspbian 8.3.0 with some modifications done for our purposes.

The ESP8266-12E system on a chip (SOC) was adopted for the remote devices. This SOC integrates a Wi-Fi interface and full support for TCP/IP. The SOC is also equipped with a 80 MHz 32-bit RISC CPU, 64 KiB RAM memory for instructions and 96 KiB RAM for data, 4 MiB flash memory, and 16 general-purpose I/O (GPIO) pins. Installed on the SOC, PunyForth, an open source FORTH implementation, provides a Read Evaluation Print Loop (REPL) shell enabling interactive programming.

The rule-based system has been evaluated in terms of lines of code (LOC) and source code size, as provided in Table 1.

Table 1. LOC and file size for all the components of the system

Knowledge representation	LOC	File size [KB]
Physical world	28	0.875
High-level actions	25	2
High-level domain	124	2 + 2 + 1
Hardware	201	19 + 0.797
Software generators	256	6 + 8
Networking	64	3
Security	74	2 + 0.703
Utilities	151	4
Total	923	

Code transmission using an encryption algorithm was also assessed. The implementation of security algorithms directly through a symbolic approach highlighted some limitations, mostly due to the required memory. For instance, the DES algorithm performs permutations and rotations of relatively large matrices. Therefore, we opted for a C implementation of the algorithm, and then the MCU image was reflashed to include secure exchange of code. MCU binary images, with and without secure exchange, differs by 8 KiB. We also compared DES-CBC and AES128-CBC in terms of encryption speed as message length increases. Message length was measured as the number of chars composing the message itself. Results are provided in Table 2.

Table 2. Comparison in terms of speed of DES-CBC and AES128-CBC as message length increases

Message length	DES speed [s]	AES speed [s]
16	0.0000111	0.0000131
32	0.0000071	0.0000081
48	0.0000091	0.0000111
64	0.0000121	0.0000151
80	0.0000131	0.0000181
96	0.0000151	0.0000231
112	0.0000171	0.0000251
128	0.0000201	0.0000281

9   Conclusions

In this work, a rule-based system for automatic IoT application configuration and programming was proposed. The required knowledge is formally modeled through a knowledge base holding facts and rules from different domains. The proposed system automatically generates symbolic code either for application configuration and for its execution. The code is sent via TCP as a sequence of symbols that are executable by devices without any other intermediate representation. As a further functionality, the automatic generation of possible correct connections among hardware components and the MCU is supported.

The rule-base system was implemented in Prolog while the symbolic environment running on devices was built atop PunyForth. A prototype implementation and experimental evaluation supported the feasibility of the approach. Our tool also permits secure code exchange using DES-CBC and AES-CBC encryption protocols. Such a functionality can be deactivated by the user when desired. Currently, the system interfaces with remote nodes via TCP, while other protocol specifications can be added provided that enough resources on remote nodes are available. Future work will focus on expanding the experimental evaluation, as well as on enabling UDP and broadcast code exchange.

References

1. Al Farooq, A., Al-Shaer, E., Moyer, T., Kant, K.: IoTC2: a formal method approach for detecting conflicts in large scale IoT systems. In: 2019 IFIP/IEEE Symposium on Integrated Network and Service Management (IM), pp. 442–447, April 2019
2. Berrani, S., Yachir, A., Aissani, M.: Towards a new framework for service composition in the internet of things. In: Demigha, O., Djamaa, B., Amamra, A. (eds.) CSA 2018. LNNS, vol. 50, pp. 57–66. Springer, Cham (2019). https://doi.org/10. 1007/978-3-319-98352-3_7
3. Calegari, R., Denti, E., Mariani, S., Omicini, A.: Logic programming as a service (LPaaS): intelligence for the IoT. In: 2017 IEEE 14th International Conference on Networking, Sensing and Control (ICNSC), pp. 72–77, May 2017. https://doi.org/ 10.1109/ICNSC.2017.8000070
4. Fortino, G., Russo, W., Savaglio, C., Shen, W., Zhou, M.: Agent-oriented cooperative smart objects: from IoT system design to implementation. IEEE Trans. Syst. Man Cybern.: Syst. **48**(11), 1939–1956 (2018). https://doi.org/10.1109/TSMC. 2017.2780618
5. Gaglio, S., Lo Re, G., Martorella, G., Peri, D.: DC4CD: a platform for distributed computing on constrained devices. ACM Trans. Embed. Comput. Syst. **17**(1), 27:1–27:25 (2017). https://doi.org/10.1145/3105923
6. Kovatsch, M., Hassan, Y.N., Mayer, S.: Practical semantics for the internet of things: physical states, device mashups, and open questions. In: 2015 5th International Conference on the Internet of Things (IOT), pp. 54–61, October 2015. https://doi.org/10.1109/IOT.2015.7356548
7. Lee, Y., Nair, S.: A smart gateway framework for IoI services. In: 2016 IEEE International Conference on Internet of Things (iThings) and IEEE Green Computing and Communications (GreenCom) and IEEE Cyber, Physical and Social Computing (CPSCom) and IEEE Smart Data (SmartData), pp. 107–114, December 2016. https://doi.org/10.1109/iThings-GreenCom-CPSCom-SmartData.2016.44
8. Nagowah, S.D., Ben Sta, H., Gobin-Rahimbux, B.: An overview of semantic interoperability ontologies and frameworks for IoT. In: 2018 Sixth International Conference on Enterprise Systems (ES), pp. 82–89, October 2018. https://doi.org/10. 1109/ES.2018.00020
9. Nguyen, X.T., Tran, H.T., Baraki, H., Geihs, K.: FRASAD: a framework for model-driven IoT application development. In: 2015 IEEE 2nd World Forum on Internet of Things (WF-IoT), pp. 387–392, December 2015. https://doi.org/10.1109/WF-IoT.2015.7389085
10. Patel, P., Cassou, D.: Enabling high-level application development for the internet of things. J. Syst. Softw. **103**, 62–84 (2015). https://doi.org/10.1016/j.jss.2015.01. 027. http://www.sciencedirect.com/science/article/pii/S0164121215000187
11. Rana, A.I., Jennings, B.: Semantic aware processing of user defined inference rules to manage home networks. J. Netw. Comput. Appl. **79**, 68–87 (2017). https://doi. org/10.1016/j.jnca.2016.11.020. http://www.sciencedirect.com/science/article/ pii/S1084804516302892

12. Santana, E.F.Z., Chaves, A.P., Gerosa, M.A., Kon, F., Milojicic, D.S.: Software platforms for smart cities: concepts, requirements, challenges, and a unified reference architecture. ACM Comput. Surv. **50**(6), 78:1–78:37 (2017). https://doi.org/10.1145/3124391

13. Soukaras, D., Patel, P., Song, H., Chaudhary, S.: IoTSuite: a ToolSuite for prototyping internet of things applications, January 2015

14. Tao, M., Ota, K., Dong, M.: Ontology-based data semantic management and application in IoT- and cloud-enabled smart homes. Future Gener. Comput. Syst. **76**, 528–539 (2017). https://doi.org/10.1016/j.future.2016.11.012. http://www.sciencedirect.com/science/article/pii/S0167739X1630615X

First Approach to Semantics of Silence in Testimonies

Alfonso Garcés-Báez$^{(\boxtimes)}$ and Aurelio López-López$^{(\boxtimes)}$

Computational Sciences Department, Instituto Nacional de Astrofísica,
Óptica y Electrónica, Sta. Ma. Tonantzintla, Puebla, Mexico
agarces@ccc.inaoep.mx, allopez@inaoep.mx

Abstract. The right to silence is considered in several legal systems. However, this phenomenon has not been sufficiently studied from a logic perspective. After reviewing some previous studies of intentional silence, Grice's conversational implicature, and omissive implicature, we formulated three interpretations of silence. Once the semantics are stated, we explore the consequences of such interpretations in puzzles as a case study involving testimonies, expressing them in answer set programming. Several conclusions are derived from the different possibilities that were opened for the analysis. Finally, we propose a strategy to generalize the use of semantics in contexts related to testimonies or interviews.

Keywords: Silence · Interpretation · Testimonies · Intention · Implicature · Omissive implicature · Says predicate

1 Introduction

Silence has been the subject of study in various scientific disciplines, which have provided insights for its understanding. However, we have not found an approach to formalize it in terms of logic, where the closest attempt was that of [6] with an "informal" logic. Next, we review some concepts related to this matter.

According to Kurzon [7], there are two types of silence, intentional and unintentional. Intentional silence is a deliberate action not to cooperate with the other party and unintentional silence is psychological in nature. The intentional silence is also a sign of group loyalty.

To interpret intentional silence, first we have to discard the modal "can" that may express unintentional silence, as in "I can not speak". Then, intentional silence can be interpreted according to four manners [7]:

1. I may not tell you
2. I must not tell you
3. I shall not tell you
4. I will not tell you

© Springer Nature Switzerland AG 2019
M. Alviano et al. (Eds.): AI*IA 2019, LNAI 11946, pp. 73–86, 2019.
https://doi.org/10.1007/978-3-030-35166-3_6

Where manners 1 and 2 are intentional external silences involving some "order" by a third party to do so. And manners 3 and 4 are intentional internal silences expressing a "will" at different degrees of the speaker to keep quiet.

The interpretation of silence must be contextual. For example, in a normal conversation, in court, silence is interpreted to the detriment of the person who is silent. The immediate reaction is that she hides something. For Kurzon the silence is defined by language and points to three types of silence:

- Psychological silence. The help of a decoder is necessary.
- Interactive silence. It occurs as an intentional pause in the conversation allowing the other person to draw inferences related to the meaning of the conversation.
- Socio-cultural silence. When silence is interpreted based on specific cultural codes.

Dyne, Ang and Botero [1] identify three types of silence manifested by employees in work organizations: Acquiescent, Defensive and ProSocial. The intentional acquiescent silence suggests disengaged behaviour that is more passive than active. The silence is defensive when this silence is proactive, involving awareness and consideration of alternatives, followed by a conscious decision to withhold ideas, information, and opinions as the best personal strategy at the moment. The prosocial silence is defined as withholding work-related ideas, information, or opinions with the goal of benefiting other people or the organization - based on altruism or cooperative motives. In this work, we focus on two of these types of silence, Acquiescent silence which reflects "silence is consent" and as such is modeled; and Defensive silence with a simpler interpretation in two variants.

The analysis and evaluation of witness testimonies in Law have been done before with artificial intelligence and argumentation theory. Walton [14] argues that testimonies can provide reasonable evidence to accept or reject a claim, leading to a logically guided decision making process. In this direction, we formulate a first logical approach to take into account silence in testimonies in a limited context, considering the definition of omissive implicature, i.e. "In some contexts, not saying p generates a conversational implicature: that the speaker didn't have sufficient reason, all things considered, to say p [12]."

Also in Law, the right to silence has been studied with a game-theoretic analysis, showing that can help to distinguish between innocent and guilty suspects [10]. In contrast, our analysis shows that defensive silence can be advantageous to guilty suspects, in the particular context of our case study.

The main contributions of this paper are: (1) we approach the interpretation of silence in interaction from an artificial intelligence perspective, specifically oriented to testimonies; (2) we model three types of silence; (3) these logical interpretations are explored in terms of a case study to check their implications; and (4) some guidelines are sketched to bring the interpretation into analysis.

This paper is organized as follows: Sect. 2 provides some preliminaries for further development of the approach. Section 3 details a case study to explore silence interpretations and consequences. We conclude in Sect. 4, discussing in addition work in progress.

2   Preliminaries

The conversational implicature is a potential inference that is not a logical implication and is closely connected with the meaning of the word "says", as explained in [5]. A formulation of implicature goes as follows, with S the speaker and H the hearer (also referred as addressee) [15]:

S conversationally implicates p iff S implicates p when:

1. S is presumed to be observing the Cooperative Principle (cooperative presumption);
2. The supposition that S believes p is required to make $S's$ utterance consistent with the Cooperative Principle (determinacy); and
3. S believes (or knows), and expects H to believe that S believes, that H is able to determine that (2) is true (mutual knowledge).

The Cooperative Principle consists of the participants making their conversational contribution as required in the scenario in which this occurs for the accepted purpose or direction of the speech exchange in which they were engaged [5]. In this sense, we employ the predicate "says", that has previously emerged in a logic formulation for access control [3]. However, we are using it more freely, i.e. with less constraints, considering in this case that intentional silence "says" something when is interpreted in its context for decision making.

We define the predicate "Says" in the sense of Grice, as:

Definition 1. *Says(X, Y), it expresses that the agent X says Y (predicate).*

Next, we define informally Defensive and Acquiescent Silence, as described by Dyne, Ang, and Botero, and then formalize such types of silence for further application and analysis.

Defensive Silence is characterized in [1] as "withholding relevant ideas, information, or opinions as a form of self-protection, based on fear." Before proceeding to a logical formulation of two variants of this silence, we state some notation regarding a group of agents doing some assertions.

Let P be a logic program or knowledge base (KB); $A_1, A_2, \ldots, A_n$ are agents; $p_1, p_2, \ldots, p_m$ are predicates. $X_{A_1} = \{\text{Says}(A_1, p_1), \ldots, \text{Says}(A_1, p_l)\} = \{\text{Says}(A_1, *)\}; \ldots; X_{A_k} = \{\text{Says}(A_k, *)\}; (1 \leq l \leq m); (1 \leq k \leq n); X = X_{A_1} \cup X_{A_2} \cup \ldots \cup X_{A_n}; X \subset P.$

Definition 2. P_{A_i} *is Total Defensive Silence (TDS) of A_i understood as:*

$$P_{A_i} = P - X_{A_i}$$

Where $(1 \leq i \leq n)$, n number of interacting agents; P is a logic program or knowledge base, and $X_{A_i} = Says(A_i, *)$ is all that the agent A_i Says (asserts), represented as predicates.

Definition 3. $P_{A_i,pj}$ *is Partial Defensive Silence (PDS) of A_i understood as:*

$$P_{A_i,pj} = P - \{Says(A_i, p_j)\}$$

Where $(1 \leq i \leq n)$, n number of interacting agents; $(1 \leq j \leq m)$; A_i is an agent; m number of utterances/assertions done by A_i, and p_j is a utterance of A_i.

Other type of silence identified in [1] is *Acquiescent Silence*, explained as "witholding relevant ideas, information, or opinions, based on resignation", that is in some sense equivalent to the saying "silence is consent". This silence is logically formulated as follows.

Definition 4. P'_{A_i} *is Total Acquiescent Silence (TAS) of A_i understood as:*

$$P'_{A_i} = P_{A_i} \cup (\{Says(A_k, *)\} \circ \lambda)$$

Where $i \neq k$, $(1 \leq i, k \leq n)$, n number of interacting agents; P_{A_i} is the TDS of A_i; $\lambda = \{A_k / A_i\}$, and the operator $\circ$ with λ substitution denotes the replacement of A_k for A_i on Says subset of agent A_i.

Answer-Set Programming (ASP). Once these three definitions of silence are formulated, we proceed to explore their implications in a case study. For this purpose, we employed the ASP paradigm, given that is closely related to intuitionistic logic [9], i.e. both are based on the concept of *proof* rather than *truth*. This is a logic programming branch that computes stable models for difficult problems [4], where a stable model is a belief system that holds for a rational agent. This approach:

- Goes beyond answering queries.
- Is used to solve computational problems by reducing them to finding answer sets of programs.
- In principle, any NP-complete problem can be solved in this way using ASP without disjunction.
- With disjunction, we can solve more-complex problems.

For self-containment sake, we provide next a brief introduction to ASP, based on [8]. A *clause* is a formula of the form $H \leftarrow B$ where H and B are arbitrary formulas in principle, called head and body of the clause respectively. There are several types of clauses. If $H = \{\}$ the clause is called a constraint and we can write that clause as $\leftarrow B$. Analogously, if $B = \{\}$ then the clause is called a fact and can be written as $H \leftarrow$. A free clause is a clause where H contains disjunctions of positive atoms and B consists of conjunctions of negative atoms.

A *logic program* is then a finite set of clauses, also called rules. If all the clauses in a program are of a certain type, we say that the program is also of that type. For example, a set of free clauses (rules) is a free program.

A set consisting of literals X, *satisfies* a basic formula F (symbolically, $X \models F$) recursively, as follows:

- For F elemental, $X \models F$ if $F \in X$ or $F = \top$.
- $X \models (F, G)$ if $X \models F$ and $X \models G$.
- $X \models (F; G)$ if $X \models F$ or $X \models G$.

Let Π be a basic program. A consistent set of literals X is *closed* under Π if, for each rule $F \leftarrow G$ in Π, $X \models F$ when $X \models G$.

X is a *answer set* for the basic program Π if X has the minimum cardinality of the consistent set of literals closed under Π.

For example, let consider the program: $q \leftarrow p \vee -p$. The closure under this program is characterized by the following condition: if $p \in X$ or $-p \in X$ then $q \in X$. It is clear that the answer set for that program is empty. If we add the rule p (that is, $p \leftarrow \top$) to this program then $\{p, q\}$ will be the answer set.

Clingo (https://potassco.org/clingo/) is an implementation of ASP that allows to find, if there exists, the answer set or stable model of a logic program. This was employed to generate the answer sets for the case study.

3   A Case Study for Testimonies and Silence

Puzzles are a form of entertainment that often involve mathematical or logical challenges. Here we focus on logic puzzles [11] involving deduction, and specifically some kind of testimonies of several people, as a test ground for our interpretations of silence and their implications. First, we analyze the implications of (total) defensive silence in the classic "knights and knaves" puzzle, and then we turn to a little more challenging puzzle involving more than two testimonies.

3.1   Knights and Knaves

"Knights and knaves" is a riddle that has many forms but all start from the following knowledge: there exists a place where every inhabitant is a knight or is a knave but not both. The knights always tell the truth and knaves always lie. Here we present a version taken from Smullyan [11]: *The Island of Knights and Knaves has two types of inhabitants: knights, who always tell the truth, and knaves, who always lie. One day, three inhabitants (A, B, and C) of the island met a foreign tourist and gave the following information about themselves:*

1. *A said that B and C are both knights.*
2. *B said that A is a knave and C is a knight.*

What types are A, B, and C?.

The solution to the puzzle as formulated is: *knave(A), knave(B), knave(C).*

The logic program that solves the puzzle can be found in Syrjanen [13] and shown in Appendix. In Fig. 1, we show a table including the solution of the original problem and symbols we will use hereon to analyze the implications of silence.

We now turn to explore what would happen if one of the inhabitants remains silent. We can assume a defensive silence to analyze each inhabitant silence

Knight

Knave

Agent	Unique model
A	
B	
C	

Fig. 1. Symbols and solution of the original problem.

(A or B) at a time, generating the corresponding models. This problem only allows to consider a total defensive silence. So, as defensive silence was defined (Definition 2) and considering P the logic program detailed in Appendix, where:

$$X_A = \{Says(A, knight(B)), Says(A, knight(C))\}$$
$$X_B = \{Says(B, knave(A)), Says(B, knight(C))\}$$

were expressed in the corresponding rules:

```
2{knight(b),knight(c)}2 :- knight(a)
2{knave(a),knight(c)}2 :- knight(b)
```

So, the *TDS* for inhabitant A is:

$$P_A = P - X_A$$

And the *TDS* for inhabitant B is:

$$P_B = P - X_B$$

Now, we find the models and analyze each case separately:

1. Running the model generator for P_A, we obtain the following solutions:

```
Answer: 1
agent(a) agent(b) agent(c) knight(c) knave(a) knight(b)
Answer: 2
agent(a) agent(b) agent(c) knave(a) knave(c) knave(b)
Answer: 3
agent(a) agent(b) agent(c) knight(c) knave(b) knight(a)
Answer: 4
agent(a) agent(b) agent(c) knave(c) knave(b) knight(a)
SATISFIABLE
```

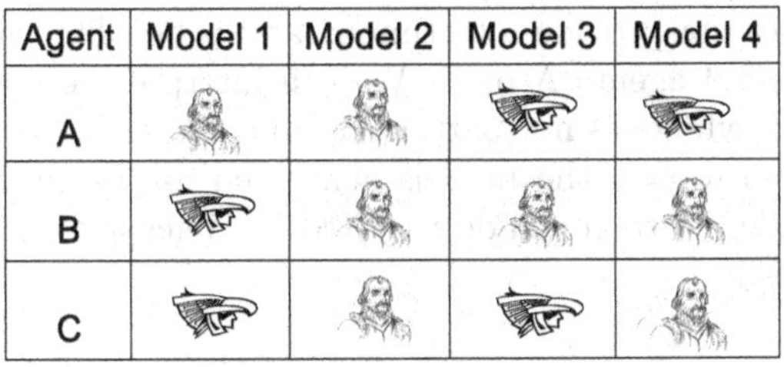

Fig. 2. Possibilities with the defensive silence of Agent A.

These are four different models, which contain the distribution of knights and knaves for each of the three inhabitants or agents. As expected, with less information, the possibilities expand. Figure 2 shows this distribution where we can notice that everybody, to a lesser or greater degree, have the possibility of being a knight. Analyzing the four Models in terms of Agents, we have:

- In the first row, the Agent A, that is silenced defensively, has the possibility of being considered a knight, and in this way halves the chances of being a knave.
- For agent B (second row) a possibility also opens of being considered a knight.
- Agent C, similarly as A, distributes its possibilities in two and two.

2. Running the model generator for P_B we get again four models. However, these models are different to those obtained when Agent A is silent. Figure 3 depicts this distribution where we can notice that:

- A model arises where every agent could be considered a knight.
- For Agent A, a possibility opens of being considered a knight.
- In the second row, the Agent B, that is silenced defensively, opens options to be a knight, and in this way halves the chances of being a knave.
- Agent C, similarly now as B, distributes its possibilities in two and two.

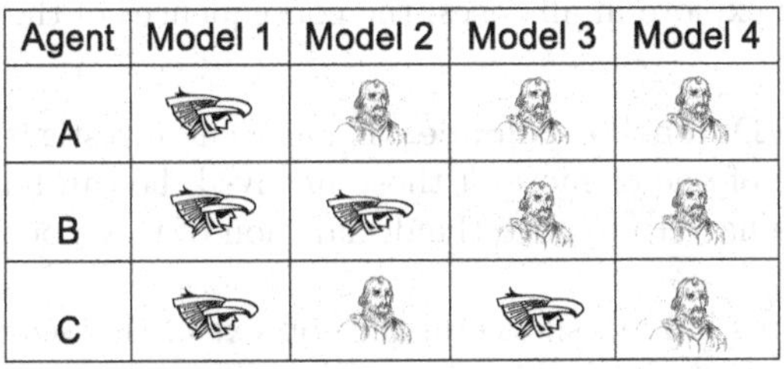

Fig. 3. Possibilities with the defensive silence of Agent B.

Under both scenarios analyzed, we got the solution of the original puzzle, i.e. the three agents are knaves. We can notice that in the statement of the puzzle, agent C does not provide a testimony and is benefited indistinctly, with the defensive silence of agents A or B. We can interpret here an unintentional silence. So Agent C, who does not participate in a speech act or in a silence act, appears in the same way in the models generated for P_A or P_B. Considering silence in this puzzle led to conclude that (total) defensive silence benefits the agent who practices it.

3.2 A Mystery with Several Testimonies

There is a second puzzle, previously modeled and solved in [4] (but unfortunately omitted here for lack of space), that includes testimonies of different people, and allows to model and explore our two interpretations of silence and variants.

In this puzzle, a mystery related to a murder is raised:

Vinny has been murdered, and Andy, Ben, and Cole are suspects.
Andy says he did not do it. He says that Ben was the victim's friend but that Cole hated the victim.
Ben says he was out of town the day of the murder, and besides he didn't even know the guy.
Cole says he is innocent and he saw Andy and Ben with the victim just before the murder.

We must assume that all the people involved tell the truth except, possibly, the murderer. The story and testimony of these three people are formulated in a program for Clingo.

The program for the puzzle produces as a result: murderer (ben). This means that according to the testimonies and the rules of commonsense knowledge provided, the murderer is Ben.

Based on the formulation of the puzzle previously described, we proceed to explore the two interpretations of intentional silence, expressed in the three definitions, linked to such context. The first interpretation is a Defensive Silence, in its Total and Partial variant, while the second corresponds to Acquiescent Silence, understood as asserting with silence what others have said, commonly by resignation. We explore in all cases, the consequences of the interpretation.

Exploring Total Defensive Silence. If an agent investigating a case faces this kind of silence of one or more of those involved, he can not count on their testimonies. So, we have to remove the declaration of those people, as stated in Definition 2.

So expressing this kind of silence in the context of this second puzzle; what would happen if silence with common sense is presented as a possibility? What conclusions the interrogator or judge can reach if some of the suspects decide to intentionally shut up?

Applying this first rule to each person giving his testimony and executing the programs, we get those presumable guilty. That is, as a result of the silence of a person, we can analyze who becomes a candidate to blame.

The possible outcomes (guilty) when a one or more suspects decide intentionally to omit their testimonies are presented in Table 1, illustrating the right to remain silent. In this, we can notice that the culprit can be anyone depending on who decides to shut up. For the possibilities, we can comment:

1. {} corresponds to the original scheme where nobody is silent, i.e. every testimony is taken into account. The only model for this case is Ben, as before.
2. When Andy is silent, the offender turns out to be either Ben or Cole. Each answer corresponds to a model, as shown below.

```
Answer: 1
murderer(ben).
Answer: 2
murderer(cole).
SATISFIABLE
```

3. When Ben is silent, any of the three suspects may be guilty. Intuitively we can think that Ben's silence has more decision capability since anyone involved can turn out as guilty.
4. Cole's silence can turn Andy or Ben guilty.
5. With the remaining possibilities, related to more than one person, any of the three involved may be guilty.

Table 1. Defensive Silence (DS) model for agent.

Silent agent(s)	Presumable culprit
{}	{ben}
{andy}	{ben, cole}
{ben}	{cole, andy, ben}
{cole}	{andy, ben}
{andy, ben}	{cole, ben, andy}
{ben, cole}	{cole, andy, ben}
{andy, cole}	{cole, ben, andy}
{andy, ben, cole}	{cole, ben, andy}

Analyzing Partial Defensive Silence. For this variant of silence, what would happen if only part of the information about the case is omitted? At the atomic level, which of the arguments of each one of the suspects has more impact on their total silence? That is, we can bring into consideration Partial Defensive Silence, as detailed in Definition 3. Here we briefly provide some results:

Table 2. Partial Defensive Silence models for Andy

Silenced testimony (predicate)	Presumable culprit
{says(andy, innocent(andy))}	{ben}
{says(andy, hated(cole, vinny))}	{ben}
{says(andy, friends(ben, vinny))}	{ben, cole}

Table 3. Partial Defensive Silence models for Ben

Silenced testimony (predicate)	Presumable culprit
{says(ben, out-of-town(ben))}	{andy, ben}
{says(ben, know(ben, vinny))}	{ben, cole}

1. In the Andy case, with the silence of his first or second statement the culprit can be Ben, with the silence of the third one, Cole also appears as presumably guilty. Table 2 details the consequences of partial silence of Andy.
2. Ben is the most affected with his silence, either total or partial since he comes out in every model, as Table 3 shows.
3. Cole can also decide, without incriminating himself, whom to reveal as guilty. Table 4 shows the different answers obtained.

Exploring Total Acquiescent Silence. The second type of silence is related with the old saying "silence is consent", expressing a passive disengaged attitude. In this interpretation, we operationalize it by deleting the person's testimony and inserting new assertions related with what he is implicitly assuming with his silence (Definition 4). For example, in the case of Ben, we have to:

1. Ignore the following assertions, since he is not declaring anything:

```
says(ben, outoftown(ben)).
says(ben, didnotknow(ben, vinny)).
```

2. Add the following assertions, to model his consent on what others say:

```
1   says(ben, innocent(andy)).
2   says(ben, together(andy, vinny)).
3   says(ben, together(ben, vinny)).
4   says(ben, friends(ben, vinny)).
5   says(ben, hated(cole, vinny)).
6   says(ben, innocent(cole)).
```

Table 5 shows the solutions reached for the case when one or several persons are silenced under the interpretation of Acquiescent Silence, i.e. silence as consent. Again, the first line corresponds to the original situation where everybody

Table 4. Partial Defensive Silence models for Cole

Silenced testimony (predicate)	Presumable culprit
{says(cole, innocent(cole))}	{ben}
{says(cole, together(andy, vinny))}	{ben}
{says(cole, together(ben, vinny))}	{andy, ben}

Table 5. Acquiescent Silence (AS) for agent.

Row	Silent agent(s)	Presumable culprit
1	{}	{ben}
2	{andy}	UNSATISFIABLE
3	{ben}	{ben}
4	{cole}	UNSATISFIABLE
5	{andy, ben}	{ben, andy}
6	{ben, cole}	{ben, cole}
7	{andy, cole}	{cole, andy}
8	{andy, ben, cole}	{cole, ben, andy}

has declared, leading to Ben as the murderer. Notice that there is no model (solution) in cases 2 and 4, where UNSATISFIABLE is produced. These situations can be interpreted that there is no evidence to blame any of the suspects, possibly leading to a mistrial. So, under this scheme, Andy and Cole are those who could benefit from remaining silent. In cases 5, 6 and 7, the person who speaks can become out of suspicion. In the latter case, as expected from common sense, when everybody is silent (no one has revealed any information), anyone can be the culprit.

Combination of Two Types of Silence. Another situation that can occur in legal cases is that those involved (witnesses) display different types of silence.

Table 6. Combining types of silences

Defensive silent	Acquiescent silent	Declarant	Presumable culprit
andy	ben	cole	{ben}
andy	cole	ben	{cole}
ben	andy	cole	{andy}
ben	cole	andy	{cole}
cole	andy	ben	{andy}
cole	ben	andy	{cole, andy, ben}

If we find that some of those declaring recur to different types of silence, what would be the consequences in the case under consideration? In particular, for the mystery, who will be guilty if the Defensive and Acquiescent silences are combined in the testimony? Table 6 shows the possibilities when Total Defensive Silence and Acquiescent Silence are combined among the three agents involved.

We can notice that under these different scenarios, the models reduce to point to only one person, that who keeps silent as consent, except in the case of the last row.

3.3   Discussion

It is evident that the silence in the testimony of the agents is an important factor in decision making of a jury or judge to assign a qualification to one of them, followed by the corresponding sentence in the cases that merits it. For instance, [2] provides an account of the use of the phrase *no comment* in police interviews, as a way to invoke the right to silence. The proposed formulations of silence can serve as a basis for the interpretation of the possible intentions of the testimonies in these cases.

Applying the interpretations to an actual case, some situations can occur. For instance, the obvious case is when one of those involved recurs to his right to remain silent. We can then proceed to consider, one at a time, the two types of silence for such person. However, other situations can emerge, for instance when two declarants A and B separately coincide in statements p and q, but let say A in addition declares r. We can then hypothesize an acquiescent silence of B, or even a partial defensive silence, since he is omitting r, and proceed accordingly to represent and analyze the case.

4   Conclusion

The silence was before the word and the acts of silence emerge from the acts of speech.

Silence expresses valuable information that can be employed for decision making. In particular, when the intentional silent is interpreted according to its context, we achieve implicatures.

Understanding and modeling the implications of silence can be useful as we have shown in a case study. A collection of actual testimonies has been elusive, meanwhile we continue exploring other puzzles involving testimonies with new challenging features. We foresee a valuable analysis of different scenarios in legal cases involving testimonies and different kinds of silence.

As future work, we plan to extend the interpretations to incorporate prosocial silence, i.e. retaining work-related information or opinions with the goal of benefiting other people or an organization.

It remains to bring the interpretations of silence to a more general framework for agent interaction, beyond testimonies and puzzles. In this direction, we are also exploring to consider payoffs of agents involved in the interaction, as well as to the predicates to know who or what has more gains with silence, as an instrument in making decisions.

The silence can be intentional, active, conscious, strategic, purposeful, powerful and completely brief.

Acknowledgements. The first author thanks the support provided by Consejo Nacional de Ciencia y Tecnología and Benemérita Universidad Autónoma de Puebla.

Appendix. Knights-and-Knaves.pl Program

```
agent(a;b;c).
1{knight(P),knave(P)}1 :- agent(P).

2{knight(b),knight(c)}2 :- knight(a).
:- knave(a),knight(b),knight(c).

2{knave(a),knight(c)}2 :- knight(b).
:- knave(b),knave(a),knight(c).
```

References

1. Dyne, L.V., Ang, S., Botero, I.C.: Conceptualizing employee silence and employee voice as multidimensional constructs. J. Manag. Stud. **40**(6), 1359–1392 (2003)
2. Garbutt, J.: The use of no comment by suspects in police interviews. In: Schröter, M., Taylor, C. (eds.) Exploring Silence and Absence in Discourse. PSD, pp. 329–357. Springer, Cham (2018). https://doi.org/10.1007/978-3-319-64580-3_12
3. Garg, D., Abadi, M.: A modal deconstruction of access control logics. In: Amadio, R. (ed.) FoSSaCS 2008. LNCS, vol. 4962, pp. 216–230. Springer, Heidelberg (2008). https://doi.org/10.1007/978-3-540-78499-9_16
4. Gelfond, M., Kahl, Y.: Knowledge Representation, Reasoning, and the Design of Intelligent Agents: The Answer-Set Programming Approach. Cambridge University Press, Cambridge (2014)
5. Grice, H.P.: Logic and conversation. In: Cole, P., et al. (ed.) Syntax and Semantics, vol. 3, pp. 41–58. Speech Acts (1975)
6. Khatchadourian, H.: How to Do Things with Silence, vol. 63. Walter de Gruyter GmbH & Co KG, Berlin (2015)
7. Kurzon, D.: The right of silence: a socio-pragmatic model of interpretation. J. Pragmat. **23**(1), 55–69 (1995)
8. Lifschitz, V.: What is answer set programming? In: AAAI, vol. 8, pp. 1594–1597 (2008)
9. Pearce, D.: Stable inference as intuitionistic validity. J. Log. Program. **38**(1), 79–91 (1999)
10. Seidmann, D.J., Stein, A.: The right to silence helps the innocent: a game-theoretic analysis of the fifth amendment privilege. Harv. Law Rev. **114**, 430–510 (2000)
11. Smullyan, R.M.: Forever Undecided. Knopf, New York (2012)
12. Swanson, E.: Omissive implicature. Philos. Top. **45**(2), 117–138 (2017)
13. Syrjänen, T.: Lparse 1.0 user's manual. Citeseer (2000)

14. Walton, D.: Witness Testimony Evidence: Argumentation, Artificial Intelligence, and Law. Cambridge University Press, Cambridge (2008)
15. Zalta, E.N., Nodelman, U., Allen, C., Perry, J.: Stanford Encyclopedia of Philosophy (2003)

Hybrid Semantics-Aware Recommendations Exploiting Knowledge Graph Embeddings

Cataldo Musto[✉], Pierpaolo Basile, and Giovanni Semeraro

Department of Computer Science, University of Bari Aldo Moro, Bari, Italy
{cataldo.musto,pierpaolo.basile,giovanni.semeraro}@uniba.it

Abstract. Graph-based recommendation methods represent an established research line in the area of recommender systems. Basically, these approaches provide users with personalized suggestions by modeling a *bipartite* graph that connects the users to the items they like and exploit such connections to identify items that are interesting for the target user.

In this work we propose a *hybrid semantics-aware* recommendation method that aims to improve classical graph-based approaches in a twofold way: *(i)* we extend and enhance the representation by modeling a *tripartite* graph, that also includes descriptive properties of the items in the form of DBPEDIA entities. *(ii)* we run graph embedding techniques over the resulting graph, in order to obtain a vector-space representation of the items to be recommended.

Given such a representation, we use the resulting embeddings to *cast* the recommendation problem to a classification one. In particular, we learn a classification model by exploiting *positive* and *negative* embeddings (the items the user liked and those she did not like, respectively), and we use such a model to classify new items as *interesting* or *not interesting* for the target user.

In the experimental evaluation we evaluated the effectiveness of our method on varying of different graph embedding techniques and on several topologies of the graph. Results show that the embeddings learnt by combining collaborative data points with the information gathered from DBPEDIA led to the best results and also beat several state-of-the-art techniques.

Keywords: Recommender system · Graph embedding · Linked data

1 Introduction

The concept of Linked Open Data (LOD) cloud [4] was introduced to describe the huge set of datasets (see Fig. 1) released throughout the Linked Open Data initiative, a project started in the late 2000s that inherited some of the ideas originally spread by the name of *Semantic Web*.

© Springer Nature Switzerland AG 2019
M. Alviano et al. (Eds.): AI*IA 2019, LNAI 11946, pp. 87–100, 2019.
https://doi.org/10.1007/978-3-030-35166-3_7

As proved by recent statistics[1], thanks to the collaborative effort behind the Linked Open Data initiative, the goal of the project is nearly to be reached. Indeed, a huge amount of *RDF triples* has been released on the Web in the last few years, thus contributing to the creation of the so-called *Web of Data*.

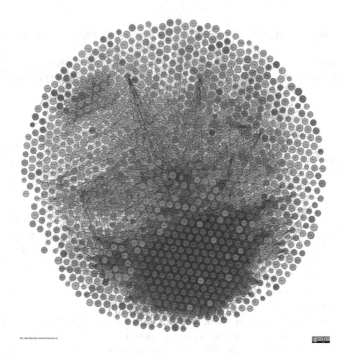

Fig. 1. The Linked Open Data cloud. Each bubble represents a dataset (a set of RDF statements). Datasets encoding similar or related information are represented with the same colors. (Color figure online)

Such a huge availability of semantics-aware machine-readable data attracted researchers and practitioners willing to investigate how these information can be exploited to develop new services and to improve the effectiveness of existing algorithms. Specifically, in the area of recommender systems (RS), data extracted from knowledge graphs such as DBPEDIA [1] or FREEBASE [6] can be helpful to tackle two of the classical problems of RS [12], as the *limited content analysis problem*, namely, the absence of content-based features that describe the items, and the *over-specialization problem*, namely, the triviality of the recommendations which are often too similar to the items the user already liked.

In the first case, *descriptive* features of the items can be freely collected from knowledge graphs and can be exploited, even when no textual content that describe the item is available. As an example, Fig. 2 shows a tiny portion of

---

[1] http://stats.lod2.eu/.

the properties available in DBPEDIA that describe the band *The Coldplay*. Such features range from very basic information, as the fact that *Chris Martin* is one of the members of the band, to more interesting and less trivial data points, as the fact that the group won a *Grammy Award*.

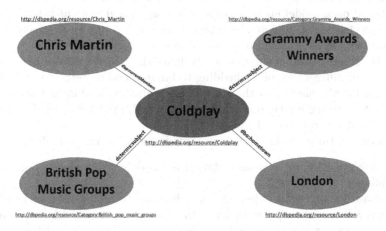

Fig. 2. A (small) part of the properties available in the DBPEDIA describing the band *The Coldplay*

In the latter - as we will show in this work - the features gathered from a knowledge graph, such as DBPEDIA, can be used to learn a graph-based data model that relies on the connections between users, items and descriptive properties gathered from the knowledge graph. This can lead to a more precise representation of the interests of the user and to more accurate (and maybe surprising) recommendations.

In parallel, graph embedding (GE) techniques emerged as an effective mean to encode the information modeled in knowledge graphs. Basically, these approaches take as input a graph and return as output a set of vectors representing its nodes. Such a representation tends to preserve the structural equivalence between nodes, that is to say, nodes having a similar "role" in the graph (*e.g.,* nodes acting as hubs) or nodes having similar neighborhoods tend to have similar embeddings. As shown in the literature, such techniques obtained very good performance in a broad range of scenarios where data can be modeled as a graph, as biology, social networks and so on [8].

Given that the information encoded in recommendation tasks can be easily modeled as a *graph* that connects users, items and descriptive properties of the items, through this paper we want to assess to what extent GE techniques can be useful to tackle the problem of learning a representation of the items in a recommendation scenario.

To this end, we propose a recommendation strategy based on the following steps: (1) a tripartite graph-based data model connecting users, items and entities gathered from DBPEDIA is built; (2) GE techniques as Node2Vec [9] and

Laplacian Eigenmaps (LE) [3] are applied over the tripartite graph, and a set of vectors is obtained as output; (3) the resulting vectors are used to train a *classification model* with positive and negative examples, that is to say, the item the user liked and those she did not like. Finally, such a model is used to predict whether a new and unseen item is interesting or not for the target user. Given that our graph-based data model encodes both *collaborative* and *content-based* information coming from user-item and item-properties connections, respectively, we can label our method as a *hybrid* recommendation strategy.

In the experimental evaluation we evaluate the effectiveness of our method on varying of different graph embedding techniques and on several topologies of the graph. Results show that the embeddings learnt by combining collaborative data points with the information gathered from DBPEDIA led to the best results and also beat several state-of-the-art techniques.

To sum up, through this article we provide the following contributions:

- We develop a hybrid recommendation methodology based on classification techniques;
- We investigate to what extent graph embedding techniques can be helpful to learn a vector space representation of the items in a recommendation scenario;
- We validate our methodology by evaluating its effectiveness with respect to several state-of-the-art baselines.

The rest of the article is organized as follows: Sect. 2 provides an overview of the state of the art in the area. Section 3 describes the basics of the proposed recommendation framework by introducing both our graph-based data model and the techniques used to create our embeddings. Next, in Sect. 4 we show the results of our experiments and in Sect. 5 we discuss the main findings of this work.

2   State of the Art

This work investigates two different research lines: *(i)* the impact of features gathered from knowledge graphs on the overall accuracy of a RS and *(ii)* the effectiveness of graph embedding techniques in the task of learning a vector space representation of the items in a recommendation scenario. In the following, we provide an overview of relevant research in the areas.

Research in the area of semantics-aware recommender systems [7] showed several attempts of investigating the impact of data available in the LOD cloud on the overall accuracy of recommendation models. These attempts include the definition of semantic similarity measures [17,20], the injection of the exogenous knowledge available in DBPEDIA [14,15] (*e.g.*, the *actor* of a movie or the *genre* of a book), or the introduction of features based on the paths that exist in the tripartite graph connecting users, items and entities available in DBPEDIA [18]. In all these cases, the literature confirmed that recommendation methods exploiting knowledge graphs tend to beat basic collaborative and content-based recommendation algorithms [2].

As for graph-based recommendation, the idea of tackling a recommendation task through a graph-based data model is not new, since Huang et al. [11], Bogers et al. [5] and Zhang et al. [24] gave evidence of the validity of the intuition in several domains. Conversely, the insight of applying GE techniques is relatively newer. As an example, in [23] the authors implement a RS for Points-of-Interests (POI) that applies embedding techniques over the graph modeling the available POIs. Similarly, [19] applied GE techniques on a tripartite graph in order to calculate user/item and item/item similarity, and uses these similarities to feed a learning to rank framework. With respect to these work, the novelty of this paper lies in the current aspects:

- Differently from [23], where graph embedding techniques are applied to the bipartite graph connecting users and POIs, in our approach nodes coming from DBPEDIA are included in the representation. Accordingly, we can state that we used GE techniques to learn richer and hybrid embeddings that encode both collaborative and content-based information.
- Differently from [19], we tackled the recommendation problem as a classification one, by using the resulting embeddings as input to build a classification model. Moreover, another distinguishing aspect is the comparison of two different methodologies (Node2Vec and LE) in a recommendation task.

To conclude, through this work we provide a preliminary investigation to assess the effectiveness of knowledge graph embeddings in recommendation tasks. Our expectation is that through this work we will trigger similar research in the area. Indeed, many more graph embedding techniques currently exist, and a comparative and empirical analysis of the accuracy of such methods can be really helpful to improve the understanding of the efficacy of GE embedding methods in recommendation scenarios.

3 Methodology

In this section we outline our methodology for semantics-aware recommendations based on GE techniques. In particular, in the following we will first introduce our graph-based data model that relies on users, items and data available in DBPEDIA, next we will show how GE techniques can be applied to obtain a vector space representation of the items to be recommended.

3.1 Data Model

The main idea behind our methodology is to represent *users* and *items* as *nodes* in a graph. Formally, given a set of users $U = \{u_1 \ldots u_n\}$ and a set of items $I = \{i_1 \ldots u_m\}$, a *bipartite* graph $G = \langle V, E \rangle$ is instantiated. Given that a node is created for each user and for each item, then $|V| = |U| + |I|$. Next, an (undirected) edge connecting a user u with an item i is created for each positive feedback expressed by that user, thus $E = \{(u, i)|likes(u, i) = true\}$. In other terms, we connect the users to the items they like through an unweighted undirected edge.

Such a basic formulation, built on the ground of simple *collaborative* data points (we just modelled user-item pairs as in collaborative filtering), can be enriched by introducing *additional* nodes and edges extracted from DBPE-DIA. Formally, we define an extended graph $G_{DB} = \langle V_{DB_{ALL}}, E_{DB_{ALL}} \rangle$, where $V_{DB_{ALL}} = V \cup V_{DB}$ and $E_{DB_{ALL}} = E \cup E_{DB}$.

E_{DB} represents the new connections resulting from the properties encoded in DBPEDIA (e.g. *subject, genre, ...*), while V_{DB} represents the new set of nodes which are connected to the items $i_1 \ldots i_m \in I$ through the properties in DBPE-DIA. Accordingly, G_{DB} becomes a *tripartite* graph, containing users, items and entities describing the items extracted from DBPEDIA.

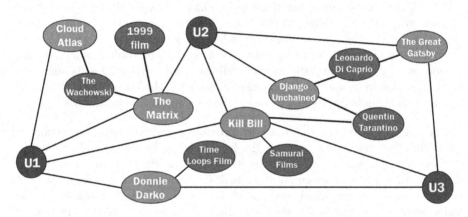

Fig. 3. Toy example of a graph-based data model. *Blue* nodes represent users, *green* nodes represent items, *red* nodes represent data gathered from DBPEDIA. In our setting, each item and each entity from DBPEDIA is mapped to a unique URI (*e.g.,* http://dbpedia.org/resource/Donnie_Darko or http://dbpedia.org/resource/ 1999_films), while each edge connected to a red node is labelled with the descriptor of the property (*e.g.,* dct:subject or dbo:starring) For the sake of readability, we did not explicitly reported the URIs. (Color figure online)

An example of our complete graph-based data model is provided in Fig. 3. If we consider the movie *Kill Bill*, the information about the director of the movie is available in DBPEDIA and encoded through the property http://dbpedia.org/ property/director. Consequently, an extra node *Quentin Tarantino* is added to V_{DB} and an extra edge, labelled with the name of the property, is instantiated in E_{DB} to connect the movie with its director. Similarly, if we consider the property http://dbpedia.org/property/starring, new nodes and edges are defined in order to model the relationship between *Kill Bill* and the main actors, such as *Leonardo di Caprio*. In turn, given that *Leonardo di Caprio* acted in several movies, many new edges are added to the graph and many new paths now connect different movies. These paths would not have been available if only *collaborative data points* were instantiated.

Given the above presented data model, in this work we compared the effectiveness of the embeddings learnt by evaluating three different topologies of the graph. The first one, referred to as *collaborative data model*, only includes user-item edges (those connecting blue and green nodes). The second one, referred to as DBPEDIA-*based data model*, models item-entity edges built on the ground of data gathered from DBPEDIA (green and red nodes). Finally, the third one is the *complete data model*, that encodes both collaborative data points and information gathered from DBPEDIA in a unique representation.

In the experimental session the effectiveness of our recommendation framework on varying of these topologies will be evaluated. It is worth to note that in this first setting we did not apply any feature selection algorithm on the properties available in DBPEDIA and we injected all of them in our data model[2].

3.2 Graph Embedding Techniques

The aim of graph embedding techniques is to represent nodes in a graph as dense vectors by projecting them in a vector space. The task is challenging since the vector representation of the nodes should preserve the structure of the graph and the connections between individual nodes. In the past decade, several methods have been proposed to solve this problem. Basically, they can be categorized in three main classes: (1) Factorization-based methods; (2) Random Walk-based methods and (3) Deep Learning-based methods.

In this work takes into account two GE algorithms: a Factorization-based method, namely Laplacian Eigenmaps (LE) [3], and a Random Walk-based approach as Node2Vec [9]. Due to space reasons, we cannot provide many details about the techniques. We suggest to refer to [8] for a complete discussion of the topic.

In a nutshell, the idea behind Factorization-based methods is to factorize a matrix that models the connections between nodes. LE constructs a weighted graph of nodes and a set of edges connecting neighbors. The embedding map is then provided by computing the eigenvectors of the Laplacian graph. The dimension d of the embedding is obtained by taking the eigenvectors corresponding to the d smallest eigenvalues of the normalized Laplacian. Typically, embeddings constructed by LE tend to preserve the 1st order proximity, that is to say, *two nodes with very similar neighbourhood will have a similar representation*. More details are reported in [3].

On the other side, Node2Vec tries to preserve higher order proximity between nodes. This is done by maximizing the probability of occurrence of subsequent nodes in fixed length random walks. This feature is important when we observe only a portion of the graph or the graph is too large to measure in its entirety. Differently from other approaches based on Random Walk, it defines a flexible

---

[2] As future work, we will investigate the effectiveness of feature selection algorithm on the quality of the embeddings.

notion of a node's network neighbourhood and implements a biased random walk procedure, which efficiently explores diverse neighbourhoods. Such a flexibility makes Node2vec able to generalize basic Random Walk-based approaches that rely on more rigid notions of network neighbourhoods, and let the methodology obtain richer representations. Generally speaking, such a representation is able to learn the concept of structural equivalence between nodes, that is to say, *two nodes having the same "role" in the graph (e.g., nodes acting as hubs) will have a similar representation* even if they do not share any (or just a few) neighbours.

To sum up, in this work we compared two different methodologies for building embeddings based on knowledge graphs: A *community-preserving technique* that learns similar embeddings for nodes having similar neighbourhoods, as LE, and a *structural-preserving technique* as Node2Vec, that uses random walks to take also into account structural information about the topology of the graph. In our specific setting, we used such techniques to learn a vector-space representation of the items to be recommended, built on the ground of the tripartite graph connecting users, items and descriptive properties gathered from DBPEDIA. In the experimental session the effectiveness of resulting vectors in a recommendation scenario will be evaluated.

3.3   Recommendation Framework

In this work we *casted* the recommendation task to a classification one, that is to say, we used the vectors representing the items the user liked as *positive examples* and those she did not like as *negative examples*. Next, we trained the classifiers and we used the models to classify all the items the user did not yet consume as *interesting* or not *interesting* for her.

Formally, we define a predicate $rate(u, i) = true$ if user $u \in U$ rated item $i \in I$. Thus, we can define the training set for the target user as $TR(u) = \{i_j \in I | rate(u, i_j) = true\}$ and the corresponding test set as $TE(u) = I - TR(u)$. Next, for each item i we define a *representation function* ϕ that takes as input the item and a specific *topology* of the graph, and returns as output the representation returned by the GE algorithm. Formally, given a specific topology T chosen among those we previously presented, we define the representation function as $\phi(i, T) = i_T$.

To sum up, given a target user u, a training set $TR(u)$, and topology T, our classifier is fed with the examples $i_T \in TR(u)$ and we use the classification model to predict the most interesting items for the target user. Specifically, items in the test set are ranked according to the *confidence* of the prediction returned by the classification algorithm and the *top-K* items are returned to the target user. In the experimental session the overall effectiveness of our recommendation framework has been evaluated by varying different topologies. This aspect will be thoroughly described in the experimental protocol.

Table 1. Statistics for MovieLens (ML), LibraryThing (LT) and Last.fm (LFM) datasets.

	ML	LT	LFM
#Users	6,040	7,112	1,892
#Items	3,883	37,231	17,632
Ratings	1,000,209	626,000	92,834
%Positive	57.51%	64.84%	53,10%
Sparsity	96.42%	99,99%	99.80%
#Mapped	3,301	11,695	10,180
#Properties	60	70	81
#Triples	397,655	601,245	844,208
#Entities	139,629	211,187	313,575

4 Experimental Evaluation

The experimental session was designed to answer to the following research questions:

- What is the impact of graph embedding techniques on the overall accuracy of our recommendation model? *(Experiment 1)*
- How does our framework perform with respect to other state-of-the-art techniques? *(Experiment 2)*.

4.1 Experimental Protocol

Experiments were carried out on three state-of-the-art datasets, i.e. MOVIELENS-1M (ML1M), LIBRARYTHING and LAST.FM. Statistics about the datasets are reported in Table 1. For all the datasets, we used a 80%–20% training-test split. Data were split in order to maintain the ratio between positive and negative ratings for each fold. Different protocols were adopted to build user profiles: in MOVIELENS-1M, user preferences are expressed on a 5-point discrete scale, thus we decided to consider as *positive* only those ratings equal to 4 and 5. For LAST.FM we considered as positive ratings those that were greater than the median of the users' listening count, negative otherwise. Finally, LIBRARYTHING ratings are expressed on a 10-point scale, so we considered as *positive* only the ratings greater or equal to 8. In all these cases, we followed the protocols already adopted in literature [18].

Mapping Data to DBPEDIA. In order to extract information from DBPEDIA, we carried out a *mapping* procedure aiming at identifying a URI in DBPEDIA for all the items (movies, books, artists). For each dataset, we exploited a mapping already available[3] which is obtained by launching a SPARQL query based on

---

[3] Github repository of LOD-aware datasets - https://github.com/sisinflab/LODrecsys-datasets.

descriptive properties of the item (*e.g.*, the name of the movie). After the mapping, a huge set of new entities and new edges is encoded in the graph. Some statistics is reported in Table 1. The values beside #*entities* and #*triples* refer to the new nodes (*e.g.*, *Leonardo di Caprio*) and the new edges (*e.g.*, the relation dbo:starring existing between *Leonardo di Caprio* and *Django Unchained*) created in the graph. Finally, #properties refers to the different properties that can be used to connect items and entities (*e.g.*, dbo:starring).

Experimental Parameters. As previously stated, we took into account three different graph topologies: *collaborative, DBpedia-based and complete*. For each topology, graph embedding were built by relying on two different GE techniques, namely *Node2Vec and LE*. We also compared three different sizes of the embeddings (128, 256 and 512), to state whether larger embeddings lead to an improvement of the accuracy. Given that we cast the recommendation problem to a classification one, the effectiveness of the different configurations is calculated in terms of F1-measure. Logistic Regression was used as classification algorithm.

Implementation Details. Embeddings are calculated by using the implementation of the abovementioned methods available in the GEM library[4]. Node2Vec is run with the following parameters: *iterations* = 1, *walkLength* = 80, *numberWalks* = 10, *contextSize* = 10, $ret_p = 1$, $inout_q = 1$, while no parameter had to be set for LE.

4.2   Discussion of the Results

Results of Experiment 1 are reported in Table 2. The first finding emerging from the experiment is that the size of the embeddings did not affect the overall accuracy of the model. Indeed, by comparing the results a very tiny difference among the configurations typically emerges. This is a first interesting outcome that is valid for all the datasets, and shows that also *small embeddings* can be used to learn an item representation based on both collaborative and DBPEDIA-based data points.

As regards the techniques we compared, *Node2Vec tended to obtain better results than LE on all the datasets* as well as for all the dimensions of the embeddings. Even if this finding was somehow expected, since Node2Vec can learn a richer representation that preserves both community-based and topology-based information, it is not trivial that such a representation can be more effective also for recommendation tasks. In this case, results showed that the use of Node2Vec always leads to better results, and this is an useful finding to foster future research in the area.

Interesting findings also emerged by analyzing the results obtained on varying of the different topologies of the graph. Indeed, we noticed that the information gathered from DBPEDIA did not always lead to an effective representation of items: if we compare the results obtained through the DBPEDIA-based topology to those relying on the collaborative topology, it emerges that the embeddings

---

[4] Github repository of the GEM library - https://github.com/palash1992/GEM.

learnt by exploiting the collaborative data points obtained the best results in almost every comparison. However, the overall best results are obtained when *both* the information sources are took into account, as shown for the *Complete* configuration. This finding shows that the content-based features extracted from DBPEDIA do a great job when merged with other data points, thus they resulted as very useful to integrate and complete the information coming from other heterogeneous data points. This result is in line with previous work investigating the impact of features gathered from the LOD cloud in recommender systems [14,15].

Table 2. Results of Experiment 1. Configurations that beat the basic collaborative data model are reported in **bold**. The best performing configurations for each dataset are reported in **bold** and **underlined**.

	ML1M			LibraryThing			Last.fm		
Collaborative	*128*	*256*	*512*	*128*	*256*	*512*	*128*	*256*	*512*
Node2Vec	0.6831	0.6804	0.6829	0.6586	0.6575	0.6581	0.6100	0.6113	0.6089
LE	0.6624	0.6625	0.6623	0.6541	0.6540	0.6537	0.6079	0.6073	0.6067
DBPEDIA-based	*128*	*256*	*512*	*128*	*256*	*512*	*128*	*256*	*512*
Node2Vec	0.6590	0.6583	0.6581	0.6524	0.6527	0.6521	0.6066	0.6071	0.6078
LE	0.6585	0.6590	0.6592	0.6538	0.6534	**0.6546**	0.6064	0.6062	0.6065
Complete	*128*	*256*	*512*	*128*	*256*	*512*	*128*	*256*	*512*
Node2Vec	**__0.6886__**	**__0.6886__**	**0.6879**	**0.6592**	**__0.6599__**	**0.6585**	**__0.6117__**	0.6114	**0.6111**
LE	0.6604	0.6607	0.6604	0.6553	0.6540	**0.6539**	0.6067	0.6068	0.6067

Finally, we compared our methodology to several baselines. As reported in Table 3, our approach beats both classic baselines (as collaborative filtering algorithms and matrix factorization ones) as well as other techniques that also encode the information coming from DBPEDIA. Specifically, we compared our method to User-to-User (U2U) and Item-to-Item (I2I) CF algorithms, Bayesian Personalized Ranking Matrix Factorization (BPRMF) and a graph-based algorithm as Personalized PageRank [10]. As regards collaborative baselines, we used the implementations available in MyMediaLite library[5], while for PageRank we exploited the Jung library[6].

Due to space reasons, we just reported the best-performing configurations of parameters, that is to say, 80 neighbours for CF on ML1M and Last.fm and 30 neighbours on Librarything, and 20 factors for BPRMF for all the datasets. Moreover, we also evaluated two variants of BPRMF and PR that encode in the model the information extracted from DBPEDIA. Specifically, the features encoded are side features that enrich the original model, as shown in previous research [21].

---

[5] http://www.mymedialite.net/.
[6] http://jung.sourceforge.net/.

Table 3. Results of Experiment 2: comparison to baselines.

	ML1M	LibraryThing	Last.fm
I2I	0.5835	0.5935	0.5092
U2U	0.5970	0.5935	0.5115
BPRMF	0.5297	0.5961	0.5117
PR	0.6023	0.6034	0.5990
BPRMF+LOD	0.6032	0.5964	0.5642
PR+LOD	0.6083	0.6152	0.6107
GE+LOD	**0.6886**	**0.6599**	**0.6117**

5   Conclusions and Future Work

In this paper we presented a semantics-aware recommendation strategy that uses graph embedding techniques to learn a vector space representation of the items to be recommended. Such a representation relies on the tripartite graph which connects users, items and entities gathered from DBPEDIA, thus it encodes both *collaborative* and *content-based information*.

Two main outcomes emerged from the experiment: first, our methodology showed that graph embedding techniques can learn an effective vector space representation that rely on the knowledge graph that connects users, items and entities gathered from DBPEDIA, since our approach overcame all the baselines we took into account. Next, results also showed the good impact of the properties extracted from DBPEDIA on the overall effectiveness of the model.

As future work, we will investigate two different directions: first, we will evaluate more graph embedding techniques since a larger overview of such techniques in recommendation scenarios is needed. On the other hand, we will evaluate features selection techniques as those proposed in [22] to filter out non-relevant properties gathered from DBPEDIA. Moreover, a broader comparison with other techniques to learn semantics-aware representations (*e.g.,* distributional semantics models [16] or representation exploiting user-generated content [13]) can be helpful to completely understand the effectiveness of such strategies.

References

1. Auer, S., Bizer, C., Kobilarov, G., Lehmann, J., Cyganiak, R., Ives, Z.: DBpedia: a nucleus for a web of open data. In: Aberer, K., et al. (eds.) ASWC/ISWC-2007. LNCS, vol. 4825, pp. 722–735. Springer, Heidelberg (2007). https://doi.org/10.1007/978-3-540-76298-0_52
2. Basile, P., Musto, C., de Gemmis, M., Lops, P., Narducci, F., Semeraro, G.: Aggregation strategies for linked open data-enabled recommender systems. In: European Semantic Web Conference (2014)
3. Belkin, M., Niyogi, P.: Laplacian eigenmaps and spectral techniques for embedding and clustering. In: Advances in Neural Information Processing Systems, pp. 585–591 (2002)

4. Bizer, C.: The emerging web of linked data. IEEE Intell. Syst. **24**(5), 87–92 (2009)
5. Bogers, T.: Movie recommendation using random walks over the contextual graph. In: Proceedings of the 2nd International Workshop on Context-Aware Recommender Systems (2010)
6. Bollacker, K., Evans, C., Paritosh, P., Sturge, T., Taylor, J.: Freebase: a collaboratively created graph database for structuring human knowledge. In: Proceedings of the 2008 ACM SIGMOD International Conference on Management of Data, pp. 1247–1250. ACM (2008)
7. de Gemmis, M., Lops, P., Musto, C., Narducci, F., Semeraro, G.: Semantics-aware content-based recommender systems. In: Ricci, F., Rokach, L., Shapira, B. (eds.) Recommender Systems Handbook, pp. 119–159. Springer, Boston (2015). https://doi.org/10.1007/978-1-4899-7637-6_4
8. Goyal, P., Ferrara, E.: Graph embedding techniques, applications, and performance: a survey. arXiv preprint arXiv:1705.02801 (2017)
9. Grover, A., Leskovec, J.: node2vec: scalable feature learning for networks. In: Proceedings of the 22nd ACM SIGKDD International Conference on Knowledge Discovery and Data Mining, pp. 855–864. ACM (2016)
10. Haveliwala, T.H.: Topic-sensitive pagerank: a context-sensitive ranking algorithm for web search. IEEE Trans. Knowl. Data Eng. **15**(4), 784–796 (2003)
11. Huang, Z., Chung, W., Ong, T.-H., Chen, H.: A graph-based recommender system for digital library. In: Proceedings of the 2nd ACM/IEEE-CS Joint Conference on Digital Libraries, pp. 65–73. ACM (2002)
12. Lops, P., de Gemmis, M., Semeraro, G.: Content-based recommender systems: state of the art and trends. In: Ricci, F., Rokach, L., Shapira, B., Kantor, P.B. (eds.) Recommender Systems Handbook, pp. 73–105. Springer, Boston (2011). https://doi.org/10.1007/978-0-387-85820-3_3
13. Lops, P., de Gemmis, M., Semeraro, G., Musto, C., Narducci, F., Bux, M.: A semantic content-based recommender system integrating folksonomies for personalized access. In: Castellano, G., Jain, L.C., Fanelli, A.M. (eds.) Web Personalization in Intelligent Environments. Studies in Computational Intelligence, vol. 229, pp. 27–47. Springer, Heidelberg (2009). https://doi.org/10.1007/978-3-642-02794-9_2
14. Musto, C., Basile, P., Lops, P., de Gemmis, M., Semeraro, G.: Introducing linked open data in graph-based recommender systems. Inf. Process. Manag. **53**(2), 405–435 (2017)
15. Musto, C., Lops, P., de Gemmis, M., Semeraro, G.: Semantics-aware recommender systems exploiting linked open data and graph-based features. Knowl.-Based Syst. **136**, 1–14 (2017)
16. Musto, C., Semeraro, G., Lops, P., de Gemmis, M.: Random indexing and negative user preferences for enhancing content-based recommender systems. In: Huemer, C., Setzer, T. (eds.) EC-Web 2011. LNBIP, vol. 85, pp. 270–281. Springer, Heidelberg (2011). https://doi.org/10.1007/978-3-642-23014-1_23
17. Musto, C., Semeraro, G., Lops, P., de Gemmis, M., Narducci, F.: Leveraging social media sources to generate personalized music playlists. In: Huemer, C., Lops, P. (eds.) EC-Web 2012. LNBIP, vol. 123, pp. 112–123. Springer, Heidelberg (2012). https://doi.org/10.1007/978-3-642-32273-0_10
18. Ostuni, V.C., Di Noia, T., Di Sciascio, E., Mirizzi, R.: Top-N recommendations from implicit feedback leveraging linked open data. In: Proceedings of the 7th ACM Conference on Recommender Systems, pp. 85–92. ACM (2013)

19. Palumbo, E., Rizzo, G., Troncy, R.: Entity2rec: learning user-item relatedness from knowledge graphs for top-N item recommendation. In: Proceedings of the Eleventh ACM Conference on Recommender Systems, pp. 32–36. ACM (2017)
20. Piao, G., Breslin, J.G.: Measuring semantic distance for linked open data-enabled recommender systems. In: Proceedings of the 31st Annual ACM Symposium on Applied Computing, pp. 315–320. ACM (2016)
21. Shi, Y., Larson, M., Hanjalic, A.: Collaborative filtering beyond the user-item matrix: a survey of the state of the art and future challenges. ACM Comput. Surv. (CSUR) **47**(1), 3 (2014)
22. Wever, T., Frasincar, F.: A linked open data schema-driven approach for top-N recommendations. In: Proceedings of the Symposium on Applied Computing, pp. 656–663. ACM (2017)
23. Xie, M., Yin, H., Wang, H., Xu, F., Chen, W., Wang, S.: Learning graph-based POI embedding for location-based recommendation. In: Proceedings of the 25th ACM International on Conference on Information and Knowledge Management, pp. 15–24. ACM (2016)
24. Zhang, Z.-K., Zhou, T., Zhang, Y.-C.: Personalized recommendation via integrated diffusion on user-item-tag tripartite graphs. Phys. A **389**(1), 179–186 (2010)

Strongly Equivalent Epistemic Answer Set Programs

Ezgi Iraz Su$^{(\boxtimes)}$ (iD)

University of Toulouse, IRIT, Toulouse, France
Ezgi-Iraz.Su@irit.fr

Abstract. Epistemic answer set programming (EASP) is a recent epistemic extension of answer set programming (ASP), endowed with the epistemic answer set (EAS) semantics. EASs propose a straightforward generalisation of ASP's original answer set semantics. Moreover, they provide intended results both for cyclic and acyclic programs, possibly containing arbitrary constraints. Epistemic here-and-there logic (EHT) is also a recent epistemic extension of a well-known nonclassical logic called here-and-there logic (HT), which is intermediate between classical logic and intuitionistic logic. In this paper, we discuss a strong equivalence characterisation for EASP programs, which is identified on EHT.

Keywords: Answer set programming · Epistemic specifications · Modal logic S5 · Epistemic logic programs · Answer sets · World views · Strong equivalence

1 Introduction

Answer set programming (ASP) [5] is a declarative problem solving approach, and its semantics is given by *answer sets*. Answer set semantics provided a correct interpretation of negation as failure (NAF) and related ASP to nonmonotonic reasoning. Today, ASP has a wide range of applications in science and technology. However, the NAF operator of ASP cannot reason about over a whole range of answer sets. Especially in situations where there are multiple answer sets of a program, ASP requires a more powerful introspective reasoning, as first recognised by Gelfond [3]. To this end, Su has recently introduced an epistemic extension of ASP called *epistemic ASP* (EASP) [13].

EASP extended ASP with epistemic operators K and K̂, able to quantify over S5 models (sets of valuations). The interpretation of this new language is in terms of an *epistemic answer set* (EAS)—an S5 model minimising both truth (as in ASP) and also knowledge. Similar to the answer set semantics, the EAS semantics is also reduct-based, which is oriented to exclusively eliminate NAF. Thus, the reduct $\Pi^{\mathcal{A}}$ of an epistemic logic program Π w.r.t. an EAS candidate $\mathcal{A}$ is a positive (excluding NAF) EASP program. The selection of EASs from among all S5 models of a program is in two steps: first, we compute the reduct of a program by a candidate model; second, we search for the EASs of this reduct.

© Springer Nature Switzerland AG 2019
M. Alviano et al. (Eds.): AI*IA 2019, LNAI 11946, pp. 101–115, 2019.
https://doi.org/10.1007/978-3-030-35166-3_8

If the candidate model equals one of these EASs, then we call it an *EAS* of the original program. EASs perform well both with cyclic and acyclic programs, giving intuitive results. Moreover, they behave regularly with epistemic logic programs including constraints (headless rules) as in ASP[1]. To spell it out, in EASP, aligning with ASP, constraints are used to eliminate possible worlds of EASs—we can refute an EAS as a whole or remove just some of its worlds, violating the constraint.

The logic of here-and-there (HT) [6] is a well-known nonclassical (3-valued) logic, which is intermediate between classical logic and intuitionistic logic. Lifschitz et al. [7] used this monotonic logic to verify the strong equivalence of nonmonotonic ASP programs. Fariñas et al. [1] have recently extended HT with the epistemic modalities K and $\hat{K}$ in which K and $\hat{K}$ are non-dual (i.e., $\hat{K}$ is not equivalent to $\neg K \neg$). The resulting formalism is called *epistemic here-and-there logic* (EHT). As a result, EHT is a particular intuitionistic logic in which duality of necessity and possibility fails. Keeping track of the approach of [7], we here propose a strong equivalence characterisation by pointing out the relation between the strong equivalence of programs in nonmonotonic EASP and the logical equivalence of the corresponding theories in monotonic EHT. Two EASP programs Π_1 and Π_2 are said to be *equivalent* in the sense of the EAS semantics if they have the same EASs. Π_1 and Π_2 are further *strongly equivalent* if $\Pi_1 \cup \Pi$ and $\Pi_2 \cup \Pi$ are equivalent for every EASP program Π. Thus, our main goal in this paper is to prove that the strong equivalence concept in EASP can be captured by the logical equivalence concept in monotonic EHT. To spell it out, Π_1 and Π_2 are strongly equivalent in EASP if and only if their translations into EHT are logically equivalent.

The rest of the paper is organised as follows. Section 2 introduces a recent epistemic extension of ASP called EASP, whose semantics is given by epistemic answer sets. Section 3 recalls an epistemic extension of HT called EHT. Section 4 first defines strong equivalence of EASP programs and then prepare us for the main result of this paper by introducing some lemmas. Finally, we prove that the strong equivalence of EASP programs can be verified by checking the equivalence of their corresponding theories (finite sets of formulas) in EHT. Section 5 concludes the paper with some discussion.

2   Epistemic Answer Set Programming (**EASP**)

This section briefly recalls *epistemic ASP* (EASP), recently proposed by Su [13].

2.1   The Language of **EASP** ($\mathcal{L}_{\mathsf{EASP}}$)

The language $\mathcal{L}_{\mathsf{EASP}}$ extends that of ASP by epistemic modal operators K and $\hat{K}$. Literals (λ) of $\mathcal{L}_{\mathsf{EASP}}$ are of two types: *objective literals (l)* and *subjective literals (g)*.

---

[1] In ASP, constraints function to rule out answer sets violating them or they have a neutral effect.

l		g	
p	$\sim p$	$\mathsf{K}\, l$	$\hat{\mathsf{K}}\, l$

in which p ranges over a set $\mathbb{P}$ of atoms. $\mathcal{L}_{\mathsf{EASP}}$ has two negations; strong negation $\sim$ and NAF (aka, default negation) $\mathbf{not}$: $\mathbf{not}\,\lambda$ is read "λ is false by default" which means that *there is not enough evidence to infer λ, and so the query λ? is undetermined.*

An *EASP rule* r is a logical statement $head(r) \leftarrow body(r)$ of the explicit structure

$$\lambda_1 \,\mathbf{or}\, \dots \,\mathbf{or}\, \lambda_k \leftarrow \lambda_{k+1}, \dots, \lambda_m, \mathbf{not}\,\lambda_{m+1}, \dots, \mathbf{not}\,\lambda_n$$

in which λ_i's are arbitrary (objective or subjective) literals for every i, $0 \leq i \leq n$ with $0 \leq k \leq m \leq n$. When $k = 0$, we suppose $head(r)$ to be $\bot$ and call r a *constraint*. In particular, a constraint which is exclusively composed of (default-negated) subjective literals is called a *subjective constraint*. When $n = k$, we suppose $body(r)$ to be $\top$ and call r a *fact*. When $n = m$, i.e., r does not contain NAF, we call it a *positive* rule.

A (positive) *EASP program* is a finite collection of (positive) rules of EASP.

2.2   The Semantics of EASP: Epistemic Answer Sets (EASs)

The semantics of EASP is given by *epistemic answer sets* (EASs): given a positive EASP program Π, we first partition Π into two disjoint subprograms; Π_m and Π_c. The set of all *constraints* $r_c \in \Pi$ constitutes Π_c. The rest, i.e., the set $\Pi \setminus \Pi_c$ forms Π_m, which is the *main* part of the program Π. We begin with computing the ESMs of Π_m, each of which is then involved in an evaluation process carried out w.r.t. the constraints in Π_c.

Truth Conditions. Let $\mathbb{O}\text{-}Lit$ be the set of all objective literals of $\mathcal{L}_{\mathsf{EASP}}$. Let $\mathcal{A}$ be a nonempty collection of consistent sets of objective literals, and let $\mathcal{A}_0 \subseteq \mathcal{A}$. Then, we call the pair $\langle \mathcal{A}, \mathcal{A}_0 \rangle$ a *pointed* S5 model with $\mathcal{A}_0$ being the set of *designated* worlds. When $\mathcal{A}_0 = \{A\}$, we simply denote it by $\langle \mathcal{A}, A \rangle$. In an explicit representation, we underline the designated worlds. Satisfaction of literals is defined by: for $l \in \mathbb{O}\text{-}Lit$,

$\mathcal{A}, A \models l$	if $l \in A$;	$\mathcal{A}, A \models \mathbf{not}\,l$	if $l \notin A$.
$\mathcal{A}, A \models \mathsf{K}\,l$	if $l \in A'$ for every $A' \in \mathcal{A}$,	$\mathcal{A}, A \models \mathbf{not}\,\mathsf{K}\,l$	if $l \notin A'$ for some $A' \in \mathcal{A}$.
$\mathcal{A}, A \models \hat{\mathsf{K}}\,l$	if $l \in A'$ for some $A' \in \mathcal{A}$,	$\mathcal{A}, A \models \mathbf{not}\,\hat{\mathsf{K}}\,l$	if $l \notin A'$ for any $A' \in \mathcal{A}$.

Note that satisfaction of an objective literal l is independent of $\mathcal{A}$, while satisfaction of subjective literals $\mathsf{K}\,l$ and $\hat{\mathsf{K}}\,l$ is independent of A. Thus, we write $\mathcal{A} \models \mathsf{K}\,l$ or $A \models l$. Then, satisfaction of an EASP program Π is defined by: for every rule $r \in \Pi$, $\mathcal{A}, A \models r$ viz.

$$\text{``}\mathcal{A}, A \models body(r) \quad \text{implies} \quad \mathcal{A}, A \models head(r)\text{''}.$$

Definition 1 (weakening of a point in an S5 model). Given $\mathcal{A} \subseteq 2^{\text{0-}Lit}$, let $\mathbf{s} : \mathcal{A} \to 2^{\text{0-}Lit}$ be a *subset* map such that $\mathbf{s}(A) \subseteq A$ for every $A \in \mathcal{A}$. Then, a *weakening* of $\mathcal{A}$ at a point $A \in \mathcal{A}$ is identified with $\langle \mathbf{s}[\mathcal{A}], \mathbf{s}(A)\rangle^2$ such that $\mathbf{s} \neq id$ on $\mathcal{A}$ and $\mathbf{s}|_{\mathcal{A} \setminus \{A\}} = id$, by which we take a strict subset of $A \in \mathcal{A}$ and do not modify the rest. Formally, we say that $\langle \mathbf{s}[\mathcal{A}], \mathbf{s}(A)\rangle$ is *weaker* than $\langle \mathcal{A}, A\rangle$ at $A \in \mathcal{A}$ if

- $\mathbf{s}(A) \subset A$ and
- $\mathbf{s}[\mathcal{A}] = (\mathcal{A} \setminus \{A\}) \cup \{\mathbf{s}(A)\}$.

Then, we denote it by $\langle \mathbf{s}[\mathcal{A}], \mathbf{s}(A)\rangle \lhd \langle \mathcal{A}, A\rangle$.

We now introduce a nonmonotonic satisfaction relation for pointed S5 models $\langle \mathcal{A}, A\rangle$, involving a *truth-minimality* property based on set inclusion over the designated point A. This condition says that none of the weakenings of $\langle \mathcal{A}, A\rangle$ at $A \in \mathcal{A}$ is a model of Π.

Definition 2 (generalisation of the answer set definition of ASP to EASP). Let $\mathcal{A} \subseteq 2^{\text{0-}Lit}$ and $A \in \mathcal{A}$. Let Π be a positive EASP program. Then, we have: $\mathcal{A}, A \models^* \Pi$ iff

- $\mathcal{A}, A \models \Pi$ and
- $\mathbf{s}[\mathcal{A}], \mathbf{s}(A) \not\models \Pi$ for every subset map $\mathbf{s}$ such that $\langle \mathbf{s}[\mathcal{A}], \mathbf{s}(A)\rangle \lhd \langle \mathcal{A}, A\rangle$.

Thus, $\mathcal{A}$ is a *truth-minimal* (T-minimal) model of Π if $\mathcal{A}, A \models^* \Pi$ for every $A \in \mathcal{A}$.

Truth-minimality takes place locally, i.e., at each point of a model separately. So, it is not strong enough to give intuitive results. Thus, we need other orderings to choose intended ones among all T-minimal models of Π. Inspired by [10], we first define the set $\text{Ep}(\Pi)$ of subjective literals occurring in Π and taking the form of $\mathsf{not}\,\mathsf{K}\,l$ and $\hat{\mathsf{K}}\,l$:

$$\text{Ep}(\Pi) = \{\mathsf{not}\,\mathsf{K}\,l \ : \ \mathsf{K}\,l \text{ appears in } \Pi\} \cup \{\hat{\mathsf{K}}\,l \ : \ \hat{\mathsf{K}}\,l \text{ appears in } \Pi\}$$

Then, we take its subset $\Phi_{\mathcal{A}} = \{g \in \text{Ep}(\Pi) \ : \ \mathcal{A} \not\models g\}$ w.r.t. a collection $\mathcal{A} \subseteq 2^{\text{0-}Lit}$. Using this set, we define a Π-indexed partial preorder $\preceq_\Pi$ between S5 models as:

$$\mathcal{A} \preceq_\Pi \mathcal{A}' \quad \text{iff} \quad \Phi_{\mathcal{A}} \subseteq \Phi_{\mathcal{A}'}.$$

The strict version of $\preceq_\Pi$ is given as usual: $\mathcal{A} \prec_\Pi \mathcal{A}'$ iff $\mathcal{A} \preceq_\Pi \mathcal{A}'$ and $\mathcal{A}' \not\preceq_\Pi \mathcal{A}$. If $\mathcal{A} \preceq_\Pi \mathcal{A}'$ and $\mathcal{A}' \preceq_\Pi \mathcal{A}$, then $\mathcal{A}$ is *equivalent* to $\mathcal{A}'$ w.r.t. $\preceq_\Pi$ (denoted by $\mathcal{A} \approx_\Pi \mathcal{A}'$).

Definition 3 (epistemic answer set (EAS)). Let $\mathcal{A}$ be a nonempty collection of consistent sets of objective literals. Then $\mathcal{A}$ is an *EAS* of a constraint-free program Π if

---

^{2} $\mathbf{s}[\mathcal{A}]$ represents the image of $\mathcal{A} \subseteq 2^{\text{0-}Lit}$ under $\mathbf{s}$, and $\mathbf{s}(A)$ represents the value of $\mathbf{s}$ at $A \in \mathcal{A}$.

1. $\mathcal{A}$ is a T-minimal model of Π;
2. there is no T-minimal model $\mathcal{A}'$ of Π such that $\mathcal{A} \prec_\Pi \mathcal{A}'$;
3. there is no T-minimal model $\mathcal{A}'$ of Π such that $\mathcal{A} \subset \mathcal{A}'$.

The 2nd and 3rd items say that $\mathcal{A}$ is maximal w.r.t. $\preceq_\Pi$ and $\subseteq$ respectively. They are used together to minimise *knowledge*. In particular, item 2 also suggests a preference order over subjective literals as: $\hat{K} l > K l$ and the reverse way for the default-negated ones.

When Π contains constraints (i.e., when $\Pi_c \neq \emptyset$), we first compute $\mathbf{EAS}(\Pi_m)^3$ as explained above. Then, we evaluate each $\mathcal{A} \in \mathbf{EAS}(\Pi_m)$ with respect to their behaviour on Π_c: let $\varphi = \bigvee_{r_c \in \Pi_c} body(r_c)$. Then for every $\mathcal{A} \in \mathbf{EAS}(\Pi_m)$ and every $A \in \mathcal{A}$,

- if $\mathcal{A}, A \not\models \varphi$, then we *accept* $\mathcal{A}$ and call it $\mathcal{A}_{accept}$;
- if $\mathcal{A}, A \models \varphi$, then we *eliminate* $\mathcal{A}$.
- Finally, we reorganise the rest in such a way that we take the biggest possible subset $\mathcal{A}_{new} \subseteq \mathcal{A}$ viz. $\mathcal{A}_{new}$ is still a minimal model of Π_m and $\mathcal{A}_{new}, A \not\models \varphi$ for every $A \in \mathcal{A}_{new}$. In other words, $\mathcal{A}_{new}$ turns into $\mathcal{A}_{accept}$.

As a result, $\mathbf{EAS}(\Pi)$ is the collection of all $\mathcal{A}_{accept}$'s and $\mathcal{A}_{new}$'s. If Π_c exclusively contains subjective constraints, then we either refute or accept the EASs of Π_m. Now, we see how to find EASs of an arbitrary EASP program (which may include NAF as well).

Definition 4 (generalisation of the reduct definition of ASP to EASP). Let Π be an EASP program. Let $\mathcal{A} \subseteq 2^{\mathcal{O}\text{-}Lit}$ and $A \in \mathcal{A}$. Then, the reduct $\Pi^{\langle \mathcal{A}, A \rangle}$ of Π with respect to $\langle \mathcal{A}, A \rangle$ is given by replacing every occurrence of default-negated literals $\mathbf{not}\, \lambda$ in Π by

R1. $\bot$ if $\mathcal{A}, A \models \lambda$ (i.e., for $\lambda = l$ if $A \models l$; for $\lambda = K l/\hat{K} l$ if $\mathcal{A} \models K l/\hat{K} l$);
R2. $\top$ if $\mathcal{A}, A \not\models \lambda$ (i.e., for $\lambda = l$ if $A \not\models l$; for $\lambda = K l/\hat{K} l$ if $\mathcal{A} \not\models K l/\hat{K} l$).

Thus, $\mathcal{A}$ is a *truth-minimal (T-minimal)* model of Π if $\mathcal{A}, A \models^* \Pi^{\langle \mathcal{A}, A \rangle}$ for every $A \in \mathcal{A}$.

Example 1. Consider the program Σ, given in the following split form:

$$\Sigma = \quad p \,\mathbf{or}\, q \leftarrow \Big\} \Sigma_m \quad \cup \quad \begin{matrix} \leftarrow K p \\ \leftarrow \mathbf{not}\, \hat{K} q \end{matrix} \Big\} \Sigma_c$$

Σ_m is a positive program, and it has three T-minimal models: $\{\{p\}\}, \{\{q\}\}$ and $\{\{p\}, \{q\}\}$. Among these, only the last is an EAS of Σ_m due to set inclusion. First consider the program Σ_c. Note that Σ_c is equivalent to $\leftarrow K p \,\mathbf{or}\, \mathbf{not}\, \hat{K} q$. Then since $\{\{p\}, \{q\}\} \not\models K p \,\mathbf{or}\, \mathbf{not}\, \hat{K} q$ at each point, we accept $\{\{p\}, \{q\}\}$. Consequently, $\mathbf{EAS}(\Sigma) = \{\{\{p\}, \{q\}\}\}$.

---

[3] $\mathbf{EAS}(\Pi)$ denotes the set of all epistemic answer sets (EASs) of an EASP program Π.

Example 2. Consider the program Δ, given in the following split form:

$$\Delta = \left.\begin{array}{l} p \text{ or } q \leftarrow \\ r \leftarrow \mathsf{K}\,p \\ s \leftarrow \mathsf{not}\,\mathsf{K}\,q \end{array}\right\} \Delta_m \quad \cup \quad \leftarrow \mathsf{not}\,p \,\bigr\} \Delta_c$$

Δ_m has three minimal models; $\{\{p,r,s\}\}$, $\{\{q\}\}$ and $\{\{p,s\},\{q,s\}\}$. Indeed, we have:

$$\left.\begin{array}{l} p \text{ or } q \\ r \leftarrow \mathsf{K}\,p \\ s \leftarrow \top \end{array}\right\} \Delta_m^{\{\{p,r,s\}\}} \quad \left.\begin{array}{l} p \text{ or } q \\ r \leftarrow \mathsf{K}\,p \\ s \leftarrow \bot \end{array}\right\} \Delta_m^{\{\{q\}\}} \quad \left.\begin{array}{l} p \text{ or } q \\ r \leftarrow \mathsf{K}\,p \\ s \leftarrow \top \end{array}\right\} \Delta_m^{\{\{p,s\},\{q,s\}\}} \quad \left.\begin{array}{l} p \text{ or } q \\ r \leftarrow \mathsf{K}\,p \\ s \leftarrow \top \end{array}\right\} \Delta_m^{\{\{p,s\},\{q,s\}\}}$$

and for instance, while $\{\{p,r,s\}\} \models \Delta_m^{\{\{p,r,s\}\}}$, its weakenings, i.e., $\{\{p,r\}\}$, $\{\{p,s\}\}$, $\{\{r,s\}\}$, $\{\{p\}\}$, $\{\{r\}\}$, $\{\{s\}\}$ and $\{\emptyset\}$ do not satisfy $\Delta_m^{\{\{p,r,s\}\}}$. The rest is similar. Now consider $\mathrm{Ep}(\Gamma_m) = \{\mathsf{not}\,\mathsf{K}\,p, \mathsf{not}\,\mathsf{K}\,q\}$. It is easy to see that $\Phi_{\{\{p,r,s\}\}} = \{\mathsf{not}\,\mathsf{K}\,q\}$, $\Phi_{\{\{q\}\}} = \{\mathsf{not}\,\mathsf{K}\,p\}$ and $\Phi_{\{\{p,s\},\{q,s\}\}} = \mathrm{Ep}(\Delta_m)$. So, we have the following order: $\{\{p,r,s\}\} \prec_{\Delta_m} \{\{p,s\},\{q,s\}\}$ and $\{\{q\}\} \prec_{\Delta_m} \{\{p,s\},\{q,s\}\}$. As a result, $\mathrm{EAS}(\Delta_m) = \{\{\{p,s\},\{q,s\}\}\}$. However, since $\{\{p,s\},\{q,s\}\} \models \mathsf{not}\,p$, we reorganise this S5 model by deleting its point $\{q,s\}$. The resulting model $\{\{p,s\}\}$ is not a T-minimal model of Δ_m. Thus, we conclude that $\mathrm{EAS}(\Delta) = \emptyset$.

Example 3. Consider the program Γ, given in the following partitioned form:

$$\Gamma = \left.\begin{array}{l} p \leftarrow \mathsf{not} \sim q \\ \sim q \leftarrow \mathsf{not}\,p \\ r \leftarrow \hat{\mathsf{K}}\,p \end{array}\right\} \Gamma_m \quad \cup \quad \left.\begin{array}{l} \leftarrow p \\ \leftarrow \mathsf{not}\,\hat{\mathsf{K}}\,q \end{array}\right\} \Gamma_c$$

Then, $\{\{p,r\},\{\sim q,r\}\}$ is a T-minimal model of Γ_m. Indeed, we have the following reducts:

$$\left.\begin{array}{l} p \leftarrow \top \\ \sim q \leftarrow \bot \\ r \leftarrow \hat{\mathsf{K}}\,p \end{array}\right\} \Gamma_m^{\{\{p,r\},\{\sim q,r\}\}} \quad \text{and} \quad \left.\begin{array}{l} p \leftarrow \bot \\ \sim q \leftarrow \top \\ r \leftarrow \hat{\mathsf{K}}\,p \end{array}\right\} \Gamma_m^{\{\{p,r\},\{\sim q,r\}\}}$$

and while $\{\{p,r\},\{\sim q,r\}\} \models \Gamma_m^{\{\{p,r\},\{\sim q,r\}\}}$, all its weakenings, i.e., $\{\{p\},\}$ $\{\sim q,r\}$, $\{\{r\},\{\sim q,r\}\}$ and $\{\emptyset,\{\sim q,r\}\}$ refute it. Similarly, $\{\{p,r\},\{\sim q,r\}\} \models$ $\Gamma_m^{\{\{p,r\},\{\sim q,r\}\}}$, while all its weakenings refute it. Obviously, $\{\{\sim q\}\}$ and $\{\{p,r\}\}$ are the other T-minimal models of Γ_m. Take $\mathrm{Ep}(\Gamma_m) = \{\hat{\mathsf{K}}\,p\}$. While $\{\{p,r\}\} \models$ $\hat{\mathsf{K}}\,p$ and $\{\{p,r\},\{\sim q,r\}\} \models \hat{\mathsf{K}}\,p$, $\{\{\sim q\}\}$ do not satisfy it. Thus, we have the following order: $\{\{\sim q\}\} \prec_{\Gamma_m} \{\{p,r\}\} \approx_{\Gamma_m} \{\{p,r\},\{\sim q,r\}\}$. Then, by using subset inclusion, we conclude that $\mathrm{EAS}(\Gamma_m) = \{\{\{p,r\},\{\sim q,r\}\}\}$. Now consider Γ_c: it is equivalent to $\leftarrow p \text{ or } \mathsf{not}\,\hat{\mathsf{K}}\,q$. Clearly, $\{\{p,r\},\{\sim q,r\}\} \models p \text{ or } \hat{\mathsf{K}}\,q$ while $\{\{p,r\},\{\sim q,r\}\} \not\models p \text{ or } \mathsf{not}\,\hat{\mathsf{K}}\,q$. Thus we reorganise the model by deleting $\{p,r\}$. The resulting model $\{\{\sim q,r\}\}$ is not a T-minimal model of Γ_m. So, we have $\mathrm{EAS}(\Gamma) = \emptyset$.

3   Epistemic Here-and-There Logic (EHT)

The logic of here-and-there (HT) is a 3-valued monotonic logic that is intermediate between classical logic and intuitionistic logic. An HT model is an ordered
pair (H, T) of valuations satisfying the *heredity constraint*: $H \subseteq T$. Pearce [8,9]
was the first to realise that this logic provides a logical and mathematical basis
for ASP. More recently, the strong equivalence of ASP programs was characterised by means of HT [7].

EHT extends HT by epistemic modal operators K and $\hat{\mathsf{K}}$ in the spirit of
intuitionistic modal logics [11]. EHT models generalise HT models (H, T) to
collections $\left\{ (H_i, T_i) \right\}_i$ of such models. From the perspective of modal logic, an
EHT model can be viewed as a refinement of S5 models in which valuations are
replaced by HT models.

3.1   The Language of EHT ($\mathcal{L}_{\mathsf{EHT}}$)

The language $\mathcal{L}_{\mathsf{EHT}}$ is given by the following grammar: for $p \in \mathbb{P}$,

$$\varphi ::= p \mid \bot \mid \varphi \wedge \varphi \mid \varphi \vee \varphi \mid \varphi \rightarrow \varphi \mid \mathsf{K}\,\varphi \mid \hat{\mathsf{K}}\,\varphi$$

Note that K and $\hat{\mathsf{K}}$ are not dual: $\hat{\mathsf{K}}\,\varphi$ is not equivalent to $\neg\mathsf{K}\,\neg\varphi$. As usual, $\top$,
$\neg\varphi$ and $\varphi \leftrightarrow \psi$ respectively abbreviate $\bot \rightarrow \bot$, $\varphi \rightarrow \bot$ and $(\varphi \rightarrow \psi) \wedge (\psi \rightarrow \varphi)$.
A finite set of EHT formulas is called an EHT *theory*, noted $\Phi, \Psi, \ldots$. The set
of atoms occurring in a formula φ is symbolised by $\mathbb{P}_\varphi$. For example, $\mathbb{P}_{\mathsf{K}(p \rightarrow q)} =$
$\{p, q\}$. This generalises to EHT theories: $\mathbb{P}_\Phi = \bigcup_{\varphi \in \Phi} \mathbb{P}_\varphi$. A formula (theory) is
nonmodal if it does not contain modalities.

3.2   The Semantics of EHT: EHT Models

The semantics of EHT is given via EHT models. An EHT model is a pair $\langle \mathcal{T}, \mathsf{s} \rangle$:

- $\mathcal{T} \subseteq 2^{\mathbb{P}}$ is a nonempty set of valuations;
- $\mathsf{s} : \mathcal{T} \rightarrow 2^{\mathbb{P}}$ is a subset map such that $\mathsf{s}(T) \subseteq T$ for every $T \in \mathcal{T}$.

The map s associates a subset-valuation to each valuation in its domain. Thus, an
EHT model $\langle \mathcal{T}, \mathsf{s} \rangle$ can alternatively be described as a collection $\left\{ (\mathsf{s}(T), T) \right\}_{T \in \mathcal{T}}$
of HT models. The inclusion constraint on s generalises the heredity constraint
of HT to EHT.

We say that $\langle \mathcal{T}, \mathsf{s} \rangle$ is *total on* $\mathcal{S} \subseteq \mathcal{T}$ if $\mathsf{s}(T) = T$ for every $T \in \mathcal{S}$. If
$\langle \mathcal{T}, \mathsf{s} \rangle$ is total on $\mathcal{T}$, then s is the identity function id, that is, $\mathsf{s}(T) = T$ for
every $T \in \mathcal{T}$. We identify $\langle \mathcal{T}, id \rangle$ simply with the S5 model $\mathcal{T} \subseteq 2^{\mathbb{P}}$. A *pointed*
EHT model is an ordered pair $(\langle \mathcal{T}, \mathsf{s} \rangle, \mathcal{T}_0)$ in which $\langle \mathcal{T}, \mathsf{s} \rangle$ is an EHT model and
$\mathcal{T}_0 \subseteq \mathcal{T}$ is the nonempty set of *designated* worlds. When $\mathcal{T}_0 = \{T_0\}$, we simply
denote it by $(\langle \mathcal{T}, \mathsf{s} \rangle, T_0)$. We display pointed models explicitly as collections
$\left\{ (\mathsf{s}(T), T) \right\}_{T \in \mathcal{T}}$ where the designated worlds are underlined. For example, we
write $\{(\emptyset, \underline{\{p\}}), (\emptyset, \{q\})\}$ for the pointed EHT model $\langle \langle \mathcal{T}, \mathsf{s} \rangle, \{T_0\} \rangle$, where $\mathcal{T} =$
$\{\{p\}, \{q\}\}$, $T_0 = \{p\}$ and $\mathsf{s}(\{p\}) = \mathsf{s}(\{q\}) = \emptyset$.

3.3   The Truth Conditions of **EHT**

In this section, we define the EHT truth conditions. Those for $\bot$, $\wedge$ and $\vee$ are standard.

$$\langle \mathcal{T}, s\rangle, T \models_{\mathsf{EHT}} p \qquad \text{if } p \in s(T);$$
$$\langle \mathcal{T}, s\rangle, T \models_{\mathsf{EHT}} \varphi \to \psi \quad \text{if } \langle \mathcal{T}, s\rangle, T \models_{\mathsf{EHT}} \varphi \text{ implies } \langle \mathcal{T}, s\rangle, T \models_{\mathsf{EHT}} \psi \text{ and}$$
$$\langle \mathcal{T}, id\rangle, T \models_{\mathsf{EHT}} \varphi \text{ implies } \langle \mathcal{T}, id\rangle, T \models_{\mathsf{EHT}} \psi;$$
$$\langle \mathcal{T}, s\rangle, T \models_{\mathsf{EHT}} \mathsf{K}\,\varphi \quad \text{if } \langle \mathcal{T}, s\rangle, T' \models_{\mathsf{EHT}} \varphi \text{ for every } T' \in \mathcal{T};$$
$$\langle \mathcal{T}, s\rangle, T \models_{\mathsf{EHT}} \hat{\mathsf{K}}\,\varphi \quad \text{if } \langle \mathcal{T}, s\rangle, T' \models_{\mathsf{EHT}} \varphi \text{ for some } T' \in \mathcal{T}.$$

It follows that $\langle \mathcal{T}, s\rangle, T \models_{\mathsf{EHT}} \neg\varphi$ if and only if $\langle \mathcal{T}, s\rangle, T \not\models_{\mathsf{EHT}} \varphi$ and $\langle \mathcal{T}, id\rangle$, $T \not\models_{\mathsf{EHT}} \varphi$. This statement will be further simplified in Proposition 3.1 below.

Example 4. $\langle \mathcal{T}, s\rangle, T_0 \models_{\mathsf{EHT}} p \vee \neg p$ if and only if $p \in s(T_0)$ or $p \notin T_0$. Moreover, $\langle \mathcal{T}, s\rangle, T_0 \models_{\mathsf{EHT}} \mathsf{K}\,(p \vee \neg p) \to \hat{\mathsf{K}}\,\neg\neg p$ if and only if $p \in T$ for some $T \in \mathcal{T}$. Finally, $\langle \mathcal{T}, s\rangle, T \models_{\mathsf{EHT}} \neg\mathsf{K}\,\neg\neg\varphi \to \neg\mathsf{K}\,\varphi$ for every EHT model $\langle \mathcal{T}, s\rangle$ and every $T \in \mathcal{T}$.

Given an EHT model $\langle \mathcal{T}, s\rangle$ and a set $\mathcal{T}_0 \subseteq \mathcal{T}$ of designated worlds, if $\langle \mathcal{T}, s\rangle, T \models_{\mathsf{EHT}} \varphi$ for every $T \in \mathcal{T}_0$, then we write $\langle \mathcal{T}, s\rangle, \mathcal{T}_0 \models_{\mathsf{EHT}} \varphi$ for short. Finally, we write $\langle \mathcal{T}, s\rangle, \mathcal{T}_0 \models_{\mathsf{EHT}} \Phi$ if $\langle \mathcal{T}, s\rangle, \mathcal{T}_0 \models_{\mathsf{EHT}} \varphi$ for every $\varphi \in \Phi$. Here are some examples:

1. $\{(\emptyset, \{p\}), (\emptyset, \{q\})\} \models_{\mathsf{EHT}} \neg p$ as $\{(\emptyset, \{p\}), (\emptyset, \{q\})\} \not\models_{\mathsf{EHT}} p$ and $\{(\{p\}, \{p\}), (\{q\}, \{q\})\} \not\models_{\mathsf{EHT}} p$.
2. $\{(\emptyset, \{p\}), (\emptyset, \{q\})\} \models_{\mathsf{EHT}} \neg\neg p$.
3. $\{(\emptyset, \{p\}), (\emptyset, \{q\})\} \models_{\mathsf{EHT}} \mathsf{K}\,\neg r$ since $\{(\emptyset, \{p\}), (\emptyset, \{q\})\} \models_{\mathsf{EHT}} \neg r$.
4. $\{(\emptyset, \{p\}), (\emptyset, \{q\})\} \not\models_{\mathsf{EHT}} \neg\hat{\mathsf{K}}\,p$ since $\{(\emptyset, \{p\}), (\emptyset, \{q\})\} \not\models_{\mathsf{EHT}} \neg p$.

Observe that the satisfaction of the formulas of the form $\mathsf{K}\,\varphi$ and $\hat{\mathsf{K}}\,\varphi$ does not depend on the set of designated worlds: if $\langle \mathcal{T}, s\rangle, \mathcal{T}_0 \models_{\mathsf{EHT}} \mathsf{K}\,\varphi$ for *some* $\mathcal{T}_0 \subseteq \mathcal{T}$, then $\langle \mathcal{T}, s\rangle, \mathcal{T}_0 \models_{\mathsf{EHT}} \mathsf{K}\,\varphi$ for *every* $\mathcal{T}_0 \subseteq \mathcal{T}$. Also note that the satisfaction of the formulas of the form $\neg\varphi$ is independent of the map s. Moreover, the satisfaction of the formulas of the form $\neg\mathsf{K}\,\varphi$, $\neg\neg\mathsf{K}\,\varphi$, $\neg\hat{\mathsf{K}}\,\varphi$ and $\neg\neg\hat{\mathsf{K}}\,\varphi$ depends on neither s nor the set of designated worlds. This fact can be justified by using Propositions 1 and 3 below.

Proposition 1. *The following items are equivalent: for an* EHT *theory* Φ,

- $\langle \mathcal{T}, s\rangle, \mathcal{T} \models_{\mathsf{EHT}} \Phi$;
- $\langle \mathcal{T}, s\rangle, T \models_{\mathsf{EHT}} \mathsf{K}\,(\bigwedge \Phi)$ *for every* $T \in \mathcal{T}$;
- $\langle \mathcal{T}, s\rangle, T \models_{\mathsf{EHT}} \mathsf{K}\,(\bigwedge \Phi)$ *for some* $T \in \mathcal{T}$.

The following result is the heredity (monotonicity) property in EHT: if a formula has an EHT model, then it also has a total EHT model, i.e., it has a classical S5 model.

Proposition 2. *If* $\langle \mathcal{T}, s\rangle, T \models_{\mathsf{EHT}} \varphi$ *then* $\langle \mathcal{T}, id\rangle, T \models_{\mathsf{EHT}} \varphi$, *that is,* $\mathcal{T}, T \models \varphi$.

The list below helps us clarify the satisfaction of negated formulas.

Proposition 3. *For an* EHT *model* $\langle \mathcal{T}, s \rangle$ *and* $\varphi \in \mathcal{L}_{\mathsf{EHT}}$,

1. $\langle \mathcal{T}, s \rangle, T \models_{\mathsf{EHT}} \neg\varphi$ *iff* $\langle \mathcal{T}, id \rangle, T \not\models_{\mathsf{EHT}} \varphi$;
2. $\langle \mathcal{T}, s \rangle, T \models_{\mathsf{EHT}} \neg\neg\varphi$ *iff* $\langle \mathcal{T}, id \rangle, T \models_{\mathsf{EHT}} \varphi$;
3. $\langle \mathcal{T}, s \rangle, T \models_{\mathsf{EHT}} \neg\mathsf{K}\varphi$ *iff* $\langle \mathcal{T}, id \rangle, T' \not\models_{\mathsf{EHT}} \varphi$ *for some* $T' \in \mathcal{T}$;
4. $\langle \mathcal{T}, s \rangle, T \models_{\mathsf{EHT}} \neg\hat{\mathsf{K}}\varphi$ *iff* $\langle \mathcal{T}, id \rangle, T' \not\models_{\mathsf{EHT}} \varphi$ *for every* $T' \in \mathcal{T}$.

3.4 The EHT Validity

A formula φ is called EHT *satisfiable* if $\langle \mathcal{T}, s \rangle, \mathcal{T}_0 \models_{\mathsf{EHT}} \varphi$ for some EHT model $\langle \mathcal{T}, s \rangle$ and $\mathcal{T}_0 \subseteq \mathcal{T}$. We call $(\langle \mathcal{T}, s \rangle, \mathcal{T}_0)$ a pointed EHT model of φ. Then, φ is EHT *valid* if $\langle \mathcal{T}, s \rangle, \mathcal{T} \models_{\mathsf{EHT}} \varphi$ for every EHT model $\langle \mathcal{T}, s \rangle$.

Example 5. $\mathsf{K}\varphi \to \neg\hat{\mathsf{K}}\neg\varphi$, $\neg\hat{\mathsf{K}}\neg\varphi \to \neg\neg\hat{\mathsf{K}}\varphi$ and $\neg\neg\mathsf{K}\varphi \to \neg\mathsf{K}\neg\varphi$ are all valid while their converses are not. On the other hand, none of $\neg\neg\mathsf{K}\varphi \to \mathsf{K}\varphi$ and $\mathsf{K}\neg\neg\varphi \to \mathsf{K}\varphi$ is EHT valid. The same holds if we replace K by $\hat{\mathsf{K}}$. (Take $\varphi = p$. Then the EHT model $\{\langle \emptyset, \{p\} \rangle\}$ provides a counterexample for all these implications except $\neg\neg\hat{\mathsf{K}}p \to \neg\hat{\mathsf{K}}\neg p$ and $\neg\mathsf{K}\neg p \to \neg\neg\mathsf{K}p$. For these two, $\{\langle \emptyset, \emptyset \rangle, \langle \emptyset, \{p\} \rangle\}$ works as a counterexample.)

The following EHT validities help us grasp the above examples more easily.

Proposition 4. *The equivalences* $\neg\mathsf{K}\varphi \leftrightarrow \hat{\mathsf{K}}\neg\varphi$ *and* $\neg\hat{\mathsf{K}}\varphi \leftrightarrow \mathsf{K}\neg\varphi$ *are* EHT *valid.*

As an immediate corollary of this proposition, we also have:

Corollary 1. *The equivalences* $\neg\neg\mathsf{K}\varphi \leftrightarrow \mathsf{K}\neg\neg\varphi$ *and* $\neg\neg\hat{\mathsf{K}}\varphi \leftrightarrow \hat{\mathsf{K}}\neg\neg\varphi$ *are* EHT *valid.*

3.5 Translating EASP Programs into EHT Theories

Let Π be an ELP. Our translation $(.)^*$ replaces '$\leftarrow$', ' or ', ',' and 'not' respectively by '$\to$', '$\vee$', '$\wedge$' and '$\neg$'. Then the translations of K and $\hat{\mathsf{K}}$ are direct. Furthermore, it introduces a fresh atom $\tilde{p}$ for each $\sim p$ occurring in Π. For these new atoms, the formula $\mathsf{Cons}(\Pi) = \bigwedge_{p \in \mathbb{P}_\Pi} \neg(p \wedge \tilde{p})$ ensures that p and $\tilde{p}$ cannot be true at the same time. (We only need it for those p that are prefixed by a strong negation in Π.) Here is an example:

$$\Pi = \{ p \text{ or } \sim q \leftarrow \hat{\mathsf{K}}r, \text{not } s \ , \ q \leftarrow \text{not } \mathsf{K}p \}.$$
$$\Pi^* = \big((\hat{\mathsf{K}}r \wedge \neg s) \to (p \vee \tilde{q}) \big) \wedge \big(\neg\mathsf{K}p \to q \big) \wedge \neg(q \wedge \tilde{q}).$$

4   Strong Equivalence

We here discuss a strong equivalence characterisation for EASP programs, defined as their logical equivalence in EHT. We will keep track of the approach proposed by [7].

Definition 5. For EASP programs Π_1 and Π_2, Π_1 is *equivalent* to Π_2 in the sense of the EAS semantics if $\mathbf{EAS}(\Pi_1) = \mathbf{EAS}(\Pi_2)$. Then, Π_1 is *strongly equivalent* to Π_2 if $\Pi_1 \cup \Pi$ is equivalent to $\Pi_2 \cup \Pi$, i.e., $\mathbf{EAS}(\Pi_1 \cup \Pi) = \mathbf{EAS}(\Pi_2 \cup \Pi)$ for every EASP program Π.

Note that strong equivalence implies equivalence (simply take $\Pi = \emptyset$). The strong equivalence concept is important because it enables us to simplify a subprogram regardless of the rest because the meaning of the whole program would not change.

4.1   Characterisation of Strong Equivalence in EHT

In this section we see that the strong equivalence of EASP programs can be verified by checking the logical equivalence of corresponding EHT theories in (monotonic) EHT.

Let $\|\varphi\|_{EHT}$ denote the collection of all EHT models of a formula $\varphi \in \mathcal{L}_{\mathsf{EHT}}$. We generalise this notation to an EHT theory Φ as follows: $\|\Phi\|_{EHT} = \|\bigwedge_{\varphi \in \Phi} \varphi\|_{EHT}$. To get prepared for our main theorem, we now generalise some well-known lemmas from HT and ASP to EHT and EASP. The first is a generalisation of Lemma 1 given in [7]:

Lemma 1. *Let $\langle \mathcal{T}, s \rangle$ be an EHT model and $T_0 \in \mathcal{T}$. For a positive EASP program Π,*

$$\langle \mathcal{T}, s \rangle, T_0 \models_{\mathsf{EHT}} \Pi^* \text{ if and only if } \{s(T) \ : \ T \in \mathcal{T}\}, s(T_0) \models \Pi^* \text{ and } \mathcal{T}, T_0 \models \Pi^*.$$

Proof. Let Π be a positive (without NAF) EASP program. Let $\langle \mathcal{T}, \mathbf{s} \rangle$ be an EHT model, and let $T_0 \in \mathcal{T}$. Then, $\langle \mathcal{T}, \mathbf{s} \rangle, T_0 \models_{\mathsf{EHT}} \Pi^*$ iff for every rule $r : head(r) \leftarrow body(r)$ in Π,

$$\langle \mathcal{T}, \mathbf{s} \rangle, T_0 \models_{\mathsf{EHT}} (body(r))^* \text{ implies } \langle \mathcal{T}, \mathbf{s} \rangle, T_0 \models_{\mathsf{EHT}} (head(r))^* \tag{1}$$

$$\text{and}$$

$$\langle \mathcal{T}, id \rangle, T_0 \models_{\mathsf{EHT}} (body(r))^* \text{ implies } \langle \mathcal{T}, id \rangle, T_0 \models_{\mathsf{EHT}} (head(r))^*. \tag{2}$$

By assumption, we know that $body(r)$ and $head(r)$ do not contain NAF for any $r \in \Pi$. As a result of this, for every $r \in \Pi$, (1) and (2) are respectively equivalent to:

$$\{\mathbf{s}(T) \ : \ T \in \mathcal{T}\}, \mathbf{s}(T_0) \models (body(r))^* \text{ implies } \{\mathbf{s}(T) \ : \ T \in \mathcal{T}\}, \mathbf{s}(T_0) \models (head(r))^*$$
$$\text{and}$$
$$\mathcal{T}, T_0 \models (body(r))^* \text{ implies } \mathcal{T}, T_0 \models (head(r))^*.$$

These implications can be combined and phrased as follows: $\langle \{\mathbf{s}(T) \ : \ T \in \mathcal{T}\}, \mathbf{s}(T_0) \rangle$ and $\langle \mathcal{T}, T_0 \rangle$ are (classical) pointed S5 models of Π^*. So, we are done.

Second, we generalise Lemma 2, again proposed in [7], as described below:

Lemma 2. *Let $\langle \mathcal{T}, s \rangle$ be an EHT model and $T_0 \in \mathcal{T}$. For an EASP program Π, we have:*

$$\langle \mathcal{T}, s \rangle, T_0 \models_{\mathsf{EHT}} \Pi^* \quad \text{if and only if} \quad \langle \mathcal{T}, s \rangle, T_0 \models_{\mathsf{EHT}} (\Pi^{\langle \mathcal{T}, T_0 \rangle})^*.$$

Proof. By the definition of reduct (see Definition 4), $\Pi^{\langle \mathcal{T}, T \rangle}$ is a positive (without NAF) program obtained from Π by the simultaneous replacement of some subformulas of the form $\mathbf{not}\,\lambda$ (where λ is an arbitrary literal; objective or subjective literal) with $\top$ and of all other subformulas of this form with $\bot$. Thus, it will be sufficient to check that for an arbitrary point $T_0 \in \mathcal{T}$, a subformula $\mathbf{not}\,\lambda$ and the formula α that replaces it,

$$\langle \mathcal{T}, \mathbf{s} \rangle, T_0 \models_{\mathsf{EHT}} (\mathbf{not}\,\lambda)^* \text{ if and only if } \langle \mathcal{T}, \mathbf{s} \rangle, T_0 \models_{\mathsf{EHT}} (\alpha)^*.$$

Since α is $\top$ or $\bot$, its translation α^* equals itself. Then, this claim can be rewritten as

$$\langle \mathcal{T}, \mathbf{s} \rangle, T_0 \models_{\mathsf{EHT}} (\mathbf{not}\,\lambda)^* \text{ if and only if } \alpha = \top.$$

Remember that $(\mathbf{not}\,\lambda)^* = \neg\lambda$ since λ is an objective or subjective literal (see Sect. 3.5 for the translation rules). Thus, we have: for every $T_0 \in \mathcal{T}$,

$$
\begin{aligned}
\langle \mathcal{T}, \mathbf{s} \rangle, T_0 \models_{\mathsf{EHT}} \neg\lambda \quad &\text{iff} \quad \langle \mathcal{T}, id \rangle, T_0 \not\models_{\mathsf{EHT}} \lambda \quad &&\text{(by Proposition 3.1)} \\
&\text{iff} \quad \mathcal{T}, T_0 \not\models \lambda \quad &&\text{(see Proposition 2)} \\
&\text{iff} \quad \alpha = \top \quad &&\text{(by Definition 4).}
\end{aligned}
$$

Finally, we generalise Lemma 1 in [2] to EHT and EASP as follows:

Proposition 5. *Let $\langle \mathcal{T}, s \rangle$ be an EHT model and $T_0 \in \mathcal{T}$. For an EASP program Π,*

$$\langle \mathcal{T}, s \rangle, T_0 \models_{\mathsf{EHT}} \Pi^* \text{ if and only if } \{s(T) \; : \; T \in \mathcal{T}\}, s(T_0) \models (\Pi^{\langle \mathcal{T}, T_0 \rangle})^*.$$

Proof. Let $\langle \mathcal{T}, \mathbf{s} \rangle$ be an EHT model and $T_0 \in \mathcal{T}$. Then, by the definition of reduct (see Definition 4), $\Pi^{\langle \mathcal{T}, T_0 \rangle}$ is a positive EASP program excluding NAF ($\bullet$). Thus, we have:

$$
\begin{aligned}
&\langle \mathcal{T}, \mathbf{s} \rangle, T_0 \models_{\mathsf{EHT}} \Pi^* \quad &&\text{iff} \quad &&\text{(by Lemma 2)} \\
&\langle \mathcal{T}, \mathbf{s} \rangle, T_0 \models_{\mathsf{EHT}} (\Pi^{\langle \mathcal{T}, T_0 \rangle})^* \quad &&\text{iff} \quad &&\text{(by ($\bullet$) and Lemma 1)} \\
&\{\mathbf{s}(T) : T \in \mathcal{T}\}, \mathbf{s}(T_0) \models (\Pi^{\langle \mathcal{T}, T_0 \rangle})^* \text{ and} \\
&\mathcal{T}, T_0 \models (\Pi^{\langle \mathcal{T}, T_0 \rangle})^* \quad &&\text{iff} \quad &&\text{(by Proposition 2)} \\
&\{\mathbf{s}(T) : T \in \mathcal{T}\}, \mathbf{s}(T_0) \models (\Pi^{\langle \mathcal{T}, T_0 \rangle})^*.
\end{aligned}
$$

The following result is our main goal in this paper. It (partly) generalises Theorem 1 proposed in [7] and shows the relation between the strong equivalence of EASP programs and the logical equivalence of their corresponding EHT theories.

Theorem 1. *The following conditions are equivalent: for* EASP *programs* Π_1 *and* Π_2,

(a) $EAS(\Pi_1 \cup \Pi) = EAS(\Pi_2 \cup \Pi)$ *for every* EASP *program* Π.
(b) Π_1^* *is equivalent to* Π_2^* *in* EHT, *that is,* $\|\Pi_1^*\|_{EHT} = \|\Pi_2^*\|_{EHT}$.

This theorem above corresponds to the standard strong equivalence results of ASP discussed in [7] for nonmodal EASP programs in which subjective literals do not appear. The proof below is a non-trivial generalisation of the proof of Lemma 4 given in [7].

Proof. To see that (b) implies (a), we first assume that Π_1^* is equivalent to Π_2^* in EHT. We know that EHT is a monotonic logic. Thus, we also have $\|\Pi_1^* \cup \Gamma\|_{EHT} = \|\Pi_2^* \cup \Gamma\|_{EHT}$ for every EHT theory Γ. Clearly, our translation $(.)^*$ is a 1–1 and into map, so it is easy to conclude that $\|(\Pi_1 \cup \Pi)^*\|_{EHT} = \|(\Pi_2 \cup \Pi)^*\|_{EHT}$ (⋆) for every EASP program Π. Thus, $(\Pi_1 \cup \Pi)^*$ and $(\Pi_2 \cup \Pi)^*$ have the same (total) EHT models. Obviously, they also have the same classical S5 models because we know that any S5 model can be reformulated as a total EHT model and vice versa. Then, from Proposition 5, we obtain that: for every EHT model $\langle \mathcal{T}, \mathbf{s} \rangle$ and for every $T \in \mathcal{T}$,

$$
\begin{array}{lll}
\{\mathbf{s}(T) : T \in \mathcal{T}\}, \mathbf{s}(T) \models \left((\Pi_1 \cup \Pi)^{\langle \mathcal{T},T \rangle}\right)^* & \text{iff} & \text{(by Proposition 5)} \\
\langle \mathcal{T}, \mathbf{s} \rangle, T \models_{\mathsf{EHT}} (\Pi_1 \cup \Pi)^* & \text{iff} & \text{(by (⋆) above)} \\
\langle \mathcal{T}, \mathbf{s} \rangle, T \models_{\mathsf{EHT}} (\Pi_2 \cup \Pi)^* & \text{iff} & \text{(by Proposition 5)} \\
\{\mathbf{s}(T) : T \in \mathcal{T}\}, \mathbf{s}(T) \models \left((\Pi_2 \cup \Pi)^{\langle \mathcal{T},T \rangle}\right)^*.
\end{array}
$$

Thus, for every $\mathbf{s} : \mathcal{T} \to 2^{\mathbb{P}}$ such that $\mathbf{s}(T) \subseteq T$ for every $T \in \mathcal{T}$ and for every $T \in \mathcal{T}$,

$$
\begin{array}{ll}
\{\mathbf{s}(T) \ : \ T \in \mathcal{T}\}, \mathbf{s}(T) \models \left((\Pi_1 \cup \Pi)^{\langle \mathcal{T},T \rangle}\right)^* & \text{iff} \\
\{\mathbf{s}(T) \ : \ T \in \mathcal{T}\}, \mathbf{s}(T) \models \left((\Pi_2 \cup \Pi)^{\langle \mathcal{T},T \rangle}\right)^*.
\end{array}
$$

Taking $\mathbf{s} = id$ will then give us: for every $T \in \mathcal{T}$,

$$
\mathcal{T}, T \models \left((\Pi_1 \cup \Pi)^{\langle \mathcal{T},T \rangle}\right)^* \quad \text{iff} \quad \mathcal{T}, T \models \left((\Pi_2 \cup \Pi)^{\langle \mathcal{T},T \rangle}\right)^* \qquad (\blacktriangle).
$$

Moreover, this equivalence also holds for every $\mathbf{s} \neq id$ such that $\mathbf{s}(T) \subset T$ and $\mathbf{s}|_{\mathcal{T} \setminus \{T\}} = id$ for every $T \in \mathcal{T}$. Thus, we have: for every $\mathbf{s} \neq id$ such that $\mathbf{s}(T) \subset T$, but $\mathbf{s}|_{\mathcal{T} \setminus \{T\}} = id$,

$$
\mathbf{s}[\mathcal{T}], \mathbf{s}(T) \models \left((\Pi_1 \cup \Pi)^{\langle \mathcal{T},T \rangle}\right)^* \quad \text{iff} \quad \mathbf{s}[\mathcal{T}], \mathbf{s}(T) \models \left((\Pi_2 \cup \Pi)^{\langle \mathcal{T},T \rangle}\right)^* \qquad (\blacktriangledown)
$$

for every $T \in \mathcal{T}$. From ($\blacktriangle$) and ($\blacktriangledown$), we obtain that for every $T \in \mathcal{T}$ (see Definition 2),

$$
\mathcal{T}, T \models^* (\Pi_1 \cup \Pi)^{\langle \mathcal{T},T \rangle} \quad \text{iff} \quad \mathcal{T}, T \models^* (\Pi_2 \cup \Pi)^{\langle \mathcal{T},T \rangle}.
$$

Again using Definition 2, we deduce that $\Pi_1 \cup \Pi$ and $\Pi_2 \cup \Pi$ have the same T-minimal models in EASP. Since $\|\Pi_1^*\|_{EHT} = \|\Pi_2^*\|_{EHT}$ by assumption, the sets of (default-negated) subjective literals appearing in Π_1 and Π_2 are the same, i.e., $\text{Ep}(\Pi_1) = \text{Ep}(\Pi_2)$. Then, it is easy to conclude that $\Pi_1 \cup \Pi$ and $\Pi_2 \cup \Pi$ have the same T-minimal models which are maximal w.r.t. the orderings $\subseteq$ and $\preceq_{\Pi_1 \cup \Pi}$, and $\subseteq$ and $\preceq_{\Pi_2 \cup \Pi}$ respectively. As a result, they have the same EASs, i.e., $\text{EAS}(\Pi_1 \cup \Pi) = \text{EAS}(\Pi_2 \cup \Pi)$.

To see that (a) implies (b), we first assume that Π_1^* and Π_2^* are not logically equivalent in EHT, i.e., $\|\Pi_1^*\|_{EHT} \neq \|\Pi_2^*\|_{EHT}$. Then, Π_1^* has an EHT model $(\langle \mathcal{T}, s \rangle, \mathcal{T})$ ($\bullet$), which is not a model of Π_2^* ($\bullet\bullet$). Now, we will find an EASP program Π such that $\mathcal{T}$ is an EAS for one of the programs $\Pi_1 \cup \Pi$ and $\Pi_2 \cup \Pi$, but not an EAS of the other.

Case 1: suppose that $\langle \mathcal{T}, id \rangle, \mathcal{T} \not\models_{EHT} \Pi_2^*$. However, by monotonicity property of EHT (see Proposition 2), ($\bullet$) implies that $\langle \mathcal{T}, id \rangle, T \models_{EHT} \Pi_1^*$ for every $T \in \mathcal{T}$. Then, by taking $s = id$ in Proposition 5, we deduce that $\mathcal{T}, T \models (\Pi_1^{\langle \mathcal{T}, T \rangle})^*$ for every $T \in \mathcal{T}$ ($\blacktriangleleft$).

We first consider the collection $\bigcup \mathcal{T} = \bigcup \{T_i\}_i$ of atoms appearing in at least one $T_i \in \mathcal{T}$. Then, we construct the following set of EHT formulas: for each i, let

$$\Pi_i = \{ p \vee \bigvee \overline{T_i} \ : \ p \in T_i \}$$

where $\overline{T_i} = \bigcup \mathcal{T} \setminus T_i$ is the relative complement of T_i w.r.t. $\bigcup \mathcal{T}$. Note that we can regard each Π_i as a set of facts in EASP. Then we take the union of such Π_i's, and we define

$$\Pi = \bigcup \{\Pi_i\}_i.$$

Since Π_i does not include NAF, we have $\Pi^{\langle \mathcal{T}, T_i \rangle} = \Pi$. Thanks to our construction, it is obvious that $\mathcal{T}, T_i \models \Pi_i$. Moreover, it is not difficult to see that $\mathcal{T}, T_i \models \Pi_j$ for every $j \neq i$ (w.l.o.g., we assume each T_i to be nonempty and not to be a subset of another T_j (for some j) in the collection $\mathcal{T}$). Thus, $\mathcal{T}, T_i \models \Pi$. Since Π is positive, $\mathcal{T}, T_i \models \Pi^{\langle \mathcal{T}, T_i \rangle}$. Then, using ($\blacktriangleleft$) we conclude that $\mathcal{T}, T_i \models (\Pi_1 \cup \Pi)^{\langle \mathcal{T}, T_i \rangle}$, for every $T_i \in \mathcal{T}$.

It remains to show that $s[\mathcal{T}], s(T_i) \not\models (\Pi_1 \cup \Pi)^{\langle \mathcal{T}, T_i \rangle}$ for every s viz. $\langle s[\mathcal{T}], s(T_i) \rangle \lhd \langle \mathcal{T}, T_i \rangle$ (see Definition 2). Again, thanks to our construction, $s[\mathcal{T}], s(T_i) \not\models \Pi_i$ for any such s (i.e., for every $s \neq id$ such that $s|_{\mathcal{T} \setminus \{T_i\}} = id$). Also notice that $\Pi_i^{\langle \mathcal{T}, T_i \rangle} = \Pi_i$ since it does not include NAF. As a result, $\mathcal{T}, T_i \models^* (\Pi_1 \cup \Pi)^{\langle \mathcal{T}, T_i \rangle}$. Since $T_i \in \mathcal{T}$ is arbitrary, by Definition 4 we conclude that $\mathcal{T}$ is a T-minimal model for $\Pi_1 \cup \Pi$. Moreover, the choice of Π guarantees that $\mathcal{T}$ is the unique T-minimal model of $\Pi_1 \cup \Pi$. So, $\mathcal{T} \in \text{EAS}(\Pi_1 \cup \Pi)$. On the other hand, using our initial assumption we easily conclude that $\langle \mathcal{T}, id \rangle, \mathcal{T} \not\models_{EHT} (\Pi_2 \cup \Pi)^*$, so $\mathcal{T}$ cannot be an epistemic answer set (EAS) for $\Pi_2 \cup \Pi$ because $\mathcal{T}$ is not even an S5 model of $(\Pi_2 \cup \Pi)^*$.

Case 2: suppose that $\langle \mathcal{T}, id \rangle, \mathcal{T} \models_{EHT} \Pi_2^*$. Then, using ($\bullet\bullet$) we conclude that $s \neq id$ (because otherwise ($\bullet\bullet$) would contradict our initial assumption). Thus, $s(T_0) \subset T_0$ for some $T_0 \in \mathcal{T}$. Then, by monotonicity property of EHT (see Proposition 2) and using ($\bullet$) we guarantee the existence of s' such that $s'(T_0) =$

$\mathbf{s}(T_0) \subset T_0$, but $\mathbf{s}'|_{\mathcal{T} \setminus \{T_0\}} = id$ and also satisfying the condition $\langle \mathcal{T}, \mathbf{s}' \rangle, \mathcal{T} \models_{\mathsf{EHT}}$ Π_1^*. We now define a set $\Pi = \bigcup \{\Pi_i\}_i$ of EHT formulas such that each Π_i is defined as below: taking $\mathcal{H} = \bigcup \{\mathbf{s}(T_i)\}_i$, we let

$$\Pi_i = \{p \vee \bigvee \left(\mathcal{H} \setminus \mathbf{s}(T_i) \right) : p \in \mathbf{s}(Ti)\} \cup \{q \leftarrow r : q, r \in \left(T_i \setminus \mathbf{s}(T_i) \right) \setminus \bigcup \{T_j\}_{j \neq i} \text{ and } q \neq r\}.$$

Note that we can also consider Π as a set of positive EASP rules, i.e., a positive EASP program. Thanks to our choice, $\langle \mathcal{T}, \mathbf{s}' \rangle, T_0 \models_{\mathsf{EHT}} (\Pi_1 \cup \Pi)^*$. Then, by Proposition 5, we moreover have $\{\mathbf{s}'(T) : T \in \mathcal{T}\}, \mathbf{s}'(T_0) \models (\Pi_1 \cup \Pi)^{\langle \mathcal{T}, T_0 \rangle}$ (note that $\Pi^{\langle \mathcal{T}, T_0 \rangle} = \Pi$ since it is a positive program). Thus, $\mathcal{T}$ cannot be an EAS of $\Pi_1 \cup \Pi$: it is easy to see that $\mathcal{T}$ is not even a T-minimal model of $\Pi_1 \cup \Pi$ since $\mathcal{T}, T_0 \not\models^* (\Pi_1 \cup \Pi)^{\langle \mathcal{T}, T_0 \rangle}$.

By the hypothesis, we know that $\mathcal{T}, T \models \Pi_2$ for every $T \in \mathcal{T}$. Then, clearly $\langle \mathcal{T}, id \rangle, T \models_{\mathsf{EHT}} (\Pi_2 \cup \Pi)^*$ for every $T \in \mathcal{T}$. By using Lemma 2, we also get $\mathcal{T}, T \models (\Pi_2 \cup \Pi)^{\langle \mathcal{T}, T \rangle}$ for every $T \in \mathcal{T}$. We now take an arbitrary weakening $\langle \mathbf{s}''[\mathcal{T}], \mathbf{s}''(T_i) \rangle$ of $\langle \mathcal{T}, T_i \rangle$ for a function $\mathbf{s}'' : \mathcal{T} \to 2^{\mathbb{P}}$ such that $\mathbf{s}''|_{\mathcal{T} \setminus \{T_i\}} = id$ and $\mathbf{s}''(T_i) \subset T_i$. Assume for a contradiction that $\mathbf{s}''[\mathcal{T}], \mathbf{s}''(T_i) \models (\Pi_2 \cup \Pi)^{\langle \mathcal{T}, T_i \rangle}$. Then, by Proposition 5, $\langle \mathcal{T}, \mathbf{s}'' \rangle, T_i \models_{\mathsf{EHT}} (\Pi_2 \cup \Pi)^*$. Since $\langle \mathcal{T}, \mathbf{s}'' \rangle, T_i \models_{\mathsf{EHT}} \Pi^*$, we have $\mathbf{s}(T_i) \subseteq \mathbf{s}''(T_i)$, but since $\langle \mathcal{T}, \mathbf{s}'' \rangle, T_i \models_{\mathsf{EHT}} \Pi_2^*$, we have $\mathbf{s}(T_i) \neq \mathbf{s}''(T_i)$ (i.e., $\mathbf{s}(T_i) \subset \mathbf{s}''(T_i)$) because by ($\bullet\bullet$) we know that $(\langle \mathcal{T}, \mathbf{s} \rangle, \mathcal{T})$ is not an EHT model of Π_2^*, so for some T_0, $\langle \mathcal{T}, \mathbf{s} \rangle, T_0 \not\models_{\mathsf{EHT}} \Pi_2^*$. Thus, we have the following order: $\mathbf{s}(T_i) \subset \mathbf{s}''(T_i) \subset T_i$. Now, take an atom $q \in \mathbf{s}''(T_i) \setminus \mathbf{s}(T_i)$ and an atom $r \in T_i \setminus \mathbf{s}''(T_i)$. For these atoms, $q \to r \in \Pi$, but clearly $\langle \mathcal{T}, \mathbf{s}'' \rangle, T_i \not\models_{\mathsf{EHT}} q \to r$ (contradiction!). As a result, $\mathcal{T}$ is a T-minimal model of $\Pi_2 \cup \Pi$. Thanks to our choice, $\mathcal{T}$ is also an EAS of $\Pi_2 \cup \Pi$.

Closed world assumption (CWA), saying that *p is assumed to be false if there is no evidence to the contrary*, is expressed in ASP by $\sim p \leftarrow \mathsf{not}\, p$. However, this representation was then discovered to cause problems (consider the program $\Pi = \{p \,\mathsf{or}\, q,\ \sim p \leftarrow \mathsf{not}\, p\}$ [10]). We have two options in EASP to express CWA: $\mathsf{not}\, \mathsf{K}\, p \to p$ and $\mathsf{not}\, \hat{\mathsf{K}}\, p \to p$. However, $\|\neg \mathsf{K}\, p \to p\|_{EHT} \neq \|\neg \hat{\mathsf{K}}\, p \to p\|_{EHT}$. This fact can be easily verified by taking the pointed EHT model $\{\emptyset, \{p\}\}$. By using the theorem above we conclude that $\mathsf{not}\, \mathsf{K}\, p \to p$ and $\mathsf{not}\, \hat{\mathsf{K}}\, p \to p$ are not strongly equivalent in EASP.

5   Conclusion

In this paper, we first recall a recent epistemic extension of ASP called epistemic ASP (EASP). Then, we characterise in EHT the strong equivalence of EASP programs in a more direct way, compared to (i) [14] and (ii) [1]: these approaches have a general setting and so it may be a bit difficult to get the intuition lying under their abstract characterisations. Moreover, (i) defines a problematic version of EHT as discussed by Su in [12]. Also, the equilibrium view approach of (i) embeds Gelfond's semantics [4], which has been no longer in use since improved versions were suggested. Similarly, the AEEM semantics of (ii) is also partly obsolete nowadays since it suffers from unintended results for ELPs containing arbitrary constraints. Thus, as future work, we would like to propose a new epistemic extension of equilibrium logic, embedding EASP as well.

References

1. Fariñas del Cerro, L., Herzig, A., Su, E.I.: Epistemic equilibrium logic. In: Yang, Q., Wooldridge, M. (eds.) Proceedings of the 24th International Joint Conference on Artificial Intelligence, pp. 2964–2970. AAAI Press (2015). http://ijcai. org/papers15/Abstracts/IJCAI15-419.html
2. Ferraris, P.: Answer sets for propositional theories. In: Baral, C., Greco, G., Leone, N., Terracina, G. (eds.) LPNMR 2005. LNCS (LNAI), vol. 3662, pp. 119–131. Springer, Heidelberg (2005). https://doi.org/10.1007/11546207_10
3. Gelfond, M.: Strong introspection. In: Dean, T.L., McKeown, K. (eds.) Proceedings of the 9th National Conference on Artificial Intelligence, Anaheim, CA, USA, 14–19 July 1991, vol. 1, pp. 386–391. AAAI Press/The MIT Press (1991)
4. Gelfond, M.: Logic programming and reasoning with incomplete information. Ann. Math. Artif. Intell. **12**(1–2), 89–116 (1994)
5. Gelfond, M., Lifschitz, V.: The stable model semantics for logic programming. In: ICLP/SLP, vol. 88, pp. 1070–1080 (1988)
6. Heyting, A.: Die formalen Regeln der intuitionistischen Logik. Sitzungsber. Preuss. Akad. Wiss. **42–71**, 158–169 (1930)
7. Lifschitz, V., Pearce, D., Valverde, A.: Strongly equivalent logic programs. ACM Trans. Comput. Log. **2**(4), 526–541 (2001). https://doi.org/10.1145/383779.383783
8. Pearce, D.: A new logical characterisation of stable models and answer sets. In: Dix, J., Pereira, L.M., Przymusinski, T.C. (eds.) NMELP 1996. LNCS, vol. 1216, pp. 57–70. Springer, Heidelberg (1997). https://doi.org/10.1007/BFb0023801
9. Pearce, D.: Equilibrium logic. Ann. Math. Artif. Intell. **47**(1–2), 3–41 (2006)
10. Shen, Y., Eiter, T.: Evaluating epistemic negation in answer set programming. Artif. Intell. **237**, 115–135 (2016). https://doi.org/10.1016/j.artint.2016.04.004
11. Simpson, A.K.: The proof theory and semantics of intuitionistic modal logic. Ph.D. thesis, University of Edinburgh, College of Science and Engineering, School of Informatics, November 1994
12. Su, E.I.: Extensions of equilibrium logic by modal concepts. (Extensions de la logique d'équilibre par des concepts modaux). Ph.D. thesis, Institut de Recherche en Informatique de Toulouse, France (2015). https://tel.archives-ouvertes.fr/tel-01636791
13. Su, E.I.: Epistemic answer set programming. In: Calimeri, F., Leone, N., Manna, M. (eds.) JELIA 2019. LNCS (LNAI), vol. 11468, pp. 608–626. Springer, Cham (2019). https://doi.org/10.1007/978-3-030-19570-0_40
14. Wang, K., Zhang, Y.: Nested epistemic logic programs. In: Baral, C., Greco, G., Leone, N., Terracina, G. (eds.) LPNMR 2005. LNCS (LNAI), vol. 3662, pp. 279–290. Springer, Heidelberg (2005). https://doi.org/10.1007/11546207_22

From Simplified Kripke-Style Semantics to Simplified Analytic Tableaux for Some Normal Modal Logics

Yaroslav Petrukhin and Michał Zawidzki$^{(\boxtimes)}$

Department of Logic, University of Łódź, Łódź, Poland
yaroslav.petrukhin@mail.ru, michal.zawidzki@filozof.uni.lodz.pl

Abstract. Modal logics K45, KB4, KD45 and S5 are of particular interest in knowledge representation, especially in the context of knowledge and belief modelling. Pietruszczak showed that these logics are curious for another reason, namely for the fact that their Kripke-style semantics can be simplified. A simplified frame has the form $\langle W, A \rangle$, where $A \subseteq W$. A reachability relation R may be defined as $R = W \times A$, which, however, makes it superfluous to explicitly refer to it. It is well-known that S5 is determined by Kripke frames with $R = W \times W$, i.e., $A = W$. Pietruszczak showed what classes of simplified frames determine K45, KD45, and KB4. These results were generalized to the extensions of these logics by Segerberg's formulas. In this paper, we devise sound, complete and terminating prefixed tableau algorithms based on simplified semantics for these logics. Since no separate rules are needed to handle the reachability relation and prefixes do not store any extra information, the calculi are accessible and conceptually simple and the process of countermodel-construction out of an open tableau branch is straightforward. Moreover, we obtain a nice explanation of why these logics are computationally easier than most modal logics, in particular NP-complete.

Keywords: Modal logic · Automated reasoning · Decision procedures · Analytic tableaux · Simplified Kripke-style semantics

1 Introduction

Overview. Modal logics are a handy tool often used in knowledge representation. The most popular field in which logics such as S5, KD45, or K45 are employed is modelling human knowledge and belief [19,31,32]. In many cases the modelling task also involves a reasoning component. For example, we would like to know whether from the assumptions:

Research reported in this paper is supported by the National Science Centre, Poland (grant number: DEC-2017/25/B/HS1/01268).

ⓒ Springer Nature Switzerland AG 2019
M. Alviano et al. (Eds.): AI*IA 2019, LNAI 11946, pp. 116–131, 2019.
https://doi.org/10.1007/978-3-030-35166-3_9

A1: [JohnBelieves]Truth,
A2: $\forall_\varphi([\text{JohnBelieves}]\varphi \rightarrow [\text{JohnBelieves}][\text{JohnBelieves}]\varphi)$,
A3: $\forall_\varphi(\neg[\text{JohnBelieves}]\varphi \rightarrow [\text{JohnBelieves}]\neg[\text{JohnBelieves}]\varphi)$

follows the conclusion:

C: $\forall_\varphi([\text{JohnBelieves}]([\text{JohnBelieves}]\varphi \rightarrow \varphi))$ [1].

To solve such reasoning task, we usually employ so-called *decision procedures*, i.e., algorithms which confronted with such a problem yield a yes/no answer. In the context of modal logics tableau-based decision procedures gained high popularity thanks to their conceptual simplicity and computational properties. Moreover, *labelled* tableau calculi for modal logics allow for straightforward synthesis of countermodels for non-valid formulas from the information stored on a branch of derivation. Model generation itself is widely used in, i.a., fault analysis, system verification [1,26] or ontology debugging [21]. A particular focus are minimal models or models with a restricted cardinality of the universe [20]. Tableau-based algorithms which can be applied to the most widespread modal logics and which facilitate constructing a model with an arbitrarily small universe out of a derivation branch are then a very useful tool which can be exploited in various areas of AI in a broad sense.

Modal Logics K45, KB4, KD45, and S5. It is well-known that the modal logic S5 is determined by the class of *universal* frames, i.e., frames of the form $\langle W, R \rangle$, where W is a non-empty set of possible words and R is a binary reachability relation such that $R = W \times W$ (R is said to be *universal* in this case). Thus, S5 is determined by the class of frames of the form $\langle W, W \times W \rangle$. As a consequence, we do not have to refer to R at all in the case of S5. Moreover, the first version of Kripke's semantics for S5 is formulated without using R [16]. The reachability relation appeared in a later Kripke's paper [17] and its aim was to make it possible to formulate semantics for other modal logics. It turns out, however, that S5 is not the only modal logic for which we can construct Kripke-style semantics without using the reachability relation.

Pietruszczak [23] introduced the concepts of *semi-universal* and *simplified* frames. The former have the form $\langle W, R \rangle$, where $R = W \times A$ and $A \subseteq W$ (R is said to be *semi-universal* and A is called *set of common alternatives to the worlds from W*). Thus, they can also be presented as follows: $\langle W, W \times A \rangle$. Hence, we can alternatively define a frame as a pair $\langle W, A \rangle$ and refer to it as *simplified frame*. Pietruszczak showed in [23] that the logic determined by the class of all simplified frames is K45. Moreover, he proved that the class of non-empty simplified frames (the ones with $A \neq \emptyset$) determines the logic KD45; the class of simplified frames which are empty or universal (the ones with $A = \emptyset$ or $A = W$)

---

[1] The assumptions can be read in the following way: A1: John believes in whatever is (logically) true, A2: If John believes that φ is true, then he believes that he believes that φ is true, A3: If John disbelieves that φ is true, then he believes that he disbelieves that φ is true. The conclusion can be read as follows: C: John believes that whatever he believes is true.

determines the logic KB4. In his follow-up paper, [24], Pietruszczak generalized this result onto the extensions of the above-mentioned logics with Segerberg's axioms [29] (Alt_k) and (Talt_k) which constrain the number of elements in A.

In this paper, we present sound, complete and terminating prefixed tableaux for these logics, based on simplified Kripke-style semantics. First, we discuss simplified tableaux for S5. Second, on the basis of Pietruszczak's results on simplified semantics, we devise tableau systems for K45, KD45, and KB4 along the same lines. The only rule that tells all these calculi apart is the rule for $\neg\Box$. What constitutes a substantial difference between our framework and some alternative approaches, such as Massacci's [18] or Goré's [8], is that they use prefixes to store information about the reachability relation. Consequently, prefixes have a complex structure which reflects all reachability links between worlds labelled by them. The rules for $\Box$-formulas are therefore designed to keep track of the "shape" of the reachability relation. In our case, however, there is no reference whatsoever to the reachability relation. From the beginning of every run of any of our tableau calculi we know what simplified model we are aiming for. As a result, the rules for $\Box$-formulas serve to obtain the desired model (i.e., the desired inclusion relations between $\emptyset$, A, and W). The internal structure of prefixes is simple and we know in advance which prefixes will label worlds from A. One consequence of this fact is that the completeness proof for our calculi is straightforward and models can be extracted directly from an open branch.

We also extended Pietruszczak's results by showing that the missing two classes of simplified frames, namely frames with $A \neq W$, and frames with $\emptyset \neq A \neq W$, which Pietruszczak does not consider in his papers, determine the modal logics of, respectively, non-reflexive, transitive, and Euclidean (standard) Kripke frames and non-reflexive, transitive, Euclidean, and serial (standard) Kripke frames. We then prove that these logics are equal to K45 and KD45, respectively, which means that both of them can be characterized by narrower simplified frame classes than the ones indicated in [23]. This complete characterization of modal logics determined by different classes of simplified frames, transposed into a tableau framework, has another interesting effect. It allows us to show, in a very simple way, why both problems: satisfiability and modal consequence are NP-complete (rather than PSPACE-complete like in the case of many other modal logics) for all these logics. Finally, we formulate a special rule which restricts the number of distinct prefixes on a branch to accommodate Segerberg's axioms. We show that when we add this rule to our calculi it does not affect their complexity.

The structure of the paper is as follows. In Sect. 2, we briefly introduce modal logics semantically and syntactically, then we describe simplified semantics for them following [23,24]. In Sect. 3, we introduce our simplified tableaux, establish their soundness, completeness, and termination, and introduce a rule that accommodates Segerberg's axioms. Section 4 is devoted to the discussion of related work. We briefly conclude the paper in Sect. 5.

2 Preliminaries. Simplified Kripke-Style Semantics

Syntax. Let $\mathscr{L}$ be a modal language with the alphabet $\langle \mathrm{PROP}, \Box, \neg, \wedge \rangle$, where $\mathrm{PROP} = \{\mathsf{p}, \mathsf{q}, \mathsf{r}, \mathsf{p}_1, \ldots\}$ is a countable set of propositional variables. The set FORM of well-formed formulas of $\mathscr{L}$ is defined inductively:

$$\varphi ::= p \mid \neg\varphi \mid \varphi \wedge \varphi \mid \Box\varphi,$$

where $p \in \mathrm{PROP}$. We define the connectives $\vee, \rightarrow, \Diamond$ as standard abbreviations, i.e, for any $\varphi, \psi \in \mathrm{FORM}$: $\varphi \vee \psi := \neg(\neg\varphi \wedge \neg\psi)$, $\varphi \rightarrow \psi := \neg\varphi \vee \psi$, $\Diamond\varphi := \neg\Box\neg\varphi$.

Axiomatization. Let us recall some basic modal axioms:

(K)	$\Box(\mathsf{p} \rightarrow \mathsf{q}) \rightarrow (\Box\mathsf{p} \rightarrow \Box\mathsf{q})$,	
(T)	$\Box\mathsf{p} \rightarrow \mathsf{p}$,	(reflexivity)
(D)	$\Box\mathsf{p} \rightarrow \Diamond\mathsf{p}$,	(seriality)
(4)	$\Box\mathsf{p} \rightarrow \Box\Box\mathsf{p}$,	(transitivity)
(5)	$\Diamond\mathsf{p} \rightarrow \Box\Diamond\mathsf{p}$,	(Euclideaness)
(B)	$\mathsf{p} \rightarrow \Box\Diamond\mathsf{p}$,	(symmetry)
(Q)	$\Box\mathsf{q}$,	(emptiness of R)
($\mathsf{T_Q}$)	$(\Box\mathsf{p} \rightarrow \mathsf{p}) \vee \Box\mathsf{q}$.	(quasi-reflexivity)

Segerberg's axioms [29] are as follows:

(Alt_k)	$\Box\mathsf{q}_1 \vee \Box(\mathsf{q}_1 \rightarrow \mathsf{q}_2) \vee \ldots \vee \Box((\mathsf{q}_1 \wedge \ldots \wedge \mathsf{q}_k) \rightarrow \mathsf{q}_{k+1})$,
(Talt_k)	$(\Box\mathsf{p} \rightarrow \mathsf{p}) \vee (\mathsf{Alt}_k)$.

Clearly, $(\mathsf{Q}) = (\mathsf{Alt}_0)$ and $(\mathsf{T_Q}) = (\mathsf{Talt}_0)$. Let Taut be the set of all classical tautologies. Recall that (Alt_k) and (Talt_k) correspond to the following conditions, respectively, $\forall_{w \in W} \mathsf{card}(R[w]) \leq k$ and $\forall_{w \in W}(R(w,w)$ or $\mathsf{card}(R[w]) \leq k)$. As follows from Segerberg's work [29], $\mathsf{S5} \oplus (\mathsf{Alt}_k)$ is determined by universal frames with $\mathsf{card}(W) \leq k$. The basic modal logic K is the smallest set of formulas such that $\mathsf{Taut} \subseteq K$, $(\mathsf{K}) \in \mathsf{K}$, and K is closed under modus ponens, uniform substitution, and the necessity rule. $\mathsf{KX}_1 \ldots \mathsf{X}_k := \mathsf{K} \oplus \{\mathsf{X}_1, \ldots, \mathsf{X}_k\}$ is the smallest extension of K by the formulas $\mathsf{X}_1, \ldots, \mathsf{X}_k$.

Semantics. The notion of *Kripke frame* is defined in a standard way, i.e., as a pair $\mathscr{F} = \langle W, R \rangle$, where $W \neq \emptyset$ and $R \subseteq W \times W$. A *Kripke model* is a pair $\mathscr{M} = \langle \mathscr{F}, V \rangle$, where $\mathscr{F}$ is a Kripke frame and $V : \mathrm{PROP} \longrightarrow 2^W$. W, R, V are called, respectively, *universe*, *reachability relation*, and *valuation*. For a given model $\mathscr{M} = \langle W, R, V \rangle$ and a world $w \in W$ we define the *satisfaction relation* $\Vdash$ in a standard way:

$$\begin{aligned}
\mathscr{M}, w \Vdash p \quad &\text{iff} \quad w \in V(p), \\
\mathscr{M}, w \Vdash \neg\varphi \quad &\text{iff} \quad \mathscr{M}, w \nVdash \varphi, \\
\mathscr{M}, w \Vdash \varphi \wedge \psi \quad &\text{iff} \quad \mathscr{M}, w \Vdash \varphi \text{ and } \mathscr{M}, w \Vdash \psi, \\
\mathscr{M}, w \Vdash \Box\varphi \quad &\text{iff} \quad \forall_{v \in R[w]} \mathscr{M}, v \Vdash \varphi,
\end{aligned}$$

where $p \in \mathrm{PROP}$, $\varphi, \psi \in \mathrm{FORM}$ and $R[w] = \{v \mid wRv\}$.

When we consider *simplified frames*, i.e., as mentioned in Sect. 1, frames of the form $\langle W, A \rangle$, where $A \subseteq W$, the last condition takes the following form:

$$\mathscr{M}, w \Vdash \Box \varphi \quad \text{iff} \quad \forall_{v \in A} \mathscr{M}, v \Vdash \varphi. \tag{1}$$

In [23] Pietruszczak provided a characterization of the logics K45, KD45, and KD45 and their extensions with Segerberg's axioms in terms of simplified frames (SF for short), which is expressed in the following theorem:

Theorem 1 ([23, Theorem 2.5], [24, Theorem 3.3]). *The following logics are determined by the following frame classes:*

K45: *finite SF;*
KD45: *finite SF with $A \neq \emptyset$;*
KB4: *finite SF with $A = \emptyset$ or $A = W$;*
K45 $\oplus$ (Alt$_k$): *SF with card$(A) \leq k$;*
KD45 $\oplus$ (Alt$_k$): *SF with $0 < $ card$(A) \leq k$;*
KB4 $\oplus$ (Alt$_k$): *SF with $A = \emptyset$ or both $A = W$ and card$(W) \leq k$;*
K45 $\oplus$ (Talt$_k$): *SF with $A = W$ or card$(A) \leq k$;*
KD45 $\oplus$ (Talt$_k$): *SF with $A = W$ or $0 < $ card$(A) \leq k$.*

If $k > l$, then:
K45 $\oplus$ {(Alt$_k$), (Talt$_l$)}: *SF with card$(A) \leq l$ or $(A = W$ and card$(W) \leq k)$;*
KD45 $\oplus$ {(Alt$_k$), (Talt$_l$)}: *SF with $0 < $ card$(A) \leq l$ or $(A = W$ and card$(W) \leq k)$.*

Recall that $(T_Q) \in$ KB4 and $(T_Q) \in$ S5 which implies, respectively, KB4 = KB4 $\oplus (T_Q) = $ KB4 $\oplus$ (Talt$_k$) and S5 = S5 $\oplus (T_Q) = $ S5 $\oplus$ (Talt$_k$). Furthermore, KB4 $\oplus$ {(Alt$_k$), (Talt$_l$)} = $KB4 \oplus$ (Alt$_k$) and S5 $\oplus$ {(Alt$_k$), (Talt$_l$)} = $S5 \oplus$ (Alt$_k$). Besides, if $l \geq k$, then K $\oplus$ (Alt$_k$) = $K \oplus$ {(Alt$_k$), (Talt$_l$)}.

Note that in the case of simplified frames for which $A \neq W$ we can assume that card$(W \setminus A) = 1$, i.e., that these frames contain only one world outside of the set A. Indeed, since Kripke models are closed under generated submodels (see [2, Proposition 2.5]), we can discard from a model based on a simplified frame all worlds $w \in W \setminus A$ save the one at which a formula of our interest holds.

Consequently, simplified frames of the form $\langle W, A \rangle$ can be divided into three 'pure' types:

(a) frames in which $A = \emptyset$, i.e., $W = \{w\}$,
(b) frames in which $W = A$,
(c) frames in which $A \neq \emptyset$ and $W = A \cup \{w\}$ for some $w \notin A$.

These types are depicted below:

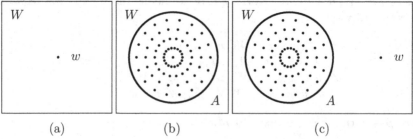

(a)   (b)   (c)

Now let's recall one basic concept. Let L be a modal logic. A formula φ is L-*satisfiable* if there exists a model $\langle \mathscr{F}, V \rangle$, such that $\mathscr{F} = \langle W, A \rangle$ belongs to the class of frames which determines L, and a world $w \in W$, such that $\mathscr{M}, w \Vdash \varphi$. If a formula φ is not L-satisfiable, then $\neg\varphi$ is L-valid.

Remark 1. Using labels: (a), (b), and (c) for frame types we can re-define the classes of simplified frames characterizing logics from Theorem 1 by indicating the types of frames a model of a satisfiable formula can be based on:

K45: (a) ∪ (b) ∪ (c);
KD45: (b) ∪ (c);
KB4: (a) ∪ (b);
K45 $\oplus$ (Alt$_k$): (a) ∪ [((b) ∪ (c))+card(A)$\leq k$];
KD45 $\oplus$ (Alt$_k$): ((b) ∪ (c))+card(A) $\leq k$;
KB4 $\oplus$ (Alt$_k$): (a) ∪ [(b)+card(A) $\leq k$];
K45 $\oplus$ (Talt$_k$): (a) ∪ (b) ∪ [(c)+card(A)$\leq k$];
KD45 $\oplus$ (Talt$_k$): (b) ∪ [(c)+card(A) $\leq k$].

If $k > l$, then:
K45 $\oplus$ {(Alt$_k$), (Talt$_l$)}: (a) ∪ [(b)+card(A)$\leq k$] ∪ [(c)+card(A) $\leq l$];
KD45 $\oplus$ {(Alt$_k$), (Talt$_l$)}: [(b)+card(A) $\leq k$] ∪ [(c)+card(A) $\leq l$].

By that means we have an almost complete characterization of logics determined by (various classes of) simplified frames. We know that the logic S5 is determined by the class of frames of the form (b) and the logic Ver is determined by the class of frames of the form (a). The only two pieces that are missing from this picture are the logics determined by the classes of frames, respectively, of the form (b) ∪ (c) and of the form (c). Before we provide a theorem that fills this gap, we introduce the following notation. Let K45* denote the logic determined by non-reflexive, transitive, and Euclidean frames, where a non-reflexive frame is a frame for which the following condition holds: $\neg\forall_{w \in W} wRw$, and let KD45* denote the logic determined by serial K45*-frames. Non-reflexivity is not modally definable since the class of non-reflexive frames is not closed under surjective bisimulations (conf. [2], it is, however, *modally $\exists$-definable* – see [22]), so neither of the above-mentioned logics is axiomatizable. The following theorem shows that these logics are our missing pieces:

Theorem 2. *1.* K45* *is determined by the class of semi-universal frames* $\langle W, W \times A \rangle$, *as well as by the class of simplified frames* $\langle W, A \rangle$, *where* $A \neq W$.
2. KD45* *is determined by the class of semi-universal frames* $\langle W, W \times A \rangle$, *as well as by the class of simplified frames* $\langle W, A \rangle$, *where* $\emptyset \neq A \neq W$.

The next theorem shows, however, that by introducing K45* and KD45* we do not go beyond the set of logics we have already presented as they collapse to K45 and KD45, respectively.

Theorem 3. *1.* K45* = K45.
2. KD45* = KD45.

Thus, we can replace the respective part of Remark 1 with the following:

Remark 2. Using labels: (a), (b), and (c) for frame types and exploiting Theorem 3, we can again re-define the classes of simplified frames characterizing the aforementioned normal modal logics in the following way:

K45: (a) $\cup$ (c),
KD45: (c),
K45 $\oplus$ (Alt$_k$): (a) $\cup$ [(c)+card(A) $\leq k$],
KD45 $\oplus$ (Alt$_k$): (c)+card(A) $\leq k$.

If $k > l$, then:
K45 $\oplus$ {(Alt$_k$), (Talt$_l$)}: (a) $\cup$ [(c)+card(A) $\leq l$];
KD45 $\oplus$ {(Alt$_k$), (Talt$_l$)}: (c)+card(A) $\leq l$.

Note that K45 $\oplus$ (Alt$_k$) = K45 $\oplus$ (Talt$_k$) and KD45 $\oplus$ (Alt$_k$) = KD45 $\oplus$ (Talt$_k$), and for $k > l$ we have K45 $\oplus$ {(Alt$_k$), (Talt$_l$)} = K45 $\oplus$ (Alt$_l$) and KD45 $\oplus$ {(Alt$_k$), (Talt$_l$)} = KD45 $\oplus$ (Alt$_l$). This is a consequence of the fact that frames of type (b) no longer define the logics K45 and KD45.

3   Simplified Analytic Tableaux

In this section we provide a characterization of sound, complete and terminating *prefixed* tableau calculi[2] for the logics mentioned in Theorem 1 determined by suitable classes of simplified frames described in Sect. 1. The notion of reachability relation is discarded in simplified semantics, so we will not refer to it in the construction of our tableau systems. Instead, we will apply Theorem 1 and devise our calculi in such a way that they return a suitable simplified model for each satisfiable formula.

We will now describe the structure of a tableau generated by our calculi. Let an expression of the form $n : \varphi$, where $n \in \mathbb{N}_0$ and $\varphi \in$ FORM, be called *prefixed formula*. Contrary to, e.g., [8,18], prefixes have a uniform structure since no information about reachability links needs to by stored by them.

Rules of our tableau calculi will have the following general form:

$$\frac{n : \varphi}{m_1^1 : \psi_1^1, \ldots, m_1^{l_1} : \psi_1^{l_1} \mid \ldots \mid m_k^1 : \psi_k^1, \ldots, m_k^{l_k} : \psi_k^{l_k}} \quad (\text{R})$$

where the '$\mid$' symbol should be read as a meta-disjunction and the ',' symbol can be conceived of as a meta-conjunction. If no '$\mid$' symbol occurs in the denominator of a rule, then it is *non-branching*. Otherwise it is called *branching rule*.

A tableau T generated by the calculus for a logic L is a *tree* whose nodes are labelled by prefixed formulas. A simple path from the root to a leaf of T is called

---

[2] For a thorough survey of prefixed tableau calculi for various modal logics between K and S5 see, e.g., [8,18].

branch of T. A branch $\mathscr{B}$ of T is extended by applying rules of the calculus to formulas that are on $\mathscr{B}$. A prefix n is *present* on $\mathscr{B}$ if there exists a formula φ, such that $n : \varphi$ is on $\mathscr{B}$. Otherwise n is *fresh* on $\mathscr{B}$. If we have a rule (R) and a prefixed formula $n : \varphi$ is present on a branch $\mathscr{B}$, then we call $n : \varphi$ (R)-*expanded* on $\mathscr{B}$ if one of the sets of formulas $m_i^1 : \psi_i^1, \ldots, m_1^{l_i} : \psi_i^{l_i}$, $1 \leq i \leq k$, is also present on $\mathscr{B}$. A rule (R) can only be applied to a prefixed formula that is not (R)-expanded.

A branch $\mathscr{B}$ is called *closed* if the closure rule ($\bot$) has been applied to it, that is, there exists a formula φ and a prefix n, such that both $n : \varphi$ and $n : \neg\varphi$ are present on $\mathscr{B}$. A branch that is not closed, is *open*. An open branch is *fully expanded* if no rules are applicable to it. A tableau T is called *closed* if all its branches are closed. Otherwise T is called *open*.

Analytic tableaux are satisfiability checkers, so a tableau proof of a formula φ is a closed tableau with the prefix formula $0 : \neg\varphi$ at its root. Our tableau calculi are designed to also check *modal consequence*. A formula φ is a modal consequence of a set of global premises G and a set of local premises U in a logic L if in all models $\langle \mathscr{F}, V \rangle$, such that $\mathscr{F} = \langle W, A \rangle$ belongs to the class of frames which determines L, whenever for every $w \in W$ it holds that $\mathscr{M}, w \Vdash$ G, then for all $w \in W$ $\mathscr{M}, w \Vdash$ U implies $\mathscr{M}, w \Vdash \varphi$. If G $\neq \emptyset$, then the modal consequence is called *global*, otherwise it is called *local*. A tableau proof that φ is a modal consequence of a set of global premises G and a set of local premises U, is a closed tableau with the prefix formula $0 : \bigwedge U \wedge \neg\varphi$ ($\bigwedge U$ is the conjunction of all the formulas from U) at its root and the rule (G) among the calculus' rules.

A tableau calculus is (*weakly*) *sound* iff for each satisfiable input formula φ there exists an open tableau generated by the calculus. It is (*strongly*) *sound* iff for φ not being a modal consequence of the sets G and U, there exists an open tableau generated by the calculus with φ and U as input formulas and G as the basis for the (G)-rule. It is (*weakly*) *complete* iff for each valid input formula φ there exists a tableau proof of φ. It is (*strongly*) *complete* iff for φ being a modal consequence of the sets G and U, there exists a tableau proof of this fact. It is *terminating* iff all tableaus generated by the calculus are finite. Finally, a tableau calculus is a *decision procedure* if it is sound, complete and terminating.

Simplified Tableau Calculus for S5. Our point of departure is a simple tableau calculus for the logic S5, presented in, e.g., [25], where S5 frames are assumed to be universal frames, i.e., they involve no reachability relation and the $\Box$-operator behaves like the universal modality. The rules of this tableau system are presented in Fig. 1(a).

Tableau Calculi for K45, KB4, and KD45. In all tableau calculi that will appear in the sequel, the Boolean rules, closure rule, prefix-generating rule, and global premise rule from Fig. 1a, i.e., ($\bot$), ($\neg\neg$), ($\wedge$), ($\neg\wedge$), ($\neg\Box$), and (G), remain unchanged[3]. Keeping that in mind, we will only list calculus-specific rules, that is propagation rules for the $\Box$-operator, when describing each of them. The order of rule application can be arbitrary since the calculus is *confluent*, however,

---

[3] Henceforth, we will refer to these rules as *common rules*.

$$(\bot) \ \frac{n : \varphi, n : \neg\varphi}{\bot} \quad (\wedge) \ \frac{n : \varphi \wedge \psi}{n : \varphi, n : \psi} \quad (\neg\wedge) \ \frac{n : \neg(\varphi \wedge \psi)}{n : \neg\varphi \mid n : \neg\psi}$$

$$(\neg\neg) \ \frac{n : \neg\neg\varphi}{n : \varphi} \quad (\Box) \ \frac{n : \Box\varphi}{m : \varphi^*} \quad (\neg\Box) \ \frac{n : \neg\Box\varphi}{m : \neg\varphi^\dagger}$$

*m is present on a   †m is the least non-negative
branch   integer fresh on a branch

$$(G) \ \frac{n : \varphi}{n : \gamma^\S}$$

$^\S\gamma \in G$

(a)

K45	KB4	KD45
$(\Box_{(a)\cup(c)}) \ \dfrac{n : \Box\varphi}{m : \varphi^*}$	$(\Box_{(a)\cup(b)}) \ \dfrac{n : \Box\varphi}{m : \varphi^*}$	$(\Box_{(c)^1}) \ \dfrac{0 : \Box\varphi}{1 : \varphi^*}$
*m is present on $\mathscr{B}$ and $m \neq 0$	*m is present on $\mathscr{B}$ and some $k \neq 0$ is present on $\mathscr{B}$	*1 is fresh on $\mathscr{B}$ and there is no $k \neq 0$ on $\mathscr{B}$
		$(\Box_{(c)^2}) \ \dfrac{n : \Box\varphi}{m : \varphi^{**}}$
		**m is present on $\mathscr{B}$ and $m \neq 0$

(b)

Fig. 1. Simplified tableau calculus for S5 (a) and K45, KB4, and KD45 (b).

as usual, to obtain the shortest derivation it is recommended that the prefix generating rule ($\neg\Box$) is only applied when no other rules are applicable.

K45. As we know from Remark 2, the logic K45 is determined by the class of simplified frames of type (a) and (c). For a given formula $\neg\varphi$ the tableau algorithm for K45 searches a model of, subsequently, type (a) and (c). To that end it uses the common rules and the ($\Box_{(a)\cup(c)}$)-rule. The intuitive sense of the latter is the following. As long as no prefix-generating rule was applied, the only prefix present on the branch is 0. Consequently, as long as no other prefix was introduced to the branch, we assume that φ has a model of type (a) consisting of only 0. Since $0 \notin A$, ($\Box_{(a)\cup(c)}$) does not allow to propagate any formulas to 0. Once any prefix other than 0 has been introduced to the branch by an application of the ($\neg\Box$)-rule, we know that φ does not have a model of type (a). Consequently, we assume that there can exist a model of type (c), i.e., a model based on a frame $\langle W, A \rangle$, where $A = W \setminus \{0\}$. ($\Box_{(a)\cup(c)}$) acts in accordance with this assumption by propagating formulas only to those prefixes which are distinct from 0. If our search turns out unsuccessful, that is we obtain a closed tree, it means that $\neg\varphi$ is K45-unsatisfiable, i.e., φ has a tableau proof in K45.

KB4. The logic KB4 is determined by the class of simplified frames of type (a) and (b). For a given formula $\neg\varphi$ the tableau algorithm for KB4 first looks for a model of type (a), that is a singleton model with an empty set of common alternatives. As long as 0 is the only prefix present on the branch, the $(\Box_{(a)\cup(b)})$-rule does not allow to propagate any formulas under the scope of $\Box$ to 0, assuming that $0 \notin A$. Once another prefix has been introduced to a branch, it tells us that no model of type (a) satisfies $\neg\varphi$. It means that $\neg\varphi$ can have only a model of type (b), that is a model based on a universal frame. After introducing at least one prefix other than 0 to the branch $(\Box_{(a)\cup(b)})$ starts to behave like the $(\Box)$-rule from the calculus for S5. If the run of the algorithm returns a closed tree, it proves that $\neg\varphi$ has neither a model of type (a), nor of type (b) and cardinality greater than 1. However if no model based on a universal frame of cardinality greater than 1 satisfies φ, then there exists no such model of cardinality 1 on which $\neg\varphi$ is satisfied, so no model of type (b) at all. Consequently, $\neg\varphi$ is KB4-unsatisfiable and thus φ has a tableau proof in KB4.

KD45. As mentioned in Remark 2, KD45 is determined by the class of simplified frames of type (c). For a given formula $\neg\varphi$ the tableau algorithm for KD45 searches a model of type (c), that is a model based on a simplified frame $\langle W, A \rangle$, where $A \neq \emptyset$ and $0 \notin A$. We know that a model our algorithm attempts to construct should consist of at least two prefixes: 0 and 1. If all possible rules were applied to formulas with the prefix 0 and no fresh prefix was introduced to the branch, we apply $(\Box_{(c)^1})$ (if possible) which is a prefix-generating rule, although it is not applied to any $\neg\Box$-formula. Of course, if neither $(\neg\Box)$, nor $(\Box_{(c)^1})$ is applicable, it means that $\neg\varphi$ is a Boolean formula and if it is propositionally consistent, it is also modally satisfiable. Clearly, $(\Box_{(c)^1})$ can be applied at most once and if it was done, $(\Box_{(c)^2})$ takes over the role of the propagating rule. $(\Box_{(c)^1})$ allows to propagate formulas in the scope of $\Box$ only to those prefixes which are distinct than 0, which follows from the fact that $0 \notin A$. If the algorithm ends up in a closed tableau, it tells us that $\neg\varphi$ is KD45-unsatisfiable, so φ has a tableau proof in KD45.

For the sake of example, in Fig. 2 we show a *dis*proof of the axiom (B) ($p \rightarrow \Box\Diamond p$) in the calculus for K45, as well as a *dis*proof of the axiom (D) ($\Box p \rightarrow \Diamond p$) in the calculus for KB4. Moreover, we get back to the example from Sect. 1 for which the logic KD45 is an adequate formalization, and show that the formula $\Box(\Box p \rightarrow p)$ is KD45-valid. All formulas are rewritten, so that they include only primitive (not defined) connectives. In the first case the tableau derivation yields the following K45-simplified countermodel $\mathcal{M}_1 = \langle W_1, A_1, V_1 \rangle$ for the formula $p \rightarrow \Box\Diamond p$: $W_1 = \{0, 1\}$, $A_1 = \{1\}$, $V_1(p) = \{0\}$. In the second case the tableau derivation yields the following KB4-simplified countermodel $\mathcal{M}_2 = \langle W_2, A_2, V_2 \rangle$ for the formula $\Box p \rightarrow \Diamond p$: $W_2 = \{0\}$, $A_2 = \emptyset$, $V_2(p) = \emptyset$.

Soundness and Completeness. In order to prove soundness and completeness of tableau algorithms from Fig. 1(b) we take the conditions listed in the beginning of this section in the contrapositive form. Thus, establishing soundness amounts to showing that each tableau rule of a calculus preserves satisfiability, i.e., if a set of formulas in the numerator of a rule is satisfiable, so is one of the sets in the denominator. To prove completeness of the calculi for K45, KB4, and KD45 we need to show that:

K45 $p \to \Box\Diamond p$	KB4 $\Box p \to \Diamond p$	KD45 $\Box(\Box p \to p)$
$0 : \neg\neg(p \land \neg\Box\neg\Box\neg p)$	$0 : \neg\neg(\Box p \land \neg\neg\Box\neg p)$	$0 : \neg\Box(\neg(\Box p \land \neg p))$
$\downarrow (\neg\neg)$	$\downarrow (\neg\neg)$	$\downarrow (\neg\Box)$
$0 : p \land \neg\Box\neg\Box\neg p$	$0 : \Box p \land \neg\neg\Box\neg p$	$1 : \neg\neg(\Box p \land \neg p)$
$\downarrow (\land)$	$\downarrow (\land)$	$\downarrow (\neg\neg)$
$0 : p$	$0 : \Box p$	$1 : \Box p \land \neg p$
$0 : \neg\Box\neg\Box\neg p$	$0 : \neg\neg\Box\neg p$	$\downarrow (\land)$
$\downarrow(\neg\Box)$	$\downarrow (\neg\neg)$	$1 : \Box p$
$1 : \neg\neg\Box\neg p$	$0 : \Box\neg p$	$1 : \neg p$
$\downarrow (\neg\neg)$		$\downarrow (\Box_{(c)}2)$
$1 : \Box\neg p$		$1 : p$
$\downarrow (\Box_{(a)\cup(c)})$		$\downarrow (\bot)$
$1 : \neg p$		$\bot$

Fig. 2. Tableau derivations in the calculi for the logics K45, KB4, and KD45.

in the case of checking satisfiability: if for a given formula φ an algorithm returned an open tableau, then φ is satisfiable;

in the case of checking modal consequence: if for a given formula φ and sets G and U of, respectively, global and local premises an algorithm returned an open tableau, then φ does not modally follow from G and U, i.e., there exist a (simplified) model $\mathscr{M} = \langle W, A, V \rangle$, such that $\mathscr{M}, w \Vdash \gamma$ for all $w \in W$ and all $\gamma \in G$, and a world $v \in W$, such that $\mathscr{M}, v \Vdash \nu$, for all $\nu \in U$, and $\mathscr{M}, v \nVdash \varphi$.

Theorem 4 (Soundness and completeness). *The tableau calculi for* K45, KB4, *and* KD45, *presented in Fig. 1b, are (strongly) sound and complete.*

Termination. Although the calculi for the logics K45, KB4, and KD45, presented in the previous section, are sound and complete, no termination is ensured yet. So far, if we run any of these algorithms on a satisfiable formula such as $\Diamond p \land \Box\Diamond p$, in all cases we will end up in an infinite loop despite the fact that the formula is satisfiable in a finite (and small) model in all three logics. The culprit is the $(\neg\Box)$-rule which is the only rule that generates new prefixes and introduces them to a branch (save $(\Box_{(c)}1)$ which generates and introduces to a branch at most one fresh prefix and as such is not a threat to termination). We need to limit its applicability. To that end we employ a so-called *blocking mechanism*. The simplified semantics underlying our calculi allows us to formulate a very simple condition restricting the number of prefixes introduced to a branch:

(B) The $(\neg\Box)$-rule cannot be applied to a prefixed formula $n : \neg\Box\varphi$ if there exists a prefix m on the branch, such that $(\neg\Box)$ has already been applied to $m : \neg\Box\varphi$[4].

Intuitively, (B) disallows to apply $(\neg\Box)$ to a prefixed formula $n : \neg\Box\varphi$ and generate new prefixes if it is known that there already exists a prefix on a branch, which satisfies (B) for $\neg\Box\varphi$.

Theorem 5 (Termination and complexity). *The tableau calculi for K45, KB4, and KD45, augmented with (B), are sound, complete and terminating. Moreover, they run in NP with respect to checking satisfiability and disproving modal consequence. As a result, they are worst-case complexity-optimal.*

By that means we obtain a nice general property of the class of normal modal logics determined by (various classes of) simplified frames: for all of them both the satisfiability problem and modal consequence are NP-complete.

Adding Segerberg's Axioms. If we want to extend our logics with Segerberg's axioms, we need to augment the calculi with a rule that appropriately constrains the number of prefixes labelling elements of A that occur on a branch. In each calculus this rule will have the same form, but a different side condition following directly from Remarks 1 and 2. First, let's introduce several auxiliary notions. Let $\mathscr{B}$ be a branch of a tableau and let n, m be prefixes occurring on $\mathscr{B}$. We define the following symbols: $\tau_{\mathscr{B}}(n) = \{\varphi \mid n : \varphi$ occurs on $\mathscr{B}\}$, $\mu_{\mathscr{B}}(n, m) = \{m : \varphi \mid \varphi \in \tau_{\mathscr{B}}(n)\} \cup \{n : \varphi \mid \varphi \in \tau_{\mathscr{B}}(m)\}$. Then, our rule has the form:

$$(\downarrow_k) \quad \frac{n_1 : \varphi_1, \ldots, n_{k+1} : \varphi_{k+1}}{\mu_{\mathscr{B}}(n_1, n_2) \mid \mu_{\mathscr{B}}(n_1, n_3) \mid \ldots \mid \mu_{\mathscr{B}}(n_k, n_{k+1})},$$

where $\tau_{\mathscr{B}}(n_i) \neq \tau_{\mathscr{B}}(n_j)$ whenever $i \neq j$, and $\mathscr{B}$ is a branch to which $(\downarrow_k)$ is applied. Intuitively, if more prefixes representing elements of the set A occur on a branch than it is allowed by the (Alt_k) and/or (Talt_k) axiom, then $(\downarrow_k)$ non-deterministically checks whether a pair of prefixes can label the same world. The tableau identification of prefixes is done by merging the sets of formulas occurring with either of these prefixes and adding to the branch all elements of this set with both prefixes (unless a given prefixed formula is already there). In each calculus we apply $(\downarrow_k)$ *with the lowest priority*, i.e., only when no other rules are applicable. Note that the branching factor of $(\downarrow_k)$ is quadratic in k.

Below, we provide a characterization of the tableau calculi for the suitable Segerberg extensions of the calculi for K45, KB4, and KD45 with the $(\downarrow_k)$-rule augmented with an appropriate side condition (SC for short).

K45 $\oplus$ (Alt_k): $(\downarrow_k)$-rule and SC: $n_i \neq 0$ *is present on* $\mathscr{B}$, $1 \leq i \leq k + 1$;
KD45 $\oplus$ (Alt_k): $(\downarrow_k)$-rule and SC: $n_i \neq 0$ *is present on* $\mathscr{B}$, $1 \leq i \leq k + 1$;
KB4 $\oplus$ (Alt_k): $(\downarrow_k)$-rule and SC: n_i *is present on* $\mathscr{B}$, $1 \leq i \leq k + 1$;

---

[4] Note that it is an analogous condition to Technique 9.1 from [18], however using it in the framework of simplified tableaux shows explicitly why it does not violate completeness.

S5 $\oplus$ (Alt$_k$): ($\downarrow_k$)-rule and SC: n_i *is present on* $\mathscr{B}$, $1 \leq i \leq k+1$;
K45 $\oplus$ (Talt$_k$): ($\downarrow_k$)-rule and SC: $n_i \neq 0$ *is present on* $\mathscr{B}$, $1 \leq i \leq k+1$;
KD45 $\oplus$ (Talt$_k$): ($\downarrow_k$)-rule and SC: $n_i \neq 0$ *is present on* $\mathscr{B}$, $1 \leq i \leq k+1$.

For $k > l$:

K45 $\oplus$ {(Alt$_k$), (Talt$_l$)}: ($\downarrow_l$)-rule and SC: $n_i \neq 0$ *is present on* $\mathscr{B}$, $1 \leq i \leq l+1$;
KD45 $\oplus$ {(Alt$_k$), (Talt$_l$)}: ($\downarrow_l$)-rule and SC: $n_i \neq 0$ *is present on* $\mathscr{B}$, $1 \leq i \leq l+1$.

Theorem 6. *The tableau calculi for* K45$\oplus$(Alt$_k$), KD45$\oplus$(Alt$_k$), KB4$\oplus$(Alt$_k$), S5 $\oplus$ (Alt$_k$), K45 $\oplus$ (Talt$_k$), KD45 $\oplus$ (Talt$_k$), K45 $\oplus$ {(Alt$_k$), (Talt$_l$)}, KD45 $\oplus$ {(Alt$_k$), (Talt$_l$)} *are (strongly) sound, complete, terminating and run in* NP.

4 Related Work

There are multiple general methodologies of devising labelled proof systems for modal logics present on the market, such as Gabbay and Governatori's *fibred tableaux* [6,7,9], Massacci's *single-step tableaux* [18], Viganò's *labelled natural deduction* [33] or Schmidt and Tishkovsky's *tableau-generation framework* [27,28]. Our framework is, however, more focused as it involves only those modal logics whose semantics can be simplified. Since S5 is in a sense archetypal for all modal logics with simplified semantics, let us start from a reference to one of the first tableau calculi for S5. In [3,4] Fitting provides a *non*-prefixed analytic tableau algorithm for S5. In his system the semantics of the logic is fully implicit in the sense that no rules for the reachability relation or prefixes are used. However, his system supposes crossing out of the formulas which are not of the form $\Box\varphi$ or $\neg\Diamond\varphi$, if the rules for $\Diamond\varphi$ or $\neg\Box\varphi$ are applied. This can be interpreted as traversing between different worlds of a model. Due to the fact that the whole semantic machinery is 'hidden', it cannot be called *simplified* in our sense, however it is in fact very accessible. In one of his later papers, [5], Fitting mentions that S5 is peculiar with respect to both its semantics and tableau-formalization, because we can assume that there is no reachability relation and an S5-frame takes the form $\langle W, \Vdash \rangle$, where $\Vdash$ is defined as in Sect. 2, with the proviso that we change $\forall_{v \in R[w]}$ for $\forall_{v \in W}$.

Priest follows up this line of thought in [25] by presenting a tableau algorithm for S5 which is simplified in our sense, i.e., does not refer to the reachability relation (although Priest himself does not use the term 'simplified tableaux'). Priest also demonstrates a general approach for the construction of prefixed tableaux for modal logics (including K45, KB4, and KD45), however in other tableau systems reachability relation is explicitly mentioned in derivation trees.

Reachability relation is handled slightly differently in prefixed modal tableaux presented by Goré in [8] and Massacci in [18]. It does not occur in the rules explicitly, that is as expressions of the form nRm, where n and m are prefixes, but is encoded in a special system of prefixes. For example, if the prefix 3.2.1 occurs on a branch, it means that it labels a world which is an R-successor of a world denoted by 3.2. By that means a tableau branch keeps track of the structure of R. Massacci's general framework of tableaux generating is modular in the sense that each semantic constraint on the reachability relation (such as symmetry, transitivity etc.) is reflected by a ($\square$)-tableau rule. Consequently, when we want to devise a tableau calculus for an extension of a given logic, we just need to add a rule-counterpart of the semantic condition defining this extension without putting the completeness of the calculus at risk. No rules need to be discarded. On the one hand, when in a logic multiple conditions are imposed on the reachability relation, it automatically leads to an expansion of the tableau calculus for this logic. On the other hand, adding subsequent rules to a calculus does not violate its completeness. An interesting fact is that Massacci notices a special status of S5, K45 and KD45 and shows that in tableaux for them applications of ($\neg\square$) can be constrained in a way that yields the NP-upper bound on the complexity of the algorithms for both the satisfiability problem and (disproving) modal consequence (which makes the tableaux complexity-optimal, as these logics are NP-complete with respect to these problems, see [10]). The cost of modularity is an expansion of the set of rules – each condition imposed on R is reflected by one or several ($\square$)-rules.

Some analogues of the ($\downarrow_k$)-rule can be found in, e.g., [11–15, 34]. Nevertheless, the context of their use is slightly different than the one presented in this paper. In our framework, ($\downarrow_k$) reflects a global restriction imposed in advance on the cardinality of the model, whereas in the cited works it handles formulas with cardinality constraints added as modal operators.

In our tableau calculi we do not have to keep track of any information related to the reachability relation. Consequently, we do not need any Gabbay-style extra rules for R. Moreover, unlike Goré's and Massacci's approaches, ours does not involve any complex prefixes and multiple ($\square$)-rules. In each tableau calculus prefixes are simply natural numbers and $\square$-formulas are handled by a single ($\square$)-rule (($\square_{(c)^1}$) is not a $\square$-rule in the classical sense). There is, however, a downside to the overall simplicity of the presented tableaux, namely the lack of modularity, contrary to all of the above-mentioned frameworks. The tableau framework presented in this paper is tailored to a particular set of modal logics, so it cannot be easily extended onto the logics outside of this set. On the other hand, the set of modal logics defined by classes of simplified frames seems rather natural due to the fact that all of its elements are NP-complete with respect to the satisfiability problem, as opposed to other modal logics (which are usually PSPACE-complete).

5   Conclusions

In this paper, we introduced a new tableau formalization of the logics K45, KB4, KD45 and their extensions with Segerberg's axioms, based on the so-called simplified semantics. We also showed that K45 = K45* and KD45 = KD45*, thanks to which we were able to further simplify the tableaux. The presented calculi are conceptually simple and make completeness and complexity proofs straightforward. Moreover, they help easily see why the logics determined by simplified frames are NP-complete.

In the future we would like to investigate whether modal logics with simplified semantics give rise to a class of sequent or hypersequent calculi which is uniform in any respect. Interestingly, it is known that the cut-elimination theorem holds for the sequent calculi for K45 and KD45 but fails for KB4 and S5 [30]. A detailed analysis of the interrelations between the calculi and the simplified semantics of the underlying logics might provide an explanation for this divergence.

Acknowledgements. We would like to thank the anonymous reviewers whose comments helped substantially improve this paper.

References

1. Baumgartner, P., Fröhlich, P., Furbach, U., Nejdl, W.: Tableaux for diagnosis applications. In: Galmiche, D. (ed.) TABLEAUX 1997. LNCS, vol. 1227, pp. 76–90. Springer, Heidelberg (1997). https://doi.org/10.1007/BFb0027406
2. Blackburn, P., de Rijke, M., Venema, Y.: Modal Logic. No. 53 in Cambridge Tracts in Theoretical Computer Science. Cambridge University Press, Cambridge (2001)
3. Fitting, M.: A tableau system for propositional S5. Notre Dame J. Formal Logic **18**(2), 292–294 (1977). https://doi.org/10.1305/ndjfl/1093887933
4. Fitting, M.: Proof Methods for Modal and Intuitionistic Logic. No. 169 in Synthese Library. Springer, Dordrecht (1983). https://doi.org/10.1007/978-94-017-2794-5
5. Fitting, M.: A simple propositional S5 tableau system. Ann. Pure Appl. Logic **96**(1), 107–115 (1999)
6. Gabbay, D.M.: Labelled Deductive Systems. Oxford University Press, Oxford (1996)
7. Gabbay, D.M., Governatori, G.: Fibred modal tableaux. In: Basin, D., D'Agostino, M., Gabbay, D.M., Matthews, S., Viganò, L. (eds.) Labelled Deduction. Applied Logic Series, vol. 17, pp. 161–191. Springer, Netherlands, Dordrecht (2000). https://doi.org/10.1007/978-94-011-4040-9_7
8. Goré, R.: Tableau methods for modal and temporal logics. In: D'Agostino, M., Gabbay, D.M., Hähnle, R., Posegga, J. (eds.) Handbook of Tableau Methods, pp. 297–396. Springer, Dordrecht (1999). https://doi.org/10.1007/978-94-017-1754-0_6
9. Governatori, G.: On the relative complexity of labelled modal tableaux. Electron. Notes Theor. Comput. Sci. **78**, 40–57 (2003)
10. Halpern, J.Y., Moses, Y.: A guide to completeness and complexity for modal logics of knowledge and belief. Artif. Intell. **54**(3), 319–379 (1992)
11. Horrocks, I., Kutz, O., Sattler, U.: The even more irresistible SROIQ. In: Doherty, P., Mylopoulos, J., Welty, C.A. (eds.) Proceedings, Tenth International Conference on Principles of Knowledge Representation and Reasoning, Lake District of the United Kingdom, 2–5 June 2006, pp. 57–67. AAAI Press (2006)
12. Horrocks, I., Sattler, U.: A tableaux decision procedure for SHOIQ. In: Kaelbling, L.P., Saffiotti, A. (eds.) IJCAI-05, Proceedings of the Nineteenth International Joint Conference on Artificial Intelligence, Edinburgh, Scotland, UK, 30 July–5 August 2005, pp. 448–453. Professional Book Center (2005)
13. Indrzejczak, A., Zawidzki, M.: Decision procedures for some strong hybrid logics. Logic Log. Philos. **22**(4), 389–409 (2013)
14. Kaminski, M., Schneider, S., Smolka, G.: Terminating tableaux for graded hybrid logic with global modalities and role hierarchies. In: Giese, M., Waaler, A. (eds.) TABLEAUX 2009. LNCS (LNAI), vol. 5607, pp. 235–249. Springer, Heidelberg (2009). https://doi.org/10.1007/978-3-642-02716-1_18

15. Kaminski, M., Schneider, S., Smolka, G.: Terminating tableaux for graded hybrid logic with global modalities and role hierarchies. Logical Methods Comput. Sci. **7**(1), 1–21 (2011)
16. Kripke, S.A.: A completeness theorem in modal logic. J. Symb. Logic **24**(1), 1–14 (1959)
17. Kripke, S.A.: Semantical considerations on modal logic. Acta Philosophica Fennica **16**, 83–94 (1963)
18. Massacci, F.: Single step tableaux for modal logics. J. Autom. Reason. **24**(3), 319–364 (2000)
19. Meyer, J.J.C., van der Hoek, W.: Epistemic Logic for AI and Computer Science. Cambridge Tracts in Theoretical Computer Science. Cambridge University Press, Cambridge (1995)
20. Papacchini, F.: Minimal model reasoning for modal logic. Ph.D. thesis, University of Manchester (2015)
21. Parsia, B., Sirin, E., Kalyanpur, A.: Debugging OWL ontologies. In: Proceedings of the 14th International Conference on World Wide Web, pp. 633–640. WWW 2005. ACM, New York (2005)
22. Perkov, T.: A generalization of modal frame definability. In: Colinet, M., Katrenko, S., Rendsvig, R.K. (eds.) ESSLLI Student Sessions 2013. LNCS, vol. 8607, pp. 142–153. Springer, Heidelberg (2014). https://doi.org/10.1007/978-3-662-44116-9_10
23. Pietruszczak, A.: Simplified Kripke-style semantics for modal logics K45, KB4 and KD45. Bull. Sect. Logic **38**(3–4), 163–171 (2009)
24. Pietruszczak, A., Klonowski, M., Petrukhin, Y., Simplified Kripke-style semantics for some normal modal logics. Studia Logica (2019). https://doi.org/10.1007/s11225-019-09849-2
25. Priest, G.: An Introduction to Non-Classical Logic: From If to Is. Cambridge Introductions to Philosophy, 2nd edn. Cambridge University Press, Cambridge (2008). https://doi.org/10.1017/CBO9780511801174
26. Reiter, R.: A theory of diagnosis from first principles. Artif. Intell. **32**(1), 57–95 (1987)
27. Schmidt, R.A., Tishkovsky, D.: Automated synthesis of tableau calculi. In: Giese, M., Waaler, A. (eds.) TABLEAUX 2009. LNCS (LNAI), vol. 5607, pp. 310–324. Springer, Heidelberg (2009). https://doi.org/10.1007/978-3-642-02716-1_23
28. Schmidt, R.A., Tishkovsky, D.: Automated synthesis of tableau calculi. Logical Methods Comput. Sci. **7**(2) (2011). https://doi.org/10.2168/LMCS-7(2:6)2011
29. Segerberg, K.K.: An Essay in Classical Modal Logic. Filosofiska Föreningen Och Filosofiska Institutionen Vid Uppsala Universitet, Uppsala (1971)
30. Takano, M.: A modified subformula property for the modal logics K5 and K5D. Bull. Sect. Logic **30**(2), 115–122 (2001)
31. van Benthem, J.: Modal Logic for Open Minds. CSLI Lecture Notes, vol. 199. CSLI Publications, Stanford (2010)
32. van Dietmarsch, H., Halpern, J.Y., van der Hoek, W., Kooi, B. (eds.): Handbook of Epistemic Logic. College Publications, Milton Keynes (2015)
33. Viganò, L.: Labelled Non-Classical Logics. Kluwer, Dordrecht (2000)
34. Zawidzki, M.: Deductive Systems and the Decidability Problem for Hybrid Logics. Łódź University Press/Jagiellonian University Press, Łódź/Kraków (2014)

AI and Computation

Automated Planning Encodings for the Manipulation of Articulated Objects in 3D with Gravity

Riccardo Bertolucci[1] [iD], Alessio Capitanelli[2] [iD], Marco Maratea[2(✉)] [iD],
Fulvio Mastrogiovanni[2] [iD], and Mauro Vallati[3] [iD]

[1] DeMaCS, University of Calabria, Rende, Italy
bertolucci@mat.unical.it
[2] DIBRIS, University of Genova, Genova, Italy
{alessio.capitanelli,marco.maratea,fulvio.mastrogiovanni}@unige.it
[3] University of Huddersfield, Huddersfield, UK
m.vallati@hud.ac.uk

Abstract. The manipulation of articulated objects plays an important role in real-world robot tasks, both in home and industrial environments. A lot of attention has been devoted to the development of *ad hoc* approaches and algorithms for generating the sequence of movements the robot has to perform in order to manipulate the object. Such approaches can hardly generalise on different settings, and are usually focused on 2D manipulations.

In this paper we introduce a set of PDDL+ formulations for performing automated manipulation of articulated objects in a three-dimensional workspace by a dual-arm robot. Presented formulations differ in terms of how gravity is modelled, considering different trade-offs between modelling accuracy and planning performance, and between human-readability and parsability by planners. Our experimental analysis compares the formulations on a range of domain-independent planners, that aim at generating plans for allowing a dual-arm robot to manipulate articulated objects of different sizes. Validation is performed in simulation on a Baxter robot.

Keywords: Mixed discrete-continuous planning · Robotics application

1 Introduction

The manipulation of articulated objects plays an important role in real-world robot tasks, both in home and industrial environments [20,23]. In literature, the problem of determining the two- or three-dimensional (2D or 3D) configuration of articulated or flexible objects has received much attention in the past few years [3,7,8,26,33], whereas the problem of obtaining a target configuration via manipulation has been explored in motion planning [4,31,35]. However, the employed manipulation strategies are often crafted specifically for the problem at

© Springer Nature Switzerland AG 2019
M. Alviano et al. (Eds.): AI*IA 2019, LNAI 11946, pp. 135–150, 2019.
https://doi.org/10.1007/978-3-030-35166-3_10

hand, with the relevant characteristics of the object and robot capabilities being either hard coded or assumed, thus undermining generalisation and scalability. More general solutions [1,8] are limited to 2D configuration, with a partial exception for the work in [1], where the notion of *overlap* between different parts of a cable is explicitly considered. A challenging aspect of identifying the movements needed to achieve a desired 3D configuration of an articulated object manipulation is that the effect of gravity has to be explicitly modelled and taken into account.

In this paper we introduce a set of PDDL+ [13] models for performing an automated manipulation of articulated objects in a 3D workspace by a dual-arm robot. Presented models differ in terms of how gravity is modelled, considering different levels of accuracy, and in the design of the formulation itself, by trading-off between human-readability and usability by planners. Three different levels of complexity are designed and described for modelling the impact of gravity on the articulated object.

Our experimental analysis compares the proposed models on a range of domain-independent PDDL+ planners, taking into account articulated objects with different sizes and different variable parameters (e.g., acceleration value) for each level of complexity. As a matter of fact, the empirical analysis highlights that the proposed models, designed following the more natural and concise representation of the considered problem, can not be handled by most of the selected PDDL+ planning engines. For this reason, we then modify the introduced PDDL+ models, providing a formulation which trades the intuitiveness of the model for the acceptability by planning engines.

Results of our extensive experimental analysis show to which degree the proposed PDDL+ models allow domain-independent PDDL+ planning engines to solve tasks that model practical, real-world applications, i.e., in terms of robot workspace and the number of links and physical features characterising the articulated object. Moreover, it gives also an indication about what is the most suited formulation and planner to solve these specific problem instances.

To sum up, the main contributions of this paper are:

- We define two sets of PDDL+ models for the task of automated, robot-based manipulation of articulated objects in a 3D workspace. Each set of models considers three different levels of complexity for representing the effect of gravity.
- We analyse the performance of a number of domain-independent PDDL+ planners on realistic articulated object manipulation tasks.

We also validate generated plans using a robot control architecture for a dual-arm robot manipulator in simulation. As a side effect of our work, we provide a challenging domain, and its PDDL+ models, to the planning community.

2   Problem Statement

Among the tasks typically carried out in shop-floor environments, the manipulation of flexible objects, e.g., cables [19,29], is particularly challenging. On the one hand, it is beneficial to plan the target cable configuration in advance; on the other hand, it is often necessary to keep a cable firmly using one grasping point to be able to manipulate other parts. A robot capable of manipulating flexible objects in its 3D workspace must be able to: (i) represent object configurations adopting suitable modelling assumptions, and then segment the whole manipulation problem in simpler actions to be sequenced and performed, each action operating in-between two intermediate 3D object configurations; and (ii) represent the actions to carry out using a formalism which allows for robust plan execution and modelling inaccuracies.

These requirements lead to a robot perception and control architecture characterized by the following features: (a) similarly to the approach described in [1], the robot plans an appropriate sequence of actions to determine relevant 3D intermediate configurations for articulated objects (i.e., a suitable *simplified* model for a flexible object like a cable) in order to determine a target 3D configuration; and (b) during plan execution, the robot monitors the outcome of each action, and compares it with the intermediate target configuration to achieve. The problem we consider in this paper can be defined as follows: given a target object configuration in 3D space, determining a plan $\mathcal{P}$ to obtain it as an ordered set of actions $\mathcal{P} = \{a_1, \ldots, a_i, \ldots, a_N; \prec\}$, where each action a_i involves one or more 3D manipulation operations to be executed by a dual-arm robot. We pose a number of assumptions described as follows:

1. flexible objects are modelled as articulated objects with a given number of links and joints, as it is customary for computational reasons [35]; we assume an inertial behaviour, i.e., rotating one link causes the movement of all upstream and downstream links, depending on the rotation joint;
2. the effects of gravity on all articulated object's 3D configurations are explicitly considered;
3. we do not assume any specific grasping or manipulation strategy to obtain a target 3D object configuration starting from another configuration;
4. the perception of articulated objects, although affected by noise, is considered *perfect*, i.e., data association is given.

We define an articulated object as a 2-ple $\alpha = \langle \mathcal{L}, \mathcal{J} \rangle$, where $\mathcal{L}$ is the ordered set of its L links, i.e.,

$$\mathcal{L} = \{l_1, \ldots, l_j, \ldots, l_L; \prec\}, \tag{1}$$

and $\mathcal{J}$ is the ordered set of its $J = L - 1$ joints, i.e.,

$$\mathcal{J} = \{j_1, \ldots, j_k, \ldots, j_J; \prec\}. \tag{2}$$

Each link l is characterised by three parameters, namely a length, and two orientations θ_l and γ_l, expressed with respect to a robot-centred reference frame (Fig. 1). We allow only for a limited number of discrete orientation values, i.e., θ_l and γ_l can take values from a pre-determined set of possible values. Given a link l_j, upstream links are those from l_1 to l_{j-1}, whereas downstream links range from l_{j+1} to l_L. Such absolute representation leads to the direct perception of links and their orientations. When a sequence of manipulation actions is

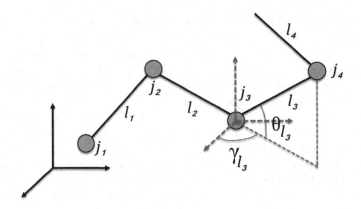

Fig. 1. A 3D articulated object configuration.

planned, changing one absolute orientation requires, in principle, the propagation of such change upstream or downstream the object via joint connections. Given an articulated object α, its configuration is a L-ple:

$$\mathcal{C}_\alpha = \{(\theta,\gamma)_1,\ldots,(\theta,\gamma)_l,\ldots,(\theta,\gamma)_L\}, \tag{3}$$

where it is intended that the orientations θ and γ are expressed with respect to an *absolute*, robot-centred, reference frame.

3   Formulation

In order to address the problem introduced above, we exploited PDDL+ to formulate three different domain models, corresponding to three different levels of abstraction of the impact of gravity on the articulated object.

PDDL+ [13] is an extension of the standard planning domain modelling language, PDDL, to model mixed discrete-continuous domains. In addition to instantaneous and durative actions, PDDL+ introduces *continuous processes* and *exogenous events*, that are triggered by changes in the environment. Processes are used to model continuous change, and therefore are well suited in this context to model the impact of gravity on articulated objects.

The absolute representation of angles we employ, on the one hand reduces the burden on the robotic framework, because the orientations of links is directly observable by the robot perception system and does not require any additional calculation. On the other hand, the complexity of the planning process is increased, due to the fact that any manipulation action has to be propagated to all the upstream or downstream link orientations. The interested reader is referred to [8] for an extensive comparison of different joint angles representation techniques in 2D setting.

In the proposed PDDL+ models, a `connected` predicate is used to describe the fact that two links are jointed. Joints are not explicitly modelled: the `connected` predicate indicates the presence of a joint between the two involved links, and the orientation is given via the `angle` function, which indicates the absolute orientation of the link l_i with regards to a plane j. The value of angles ranges between 0 and 359 degrees. The effect of the manipulation of two `connected` links are propagated via a corresponding `affects` predicate. In order to reduce the computational complexity, we fixed the way in which the robot can manipulate two connected links, so that propagation can only happen upstream. In other words, given two consecutive links, we allow the robot to move only the upstream link, while the other one is kept fixed. It should be noted that, if needed, the model can be easily extended to deal with both up and downstream manipulation by adding the appropriate predicates. The number of planes that can be represented is not fixed and can be easily modified: in our evaluation we considered 2 planes, vertical and horizontal, corresponding to a 3D space.

The planner can modify the orientation of links using the following constructs:

- An operator `start-increase(l1,l2,plane)` is used by the planner to manipulate the orientation of the link l_2 on the plane $plane$, by using a gripper for keeping l_1 still, and another gripper for moving l_2.
- A process `move-increase(l2, plane)` is used for modelling the continuous movement performed by the robot to increase the absolute angle related to l_2 on the corresponding $plane$. This process is activated by the above operator.
- An operator `stop-increase(l1,l2,plane)` is activated by the planner to stop the modification of the orientation of the l_1 and l_2 links. The robot is therefore releasing the two links.
- The events `back-to-zero(l, plane)` and `back-to-360(l, plane)` are triggered when the value of the angle of link l on $plane$ reaches, respectively, 360 or 0. In the former (latter) case, the value of the angle is reset to 0 (359).
- A process `propagate-increase(l1,l2,plane)` is activated when a process `move-increase(l2, plane)` is ongoing, and it allows to propagate the effects of the current manipulation on all the affected upstream angles.

In a nutshell, the planning engine can modify the angle between two connected links via the operator `start-increase(l1,l2,plane)`: this starts the movement process, that can be stopped by the engine using another dedicated operator. The movement process is also impacting a (potentially long) cascade of processes that models the propagation of the manipulation to affected upstream angles.

The above-listed constructs are in charge of performing and modelling manipulations aimed at increasing angles. A corresponding set of constructs is used to allow the planner to decrease some specified angles. Figure 2 shows the PDDL+ encoding of the `start-increase` operator and the `back-to-zero` event. Notably, the predicate `in-use` is exploited to avoid parallel manipulations of the articulated object by the robot. This is because the robot's grippers are not explicitly modelled, therefore many different actions could potentially be planned in parallel by the planning engine. The `freeToMove` predicates are used to indicate if a link is currently being manipulated or not; these predicates are a sort of token for grasping a specific link.

```
(:action start-increase
:parameters (?l1 -link ?l2 -link ?x -plane)
:precondition (and   (connected ?l1 ?l2)
     (not (in-use)))
:effect (and   (in-use)
     (not (freeToMove ?l2))
     (not (freeToMove ?l1))
     (increasing_angle-robot ?l2 ?x)))

(:process move-increase
:parameters (?l2 -link ?x -plane)
:precondition
     (increasing_angle-robot ?l2 ?x)
:effect
     (increase (angle ?l2 ?x)(* #t (speed-i))))

(:event back-to-zero
:parameters (?l3 -link ?x -plane)
:precondition
     (>= (angle ?l3 ?x) 360)
:effect
     (assign (angle ?l3 ?x) 0))
```

Fig. 2. Part of the proposed PDDL+ formulation.

3.1   Modelling Gravity

Gravity is one of the main reasons for encoding a model in PDDL+, as gravity effects are (i) continuous in nature, and (ii) not under the direct control of the planning engine. For these reasons, PDDL+ constructs such as continuous processes and events are extremely handy for describing the impact of gravity on the 3D manipulation of an articulated object.

The representation of the effects of gravity on an articulated object can be cumbersome, and may prevent the generation of valid plans in a reasonable amount of time. Because of that, we introduce three different levels of complexity that can be implemented in the proposed PDDL+ model. It is worth noting that the typical articulated object, in order to support the manipulation via a robot, has quite stiff joints, which are therefore resisting –up to some degrees– to the gravity effect.

No Gravity (NoG). The most trivial way to reduce the complexity burden due to the computation of the effects of gravity on the articulated object is, of course, to completely ignore gravity. In cases where the joints of the articulated objects are extremely stiff, this model can still give some useful information to the robot. Notably, the reduced complexity may allow to quickly re-plan in cases where the robot observes that gravity has significantly modified the configuration of the object.

Uniform Circular Motion (MCU). A more sophisticated way of modelling the impact of gravity on an articulated object can be obtained by taking a joint-by-joint perspective. As links are connected by joints, they can not fall to the ground, but are bounded to each other by the joints. The impact of gravity on a joint angle can be modelled as a uniform circular motion that moves the angle towards a value of 360 (if we consider a 180-degree angle to be on the z axis). In this encoding, the angular speed is constant. The impact of gravity on an angle is modelled using a pair of dedicated processes (according to the fact that the initial angle is lower or higher than 180) and, due to the fact that angles are absolute, such motion is also propagated to all the affected joints via a different PDDL+ process. The effects of gravity on a joint can be stopped for two reasons: (i) the angle has reached the rest position (360/0 degrees), or (ii) the corresponding link has been grabbed by the gripper of the robot.

Uniformly Accelerated Circular Motion (MCUA). Building on top of the MCU formalisation, we introduce a more advanced representation of the impact of gravity by modelling it as a uniformly accelerated circular motion. As before, all joints angle tend to return to a 360° position on the z axis. However, their initial angular speed is 0, but it is uniformly accelerated. The acceleration is encoded in PDDL+ by means of an additional process, that is in charge of increasing the angular speed while the gravity effect is active on a specific joint, and an appropriate event that "resets" the speed value when the effect of gravity ends.

As for the manipulation of angles performed by the robot, also in the MCU and MCUA formulations the effect of gravity on an angle are propagated to all the affected joints by a set of dedicated processes and events. An example of the process exploited in the MCU formulation for modelling gravity is provided in Fig. 3.

3.2   Alternative Formulations

The process presented in Fig. 3, as the dual `gravity-decrease` and those exploited in the MCUA formulation, has been modelled in the most human-readable way, due to the fact that robotics experts have to be involved in the modelling process. For this reason, the process keeps true a Boolean predicate, that is used to represent the fact that gravity is impacting the corresponding link. Semantically, this implies that every time step in which the process is active, the corresponding predicate is set to true. While this can be interpreted as an abuse of PDDL+ language features, it is supported by some state-of-the-art planning engines, and provides a good ground for describing and discussing the model with robotics experts.

```
(:process gravity-increase
:parameters (?ll - link)
:precondition (and   (freeToMove ?ll)
      (> (angle ?ll ZAXES) 180)
      (< (angle ?ll ZAXES) 360))
:effect (and
      (increase
          (angle ?ll ZAXES) (* #t (speed-g)))
      (increasing_angle-gravity ?ll)))
```

Fig. 3. The process used in the MCU formulation to model the effect of gravity on angles between 180 and 359°.

Furthermore, in a preliminary set of experiments, we observed that some aspects of the modelling of processes and events of the presented PDDL+ models were not accepted by some of the planning engines at the state of the art. With regards to events, an example of an unaccepted event is provided in Fig. 2. The back-to-zero event is used to reset an angle to 0° as soon as the value of 360° is reached. While it is easy to see that the effect of the event is making the precondition false, preventing the event to be re-applied immediately, some planning engines do not accept this formulation. Instead, they require that a Boolean precondition is falsified by the list of effects. We therefore modified the formulations with an additional predicate: it is initially set to true to allow events to be triggered. As soon as an event is triggered, its effects falsify the predicate, that is then reset to true by a subsequent reset event.

For the sake of completeness, and to exploit the opportunity to investigate how planning engines performance are affected by different models, we consider in our experimental analysis both formulations. We will refer to the "Original" formulation as the formulation that is not well-supported by planning engines but maximises human readability. The other formulation will be referred to as "Modified", and it aims at maximising the parsability by planning engines. Both versions of the models, and the corresponding problem instances can be found at https://github.com/Flaudia/AMAO.

4   Experimental Analysis

This section presents the PDDL+ benchmarks and the planners employed in our analysis, as well as the results of the experiments we conducted. The main aim of this analysis is to test whether our overall PDDL+ solution can solve tasks that model practical, real-world applications, i.e., in terms of robot workspace and the number of links and physical features characterising the articulated object.

For each set of formulations, we have generated planning instances by varying the following parameters: (i) number of links of the articulated object: 3, 4, 5, 6, 7, 8, 10, 12; (ii) in MCU: angular speed of 0.1, 0.5, and 1.0 grades per second; and (iii) in MCUA: acceleration of 0.1 and 0.5 grades per second.

In order to guarantee a fair assessment of the performance of planners according to the level of complexity used for encoding the impact of gravity, for each size of the articulated object 5 manipulation tasks were created by randomly generating initial and final configurations (while ensuring that a plan is possible). Those instances are then encoded in PDDL+ according to the complexity level and to the value of the corresponding MCU or MCUA parameter. Beside the size of the object, no additional parameters have to be set for the NoG formulation. Therefore, for each size of the object there are 5 tasks, encoded in 30 different problem models. The total number of problem models considered in our experimental analysis is 240.

As a reference robot we considered a Baxter dual-arm manipulator, which is widely used for research purposes and for performing manipulation tasks. This type of robot is directly supported by the presented PDDL+ formulation, and has been used –in simulation– to validate the generated plans. Moreover, it takes care also of the motion planning part. An example is shown in Fig. 4.

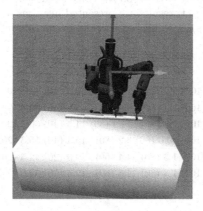

Fig. 4. A simulated Baxter robot manipulating a four link articulated object. The robot-centred reference frame is highlighted with different colours for the three reference axes.

In our analysis we have employed the following state-of-the-art PDDL+ solvers: UPMurphi [11] is possibly the most popular domain-independent PDDL+ planner, and is based on a model-checker adapted to deal with PDDL+; DiNo [27], which adds heuristics to the UPMurphi approach; and ENHSP [28,30], a numeric planner with heuristics extended to process PDDL+ problems. Those planners have been selected due to their widespread use in literature and in applications of PDDL+ planning.

Experiments have been run on a machine equipped with i7-6900K 3.20 Ghz CPU, 32 GB of RAM, running Ubuntu 16.04.3.LTS OS. 8 GB of memory were made available for each planner run, and a 5 CPU-time minutes cut-off time limit was enforced. All such planners do not utilize multiple cores.

Table 1. Results achieved by DiNo on the considered benchmarks. Sizes greater than 7 are omitted, as the planner did not solve any benchmark of these sizes. For each dimension of the articulated object, results are presented in terms of average runtime (percentage of solved instances). Average is calculated by considering solved instances only.

		Size – Number of links of the articulated object				
		3	4	5	6	7
NoG		0.5 (40)	88.1 (40)	8.9 (20)	22.0 (40)	– (0)
MCU	0.1	0.6 (40)	130.1 (40)	13.4 (20)	27.2 (40)	– (0)
	0.5	0.6 (40)	130.2 (40)	13.5 (20)	26.8 (40)	– (0)
	1.0	0.6 (40)	125.5 (40)	13.4 (20)	26.7 (40)	– (0)
MCUA	0.1	0.6 (40)	0.9 (20)	15.4 (20)	36.2 (40)	– (0)
	0.5	0.6 (40)	1.1 (20)	15.4 (20)	36.0 (40)	– (0)

Table 2. Results achieved by ENHSP on the considered benchmarks. For each dimension of the articulated object, results are presented in terms of average runtime (percentage of solved instances). Average is calculated by considering solved instances only.

		Size – Number of links of the articulated object							
		3	4	5	6	7	8	10	12
NoG		0.4 (100)	0.6 (100)	0.7 (80)	7.3 (80)	15.5 (40)	3.8 (20)	108.4 (60)	4.5 (20)
MCU	0.1	0.5 (100)	1.9 (100)	1.3 (80)	4.4 (60)	63.9 (40)	36.0 (20)	– (0)	198.5 (20)
	0.5	0.5 (100)	1.9 (100)	1.3 (80)	14.9 (80)	14.5 (40)	60.7 (20)	– (0)	– (0)
	1.0	0.5 (100)	1.7 (100)	40.0 (80)	3.2 (80)	15.4 (40)	55.3 (20)	– (0)	– (0)
MCUA	0.1	0.5 (100)	1.2 (100)	1.3 (80)	4.4 (60)	19.3 (20)	42.5 (20)	50.3 (20)	– (0)
	0.5	0.5 (100)	1.2 (100)	1.3 (80)	4.8 (60)	19.4 (20)	50.0 (20)	55.3 (20)	– (0)

To be as inclusive as possible in terms of planning engines, in the rest of this section we will discuss results obtained with the Modified version of the PDDL+ models.

Tables 1, 2 and 3 present the results of DiNo, ENHSP, and UPMurphi, respectively. All tables are organised as follows. The columns report the various number of links, while in the rows there are the different formulations, with their variants. For each introduced gravity encoding and number of links, it is reported the average runtime for solved instances, while in parenthesis it is reported the percentage of solved instances. In general, it is easy to derive from the results presented in the tables that, of course, the difficulty in solving the instances increases with the number of links. With regards to the level of complexity of the gravity, the NoG model –which completely ignores gravity– seems to be the easiest (relatively) to solve, followed by MCUA, while MCU seems to be the hardest. Intuitively, the fact that MCUA is easier than MCU can be due to the fact that in the MCUA model the effect of gravity slowly builds up, while in the MCU formulation the impact of gravity starts immediately at full speed.

Table 3. Results achieved by UPMurphi on the considered benchmarks. Sizes greater than 5 are omitted, as the planner did not solve any benchmark as well. For each dimension of the articulated object, results are presented in terms of average runtime (percentage of solved instances). Average is calculated by considering solved instances only.

		Size – Number of links		
		3	4	5
NoG		29.2 (40)	170.2 (20)	– (0)
MCU	0.1	33.1 (40)	180.3 (20)	– (0)
	0.5	32.5 (40)	178.9 (20)	– (0)
	1.0	32.1 (40)	175.6 (20)	– (0)
MCUA	0.1	2.4 (20)	– (0)	– (0)
	0.5	45.6 (40)	214.8 (20)	– (0)

Considering the MCU and MCUA formulations separately, the performance of the planning engines are not significantly affected by the employed parameters for MCUA, while for MCU the situation looks different: DiNo and UPMurphi do not look to be affected by the employed parameters, while the performance of ENHSP can significantly differ, also in the percentage of solved instances (see, e.g., analysis for 6 links). Our analysis suggests that this is due to the fact that DiNo and UPMurphi tend to solve only the easiest instances, for each considered size of the object, that requires short and quick to execute plans to be solved. In that, the impact of using the MCU or MCUA model is limited. Instead, as ENHSP can solve also some more complicated instances, taking into account gravity becomes pivotal. Moreover, we can see that ENHSP can solve instances up to 12 links, while DiNo and UPMurphi stops at 6 and 2, respectively. ENHSP is also the only solver able to solve all instances up to 4 links, and the majority of the instances up to 6 links.

About the plans returned by solvers, we noticed no significant difference in terms of both quality and structure for the three approaches. It may be the case that DiNo is able to take better into account the upstream propagation of the effects of the manipulation on angles. While ENHSP tends to provide plans where the robot operates directly on the links of the joint that needs to be modified for reaching the goal position, DiNo seems to prefer the robot to work on different links, and to exploit the use of propagation processes to reach the goal position. However, given the small number of instances solved by DiNo, it is hard to assess whether this behaviour emerged by chance, or it is due to the characteristics of the planning approach exploited by the engine.

Validation. The validation performed by simulating the execution of generated plans on a Baxter robot suggests that the MCU representation provides a reasonably accurate way to encode the gravity effect, as the generated plans can be executed in the simulation environment without further adjustments. An example can be found at https://github.com/Flaudia/AMAO.

4.1   Comparison of PDDL+ Models

Out of the considered planners, only ENHSP does support the Original formulation encodings, and provides valid plans. In this section we therefore exploit this planner to compare the impact of the two formulations on its performance.

Figure 5 shows how the performance of ENHSP are affected by the two sets of PDDL+ models, i.e., the Original and Modified models introduced in Sect. 3.

In Fig. 5, performance are compared in terms of Penalised Average Runtime 10 (PAR10). PAR10 is the average runtime where unsolved instances count as 10*cutoff time. PAR10 is a metric usually exploited in machine learning and algorithm configuration techniques, as it allows to consider coverage and runtime at the same time.

In our analysis, PAR10 is calculated considering all instances of the same size, in terms of number of links, regardless of the way in which gravity is modelled. In other words, each point of the graph corresponds to the PAR10 score obtained by the planner on the 30 planning instances generated for the considered size of the object. It can be noted that when considering objects with more than 5 links, the use of the Original formulation allows to improve the performance of ENHSP. According to the Wilcoxon signed rank test [34], performed by considering all the instances, the performance improvement obtained by using the Original models is substantial and statistically significant ($p < 0.05$). In terms of quality of the generated plans, there is still no significant difference between plans generated using the Original or the Modified models.

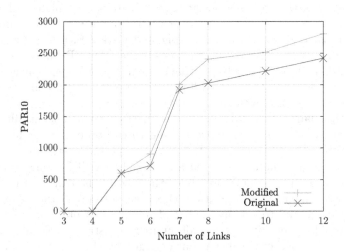

Fig. 5. Comparison of ENHSP performance, in terms of PAR10, when run on the Original formulation and on the Modified models.

While this may be due to the way in which the specific planner has been designed, and it is not easy to generalise, it is still interesting to note that the most human-friendly encoding is the one that allows to deliver the best performance.

5   Related Work, Conclusions and Future Work

Being able to model continuous quantities in the planning process has been subject to extensive research in Robotics, with particular reference to combined task-motion planning. In fact, combined task-motion planning may overcome those situations in which a high-level plan may not be executable in practice due to the nature of the robot workspace [6,22,32]. The approach in [6] integrates Metric-FF [21] and a sampling-based motion planner. Skolem symbols are used in [32] to incorporate workspace knowledge in predicates, which implies a symbolic-geometric mapping to be checked at run-time. Modelling the planning problem in the so-called *belief space* allows for the integration between a Markov decision process and logic-based planning [14], specifically by performing a search over finite sets of robot configurations. An interesting approach to consider is termed *Iteratively Deepened Task and Motion Planning* [10], which incorporates workspace-related information at the task planning level. Therein, task-motion interaction is done using the notion of *semantic attachment* [12], i.e., procedural functions activated during the planning process. It is noteworthy that in our case we do not consider robot motion at the continuous level in the planning process. Rather, we aim at modelling the effects of a continuous, exogenous process, i.e., gravity, on the configuration of the object the robot manipulates.

In this paper we presented two sets of PDDL+ models for the problem of robot manipulation of articulated object in a 3D workspace. Each model can then consider three levels of complexity for representing the impact of gravity. An experimental analysis, considering state-of-the-art PDDL+ planners and articulated objects of different sizes, have shown that with our PDDL+ formulations it is possible to solve tasks that model practical, real-world applications, i.e., in terms of robot workspace and the number of links and physical features characterising the articulated object. The simulation of generated plans on a Baxter dual-arm manipulator confirmed that the plans generated using the MCU formulation is a good compromise to successfully manipulate an object.

As a side effect of our work, we also designed a set of challenging PDDL+ models, that can be used to compare the performance of planning engines. We also believe they provide a good ground for testing and exploiting knowledge engineering techniques for evaluating the quality of different planning encodings [24]. As future work, we would like to inject some heuristic in the best performing planner (e.g., [17,18] from SAT) to possibly further improve performance, and to test our approach on different robots models, and to evaluate more PDDL+ planners, namely SMTPlan+ [9], DReal [5] and EZCSP [2]. Both SMTPlan+ and Dreal rely on an SMT module for solving problems described using PDDL+, while EZCSP exploits Constraint Answer Set Programming (CASP) [25], which extends ASP [15,16] to model continuous behaviors. SMTPlan+ has not been evaluated given that we were not able to compile it under the machines at our disposal, while EZCSP is not included because currently it does not directly support PDDL+, and the problem needs to be expressed in CASP. Finally, DReal does not seem to be capable of generating a plan for any of the models.

References

1. Agostini, A., Torras, C., Worgotter, F.: Integrating task planning and interactive learning for robots to work in human environments. In: Proceedings of the 22nd International Joint Conference on Artificial Intelligence (IJCAI 2011), pp. 2386–2391. IJCAI/AAAI (2011)
2. Balduccini, M., Magazzeni, D., Maratea, M., Leblanc, E.: CASP solutions for planning in hybrid domains. Theory Practice Logic Program. **17**(4), 591–633 (2017)
3. Bertolucci, R., et al.: An ASP-based framework for the manipulation of articulated objects using dual-arm robots. In: Balduccini, M., Lierler, Y., Woltran, S. (eds.) LPNMR 2019. LNCS, vol. 11481, pp. 32–44. Springer, Heidelberg (2019). https://doi.org/10.1007/978-3-030-20528-7_3
4. Bodenhagen, L., et al.: An adaptable robot vision system performing manipulation actions with flexible objects. IEEE Trans. Autom. Sci. Eng. **11**(3), 749–765 (2014)
5. Bryce, D., Gao, S., Musliner, D.J., Goldman, R.P.: SMT-based nonlinear PDDL+ planning. In: Proceedings of the 29th AAAI Conference on Artificial Intelligence (AAAI 2015), pp. 3247–3253. AAAI Press (2015)
6. Cambon, S., Alami, R., Gravot, F.: A hybrid approach to intricate motion, manipulation and task planning. Int. J. Robot. Res. **28**(1), 104–126 (2009)
7. Capitanelli, A., Maratea, M., Mastrogiovanni, F., Vallati, M.: Automated planning techniques for robot manipulation tasks involving articulated objects. In: Esposito, F., Basili, R., Ferilli, S., Lisi, F. (eds.) AI*IA 2017. LNCS, vol. 10640, pp. 483–497. Springer, Heidelberg (2017). https://doi.org/10.1007/978-3-319-70169-1_36
8. Capitanelli, A., Maratea, M., Mastrogiovanni, F., Vallati, M.: On the manipulation of articulated objects in human-robot cooperation scenarios. Robot. Auton. Syst. **109**, 139–155 (2018)
9. Cashmore, M., Fox, M., Long, D., Magazzeni, D.: A compilation of the full PDDL+ language into SMT. In: Proceedings of the 26th International Conference on Automated Planning and Scheduling (ICAPS 2016), pp. 79–87. AAAI Press (2016)
10. Dantam, N., Kingstone, Z., Chaudhuri, S., Kavraki, L.: An incremental constraint-based framework for task and motion planning. Int. J. Robot. Res. **37**(10), 1134–1151 (2018)
11. Della Penna, G., Magazzeni, D., Mercorio, F., Intrigila, B.: Upmurphi: a tool for universal planning on PDDL+ problems. In: Proceedings of the 19th International Conference on Automated Planning and Scheduling (ICAPS 2009). AAAI (2009)
12. Dornhege, C., Eyerich, P., Keller, T., Trug, S., Brenner, M., Nebel, B.: Semantic attachments for domain-independent planning systems. In: Proceedings of the 19th International Conference on Automated Planning and Scheduling (ICAPS 2009). AAAI (2009)
13. Fox, M., Long, D.: Modelling mixed discrete-continuous domains for planning. J. Artif. Intell. Res. **27**, 235–297 (2006)
14. Garrett, C., Perez, T., Kaelbling, L.: FF-Rob: leveraging symbolic planning for efficient task and motion planning. Int. J. Robot. Res. **37**(1), 104–136 (2018)

15. Gebser, M., Leone, N., Maratea, M., Perri, S., Ricca, F., Schaub, T.: Evaluation techniques and systems for answer set programming: a survey. In: Proceedings of the 27th International Joint Conference on Artificial Intelligence (IJCAI 2018), pp. 5450–5456. ijcai.org (2018)
16. Gebser, M., Maratea, M., Ricca, F.: The design of the seventh answer set programming competition. In: Balduccini, M., Janhunen, T. (eds.) LPNMR 2017. LNCS (LNAI), vol. 10377, pp. 3–9. Springer, Cham (2017). https://doi.org/10.1007/978-3-319-61660-5_1
17. Giunchiglia, E., Maratea, M., Tacchella, A.: Dependent and independent variables in propositional satisfiability. In: Flesca, S., Greco, S., Ianni, G., Leone, N. (eds.) JELIA 2002. LNCS (LNAI), vol. 2424, pp. 296–307. Springer, Heidelberg (2002). https://doi.org/10.1007/3-540-45757-7_25
18. Giunchiglia, E., Maratea, M., Tacchella, A.: (In)effectiveness of look-ahead techniques in a modern SAT solver. In: Rossi, F. (ed.) CP 2003. LNCS, vol. 2833, pp. 842–846. Springer, Heidelberg (2003). https://doi.org/10.1007/978-3-540-45193-8_64
19. Henrich, D., Worn, H.: Robot Manipulation of Deformable Objects. Advanced Manufacturing. Springer, Heidelberg (2000). https://doi.org/10.1007/978-1-4471-0749-1
20. Heyer, C.: Human-robot interaction and future industrial robotics applications. In: Proceedings of IEEE International Conference on Intelligent Robots and Systems (IROS 2010), pp. 4749–4754. IEEE (2010)
21. Hoffmann, J.: The metric-FF planning system: translating íngnoring delete listsťo numeric state variables. J. Artif. Intell. Res. **20**, 291–341 (2003)
22. Kaelbling, L., Perez, T.: Integrated task and motion planning in the belief space. Int. J. Robot. Res. **32**(9–10), 1194–1227 (2013)
23. Krüger, J., Lien, T., Verl, A.: Cooperation of humans and machines in the assembly lines. CIRP Ann. - Manuf. Technol. **58**(2), 628–646 (2009)
24. McCluskey, T.L., Vaquero, T.S., Vallati, M.: Engineering knowledge for automated planning: towards a notion of quality. In: Proceedings of the Knowledge Capture Conference (K-CAP 2017), pp. 14:1–14:8 (2017)
25. Mellarkod, V.S., Gelfond, M., Zhang, Y.: Integrating answer set programming and constraint logic programming. Ann. Math. Artif. Intell. **53**(1–4), 251–287 (2008)
26. Nair, A., et al.: Combining self-supervised learning and imitation for vision-based rope manipulation. In: Proceedings of the 2017 IEEE International Conference on Robotics and Automation (ICRA 2017), pp. 2146–2153. IEEE (2017)
27. Piotrowski, W.M., Fox, M., Long, D., Magazzeni, D., Mercorio, F.: Heuristic planning for PDDL+ domains. In: Proceedings of the 25th International Joint Conference on Artificial Intelligence (IJCAI 2016), pp. 3213–3219. IJCAI/AAAI Press (2016)
28. Ramírez, M., et al.: Integrated hybrid planning and programmed control for real time UAV maneuvering. In: Proceedings of the 17th International Conference on Autonomous Agents and MultiAgent Systems (AAMAS 2018), pp. 1318–1326. International Foundation for Autonomous Agents and Multiagent Systems, Richland, SC, USA/ACM (2018)
29. Saadat, M., Nan, P.: Industrial applications of automatic manipulation of flexible materials. Ind. Robot: Int. J. **29**(5), 434–442 (2002)
30. Scala, E., Haslum, P., Thiébaux, S., Ramírez, M.: Interval-based relaxation for general numeric planning. In: Proceedings of the 22nd European Conference on Artificial Intelligence (ECAI 2016). Frontiers in Artificial Intelligence and Applications, vol. 285, pp. 655–663. IOS Press (2016)

31. Schulman, J., Ho, J., Lee, C., Abbeel, P.: Learning from demonstrations through the use of non-rigid registration. In: Inaba, M., Corke, P. (eds.) Robotics Research. STAR, vol. 114. Springer, Cham. https://doi.org/10.1007/978-3-319-28872-7_20
32. Srivastava, S., Fang, E., Riano, L., Chitnis, R., Russell, S., Abbeel, P.: Combined task and motion planning through an extensible planner-independent interface layer. In: Proceedings of the 2014 IEEE International Conference on Robotics and Automation (ICRA 2014), pp. 639–646. IEEE (2014)
33. Wakamatsu, H., Arai, E., Hirai, S.: Knotting and unknotting manipulation of deformable linear objects. Int. J. Robot. Res. 25(4), 371–395 (2006)
34. Wilcoxon, F.: Individual comparisons by ranking methods. Biometrics Bull. 1(6), 80–83 (1945)
35. Yamakawa, Y., Namiki, A., Ishikawa, M.: Dynamic high-speed knotting of a rope by a manipulator. Int. J. Adv. Robot. Syst. 10, 1–12 (2013)

Frequency Assignment in High Performance Computing Systems

Andrea Borghesi[1]([✉]), Michela Milano[1], and Luca Benini[1,2]

[1] DISI/DEI, University of Bologna, Bologna, Italy
{andrea.borghesi3,michela.milano,luca.benini}@unibo.it
[2] Integrated System Laboratory, ETHZ, Zürich, Switzerland

Abstract. Power consumption is an increasingly limiting factor in modern ICT infrastructure, especially in the context of High Performance Computing. Common strategies to curb energy consumption are power capping, i.e. constraining the system power consumption within certain power budget, and Dynamic Voltage/Frequency Scaling, i.e. reducing the computing elements operating clock to decrease power usage. In this paper we tackle the frequency assignment problem in the context of a power capped system. We propose three approaches to solve the problem, a greedy algorithm, a CP model and MIP model. As a case study, we consider the Eurora supercomputer, hosted at CINECA computing center in Bologna. The experimental results show that the MIP approach outperforms the other methods when the problem is loosely constrained. With tighter bounds, the CP method can always find a solution, whereas the MIP fails to provide a solution for half of the considered instances.

1 Introduction

Supercomputers peak performance[1] is expected to reach the ExaFlops (10^{18}) scale in 2023 [21], as revealed by the rise of the worldwide supercomputer installation [10]. A key factor limiting further growth is the power consumption. According to [1] an acceptable range for an Exascale supercomputer is 20 MW. Reaching the Exascale with current technologies would lead to unacceptable power consumption, in the order of hundreds of MWatts, hence new solutions for power awareness are needed.

A commonly used technique to reduce the power consumption of the processing units (especially CPUs) is Dynamic Voltage and Frequency Scaling (DVFS) [13,20], a method that trades processor performance for lower power consumption. With DVFS a processor can run at one of the supported frequency/voltage pairs lower than the maximum rated one. Lower frequency and voltage lead to significantly lower power consumption allowing more jobs to run simultaneously. One of the key practical problems limiting the adoption of DVFS is the trade-off between reduced power consumption and increase of execution time, which create accounting problems and user dissatisfaction [6]. Consequently, many works try

---

[1] Measured as FLOPS (floating point operations per second).

© Springer Nature Switzerland AG 2019
M. Alviano et al. (Eds.): AI*IA 2019, LNAI 11946, pp. 151–164, 2019.
https://doi.org/10.1007/978-3-030-35166-3_11

to exploit frequency reduction without impacting, as far as possible, the applications duration [8,25]. Another widespread approach to limit the amount of power consumed by HPC systems is *power capping* [14,22], i.e. forcing a system not to consume more than a certain amount of power at any given time. Power capping approaches are gaining popularity due the relatively simple implementation. Currently, power capping features are typically implemented via hardware solutions, that is the runtime power consumption is reduced through limiting the computing node performance (DVFS) [24].

An alternative approach for power capping is to act on the jobs execution order, as shown by numerous works in recent years [3,4,11,12,16], and even better results can be obtained by combining both methods [5]. In many cases the system power cap value can vary during the course of time, e.g. the power budget can decrease during hot days when the cooling system is running at full regime. When the power available is reduced the power constraint can be violated. If the current workload power consumption does not exceed the reduced power cap we can simply respect the new constraint by postponing the execution of new applications. Conversely, if the current power consumption is larger than the new power budget we may be required to take more drastic actions. In this paper we study the possibility to employ DVFS and act on the frequencies of the jobs currently running in the system, in order to slow them down and reduce the overall power consumption. We propose three different methods to deal with the frequency reassignment problem on a real supercomputer: (1) a greedy algorithm, (2) a CP model with a dedicated search strategy and (3) a MIP model.

Section 2 describes the target HPC system and Sect. 3 formally defines the tackled problem. The greedy method, the CP approach and the MIP model are respectively introduced in Sects. 4, 5 and 6. Section 7 shows the results of our experiments; final remarks can be found in Sect. 8.

2   System Description

The Eurora supercomputer [2] has a heterogeneous architecture composed by 64 nodes, each one with 2 CPUs (8 cores each) and 2 HW accelerators, plus 16 GB of RAM. The tool currently used to manage the workload on Eurora system is PBS [26] (Portable Batch System). Jobs are submitted by the users into one of multiple queues, each one characterized by different access requirements and by a different estimated waiting time. Each queue has a priority and there is a special one, the *reservation* queue, that contains jobs with highest priority and preferred treatment. In this work we do not consider the jobs dispatching problem, but rather we tackle the issue of how to optimally reassign the frequencies of a set of jobs running on the supercomputer and consuming a certain amount of power, if the overall power budget changes. In the rest of the paper we assume that schedule and allocation have already been decided.

2.1 Frequency Variability Impact

DVFS implies changing the frequency while tasks run on a supercomputer, thus modifying its power consumption and duration (e.g. lower frequency leads to longer duration and smaller consumed power). The entity of this change depends on technological characteristics; Fraternali et al. [15] quantified this effect on the Eurora supercomputer – their results guided our frequency assignment strategy.

There are two main factors determining the impact of changing a job frequency: (1) the application type and (2) the execution node. The cited paper studies three kind of jobs: a real HPC application (Quantum EXPRESSO [17]), a synthetic CPU-bound benchmark (i.e. a task which particularly stresses the CPU) and a synthetic MEM-bound benchmark (i.e. memory intensive application). In our work we follow this distinction. Clearly, slowing down a CPU-intensive application would cause a larger increase in duration w.r.t. to the same slow down for a memory-bound job. The second factor is the node on which the application is running: the frequency variations have different impact depending on the node type. In Eurora we have *high frequency* nodes, with frequency ranging from 1.2 GHz up to 3.4 GHz, and *low frequency* nodes, with frequency from 1.2 GHz up to 2.1 GHz. The current system always runs the applications at the maximum speed allowed by the execution nodes.

3 Problem Definition

We assume a set of jobs is running in the system consuming a total power P_{sys}; that power budget is then reduced (e.g $P'_{sys} = 0.7 * P_{sys}$). The goal is to assign a frequency to each job to respect the new power constraint. The main objective is not to disrupt the performance in term of Quality-of-Service (QoS) for the users while at the same time saving energy; both these goals can be reached by minimizing the job durations increase due to the jobs slow down. Each job i is already running, with a start time st_i and an expected end time et_i, with $et_i = st_i + d_i$ where d_i is the expected duration at the current running frequency[2]. If we define the current time as ct, $d_i^{el} = ct - st_i$ represents the elapsed duration of a job so far. Each job belongs to a specific queue (depending on the user choice and on the job characteristics). By analyzing existing execution traces coming from PBS, we have determined an estimated waiting time for each queue, which applies to each job it contains: we refer to this value as ewt_i.

We assume that each job is running at frequency f_i; the default dispatcher always assigns the maximum frequency possible when scheduling, but the dispatcher can deal with different frequencies as input. Every job is also characterized by the type of the node it is running on nt_i and the application type at_i. The node type could assume two different values: 0, corresponding to a low frequency node, and 1, corresponding to a high frequency node. The application type can assume three values: 0 for average applications, 1 for CPU-bound

---

[2] This duration is the maximum allowed execution time declared by the user at submission time.

applications and 2 for memory-bound applications. As seen in Sect. 2.1 both node type and application type have a strong impact on the variation of power and duration given a frequency change. Each job has a related power consumption p_i, which is the power consumed by the job running at the frequency decided by the dispatcher.

3.1 Model Extensions

The original problem is not particularly constrained but this is an artifact due to the relative simple HPC system used as case study. Hence, we considered a set of extensions, i.e. additional constraints that are typical requirements in supercomputers. We first added job deadlines, i.e. each job i has a deadline dl_i and it must finish within that deadline (thus constraining the allowed duration increase). This will be referred as *Extension D*. Then, we implemented a second extension (*Extension R*), namely we set dependencies among jobs (in particular end-to-end relationships). Each job i may have a set of "related" jobs Rel_i whose end needs to come after job i ends[3]. Finally, we considered the case with both the deadlines and the job relations constraints, *Extension D-R*.

4   Greedy Algorithm

The first proposed approach is a greedy algorithm: we decrease the frequency of few jobs as much as possible until reaching the desired power saving. The main advantage of this simple algorithm is its efficiency: even on the larger instances (up to 2000 jobs) the time required to produce a solution is negligible. Our purpose is to implement our techniques on real systems with tight real-time requirement, hence we disregard optimal solutions but rather look for the best ones given a time limit.

The pseudo-code for the greedy algorithm is presented in Algorithm 1. The set of running jobs is called *running_jobs*, *current_power* is the sum of the jobs powers, *desired_power* is an input of the algorithm and defines the new power budget; lines 1–3 initialize the algorithm. Line 4 sorts the jobs according to a combination of different factors: (I) the job power consumption (we try to slow down big applications first in order to slow fewer jobs); (II) the remaining duration of the job compared to the overall duration (not to slow down jobs closer to completion); (III) the job priority, computed w.r.t. the expected waiting time (activities in queue with higher priorities should wait shorter times). The actual equation computing the weight w_i of a job i is $w_i = p_i * (\alpha w_i^D + (1 - \alpha)w_i^Q)$, where p_i is the power consumption, $w_i^D = d_i/d_i^{el}$ is the ratio between total and elapsed duration and $w_i^Q = ewt_i/\max_{i \in J}(ewt_i)$ is the queue priority factor. α modulates the factors impact (in our experiments $\alpha = 0.6$).

Once jobs are sorted, the first one is selected and its frequency is set at the minimum value (lines 8–9) – modified power and duration are computed

---

[3] We suppose that all jobs have already started, hence start-to-end relationships must already hold.

accordingly (lines 10–11). These functions are based on the value derived from [15] and depend on the job features. Line 12 notifies changes (modified power consumption and new end time et'_i); finally, the power consumption decrease is computed and the job is removed from the sorted list (lines 13–14), since it cannot be slowed down anymore. Jobs are selected for power reduction until reaching the desired goal (line 5); if the goal is unattainable (after slowing down all jobs) the algorithm fails (lines 6–7)[4].

Algorithm 1. Greedy Algorithm

---

1 $J \leftarrow running\_jobs$
2 $power\_goal \leftarrow current\_power - desired\_power$
3 $power\_saved \leftarrow 0$
4 $Sort(J)$
5 **while** $power\_saved < power\_goal$ **do**
6   **if** $J = \emptyset$ **then**
7   **return** 0
8      $j \leftarrow J[0]$
9      $new\_freq \leftarrow GetMinFreq(j)$
10      $power\_gain \leftarrow FindPowerGain(j, new\_freq)$
11      $new\_duration \leftarrow FindNewDur(j, new\_freq)$
12      $Update(running\_jobs, j, new\_freq)$
13      $J \leftarrow J - \{j\}$
14      $power\_saved \leftarrow power\_saved + power\_gain$
15 **return** 1

Modifying the greedy algorithm to cope with the problem extensions proved to be ineffective (e.g. setting the job frequency to the minimum only if this action does not violate the deadline), since the extended algorithm was not able to solve the majority of instances. This happens because with additional constraints a solution can be found only "spreading" the slow down among several jobs, contrary to the greedy algorithm behaviour (maximum slowing down of as few job as possible).

5   The CP Model

The greedy algorithm is very fast but it lacks reasoning power, thus we propose a CP model to optimally reassign the job frequencies. There is a decision (integer) variable for each job F_i $\forall i \in J$; the variables represent the frequency assigned to each job. The frequency domains depend on the execution node: for low power nodes the allowed values are [1.2, 1.3, 1.4, .., 2.1] GHz and for high power nodes the range is [1.2, 1.4, 1.6, .., 2.8, 3.1, 3.4] GHz. Consequently, the domain of F_i

---

[4] In the current system running applications cannot be interrupted/restarted.

could either be [0, ..,9] if the job runs on a 2.1 GHz node or [0, .., 10] otherwise. The duration of job i can be seen as $d_i = d_i^{el} + d_i^R$, the duration elapsed so far plus the remaining duration.

The relationship between the different frequencies and the changes in power (duration) is encoded in a set of vectors. Given a job i we can identify the correct vector for the durations DM and the powers PM, depending on the job application type ai_i and node type nt_i. Each vector contains as many elements as the possible frequencies; each element specifies the duration/power change w.r.t. a base frequency (the maximum one) – e.g. if a job has a duration of d_i at maximum frequency, the duration at frequency F_i' becomes $d_i' = DM[F_i'] * d_i$. The method for obtaining the new power is analogous. To encode these relations we introduce two auxiliary variables for each job, P_i^{Mul} for power and D_i^{Mul} for duration. These variables are related to the frequency by the equations $D_i^{Mul} = DM[F_i]$ and $P_i^{Mul} = PM[F_i]$. These relations are expressed in the CP model via *element* constraints [19]:

$$element(F_i, DM, D_i^{Mul}) \quad \forall i \in J \tag{1}$$

$$element(F_i, PM, P_i^{Mul}) \quad \forall i \in J \tag{2}$$

We use two additional auxiliary variables to represent the new power NP_i and duration ND_i for each job:

$$NP_i = P_i^{Mul} * p_i \qquad\qquad \forall i \in J \tag{3}$$

$$ND_i = D_i^{Mul} * d_i^R + d_i^{el} \qquad\qquad \forall i \in J \tag{4}$$

The duration increase DI_i of a job can be expressed as:

$$DI_i = (ND_i - d_i) = (D_i^{Mul} - 1)d_i^R \quad \forall i \in J \tag{5}$$

Now we need to impose the constraint on the new powers, i.e. their sum must not be greater than the new power cap p_{cap}:

$$\sum_{\forall i \in J} NP_i \leq p_{cap} \tag{6}$$

We also want to set special constraints for the duration increase of jobs in the reservation queue (JR), namely we want the maximum and the average duration increase of those jobs to be less or equal of, respectively, di_{res}^{max} and di_{res}^{avg}:

$$\frac{1}{|JR|} \sum_{\forall i \in JR} DI_i \leq di_{res}^{avg} \tag{7}$$

$$max_{\forall i \in JR} DI_i \leq di_{res}^{max} \tag{8}$$

The frequency reassignment problem has a dual goal: on one hand we want to reduce the energy consumed by the HPC system, on the other hand we want to maintain a good performance for the end users – i.e. we want to keep the duration increases as low as possible. After a preliminary evaluation phase where we experimented with different objective functions, we opted to minimize the duration increase since this always guarantees an improvement in terms of consumed energy and users' satisfaction. This objective is expressed with this equation: $\min \sum_{\forall i \in J} DI_i$.

5.1   Search Strategy

As a reminder, we do not look for optimal solutions hence we do not use a complete strategy; all the proposed search strategies are implemented with a realistic time limit of 5 s. The first search strategy we used is a basic version of the common strategy used for integer variables in CP. The variable selection proceeds among unbound variables and chooses the one with the smallest domain. Ties are broken by selecting the variable with lower min value. For the value selection, we first try to assign the maximum allowed value for the selected variable. In the rest of the paper we will call this strategy *CP Standard*.

Heuristic-Based Search. The CP standard search can produce good results but it requires a much longer time than the greedy algorithm - during the 5 s time limit the greedy algorithm was often able to produce better solutions, especially on instances of non-trivial size. We then devised a new search strategy able to produce solutions at least as good as the greedy ones and in a much shorter time than the standard strategy. The new search strategy combines both the benefit of the greedy algorithm and the capacity of exploring a larger search space typical of CP search strategies. Namely, our strategy starts from the solution generated by the greedy algorithm – hence we can quickly obtain a first, feasible solution – then performs backtracking and tries to improve the current solution.

The backtracking is performed in typical CP fashion: at each decision point a variable is selected and a new value is assigned. The variable selection procedure exploits the heuristic too: the variables are ordered with the same method used for the greedy algorithm and then the first variable in the ranking is chosen. The idea is to consider first the variables that will have a greater impact on the objective function. Once a variable is selected we set its value to the maximum allowed. We will refer to this strategy as *CP + Heuristic*.

Large Neighborhood Search. We also implemented a Large Neighborhood Search strategy [7]. Similarly to local search, with LNS we modify an existing solution to the problem. However, instead of making small changes to a solution, a subset of variables (called *fragment*) from the problem is selected and relaxed. A search is then performed on these relaxed variables. To perform this complete search we used the heuristic-based search described in the previous section.

The three main aspects which impact the LNS efficacy are the fragment selection procedure, the fragment size and the search limit. After a preliminary evaluation, the best selection criterion was combining complete random selection and weighted selection[5]. We decide the fragment size and the search limit (expressed as failures and branches limit) through a reinforced learning method which changes these parameters based on the quality of the solutions found by previous LNS iterations; this strategy was inspired by a previous work [23].

5.2 Extensions

The extensions described in Sect. 3.1 are modeled by the following equations (deadlines and the relations):

$$ET_i \leq dl_i \qquad\qquad\qquad \forall i \in J \qquad (9)$$
$$ET_i \leq ET_j \qquad \forall j \in Rel_i \qquad\qquad \forall i \in J \qquad (10)$$

where $ET_i = st_i + d_i^{el} + D_i^M d_i^R$ is the variable which represents a job end time and Rel_i is the set of jobs related to i.

The search strategy still belongs to the LNS framework but with a different way to find the solution of the relaxed fragment. If job relations are involved as well (Extensions R and D-R) the CP standard search strategy is used. Conversely, with deadlines a modified version of the heuristic described in Sect. 5.1 is used. The first solution is obtained with a variant of the greedy algorithm: instead of indiscriminately setting the frequencies to their minimum levels, the modified version does that only if it will not force the slowed job to go beyond its deadline. Note that this first solution may be infeasible, i.e. could violate the power constraint. After the first solution is found the second phase is performed as before.

6   The MIP Model

We describe now a third approach to solve the frequency assignment problem, namely a Mixed Integer Program (MIP) model. This kind of method is generally well suited to deal with assignment problems. In the MIP model we have a set of binary variables X where X_{if} assumes value 1 if job i has frequency f, 0 otherwise; index i has the whole set of jobs J as a range and f can vary in the job frequency range F, defined as before based on node type. Each job has exactly one frequency (Eq. 12). For each job i we have a set of power and duration multipliers, one for each allowed frequency, respectively d_{if}^{Mul} and p_{if}^{Mul}. These multipliers combined with the current job power p_i and the binary variable express the power constraint (Eq. 13). Equations 14 and 15 specify the constraints on the jobs duration increase, respectively, on the maximum increase ($\leq di_{res}^{max}$) and on the average increase ($\leq di_{res}^{avg}$). Variable r_i indicates if job i belongs to the reservation queue (1 means reservation, 0 otherwise). $(d_{if}^{Mul} - 1)d_i^R X_{if}$ represents the duration increase of job i. Finally, Eq. 12 sets the objective, i.e. minimization of the duration increase.

---

[5] A variable i is relaxed with probability $P = \psi \frac{w_i}{\sum_{\forall i \in J} w_i} + (1 - \psi)\frac{1}{|J|}$ where w_i is the weight and $\psi \in [0, 1]$ is a real number.

$$\min \sum_{i \in J} \sum_{f \in F} (d_{if}^{Mul} - 1) d_i^R X_{if} \tag{11}$$

$$\sum_{f \in F} X_{if} = 1 \qquad \forall i \in J \tag{12}$$

$$\sum_{i \in J} \sum_{f \in F} p_{if}^{Mul} p_i X_{if} \leq p_{cap} \tag{13}$$

$$\sum_{i \in J} \sum_{f \in F} r_i (d_{if}^{Mul} - 1) d_i^R X_{if} \leq di_{res}^{avg} \sum_{i \in J} r_i \tag{14}$$

$$\sum_{f \in F} r_i (d_{if}^{Mul} - 1) d_i^R X_{if} \leq di_{res}^{max} \qquad \forall i \in J \tag{15}$$

The constraints for the extensions are the same of the CP model, namely Eqs. 9 and 10. The end time is expressed as $ET_i = st_i + d_i^{el} + \sum_{f \in F} d_{if}^{Mul} d_i^R X_{if}$.

7 Results

The experiments were carried out on a computer with a 2.4 Ghz CPU (4 i7 cores) and 16 GB of RAM. The proposed methods were implemented using *or-tools* [18], Google's software suite for combinatorial optimization. The MIP solver used on top of or-tools is the open-source *Cbc* (Coin-or branch and cut) MILP solver [9]. We evaluated all the approaches on instances which represent realistic workloads, derived from traces collected on Eurora in a timespan of several months. We have instances of several sizes, from smaller ones composed of 50 jobs up to the bigger ones with 2000 jobs. As told before, we have strict time constraints to produce a solution due to the real-time nature of our application. Therefore we set a time limit of 5 s to the solvers in all the experiments. The time limit is not a problem for the greedy algorithm on any of our instances; the time required by this method is always around a few hundreds of milliseconds.

7.1 Models Evaluation

In this section we compare the performance of the different approaches when dealing with the base version of the problem (without extension). In particular we show the results obtained by: (1) the greedy algorithm, (2) the CP model using standard search, (3) the CP model using heuristic-based search, (4) the CP model using LNS and (5) the MIP model. For the LNS we used the technique with the best performance, namely the combination of weighted and random fragment selection (fragment size with reinforced learning) and the heuristic-based search to solve the relaxed fragments. For every model we run experiments on 30 instances. For each instance we first compute the initial power (the power consumed by all jobs in the instance) then we try to reduce the power available and assign new frequencies; as power cap levels we tested decreasing percentages of the initial power (the power levels are identified by the markers in the following graphs).

To briefly summarize our experiments, when the MIP solver manages to find a solution within the time limit it also proves that the solution is optimal, so the remaining models can at best try to get as close as possible. In particular, in the case of the base problem the MIP approach can solve all the instances to optimality and clearly outperforms the other models, especially on larger instances. If we start to consider the problem extensions the MIP solver struggles more to find a solution for larger instances (obviously always within the time limit) w.r.t. to the CP solvers. Nevertheless, when it does find a one, the solution is optimal (or very close to the optimal one) and still outperforms the remaining models on the corresponding instance.

In the following graphs we report the duration increases and the energy differences; these values are the normalized averages for all instances. Figure 1 presents two graphs. On the left we can see the average duration increase (as a percentage) obtained when decreasing the power budget available (from the right, maximum power, to the left). The right graph depicts instead the energy difference (in percentage) w.r.t. to the maximal power budget. Although the objective function considers only the job durations, we report also the energy differences to prove that we obtain significant energy savings, even without explicitly focusing on it. For lack of space, we show this only in the 100 jobs case but the results are analogous with larger instances.

All the results we obtained clearly reveal that when we reduce the power budget the average duration of the jobs increases, as a large fraction of jobs need to be slowed down. As we can see in Fig. 1a when we consider small instances (from 50 to 200 jobs) the MIP solver and CP plus LNS both provide optimal solutions - their lines completely overlap. It is very easy to observe that already with smaller instances there is a great gap between CP plus LNS and CP methods without LNS: in particular CP with the standard search provides the worst results, even worse than the greedy algorithm - except when the power becomes very tight (50%–55%). CP with the heuristic search is able to find solutions equal or better than the greedy algorithm ones - as we expected since it starts from the greedy solution and then improves it. In Fig. 1b we can see that while both CP plus LNS and MIP find solutions very close to the optimal, these solutions are not the same: their related energy savings slightly differ.

When the instances become larger (400 to 800 jobs) we start to see the gap which separates the solutions found by the MIP solver from those provided by the CP methods: Fig. 2a reveals that even CP plus LNS is not able to find the optimal solution provided by MIP. However, the gap is minimal (at least for the 600 jobs case) and LNS still performs much better than the remaining methods. The situation worsens for CP and greedy approaches when the instances grow larger (more than 1000 jobs): in Fig. 2b we can see how the MIP now definitely outperforms all other methods, CP and LNS included. We can also see that with larger instances it is very difficult for the heuristic-based search to improve the first solution obtained by the greedy method. LNS manages to explore the search space more effectively but not enough to reach an optimal solution. With even bigger instances the optimality gap grows even further. The main reason is

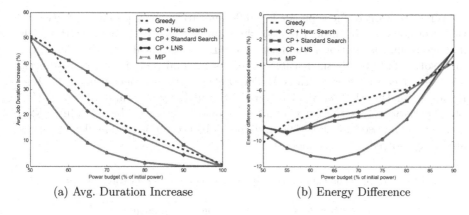

(a) Avg. Duration Increase   (b) Energy Difference

Fig. 1. Base problem - 100 jobs (duration increase and energy difference)

the fact that the base problem is rather loosely constrained and, as it is known from the literature, MIP techniques are very effective when dealing with pure assignment problems.

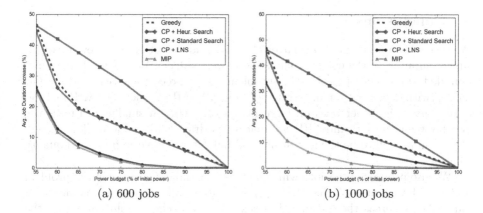

(a) 600 jobs   (b) 1000 jobs

Fig. 2. Base problem - 600 and 1000 jobs (duration increase)

Problem Extensions. The problem extensions we considered have the implication of raising the difficulty of the problem. As mentioned before we did not consider a greedy algorithm to deal with the extensions. Our experiments with the extended model reveal a behaviour comparable to the base problem: the MIP approach is again the one able to find the best solutions, CP plus LNS approaches the quality of MIP with smaller instances and the gap gradually increases with larger instances. The remaining CP methods perform far worse then the previous models. The plots for all the extended models are extremely similar to those previously seen, hence we are not going to show them.

What we want to focus on is a key difference to the base problem, at least for the extensions which consider relationships among jobs. While all the CP models manage to find a solution for almost all the instances within the time limit, the MIP solver fails to obtain feasible solutions for many of the larger instances. This aspect can be seen in Table 1. The table reports the percentages of solved instances for the MIP solver, CP plus LNS and CP with standard search (CP plus heuristic solves the same number of instances solved by CP plus LNS). Instances composed by 600, 1500 and 2000 jobs are reported (smaller instances are always solved by every model).

Table 1. Extensions experiments summary; percentages of solved instance.

Solver	600 Jobs			1500 Jobs			2000 Jobs		
	D	R	D-R	D	R	D-R	D	R	D-R
MIP	100	100	95	100	50	70	100	35	45
CP + LNS	100	100	95	100	100	90	100	95	95
CP + Std	100	100	100	100	100	100	100	100	100

8   Conclusions

We tackled the problem of regulating the workload execution on a power capped supercomputer, in the case of a changing power budget. We propose three time-bounded approaches to solve this problem: (1) a greedy algorithm, (2) a CP model (with dedicated solving strategies) and (3) a MIP model. The MIP method outperforms the other ones on large instances, while on smaller instances the gap between the CP and MIP approaches is drastically reduced. The greedy algorithm proved to be the fastest method but often unable to find good quality solutions.

We also propose extensions which increase the difficulty of the initial problem and reveal weakness of the MIP approach, especially on larger instances. In particular, whereas the CP model almost always reaches a solution within the time limit, the MIP solver struggles with the job relations extension and finds a solution only in about half of the test instances (although it still outperforms the other approaches when it does find a solution).

Acknowledgement. This work has been partially supported by European H2020 FET project OPRECOMP (g.a. 732631). We also want to thank CINECA and for granting us the access to their systems.

References

1. Ashraf, M.U., Eassa, F.A., Albeshri, A.A., Algarni, A.: Toward exascale computing systems: an energy efficient massive parallel computational model. Int. J. Adv. Comput. Sci. Appl. **9**(2), 118–126 (2018)

2. Bartolini, A., Cacciari, M., Cavazzoni, C., Tecchiolli, G., Benini, L.: Unveiling eurora - thermal and power characterization of the most energy-efficient supercomputer in the world. In: Design, Automation Test in Europe Conference Exhibition (DATE), March 2014

3. Borghesi, A., Collina, F., Lombardi, M., Milano, M., Benini, L.: Power capping in high performance computing systems. In: Pesant, G. (ed.) CP 2015. LNCS, vol. 9255, pp. 524–540. Springer, Cham (2015). https://doi.org/10.1007/978-3-319-23219-5_37

4. Borghesi, A., Conficoni, C., Lombardi, M., Bartolini, A.: MS3: a mediterranean-stile job scheduler for supercomputers - do less when it's too hot! In: 2015 International Conference on High Performance Computing & Simulation, HPCS 2015, 20–24 July 2015, Amsterdam, Netherlands, pp. 88–95 (2015). https://doi.org/10.1109/HPCSim.2015.7237025

5. Borghesi, A., Bartolini, A., Lombardi, M., Milano, M., Benini, L.: Scheduling-based power capping in high performance computing systems. Sustainable Comput.: Inform. Syst. **19**, 1–13 (2018)

6. Borghesi, A., Bartolini, A., Milano, M., Benini, L.: Pricing schemes for energy-efficient HPC systems: design and exploration. Int. J. High Perform. Comput. Appl. **33**(4), 716–734 (2019)

7. Carchrae, T., Beck, J.: Principles for the design of large neighborhood search. J. Math. Model. Algorithms **8**(3), 245–270 (2009). https://doi.org/10.1007/s10852-008-9100-2

8. Cesarini, D., Bartolini, A., Bonfà, P., Cavazzoni, C., Benini, L.: Countdown-a runtime library for application-agnostic energy saving in MPI communication primitives. In: 2nd Workshop on AutotuniNg and aDaptivity AppRoaches for Energy Efficient HPC Systems (ANDARE 2018), June 2018. http://arxiv.org/abs/1806.07258

9. COIN-OR: Cbc (coin-or branch and cut) milp solver. https://projects.coin-or.org/Cbc

10. Dongarra, J.J., Meuer, H.W., Strohmaier, E.: 29th top500 Supercomputer Sites. Technical report, Top500.org, November 1994

11. Etinski, M., Corbalan, J., Labarta, J., Valero, M.: Optimizing job performance under a given power constraint in HPC centers. In: Green Computing Conference, 2010 International, August 2010. https://doi.org/10.1109/GREENCOMP.2010.5598303

12. Etinski, M., Corbalan, J., Labarta, J., Valero, M.: Parallel job scheduling for power constrained HPC systems. Parallel Comput. **38**(12), 615–630 (2012). https://doi.org/10.1016/j.parco.2012.08.001, http://www.sciencedirect.com/science/article/pii/S0167819112000610

13. Etinski, M., Corbalan, J., Labarta, J., Valero, M.: Understanding the future of energy-performance trade-off via DVFS in HPC environments. J. Parallel Distrib. Comput. **72**(4), 579–590 (2012). https://doi.org/10.1016/j.jpdc.2012.01.006, http://www.sciencedirect.com/science/article/pii/S0743731512000172

14. Fan, X., Weber, W.D., Barroso, L.A.: Power provisioning for a warehouse-sized computer. In: ACM SIGARCH Computer Architecture News, vol. 35, pp. 13–23. ACM (2007)

15. Fraternali, F., Bartolini, A., Cavazzoni, C., Benini, L.: Quantifying the impact of variability and heterogeneity on the energy efficiency for a next-generation ultra-green supercomputer. IEEE Trans. Parallel Distrib. Syst. **29**(7), 1575–1588 (2017)

16. Galleguillos, C., Sîrbu, A., Kiziltan, Z., Babaoglu, O., Borghesi, A., Bridi, T.: Data-driven job dispatching in HPC systems. In: Nicosia, G., Pardalos, P., Giuffrida, G., Umeton, R. (eds.) MOD 2017. LNCS, vol. 10710, pp. 449–461. Springer, Cham (2018). https://doi.org/10.1007/978-3-319-72926-8_37

17. Giannozzi, P., Baroni, S., Bonini, N., et al.: Quantum espresso: a modular and open-source software project for quantum simulations of materials. J. Phys.: Condensed Matter **21**(39), 395502 (19pp) (2009). http://www.quantum-espresso.org

18. Google: or-tools. https://developers.google.com/optimization/

19. Hentenryck, P.V., Carillon, J.: Generality versus specificity: an experience with AI and OR techniques. In: Proceedings of the 7th National Conference on Artificial Intelligence, 21–26 August 1988, St. Paul, MN, pp. 660–664 (1988). http://www.aaai.org/Library/AAAI/1988/aaai88-117.php

20. Hsu, C.H., Feng, W.C.: A power-aware run-time system for high-performance computing. In: Proceedings of the 2005 ACM/IEEE Conference on Supercomputing, SC 2005, p. 1. IEEE Computer Society, Washington, DC (2005). https://doi.org/10.1109/SC.2005.3

21. Kogge, P., Resnick, D.R.: Yearly update: exascale projections for 2013 (2013). https://doi.org/10.2172/1104707, http://www.osti.gov/scitech/servlets/purl/1104707

22. Lefurgy, C., Wang, X., Ware, M.: Power capping: a prelude to power shifting. Cluster Comput. **11**(2), 183–195 (2008)

23. Mairy, J.B., Deville, Y., Van Hentenryck, P.: Reinforced adaptive large neighborhood search. In: The Seventeenth International Conference on Principles and Practice of Constraint Programming (CP 2011), p. 55 (2011)

24. Maiterth, M., et al.: Energy and power aware job scheduling and resource management: global survey initial analysis. In: 2018 IEEE International Parallel and Distributed Processing Symposium Workshops (IPDPSW), pp. 685–693. IEEE (2018)

25. Rountree, B., Lownenthal, D.K., de Supinski, B.R., et al.: Adagio: making DVS practical for complex HPC applications. In: Proceedings of the 23rd International Conference on Supercomputing, ICS 2009, pp. 460–469. ACM, New York (2009). https://doi.org/10.1145/1542275.1542340

26. Works, A.P.: Pbs professional®18.2 administrator's guide (2019). https://www.pbsworks.com/pdfs/PBSAdminGuide18.2.pdf

PRONOM: Proof-Search
and Countermodel Generation
for Non-normal Modal Logics

Tiziano Dalmonte[1], Sara Negri[2], Nicola Olivetti[1],
and Gian Luca Pozzato[3]([⊠])

[1] Aix Marseille Univ, Université de Toulon, CNRS, LIS, Marseille, France
{tiziano.dalmonte,nicola.olivetti}@lis-lab.fr
[2] Department of Philosophy, University of Helsinki, Helsinki, Finland
sara.negri@helsinki.fi
[3] Dipartimento di Informatica, Universitá degli Studi di Torino, Turin, Italy
gianluca.pozzato@unito.it

Abstract. We present PRONOM, a theorem prover and countermodel generator for non-normal modal logics. PRONOM implements some labelled sequent calculi recently introduced for the basic system **E** and its extensions with axioms M, N, and C based on bi-neighbourhood semantics. PRONOM is inspired by the methodology of lean $T^A P$ and is implemented in Prolog. When a modal formula is valid, then PRONOM computes a proof (a closed tree) in the labelled calculi having that formula as a root in the labelled calculi, otherwise PRONOM is able to extract a model falsifying it from an open, saturated branch. The paper shows some experimental results, witnessing that the performances of PRONOM are promising.

Keywords: Non-normal modal logics · Labelled sequent calculi · Theorem proving

1 Introduction

Non-Normal Modal Logics (NNML for short) have been studied since the seminal works by C.I. Lewis, Scott, Lemmon, and Chellas (for an introduction see [3]) in the 1960s. They are a generalization of ordinary modal logics that do not satisfy some axioms or rules of minimal normal modal logic **K**. They have gained interest in several areas such as epistemic and deontic reasoning, reasoning about games, and reasoning about "truth in most of the cases".

In epistemic reasoning, where $\Box A$ is read as "the agent knows/believes A", it was early observed [21] that NNML offers a partial solution to the problem of omniscience: a non-omniscient agent would not necessarily be able to conclude

Supported by the ANR project TICAMORE ANR-16-CE91-0002-01, the Academy of Finland project 1308664 and INdAM project GNCS 2019 "METALLIC #2".

M. Alviano et al. (Eds.): AI*IA 2019, LNAI 11946, pp. 165–179, 2019.
https://doi.org/10.1007/978-3-030-35166-3_12

that she knows (or believes) B from that fact that she knows both A and $A \to B$, that is $\Box B$ does not follows from $\Box A$ and $\Box A \to \Box B$. This corresponds to rejecting the K-axiom, or even more strongly, the rule of monotonicity (RM) $A \to B$ implies $\Box A \to \Box B$ and possibly also the rule of necessitation (if B is valid then also $\Box B$ is valid) as it corresponds to the assumption that the agent knows every logical validity.

In deontic logic, where $\Box A$ is interpreted as "it is obligatory that A", NNML may offer a way-out to some well-known paradoxes caused by standard (normal) deontic logic. The simplest example is Ross' paradox [20]: let M denotes "the letter is mailed" and B "the letter is burnt", obviously $M \to (M \lor B)$, but from $\Box M$, i.e. the obligation of send the letter, it seems odd to conclude $\Box(M \lor B)$, that is the obligation to send the letter or to burn it. Again, in this case the "culprit" is the (RM) rule mentioned above. A similar analysis underlies the *gentle-murder* paradox. Moreover normal deontic logic does not allow one to represent conflicting obligations: for instance let A be "you go to the faculty meeting", it may hold both $\Box A$ and $\Box \neg A$ (the former because you are a member of the academic staff, the latter because you have a more important thing to do), without wanting $\Box \bot$, that by (RM) would trivialize obligations. Here the critical point is axiom C which allows one to conclude $\Box(A \land \neg A)$ from $\Box A$ and $\Box \neg A$. Moreover, also $\Box \top$ (whence the necessitation rule) has been rejected by some authors, on the base that a logical truth cannot be the object of an obligation.

A non-normal interpretation of modal operators has been considered in logics of Ability (see [18] and references therein) where the formula $\Diamond A$ is interpreted as "the agent has the ability of doing something which makes A true"; let R denote "Ann draws a red card" and B "Ann draws a black card", clearly $\Diamond(R \lor B)$ holds as Ann can choose a card from a normal deck of cards that will be either red or black, but unless she has a "magical" ability, she cannot ensure that she will pick a red card or a black one, thus it is reasonable (or at least consistent) to assume both $\neg \Diamond R$ and $\neg \Diamond B$. But this shows that the logic of ability does not satisfy the C axiom (in the dual form): $\Diamond(A \lor B) \to \Diamond A \lor \Diamond B$. NNML have also some interest in the area of game logic, more precisely it turns out that Monotonic logic extended with axiom $\Diamond \top$ is a particular case of *coalition logics*, see [19].

Finally, $\Box A$ can be interpred as "A is true in almost all cases" [2], with this interpretation axiom C clearly fails, as the fact that A and B are independently true in "almost all cases" does not entail that $A \land B$ will also be such; a similar situation arises with a probabilistic reading of $\Box A$ as "A is true with high probability" [18].

Non-normal modal logics enjoy a simple semantic characterization in terms of Neighbourhood models: these are possible world models where each world is equipped with a set of neighbourhoods, each one being itself a set of worlds; the basic stipulation is that a modal formula $\Box A$ is true at a world w if the set of worlds which make A true belongs to the neighbourhoods of w. A family of logics is obtained by imposing further closure conditions on the set of neighbourhoods.

In this paper we describe PRONOM (theorem PROver for NOnnormal Modal logics) a Prolog theorem prover for the classical cube of non-normal modal logic[1]. Not many theorem provers for NNML have been developed so far. Here is a brief account: in [8] optimal decision procedures are presented for the whole cube of NNML; these procedures reduce a validity/satisfiability checking in NNML to a set of SAT problems and then call an efficient SAT solver. For this reason they probably outperform any (implementation of) specific calculi for these logics, but they do not provide explicitly "proofs", nor countermodels. A theorem prover for logic EM based on a tableaux calculus (very similar to the one in [10]) is presented in [9]: the system handles more complex Coalition Logic and Alternating Time Temporal logic, and it is implemented in ELAN, an environment for rewriting systems. Finally [11] presents a Prolog implementation of a non-normal modal logic containing both the [∀∀] and the [∃∀] modality; the fragment with just [∃∀] coincides with the logic EM, which is covered also by our theorem prover.

The prover PRONOM implements the labelled sequent calculi presented in [4]. These calculi are based on *bi-neighbourhood* semantics, a variant of the neighbourhood semantics recalled above: in a bi-neighbourhood model each world has associated a set of *pairs* of neighbourhoods, the idea being that the two components of a pair provide independently a positive and negative support for a modal formula. The bi-neighbourhood semantics is particularly significant for logics without monotonicity and maybe of interest in itself. However the main reason to consider it, rather than the standard one, is that it is easier to generate countermodels in the bi-neighbourhood semantics than standard neighbourhood models. On the other hand, it is shown in [4] that the two semantics are equivalent, and more precisely standard neighbourhood models and bi-neighbourhood models can be constructively transformed into each other. The calculi are modular and make use of labels to represent both worlds and neighbourhoods in the syntax. They have invertible rules and provide a decision procedure for the respective logic. Because of the invertibility of the rules, a finite countermodel in the bi-neighbourhood semantics (whence in the standard one) can be directly extracted from a failed derivation.

The Prolog implementation closely corresponds to the calculi: each rule is encoded by a Prolog clause of a predicate called `terminating_proof_search`. This correspondence ensures in principle both the soundness and completeness of the theorem prover. Termination of proof search is obtained by controlling the non-redundant application of the relevant rules. PRONOM provides both proof search and countermodel generation: it searches for a derivation of an input formula, but in case of failure, it generates a countermodel (in the bi-neighbourhood semantics) of the formula.

As far as we know, PRONOM is the *first* theorem prover that provides both proof search and countermodel generation for the *whole* cube of non-normal modal logics. Although there are no benchmarks, its performance seems promising. The program PRONOM, as well as all the Prolog source files, including those

---

[1] A complete description of the whole cube of NNML will be provided in Sect. 2.

used for the performance evaluation, are available for free usage and download at http://193.51.60.97:8000/pronom/.

2   Non-normal Modal Logics, Neighbourhood Semantics and Labelled Calculi

In this section, we present the classical cube of NNMLs, both axiomatically and semantically. The latter is defined in terms of bi-neighbourhood models [4] and it is equivalent to the standard neighbourhood semantics.

Let Atm be a countable set of propositional variables. The language $\mathcal{L}$ contains formulas given by the following grammar: $A ::= p \mid \bot \mid \top \mid A \vee A \mid A \wedge A \mid A \rightarrow A \mid \Box A$, where $p \in$ Atm.

The minimal logic $\mathbf{E}$ in the language $\mathcal{L}$ is defined by adding to classical propositional logic the rule of inference

$$\text{RE} \ \frac{A \rightarrow B \qquad B \rightarrow A}{\Box A \rightarrow \Box B} \ ,$$

and can be extended further by choosing any combination of axioms M, C, and N below on the left, thus producing eight distinct logics (see the *classical cube*, below on the right).

M ▶ $\Box(A \wedge B) \rightarrow \Box A$

C ▶ $\Box A \wedge \Box B \rightarrow \Box(A \wedge B)$

N ▶ $\Box\top$

We recall that axioms M and N are respectively equivalent to the rules RM $(A \rightarrow B/\Box A \rightarrow \Box B)$ and RN $(A/\Box A)$, and that axiom K $(\Box(A \rightarrow B) \rightarrow \Box A \rightarrow \Box B)$ is derivable from M and C. As a consequence, we have that the top system **EMCN** is equivalent to the weakest normal modal logic **K**.

We consider here a variant of the standard neighbourhood semantics for NNMLs, called bi-neighbourhood semantics [4].

Definition 1. *A* bi-neighbourhood model *is a tuple*

$$\mathcal{M} = \langle \mathcal{W}, \mathcal{N}_b, \mathcal{V} \rangle,$$

where:

- *$\mathcal{W}$ is a non-empty set of worlds (states)*
- *$\mathcal{V}$ is a valuation function*
- *$\mathcal{N}_b$ is a bi-neighbourhood function $\mathcal{W} \longrightarrow \mathcal{P}(\mathcal{P}(\mathcal{W}) \times \mathcal{P}(\mathcal{W}))$, where $\mathcal{P}$ denotes the power set.*

We say that $\mathcal{M}$ is a M-model *if $(\alpha, \beta) \in \mathcal{N}_b(w)$ implies $\beta = \emptyset$, it is a* N-model *if for all $w \in \mathcal{W}$ there is $\alpha \subseteq \mathcal{W}$ such that $(\alpha, \emptyset) \in \mathcal{N}_b(w)$, and it is a* C-model *if $(\alpha_1, \beta_1), (\alpha_2, \beta_2) \in \mathcal{N}_b(w)$ implies $(\alpha_1 \cap \alpha_2, \beta_1 \cup \beta_2) \in \mathcal{N}_b(w)$. The forcing relation for boxed formulas is as follows:*

$$w \Vdash \Box A \quad \textit{iff} \quad \text{there is } (\alpha, \beta) \in \mathcal{N}_b(w) \text{ s.t. } \alpha \subseteq [A] \text{ and } \beta \subseteq [\neg A],$$

where $[A]$ *is, as usual, the truth set of* A *in* $\mathcal{W}$ *obtained by the valuation* $\mathcal{V}$.

In [4] it is shown that the bi-neighbourhood semantics characterises the whole cube of NNMLs, in the sense that:

Theorem 1. *A formula* A *is a theorem of* **E** *iff it is valid in all bi-neighbourhood models. The correspondence carries over to the extensions:* A *is a theorem of* **E**+(M/C/N) *iff it is valid respectively in all bi-neighbourhood M/N/C-models (including any combination of axioms/corresponding model conditions).*

It is instructive to recall also the standard neighbourhood semantics and see how the two semantics are related. A standard *neighbourhood model* has the form $\mathcal{M} = \langle \mathcal{W}, \mathcal{N}_s, \mathcal{V} \rangle$, where $\mathcal{W}, \mathcal{V}$ are as before, and $\mathcal{N}_s$ has type $\mathcal{W} \longrightarrow \mathcal{P}(\mathcal{P}(\mathcal{W}))$. The forcing relation for boxed formulas is: $w \Vdash \Box A$ iff $[A] \in \mathcal{N}_s(w)$. In addition we may consider the following conditions: a model $\mathcal{M}$ is *supplemented* if $\alpha \in \mathcal{N}_s(w)$ and $\alpha \subseteq \beta$ implies $\beta \in \mathcal{N}_s(w)$, it *contains the unit* if $\mathcal{W} \in \mathcal{N}_s(w)$ for all $w \in \mathcal{W}$, and it is *closed under intersection* if $\alpha, \beta \in \mathcal{N}_s(w)$ implies $\alpha \cap \beta \in \mathcal{N}_s(w)$.

It is easy to see that every standard model gives rise to a bi-neighbourhood model, by taking for each neighbourhood $\alpha \in \mathcal{N}_s(x)$, the pair $(\alpha, \mathcal{W} \setminus \alpha)$. Moreover if the model is supplemented, contains the unit, or is closed under intersection the corresponding bi-neighbourhood model is a M/N/C model respectively.

On the other hand every bi-neighbourhood model can be transformed into a standard model [4]: given a bi-neighbourhood model $\mathcal{M} = \langle \mathcal{W}, \mathcal{N}_b, \mathcal{V} \rangle$ we can define the standard neighbourhood model $\mathcal{M}' = \langle \mathcal{W}, \mathcal{N}_s, \mathcal{V} \rangle$ by taking for all $w \in \mathcal{W}$, $\mathcal{N}_s(w) = \{\gamma \subseteq \mathcal{P}(\mathcal{W}) \mid \text{there is } (\alpha, \beta) \in \mathcal{N}_b(w) \text{ s.t. } \alpha \subseteq \gamma \text{ and } \beta \subseteq \mathcal{W} \setminus \gamma\}$. It can be proved that the two models are equivalent and that the transformation preserves additional properties (supplementation etc.) whenever the bi-neighbourhood model is a M/N/C model. For logics without monotonicity the above transformation can be optimized in order to obtain a model whose size is polynomially bounded by the size of the original one [4].

We turn now to present the labelled calculi for NNMLs based on the bi-neighbourhood semantics. The language $\mathcal{L}_{LS}$ of labelled calculi extends $\mathcal{L}$ with a set $WL = \{x, y, z, ...\}$ of *world labels*, and a set $NL = \{a, b, c, ...\}$ of *neighbourhood labels*. We define *positive neighbourhood terms*, written $[a_1, ..., a_n]$, as finite multisets[2] of neighbourhood labels, with the unary multiset $[a]$ representing an atomic term. Moreover, if t is a positive term, then $\bar{t}$ is a negative term. Negative terms $\bar{t}$ cannot be proper subterms, in particular cannot be negated. The term τ and its negative counterpart $\bar{\tau}$ are neighbourhood constants.

Intuitively, positive (resp. negative) terms represent the intersection (resp. the union) of their constituents, whereas t and $\bar{t}$ are the two members of a pair of neighbourhoods in bi-neighbourhood models.

The formulas of $\mathcal{L}_{LS}$ are of the following kinds:

$$\phi ::= x : A \mid t \Vdash^{\forall} A \mid t \Vdash^{\exists} A \mid x \in t \mid t \in \mathcal{N}(x).$$

---

[2] As a difference with [4] here terms are multisets rather than sets. This is ininfluent for the properties of the calculi.

Sequents are pairs $\Gamma \Rightarrow \Delta$ of multisets of formulas of $\mathcal{L}_{LS}$. The fully modular calculi LSE* are defined by the rules in Fig. 1.

Initial sequents: $x : p, \Gamma \Rightarrow \Delta, x : p$ $x : \bot, \Gamma \Rightarrow \Delta$ $\Gamma \Rightarrow \Delta, x : \top$

Propositional rules: As for **G3K** [12].

$$\frac{x \in t, x : A, t \Vdash^\forall A, \Gamma \Rightarrow \Delta}{x \in t, t \Vdash^\forall A, \Gamma \Rightarrow \Delta} \; L \Vdash^\forall \qquad \frac{x \in t, \Gamma \Rightarrow \Delta, x : A}{\Gamma \Rightarrow \Delta, t \Vdash^\forall A} \; R \Vdash^\forall$$

$$\frac{x \in t, x : A, \Gamma \Rightarrow \Delta}{t \Vdash^\exists A, \Gamma \Rightarrow \Delta} \; L \Vdash^\exists \qquad \frac{x \in t, \Gamma \Rightarrow \Delta, x : A, t \Vdash^\exists A}{x \in t, \Gamma \Rightarrow \Delta, t \Vdash^\exists A} \; R \Vdash^\exists$$

$$\frac{[a] \in \mathcal{N}(x), [a] \Vdash^\forall A, \Gamma \Rightarrow \Delta, \overline{[a]} \Vdash^\exists A}{x : \Box A, \Gamma \Rightarrow \Delta} \; L\Box$$

$$\frac{t \in \mathcal{N}(x), \Gamma \Rightarrow \Delta, x : \Box A, t \Vdash^\forall A \qquad t \in \mathcal{N}(x), \bar{t} \Vdash^\exists A, \Gamma \Rightarrow \Delta, x : \Box A}{t \in \mathcal{N}(x), \Gamma \Rightarrow \Delta, x : \Box A} \; R\Box$$

$$\frac{}{t \in \mathcal{N}(x), y \in \bar{t}, \Gamma \Rightarrow \Delta} \; M \qquad \frac{\tau \in \mathcal{N}(x), \Gamma \Rightarrow \Delta}{\Gamma \Rightarrow \Delta} \; N\tau \qquad \frac{}{x \in \bar{\tau}, \Gamma \Rightarrow \Delta} \; N\bar{\tau}$$

$$\frac{[a_1, ..., a_n] \in \mathcal{N}(x), [a_1] \in \mathcal{N}(x), ..., [a_n] \in \mathcal{N}(x), \Gamma \Rightarrow \Delta}{[a_1] \in \mathcal{N}(x), ..., [a_n] \in \mathcal{N}(x), \Gamma \Rightarrow \Delta} \; C$$

$$\frac{x \in [a_1], ..., x \in [a_n], \Gamma \Rightarrow \Delta}{x \in [a_1, ..., a_n], \Gamma \Rightarrow \Delta} \; dec \qquad \frac{x \in \overline{[a_1]}, \Gamma \Rightarrow \Delta \quad ... \quad x \in \overline{[a_n]}, \Gamma \Rightarrow \Delta}{x \in \overline{[a_1, ..., a_n]}, \Gamma \Rightarrow \Delta} \; \overline{dec}$$

Application conditions:

x is fresh in $R \Vdash^\forall$ and $L \Vdash^\exists$, a is fresh in $L\Box$, and x occurs in the conclusion of $N\tau$.

Fig. 1. The rules of LSE*.

The above version of the calculi are sound and complete for sequents that may appear in a backward proof search having at the root a single formula (these sequents belong to the class of regular sequents, see [4] for details). It is easy to see that in case of monotonic logics (i.e. logics containing M) the rule $R\Box$ can be simplified by eliminating the second premise. The reason is that an application of the rule $L \Vdash^\exists$ to the term $\bar{t}$ will introduce an element $y \in \bar{t}$ in the antecedent, so that the sequent immediately succeeds by rule M. So we can replace the rule $R\Box$ with the following:

$$\frac{t \in \mathcal{N}(x), \Gamma \Rightarrow \Delta, x : \Box A, t \Vdash^\forall A}{t \in \mathcal{N}(x), \Gamma \Rightarrow \Delta, x : \Box A} \; R\Box M$$

Moreover the rule M can also be deleted as it is not applicable anymore.

3 Design of PRONOM

In this section we present a Prolog implementation of the labelled calculi recalled in Sect. 2. The program, called PRONOM, is inspired by the "lean" methodology of lean $T^A P$, even if it does not follow its style in a rigorous manner. The program comprises a set of clauses, each one of them implementing a sequent rule or an axiom of LSE and its extensions. The proof search is provided for free by the mere depth-first search mechanism of Prolog, without any additional ad hoc mechanism, following the line of the theorem provers for modal and conditional logics in [1,7,13–17] and for preferential reasoning [5] in [6]. In the case of **EM** we consider both the modular version like in Fig. 1, and the optimised version in which the rule $R\Box$ is replaced by $R\Box_M$.

PRONOM represents a sequent with Prolog lists Spheres, Gamma and Delta. Lists Gamma and Delta represent the left-hand side and the right-hand side of the sequent, respectively. Elements of Gamma and Delta are labelled formulas, implemented by Prolog lists with two, three or four elements, as follows:

- standard formulas are pairs [x,f], where x is a label and f is a formula;
- formulas of the form either $x \in t$ or $x \in \overline{t}$ are triples [x,0,t] ([x,1,t], respectively), where x is a label and t represents term t; the inner value, either 0 or 1, is used to distinguish between positive and negative terms, t and $\overline{t}$, respectively;
- formulas of the form $t \models^{\exists} A$, or $t \models^{\forall} A$, or $\overline{t} \models^{\exists} A$, or $\overline{t} \models^{\forall} A$ are represented by quadruples [exists,t,0,a], [forall,t,0,a], [exists,t,1,a], [forall,t,1,a], respectively.

The list Spheres contains pairs of the form [x,Items], where Items is the list of terms belonging to $N(x)$. Symbols $\top$ and $\bot$ are represented by constants true and false, respectively, whereas connectives $\neg$, $\wedge$, $\vee$, $\rightarrow$, and $\Box$ are represented by -, ^, ?, ->, and box. Propositional variables are represented by Prolog atoms. As an example, the Prolog lists

```
[ [x,[t]] ]
[ [y,1,t], [y,a], [forall,t,0,a^b] ]
[ [exists,t,1,a^b], [x,box(a)] ]
```

are used to represent the sequent $t \in N(x), y \in \overline{t}, y : A, t \models^{\forall} A \wedge B \Rightarrow \overline{t} \models^{\exists} A \wedge B, x : \Box A$.

Given a non-normal modal formula F represented by the Prolog term f, PRONOM executes the main predicate of the prover, called prove[3], whose only two clauses implement the functioning of PRONOM: the first clause checks whether F is valid and, in case of a failure, the second one computes a model falsifying F. In detail, the predicate prove first checks whether the formula is valid by executing the predicate:

---

[3] The user can run PRONOM without using the interface of the web application. To this aim, he just need to invoke the goal prove(f).

```
terminating_proof_search(Spheres,Gamma,Delta,ProofTree,RBox,RExist,LAll).
```

This predicate succeeds if and only if the sequent represented by the lists Spheres, Gamma and Delta is derivable. When it succeeds, the output term ProofTree matches with a representation of the derivation found by the prover. Further arguments RBox,RExist, and LAll are used in order to control the application of rules $R\square$, $R \Vdash^{\exists}$, and $L \Vdash^{\forall}$, for obtaining a terminating proof search. More in detail, let us consider the rule $R\square$, which is applied (backward) to a sequent of the form $t \in N(x), \Gamma \Rightarrow \Delta, x : \square A$: both the principal formulas $t \in N(x)$ and $x : \square A$ are copied into the premises, then we need to prevent further applications of the same rule in a backward proof search. In order to control the application of this rule, the list RBox contains triples of the form [x,a,t] in order to keep trace of the fact that, in the current branch of the tree, the rule $R\square$ has been already applied to $x : \square A$ by using $t \in N(x)$. Therefore, the application of the rule is restricted by instantiating a Prolog variable T such that [X,A,T] does not belong to RBox. Similarly for RExist and LAll.

As an example, in order to prove that the sequent $x : \square(A \wedge (B \vee C)) \Rightarrow x : \square((A \wedge B) \vee (A \wedge C))$ is valid in **E**, one queries PRONOM with the goal:

```
terminating_proof_search([x, [ ]], [[x, (box (a ^ (b ? c)))]],
    [[x, (box ((a ^ b) ? (a ^ c)))]], ProofTree, [ ], [ ], [ ]).
```

Each clause of terminating_proof_search implements an axiom or rule of the sequent calculi LSE and extensions. To search for a derivation of a sequent $\Gamma \Rightarrow \Delta$, PRONOM proceeds as follows. First of all, if $\Gamma \Rightarrow \Delta$ is an instance of an axiom, the goal will succeed immediately by using the following clause:

```
terminating_proof_search(Spheres,Gamma,Delta,tree(axiom),_,_,_):-
    member([X,A],Gamma),
    member([X,A],Delta),!.
```

The modular, unoptimised, version for logic **EM** has also the following clause:

```
terminating_proof_search(Spheres,Gamma,Delta,tree(m),_,_,_):-
    member([_,List],Spheres),
    member(T,List),
    member([_,1,T],Gamma),!.
```

If $\Gamma \Rightarrow \Delta$ is not an instance of the axioms, then the first applicable rule will be chosen, e.g. if Spheres contains an element [X, List], such that List contains T, representing that $t \in N(x)$, and Delta contains a formula [X,box A], representing that $x : \square A$ belongs to the right hand side of the sequent, then the clause implementing the $R\square$ rule will be chosen, and PRONOM will be recursively invoked on the premises of such a rule. PRONOM proceeds in a similar way for the other rules. The ordering of the clauses is such that the application of the branching rules is postponed as much as possible. As an example, the clause implementing $R\square$ is as follows:

```
1.  terminating_proof_search(Spheres,Gamma,Delta,
                  tree(rbox,LeftTree,RightTree),RBox,RExist,LAll):-
2.      member([X,box A],Delta),
3.      member([X,SpOfX],Spheres),
4.      member(T,SpOfX),
5.      \+member([X,A,T],RBox),
6.      !,
7.      terminating_proof_search(Spheres,Gamma,[[forall,T,0,A]|Delta],
                          LeftTree,[[X,A,T]|RBox],RExist,LAll),
8.      terminating_proof_search(Spheres,[[exists,T,1,A]|Gamma],Delta,
                          RightTree,[[X,A,T]|RBox],RExist,LAll).
```

Line 5 implements the restriction on the application of the rule described above, and used in order to ensure a terminating proof search: given an instantiation of the Prolog variable T, the rule is applied only in case it has not been already applied by using the same T for the formula $x : \Box A$ in the current branch, namely [X,A,T] does not belong to RBox. Since the rule is invertible, Prolog cut ! is used in line 6 to eventually block backtracking.

When the predicate terminating_proof_search fails, then the initial formula is not valid, and PRONOM extracts a model falsifying such a formula from an open saturated branch. This is computed by executing the predicate:

build_saturate_branch(Spheres,Gamma,Delta,Model,RBox,RExist,LAll).

This predicate has the same arguments of terminating_proof_search, with the exception of the fourth one: here the variable Model matches a description of an open, saturated branch obtained by applying the rules of the calculi to the initial formula. Since the very objective of this predicate is to build an open, saturated branch in the sequent calculus, its clauses are essentially the same as the ones for the predicate terminating_proof_search, however rules introducing a branch in a backward proof search are implemented by *pairs* of (disjoint) clauses, each one representing an attempt to build an open saturated branch. As an example, the following clauses implement the saturation in presence of a boxed formula $x : \Box A$ in the right hand side of a sequent:

```
1.   build_saturate_branch(Spheres,Gamma,Delta,Model,RBox,RExist,LAll):-
2.       member([X,box A],Delta),
3.       member([X,SpOfX],Spheres),
4.       member(T,SpOfX),
5.       \+member([X,A,T],RBox),
6.       build_saturate_branch(Spheres,Gamma,[[forall,T,0,A]|Delta],Model,
                          [[X,A,T]|RBox],RExist,LAll).
7.   build_saturate_branch(Spheres,Gamma,Delta,Model,RBox,RExist,LAll):-
8.       member([X,box A],Delta),
9.       member([X,SpOfX],Spheres),
10.      member(T,SpOfX),
11.      \+member([X,A,T],RBox),
12.      build_saturate_branch(Spheres,[[exists,T,1,A]|Gamma],Delta,Model,
                          [[X,A,T]|RBox],RExist,LAll).
```

PRONOM will first try to build a countermodel by considering the left premise of the rule $R\square$, corresponding to recursively invoking the predicate build_saturate_branch on the premise introducing $t \models^\forall A$ in the right hand side of the sequent in line 6. In case of a failure, the saturation process is completed by considering the right premise of $R\square$ introducing $\bar{t} \models^\exists A$ by the recursive call of line 12.

Clauses implementing axioms for the predicate terminating_proof_search are replaced by the last clause, checking whether the current sequent represents an open and saturated branch:

```
build_saturate_branch(Spheres,Gamma,Delta,model(Spheres,Gamma,Delta),_,_,_):-
    \+instanceOfAnAxiom(Spheres,Gamma,Delta).
instanceOfAnAxiom(_,Gamma,Delta):-member([X,A],Gamma),member([X,A],Delta),!.
```

Since this is the very last clause of the predicate build_saturate_branch, it is considered by PRONOM only if no other clause/rule is applicable, therefore the branch is saturated. The auxiliary predicate instanceOfAnAxiom checks whether the branch is open by proving that it is not an instance of the axioms. The third argument matches a term model representing the countermodel extracted from the lists Spheres, Gamma, and Delta.

The implementation of the calculi for extensions of **E** is very similar: given the modularity of the calculi LSE*, the systems implementing the extensions are easily obtained by adding clauses for both the predicates terminating_proof_search and build_saturate_branch corresponding to the rules specifically tailored for the extensions under consideration. The only exception is logic **EM**, for which we give also an optimised version containing the rule $R\square_M$ instead of $R\square$. For the extensions of **EM** we only propose the version with $R\square_M$ in place of $R\square$.

PRONOM can be used by means of a simple web interface, implemented in php and allowing the user to check whether a non-normal modal formula is valid by using a computer or a mobile device. The web interface also allows the user to choose the modal system to adopt, namely **E** or one of the extensions mentioned in Sect. 2. When a formula is valid, PRONOM builds a pdf file showing a derivation in the sequent calculus LSE (or one of its extensions) as well as the LATEX source file. Otherwise, a countermodel falsifying the initial formula is displayed. Prolog source codes and experimental results are also available. Some pictures of PRONOM are shown in Figs. 2, 3 and 4.

4   Performance of PRONOM

The performance of PRONOM seems to be promising. We have tested it by running SWI-Prolog, version 7.6.4, on an Apple MacBook Pro, 2.7 GHz Intel Core i7, 8GB RAM machine. We have performed two kinds of experiments: 1. We have tested PRONOM over sets of valid formulas in the basic system **E** as well as in each considered extension; 2. We have tested PRONOM on randomly generated formulas, fixing different time limits, numbers of propositional variables, and levels of nesting of connectives.

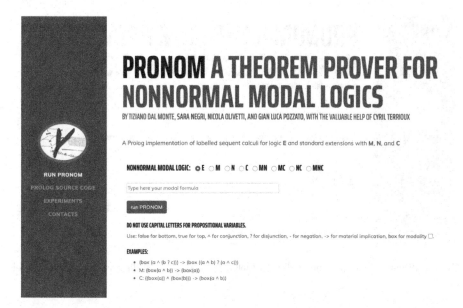

Fig. 2. Home page of PRONOM. When the user wants to check whether a formula F is valid, then (i) he selects the non-normal modal logic to use, (ii) he types F in the form and (iii) clicks the button in order to execute the calculi.

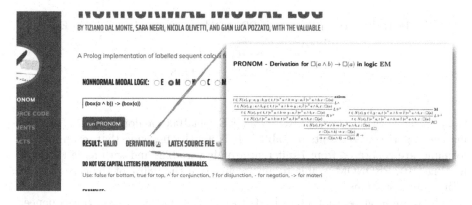

Fig. 3. When a formula is valid, PRONOM computes a pdf file as well as a LaTeX source file of a derivation.

Concerning 1, we have considered around hundred valid formulas obtained by generalizing schemas of valid formulas by varying some crucial parameters, like the modal degree of a formula (the level of nesting of the $\square$ connective). For instance, we have considered the following schemas (valid in all systems):

$$(\square(\square(A_1 \wedge (B_1 \vee C_1)) \wedge \cdots \wedge \square(A_n \wedge (B_n \vee C_n)))) \rightarrow$$
$$(\square(\square((A_1 \wedge B_1) \vee (A_1 \wedge C_1)) \wedge \cdots \wedge \square((A_n \wedge B_n) \vee (A_n \wedge C_n))))$$

$$(\square^n C_1 \wedge \cdots \wedge \square^n C_j \wedge \square^n A) \rightarrow (\square^n A \vee \square^n D_1 \vee \cdots \vee \square^n D_k)$$

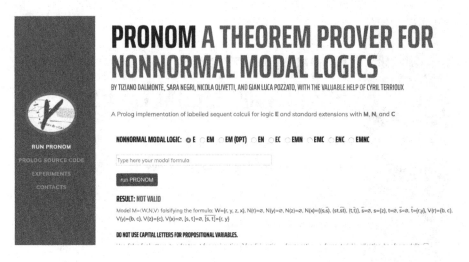

Fig. 4. When a formula is not valid, PRONOM computes and displays a counter model falsifying it.

We have obtained encouraging results: Table 1 reports results for **E**, from which it can be observed that PRONOM is able to answer in less than one second on more than the 75% of the tests, also on valid formulas with high modal degrees.

Table 1. Number of timeouts of PRONOM over 91 valid formulas in **E**.

0.1 ms	1 ms	100 ms	1 s	5 s
51	32	26	22	18

Concerning 2, we have tested PRONOM for **E** over 1000 random formulas, obtaining the experimental results of Table 2. It is worth observing that, even in case formulas are generated from 7 different atomic variables and with a high level of nesting (10), PRONOM is able to answer in more than 80% of the cases within a time limit of 10 ms.

The random generation often leads to not valid formulas; as a consequence, this kind of tests has been useful also in order to evaluate the performance of PRONOM in computing countermodels: indeed, we have considered the number of timeouts in the execution of the top-level predicate **prove** described in the previous section, including the extraction of a countermodel in case of a failure in the proof search. Again, the experimental results seems to be adequate, and the time required for the generation of a counter model of a not valid formula is negligible with respect to the time needed to perform the whole computation.

We have repeated the above experiments also for all the extensions of **E** considered by PRONOM, and we have obtained the results in Figs. 5 and 6.

It is worth noticing that the above experimental results refer to the Prolog component of PRONOM only, thus they do not take into account the effort of

Table 2. Percentage of timeouts in 1000 random tests (system **E**).

Number of variables/depth	1 ms	10 ms	1 s	10 s
3 variables - depth = 5	3%	2%	0	0
3 variables - depth = 7	29%	16%	14%	12%
7 variables - depth = 10	27%	19%	14%	9%

the graphical interface in computing the pdf file of the derivation. Since the web application often requires a long time to answer, we are currently working on improving the performances of PRONOM in such a way that the interface will first provide an answer about the validity of the formula, whereas the generation of the LaTeX/pdf file will be performed only if this option is explicitly selected by the user by clicking a suitable button. Moreover, we are planning to perform more

System EN

0.1ms	1ms	100ms	1s	5s
76,92%	38,46%	34,07%	30,77%	29,67%

System EC

0.1ms	1ms	100ms	1s	5s
80,41%	69,59%	64,43%	61,34%	58,76%

System EM (optimized version)

0.1ms	1ms	100ms	1s	5s
79,06%	63,87%	28,80%	8,90%	8,90%

System ENC

0.1ms	1ms	100ms	1s	5s
82,98%	54,52%	51,06%	48,67%	47,34%

System EMN

0.1ms	1ms	100ms	1s	5s
72,92%	52,82%	32,98%	18,23%	15,28%

System EMC

0.1ms	1ms	100ms	1s	5s
87,41%	75,85%	51,36%	38,78%	37,76%

System EMNC

0.1ms	1ms	100ms	1s	5s
79,62%	63,24%	46,01%	33,40%	32,35%

Fig. 5. Percentages of timeouts of PRONOM over valid formulas in extensions of **E**.

EN

Number of variables/Depth	1ms	10ms	1s	10s
3 variables - Depth = 5	27	17	8	3
3 variables - Depth = 7	59	47	43	33
7 variables - Depth = 10	65	43	40	38

EC

Number of variables/Depth	1ms	10ms	1s	10s
3 variables - Depth = 5	7	5	2	2
3 variables - Depth = 7	31	31	23	19
7 variables - Depth = 10	28	26	27	20

EM (optimized version)

Number of variables/Depth	1ms	10ms	1s	10s
3 variables - Depth = 5	6	1	0	0
3 variables - Depth = 7	21	21	8	8
7 variables - Depth = 10	20	15	14	7

EMN

Number of variables/Depth	1ms	10ms	1s	10s
3 variables - Depth = 5	12	3	1	0
3 variables - Depth = 7	48	25	18	14
7 variables - Depth = 10	45	18	16	13

ENC

Number of variables/Depth	1ms	10ms	1s	10s
3 variables - Depth = 5	57	48	45	41
3 variables - Depth = 7	67	58	52	50
7 variables - Depth = 10	69	64	55	48

EMNC

Number of variables/Depth	1ms	10ms	1s	10s
3 variables - Depth = 5	36	34	20	12
3 variables - Depth = 7	62	54	48	34
7 variables - Depth = 10	68	55	53	44

EMC

Number of variables/Depth	1ms	10ms	1s	10s
3 variables - Depth = 5	11	1	1	1
3 variables - Depth = 7	25	18	17	12
7 variables - Depth = 10	27	23	19	8

Fig. 6. Percentage of timeouts in 1000 random tests for extensions of **E**.

accurate tests following the approach of [8], where randomly generated formulas can be obtained by selecting different degrees of probability about their validity.

5 Conclusions

We have described a Prolog Theorem prover for non-normal modal logics. As far as we know ours is the first program that provides both proof-search and countermodel generation for the whole cube of NNML. It implements directly, concisely, and modularly the labelled sequent calculi presented in [4]. The system provides both proof-search and countermodel construction: given a formula to check, the system outputs either a derivation or a countermodel of the formula, the latter in the bi-neighbourhood semantics, a variant of the standard neighbourhood semantics. Although the implementation does not make use of any optimization or any sophisticated data structure, its performances are encouraging. In future research we intend to study some improvements like the use of free variables for term instantiation and other optimisations. We also intend to implement an automated and *efficient* transformation of the bi-neighbourhood countermodels into standard neighbourhood models, as shown in [4].

References

1. Alenda, R., Olivetti, N., Pozzato, G.L.: CSL-lean: a theorem-prover for the logic of comparative concept similarity. Electron. Notes Theoret. Comput. Sci. (ENTCS) **262**, 3–16 (2010)
2. Askounis, D., Koutras, C.D., Zikos, Y.: Knowledge means 'all', belief means 'most'. J. Appl. Non-Classical Logics **26**(3), 173–192 (2016)
3. Chellas, B.F.: Modal Logic. Cambridge University Press, Cambridge (1980)
4. Dalmonte, T., Olivetti, N., Negri, S.: Non-normal modal logics: bi-neighbourhood semantics and its labelled calculi. In: Bezhanishvili, G., D'Agostino, G., Metcalfe, G., Studer, T. (eds.) Advances in Modal Logic 12, Proceedings of the 12th Conference on Advances in Modal Logic, 27–31 August 2018, Held in Bern, Switzerland, pp. 159–178. College Publications (2018)
5. Giordano, L., Gliozzi, V., Olivetti, N., Pozzato, G.L.: Analytic tableaux for KLM preferential and cumulative logics. In: Sutcliffe, G., Voronkov, A. (eds.) LPAR 2005. LNCS (LNAI), vol. 3835, pp. 666–681. Springer, Heidelberg (2005). https://doi.org/10.1007/11591191_46
6. Giordano, L., Gliozzi, V., Pozzato, G.L.: KLMLean 2.0: a theorem prover for KLM logics of nonmonotonic reasoning. In: Olivetti, N. (ed.) TABLEAUX 2007. LNCS (LNAI), vol. 4548, pp. 238–244. Springer, Heidelberg (2007). https://doi.org/10.1007/978-3-540-73099-6_19
7. Girlando, M., Lellmann, B., Olivetti, N., Pozzato, G.L., Vitalis, Q.: VINTE: an implementation of internal calculi for Lewis' logics of counterfactual reasoning. In: Schmidt, R.A., Nalon, C. (eds.) TABLEAUX 2017. LNCS (LNAI), vol. 10501, pp. 149–159. Springer, Cham (2017). https://doi.org/10.1007/978-3-319-66902-1_9
8. Giunchiglia, E., Tacchella, A., Giunchiglia, F.: SAT-based decision procedures for classical modal logics. J. Automated Reason. **28**(2), 143–171 (2002)

9. Hansen, H.: Tableau games for coalition logic and alternating-time temporal logic-theory and implementation. Master's thesis, University of Amsterdam (2004)
10. Lavendhomme, R., Lucas, T.: Sequent calculi and decision procedures for weak modal systems. Studia Logica **65**, 121–145 (2000)
11. Lellmann, B.: Countermodels for non-normal modal logics via nested sequents. In: Bezhanishvili, N., Venema, Y. (eds.) SYSMICS2019 - Booklet of Abstracts, pp. 107–110. Language and Computation University of Amsterdam, Institute for Logic (2019)
12. Negri, S.: Proof theory for non-normal modal logics: the neighbourhood formalism and basic results. IfCoLog J. Log. Appl. **4**(4), 1241–1286 (2017)
13. Olivetti, N., Pozzato, G.L.: CondLean: a theorem prover for conditional logics. In: Cialdea Mayer, M., Pirri, F. (eds.) TABLEAUX 2003. LNCS (LNAI), vol. 2796, pp. 264–270. Springer, Heidelberg (2003). https://doi.org/10.1007/978-3-540-45206-5_23
14. Olivetti, N., Pozzato, G.L.: CondLean 3.0: improving condlean for stronger conditional logics. In: Beckert, B. (ed.) TABLEAUX 2005. LNCS (LNAI), vol. 3702, pp. 328–332. Springer, Heidelberg (2005). https://doi.org/10.1007/11554554_27
15. Olivetti, N., Pozzato, G.L.: Theorem proving for conditional logics: CondLean and GoalDuck. J. Appl. Non-Classical Logics **18**, 427–473 (2008)
16. Olivetti, N., Pozzato, G.L.: NESCOND: an implementation of nested sequent calculi for conditional logics. In: Demri, S., Kapur, D., Weidenbach, C. (eds.) IJCAR 2014. LNCS (LNAI), vol. 8562, pp. 511–518. Springer, Cham (2014). https://doi.org/10.1007/978-3-319-08587-6_39
17. Olivetti, N., Pozzato, G.L.: Nested sequent calculi and theorem proving for normal conditional logics: the theorem prover NESCOND. Intelligenza Artificiale **9**, 109–125 (2015)
18. Pacuit, E.: Neighborhood Semantics for Modal Logic. Springer, Heidelberg (2017). https://doi.org/10.1007/978-3-319-67149-9
19. Pauly, M.: A modal logic for coalitional power in games. J. Logic Comput. **12**(1), 149–166 (2002)
20. Ross, A.: Imperatives and logic. Theoria **7**, 53–71 (1941)
21. Vardi, M.Y.: On epistemic logic and logical omniscience. In: Theoretical Aspects of Reasoning About Knowledge, pp. 293–305. Elsevier (1986)

Partitioned Least Squares

Roberto Esposito[1]([✉]), Mattia Cerrato[1], and Marco Locatelli[2]

[1] Dipartimento di Informatica, Università di Torino, 10149 Torino, Italy
{roberto.esposito,mattia.cerrato}@unito.it
[2] Dipartimento di Ingegneria e Architettura, Università di Parma, 43124 Parma, Italy
marco.locatelli@unipr.it

Abstract. Linear least squares is one of the most widely used regression methods among scientists in many fields. The simplicity of the model allows this method to be used when data is scarce and it is usually appealing to practitioners that need to gather some insight into the problem by inspecting the values of the learnt parameters. In this paper we propose a variant of the linear least squares model that allows practitioners to partition the input features into groups of variables that they require to contribute similarly to the final result. We formally show that the new formulation is not convex and provide two alternative methods to deal with the problem: one non-exact method based on an alternating least squares approach; and one exact method based on a reformulation of the problem using an exponential number of sub-problems whose minimum is guaranteed to be the optimal solution. We formally show the correctness of the exact method and also compare the two solutions showing that the exact solution provides better results in a fraction of the time required by the alternating least squares solution (assuming that the number of partitions is small).

1 Introduction

Linear regression models are among the most extensively employed statistical methods in science and industry alike. Their simplicity, ease of use and performance in low-data regimes enables their usage in various prediction tasks. As the number of observations usually exceeds the number of variables, a practitioner has to resort to approximating the solution of an overdetermined system. Least squares approximation benefits from a closed-form solution and might be the de-facto standard in linear regression analysis. Among the benefits of linear regression models is the possibility of easily interpreting how much each variate is contributing to the approximation of the dependent variable by means of observing the magnitudes and signs of the associated parameters.

In some application domains, partitioning the variables in non-overlapping subsets is beneficial either as a way to insert human knowledge into the regression analysis task or to further improve model interpretability. When considering high-dimensionality data, grouping variables together is also a natural way to make it easier to reason about the data and the regression result. As an example,

© Springer Nature Switzerland AG 2019
M. Alviano et al. (Eds.): AI*IA 2019, LNAI 11946, pp. 180–192, 2019.
https://doi.org/10.1007/978-3-030-35166-3_13

consider a regression task where the dependent variable is the score achieved by students in an University or College exam. A natural way to group the dependent variables is to divide them into two groups where one contains the variables which represent a student's effort in the specific exam (hours spent studying, number of lectures attended...), while another contains the variables related to previous effort and background (number of previous exams passed, number of years spent at University or College, grade average...). As an another example, when analyzing complex chemical compounds, it is possible to group together fine-grained features to obtain a partition which refers to high-level properties of the compound (such as structural, interactive and bond-forming among others).

In this paper, we introduce a variation on the linear regression problem which allows for partitioning variables into meaningful groups. The parameters obtained by solving the problem allows one to easily assess the contribution of each group to the dependent variable as well as the importance of each element of the group.

Our contributions include a formal non-convexity proof for the new Partitioned Least Squares problem and two possible algorithms to solve it. One is based on the Alternating Least Squares algorithm, where the optimization of the parameters is iterative and can get trapped into local minima; the other is based on a reformulation of the original problem into an exponential number of sub-problems, where the exponent is the cardinality K of the partition. We prove that solutions found by the second approach are globally optimal and test both algorithms on data extracted from the analysis of chemical compounds. Our experimental results show that the optimal algorithm is also faster, provided that the size of the partition is small.

While to the best of our knowledge the regression problem and the algorithms we present are novel, there has been previous work dealing with alternative formulations to the linear regression problem. Partial Least Squares Regression [8] parametrizes both the dependent and independent variables; Weighted Linear Regression minimizes the residuals' *weighted* sum of squares. Partitioned variables have also been the subject of previous work dealing with *selecting* groups of features given a partitioning. Huang et al. provide a review of such methodologies [6].

2   Model Description

Let us consider the problem of inferring a linear least squares model to predict a real variable y given a vector $x \in R$. We will assume that the examples are available at learning time as an $N \times M$ matrix X and $N \times 1$ column vector y. We will also assume that the problem is expressed in homogeneous coordinates, i.e., that X has an additional column containing values equal to 1, and that the intercept term of the affine function is included into the weight vector.

The standard least squares formulation for the problem at hand is to minimize the quadratic loss over the residuals, i.e.:

$$\text{minimize}_w \|Xw - y\|_2^2$$

Table 1. Notation

Symbol(s)	Definition
$(\cdot)_n$	n-th component of a vector
k, K	k is the index for iterating over the K subsets belonging to the partition
m, M	m is the index for iterating over the M variables
$\mathbf{X}$	an $N \times M$ matrix containing the descriptions of the training instances
$\mathbf{A} \times \mathbf{B}$	matrix multiplication operation (we also simply write it $\mathbf{AB}$ when the notation appears clearer)
$\boldsymbol{y}$	a vector of length N containing the labels assigned to the examples in $\mathbf{X}$
$\bullet$	wildcard used in subscriptions to denote whole columns or whole rows: e.g., $\boldsymbol{X}_{\bullet,k}$ denotes the k-th column of matrix $\mathbf{X}$ and $\boldsymbol{X}_{m,\bullet}$ denotes its m-th row
$*$	denotes an optimal solution, e.g., $p^\star$ denotes the optimal solution of the PartitionedLS problem, while $p_b^\star$ denotes the optimal solution of the PartitionedLS-b problem
$\mathbf{P}$	a $M \times K$ partition matrix, $P_{m,k} \in \{0,1\}$, with $P_{m,k} = 1$ iff variable α_m belongs to the k-th element of the partition
P_k	the set of all indices in the k-th element of the partition: $\{m \mid P_{k,m} = 1\}$
$k[m]$	index of the partition element to which α_m belongs, i.e.: $k[m]$ is such that $m \in P_{k[m]}$
$\circ$	Hadamard (i.e., element-wise) product. When used to multiply a matrix by a column vector, it is intended that the columns of the matrix are each one multiplied (element-wise) by the column vector
$\oslash$	Hadamard (i.e., element-wise) division
$\succeq$	element-wise larger-than operator: $\boldsymbol{\alpha} \succeq 0$ is equivalent to $\alpha_m \geq 0$ for $m \in 1..M$

This is a problem that has the closed form solution $\boldsymbol{w} = (\mathbf{X}^T\mathbf{X})^{-1}\mathbf{X}^T\boldsymbol{y}$. As mentioned in Sect. 1, in many application contexts where M is large, the resulting model is hard to interpret. However, it is often the case that domain experts can partition the elements in the weights vector into a small number of groups and that a model built on this partition would be much easier to interpret. Then, let $\mathbf{P}$ be a "partition" matrix for the problem at hand (this is not a partition matrix in the linear algebra sense, it is simply a matrix containing the information needed to partition the features of the problem). More formally, let $\mathbf{P}$ be a $M \times K$ matrix where $P_{m,k} \in \{0,1\}$ is 1 iff feature number m belongs to the k-th partition element. We will also write P_k to denote the set $\{m \mid P_{m,k} = 1\}$. For the sake of reference Table 1 summarises the notation adopted in this paper.

Here we introduce the Partitioned Least Square (PartitionedLS) problem, a model where we introduce K additional variables and try to express the whole regression problem in terms of these new variables (and in terms of how the original variables contribute to the predictions made using them). The simplest way to describe the new model is to consider its regression

$$f(\mathbf{X}) = \left(\sum_{k=1}^{K} \beta_k \sum_{m \in P_k} \alpha_m x_{n,m} + t \right)_n \tag{1}$$

where $(\cdot)_n$ denotes the n-th component of the vector being built. The first summation is over the K sets in the partition that domain experts have identified as interesting, while the second one iterates over all variables in that set. We note that the m-th α weight contributes to the k-th element of the partition only if it belongs to it. As we shall see, we require that all α values are not smaller than 0 and that $\forall k : \sum_{m \in P_k} \alpha_m = 1$. Consequently, the expression returns a vector of predictions calculated in terms of two sets of weights: the β weights, which are meant to capture the magnitude and the sign of the contribution of the k-th element of the partition, and the α weights, which are meant to capture how each feature in the k-th set contributes to it. We note that the α weight vector is of the same length as the vector $\boldsymbol{w}$ in the least squares formulation. Despite this similarity, we prefer to use a different symbol because the interpretation of (and the constraints on) the α weights are different with respect to the $\boldsymbol{w}$ weights.

It is easy to verify that the definition of f in (1) can be rewritten in matrix notation as:

$$f(\mathbf{X}) = \left(\sum_{k=1}^{K} \beta_k \sum_m P_{m,k} \alpha_m x_{n,m} + t \right)_n = \mathbf{X} \times (\mathbf{P} \circ \boldsymbol{\alpha}) \times \boldsymbol{\beta} + t \tag{2}$$

where $\circ$ is the Hadamard product extended to handle column-wise products. More formally, if $\mathbf{Z}$ is a $A \times B$ matrix, $\mathbf{1}$ is a B dimensional vector with all entries equal to 1, and $\boldsymbol{a}$ is a column vector of length A, then $\mathbf{Z} \circ \boldsymbol{a} \triangleq \mathbf{Z} \circ (\boldsymbol{a} \times \mathbf{1}^T)$; where the $\circ$ symbol on the right hand side of the definition is the standard Hadamard product. Equation (2) can be rewritten in homogeneous coordinates as:

$$f(\mathbf{X}) = \mathbf{X} \times (\mathbf{P} \circ \boldsymbol{\alpha}) \times \boldsymbol{\beta} \tag{3}$$

where $\mathbf{X}$ incorporates a column of 1 and we consider an additional group (with index $K + 1$) having a single α_{M+1} variable in it. Given the constraints on α variables, α_{M+1} is forced to assume a value equal to 1 and the value of t is then totally incorporated into β_{K+1}. In the following we will assume that the problem is given in homogeneous coordinates and that the constants M and K already count the additional group and variable.

Definition 1. *The partitioned least squared (PartitionedLS) problem is formulated as:*

$$minimize_{\boldsymbol{\alpha},\boldsymbol{\beta}} \|\mathbf{X} \times (\mathbf{P} \circ \boldsymbol{\alpha}) \times \boldsymbol{\beta} - \boldsymbol{y}\|_2^2$$
$$\text{s.t.} \quad \boldsymbol{\alpha} \succeq 0$$
$$\mathbf{P}^T \times \boldsymbol{\alpha} = 1$$

In summary, we want to minimize the squared residuals of $f(\mathbf{X})$, as defined in (3), under the constraint that for each subset k in the partition, the set of weights form a distribution: they need to be all nonnegative as imposed by $\boldsymbol{\alpha} \succeq 0$ constraint and they need to sum to 1 as imposed by $\mathbf{P}^T \times \boldsymbol{\alpha} = \mathbf{1}$ constraint.

Unfortunately we do not know a closed form solution for this problem. Furthermore, the problem is not convex and hence hard to optimally solve using standard out-of-the-box solvers. The following theorem states this fact formally. Due to space constraints we do not provide the proof in full details.

Theorem 1. *The PartitionedLS problem is not convex.*

Proof. (sketch) It suffices to show that the Hessian of the objective function is not positive semidefinite. By Schwarz's theorem, since the loss function has continuous second partial derivatives, the matrix is symmetric and we can apply the Sylvester criterion for checking positive definiteness. In practice, we prove that Hessian is not positive semidefinite by showing that not all leading principal minors are larger than zero. In our specific case, the second minor can be shown to assume values smaller than zero and this proves the theorem. Let us denote with L the objective of the PartitionedLS problem

$$L = \|\mathbf{X} \times (\mathbf{P} \circ \boldsymbol{\alpha}) \times \boldsymbol{\beta} - \mathbf{y}\|_2^2$$

$$= \sum_n \left(\sum_k \beta_k \sum_{\alpha_m \in P_k} \alpha_m x_{n,m} - y_n \right)^2$$

Consider the vector containing all the variables of the PartitionedLS problem in the following order: $(\alpha_1, \beta_1, \alpha_2, \beta_2, \ldots, \alpha_K, \beta_K, \alpha_{K+1}, \alpha_{K+2}, \ldots, \alpha_M)$ and assume the problem is not trivial, i.e., that $m > 1, k > 1$. In the following, without loss of generality, we will assume that $\alpha_1 \in P_1$. Under these assumptions, to prove that the second minor is smaller than zero, amounts to prove that:

$$H_{11}H_{22} - H_{12}H_{21} = \frac{\partial^2 L}{\partial\alpha_1\partial\alpha_1} \frac{\partial^2 L}{\partial\beta_1\partial\beta_1} - \frac{\partial^2 L}{\partial\alpha_1\partial\beta_1} \frac{\partial^2 L}{\partial\beta_1\partial\alpha_1}$$

$$= \frac{\partial^2 L}{\partial^2\alpha_1} \frac{\partial^2 L}{\partial^2\beta_1} - \left(\frac{\partial^2 L}{\partial\alpha_1\partial\beta_1} \right)^2 < 0$$

By working out the details of the partial derivatives, one ends up with the expression:

$$H_{11}H_{22} - H_{12}H_{21} = \left(2\beta_1^2 \sum_n x_{n,1}^2 \right) 2 \sum_n \left(\sum_{\overline{m} \in P_1} \alpha_{\overline{m}} x_{n,\overline{m}} \right)^2$$

$$- \left[2 \sum_n x_{n,1} \left(\beta_1 \sum_{\overline{m} \in P_1} \alpha_{\overline{m}} x_{n,\overline{m}} + \rho_{\alpha,\beta}(n) \right) \right]^2, \quad (4)$$

where $\rho_{\alpha,\beta}(n)$ is a short hand for $\sum_k \beta_k \sum_{\overline{m} \in P_k} \alpha_{\overline{m}} x_{n,\overline{m}} - y_n$. To simplify the algebra, let us now assume that for all $n, k : \sum_{\overline{m} \in P_k} \alpha_{\overline{m}} x_{n,\overline{m}}$ is equal to a constant c. We notice that albeit being a strong assumption, it does not hinder the generality of the result since to prove that the Hessian is not semidefinite it suffices to find a single configuration of the problem in which it is not. Under this assumption, $\rho_{\alpha,\beta}(n) = c \sum_k \beta_k - y_n$:

$$
\begin{aligned}
(4) = &\, 4Nc^2\beta_1^2 \sum_n x_{n,1}^2 - \left[2 \sum_n x_{n,1} \left(\beta_1 c + c \sum_k \beta_k - y_n \right) \right]^2 \\
= &\, 4Nc^2\beta_1^2 \sum_n x_{n,1}^2 - \left[2\beta_1 c \sum_n x_{n,1} + 2c \left(\sum_k \beta_k \right) \left(\sum_n x_{n,1} \right) - 2 \sum_n x_{n,1} y_n \right]^2 .
\end{aligned}
$$

We end the proof by noticing that the expression on the left of the minus sign is constant w.r.t. $\beta_2 \ldots \beta_K$, while the part on the right of the minus sign can be made arbitrarily large by varying those variables. This shows that for a certain configuration of β_k values, the expression can be made negative.   □

In the following we will provide two algorithms that solve the above problem. One is an alternating least squares approach which scales well with K, but it is not guaranteed to provide the optimal solution. The other one is a reformulation of the problem through a (possibly) large number of convex problems whose minimum is guaranteed to be the optimal solution of the original problem. Even though the second algorithm does not scale well with K, we believe that this *should not be a problem* since the PartitionedLS is by design well suited for small K values (otherwise the main reason inspiring its creation would cease to exist since for large K values the new model would not be much more interpretable than the original one).

3   Algorithms

3.1   Alternating Least Squares Approach

In the PartitionedLS problem we aim at minimizing a non convex objective, where the non convexity depends on the multiplicative interaction between α and β variables in the expression $\| \mathbf{X} \times (\mathbf{P} \circ \alpha) \times \beta - y \|_2^2$. Interestingly, if one fixes α, the expression $\mathbf{X} \times (\mathbf{P} \circ \alpha)$ results in a matrix $\mathbf{X}'$ that does not depend on any variable. Then, the whole expression can be rewritten as a problem $p_\alpha = \| \mathbf{X}'\beta - y \|_2^2$ which is the convex objective of a standard least squares problem in the β variables. In a similar way, it can be shown that by fixing β one also ends up with a p_β convex optimization problem.

These observations naturally lead to the formulation of an alternating least squares solution where one alternates between solving p_α and p_β. In Algorithm 1.1 we formalize this intuition into an algorithm where, after initializing α and β randomly, we iterate T times. At each iteration we take the latest estimate for the α variables and solve the p_α problem based on that estimate, we then keep the newly found β variables and solve the p_β problem based on them. At each iteration the overall objective is guaranteed not to increase in value and we conjecture convergence to some stationary point as $T \to \infty$.

Algorithm 1.1. Alternating least squares solution to the PartitionedLS problem. The notation const(α) (respectively const(β)) is just to emphasize that the current value of α (respectively β) will be used as a constant in the following step.

```
1     function PartitionedLS-alternating(X, y, P)
2         α = random(M)
3         β = random(K)
4
5         for t in 1...T
6             a = const(α)
7             p* = minimizeβ (‖(X × (P ∘ a) × β − y‖²₂))
8
9
10            b = const(β)
11            p* = minimizeα (‖(X × (P ∘ α) × b − y‖²₂,
12                          α ⪰ 0,
13                          Pᵀ × α = 1)
14        end
15
16        return (p*, α, β)
17    end
```

3.2   Reformulation as a Set of Convex Subproblems

Here we show how the PartitionedLS problem can be reformulated as a set of convex problems such that the problem of achieving the smallest objective attains the global optimum of the original problem.

Definition 2. *The* PartitionedLS-b *problem is a PartitionedLS problem in which the β variables are substituted by a constant vector $\boldsymbol{b} \in \{-1, 1\}^K$, and the normalization constraints over the α variables are dropped:*

$$minimize_\alpha \|\mathbf{X} \times (\mathbf{P} \circ \boldsymbol{b}) \times \boldsymbol{\alpha} - \boldsymbol{y}\|_2^2$$
$$\text{s.t.} \quad \boldsymbol{\alpha} \succeq 0$$

We note that the above definition actually defines 2^K minimization problems, one for each of the possible $\boldsymbol{b}$ vectors. Interestingly, each one of the minimization problems can be shown to be convex by the same argument used in Sect. 3.1 (for fixed β variables) and we will prove that the minimum attained by minimizing those problems corresponds to the global minimum of the original problem. We also show that by simple algebraic manipulation of the result found by a PartitionedLS-b solution, it is possible to write a corresponding PartitionedLS solution attaining the same objective.

The main breakthrough here derives from noticing that in the original formulation the β variables are used to keep track of two facets of the solution: *(i)* the magnitude and *(ii)* the sign of the contribution of each subset in the partition of the variables. With the b vector keeping track of the signs, one only needs to reconstruct the magnitude of the β contributions to recover the solution of the original problem.

To do so, let us start by calculating a normalization vector $\bar{\beta}$ containing in $\bar{\beta}_k$ the normalization factor for variables in partition subset k:

$$\bar{\beta} = \left(\sum_{m \in P_k} \alpha_m \right)_k = \mathbf{P}^T \times \boldsymbol{\alpha}.$$

Then, the vector $\hat{\alpha}$ (containing the α variables as defined in the original problem) can be recovered by dividing each α_m by $\bar{\beta}_{k[m]}$:

$$\hat{\alpha} = \left(\frac{\alpha_m}{\bar{\beta}_{k[m]}} \right)_m = \sum_{k=1}^{K} \left((\mathbf{P} \circ \boldsymbol{\alpha}) \oslash \bar{\beta}^T \right)_{\bullet,k} = \left(\mathbf{P} \circ \boldsymbol{\alpha} \oslash \bar{\beta}^T \right) \times \mathbf{1},$$

and the $\hat{\beta}$ vector (containing both signs and magnitudes of the contribution of each subset in the partition) can be reconstructed simply by taking the Hadamard product of b and $\bar{\beta}$:

$$\hat{\beta} = b \circ \bar{\beta}.$$

The complete algorithm, which detects and returns the best solution of the PartitionedLS-b problems over all possible b vectors, is reported in Algorithm 1.2.

The following lemma (whose proof we omit due to space constraints) shows that a PartitionedLS solution using $\hat{\alpha}$ and $\hat{\beta}$ has the same objective value as the PartitionedLS-b solution using the given b and α values.

Lemma 1. *(Rewriting Lemma) Let $\boldsymbol{\alpha}$ be a vector of m positive values, $b \in \{-1, 1\}^K$ a vector of K signs, and $\bar{\beta}$ a vector of K non zero values. Let also $\hat{\alpha}$, $\hat{\beta}$ be such that:*

$$\hat{\alpha} = \left(\frac{\alpha_m}{\bar{\beta}_{k[m]}} \right)_m \quad \text{for } m \in \{1 \ldots M\}$$

and

$$\hat{\beta} = \left(b_k \bar{\beta}_k \right)_k \quad \text{for } k \in \{1 \ldots K\}.$$

Then:

$$\mathbf{X} \times (\mathbf{P} \circ \boldsymbol{\alpha}) \times b = \mathbf{X} \times (\mathbf{P} \circ \hat{\alpha}) \times \hat{\beta}.$$

Corollary 1. *Under the hypotheses of the Rewriting Lemma it holds:*

$$\| \mathbf{X} \times (\mathbf{P} \circ \hat{\alpha}) \times \hat{\beta} - \mathbf{y} \|_2^2 = \| \mathbf{X} \times (\mathbf{P} \circ \boldsymbol{\alpha}) \times b - \mathbf{y} \|_2^2 \tag{5}$$

Theorem 2. *Let p^* be the optimal value of the PartitionedLS problem and let p_{b^*} be the value attained by the PartitionedLS-b algorithm (Algorithm 1.2). Then, $p^* = p_{b^*}$.*

Proof. We first show that $p^* \geq p_{b^*}$, then we show that $p_{b^*} \leq p^*$ and conclude that $p^* = p_{b^*}$. In the following let:

Algorithm 1.2. PartitionedLS-b solution to the PartitionedLS problem. The function extract_min retrieves the $(\dot{p}, \dot{\alpha}, \dot{\beta})$ tuple in the results array attaining the lowest $\dot{p}$ value.

```
1     function PartitionedLS-optimal(X, y, P)
2        results = []
3
4        for b̊ in {1, −1}^K
5           p̊ = minimize_α̊ (‖(X × (P ∘ α̊) × b̊ − y‖₂²), α̊ ⪰ 0)
6
7              results += (p̊, α̊, b̊)
8        end
9
10       p*, α, b = extract_best(results)
11
12
13       β̄ = Pᵀ × α
14       α̂ = (P ∘ α ⊘ β̄ᵀ) × 1
15       β̂ = b ∘ β̄
16
17       return (p*, α̂, β̂)
18    end
```

– b^* be the best sign vector as found by Algorithm 1.2 and let α_{b^*} be the corresponding α vector (i.e., α_{b^*}, b^* attain the p_{b^*} solution);
– $\hat{\alpha}^*, \hat{\beta}^*$ be the values attaining the p^* solution.

Notice that Corollary 1 of the Rewriting Lemma implies that for sign vector $b = \hat{\beta} \oslash \bar{\beta}$ and $\alpha_b = \left(\alpha_m \bar{\beta}_{k[m]}\right)_m$:

$$p^* = \|X \times (P \circ \hat{\alpha}^*) \times \hat{\beta}^* - y\|_2^2 = \|X \times (P \circ \alpha_b) \times b - y\|_2^2.$$

Since the p_{b^*} solution is the best solution over all the possible sign vectors, it holds that:

$$\|X \times (P \circ \alpha_b) \times b - y\|_2^2 \geq \|X \times (P \circ \alpha_{b^*}) \times b^* - y\|_2^2 = p_{b^*}.$$

Vice-versa by Corollary 1 of the Rewriting Lemma it holds that for $\hat{\alpha}, \hat{\beta}$ as given in the Rewriting Lemma assumptions, it holds that:

$$p_{b^*} = \|X \times (P \circ \alpha_{b^*}) \times b^* - y\|_2^2 = \|X \times (P \circ \hat{\alpha}) \times \hat{\beta} - y\|_2^2.$$

Since p^* is the global optimum for the PartitionedLS problem, it holds:

$$\|X \times (P \circ \hat{\alpha}) \times \hat{\beta} - y\|_2^2 \geq \|X \times (P \circ \hat{\alpha}^*) \times \hat{\beta}^* - y\|_2^2 = p^* s$$

□

4 Regularization

The PartitionedLS model presented so far has no regularization mechanism in place and, as such, it risks overfitting the training set. Since the α values are normalized by definition, the only parameters that need regularization are those collected in the β vector. Then, the regularized version of the objective function simply adds a penalty on the size of the β vector:

$$\|\mathbf{X} \times (\mathbf{P} \circ \boldsymbol{\alpha}) \times \boldsymbol{\beta}\|_2^2 + \eta\|\boldsymbol{\beta}\|_2^2 \tag{6}$$

where the squared euclidean norm could be substituted with the L1 norm in case a LASSO-like regularization is preferred.

The objective expressed in (6) can be used in Algorithm 1.1 as is, but it needs to be slightly updated so to accommodate the differences in the objective function when used in Algorithm 1.2. In this second case, in fact, the correct expression for the $\|\boldsymbol{\beta}\|_2^2$ regularization term becomes: $\|\mathbf{P}^T \times \boldsymbol{\alpha}\|_2^2$ since the optimization program does not maintain an explicit list of β variables. We notice that since the regularization term is convex, it does not hinder the convexity of the optimization problems in both algorithms presented in this paper.

5 Experiments

While the main motivation of the proposed approach is interpretability, we do not provide here any direct measurement of this property. Unfortunately, interpretability is not easily measurable since its very notion has not yet been clearly defined and a multitude of different definitions coexist. Instead, we simply argue that the smaller "grouped" model better matches one interpretability definition based on *transparency* (in both the *simulatability* and *decomposability* meanings, see [7]). In the following we will focus on the algorithmic properties of the two algorithms we presented in this paper, showing how they behave so to provide some insight about when one should be preferred over the other.

In order to assess the advantages/disadvantages of the two algorithms presented in this paper, we apply them to solve the block-relevance analysis proposed in [3,4]. We will assess the two algorithms on a dataset [2] containing 82 features describing measurements over simulated (VolSurf+ [5]) models of 44 drugs. The regression task is the prediction of the lipophilicity of the 44 compounds. The 82 features are partitioned into 6 groups according to the kind of property they describe. The six groups are characterized in [3] as follows:

- **Size/Shape**: 7 features describing the size and shape of the solute;
- **OH2**: 19 features expressing the solute's interaction with water molecules;
- **N1**: 5 features describing the solute's ability to form hydrogen bond interactions with the donor group of the probe;
- **O**: 5 features expressing the solute's ability to form hydrogen bond interactions with the acceptor group of the probe;

- **DRY**: 28 features describing the solute's propensity to participate in hydrophobic interactions;
- **Others**: 18 descriptors describing mainly the imbalance between hydrophilic and hydrophobic regions.

This dataset, while not high-dimensional in the broadest sense of the term, can be partitioned into well-defined, interpretable groups of variables. Previous literature which employed this dataset has indeed focused on leveraging the data's structure to obtain explainable results [4].

We used as training/test split the one proposed in [2] and set the regularization parameter η to 1.0 (since we are not aiming at finding the most accurate regressor, we did not investigate other regularization settings).

For this particular problem, the number of groups is small and the optimal algorithm needs to solve just $2^6 = 64$ convex problems. It terminates in 0.90 s reaching a value of the regularized objective function of about 6.679. For what concerns the approximated algorithm, we ran it in a Multistart fashion with 100 randomly generated starting points. We repeated the experiment using two different configurations of parameter T (number of iterations), setting it to 20 and 100, respectively. For each configuration we kept track of the cumulative time and of the ("cumulative") best solution found. As one would expect, increasing the value of parameter T slows down the algorithm, but allows it to converge to better solutions. Figure 1 reports the best objective value found by the algorithms plotted against the time (reported on a logarithmic scale to improve visualization) necessary to get to such a solution. The experiments show that Algorithm 1.2 retrieves a more accurate (actually the globally optimal) answer in a fraction of the time. Indeed, it is straightforward to observe that, in typical scenarios[1], the only times where the alternating least squares approach outperforms the optimal algorithm in terms of running time is for cases where the total number of iterations (convex subproblems solved) is smaller than the 2^K subproblems needed by Algorithm 1.2 to compute the optimal solution. In our admittedly limited experimentation, this leads to solutions that grossly approximate the optimal one. Our conclusion is that the optimal algorithm is likely to be preferable in most cases. The exceptions are the cases where the number of groups is large or the cases where the time required to solve a single convex problem is very large and approximate solutions do not hinder the applicability of the result in the application at hand. For what concerns the cases with a large number of groups, we argue that this setting defies the main motivation behind employing a model such as the one we presented.

---

[1] In this informal argument we are assuming that each convex problem requires about the same amount of time to be solved. While this is not guaranteed, we believe that it is very unlikely that deviations from this assumption would lead to situations very different from the ones outlined in the argument.

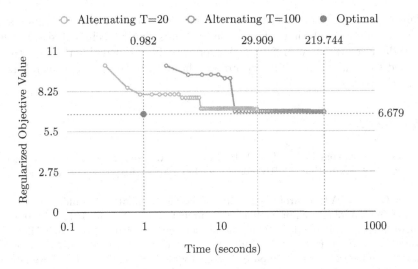

Fig. 1. Plot of the behavior of the two proposed algorithms. The PartitionedLS-alternating algorithm has been repeated 100 times following a Multistart strategy and in two settings ($T = 20$ and $T = 100$). Each point on the orange and green lines reports the cumulative time and best objective found during these 100 restarts.(Color figure online)

6 Conclusions

In this paper, we presented an alternative least squares linear regression formulation and two algorithms to solve it: one iterative, one optimal. In our experimentation, we found the optimal algorithm to be faster, although its time complexity grows exponentially with the number of groups. Our model enables scientists and practitioners to group features together into partitions modeling higher level abstractions which are easier to reason about. In the future, we would like to perform an extensive experimentation on high-dimensionality data to better understand the tradeoff between our Alternating Least Squares and exact approaches when the number of groups is higher. In contrast with the choice we made in this paper (where we focused on a dataset showcasing a real application of the methodology), in this new experimentation we will use more broadly available datasets. Even though the datasets and groupings will appear to be less justified, the new setting will allow us to better study in which cases it may be more beneficial to recover a lower-quality solution in a shorter amount of time, rather than striving for an optimal solution using the exact algorithm (Algorithm 1.2). We also plan to investigate branch-and-bound strategies to avoid the explicit computation of all 2^K sub-problems in the optimal algorithm.

A Julia [1] implementation of the algorithms is available at https://github.com/ml-unito/PartitionedLS; the code for the experiments can be downloaded from: https://github.com/ml-unito/PartitionedLS-experiments.

This latter repository also contains the dataset we used in our experiments in the format required to be loaded from the programs. Due to technical reasons, the original dataset presented in [2] is no longer available for download. The authors confirmed that they are willing to provide the data to interested researchers if contacted directly.

References

1. Bezanson, J., Karpinski, S., Shah, V.B., Edelman, A.: Julia: a fast dynamic language for technical computing. CoRR abs/1209.5145 (2012). http://arxiv.org/abs/1209.5145
2. Caron, G., et al.: A fast chromatographic method for estimating lipophilicity andionization in nonpolar membrane-like environment. Mol. Pharm. **13**(3), 1100–1110 (2016). https://doi.org/10.1021/acs.molpharmaceut.5b00910. pMID: 26767433
3. Ermondi, G., Caron, G.: Molecular interaction fields based descriptors to interpret and compare chromatographic indexes. J. Chromatogr. A **1252**, 84–89 (2012). https://doi.org/10.1016/j.chroma.2012.06.069. http://www.sciencedirect.com/science/article/pii/S0021967312009636
4. Giulia, C., Maura, V., Giuseppe, E.: The block relevance (BR) analysis to aid medicinal chemists to determine and interpret lipophilicity. Med. Chem. Commun. **4**, 1376–1381 (2013). https://doi.org/10.1039/C3MD00140G
5. Goodford, P.J.: A computational procedure for determining energetically favorable binding sites on biologically important macromolecules. J. Med. Chem. **28**(7), 849–857 (1985). https://doi.org/10.1021/jm00145a002
6. Huang, J., Breheny, P., Ma, S.: A selective review of group selection in high-dimensional models. Stat. Sci.: Rev. J. Inst. Math. Stat. **27**(4) (2012)
7. Lipton, Z.: The mythos of model interpretability. Commun. ACM **61** (2016). https://doi.org/10.1145/3233231
8. Wold, S., Sjöström, M., Eriksson, L.: PLS-regression: a basic tool of chemometrics. Chemom. Intell. Lab. Syst. **58**(2), 109–130 (2001). https://doi.org/10.1016/S0169-7439(01)00155-1. http://www.sciencedirect.com/science/article/pii/S0169743901001551. pLS Methods

Number of Minimal Hypergraph Transversals and Complexity of IFM with Infrequency: High in Theory, but Often Not so Much in Practice!

Domenico Saccà[1]([✉])[iD] and Edoardo Serra[2][iD]

[1] University of Calabria, 87036 Rende, CS, Italy
sacca@unical.it
[2] Boise State University, Boise 83725, ID, USA
edoardoserra@boisestate.edu

Abstract. Hypergraph *Dualization* (also called as *hitting set enumeration*) is the problem of enumerating all minimal transversals of a hypergraph $\mathcal{H}$, i.e., all minimal inclusion-wise hyperedges (i.e., sets of vertices) that intersect every hyperedge in $\mathcal{H}$. Dualization is at the core of many important Artificial Intelligence (AI) problems. As a contribution to a better understanding of Dualization complexity, this paper introduces a tight upper bound to the number of minimal transversals that can be computed in polynomial time. In addition, the paper presents an interesting exploitation of the upper bound to the number of minimal transversals. In particular, the problem dealt with is characterizing the complexity of the data mining problem called IFM_I (Inverse Frequent itemset Mining with Infrequency constraints), that is the problem of finding a transaction database whose frequent and infrequent itemsets satisfy a number of frequency/infrequency patterns given in input.

Keywords: Hypergraph transversal · Hypergraph dualization · Inverse data mining

1 Introduction

A *hypergraph* is a pair $\mathcal{H} = (V, E)$, where V is a non-empty finite set of vertices and $E \subseteq 2^V$ is a non-empty set of hyperedges (refer to [2] for more details on hypergraphs). Let $n = |V|$ and $m = |E|$ be the number of vertices and of hyperedges, respectively. Moreover, let $\check{E}$ be the inclusion-wise minimal hyperedges in E, $\check{m} = |\check{E}|$ and $\check{\mathcal{H}} = (V, \check{E})$ (*inclusion reduction* of $\mathcal{H}$).

A *transversal* of $\mathcal{H}$ is a hyperedge I that intersects every hyperedge in E and it is a *minimal transversal* (also called *hitting set*) if no proper subset of it is a transversal of $\mathcal{H}$. Let E^d be the set of all minimal transversals of $\mathcal{H}$ and $m^d = |E^d|$. As the minimal transversals of $\mathcal{H}$ coincide with the ones of $\check{\mathcal{H}}$, in the remainder of this section, unless it is otherwise specified, we assume that $\mathcal{H}$

© Springer Nature Switzerland AG 2019
M. Alviano et al. (Eds.): AI*IA 2019, LNAI 11946, pp. 193–209, 2019.
https://doi.org/10.1007/978-3-030-35166-3_14

is a Sperner hypergraph, i.e., $\mathcal{H}$ coincides with its inclusion reduction $\check{\mathcal{H}}$. The problem of enumerating all minimal transversals of a given hypergraph is known in the literature with the name of *hypergraph dualization* (also called *hitting set enumeration*, see, e.g., [8,10]). A hypergraph $\mathcal{H}_1$ is *dual* of a hypergraph $\mathcal{H}_2$ if the hyperedges of $\mathcal{H}_1$ are exactly all minimal transversals of $\mathcal{H}_2$ and the *duality problem* consists of deciding whether $\mathcal{H}_1$ is dual of a hypergraph $\mathcal{H}_2$. Main relevant results on dualization and duality problems can be summarized as:

- the number m^d of minimal transversals may be exponential in the number n of vertices and the number m of minimal hyperedges and, therefore, the efficiency of a dualization algorithm is measured in terms of n and of $M = m + m^d$ (i.e., the combined input and output size);
- a fast well-known dualization algorithm [12] runs in quasi-polynomial time $n \cdot M^{o(\log M)}$;
- recently, it has been proved in [14] that the *Duality problem* is in DSPACE[$\log^2 n$] and it has been devised a deterministic algorithm in [13] that, given two hypergraphs $\mathcal{H}_1$ and $\mathcal{H}_2$, computes a transversal of $\mathcal{H}_2$ missing in $\mathcal{H}_1$ in quadratic logspace.

As pointed out in [14], dualization and duality are at the core of a number of important problems in the areas of knowledge discovery, machine learning, and more generally in AI and knowledge representation. Just to mention a few: Learning monotone Boolean CNFs and DNFs with membership queries [15], model-based diagnosis [22], computing a Horn approximation to a non-Horn theory [17], computing minimal abductive explanations to observations [9], and computing of the maximal frequent and minimal infrequent sets in data mining [15,16].

In this paper we define an upper bound $\widetilde{m}^d$ to the number m^d of minimal transversals and we show that this bound can be computed in polynomial time. This bound is based on the structure of the *complement hypergraph* $\overline{\mathcal{H}} = (V, \overline{E})$ of $\mathcal{H}$, that is the hypergraph obtained from $\mathcal{H}$ by replacing every $I \in E$ with $\overline{I} = V \setminus I$. Obviously $\overline{m} = |\overline{E}|$ is equal to m. Let $\bar{n} = |\overline{V}| \leq n$, where $\overline{V} = \cup_{\overline{I} \in \overline{E}} \overline{I}$ is the set of vertices that are not included in all hyperedges in E. In addition, $\bar{n}_2 = |\overline{V}_2|$, where $\overline{V}_2 = \{\{v_1, v_2\} \mid v_1, v_2 \in V$ and $\exists \overline{I} \in \overline{E}$ s.t. $\{v_1, v_2\} \subseteq \overline{I}\}$ is the set of vertex pairs that are not included in some hyperedge in E.

The upper bound $\widetilde{m}^d$ is equal to $m_1^d + m_2^d + \widetilde{m}_{3+}^d$, where $m_1^d = n - \bar{n}$ is the number of singleton minimal transversals, $m_2^d = \bar{n}(\bar{n} - 1)/2 - \bar{n}_2$ is the number of two-vertex minimal transversals and $\widetilde{m}_{3+}^d$ is an upper bound of the overall number of minimal transversals with 3 or more vertices. The value of $\widetilde{m}_{3+}^d$ is computed in time $\mathcal{O}(n \cdot m^2)$ by means of the formula (2), reported in Sect. 2, that takes into account a particular type of intersection between any two complement hyperedges. We next give an intuition to clarify this point. Let us first introduce a parameter $\kappa(\mathcal{H}) = \log_{\bar{n}}(m_2^d + \widetilde{m}_{3+}^d)$ to better characterize the magnitude of $\widetilde{m}^d$ w.r.t. $\bar{n}$ in a hypergraph $\mathcal{H}$, so that we can write $\widetilde{m}^d = m_1^d + \bar{n}^{\kappa(\mathcal{H})} = n - \bar{n} + \bar{n}^{\kappa(\mathcal{H})}$.

For each p, $1 < p < \bar{n}$, and for each two distinct complement hyperedges $\bar{I}$ and $\bar{J}$, $\bar{I} \textcircled{p} \bar{J}$ denotes the set of vertices in $\bar{I} \cap \bar{J}$ that are contained in at least $p-2$ other complements, i.e., a vertex is in $\bar{I} \textcircled{p} \bar{J}$ if and only if it is contained in at most $m-p$ hyperedges in H and is neither in I nor in J – note that $\bar{I} \textcircled{2} \bar{J} = \bar{I} \cap \bar{J}$. Let $\mathcal{CH}$ be any family of hypergraphs for which $\widetilde{m}_{3+}^d \in \Omega(2^{(\log \bar{n})^c})$ with $c > 1$. Then there are two positive constants r_1 and r_2 and $n_0 > 0$ such that for each $\ddot{n} > n_0$, there exist $\mathcal{H} \in \mathcal{CH}$ with $\bar{n} = \ddot{n}$, two hyperedges I and J in $\mathcal{H}$ and an index p for which $r_1(\log \bar{n})^{c-1} \leq p < \bar{n}$ and $r_2(\log \bar{n})^{c-1} \leq (q-p) < \bar{n}$, where $q = |\bar{I} \textcircled{p} \bar{J}|$. In other words, a super-polynomial growth of $\widetilde{m}^d$ is determined by an (at least) logarithmically increasing number of "tangled" intersection patterns for the complement hyperedges.

The advantage of the upper bound $\widetilde{m}^d$ is that one knows in advance how complex it would be to solve Dualization. In addition, the upper bound $\widetilde{m}^d$ can be exploited to introduce some cuts during the execution of dualization algorithms. Obviously this advantage is real only if the upper bound results to be tight. The above-described necessary condition for its super-polynomial growth witnesses that the bound is not at all trivial: indeed, the condition requires that the hyperedges have intricate overlappings. Furthermore, some experiments carried out in [16] show that the upper bound is indeed tight in practice – the only case it provides a loose estimation is when the hypergraph contains singleton hyperedges but, as shown in the paper, this anomaly can be easily eliminated by suitably removing all singleton hyperedges.

The experiments conducted in [16] refer to an interesting application of Dualization: the problem of finding minimal infrequent itemsets in data mining applications, that is illustrated next. Think of V as a set of generic objects, called *items*. Then, any non-empty subset of V corresponds to an *itemset* and a (*transactional*) *database* $\mathcal{D}$ over V (also called *dataset*) is a bag of itemsets (called *transactions*), which may occur duplicated in $\mathcal{D}$ – say that the number of duplicates of a transaction $I \in \mathcal{D}$ is $\delta(I)$. Given an itemset $I \subseteq V$, the *support* of I in $\mathcal{D}$ is $\sigma^{\mathcal{D}}(I) = \sum_{J \in \mathcal{D} \wedge I \subseteq J} \delta(J)$, that is the number of transaction duplicates in $\mathcal{D}$ containing I. The so-called *anti-monotonicity property* holds: if $I \subset J$ then $\sigma^{\mathcal{D}}(I) \geq \sigma^{\mathcal{D}}(J)$. Given a support threshold $\sigma > 0$, I is called a σ-*frequent* itemset in $\mathcal{D}$ if $\sigma^{\mathcal{D}}(I) > \sigma$; otherwise I is σ-*infrequent*. To characterize the σ-frequent/infrequent itemsets, by the anti-monotonicity property, it is sufficient to enumerate the maximal (inclusion-wise) σ-frequent itemsets and the minimal σ-infrequent itemsets. Assume that the set of maximal σ-frequent itemsets, say E, is given. As evidenced in [3,15], by considering E as a set of hyperedges on V, the minimal σ-infrequent itemsets coincide with the minimal transversals of the hypergraph $(V, \overline{E})$, where $\overline{E}$ is the set of the complementary hyperedges in E.

The experiments described in Appendix A of [16] show that the parameter $\kappa(\mathcal{H}) = \log_{\bar{n}}(m_2^d + \widetilde{m}_{3+}^d)$ is small in typical frequent/infrequent applications: its value slightly exceeds 3 only in one case and for two thirds of the cases the value is less than 2. In the same appendix, an empirical analysis of the parameter κ over twelve real datasets confirms that the parameter value is greater than

3 (actually, 3.12) only for one dataset whereas is much lower for the others. This fact s uggests using the parameter κ to single out hypergraph families for which the number of minimal transversals is polynomial: fixed a rational constant k, a (not necessarily Sperner) hypergraph $\mathcal{H} = (V, E)$ is k-bounded if $\kappa(\mathcal{H}) \leq k$. If $\mathcal{H}$ is not Sperner then $\kappa(\mathcal{H})$ is defined to be equal to $\kappa(\check{\mathcal{H}})$, where $\check{\mathcal{H}}$ is the inclusion reduction of $\mathcal{H}$. Obviously recognizing whether $\mathcal{H}$ is k-bounded can be done in polynomial time. By exploiting the structure of the formula for computing the upper bound $\widetilde{m}^d$, we present an algorithm that computes the minimal transversals of a k-bounded hypergraph in polynomial time.

We stress that our k-boundedness definition is different from other definition used in the literature, in particular hypergraphs with (k, r)-bounded intersections in which the intersection of any k distinct hyperedges has size at most r. In the case that $k + r$ is less than or equal to a given constant, all minimal transversals can be computed in incremental polynomial time as proven in [18]. Thus, the complexity of a finding a first minimal transversal or a new one (duality problem) is polynomial, but the overall complexity may be exponential as the number of minimal transversals can be exponential. Instead this number is guaranteed to be polynomial for hypergraphs that are k-bounded according to our definition.

It is worth noting that there is a sort of complementarity between the two definitions of boundedness for a hypergraph $\mathcal{H}$: (k, r)-boundedness of [18] fixes bounds to the intersections of the hyperedges in $\mathcal{H}$, whereas the bounds in our definition concern the intersections of the complement hyperedges. For a (k, r)-bounded hypergraph, every duality problem instance is solved in polynomial time but this resolution must be iterated for a number of times that can be exponential. Instead, for a k- bounded hypergraph according to our definition, every duality problem cannot be in general solved in polynomial time, but the number of iterations is limited as the number of minimal transversals is polynomial.

We observe that another notion of k-bounded hypergraphs has been introduced in [5] with the goal of investigating dualization complexity in the framework of fixed-parameter tractability (FPT) – a problem with input size s and another input parameter k is in FPT if it can be solved in $O(f(k)\,p(n))$ time, where f is any computable function and p is a polynomial [7,11]. The dualization problem dealt with concerns hypergraphs with a limited rank r – the *rank* of a hypergraph $\mathcal{H}$ is the largest number of vertices in an edge of $\mathcal{H}$. The problem is stated as: given a hypergraph $\mathcal{H}$ with a fixed rank r and a number k, is there some minimal transversal with more than k vertices? In [5] it is shown that this problem is in FPT and that computing all minimal transversals with at most k vertices can be done in $O(r^k\,p(s))$, where $p(s)$ is a polynomial in the size s of $\mathcal{H}$.

We extend the notion of hypergraph by adding a function δ associating a natural number to every hyperedge, which indicates the number of occurrences of the hyperedge. We then define a *duplicated-hyperedge hypergraph* $\mathcal{H}$ as a triple (V, E, δ) and apply the notion of *support* to hyperedges: given any $K \subseteq V$ (not necessarily in E), $\sigma^{\mathcal{H}}(K) = \sum_{I \in E \wedge K \subseteq I} \delta(I)$, that is the the number of duplicated hyperedges in E containing K. It turns out that the problem of discovering σ-frequent/infrequent itemsets can be directly formulated in terms of hypergraph.

We next reverse the frequent itemset perspective of the problem in a way that the role of σ-infrequent itemsets (thus minimal transversals) becomes crucial.

We are given $\mathcal{H} = (V, E, \delta)$ together with two natural numbers $\sigma^d \geq 0$ and $\omega > 0$. The *Frequent-Infrequent Duplicated Hypergraph Problem* (FIDHy for short) consists of deciding whether there exists a duplicated hypergraph $\widehat{\mathcal{H}} = (V, \widehat{E}, \hat{\delta})$ such that (1) $\sum_{I \in \widehat{E}} \hat{\delta}(I) = \omega$, (2) for each $I \in E$, $\sigma^{\widehat{\mathcal{H}}}(I) = \delta(I)$ and (3) for each minimal transversal I of the complement hypergraph $(V, \overline{E})$ of $\mathcal{H}$, $\sigma^{\widehat{\mathcal{H}}}(I) \leq \sigma^d$.

Observe that FIDHy formulates the classical *inverse frequent itemset mining* problem (IFM) (i.e., finding a transactional database $\mathcal{D}$ satisfying given support constraints on the itemsets in E, that are typically the frequent ones, see [4,20]) with an additional infrequency constraint on the set E' of the itemsets that are neither in E nor subsets of some itemset in E. The infrequent itemsets in E' must have their supports below a given threshold, say σ^d. This version of the problem, called IFM with infrequency support constraint (IFM$_I$ for short), has been first proposed in [16][1]. By the anti-monotonicity property, it is sufficient to enforce the infrequency support constraint to the minimal itemsets in E', which correspond to the minimal transversals of the complement of the hypergraph $\mathcal{H}$. It turns out that FIDHy is the hypergraph formulation of IFM$_I$.

In this paper we prove that FIDHy (thus the decision complexity of IFM$_I$) is NEXP-complete. But this high complexity result can be scaled down as follows.

First, because of the strong relationships with frequent itemset applications, we consider the case that the input duplicated hypergraph $\mathcal{H} = (V, E, \delta)$ is k-bounded, for a given rational constant k: the set of all such instances is called the k-*Bounded* FIDHy *Problem*, k-FIDHy for short. The set of IFM$_I$ instances corresponding to the instances of k-FIDHy is called the k-IFM$_I$ problem. We prove that k-FIDHy (aka, the decision k-IFM$_I$ problem) is in PSPACE and NP-hard.

We can make a further step to reduce the complexity of the problem by relaxing the integer restriction to the range of the function $\hat{\delta}$. We call this version of the problem *relaxed k-FIDHy* and prove that it is NP-complete.

Despite we have reduced its complexity from NEXP to NP, the problem remains intractable. Nevertheless, an approximate solution approach for k-IFM$_I$ has been proposed in [16], which has been shown in a large number of experiments to be very effective in solving large instances of both synthesized and real datasets.

The remainder of this paper is organized as follows. In Sect. 2 we present the upper bound on the number of minimal transversals. In Sect. 3 we formulate IFM$_I$ and prove that deciding whether there exists a feasible database is NEXP-complete. In the same section we also introduce k-IFM$_I$, prove its complexity and illustrate our conjecture that the parameter κ is small for real transaction databases. Finally, in Sect. 4, we draw the conclusion. For space reason, the proofs of most of the theorems and propositions stated in the paper are placed in an online appendix [23].

---

[1] A preliminary version of this paper is a companion manuscript for [16].

2   Upper Bound on the Number of Minimal Transversals

Given a set of vertices V, any (possibly empty or improper) subset of V is called a *hyperedge* on V.[2] A *hypergraph* is a pair $\mathcal{H} = (V, E)$, where V is a non-empty finite set of vertices and $E \subseteq 2^V$ is a non-empty set of hyperedges on V. $\mathcal{H}$ is a *Sperner hypergraph* if for each two distinct hyperedges I and J in E, $I \not\subseteq J$ – let $n = |V| > 0$, $m = |E| > 0$. The Sperner hypergraph $\breve{\mathcal{H}} = (V, \breve{E})$ that is obtained from $\mathcal{H}$ by removing all hyperedges that are not minimal (i.e., $\breve{E} = \{I | I \in E \wedge \nexists J \in E : J \subsetneq I\}$) is called the *inclusion reduction* of $\mathcal{H}$. Obviously, if $\emptyset \in E$ then $\breve{E} = \{\emptyset\}$.

For each $I \subseteq V$, let $\bar{I} = V \setminus I$ be the *complement hyperedge* of I. Let $\overline{V}$ denote $\cup_{I \in E} \bar{I}$ and $\bar{n} = |\overline{V}| \leq n$ be the number of vertices that are not included in all hyperedges in E. In addition, $\bar{n}_2 = |\overline{V}_2|$, where $\overline{V}_2 = \{\{v_1, v_2\} | \exists I \in E : \{v_1, v_2\} \subseteq \bar{I}\}$ consists of all vertex pairs that are not included in all hyperedges.

Given a hypergraph $\mathcal{H} = (V, E)$, a subset I of V that intersects every hyperedge in E is a *transversal* (or *hitting set*) of $\mathcal{H}$ and it is a *minimal transversal* if no subset of I is a transversal. The *dual* of $\mathcal{H}$ is the hypergraph $\mathcal{H}^d = (V, E^d)$ such that E^d is the set of all minimal transversals of $\mathcal{H}$ – obviously, $\mathcal{H}^d$ is a Sperner hypergraph. We have that (i) $\mathcal{H}^d = (\breve{\mathcal{H}})^d$ and (ii) if $E^d \neq \emptyset$ then $(\mathcal{H}^d)^d = \breve{\mathcal{H}}$. Observe that $E^d = \emptyset$ if and only if E contains the empty hyperedge.

Let $\mathcal{H}^d = (V, E^d)$ be the dual of a hypergraph $\mathcal{H} = (V, E)$. We denote $m^d = |E^d|$ and for each $i > 0$, $m_i^d = |E_i^d|$, where E_i^d is the set of minimal transversals having i vertices. We point out that, if $m = 1$ (i.e., $E = \{I\}$), then the value of m^d is trivially known: $m^d = 0$ if $I = \emptyset$ or $m^d = m_1^d = |I|$ otherwise. We next focus on the case that $m > 1$ by assuming that $\mathcal{H}$ is a Sperner hypergraph – then E cannot contain the empty hyperedge.

Proposition 1. *Let $\mathcal{H} = (V, E)$ be a Sperner hypergraph with $m > 1$. Then $m_1^d = n - \bar{n}$ and $m_2^d = \bar{n}(\bar{n} - 1)/2 - \bar{n}_2$.*   ∎

An upper bound $\widetilde{m}^d$ to m^d can be defined as $\widetilde{m}^d = m_1^d + m_2^d + \widetilde{m}_{3+}^d$, where $\widetilde{m}_{3+}^d$ is an upper bound to the number of minimal transversals with at least 3 vertices. To compute $\widetilde{m}_{3+}^d$, we define an upper bound $\widetilde{m}_i^d$ to m_i^d, $\forall i \geq 3$. To this end, we first need some additional definitions and notation:

- $\forall i: 1 < i < m$, $\overline{V}[i]$ is the set of all vertices in $\overline{V}$ that are contained into at least i hyperedge complements, i.e., in at most $m - i$ hyperedges in $\mathcal{H}$;
- $\forall I, J \in E$, $J \neq I$, and $\forall i, 1 < i < m$: $\bar{I} \overline{\cap} \bar{J} = \bar{I} \cap \bar{J} \cap \overline{V}[i]$, i.e., a vertex is in $\bar{I} \overline{\cap} \bar{J}$ if and only if it is contained in at most $m - i$ hyperedges in $\mathcal{H}$ and is neither in I nor in J – note that $\bar{I} \overline{\cap} \bar{J} = \bar{I} \cap \bar{J}$;
- $\forall I \in E$ and $\forall i, 1 < i < m$, $\bar{I}[i] = \cup_{J \in E, J \neq I: |\bar{I} \overline{\cap} \bar{J}| \geq i-1} (\bar{I} \overline{\cap} \bar{J})$, i.e., the vertices in $\bar{I} \overline{\cap} \bar{J}$ are included into $\bar{I}[i]$ only if $|\bar{I} \overline{\cap} \bar{J}| \geq i - 1$.

Theorem 1. *Let a Sperner hypergraph $\mathcal{H} = (V, E)$ with $m > 1$ be given. Let J be a minimal transversal of $\mathcal{H}$ with cardinality $p + 1$, where $p \geq 2$, i.e., J is a*

---

[2] Other hypergraph definitions require a hyperedge not to be empty.

hyperedge with at least three vertices. Take any ordering of the vertices in J, say $v_1, \ldots, v_{p+1}$, and let J_i denote $J \setminus \{v_i\}$, $\forall i, 1 \leq i \leq p+1$. Then $p < m$ and there exist $p+1$ distinct hyperedges $I_1, \ldots, I_{p+1}$ in $\mathcal{H}$ such that $\forall i, 1 \leq i \leq p+1$:

1. *$J_i \subseteq \bar{I}_i$ (i.e., $J_i \cap I_i = \emptyset$) and $J \not\subseteq \bar{I}_i$ (i.e., $v_i \in I_i$);*
2. *$\forall j, 1 \leq j \leq p+1$ and $i \neq j$, $J \setminus \{v_i, v_j\} \subseteq \bar{I}_i \mathbin{\textcircled{p}} \bar{I}_j$ and $v_j \in \bar{I}_i[p]$.*

Proof. Let us first prove by contradiction that there exist $p + 1$ hyperedges $I_1, \ldots, I_{p+1}$ in E such that $\forall i, 1 \leq i \leq p + 1$, $J_i \subseteq \bar{I}_i$. Suppose not. Then for some i, J_i intersects every hyperedge $I \in E$. Hence J_i is a transversal of $\mathcal{H}$ and we get a contradiction with the hypothesis that J is a minimal transversal of H. It follows that there are $p + 1$ hyperedges $I_1, \ldots, I_{p+1}$ in E such that $\forall i, 1 \leq i \leq p+1$, $J_i \subseteq \bar{I}_i$. We again proceed by contradiction to show that the hyperedges $I_1, \ldots, I_{p+1}$ are distinct. Suppose then that there are two distinct indices i and j such that $I_i = I_j$. We have $\bar{I}_i = J \setminus \{v_i\}$, $\bar{I}_j = J \setminus \{v_j\}$ and $v_i \neq v_j$ by hypothesis. But we have previously proved that $J \setminus \{v_i\} \subseteq \bar{I}_i$ and $J \setminus \{v_j\} \subseteq \bar{I}_j$. So, from $\bar{I}_i = \bar{I}_j$ it follows that that $J \subseteq \bar{I}_i$ and, therefore, J is not a transversal of $\mathcal{H}$ as it does not intersect I_i – a contradiction. So I_i and I_j must be distinct and, then, $p < m$. In addition, as we have previously proved that $J_i \subseteq \bar{I}_j$ and $J \not\subseteq \bar{I}_i$, part (1) is proved as well.

Consider now any two I_i and I_j, with $i \neq j$. We have that $J \setminus \{v_i\} \subseteq \bar{I}_i$ and $J \setminus \{v_j\} \subseteq \bar{I}_j$ with $v_i \neq v_j$; hence, $J_{i,j} = J \setminus \{v_i, v_j\} \subseteq \bar{I}_i \cap \bar{I}_j$. Take now any $v_k \in J_{i,j}$. By part (1), I_k is different from both I_i and I_j; in addition, v_k is not contained in every I_q, with $q \neq k$ and, then, it is contained in at most $m - p$ hyperedges of H. It follows that each of the $p - 1$ vertices in $J_{i,j}$ is contained in at most $m-p$ hyperedges in H. Therefore $J_{i,j} \subseteq \bar{I}_i \mathbin{\textcircled{p}} \bar{I}_j$. It also follows that each $v_q \in J_{i,j} = J_i \setminus \{v_j\}$ is in $\bar{I}_i[p]$. To conclude the proof of part (2) we have to show that also $v_j \in \bar{I}_i[p]$. To this end, observe that $J_i \setminus \{v_j\}$ is not empty as $p \geq 2$. Then there exists some I_k, with $k \neq i$ and $k \neq j$, such that $J \setminus \{v_i, v_k\} \subseteq \bar{I}_i \mathbin{\textcircled{p}} \bar{I}_k$. It follows that $v_j \in \bar{I}_i[p]$. $\square$

We are now ready to define an upper bound $\tilde{m}^d_{p+1}$ to m^d_{p+1}, $1 < p < m$:

$$\tilde{m}^d_{p+1} = \frac{2}{p\,(p+1)} \cdot \sum_{\substack{I,J \in E, I < J: \\ |\bar{I} \mathbin{\textcircled{p}} J| \geq p-1}} \binom{|\bar{I} \mathbin{\textcircled{p}} \bar{J}|}{p-1} \cdot |\bar{I}[p] \cap J| \cdot |\bar{J}[p] \cap I|. \tag{1}$$

Note that $I < J$ refers to any lexicographic ordering of the hyperedges that simply avoids two hyperedges to be considered twice in the above summation.

Theorem 2. *For each p such that $1 < p < m$, $m^d_{p+1} \leq \tilde{m}^d_{p+1}$.*   ∎

The next proposition provides some insights on the values that can be taken by our bounds to the number of minimal transversals.

Proposition 2. *Let $f(\bar{n})$ be a function expressing $\sum_{p=2}^{m-1} \tilde{m}^d_{p+1}$ in terms of the value of $\bar{n}$ of a Sperner hypergraph $\mathcal{H}$. Then $f(\bar{n}) \in \mathcal{O}(2^{\bar{n} \log \bar{n}})$.*

Let $\mathcal{CH}$ be any family of Sperner hypergraphs for which $f(\bar{n}) \in \Omega(2^{(\log \bar{n})^c})$ with $c > 1$. Then there are two positive constants r_1 and r_2 and $n_0 > 0$ such that for each $\ddot{n} > n_0$, there exist $\mathcal{H} \in \mathcal{CH}$ with $\bar{n} = \ddot{n}$, two hyperedges I and J in $\mathcal{H}$ and an index p for which (i) $r_1(\log \bar{n})^{c-1} \le p < \bar{n}$ and $r_2(\log \bar{n})^{c-1} \le (q - p) < \bar{n}$, where $q = |\bar{I} \cap \bar{J}|$, and (ii) both $\bar{I}[p] \cap J$ and $\bar{J}[p] \cap I$ are not empty. ∎

As shown in Example 1 below, $\sum_{p=2}^{m-1} \tilde{m}_{p+1}^d$ may get a value of the order of $2^{\bar{n} \log \bar{n}}$, which is greater than $2^{\bar{n}}$ (the maximum number of minimal transversals). Thus Proposition 2 states that our estimation of the exponential growth of the number of minimal transversals may only add a logarithmic factor in the exponent. On the other hand, the proposition points out that a super-polynomial growth of the bound is determined by rather "tangled" intersection patterns for the complement hyperedges, which involve an (at least) logarithmically increasing number of them.

Example 1. Let $\mathcal{H} = (V, E)$, where $V = \{a_1, \ldots, a_n, b_1, \ldots, b_n\}$, $E = \{(a_1, b_1), (a_2, b_2), \ldots, (a_n, b_n)\}$ and $n \ge 3$. It is easy to see that a minimal transversal is an hyperedge $(x_1, \ldots, x_n)$ such that for each i, $1 \le i \le n$, x_i is either a_i or b_i. Then the number of minimal transversals is $m^d = m_n^d = 2^n$, i.e., $\mathcal{H}$ is exponential even though it is $(1, 2)$-bounded according to the definition of [18]. Let us now compute $\tilde{m}_n^d$ using the formula (1). We set $p = n - 1$ to preserve the same notation of this formula; therefore, $\tilde{m}_{p+1}^d$ is equal to $\tilde{m}_n^d$. We have that for each I, J in E, $|\bar{I} \cap \bar{J}| = 2n - 4$. Then the term inside the summation in the formula (1) becomes:

$$\binom{|\bar{I} \cap \bar{J}|}{p - 1} \cdot |\bar{I}[p] \cap J| \cdot |\bar{J}[p] \cap I| = \binom{2n - 4}{n - 2} \cdot 2 \cdot 2 = 4 \binom{2n - 4}{n - 2}.$$

Then, by multiplying the above value by $n(n - 1)/2$ (the number of pairs I, J in E), we obtain the value of the overall summation term. Further on, by multiplying this result by the initial formula term $\frac{2}{p(p+1)} = \frac{2}{(n-1)n}$, we obtain the value of $\tilde{m}_n^d$:

$$\tilde{m}_n^d = \frac{2}{(n - 1)n} \cdot \frac{(n - 1)n}{2} \cdot 4 \cdot \binom{2n - 4}{n - 2} = 4 \cdot \prod_{i=0}^{n-3} \frac{2n - 4 - i}{n - 2 - i}.$$

We have that for each i, $0 \le i \le n - 3$, $2 \le \frac{2n-4-i}{n-2-i} \le n - 1$. Therefore, $4 \cdot 2^{n-2} = 2^n < \tilde{m}_n^d < 4 \cdot (n - 1)^{n-2} = 2^{(n-2)\log(n-1)+2}$. □

Example 2. Let $V = \{a_1, \ldots, a_n, b_1, \ldots, b_n, c_1, \ldots, c_n\}$ and $E = \bigcup_{i=1}^n \{V \setminus \{a_i, b_i\}, V \setminus \{a_i, c_i\}, V \setminus \{b_i, c_i\}\}$. Then the minimal transversals are the hyperedges $\{a_i, b_i, c_i\}$, $1 \le i \le n$. To give some intuition on this property, consider the case $n = 2$. We have $V = \{a_1, a_2, b_1, b_2, c_1, c_2\}$ and $E = \{\{a_2, b_2, c_1, c_2\}, \{a_2, b_1, b_2, c_2\}, \{a_1, a_2, b_2, c_2\}, \{a_1, b_1, c_1, c_2\}, \{a_1, b_1, b_2, c_1\}, \{a_1, a_2, b_1, c_1\}\}$. It is easy to see that the minimal transversals are $\{a_1, b_1, c_1\}$ and $\{a_2, b_2, c_2\}$.

It turns out that the number of minimal transversals is $m^d = m_3^d = n$. To compute $\tilde{m}_3^d = \tilde{m}_{p+1}^d$ for $p = 2$, we set $\bar{E} = \{\bar{I} \mid I \in E\}$ equal to $\bigcup_{i=1}^n \bar{E}_i$, where

$\bar{E}_i = \{\{a_i, b_i\}, \{a_i, c_i\}, \{b_i, c_i\}\}$. It is easy to see that for any two distinct $\bar{E}_{i_1}$ and $\bar{E}_{i_2}$, every hyperedge in $\bar{E}_{i_1}$ is disjoint from all hyperedges in $\bar{E}_{i_2}$; so, only hyperedges in the same $\bar{E}_i$ contribute to the computation of the formula 1. Then, by also considering that $\bar{I} \cap \bar{J} = \overline{I \cap J}$, we can rewrite the formula as:

$$\tilde{m}_3^d = \sum_{i=1}^{n} \frac{2}{2 \cdot 3} \cdot \sum_{\bar{I}, \bar{J} \in \bar{E}_i, \bar{I} \neq \bar{J}:}^{|\bar{I} \cap \bar{J}| \geq 1} \binom{1}{1} \cdot 1 \cdot 1 = \sum_{i=1}^{n} \frac{1}{3} \cdot 3 \cdot \binom{1}{1} = n$$

Note that the above computation takes into account that $\bar{I} \cap \bar{J} = \overline{I \cap J}$. □

Example 3. Let $V = \{a_1, \ldots, a_{2n}\}$ and $E = \{\{a_1\}, \ldots, \{a_{2n}\}\}$. It is easy to see that there is a unique minimal transversal that coincides with V, i.e., $m^d = m_{2n}^d = 1$. However, $\tilde{m}_{2n}^d$ is exponential in n as shown nest. Let us compute $\tilde{m}^d \geq \tilde{m}_{2n}^d$ using the formula (1). We set $p = n - 1$ to preserve the same notation of this formula; therefore, $\tilde{m}_{p+1}^d$ is equal to $\tilde{m}_n^d$. We have that for each I, J in E, $|\bar{I} \cap \bar{J}| = 2n - 2$. Then the term inside the summation in the formula (1) becomes:

$$\binom{|\bar{I} \cap \bar{J}|}{p-1} \cdot |I[p] \cap J| \cdot |J[p] \cap I| = \binom{2n-2}{n-2} \cdot 1 \cdot 1 = \binom{2n-2}{n-2}.$$

Then, by multiplying the above value by $2n(2n-1)/2 = n(2n-1)$ (the number of pairs I, J in E), we obtain the value of the overall summation term. Further on, by multiplying this result by the initial formula term $\frac{2}{p(p+1)} = \frac{2}{(n-1)n}$, we obtain the value of $\tilde{m}_n^d$:

$$\tilde{m}_n^d = \frac{2}{(n-1)n} \cdot n \cdot (2n-1) \cdot \binom{2n-2}{n-2} = \frac{2(2n-1)}{n-1} \cdot \prod_{i=0}^{n-3} \frac{2n-2-i}{n-2-i}.$$

We have that for each i, $0 \leq i \leq n-3$, $\frac{2n-2-i}{n-2-i} \geq 2$ and $\frac{2n-i}{n-i} > 2$. Therefore, $\tilde{m}_n^d \geq 2^n$. The bound produces an anomalous overestimation in the presence of singleton hyperedges. But the anomaly can be easily eliminated by removing any singleton hyperedge and its vertex, say a_1, from the other hyperedges, thus obtaining the hypergraph $\mathcal{H}'$. The minimal transversals of $\mathcal{H}$ are obtained by adding a to every minimal transversal of $\mathcal{H}'$. The removal can be iterated for all other singleton hyperedges so that we either all hyperedges are removed (as in the example) or a hypergraph with no singleton hyperedges is eventually obtained. □

In order to introduce an overall upper bound $\tilde{m}^d$ to the number m^d of minimal transversals, as the number of minimal transversals with less than 3 vertices is exactly known, we next define an upper bound $\tilde{m}_{3+}^d$ to the number m_{3+}^d of minimal transversals with 3 or more vertices:

$$\tilde{m}_{3+}^d = \tilde{m}_3^d + \sum_{p=3}^{r-1} \ddot{m}_{p+1}^d \tag{2}$$

where $\widetilde{m}_3^d$ is defined by formula (1), $r = \min(m, \bar{n})$ and $\ddot{m}_{p+1}^d$ is defined as:

$$\ddot{m}_{p+1}^d = \frac{2}{p\,(p+1)} \cdot \sum_{\substack{I,J \in E, I < J: \\ |\bar{I}_{\!\lceil p \rceil} \bar{J}| \geq p-1}} c_{IJp} \cdot |\bar{I}[p] \cap J| \cdot |\bar{J}[p] \cap I|$$

where c_{IJp} is equal (i) to 0 if $\binom{|\bar{I}_{\lceil p\rceil}\bar{J}|}{p-1} \leq \binom{|\bar{I}_{\lceil p\rceil}\bar{J}|}{p-2}$ or (ii) to $\binom{|\bar{I}_{\lceil p\rceil}\bar{J}|}{p-1} - \binom{|\bar{I}_{\lceil p\rceil}\bar{J}|}{p-2}$ otherwise. Observe that the case (i) arises if and only if $q - 2p + 3 \leq 0$ and that the value of c_{IJp} for the case (ii) is actually equal to $\binom{|\bar{I}_{\lceil p\rceil}\bar{J}|}{p-1} \cdot \frac{q-2p+3}{q-p+2}$.

Theorem 3. *Let $\mathcal{H} = (V, E)$ be a Sperner hypergraph. If $\emptyset \in E$ then $\widetilde{m}^d = m^d = 0$, otherwise $\widetilde{m}^d = m_1^d + m_2^d + \widetilde{m}_{3+}^d$ is an upper bound to the number m^d of minimal transversals, where m_1^d and m_2^d are the numbers of minimal transversals with respectively 1 and 2 vertices (see Proposition 1) and $\widetilde{m}_{3+}^d$ is defined by formula (2) and can be computed in time $\mathcal{O}(n \cdot m^2)$.* ∎

We define a parameter κ as a function from the set of all hypergraphs $2^{\mathcal{H}}$ to $\mathcal{Q} \cup \{-\infty\}$, where $\mathcal{Q}$ is the set of rational numbers. For each $\mathcal{H} \in 2^{\mathcal{H}}$, $\kappa(\mathcal{H}) = \log_{\bar{n}}(m_2^d + \widetilde{m}_{3+}^d)$ if $\mathcal{H}$ is a Sperner hypergraph[3], or $\kappa(\mathcal{H}) = \kappa(\breve{\mathcal{H}})$ otherwise. Then we can state that an upper bound to the number m^d of minimal transversals of a hypergraph $\mathcal{H}$ is $\widetilde{m}^d = m_1^d + \bar{n}^{\kappa(\mathcal{H})}$. Note that $\kappa(\mathcal{H})$ is either equal to $-\infty$ or ≥ 0. Our conjecture is that the parameter is small in practice (between 1.5 and 3.5) for hypergraphs corresponding to maximal frequent itemsets.

Definition 1. *Let a rational number k be fixed. Then every hypergraph $\mathcal{H}$ for which $\kappa(\mathcal{H}) \leq k$ is called a k-bounded hypergraph.*

Proposition 3. *Given a rational number k and a hypergraph $\mathcal{H} = (V, E)$, deciding whether $\mathcal{H}$ is k-bounded can be done in time $\mathcal{O}(n \cdot m^2)$. In addition, if k is a constant and $\mathcal{H}$ is a k-bounded hypergraph then the number of minimal transversals of $\mathcal{H}$ is polynomial in n.* ∎

Theorem 4. *Let k be a rational constant and $\mathcal{H} = (V, E)$ be a k-bounded hypergraph. Then the minimal transversals of $\mathcal{H}$ can be computed in time polynomial in n and m.* ∎

3   Hypergraph Formulation of Inverse Frequent Itemset Mining with Infrequency Constraints

A *duplicated-hyperedge hypergraph* $\mathcal{H}$ is a triple (V, E, δ), where (V, E) is a hypergraph for which $\emptyset \notin E$ and $\delta : E \rightarrow \mathbb{N}$ is a function associating a natural number to every hyperedge in E – for each $I \in E$, $\delta(I)$ indicates the number of occurrences of the hyperedge I. Given any $K \subseteq V$ (not necessarily in E), $\sigma^{\mathcal{H}}(K) = \sum_{I \in E \wedge K \subseteq I} \delta(I)$ denotes the *support* of K in $\mathcal{H}$, that is the the number of duplicated hyperedges in E containing K. Observe that the so-called *anti-monotonicity property* holds: if $I \subset J$ then $\sigma^{\mathcal{H}}(I) \geq \sigma^{\mathcal{H}}(J)$.

---

[3] We assume that $\log_{\bar{n}} \widetilde{m}_{3+}^d$ is equal to $-\infty$ if $\widetilde{m}_{3+}^d = 0$ or it is rounded up to a fixed number of decimal places otherwise.

Definition 2. Let $\mathcal{H} = (V, E, \delta)$ be a duplicated-hyperedge hypergraph and $\sigma^d \geq 0$ and $\omega > 0$ be two natural numbers. Let $\overline{\mathcal{H}} = (V, \overline{E})$ be the complement hypergraph of (V, E), where $\overline{E} = \{\overline{I} \mid I \in E\}$. The *Frequent-Infrequent Duplicated Hypergraph Problem* (FIDHy for short) consists of deciding whether there exists a duplicated hypergraph $\widehat{\mathcal{H}} = (V, \widehat{E}, \widehat{\delta})$ such that (1) $\sum_{I \in \widehat{E}} \widehat{\delta}(I) = \omega$, (2) for each $I \in E$, $\sigma^{\widehat{\mathcal{H}}}(I) = \delta(I)$ and (3) for each $I \in \overline{E}^d$ (i.e., for each minimal transversal of the complement of $\mathcal{H}$), $\sigma^{\widehat{\mathcal{H}}}(I) \leq \sigma^d$.

This apparently "abstruse" problem has an important application in data mining, if we think of the hypergraph vertices in V as generic objects, called *items*. Then, any non-empty subset of V corresponds to an *itemset* (i.e., a set of items) and a duplicated-hyperedge hypergraph $\mathcal{H} = (V, E, \delta)$ represents a (*transactional*) database $\mathcal{D}$ over V (also called *dataset*), that is a bag of itemsets (called *transactions*), which may occur duplicated in $\mathcal{D}$ – thus, a hyperedge $I \in E$ is a transaction and $\delta(I)$ is its number of duplicates. The *size* of $\mathcal{D}$ is the total number of transaction duplicates $\sum_{I \in E} \delta(I)$. Given an itemset I, the support of I in $\mathcal{D}$, denoted by $\sigma^{\mathcal{D}}(I)$, coincides with $\sigma^{\mathcal{H}}(I)$.

Given a support threshold $\sigma > 0$, I is called a σ-*frequent* itemset in $\mathcal{D}$ if $\sigma^{\mathcal{D}}(I) > \sigma$; otherwise I is σ-*infrequent*. A popular mining task over transaction databases is to single out the set of the σ-*frequent itemsets*. This problem has attracted relevant research efforts, and several solution approaches and generalizations have indeed been discussed in the literature [1,15,19]. The problem can be formulated in terms of hypergraph as: given a duplicated-hyperedge hypergraph $\mathcal{H} = (V, E, \delta)$, find all hyperedges K on V for which $\sigma^{\mathcal{H}}(K) > \sigma$.

The perspective of the frequent itemset mining problem can be naturally inverted as follows. We are given in advance a natural number $\omega > 0$ and a set E of (frequent) itemsets together with their minimal and maximal support constraints: the goal is to decide whether there is a transaction database with size ω satisfying the above constraints (and, of course, compute the database whenever the answer is positive). This problem, called the *inverse frequent itemset mining* problem (IFM), has been introduced in the context of defining generators for benchmarks of mining algorithms [20], and its computational properties have been investigated: in particular, decision IFM has been proved to be NP-hard and in PSPACE (see, e.g., [4,20]).

Table 1. Examples of feasible databases for an IFM instance

$E_i \in E$	σ^{E_i}
$\{a, b\}$	100
$\{b, c\}$	100
$\{c, d\}$	50
ω	170

$\{a, b, c\}$	70
$\{b, c, d\}$	10
$\{a, b\}$	30
$\{b, c\}$	20
$\{c, d\}$	40

$\{a, b, c\}$	40
$\{b, c, d\}$	40
$\{a, b\}$	60
$\{b, c\}$	20
$\{c, d\}$	10

(a) Constraints   (b) Database $\mathcal{D}_1$ (c) Database $\mathcal{D}_2$

As an example, given $\mathcal{I} = \{a, b, c, d\}$ and $E = \{\{a, b\}, \{b, c\}, \{c, d\}\}$, consider the support constraints represented in Table 1-a. The itemsets $E_1 = \{a, b\}$ and $E_2 = \{b, c\}$ must occur in exactly 100 transactions (possibly as sub-transactions) and the itemset $E_3 = \{c, d\}$ must occur in exactly 50 transactions. We also assume that the database size (i.e., the total number of transactions) must be 170.

A feasible database $\mathcal{D}_1$ is shown in Table 1-b—the second column indicates the number of duplicates (occurrences) of every transaction. The first support constraint is satisfied by the transactions $\{a, b, c\}$ and $\{a, b\}$, the second one by the transactions $\{a, b, c\}$, $\{b, c, d\}$ and $\{b, c\}$ and the third one by the transactions $\{b, c, d\}$ and $\{c, d\}$.

The IFM problem can be formulated in terms of hypergraphs as follows: given a duplicated-hyperedge hypergraph $\mathcal{H} = (V, E, \delta)$, find a hypergraph $\widehat{\mathcal{H}} = (V, \hat{E}, \hat{\delta})$ such that for each $I \in E$, $\sigma^{\widehat{\mathcal{H}}}(I) = \delta(I)$. This corresponds to the FIDHy problem for the case that $\sigma^d \geq \omega$ so that condition (1) and (3) in Definition 2 trivially hold and, then, they can be removed.

IFM does not enforce any constraint on the itemsets that are neither in E nor subsets of some itemset in E – we call the set of such itemsets E'. It may therefore happen that $\mathcal{D}$ contains additional (and, perhaps, unsuspected or even undesired) frequent itemsets. For instance, the itemset $\{a, b, c\}$ in the database $\mathcal{D}_1$ of Table 1-b is in E' and turns out to be frequent with a support of 70. Note that in the example, E' consists of $\{a, b, c, d\}$ and all non-empty subsets of it, except $\{a, b\}$, $\{b, c\}$, $\{c, d\}$, $\{a\}$, $\{b\}$, $\{c\}$ and $\{d\}$.

Recently, a substantial extension to the original framework of IFM has been introduced in [16] that pertains to the role played by the itemsets I that are in E'. This formulation explicitly considers an extra input parameter σ' which defines a maximum support threshold over the itemsets in E' so that, by keeping the threshold small, itemsets in E' are constrained not to be frequent. This version of the problem is called *inverse frequent itemset mining problem with infrequency constraints* (IFM$_I$). The goal is to find a database $\mathcal{D}$ for which the supports on the itemsets both in E and in E' are satisfied. Such a solution may contain arbitrary transactions; however, by keeping the support σ' small, we can avoid these "extra" itemsets to become frequent in the solution database. Further extensions of IFM have been recently investigated in [25], including the formulation of the problem for generating NoSQL databases.

To enforce σ'-infrequency for the itemsets in E', by the anti-monotonicity property, it is sufficient to apply the constraint to the set of the minimal infrequent itemsets in E', called the *negative border* in the literature (see [15]). As evidenced in [3,15,16], the negative border coincides with the set of minimal transversals of the complement hypergraph $\overline{\mathcal{H}} = (V, \overline{E})$. It turns out that, by setting $\sigma^d = \sigma'$, the FIDHy problem is the hypergraph formulation of IFM$_I$. In the example the set of the minimal infrequent itemsets in E' is $\{\{a, c\}, \{a, d\}, \{b, d\}\}$. If we fix $\sigma' = 40$, a feasible database for IFM$_I$ is $\mathcal{D}_2$, shown in Table 1-c. The infrequency support constraint is satisfied as the supports of $\{a, c\}$, $\{a, d\}$, $\{b, d\}$ are respectively 40, 0 and 40.

The theorem below states that the Frequent-Infrequent Duplicated Hypergraph Problem is NEXP-complete. Recall that NEXP is the class of decision problems that can be solved by a non-deterministic Turing machine using time $\mathcal{O}(2^{p(n)})$ for some polynomial $p(n)$, where n is the size of the input (see [21]).

Theorem 5. *The* FIDHy *problem (aka, the decision* IFM$_I$ *problem) is* NEXP-*complete.*

Proof. The proof, included in the Appendix [23], uses some duality properties on hypergraph composition operators that we mention here for their potential general interest. Given two sets of hyperedges E_1 and E_2, let $E_1 \boxdot E_2$ denote the set of hyperedges $\{I \cup J \mid I \in E_1, J \in E_2\}$. Let $\mathcal{H}_1 = (V_1, E_1)$ and $\mathcal{H}_2 = (V_2, E_2)$ be two hypergraphs having distinct vertices, i.e., $V_1 \cap V_2 = \emptyset$. Then: (1) $\mathcal{H}_1 \cup \mathcal{H}_2$ denotes the hypergraph $(V_1 \cup V_2, E_1 \cup E_2)$ (*union*) and (2) $\mathcal{H}_1 \boxdot \mathcal{H}_2$ denotes the hypergraph $(V_1 \cup V_2, E_1 \boxdot E_2)$ (*product*). The following properties hold:

Lemma 1. *Let* $\mathcal{H}_1 = (V_1, E_1)$ *and* $\mathcal{H}_2 = (V_2, E_2)$ *be two hypergraphs with distinct vertices. Then:* $(\mathcal{H}_1 \cup \mathcal{H}_2)^d = \mathcal{H}_1^d \boxdot \mathcal{H}_2^d$ *and* $(\mathcal{H}_1 \boxdot \mathcal{H}_2)^d = \mathcal{H}_1^d \cup \mathcal{H}_2^d$. ∎

The proof of the lemma is reported in the Appendix [23] as well. We point out that the hardness proof of the Theorem is based on a reduction from the binary domain inverse OLAP problem studied in [24]. □

Consider now the case that the input duplicated hypergraph $\mathcal{H} = (V, E, \delta)$ is k-bounded, for a given rational constant k: the set of all such instances is called the *Frequent-Infrequent Duplicated k-Bounded Hypergraph Problem*, k-FIDHy for short. The set of IFM$_I$ instances corresponding to the instances of k-FIDHy is called the k-IFM$_I$ problem.

Proposition 4. *The* k-FIDHy *problem (aka, the decision* k-IFM$_I$ *problem) is in* PSPACE *and* NP-*hard.* ∎

As we argued in the Introduction, our conjecture is that $\kappa(x)$ is small in real instances of IFM$_I$ and that only very artificial instances get a parameter value much greater than 3, i.e., in practice real world instances of IFM$_I$ are indeed instances of 3-IFM$_I$. We next make a further step to reduce the complexity of the problem by relaxing the integer range of the function $\hat{\delta}$: we replace it with a function $\hat{\delta}_Q : \hat{E} \to Q^+$, where Q^+ is the set of non-negative rational numbers. We call this version of the problem *relaxed k-FIDHy*.

Proposition 5. *The relaxed* k-FIDHy *problem (aka, the decision relaxed* k-IFM$_I$ *problem) is* NP-*complete.* ∎

Despite we have reduced its complexity from NEXP of NP, the problem remains intractable. Nevertheless, a solution approach for k-IFM$_I$ has been proposed in [16], which has been shown in a large number of experiments to be very effective in solving large instances of both synthesized and real datasets. This solution is based on a version of the simplex method, called *column generation* (see, e.g., [6]), that is suitable to handle a large number of variables (large-scale linear programs). This method solves a linear program without explicitly including all columns in the coefficient matrix but only a subset of them with cardinality equal to the number of rows (i.e., constraints). Columns are dynamically generated by solving an auxiliary optimization problem called the *pricing problem*, which has been proved in [16] to be NP hard for k-FIDHy. A heuristic polynomial-time algorithm to solve the pricing problem is provided in that paper, that enables an effective solution of k-IFM$_\text{I}$ (thus k-FIDHy). The method allows us to handle linear programs with an enormous number of variables (from 10^{22} to over 10^{240} in the experiments of [16]) using a polynomial amount of space. Those experiments reveal that exponential time is not gotten in practice as it happens for the classic execution of the simplex algorithm.

4   Conclusion

Given a hypergraph $\mathcal{H} = (V, E)$ with n vertices in V and m hyperedges in E, dualization is the problem of enumerating all minimal transversals of $\mathcal{H}$. Dualization is at the core of a number of important problems in the areas of knowledge discovery, machine learning, and more generally in AI and knowledge representation.

In this paper we have defined an upper bound $\widetilde{m}^d$ to the number m^d of minimal transversals of $\mathcal{H}$ and have shown that this bound can be computed in polynomial time. This bound is based on the structure of the complement hypergraph $\overline{\mathcal{H}} = (V, \overline{E})$ of $\mathcal{H}$, that is the hypergraph obtained from $\mathcal{H}$ by replacing every $I \in E$ with $\overline{I} = V \setminus I$. Obviously $\overline{m} = |\overline{E}|$ is equal to m. Let $\bar{n} = |\overline{V}| \leq n$, where $\overline{V} = \cup_{\overline{I} \in \overline{E}} \overline{I}$ is the set of vertices that are not included in all hyperedges in E. In addition, $\bar{n}_2 = |\overline{V}_2|$, where $\overline{V}_2 = \{\{v_1, v_2\} \mid v_1, v_2 \in V$ and $\exists \overline{I} \in \overline{E}$ s.t. $\{v_1, v_2\} \subseteq \overline{I}\}$ is the set of vertex pairs that are not included in some hyperedge in E.

The upper bound $\widetilde{m}^d$ is equal to $m_1^d + m_2^d + \widetilde{m}_{3+}^d$, where $m_1^d = n - \bar{n}$ is the number of singleton minimal transversals, $m_2^d = \bar{n}(\bar{n} - 1)/2 - \bar{n}_2$ is the number of two-vertex minimal transversals and $\widetilde{m}_{3+}^d$ is an upper bound of the overall number of minimal transversals with 3 or more vertices. We have defined a formula that computes the value of $\widetilde{m}_{3+}^d$ in time $\mathcal{O}(n \cdot m^2)$, that takes into account a particular type of intersection between any two complement hyperedges. We have introduced a parameter $\kappa(\mathcal{H}) = \log_{\bar{n}}(m_2^d + \widetilde{m}_{3+}^d)$ to estimate the magnitude of $\widetilde{m}^d$ w.r.t. $\bar{n}$ in a hypergraph $\mathcal{H}$, so that we can write $\widetilde{m}^d = m_1^d + \bar{n}^{\kappa(\mathcal{H})} = n - \bar{n} + \bar{n}^{\kappa(\mathcal{H})}$.

A surprising result is that the necessary condition for a super-polynomial growth of the upper bound requires that the hyperedges in the complement hypergraph of $\mathcal{H}$ have intricate overlappings that may arise only when the hyperedges of $\mathcal{H}$ have small sizes and limited intersections. Such conditions characterize the bounded hypergraphs studied in [18], for which dualization can be computed in incremental polynomial time, i.e., finding every new minimal transversal is polynomial and a possible overall exponential complexity depends on the number of minimal transversals.

It turns out that there is a sort of complementarity between the two definitions of boundness for a hypergraph $\mathcal{H}$: the definition of [18] fixes bounds to the sizes and the intersections of the hyperedges in $\mathcal{H}$, whereas the bounds in our definition concern the size and intersections of the complement hyperedges. For a bounded hypergraph according to [18], the computation of every new minimal transversal (*duality* problem) is done in polynomial time but this step must be iterated for a number of times that can be exponential. Instead, for a bounded hypergraph according to our definition, every duality problem cannot be in general solved in polynomial time, but the number of iterations is limited as the number of minimal transversals is polynomial. It turns out that dualization may be intractable in the worst case but it is often effectively solved in practice. This is confirmed by the results of the fact that it has been devised a deterministic algorithm in [13] that solves duality in quadratic logspace and there are classes of hypergraphs for which dualization is in FPT (fixed-parameter tractability) [5]. As stated in [26], "the worst-case approach is simply too pessimistic and tells us too little about algorithmic performance in practice (...) Going beyond worst-case complexity is a key challenge in complexity theory and is the subject of much current research." Our paper follows this approach.

In addition, as dualization is at the core of important data mining problems concerned with finding itemsets in a transaction database that are frequent or infrequent w.r.t. to given frequency thresholds, we have analyzed the complexity of IFM$_I$ (Inverse Frequent itemset Mining with Infrequency constraints) by using a hypergraph formalization of the problem and by exploiting the upper bound $\tilde{m}^d$. Also in this case, despite the high worst-case complexity, the problem can be effectively solved in practice.

References

1. Agrawal, R., Imieliński, T., Swami, A.: Mining association rules between sets of items in large databases. In: Proceedings of the 1993 ACM SIGMOD International Conference on Management of Data, SIGMOD 1993, pp. 207–216. ACM, New York (1993). https://doi.org/10.1145/170035.170072
2. Berge, C.: Graphs and Hypergraphs. North-Holland Pub. Co., Amsterdam (1973)
3. Boros, E., Gurvich, V., Khachiyan, L., Makino, K.: On maximal frequent and minimal infrequent sets in binary matrices. Ann. Math. Artif. Intell. **39**, 211–221 (2003). https://doi.org/10.1023/A:1024605820527
4. Calders, T.: Itemset frequency satisfiability: complexity and axiomatization. Theoret. Comput. Sci. **394**(1–2), 84–111 (2008). https://doi.org/10.1016/j.tcs.2007.11.003
5. Damaschke, P.: Parameterized algorithms for double hypergraph dualization with rank limitation and maximum minimal vertex cover. Discret. Optim. **8**(1), 18–24 (2011). https://doi.org/10.1016/j.disopt.2010.02.006
6. Desaulniers, G., Desrosiers, J., Solomon, M.M.: Column Generation. Springer, New York (2005). https://doi.org/10.1007/b135457
7. Downey, R.G., Fellows, M.R.: Parameterized Complexity. Springer, New York (1999). https://doi.org/10.1007/978-1-4612-0515-9

8. Eiter, T., Gottlob, G.: Identifying the minimal transversals of a hypergraph and related problems. SIAM J. Comput. **24**(6), 1278–1304 (1995). https://doi.org/10.1137/S0097539793250299

9. Eiter, T., Makino, K.: Generating all abductive explanations for queries on propositional horn theories. In: Baaz, M., Makowsky, J.A. (eds.) CSL 2003. LNCS, vol. 2803, pp. 197–211. Springer, Heidelberg (2003). https://doi.org/10.1007/978-3-540-45220-1_18

10. Elbassioni, K.M., Rauf, I., Ray, S.: Enumerating minimal transversals of geometric hypergraphs. In: Proceedings of the 23rd Annual Canadian Conference on Computational Geometry, Toronto, Ontario, Canada, 10–12 August (2011)

11. Flum, J., Grohe, M.: Parameterized Complexity Theory. Texts in Theoretical Computer Science. An EATCS Series. Springer, Heidelberg (2006). https://doi.org/10.1007/3-540-29953-X

12. Fredman, M.L., Khachiyan, L.: On the complexity of dualization of monotone disjunctive normal forms. J. Algorithms **21**(3), 618–628 (1996). https://doi.org/10.1006/jagm.1996.0062

13. Gottlob, G., Malizia, E.: Achieving new upper bounds for the hypergraph duality problem through logic. SIAM J. Comput. **47**(2), 456–492 (2018). https://doi.org/10.1137/15M1027267

14. Gottlob, G.: Deciding monotone duality and identifying frequent itemsets in quadratic logspace. In: Hull, R., Fan, W. (eds.) PODS, pp. 25–36. ACM (2013). https://doi.org/10.1145/2463664.2463673

15. Gunopulos, D., Khardon, R., Mannila, H., Toivonen, H.: Data mining, hypergraph transversals, and machine learning. In: Mendelzon, A.O., Özsoyoglu, Z.M. (eds.) PODS 1997, pp. 209–216. ACM Press (1997). https://doi.org/10.1145/263661.263684

16. Guzzo, A., Moccia, L., Saccà, D., Serra, E.: Solving inverse frequent itemset mining with infrequency constraints via large-scale linear programs. ACM Trans. Knowl. Discov. Data **7**(4), 18:1–18:39 (2013). https://doi.org/10.1145/2541268.2541271

17. Kavvadias, D., Papadimitriou, C.H., Sideri, M.: On horn envelopes and hypergraph transversals. In: Ng, K.W., Raghavan, P., Balasubramanian, N.V., Chin, F.Y.L. (eds.) ISAAC 1993. LNCS, vol. 762, pp. 399–405. Springer, Heidelberg (1993). https://doi.org/10.1007/3-540-57568-5_271

18. Khachiyan, L., Boros, E., Elbassioni, K.M., Gurvich, V.: On the dualization of hypergraphs with bounded edge-intersections and other related classes of hypergraphs. Theor. Comput. Sci. **382**(2), 139–150 (2007). https://doi.org/10.1016/j.tcs.2007.03.005

19. Liu, G., Li, J., Wong, L.: A new concise representation of frequent itemsets using generators and a positive border. Knowl. Inf. Syst. **17**(1), 35–56 (2008). https://doi.org/10.1007/s10115-007-0111-5

20. Mielikainen, T.: On inverse frequent set mining. In: Proceedings of 2nd Workshop on Privacy Preserving Data Mining, PPDM 2003, pp. 18–23. IEEE Computer Society, Washington, DC (2003)

21. Papadimitriou, C.H.: Computational Complexity. Addison-Wesley, Boston (1994)

22. Reiter, R.: A theory of diagnosis from first principles. Artif. Intell. **32**(1), 57–95 (1987). https://doi.org/10.1016/0004-3702(87)90062-2

23. Saccà, D., Serra, E.: On line appendix to: number of minimal hypergraph transversals and complexity of IFM with infrequency: high in theory, but often not so much in practice! Version of 12 September 2019. http://sacca.deis.unical.it/#view=object&format=object&id=1490/gid=160

24. Saccà, D., Serra, E., Guzzo, A.: Count constraints and the inverse OLAP problem: definition, complexity and a step toward aggregate data exchange. In: Lukasiewicz, T., Sali, A. (eds.) FoIKS 2012. LNCS, vol. 7153, pp. 352–369. Springer, Heidelberg (2012). https://doi.org/10.1007/978-3-642-28472-4_20
25. Saccá, D., Serra, E., Rullo, A.: Extending inverse frequent itemsets miningto generate realistic datasets: complexity, accuracy and emerging applications. Data Min. Knowl. Discov. **33**, 1736–1774 (2019). https://doi.org/10.1007/s10618-019-00643-1
26. Vardi, M.Y.: Lost in math? Commun. ACM **62**(3), 7 (2019). https://doi.org/10.1145/3306448

Handling Modifiers in Question Answering over Knowledge Graphs

Lucia Siciliani[1], Dennis Diefenbach[2], Pierre Maret[2], Pierpaolo Basile[1(✉)], and Pasquale Lops[1]

[1] Department of Computer Science, University of Bari Moro, Bari, Italy
{lucia.siciliani,pierpaolo.basile,pasquale.lops}@uniba.it
[2] Laboratoire Hubert Curien, Saint Etienne, France
{dennis.diefenbach,pierre.maret}@univ-st-etienne.fr

Abstract. Question Answering (QA) over Knowledge Graphs (KGs) has gained its momentum thanks to the spread of the Semantic Web. However, despite the abundance of methods proposed in this field, there are still many aspects that need to be fully covered. One of them is the generation of SPARQL queries with modifiers, i.e. queries that are made up not only by triple patterns but also other terms belonging to the SPARQL syntax, such as FILTER, LIMIT, COUNT, ORDER BY. This task results difficult to accomplish in a generic way since the matching with natural language is not straightforward. Few works try to address this complex issue. In this paper, we propose a new approach to handle and to generate queries containing modifiers. Our method is able to generate queries with multiple modifiers, it is easily extendable to cover new modifiers and new languages, and it is independent of the KG structure. Our approach represents an extension of an existing work called QAnswer.

Keywords: Question answering · SPARQL · Knowledge graphs · Modifiers · Multilingual · Qanswer

1 Introduction

The research field of Question Answering (QA) aims to build a system able to automatically answer questions exploiting one o more data sources. Since the kind of data source deeply influences the methods that have to be employed to answer a question, the research on this topic is usually categorized in systems that employ unstructured data sources (books, articles, etc.) and the ones that use structured data sources (databases, knowledge graphs). Moreover, there are also hybrid approaches which try to combine the information from both data sources.

QA over structured data started in the late sixties. Then the spread of databases and the number of non-expert users of these technologies create the urge for natural language interfaces able to allow an easier access to this information [1]. After the advancement in the Semantic Web area, it was straightforward

© Springer Nature Switzerland AG 2019
M. Alviano et al. (Eds.): AI*IA 2019, LNAI 11946, pp. 210–222, 2019.
https://doi.org/10.1007/978-3-030-35166-3_15

that QA systems could undoubtedly help to access the information that is contained in Knowledge Graphs (KG).

The literature on this topic is now wide and many approaches have been proposed. Nevertheless, a definitive solution has not been reached yet due to the complexity of this task. There are three main issues that QA systems have to overcome in order to accomplish their goal: bridge the *lexical gap*, i.e. match words in the question to the right resource in the KG, resolve the *ambiguities*, i.e. choose the right resource among the others according to the context, and finally construct *complex queries*, i.e. capture the semantics of the question and its intent, and build a SPARQL query expressing the same meaning.

In this paper, we tackle the last issue: generation of SPARQL queries with modifiers for QA systems over Knowledge-Graphs. By SPARQL queries with modifiers, we refer to queries that not only contain triple patterns but also other SPARQL syntax like filters, aggregates (*sum, avg, max*) and functions. Throughout the paper we will use the terms "SPARQL modifiers" or simply "modifiers" for referring to those queries.

The idea that a QA system should also be able to support modifiers is due to the fact that some recurrent natural language requests can only be answered by these types of queries. Some example of such requests are: "Which mathematicians were born before 1600?", "In which year was Barack Obama born?", "How many cities have more than 10,000 inhabitants?".

The objective of this paper is to present an approach that is able to deal with this type of questions. It represents an extension of QAnswer [2], a QA system that allows generating queries with a fixed number of triple patterns. The approach proposed in this paper is extensible so that new modifiers can be added. It is designed to work for both keywords and natural language questions. Moreover, the approach supports multiple languages.

The paper is organised as follows. In Sect. 2 we present related works. In Sect. 3 we describe the QAnswer approach that will be extended in this work. The new approach is described in Sect. 4. We describe the experiments and the demonstrator in Sect. 5, while conclusions are reported in Sect. 6.

2 Related Work

The problem of generating queries with modifiers is a well know problem in QA over KGs as described in the most recent surveys of this domain [3,5]. In [5] the challenge of generating "complex queries" is described, i.e. generating queries that are different from a SELECT query with only one triple pattern. Queries with modifiers are included in the category of complex queries. In [3] the challenge of dealing with "Aggregations, comparison, and negation operators" is mentioned. These challenges include some specific SPARQL syntax and is, therefore, a subset of the more general problem of generating queries with modifiers.

Although being recognized as a main issue of QA over KG [3,5], handling modifiers is still poorly addressed in the literature. The interest in this topic is surely increasing as shown by the increase in the number of queries containing modifiers which are included in nowadays datasets for QA. In Table 1 we show the results of an investigation of the modifiers that appear over the last three editions of the QALD dataset[1] and the LC-QuaD dataset[2]. However, it is important to notice that the list of modifiers that appear in Table 1 is not exhaustive: they represent only a very small subset of all modifiers defined by SPARQL. Even if some modifiers are not included in any dataset at the state of the art, they are needed to answer questions posed by users.

Table 1. Distribution of modifiers over different datasets.

Modifier	QALD9 (train)	QALD9 (test)	QALD8 (train)	QALD8 (test)	QALD7 (train)	QALD7 (test)	LC-QuaD (train)	LC-QuaD (test)
ASK	37	4	34	0	29	0	285	83
FILTER	32	16	9	1	10	3	0	0
LIMIT	45	12	23	8	19	6	0	0
COUNT	26	11	8	1	7	1	535	123
GROUP BY	3	3	0	0	0	0	0	0
ORDER BY	42	12	23	3	19	6	0	0
UNION	29	17	2	0	3	1	0	0
w/o modifiers	268	98	151	30	155	34	3179	793
Total Size	408	150	219	41	215	43	4000	1000

Regarding the approaches already proposed in the literature to cope with this problem, a true evaluation of the state of the art is very difficult to accomplish. This is due to the fact that the performance of QA systems are always evaluated using metrics that take into account only the answers provided, while the SPARQL translation is ignored. Usually, this is done because there can be more than one SPARQL query capable to retrieve the same answer and calculate the accuracy of each method would be troublesome. To make a proper comparison both results and SPARQL translations of each system should be considered and properly analyzed. Moreover, since complex queries are often considered as a rarity, novel QA methods usually focus more on addressing other problems such as the lexical gap or ambiguity and handling only simple modifiers like COUNT or ASK. Only a few works discuss the possibility of generating queries with modifiers. We describe them in the following.

Pythia [10], performs an analysis of the input question to build a linguistic representation of its ontology independent part. These representations can be compositionally combined to represent the structure of complex queries. The authors state that spatial propositions, adjectival modifiers, superlatives, aggregation, comparisons, and negations can be handled by their method. However,

---

[1] http://qald.aksw.org/.
[2] http://lc-quad.sda.tech/.

the proposed approach has been tested only on a closed-domain dataset, i.e. Geosystem[3] since at the time of the publication the QALD dataset did not exist yet. In [9], the authors use a template based method to construct queries for a given question. They use the same parsing and meaning construction mechanism used in Pythia. This method implies the use of the Lexicalized Tree Adjoining Grammar (LTAG) for syntactic representation and of Dependency-based Underspecified Discourse REpresentation Structures (DUDEs) for semantic representations. Both these representations offer the advantage to be designed for compositionality, however, they appear difficult to modify to cover new kind of query structures. Moreover, they are strongly dependent on the language thus the approach is hardly adaptable to new languages.

In Intui3 [4], the syntactic and semantic information produced by two standard NLP tools is used to split the question in chunks and determine their interpretation. Among the different types of chunks there are the functional ones which correspond to lexical cues and correspond to functions such as COUNT, min or max. System CASIA [7] use pre-defined SPARQL templates to generate the final query. It can only handle the count modifier.

To summarize, there are only a few works that tried to tackle the problem of generating SPARQL queries with modifiers. Most of the state of the art is concentrating on generating triple pattern queries.

3   QAnswer: Existing Approach

In this section, we describe the existing approach we build on. It can be decomposed into four steps: Query Expansion, Query Construction, Query Ranking, and Answer Decision. A schematic description of the four steps is depicted in Fig. 1.

In the query expansion phase, all consequent n-grams in the questions are analyzed and mapped to potential resources in the KG. An important issue is how to select the right resources that actually reflect the meaning of the original question.

In the query construction step, we start from all the resources identified in the previous step. Out of the identified resources, all possible SPARQL queries are generated, i.e. all SPARQL queries whose triple patterns are made up by these resources or which gives directly back one of these resources.

For further discussion, we introduce the following notation. Each query is made up by a pair of a triple pattern and projection variable. We denote such pair as P. Thus we can say that this step returns a list of pairs P that in the following we denote as $List(P)$.

In the query ranking phase, the queries created in the previous step are ranked based on a series of features. Some of these include: how many words in the questions are associated with resources in the SPARQL queries and how similar is the label of the resource to the corresponding resource in the question. The objective is to get the correct query in the top position.

---

[3] ftp://ftp.cs.utexas.edu/pub/mooney/nl-ilp-data/geosystem/.

Finally, in the answer decision phase, the first ranked query of the previous phase is analyzed. The goal is to decide if the query matches the user intent or not. This is, for example, necessary when the KG does not contain the information requested by the user. In this case, none of the constructed queries will express the user intention and no answer should be given. For a more detailed description of this process we refer to [2].

This approach has a number of advantages over traditional methods [3]. These include:

- **Robustness**: users can ask questions using keywords (comedians turin born in), natural language questions (What are comedians born in Turin?) and even malformed questions (Comedians that born in Turin?), i.e., syntactically wrong questions. The algorithm is robust enough to deal with all these scenarios (spelling mistakes are not considered).
- **Multilingualism**: the approach can be applied to other languages, i.e.: English, German, French, Italian, Spanish, Portuguese, Arabic and Chinese.
- **Portability**: making QA system over a new dataset can be difficult. Some approaches need a lot of training data, others are not designed to be portable at all. The approach depicted above was applied to a number of different datasets including Wikidata, DBpedia, Dblp, Freebase, MusicBrainz, Scigraph, and LinkedGeoData.
- **Multi-Knowledge Base**: the algorithm allows to query multiple Knowledge Bases at the same time.
- **Precision and Recall**: the algorithm was tested on multiple benchmarks and can compete with most of the existing approaches.

The goal of this work is to extend the method described above to also cope with questions with modifiers while trying to maintain the aforementioned features.

4   Improved Approach Supporting Queries with Modifiers

In this section, we describe our approach for supporting queries with modifiers, and how we modified the existing process of QAnswer. We follow one of the principles of QAnswer which is to ignore the syntax of the question and to build interpretations of the question based on the semantics of the words. We introduce three steps in QAnswer's original process as shown in Fig. 2.

4.1   Pre-processing

The first new element in our pipeline is the pre-processing step. In this step, temporal expressions and numerical values within the natural language question are identified and normalized. For the running example "How many comedians were born in Turin after 1970" we want to identify the date "1970" and normalize it to the time interval between the "01-01-1970" and the "31-12-1970". Another example would be "Italian comedians born in the 70s." where we want to identify

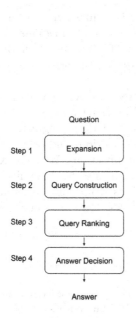

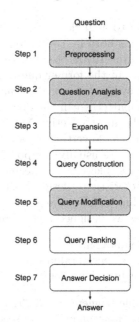

Fig. 1. Conceptual overview of the QAnswer approach

Fig. 2. Evolution of the QAnswer process to generate queries with modifiers

the expression *70s* and normalize it to the time between the "01-01-1970" and the "31-12-1979". Moreover we identify different prepositions like *before, in* or *after*. For performing this task, we decided to exploit HeidelTime [8], a multilingual temporal tagger that allows to detect and normalize temporal expressions according to the TIMEML [6] annotation standard. Given a temporal expression such as *70s*, HeidelTime assigns to it a `TIMEX3INTERVAL` tag and also retrieves the normalized interval. It is important to notice that HeidelTime only recognizes the temporal expression and does not consider the presence of expressions like "before" and "after". We take over the management of this aspect. Similarly in the pre-processing step we also identify numbers. Note that currently we do not identify expressions like: "Give me cities with more than hundred thousand inhabitants.". While this is not done yet, this step should also be used to identify and normalize units and currencies. To summarize, for our running example we would identify two expressions: (1) 1950, as a date, normalized as the time interval between "01-01-1950" and the "31-12-1950"; (2) 1950, as a number.

4.2 Question Analysis

In this step, potential modifiers are identified. The main idea behind our approach is that SPARQL modifiers are triggered by specific linguistic patterns. For example in the question "How many comedians were born in Turin after 1970?" the pattern "How many" can trigger a `COUNT` and the pattern "after 1970" a `FILTER`. There is a wide variety of patterns, and several linguistic patterns can correspond to a single modifier. For example the two questions "Total number of comedians born in Turin after 1970?." and "How many comedians were born in Turin after 1970?" require that the construct COUNT appears in the query translation: in the former question this is triggered by the noun *total*, while in the latter by the locution *How many*.

Linguistic patterns can thus be difficult to identify even when including in the pipeline the most effective Natural Language Processing tools such as dependency parsers. Nevertheless, an interesting feature of these linguistic patterns is that they are usually composed by adverbs, prepositions and other locutions which are less likely to be affected by some lexical inflections. We thus exploited this characteristic to design a set of rules able to capture these linguistic variations and link them to the proper SPARQL modifiers. To be flexible towards new expressions we designed a structure to add new rules. Here are some examples:

- COUNT,en,how many
- FILTER(=),en,literaldate
- LIMIT,it,literalnumber

The first one triggers the COUNT modifier for English questions that contain the expression "how many". The second triggers a FILTER modifier with equality operator when in an English question a date is matched. The third one triggers a LIMIT modifier in an Italian question if a number is matched.

The general structure of a rule is defined by the following items:

- Modifier: the modifier that the regex pattern indicates as potential syntax element in the final query;
- Operator (optional): an operator that may change the modifier (like the "=" in the FILTER(=) rule);
- Language: the language for which this rule is used (we adopt the format described by RFC3066[4]).
- Regex: the linguistic pattern that has to be found in the question;

In this step, all existing rules are taken into consideration and if one is matched, the corresponding modifier is attached to the question. Note that we do not impose that the final query must include all these operators, but we only take into consideration that they might be used to generate it. For the running question "How many Italian comedians were born after 1970", there are five rules that will match with the question. The phrase "How many" can indicate that the final query can contain a COUNT modifier. Moreover, the expression "1970" triggers that the final query can contain an equality filter for the date 1970, a numeric filter with the number "1970" or it could require to limit the number of results to 1970. Finally the expression "after 1970" implies that the final query could contain a filter on a date bigger or equal than "1970". To summarize, in the Question Analysis step the following modifiers are identified:

---

[4] https://tools.ietf.org/html/rfc3066.

- COUNT,en,how many
- FILTER(=),en,literaldate
- FILTER(=),en,literalnumber
- LIMIT,en,literalnumber
- FILTER(>),en,after literaldate

Once all the modifiers are recognized, they are stored in a list that we denote by $List(M)$. For the running example it includes the following modifiers: $List(M) = \{$COUNT, FILTER(=) (literaldate), FILTER(=) (literalnumber), LIMIT, FILTER(>)$\}$. The list is used in the query modification step and it does not affect the expansion and query construction steps which are described in Sect. 3.

4.3   Query Modification

The query modification step follows both the Query Analysis step and the Query Construction step. The first step returns a list of modifiers $List(M)$ while the second returns a list of pairs $List(P)$ containing triple patterns and projection variables.

For the considered example, $List(M) = \{$COUNT, FILTER(=) (literaldate), FILTER(=) (literalnumber), LIMIT, FILTER(>)$\}$. Let Q be the SPARQL query we want to generate, i.e. the one corresponding to the user's question. By construction, the list $List(P)$ generated in the query construction step contains the triple pattern of Q. Moreover, the modifiers in Q are contained in $List(M)$. This means that by combining the elements in $List(M)$ and $List(P)$ it is possible to generate Q.

The goal of this step is thus to apply the modifiers in $List(M)$ on the list of triple patterns and projection variables in $List(P)$. In this way, a list of queries with modifiers will be generated. This list by construction also contains the query Q.

The key observation in this step is the following. While in theory every element in $List(M)$ should be applied to $List(P)$, this does not necessarily mean that each modifier can be applied to each pair of a triple pattern and projection variable. This considerably reduces the complexity of the problem. We want to explain this in detail for some modifiers.

- COUNT: If the result of the triple pattern is a list of resources, it is semantically meaningful to add in the head of the query a COUNT operator. This happens for example in the question: "How many children has Barack Obama?". On the contrary, if the result of the triple pattern is a number, then it is not semantically meaningful to add a COUNT operator. For example for the question "What is the population of Boston?" the result of the projection variable is an integer. In this case, including a COUNT operator does not make sense and would lead to a wrong answer. To summarize, a COUNT can be applied to all pairs of P where the projection variable is not a number.
- FILTER(=),literalnumber: A filter with a number can only be applied if the variable that is filtered is a number. So it makes semantically sense to apply this modifier if this condition is met.

- ORDER BY: An order by can only be applied to a variable that is either numerical, expresses dates or a list of literals. It does not make sense to apply it to a list of resources.
- MAX: It is important to apply the MAX modifier only if the projection variable is numeric or a date. If the projection variable contains resources then applying the MAX modifiers does semantically not make sense.

Note that while these constraints are straightforward, they considerably reduce the number of queries that can be generated by combining $List(M)$ with $List(T)$.

If P is a pair of a triple pattern and projection variable and, M is a modifier then we denote with $query(P, M)$ the query that can be generated by combining the modifier M with the pair P.

Finally, note that to each element in $List(T)$ several modifiers in $List(M)$ can be applied. We control this with a variable K that indicates the maximum number of modifiers that can be applied to each pair P. The Algorithm 1 describes the procedure that we use to combine $List(T)$ with $List(M)$. This concludes the description of the extensions that we made to the original QAnswer algorithm.

Data: List of pairs $List(P)$, list of modifiers $List(M)$, integer K
Result: $List(Q)$ of queries that can be generated by applying at most K of the modifiers in $List(M)$ on the pairs in $List(T)$

1   $List(Q) = List(P)$; for P in $List(P)$ do
2   for $i = 0; i < K; i + +$ do
3   for M in $List(M)$ do
4             $List(Q) = List(Q) \cup query(P, M)$
5   end
6   end
7 end
8 return $List(Q)$

Algorithm 1. Algorithm to compute all queries that can be generated by applying at most K of the modifiers in $List(M)$ on the pairs in $List(T)$

4.4   Advantages and Limitations

To summarize our approach, in the first step the question is analyzed to identify candidate resources and modifiers it could refer to. In the second step, these resources and modifiers are combined by taking into consideration the information in the KG and the semantics of the modifiers. Our solution has the following main advantages, which are consistent with the ones presented in Sect. 3:

- **Robustness**: keyword questions are supported as well as full sentences. It is possible to formulate questions like "Barack Obama year born" or "British scientists 5". This is due to the fact that in the Question Analysis step we rely only on upon regular expressions and we do not use POS tagging or dependency parsing rules to extract patterns;

- **Multilingualism**: our approach is easily extensible to cover new languages. For example, the rule "how many, en, COUNT" can be adapted to other languages by simply changing the regex and the target language: the Italian equivalent for the aforementioned rule would be "quanti, it, COUNT" while for German, it would be "wie viele, de, COUNT".
- **Portability**: our proposal does not rely on how the Knowledge Graph is structured. It is thus portable to new datasets. For example, consider the question "How many children has Barack Obama?". The right SPARQL query is deeply influenced by how this information is encoded: the property to consider to get the answer could have as object either the resources identifying Obama's children or the integer "2". In the first case, the final query should contain a COUNT modifier, while in the latter, there is no need for a modifier since the object is already the answer we are looking for. Our method attempts to construct both queries and generates only the valid ones.
- **Multi-Knowledge Graph**: our approach is still valid even if multiple KG are queried. This characteristic of QAnswer is not altered by the newly introduced steps.

Regarding the disadvantages, our approach is affected by the problem of the lexical gap. This means that even if the query modifiers are correctly identified, the final SPARQL query might still be erroneous due to a mismatch between a word in the question and the resources in the KG. This is particularly true when coping with the ORDER BY modifier which is usually triggered by superlatives: in the question "Who is the tallest basketball player?" even if we correctly identify the presence of the superlative "tallest" and construct a query having the ORDER BY and LIMIT modifiers, the missing match between "tall" and the property dbp:height in the KG leads to a wrong result.

5   Implementation and Experiments

In the current implementation, we support the list of modifiers shown in Table 2. To support all linguistic expressions that trigger these modifiers, we defined 136 rules in 4 different languages.

To test our approach we carried out two experiments. The first consisted of running our algorithm over the questions in the QALD-9 test set that involve modifiers. There are 53 questions in QALD-9 that involve modifiers. We evaluated them using precision, recall and F-Measure as in the official challenges. As a result, we obtain a Precision of 0.11, a Recall of 0.12, and an F-Measure of 0.11. This means that with the current approach we are able to solve only 10% of the questions with modifiers that are contained in the QALD-9 test set. This result is caused by three particular reasons.

The main cause of failure is represented by the lexical gap, which means that the system does not map the natural language question to the right KG resources. The lexical gap problem can arise in different contexts. For example, for the question "How many seats does the home stadium of FC Porto have?" two triple patterns need to be involved in the final query, i.e. dbr:FC_Porto

Table 2. Modifiers supported in the current version.

Modifiers	Example question
ASK	Is Dante Alighieri the author of the Divine Comedy?
COUNT	How many books are written by George Orwell?
	How many inhabitants has London?
FILTER (date)	Which actors are born before 1980?
FILTER (number)	Books with more than 500 pages
FILTER (string)	Divine Comedy in Japanese
LIMIT	5 mountains in Italy?
SUM	Give me the sum of books written by Oscar Wilde
AVG	
GROUP BY	How many books did each author write ?
ORDER BY	Give me the most populated city
Temporal Functions (e.g. YEAR, MONTH)	In which year was Barack Obama born?
	How old is Barack Obama?
	How many years ago was Italy founded?

`dbo:ground ?ground.` and `?ground dbo:capacity ?capacity.` However, our system does not connect the 1-gram "seats" to the property `dbo:capacity` due to the great lexical gap and this provokes an error in the query construction step. In the question "How many grandchildren did Jacques Cousteau have?" the problem lies in the noun "grandchildren" which holds a specific semantic, i.e. "children of children". Our systems maps "grandchildren" with `dbp:children` only once and not twice as required by the correct query.

Another cause of failure is represented by the presence of modifiers which are not covered by our set of rules. For example in the question "Which countries have more than ten volcanoes?" there is the phrase "more than ten" which should trigger the modifier `GROUP BY ?uri HAVING ( COUNT(?x) > 10 )` where `?x` is a variable representing the volcanoes and `?uri` is a variable representing the countries. The `having` modifier is still not covered by our method, moreover as stated in Sect. 4, our preprocessing step is still unable to trace "ten" back to its numerical value.

Finally, there are some questions like "Which space probes were sent into orbit around the Sun?" which involve resources belonging to The Dublin Core[5] namespace that are difficult to map like http://purl.org/dc/terms/subject which is used in the triple pattern `?s dct:subject dbc:Missions_to_the_Sun`.

To summarize we can say that the questions with modifiers that appear in QALD are very hard to solve in a general manner. Moreover, many of the questions in QALD use modifiers to deal with KG problems, like dealing with

---

[5] http://dublincore.org/.

properties that express the same semantics. A detailed table showing the result for each question in the dataset can be found at https://bit.ly/2GfOwF1.

We carried out a second experiment where we constructed a dataset of question over Wikidata containing modifiers. The dataset contains 89 English questions. The dataset can be downloaded at https://bit.ly/2IsvNrs. We evaluated them using precision, recall, and F-Measure as in the official challenges. As a result, we obtain a Precision of 0.87, a Recall of 0.87 and an F-Measure of 0.87. The main source of problems is the ranking of the generated queries that is sometimes failing. All experiments were carried out by fixing the maximum number of triple patterns per query to 3 and the maximum number of modifiers per query to 2. A demo showing the system can be found under http://qanswer.eu/qa. The support of the modifiers is currently limited to English, French, Italian, and German. We plan to add the support for the other languages by extending the configuration file soon.

6   Conclusions and Future Work

In this work, we have focused on the issue of complex queries in QA over KGs and, in particular, on the task of generating queries containing modifiers. Complex queries with modifiers constitute one of the main challenges for this research field, however, at the state of the art there is no work which analyzes this problem in depth.

We have proposed a solution based on the use of a set of rules which allows robustness, multilingualism, portability, and independence from the underlying KG. The analysis of the results obtained over the QALD-9 test set shows that there is still room for improvement, and the questions proposed in current challenges are hard to tackle. In particular, the lexical gap has a deep influence over the capability of the system on handling this kind of questions. We have presented a new benchmark for this type of challenge and we could show that the presented approach is able to generate queries with modifiers for questions with a low lexical gap.

This work opens new challenges in the domain of QA over KGs. One is to inform the user about the interpretation that the system gave to the question in the case the generated SPARQL query contains modifiers. A second is the visualization of the result sets that need to be ordered or grouped. Moreover, the study of modifiers showed also the limits in current KG in the handling and normalization of units. As future work, we plan to further extend the list of our rules in order to cover more languages and modifiers, especially those triggered by the presence of superlatives in the input question.

References

1. Androutsopoulos, I., Ritchie, G.D., Thanisch, P.: Natural language interfaces to databases-an introduction. Nat. Lang. Eng. **1**(1), 29–81 (1995)
2. Diefenbach, D., Both, A., Singh, K., Maret, P.: Towards a question answering system over the semantic web (2018). arXiv:1803.00832
3. Diefenbach, D., Lopez, V., Singh, K., Pierre, M.: Core techniques of question answering systems over knowledge bases: a survey. Knowl. Inf. Syst. **55**, 529–569 (2017)
4. Dima, C.: Answering natural language questions with Intui3. In: Conference and Labs of the Evaluation Forum (CLEF) (2014)
5. Höffner, K., Walter, S., Marx, E., Usbeck, R., Lehmann, J., Ngonga Ngomo, A.C.: Survey on challenges of question answering in the semantic web. Semant. Web **8**(6), 895–920 (2017)
6. Pustejovsky, J., et al.: Timeml: robust specification of event and temporal expressions in text. New Dir. Quest. Answ. **3**, 28–34 (2003)
7. Shizhu, H., Yuanzhe, Z., Kang, L., Jun, Z., et al.: Casia@ v2: a MLN-based question answering system over linked data. In: Working Notes for CLEF 2014 Conference, pp. 1249–1259. CEUR-WS (2014)
8. Strötgen, J., Gertz, M.: Multilingual and cross-domain temporal tagging. Lang. Resour. Eval. **47**(2), 269–298 (2013)
9. Unger, C., Bühmann, L., Lehmann, J., Ngonga Ngomo, A.C., Gerber, D., Cimiano, P.: Template-based question answering over RDF data. In: Proceedings of the 21st International Conference on World Wide Web, pp. 639–648. ACM (2012)
10. Unger, C., Cimiano, P.: Pythia: compositional meaning construction for ontology-based question answering on the semantic web. In: Muñoz, R., Montoyo, A., Métais, E. (eds.) NLDB 2011. LNCS, vol. 6716, pp. 153–160. Springer, Heidelberg (2011). https://doi.org/10.1007/978-3-642-22327-3_15

A Graphical Analysis of Integer Infeasibility in UTVPI Constraints

K. Subramani[(⊠)] and Piotr Wojciechowski

LDCSEE, West Virginia University, Morgantown, USA
{k.subramani,pwojciec}@mail.wvu.edu

Abstract. In this paper, we discuss a theorem of the alternative for integer feasibility in a class of constraints called Unit Two Variable Per Inequality (UTVPI) constraints. In general, a theorem of the alternative gives two systems of constraints such that exactly one system is feasible. Theorems of the alternative for linear feasibility have been discussed extensively in the literature. If a theorem of the alternative provides a "succinct" certificate of infeasibility, it is said to be **compact**. In general, theorems of the alternative for linear feasibility are compact (see Farkas' lemma for instance). However, compact theorems of the alternative cannot exist for integer feasibility in linear programs unless **NP = coNP**. A second feature of a theorem of the alternative is its form. Typically, theorems of the alternative connect pairs of linear systems. A graphical theorem of the alternative, on the other hand, connects infeasibility in a linear system to the existence of particular paths in an appropriately constructed constraint network. Graphical theorems of the alternative are known to exist for selected classes of linear programs. In this paper, we detail a **compact**, **graphical** theorem of the alternative for integer feasibility in UTVPI constraints.

1 Introduction

In this paper, we introduce a graphical theorem of the alternative for integer feasibility in a class of constraints called Unit Two Variable Per Inequality (UTVPI) constraints. Typically, theorems of the alternative connect pairs of linear systems and have the following form: Given two linear systems **A** and **B**, exactly one of them is feasible. System **A** is called the primal system and System **B** is called the dual system. It is not hard to see that theorems of the alternative provide certificates of infeasibility. If this certificate of infeasibility is "succinct", i.e., polynomial in the size of the input, then it is said to be **compact**.

The most celebrated theorem of the alternative was proposed by Gyula Farkas in [4]. Succinctly put, the theorem states that if a given vector **c** does not lie in the positive span of a set of vectors **S**, then there must exist a hyperplane **y**, which separates the set **S** and the vector **c**. Although this theorem was proved more than a hundred years ago, new proofs of this theorem continue to be investigated and published (see [3]). In [22], Farkas' lemma is proved as a corollary of the correctness of the Fourier-Motzkin elimination method [15]. A number of

© Springer Nature Switzerland AG 2019
M. Alviano et al. (Eds.): AI*IA 2019, LNAI 11946, pp. 223–234, 2019.
https://doi.org/10.1007/978-3-030-35166-3_16

different theorems of the alternative such as Gordan's theorem [7] and Stiemke's theorem [18] have been documented in [11].

Theorems of the alternative for integer feasibility are less common. In general, a compact theorem of the alternative for integer feasibility cannot exist unless **NP = coNP**. However, the literature documents Farkas type lemmas for a number of specialized integer programs [10]. Note that the integer feasibility problem for UTVPI constraint systems (UCS) is in **P**. However, this fact by itself does not guarantee the existence of natural certificates of infeasibility.

A graphical theorem of the alternative, on the other hand, relates infeasibility in a linear system to the existence of particular paths in an appropriately constructed constraint network. Such theorems of the alternative are known to exist for selected classes of linear programs. For instance, it is well-known that a system of difference constraints (constraints of the form $x_i - x_j \leq c_{ij}$) is infeasible if and only if the corresponding constraint network contains a negative cost cycle [14]. The property of Total Unimodularity [13] ensures that a difference constraint system is linearly infeasible (does not contain any point) if and only if it is integer infeasible (does not contain an integer point). Thus, technically, a negative weight cycle is also a graphical theorem of the alternative for integer feasibility of a system of difference constraints. However, the focus of this paper is on UTVPI constraints, where linear feasibility does not imply integer feasibility.

UTVPI constraints occur in a number of problem domains including but not limited to program verification [9], abstract interpretation [2,12], real-time scheduling [6], game theory [21], and operations research. Indeed many software and hardware verification queries are naturally expressed using this fragment of integer linear arithmetic, i.e., the case in which the solutions of a UCS are required to be integral. We note that when the goal is to model indices of arrays and queues in hardware or software, rational solutions are unacceptable [9]. Other application areas include spatial databases [17] and theorem proving. UTVPI constraints are the invariants of the octagon abstract domain in [12]. For a detailed discussion on the related work in UTVPI constraints, the interested reader is referred to [9] and [1].

A graphical theorem of the alternative for UTVPI constraints was described in [9]. However, it is important to note that our work differs from the work in [9] in that the work in [9] utilizes a different graphical construction than the one used by our paper. Likewise, [16] describes an incremental implementation of [9]. Additionally, our theorem of the alternative utilizes the constraint network corresponding to the original system without any added constraints. Thus, we do not need to prove that the constraints in a certificate of infeasibility are derivable from the original system since they are guaranteed to be part of the original system.

Our result provides a different perspective on the integer infeasibility of UCSs compared to these other approaches. This is similar to the different perspective on linear infeasibility offered by Gale's theorem [5], Gordan's theorem [7], and Stiemke's theorem [18] when compared to Farkas' lemma [4].

The rest of this paper is organized as follows: In Sect. 2, we introduce the problem being studied. Section 3 briefly describes the network construction used by our theorem of the alternative. Our theorem of the alternative is presented in Sect. 4. We conclude in Sect. 5 by summarizing our contributions, and outlining avenues for future research.

2   Statement of Problem

In this section, we formally define the integer feasibility problem in UTVPI constraints and also define the various terms that will be used in the rest of the paper.

Definition 1. *A constraint of the form $x_i - x_j \leq c_{ij}$ where $c_{ij} \in \mathbb{Z}$ is called a difference constraint.*

Definition 2. *A constraint of the form $a_i \cdot x_i + a_j \cdot x_j \leq c_{ij}$ is said to be a Unit Two Variable Per Inequality (UTVPI) constraint if $a_i, a_j \in \{-1, 0, +1\}$ and $c_{ij} \in \mathbb{Z}$.*

Definition 3. *A constraint of the form $x_i \leq c_i$ or $-x_i \leq c_i$, where $c_i \in \mathbb{Z}$, is called an absolute constraint.*

Observe that an absolute constraint is a UTVPI constraint in which one of the coefficients (a_i or a_j) is 0. By adding a new variable x_0, such a constraint can be converted into constraints of the form: $a_i \cdot x_i + a_0 \cdot x_0 \leq c_i$, where both a_i and a_0 are non-zero.

Definition 4. *The constant which bounds a UTVPI constraint is called the defining constant.*

Example 1. The defining constant for the constraint $x_1 - x_2 \leq 9$ is 9.

Definition 5. *A conjunction of UTVPI constraints is called a UTVPI constraint system (UCS) and can be represented in matrix form as $\mathbf{A} \cdot \mathbf{x} \leq \mathbf{c}$. If the constraint system has m constraints over n variables, then $\mathbf{A}$ has dimensions $m \times n$.*

Observe that a UCS defines a polyhedron in n-dimensional space. Given such a system, we are interested in the following question: Does the defined polyhedron enclose an integer point? This problem is called the *Integer Feasibility problem* (IF).

Our goal is to design a graphical theorem of the alternative for the IF problem. In other words, we should be able to provide graphical refutations for infeasible UCSs. Our theorem of the alternative incorporates the following properties of UTVPI constraints:

(i) A UCS is integer feasible if and only if the corresponding constraint network does not contain certain types of cycles (see Sect. 4).

(ii) Fourier-Motzkin with rounding (FMR) is a sound and complete procedure for detecting integer feasibility in UTVPI constraints (see Sect. 4 and [19]).

While integer feasibility in a UCS immediately implies linear feasibility, the converse is not true.

Our theorem of the alternative uses the following inference rules [9].

The transitive rule is

$$\frac{a_i \cdot x_i + a_j \cdot x_j \leq c_{ij} \qquad -a_j \cdot x_j + a_k \cdot x_k \leq c_{jk}}{a_i \cdot x_i + a_k \cdot x_k \leq c_{ij} + c_{jk}},$$

and the tightening rule is

$$\frac{a_i \cdot x_i + a_j \cdot x_j \leq c_{ij} \qquad a_i \cdot x_i - a_j \cdot x_j \leq c'_{ij}}{a_i \cdot x_i \leq \lfloor \frac{c_{ij} + c'_{ij}}{2} \rfloor}.$$

The integer closure of $\mathbf{U}$ is the closure of $\mathbf{U}$ under the transitive and tightening inference rules [12]. This means that once the integer closure is computed, additional applications of the transitive and tightening inference rules do not create any additional constraints.

Note that the transitive inference rule corresponds to summing two UTVPI constraints. Thus, the transitive inference rule preserves linear solutions in addition to preserving integer solutions. In fact the closure of $\mathbf{U}$ under the transitive inference rule is the linear closure of $\mathbf{U}$ [12]. This is also true for systems of difference constraints.

3   Constraint Network Representation

In this section, we describe the constraint network representation used in this paper.

Let $\mathbf{U} : \mathbf{A} \cdot \mathbf{x} \leq \mathbf{c}$ denote the UCS, and let $\mathbf{X}$ denote the set of all (fractional and integral) solutions to $\mathbf{U}$. Corresponding to this constraint system, we construct the constraint network $\mathbf{G} = \langle V, E, \mathbf{c} \rangle$ by utilizing the network construction from [20].

The input UCS is transformed into a constraint network as follows:

For each variable, one node is added to the constraint network. Each constraint corresponds to a single edge as follows:

1. The constraint $x_i - x_j \leq c$ corresponds to the edge $x_j \overset{c}{\blacksquare} x_i$. We refer to this as a gray edge. This edge is also denoted by $x_i \overset{c}{\blacksquare} x_j$.

2. The constraint $x_i + x_j \leq c$ corresponds to the edge $x_j \overset{c}{\square} x_i$. We refer to this as a white edge.

3. The constraint $-x_i - x_j \leq c$ corresponds to the edge $x_j \overset{c}{\blacksquare} x_i$. We refer to this as a black edge.

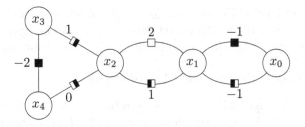

Fig. 1. Constraint network for example constraints.

Note that all of these edges can be traversed in either direction.

To handle absolute constraints we add the vertex x_0. Each absolute constraint corresponds to a pair of edges as follows:

1. The constraint $x_i \leq c$ corresponds to the edges $x_i \overset{c}{\square} x_0$ and $x_i \overset{c}{\blacksquare} x_0$.
2. The constraint $-x_i \leq c$ corresponds to the edges $x_i \overset{c}{\blacksquare} x_0$ and $x_i \overset{c}{\blacksquare} x_0$.

If **U** has n variables and m constraints, then **G** has $(n + 1)$ vertices and up to $(m + 2 \cdot n)$ edges.

Example 2. Consider the UCS defined by System (1).

$$
\begin{array}{llll}
l_1 : x_1 + x_2 \leq 2 & l_2 : & x_1 - x_2 \leq 1 & l_3 : x_3 - x_2 \leq 1 \\
l_4 : x_4 - x_2 \leq 0 & l_5 : -x_3 - x_4 \leq -2 & l_6 : & -x_1 \leq -1
\end{array}
\tag{1}
$$

This UCS has an integer solution of $x_1 = 1$, $x_2 = 1$, $x_3 = 1$, and $x_4 = 1$. The constraint network corresponding to UCS (1) is provided in Fig. 1.

This constraint network differs from the ones in [12] and [9] in several respects:

(a) In this constraint network, the edges are "undirected", i.e., the search algorithms for determining feasibility can traverse them in either direction. This is in marked contrast to potential networks, which are directed graphs and must be traversed along directed edges.
(b) This constraint network directly reflects the original input UTVPI system. Accordingly, this network retains information about constraint types explicitly.
(c) The networks in [12] and [9] are in essence a difference constraint network representation of UTVPI constraints. However, all UTVPI constraints are represented explicitly in this constraint network.

This constraint network differs from bidirected graphs as described in [15] and [8] in how we represent absolute constraints. In a bidirected graph, each absolute constraint is represented by an edge between a vertex and itself. However, this doubles the weight of the corresponding edge. In our construction we introduce the vertex x_0 to handle absolute constraints. This allows us to represent absolute constraints without doubling the weight of the corresponding edges. Thus, we do not need to use extra edges in cycles that have edges corresponding to absolute constraints.

We now introduce the notion of edge reductions.

Definition 6. *An edge reduction is an operation which takes a two-edge path and computes a single edge equivalent to that path. This operation represents summing the two UTVPI constraints corresponding to the edges in question. If this summation results in a UTVPI constraint, the reduction is said to be* valid.

Note that not every two-edge path corresponds to a valid reduction. Consider the two-edge path, $(x_1 \overset{2}{\square} x_2 \overset{2}{\blacksquare} x_3)$. This corresponds to the constraints $x_1 + x_2 \leq 2$ and $x_2 - x_3 \leq 2$. Summing these two constraints results in the constraint $x_1 + 2 \cdot x_2 - x_3 \leq 4$ which is not a valid UTVPI constraint. Thus, there is no valid reduction for this path.

Instead, consider the path $(x_1 \overset{2}{\square} x_2 \overset{2}{\blacksquare} x_3)$. This corresponds to the constraints $x_1 + x_2 \leq 2$ and $-x_2 + x_3 \leq 2$. Summing these two constraints results in the constraint $x_1 + x_3 \leq 4$ which is a valid UTVPI constraint and corresponds to the edge $(x_1 \overset{4}{\square} x_3)$. Thus, the path $(x_1 \overset{2}{\square} x_2 \overset{2}{\blacksquare} x_3)$ reduces to the edge $(x_1 \overset{4}{\square} x_3)$.

We use Definition 6 to define paths in the constraint network.

Definition 7. *We say that a path has type t, if it can be reduced to a single edge of type t, where $t \in \{ \square, \blacksquare, ◨, ◧ \}$.*

Definition 8. *The weight of a path p is the sum of the weights of the edges in p.*

A path from a vertex to itself is a cycle. Note that we allow for cycles to use edges and vertices more than once. Infeasibility of the original UCS corresponds to the presence of cycles with negative weight that reduce down to a single gray edge. We call these negative weight gray cycles.

Throughout this paper, we will utilize the following result from [20].

Theorem 1. *Let $\mathbf{U}$ be a UCS and let $\mathbf{G}$ be the corresponding constraint network. $\mathbf{U}$ is linearly feasible if and only if $\mathbf{G}$ does not contain a negative weight gray cycle.*

4   Characterizing Integer (in)feasibility in UTVPI Constraints

In this section, we present a theorem of the alternative for integer infeasibility in UTVPI constraints.

As before, let $\mathbf{U} : \mathbf{A} \cdot \mathbf{x} \leq \mathbf{c}$ denote a UCS and let $\mathbf{G} = \langle V, E, \mathbf{c} \rangle$ denote the constraint network as described in [20]. The details of this constraint network can be found in Sect. 3.

Let $\mathbf{U}'$ denote the UCS constructed by adding absolute constraints of the form $x_i \leq c_i$ and $-x_i \leq c_i$, to $\mathbf{U}$. An absolute constraint is added to $\mathbf{U}'$ under the following circumstances:

1. If the constraint $x_i + x_i \leq (2 \cdot c_i + 1)$ is derivable from $\mathbf{U}$ by the transitive inference rule, then the constraint $x_i \leq c_i$ is added to $\mathbf{U}'$.
2. If the constraint $-x_i - x_i \leq (2 \cdot c_i + 1)$ is derivable from $\mathbf{U}$ by the transitive inference rule, then the constraint $-x_i \leq c_i$ is added to $\mathbf{U}'$.

Let $\mathbf{X}'$ denote the set of feasible solutions to $\mathbf{U}'$. Let $\mathbf{G}' = \langle V', E', c' \rangle$ denote the constraint network representation of $\mathbf{U}'$.

We first prove a number of lemmata.

Lemma 1. *If $\mathbf{u}$ is an integer point in $\mathbf{X}$, then $\mathbf{u}$ is an integer point in $\mathbf{X}'$ as well.*

Proof. Observe that every constraint in $\mathbf{U}'$ is either a constraint in $\mathbf{U}$ or an absolute constraint of the form $x_i \leq c_i$ or $-x_i \leq c_i$, which was added as per the discussion above. For our purposes, it suffices to show that any integer point satisfying the constraints in $\mathbf{U}$, satisfies all the absolute constraints that are in $\mathbf{U}'$, but not in $\mathbf{U}$.

Let the constraint $l_1 : x_j \leq c_j$ denote one such constraint, i.e., l_1 is in $\mathbf{U}'$, but not in $\mathbf{U}$. As per the construction of $\mathbf{U}'$, l_1 was added to $\mathbf{U}'$ because the constraint $x_j + x_j \leq (2 \cdot c_j + 1)$ is deducible from the constraints in $\mathbf{U}$. Thus, every integer point in $\mathbf{X}$ must also satisfy the constraint $x_j + x_j \leq (2 \cdot c_j + 1)$. It follows that every integer point in $\mathbf{X}$ also satisfies the constraint $x_j \leq \lfloor \frac{2 \cdot c_j + 1}{2} \rfloor = c_j$.

Since the constraint l_1 was picked arbitrarily, the same argument applies for every constraint of the form $x_i \leq c_i$, which is present in $\mathbf{U}'$. but not in $\mathbf{U}$. Furthermore, the above argument can easily be generalized to the case where the absolute constraint in question has the form $-x_i \leq c_i$ by changing the sign on all of the variables.

Based on the above discussion, it follows that the integer points in $\mathbf{X}$ satisfy all the constraints in $\mathbf{U}'$, i.e., they satisfy all the constraints in $\mathbf{U}$ and the additional absolute constraints that define $\mathbf{U}'$. It follows that every integer point in $\mathbf{X}$ is also an integer point in $\mathbf{X}'$.   □

Observe that the converse of Lemma 1 is trivially true since $\mathbf{U}'$ is constructed by adding constraints to $\mathbf{U}$, and thus every integer point in $\mathbf{X}'$ is also in $\mathbf{X}$.

Lemma 2. *If $\mathbf{G}'$ has a negative weight gray cycle, then $\mathbf{X}$ contains no integer points.*

Proof. From Theorem 1, we know that if $\mathbf{G}'$ contains a negative weight gray cycle, then $\mathbf{X}'$ is empty. It follows that $\mathbf{X}'$ does not contain any integer points. By Lemma 1, it follows that $\mathbf{X}$ cannot contain any integer points either.   □

We have now shown that if $\mathbf{G}'$ contains a path from a vertex x_i to itself that can be reduced to a single gray edge of negative weight, then the constraint system $\mathbf{U}$ does not enclose an integer point. The following lemmata will help us establish the converse.

We need the following definition from [12].

Definition 9. *The tightened transitive closure* $\mathbf{U}^*$ *of a UCS* $\mathbf{U}$ *is the set of* **all** *UTVPI constraints (including absolute constraints) that are derivable from* $\mathbf{U}$ *by the transitive and tightening inference rules.*

We make the following observations regarding the tightened transitive closure, $\mathbf{U}^*$:

(a) The set of constraints in $\mathbf{U}$ is a subset of the set of constraints in $\mathbf{U}^*$.

(b) Every constraint in $\mathbf{U}^*$ is either a constraint in $\mathbf{U}$, or obtained by the application of either the tightening rule or the transitive rule to constraints in $\mathbf{U}^*$.

(c) $\mathbf{U}^*$ is closed under the transitive and tightening inference rules. This means that application of either the tightening rule or the transitive rule to constraints in $\mathbf{U}^*$ will not result in a UTVPI constraint that is not already in $\mathbf{U}^*$.

(d) $\mathbf{U}$ has no integral solution if and only if $\mathbf{U}^*$ contains a contradiction, i..e, a constraint of the form $0 \leq a$, where $a < 0$ [12]. Note that this means that $\mathbf{U}$ has no integral solution if and only if $\mathbf{U}^*$ has no linear solution.

Lemma 3. *If* $\mathbf{X}$ *contains no integer points, then* $\mathbf{X}'$ *is empty, i.e.,* $\mathbf{X}'$ *is linearly infeasible.*

Proof. In this proof, we will establish that the set $\mathbf{X}'$ of solutions to the constraint system $\mathbf{U}'$ (constructed as per the discussion prior to Theorem 2) is a subset of $\mathbf{X}^*$, where $\mathbf{X}^*$ is the set of all solutions to $\mathbf{U}^*$, the tightened transitive closure of $\mathbf{U}$. The lemma follows.

We first observe that every constraint in $\mathbf{U}^*$ is obtained by applications of the transitive and tightening inference rules detailed above. As stated previously, applications of the transitive inference rule correspond to edge reductions and so the constraints added in this fashion to $\mathbf{U}^*$ do not affect its linear feasibility. Thus, we are only concerned with the constraints added through application of the tightening inference rule. We will now show that each constraint added to $\mathbf{U}^*$ as a result of applying the tightening inference rule is also added to $\mathbf{U}'$.

We note that only absolute constraints are added to $\mathbf{U}^*$ through the application of the tightening inference rule. Assume that the constraint $x_i \leq c_i$ is added to $\mathbf{U}^*$ by the tightening rule. From [1], one round of tightening is sufficient to find the tightened transitive closure. Thus, we can assume without loss of generality that either $x_i + x_i \leq 2 \cdot c_i + 1$ or $x_i + x_i \leq 2 \cdot c_i$ is deducible from the original set of constraints, $\mathbf{U}$, by the transitive inference rule. In the first case, the constraint $x_i \leq c_i$ is, by definition, in $\mathbf{U}'$. In the second case, the constraint $x_i \leq c_i$ is equivalent to the constraint $x_i + x_i \leq 2 \cdot c_i$. Thus, this constraint does not remove any solutions from $\mathbf{X}$.

Likewise, assume that the constraint $-x_i \leq c_i$ is added to $\mathbf{U}^*$ by the tightening rule. It follows that $-x_i - x_i \leq 2 \cdot c_i + 1$ or $-x_i - x_i \leq 2 \cdot c_i$ is deducible from the original constraints, $\mathbf{U}$. In the first case, the constraint $-x_i \leq c_i$ is, by definition, in $\mathbf{U}'$. In the second case, the constraint $-x_i \leq c_i$ is equivalent to the constraint $-x_i - x_i \leq 2 \cdot c_i$. Thus, this constraint does not remove any solutions from $\mathbf{X}$.

We can thus conclude that every constraint added to $\mathbf{U}^*$ that removes solutions from $\mathbf{X}$ is also added to $\mathbf{U}'$. It follows that any vector $\mathbf{u}$ that satisfies $\mathbf{U}'$ also satisfies $\mathbf{U}^*$, i.e., $\mathbf{X}' \subseteq \mathbf{X}^*$. Finally, we note that if $\mathbf{X}$ contains no integer points, then $\mathbf{X}^*$ is empty [12]. Inasmuch as $\mathbf{X}' \subseteq \mathbf{X}^*$, $\mathbf{X}'$ is also empty. $\qquad\square$

Lemma 4. *If $\mathbf{X}$ contains no integer points, then $\mathbf{G}'$ contains a path from a vertex x_i to itself that can be reduced to a single gray edge of negative weight.*

Proof. By Lemma 3, if $\mathbf{X}$ contains no integer points, then $\mathbf{X}'$ is empty. Thus, by Theorem 1, $\mathbf{G}'$ contains a negative weight gray cycle from a vertex x_i to itself. However, such a cycle can be reduced to a single gray edge of negative weight. The lemma follows. $\qquad\square$

Having established the preceding lemmata, we now prove the following result.

Theorem 2. *Either the constraint system $\mathbf{U}$ encloses an integer point or (mutually exclusively) $\mathbf{G}'$ contains a path from a vertex x_i to itself that can be reduced to a single gray edge of negative weight.*

Proof. As shown in Lemma 2, if $\mathbf{G}'$ contains a path from a vertex x_i to itself that can be reduced to a single gray edge of negative weight, then $\mathbf{X}$ and hence $\mathbf{U}$ do not contain any integer points. Likewise, as per Lemma 4, if $\mathbf{X}$ contains no integer points, then $\mathbf{G}'$ contains precisely such a path. $\qquad\square$

Next we express this result in terms of the original constraint network $\mathbf{G}$. From Theorem 1, a negative weight gray cycle in $\mathbf{G}$ means that $\mathbf{X}$ is empty. Thus, $\mathbf{X}$ contains no integer points. As a result, we assume that $\mathbf{G}$ has no negative weight gray cycle.

Lemma 5. *If $\mathbf{G}$ has no negative weight gray cycle, then $\mathbf{X}$ contains no integer points if and only if $\mathbf{U}' \setminus \mathbf{U}$ contains the constraints $x_i \leq c_i$ and $-x_i \leq -c_i - 1$ for some x_i.*

Proof. The two constraints sum to produce the constraint $0 \leq -1$. This is clearly a contradiction. Thus, if $\mathbf{U}' \setminus \mathbf{U}$ has the desired constraints, then $\mathbf{X}$ has no integer points.

If $\mathbf{X}$ contains no integer points, then, by Lemma 4, $\mathbf{G}'$ contains a negative weight gray cycle. By the assumption that $\mathbf{G}$ has no negative weight gray cycles, this cycle must use edges corresponding to constraints in $\mathbf{U}' \setminus \mathbf{U}$.

All the constraints in $\mathbf{U}' \setminus \mathbf{U}$ are absolute constraints. Thus, any negative weight gray cycle in $\mathbf{G}'$ must use x_0. Since at least two edges of such a cycle must use x_0, any negative weight gray cycle in $\mathbf{G}'$ must use at least two edges corresponding to absolute constraints.

Let $p = (p_1, p_2, \ldots p_{|p|})$ be a negative weight gray cycle in $\mathbf{G}'$ with the fewest edges. Assume without loss of generality that the first edge in p, p_1, corresponds to the constraint $x_i \leq c_i \in \mathbf{U}' \setminus \mathbf{U}$ for some x_i.

If p_2 corresponds to a non-absolute constraint, then p_2 corresponds to a constraint of the form $-x_i + a_j \cdot x_j \leq c_{ij}$ where $a_j \in \{-1, 1\}$.

The constraint $x_i \leq c_i$ is in $\mathbf{U}' \setminus \mathbf{U}$. Thus, the constraint $x_i + x_i \leq 2 \cdot c_i + 1$ is derivable from $\mathbf{U}$ by the transitive inference rule. Since the constraint $-x_i + a_j \cdot x_j \leq c_{ij}$ is in $\mathbf{U}$, the constraint $a_j \cdot x_j + a_j \cdot x_j \leq 2 \cdot (c_{ij} + c_i) + 1$ is derivable from $\mathbf{U}$ by the transitive inference rule. Thus, the constraint $a_j \cdot x_j \leq c_{ij} + c_i$ is in $\mathbf{U}'$. Let p_1' be the edge in $\mathbf{G}'$ that corresponds to this constraint. Let $p' = (p_1', p_3, p_4, \ldots, p_{|p|})$. By construction p' is a gray cycle with the same weight as p. Thus p' is a negative weight gray cycle with fewer edges than p.

However, this means that there is a negative weight gray cycle in $\mathbf{G}'$ with fewer edges than p. Thus, p cannot have any edges corresponding to non-absolute constraints. This means that the edges in p correspond to the constraints $x_i \leq c_{i1}$ and $-x_i \leq c_{i2}$ where $c_{i1} + c_{i2} < 0$ for some x_i. Without loss of generality assume that $x_i \leq c_{i1} \in \mathbf{U}' \setminus \mathbf{U}$.

Thus, the constraint $x_i + x_i \leq 2 \cdot c_{i1} + 1$ is derivable from $\mathbf{U}$ by the transitive inference rule. If the constraint $-x_i \leq c_{i2} \in \mathbf{U}$, then the constraint

$$0 = x_i + x_i - 2 \cdot x_i \leq 2 \cdot c_{i1} + 1 + 2 \cdot c_{i2} = 2 \cdot (c_{i1} + c_{i2}) + 1 \leq -2 + 1 = -1$$

is derivable from $\mathbf{U}$ by the transitive inference rule. However, this means that $\mathbf{U}$ is infeasible and, by Theorem 1, $\mathbf{G}$ has a negative weight gray cycle. Thus, we must have that $-x_i \leq c_{i2} \in \mathbf{U}' \setminus \mathbf{U}$. Thus, $-x_i - x_i \leq 2 \cdot c_{i2} + 1$ is derivable from $\mathbf{U}$ by the transitive inference rule. Since $\mathbf{U}$ is feasible, we must have that $0 \leq c_{i1} + c_{i2} + 1 < 0 + 1$. Thus, we have that $c_{i1} + c_{i2} = -1$ as desired. $\qquad \square$

Theorem 3. *Either the constraint system $\mathbf{U}$ encloses an integer point or (mutually exclusively), the corresponding network $\mathbf{G}$ contains either*

(a) *a path from a vertex x_i to itself that can be reduced to a single gray edge of negative weight or*

(b) *a white path (path of type $\square$) of odd weight from x_i to itself and a black path (path of type $\blacksquare$) of odd weight from x_i to itself with total weight 0.*

Proof. If $\mathbf{G}$ contains a path of type (a), then by Theorem 1, $\mathbf{U}$ contains no rational points and thus no integer points.

If $\mathbf{G}$ contains a path of type (b), then for some c_i the constraints $x_i + x_i \leq 2 \cdot c_i + 1$ and $-x_i - x_i \leq -2 \cdot c_i - 1$ are derivable from $\mathbf{U}$ by the transitive inference rule [20]. Thus, the constraints $x_i \leq c_i$ and $-x_i \leq -c_i - 1$ are in $\mathbf{U}'$. This means that $\mathbf{U}'$ (and thus $\mathbf{U}$) contains no integer points.

If $\mathbf{U}$ does not contain an integer point, then there are two cases, either $\mathbf{U}$ contains no rational points or it contains rational, but no integer points.

If $\mathbf{U}$ contains no rational points, then, by Theorem 1, $\mathbf{G}$ has a path of type (a).

If $\mathbf{U}$ contains rational but no integer points, then, by Lemma 5, $\mathbf{U}' \setminus \mathbf{U}$ contains the constraints $x_i \leq c_i$ and $-x_i \leq -c_i - 1$ for some x_i. Thus, the constraints

$x_i + x_i \leq 2 \cdot c_i + 1$ and $-x_i - x_i \leq -2 \cdot c_i - 1$ are derivable from $\mathbf{U}$ by the transitive inference rule. The constraints used to derive $x_i + x_i \leq 2 \cdot c_i + 1$ correspond to a white path of weight $(2 \cdot c_i + 1)$ from x_i to itself [20]. Note that this path has odd weight. The constraints used to derive $-x_i - x_i \leq -2 \cdot c_i - 1$ correspond to a black path of weight $(-2 \cdot c_i - 1)$ from x_i to itself [20]. Note that this path also has odd weight. The total weight of these paths is 0. Thus, $\mathbf{G}$ has a path of type (b). $\qquad\square$

Note that our graphical theorem of the alternative differs from the one in [9] in the following ways:

1. Our theorem of the alternative utilizes the constraint network from [20], not the constraint network in [12].
2. Our theorem of the alternative is based on the constraint network corresponding to the original system without the need for constraints derived from the tightening inference rule. While the algorithm in [9] does use the unmodified graph, this is not explicitly given as a theorem of the alternative.

5 Conclusion

This paper introduced a new graphical theorem of the alternative of integer feasibility in UTVPI constraints. This graphical theorem of the alternative classifies integer infeasibility in terms of the existence of certain paths and cycles in the appropriately constructed constraint network. UTVPI constraints occur in a number of important domains, including but not limited to operations research and program verification. Our focus in this paper was the development of a graphical, compact theorem of the alternative for integer feasibility in UTVPI constraints. The literature is replete with theorems of the alternative for linear feasibility; indeed, Farkas' lemma is one of the more well-cited such theorems. Theorems of the alternative for integer feasibility are less common. In general, compact theorems of the alternative for integer feasibility in linear systems cannot exist unless $\mathbf{NP} = \mathbf{coNP}$.

Acknowledgments. This research was supported in part by the Air-Force Office of Scientific Research through grant FA9550-19-1-017.

References

1. Bagnara, R., Hill, P.M., Zaffanella, E.: Weakly-relational shapes for numeric abstractions: improved algorithms and proofs of correctness. Form. Methods Syst. Des. **35**(3), 279–323 (2009)
2. Cousot, P., Cousot, R.: Abstract interpretation: a unified lattice model for static analysis of programs by construction or approximation of fixpoints. In: POPL, pp. 238–252 (1977)
3. Dax, A.: Classroom note: an elementary proof of Farkas' lemma. SIAM Rev. **39**(3), 503–507 (1997)

4. Farkas, G.: Über die Theorie der Einfachen Ungleichungen. J. für die Reine und Angewandte Mathematik **124**(124), 1–27 (1902)
5. Gale, D.: The Theory of Linear Economic Models. McGraw-Hill, New York (1960)
6. Gerber, R., Pugh, W., Saksena, M.: Parametric dispatching of hard real-time tasks. IEEE Trans. Comput. **44**(3), 471–479 (1995)
7. Gordan, P.: Ueber die auflösung linearer gleichungen mit reellen coefficienten. Math. Ann. **6**(1), 23–28 (1873)
8. Hurkens, C.A.J.: On the existence of an integral potential in a weighted bidirected graph. Linear Algebr. Appl. **114–115**, 541–553 (1989). Special Issue Dedicated to Alan J. Hoffman
9. Lahiri, S.K., Musuvathi, M.: An efficient decision procedure for UTVPI constraints. In: Gramlich, B. (ed.) FroCoS 2005. LNCS (LNAI), vol. 3717, pp. 168–183. Springer, Heidelberg (2005). https://doi.org/10.1007/11559306_9
10. Lasserre, J.B.: Integer programming, Barvinok's counting algorithm and Gomory relaxations. Oper. Res. Lett. **32**(2), 133–137 (2004)
11. Marlow, W.H.: Mathematics for Operations Research. Wiley, Hoboken (1978)
12. Miné, A.: The octagon abstract domain. High.-Order Symb. Comput. **19**(1), 31–100 (2006)
13. Nemhauser, G.L., Wolsey, L.A.: Integer and Combinatorial Optimization. Wiley, New York (1999)
14. Schrijver, A.: Theory of Linear and Integer Programming. Wiley, New York (1987)
15. Schrijver, A.: Disjoint circuits of prescribed homotopies in a graph on a compact surface. J. Comb. Theory, Ser. B **51**(1), 127–159 (1991)
16. Schutt, A., Stuckey, P.J.: Incremental satisfiability and implication for UTVPI constraints. INFORMS J. Comput. **22**(4), 514–527 (2010)
17. Sitzmann, I., Stuckey, P.J.: O-trees: a constraint-based index structure. In: Australasian Database Conference, pp. 127–134 (2000)
18. Stiemke, E.: Über positive lösungen homogener linearer gleichungen. Math. Ann. **76**(2), 340–342 (1915)
19. Subramani, K.: On deciding the non-emptiness of 2SAT polytopes with respect to first order queries. Math. Log. Q. **50**(3), 281–292 (2004)
20. Subramani, K., Wojciechowski, P.J.: A combinatorial certifying algorithm for linear feasibility in UTVPI constraints. Algorithmica **78**(1), 166–208 (2017)
21. Vohra, R.V.: The ubiquitous Farkas' lemma. In: Alt, F.B., Fu, M.C., Golden, B.L. (eds.) Perspectives in Operations Research. ORCS, vol. 36, pp. 199–210. Springer, New York (2006). https://doi.org/10.1007/978-0-387-39934-8_11
22. Williams, H.P.: Model Building in Mathematical Programming, 4th edn. Wiley, Hoboken (1999)

Multi-agent Path Finding
with Capacity Constraints

Pavel Surynek[1]([⊠]) [ORCID], T. K. Satish Kumar[2], and Sven Koenig[3]

[1] Faculty of Information Technology, Czech Technical University in Prague,
Thákurova 9, 160 00 Praha 6, Czechia
`pavel.surynek@fit.cvut.cz`
[2] Henry Salvatori Computer Science Center, University of Southern California,
941 Bloom Walk, Los Angeles, USA
`tkskwork@gmail.com`
[3] Information Sciences Institute, University of Southern California,
4676 Admiralty Way, Marina del Rey, USA
`skoenig@usc.edu`

Abstract. In multi-agent path finding (MAPF) the task is to navigate agents from their starting positions to given individual goals. The problem takes place in an undirected graph whose vertices represent positions and edges define the topology. Agents can move to neighbor vertices across edges. In the standard MAPF, space occupation by agents is modeled by a capacity constraint that permits at most one agent per vertex. We suggest an extension of MAPF in this paper that permits more than one agent per vertex. Propositional satisfiability (SAT) models for these extensions of MAPF are studied. We focus on modeling capacity constraints in SAT-based formulations of MAPF and evaluation of performance of these models. We extend two existing SAT-based formulations with vertex capacity constraints: MDD-SAT and SMT-CBS where the former is an approach that builds the model in an eager way while the latter relies on lazy construction of the model.

Keywords: Multi agent path finding · propositional satisfiability
(SAT) · Capacity constraints · Cardinality constraints

1 Introduction

In *multi-agent path finding* (MAPF) [9,18–20,23,27,32] the task is to navigate agents from given starting positions to given individual goals. The standard version of the problem takes place in undirected graph $G = (V, E)$ where agents from set $A = \{a_1, a_2, ..., a_k\}$ are placed in vertices with at most one agent per vertex. The initial configuration of agents in vertices of the graph can be written as $\alpha_0 : A \to V$ and similarly the goal configuration as $\alpha_+ : A \to V$. The task of navigating agents can be expressed as transforming the initial configuration of agents $\alpha_0 : A \to V$ into the goal configuration $\alpha_+ : A \to V$.

© Springer Nature Switzerland AG 2019
M. Alviano et al. (Eds.): AI*IA 2019, LNAI 11946, pp. 235–249, 2019.
https://doi.org/10.1007/978-3-030-35166-3_17

Movements of agents are instantaneous and are possible across edges into neighbor vertices assuming no other agent is entering the same target vertex. This formulation permits agents to enter vertices being simultaneously vacated by other agents. Trivial case when a pair of agents swaps their positions across an edge is forbidden in the standard formulation. We note that different versions of MAPF exist where for example agents always move into vacant vertices [28]. We usually denote the configuration of agents at discrete time step t as $\alpha_t : A \to V$. Non-conflicting movements transform configuration α_t *instantaneously* into next configuration α_{t+1}. We do not consider what happens between t and $t + 1$ in this discrete abstraction. Multiple agents can move at a time hence the MAPF problem is inherently parallel.

In order to reflect various aspects of real-life applications, variants of MAPF have been introduced such as those considering *kinematic constraints* [8], *large agents* [11], or *deadlines* [14] - see [13] for a more detailed survey.

Particularly in this work we are dealing with an extension of MAPF that generalizes the constraint of having at most one agent per vertex. There are many situations where we need to model nodes that could hold more than one agent at a time. Such situations include various graph-based evacuation models where for example nodes correspond to rooms in evacuated buildings [10] which naturally can hold more than one agent. Various spatial projections could also lead to having multiple agents per vertex such as upper projection of agents representing aerial drones where a single node corresponds to x,y-coordinate that could hold multiple agents at different z-coordinates [12]. Generally the need to consider nodes capable of containing multiple agents appears in modeling of multi-agent motion planning task at higher levels of granularity.

1.1   Contributions

The contribution of this paper consists in showing how to generalize existing *propositional satisfiability* (SAT) [4] models of MAPF for finding optimal plans with general capacity constraints that bound the number of agents in vertices. Two existing SAT-based models are generalized: MDD-SAT [31] that builds the propositional model in an *eager way* and SMT-CBS [29,30] that builds the model in a *lazy way* inspired by satisfiability modulo theories (SMT) [16].

The eager style of building the propositional model means that all constraints are posted into the model in advance. Such model is *complete*, that is, it is solvable (satisfiable) if and only if the instance being modeled is solvable. In contrast to this, the lazy style does not add all constraints at once and works with *incomplete* models. The incomplete model preserve only one-sided implication w.r.t. solvability: if the instance being modeled is solvable then the incomplete model is solvable (satisfiable).

The SMT-CBS algorithm iteratively refines the incomplete model towards the complete one by eliminating conflicts. That is, a candidate solution is extracted from the satisfied incomplete model. The candidate is checked for conflicts - whether any of the MAPF rules is violated - for example if a collision between agents occurred. If there are no conflicts, we are finished as the candidate is a valid solution of the input MAPF instance. If a conflict is detected, then a constraint that eliminates this particular conflict is added to the incomplete model resulting in a new model and the process is repeated. A new candidate solution is extracted from the new model etc. Eventually the process may end up with a complete model after eliminating all possible conflicts. However, we hope that the process finishes before constructing a complete model and we solve the instance with less effort.

In the presented generalization with capacity constraints we need to distinguish between the eager and lazy variant. The capacity constraint concerning given vertex v bounding the number of agents that can simultaneously occupy v by some integer constant say 2 can be literally translated into the requirement that no 3 distinct agents can occupy v at the same time. Such a constraint can be directly posted in the eager variant: we either forbid all possible triples of agents in v or post the corresponding *cardinality constraint* [3,22].

The situation is different in the lazy variant. To preserve the nature of the lazy approach we cannot post the capacity bound entirely as conceptually at the low level we are informed only about a particular MAPF rule violation, say for example agents a_1, a_5 and a_8 occurred simultaneously in v which is forbidden in given MAPF. The information that there is a capacity constraint on v bounding the number of agents in v by 2 may even not be accessible at the low level. Hence we can forbid simultaneous occurrence of only the given triple of agents, a_1, a_5 and a_8 in this case.

The paper is organized as follows. We first introduce the standard multi-agent path finding problem formally including commonly used objectives. Then we introduce two major existing SAT-based encodings. On top of this, we show how to extend these encodings with vertex capacities. Finally we evaluate extended models on standard benchmarks including open grids and large game maps.

2   Formal Definition of MAPF and Vertex Capacities

The *Multi-agent path finding* (MAPF) problem [18,23] consists of an undirected graph $G = (V, E)$ and a set of agents $A = \{a_1, a_2, ..., a_k\}$ such that $|A| \leq |V|$. Each agent is placed in a vertex so that at most one agent resides in each vertex. The placement of agents is denoted $\alpha : A \to V$. Next we are given initial configuration of agents α_0 and goal configuration α_+.

At each time step an agent can either *move* to an adjacent vertex or *wait* in its current vertex. The task is to find a sequence of move/wait actions for each agent a_i, moving it from $\alpha_0(a_i)$ to $\alpha_+(a_i)$ such that agents do not *conflict*, i.e., do not occupy the same location at the same time nor cross the same edge in opposite directions simultaneously. The following definition formalizes the commonly used movement rule in MAPF.

Definition 1 Valid movement in MAPF. *Configuration α' results from α if and only if the following conditions hold:*

(i) *$\alpha(a) = \alpha'(a)$ or $\{\alpha(a), \alpha'(a)\} \in E$ for all $a \in A$ (agents wait or move along edges);*

(ii) *for all $a \in A$ it holds $\alpha(a) \neq \alpha'(a) \Rightarrow \neg(\exists b \in A)(\alpha(b) = \alpha'(a) \wedge \alpha'(b) = \alpha(a))$*
      (no two agents cross an edge in opposite directions);
(iii) *and for all $a, a' \in A$ it holds that $a \neq a' \Rightarrow \alpha'(a) \neq \alpha'(a')$ (no two agents share a vertex in the next configuration).*

Solving the MAPF instance is to find a sequence of configurations $[\alpha_0, \alpha_1, \ldots, \alpha_\mu]$ such that α_{i+1} results using valid movements from α_i for $i = 1, 2, \ldots, \mu - 1$, and $\alpha_\mu = \alpha_+$.

A version of MAPF with *vertex capacities* generalizes the above definition by adding capacity function $c : V \rightarrow \mathbb{Z}_+$ that assigns each vertex a positive integer capacity. The interpretation is that a vertex v can hold up to the specified number of agents $c(v)$ at any time-step.

The definition of the valid movement will change only in point (iii) where instead of permitting at most one agent per vertex we allow any number of agents not exceeding the capacity of the vertex:

Definition 2 Vertex capacities in MAPF.

(iii') *for all $v \in V$ it holds that $|a \mid \alpha'(a) = v| \leq c(v)$ (the number of agents in each vertex does not exceed the capacity in the next configuration).*

Generalized vertex capacities relax the problem in fact as illustrated in Fig. 1. Intuitively, capacities greater than one induce additional parking place in the environment which we hypothetise makes the problem easier to solve.

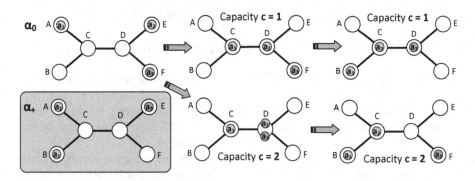

Fig. 1. Illustration of the standard MAPF ($c = 1$) and MAPF with generalized vertex capacity (uniform capacity $c = 2$ us used). With $c = 2$ two agents a_2 and a_3 can both enter vertex D. In contrast to this, a_3 must wait in vertex F in the standard MAPF.

2.1 Common Objectives in MAPF

We address here optimal MAPF solving hence we need to introduce objective functions more formally. In case of *makespan* [28] we just need to minimize μ in the aforementioned solution sequence. For introducing the *sum-of-costs* objective [7,19,20,25] we need the following notation:

Definition 3. Sum-of-costs objective *is the summation, over all agents, of the number of time steps required to reach the goal vertex. Denoted ξ, where $\xi = \sum_{i=1}^{k} \xi(path(a_i))$, where $\xi(path(a_i))$ is an individual path cost of agent a_i connecting $\alpha_0(a_i)$ and $\alpha_+(a_i)$ calculated as the number of edge traversals and wait actions.*[1]

Observe that in the sum-of-costs we accumulate the cost of wait actions for agents not yet reaching their goal vertices. For the sake of brevity we focus here on the sum-of-costs, but we note that all new concepts can be introduced for different cumulative objectives like the makespan.[2]

We note that finding a solution that is optimal (minimal) with respect to the sum-of-costs objective is NP-hard [17]. The same result holds for the variant with capacities as it is a straight generalization of the standard MAPF version.

3 Related Work

Let us now recall existing SAT-based optimal MAPF solvers. We here focus on aspects important for introducing capacities. We recall MDD-SAT, the sum-of-costs optimal solver based on *eager* SAT encoding [31], and SMT-CBS [30], the most recent SAT-based, or more precisely SMT-based, algorithm using *lazy encoding*.

3.1 SAT-based Approach

The idea behind the SAT-based approach is to construct a propositional formula $\mathcal{F}(\xi)$ such that it is satisfiable if and only if a solution of a given MAPF of sum-of-costs ξ exists [28]. Moreover, the approach is constructive; that is, $\mathcal{F}(\xi)$ exactly reflects the MAPF instance and if satisfiable, solution of MAPF can be reconstructed from satisfying assignment of the formula. We say $\mathcal{F}(\xi)$ to be a *complete propositional model* of MAPF.

Definition 4 (complete propositional model). *Propositional formula $\mathcal{F}(\xi)$ is a* complete propositional model *of MAPF Σ if the following condition holds:*

$$\mathcal{F}(\xi) \text{ is satisfiable} \Leftrightarrow \Sigma \text{ has a solution of sum-of-costs } \xi.$$

---

[1] The notation $path(a_i)$ refers to path in the form of a sequence of vertices and edges connecting $\alpha_0(a_i)$ and $\alpha_+(a_i)$ while ξ assigns the cost to a given path.

[2] Dealing with objectives is out of scope of this paper. We refer the reader to [31] for more detailed discussion.

Being able to construct such formula $\mathcal{F}$ one can obtain optimal MAPF solution by checking satisfiability of $\mathcal{F}(0)$, $\mathcal{F}(1)$, $\mathcal{F}(2)$, ... until the first satisfiable $\mathcal{F}(\xi)$ is met. This is possible due to monotonicity of MAPF solvability with respect to increasing values of common cumulative objectives like the sum-of-costs. In practice it is however impractical to start at 0; lower bound estimation is used instead - sum of lengths of shortest paths can be used in the case of sum-of-costs. The framework of SAT-based solving is shown in pseudo-code in Algorithm 1.

3.2   Details of the MDD-SAT Encoding

Construction of $\mathcal{F}(\xi)$ as used in the MDD-SAT solver relies on time expansion of underlying graph G. Having ξ, the basic variant of time expansion determines the maximum number of time steps μ (*makespan*) such that every possible solution of the given MAPF with the sum-of-costs less than or equal to ξ fits within μ timesteps. Given ξ we can calculate μ as $max_{i=1}^{k}\{\xi_0(a_i)\} + \xi - \xi_0$ where $\xi_0(a_1)$ is the length of the shortest path connecting $\alpha_0(a_i)$ and $\alpha_+(a_i)$; $\xi_0 = \sum_{i=1}^{k} \xi_0(a_i)$. The detailed justification of this equation is given in [31].

Time expansion itself makes copies of vertices V for each timestep $t = 0, 1, 2, ..., \mu$. That is, we have vertices v^t for each $v \in V$ and time step t. Edges from G are converted to directed edges interconnecting timesteps in the time expansion. Directed edges (u^t, v^{t+1}) are introduced for $t = 1, 2, ..., \mu - 1$ whenever there is $\{u, v\} \in E$. Wait actions are modeled by introducing edges (u^t, t^{t+1}). A directed path in the time expansion corresponds to trajectory of an agent in time. Hence the modeling task now consists in construction of a formula in which satisfying assignments correspond to directed paths from $\alpha_0^0(a_i)$ to $\alpha_+^\mu(a_i)$ in the time expansion.

Assume that we have time expansion $TEG_i = (V_i, E_i)$ for agent a_i. Propositional variable $\mathcal{X}_v^t(a_j)$ is introduced for every vertex v^t in V_i. The semantics of $\mathcal{X}_v^t(a_i)$ is that it is *TRUE* if and only if agent a_i resides in v at time step t. Similarly we introduce $\mathcal{E}_{u,v^t}(a_i)$ for every directed edge (u^t, v^{t+1}) in E_i. Analogously the meaning of $\mathcal{E}_{u,v}^t(a_i)$ is that is *TRUE* if and only if agent a_i traverses edge $\{u, v\}$ between time steps t and $t+1$.

Constraints are added so that truth assignment are restricted to those that correspond to valid solutions of a given MAPF. Added constraints together ensure that $\mathcal{F}(\xi)$ is a *complete propositional model* for given MAPF.

We here illustrate the model by showing few representative constraints. We omit here constraints that concern objective function. For the detailed list of constraints we again refer the reader to [31].

Collisions among agents are eliminated by the following constraint for every $v \in V$ and timestep t expressed on top of $\mathcal{X}_v^t(a_i)$ variables:

$$\sum_{a_i \in A \mid v^t \in V_i} \mathcal{X}_v^t(a_i) \leq 1 \qquad (1)$$

There are various ways how to translate the constraint using propositional clauses. One efficient way is to introduce $\neg \mathcal{X}_v^t(a_i) \vee \neg \mathcal{X}_v^t(a_j)$ for all possible pairs of a_i and a_j.

Next, there is a constraint stating that if agent a_i appears in vertex u at time step t then it has to leave through exactly one edge (u^t, v^{t+1}). This can be established by following constraints:

$$\mathcal{X}_u^t(a_i) \Rightarrow \bigvee_{(u^t, v^{t+1}) \in E_i} \mathcal{E}_{u,v}^t(a_i), \tag{2}$$

$$\sum_{v^{t+1} \mid (u^t, v^{t+1}) \in E_i} \mathcal{E}_{u,v}^t(a_i) \leq 1 \tag{3}$$

Similarly, the target vertex of any movement except wait action must be empty. This is ensured by the following constraint for every $(u^t, v^{t+1}) \in E_i$:

$$\mathcal{E}_{u,v}^t(a_i) \Rightarrow \bigwedge_{a_j \in A \mid a_j \neq a_i \wedge v^t \in V_j} \neg \mathcal{X}_v^t(a_j) \tag{4}$$

Other constraints ensure that truth assignments to variables per individual agents form paths. That is if agent a_i enters an edge it must leave the edge at the next time step.

$$\mathcal{E}_{u,v}^t(a_i) \Rightarrow \mathcal{X}_v^t(a_i) \wedge \mathcal{X}_v^{t+1}(a_i) \tag{5}$$

A common measure how to reduce the number of decision variables derived from the time expansion is the use of *multi-value decision diagrams* (MDDs) [20]. The basic observation that holds for MAPF is that an agent can reach vertices in the distance d (distance of a vertex is measured as the length of the shortest path) from the current position of the agent no earlier than in the d-th time step. Analogical observation can be made with respect to the distance from the goal position.

Above observations can be utilized when making the time expansion of G. For a given agent, we do not need to consider all vertices at time step t but only those that are reachable in t timesteps from the initial position and that ensure that the goal can be reached in the remaining $\mu - t$ timesteps.

3.3   Resolving Conflicts Lazily in SMT-CBS

SMT-CBS is inspired by the search-based algorithm CBS [19,21] that uses the idea of resolving conflicts lazily; that is, a solution of MAPF instance is not searched against the complete set of movement constraints that forbids collisions between agents but with respect to initially empty set of collision forbidding constraints that gradually grows as new conflicts appear. SMT-CBS follows the high-level framework of CBS but rephrases the process into propositional satisfiability in a similar way as done in formula satisfiability testing in the *satisfiability modulo theory* paradigm [5,15,16].

Algorithm 1. Framework of SAT-based MAPF solving

---

1   **SAT-Based** $(G = (V, E), A, \alpha_0, \alpha_+)$
2    $paths \leftarrow \{$shortest path from $\alpha_0(a_i)$ to $\alpha_+(a_i) | i = 1, 2, ..., k\}$
3    $\xi \leftarrow \sum_{i=1}^{k} \xi(N.paths(a_i))$
4   **while** $TRUE$ **do**
5      $\mathcal{F}(\xi) \leftarrow$ encode$(\xi, G, A, \alpha_0, \alpha_+)$
6      $assignment \leftarrow$ consult-SAT-Solver$(\mathcal{F}(\xi))$
7   **if** $assignment \neq UNSAT$ **then**
8        $paths \leftarrow$ extract-Solution$(assignment)$
9   **return** $paths$
10     $\xi \leftarrow \xi + 1$

The high-level of CBS searches a *constraint tree* (CT) using a priority queue in breadth first manner. CT is a binary tree where each node N contains a set of collision avoidance constraints $N.constraints$ - a set of triples (a_i, v, t) forbidding occurrence of agent a_i in vertex v at time step t, a solution $N.paths$ - a set of k paths for individual agents, and the total cost $N.\xi$ of the current solution.

The low-level process in CBS associated with node N searches paths for individual agents with respect to set of constraints $N.constraints$. For a given agent a_i, this is a standard single source shortest path search from $\alpha_0(a_i)$ to $\alpha_+(a_i)$ that avoids a set of vertices $\{v \in V | (a_i, v, t) \in N.constraints\}$ whenever working at time step t. For details see [19].

CBS stores nodes of CT into priority queue OPEN sorted according to the ascending costs of solutions. At each step CBS takes node N with the lowest cost from OPEN and checks if $N.paths$ represent paths that are valid with respect to MAPF movements rules - that is, $N.paths$ are checked for collisions. If there is no collision, the algorithms returns valid MAPF solution $N.paths$. Otherwise the search branches by creating a new pair of nodes in CT - successors of N. Assume that a collision occurred between agents a_i and a_j in vertex v at time step t. This collision can be avoided if either agent a_i or agent a_j does not reside in v at timestep t. These two options correspond to new successor nodes of N: N_1 and N_2 that inherit the set of conflicts from N as follows: $N_1.conflicts = N.conflicts \cup \{(a_i, v, t)\}$ and $N_2.conflicts = N.conflicts \cup \{(a_j, v, t)\}$. $N_1.paths$ and $N_1.paths$ inherit paths from $N.paths$ except those for agents a_i and a_j respectively. Paths for a_i and a_j are recalculated with respect to extended sets of conflicts $N_1.conflicts$ and $N_2.conflicts$ respectively and new costs for both agents $N_1.\xi$ and $N_2.\xi$ are determined. After this, N_1 and N_2 are inserted into the priority queue OPEN.

SMT-CBS compresses CT into a single branch in which the propositional model taken from MDD-SAT is iteratively refined. The high-level branching from CBS is deferred to the low level of SAT solving. In the MDD-SAT encoding collision avoidance constraints are omitted initially, only constraints ensuring that assignments form valid paths interconnecting starting positions with goals

---

Algorithm 2. SMT-CBS algorithm for solving MAPF

---

1   **SMT-CBS** $(\Sigma = (G = (V, E), A, \alpha_0, \alpha_+))$
2     $conflicts \leftarrow \emptyset$
3     $paths \leftarrow \{path^*(a_i)$ a shortest path from $\alpha_0(a_i)$ to $\alpha_+(a_i)|i = 1, 2, ..., k\}$
4     $\xi \leftarrow \sum_{i=1}^{k} \xi(paths(a_i))$
5   **while** $TRUE$ **do**
6        $(paths, conflicts) \leftarrow$ SMT-CBS-Fixed$(conflicts, \xi, \Sigma)$
7   **if** $paths \neq UNSAT$ **then**
8   **return** $paths$
9        $\xi \leftarrow \xi + 1$

10   **SMT-CBS-Fixed**$(conflicts, \xi, \Sigma)$
11     $\mathcal{H}(\xi) \leftarrow$ encode-Basic$(conflicts, \xi, \Sigma)$
12   **while** $TRUE$ **do**
13        $assignment \leftarrow$ consult-SAT-Solver$(\mathcal{H}(\xi))$
14   **if** $assignment \neq UNSAT$ **then**
15           $paths \leftarrow$ extract-Solution$(assignment)$
16           $collisions \leftarrow$ validate$(paths)$
17   **if** $collisions = \emptyset$ **then**
18   **return** $(paths, conflicts)$
19   **for** $each$ $(a_i, a_j, v, t) \in collisions$ **do**
20              $\mathcal{H}(\xi) \leftarrow \mathcal{H}(\xi) \cup \{\neg\mathcal{X}_v^t(a_i) \vee \neg\mathcal{X}_v^t(a_j)\}$
21              $conflicts \leftarrow conflicts \cup \{[(a_i, v, t), (a_j, v, t)]\}$
22   **return** $(UNSAT, conflicts)$

---

are preserved. This will result in an *incomplete propositional model* denoted $\mathcal{H}(\xi)$. The important component of SMT-CBS is a paths validation procedure that reports back the set of conflicts found in the current solution that are used for making model refinements.

SMT-CBS is shown in pseudo-code as Algorithm 2. The algorithm is divided into two procedures: SMT-CBS representing the main loop and SMT-CBS-Fixed solving the input MAPF for fixed cost ξ. The major difference from the standard CBS is that there is no branching at the high-level. The high-level SMT-CBS roughly correspond to the main loop of MDD-SAT. The set of conflicts is iteratively collected during the entire execution of the algorithm. Procedure *encode* from MDD-SAT is replaced with *encode-Basic* that produces encoding that ignores specific movement rules (collisions between agents) but in contrast to *encode* it encodes collected conflicts into $\mathcal{H}(\xi)$.

The conflict resolution in the standard CBS implemented as high-level branching is here represented by refinement of $\mathcal{H}(\xi)$ with disjunction (line 20). The presented SMT-CBS can eventually build the same formula as MDD-SAT but this is done lazily.

4   Handling Capacity Constraints in MAPF

To adapt the SAT-based approach for MAPF with capacities we need minor modifications only in both MDD-SAT and SMT-CBS. However in each algorithm the integration of capacity constraints is profoundly different. While in MDD-SAT we integrate capacity constraints eagerly in the line with the original design of the algorithm (that is, the constraint in introduced as a whole), in SMT-CBS we integrate capacity constraint lazily which means part by part as new conflicts appear.

4.1   Details of the Encoding with Capacities

We need only a small modification of the MDD-SAT encoding to handle vertex capacities. We need to replace constraint (1) with the following constraint that is again posted for every vertex v and time step t:

$$\sum_{a_i \in A \mid v^t \in V_i} \mathcal{X}_v^t(a_i) \leq c(v) \tag{6}$$

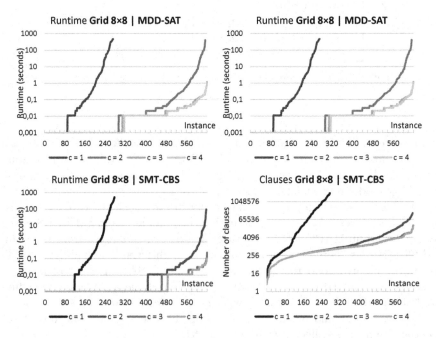

Fig. 2. Sorted runtimes and the number of clauses on the 8×8 grid. MDD-SAT and SMT-CBS are compared.

Unlike in the standard MAPF we need here a more sophisticated translation of the constraint to propositional clauses. Using the approach of forbidding individual $c(v) + 1$-tuples can be highly inefficient especially in cases when $c(v)$ is large. Therefore we use cardinality constraints encodings commonly used in SAT [3,22,24]. Generally the cardinality constraint over set of propositional variables $\{\mathcal{X}_1, \mathcal{X}_2, ..., \mathcal{X}_n\}$ permits at most a specified number of variables from the set to be *TRUE*, denoted $\leq_k \{\mathcal{X}_1, \mathcal{X}_2, ..., \mathcal{X}_n\}$ means that at most k variables from the set can be *TRUE*.

In our case of MAPF with capacities we need to introduce following cardinality constraints for every vertex v and time step t. The practical implementation of cardinality constraints is done through encoding adder circuits inside the formula [22].

$$\leq_{c(v)} \{\mathcal{X}_v^t(a_i) \mid a_i \in A \wedge v^t \in V_i\} \tag{7}$$

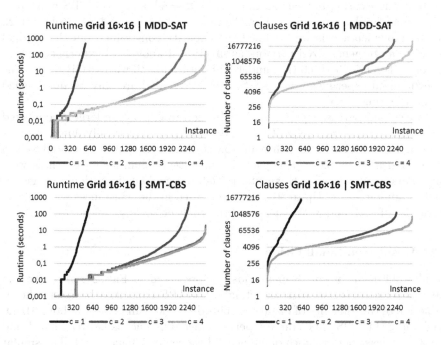

Fig. 3. Sorted runtimes and the number of clauses on the 16×16 grid. MDD-SAT and SMT-CBS are compared.

4.2 Capacities in SMT-CBS

Capacities in SMT-CBS are resolved lazily as well. That is, the capacity constraint is not posted entirely as a cardinality constraint but instead individual sets of agents that violate the capacity are forbidden one by one as they appear. That is for example if a generalized conflict occurs with agents $a_{i_1}, a_{i_2}, ..., a_{i_m}$ in vertex v (in other words if $m > c(v)$) we post a conflict elimination clause concerning the colliding set of agents: $\neg \mathcal{X}_v^t(a_{i_1}) \vee \neg \mathcal{X}_v^t(a_{i_2}) \vee ... \vee \neg \mathcal{X}_v^t(a_{i_m})$.

Hence in the SMT-CBS algorithm we modify only lines 20 and 21 that handle generalized vertex conflicts. Also we need to modify the validation procedure called at line 15 to reflect generalized vertex capacities.

5   Experimental Evaluation

To evaluate the performance of capacity handling in context of SAT-based algorithms we performed an extensive evaluation on both standard synthetic benchmarks [6,20] and large maps from games [26].

5.1   Setup of Experiments and Benchmarks

We took the existing implementations of MDD-SAT and SMT-CBS written in C++. Both implementations are built on top of the Glucose 4 SAT solver [1,2]. In the implementations we modified the capacity constraint from the original *at-most-one* to generalized variants as mentioned above. All experiments were run on a Ryzen 7 CPU 3.0 Ghz under Kubuntu linux 16 with 16 GB RAM. The timeout in all experiments was set to 500 s. Presented are only results finished within this time limit.

The second part of experimental evaluation took place on large 4-connected maps taken from *Dragon Age* [19,26]. We took three structurally different maps focusing on various aspects such as narrow corridors, large almost isolated rooms, or topologically complex open space. In contrast to small instances, these were only sparsely populated with agents. Initial and goal configuration were generated at random again. Up to 80 agents were used in these instances and uniform capacities of 1, 2, and 3. We measured the runtime on large maps.

5.2   Results on Small Grids

Results obtained for small open grids are presented in Figs. 2 and 3. We can see that in comparison with the standard MAPF capacities bring significant reduction of the difficulty of instances. This difference can be seen in both MDD-SAT and SMT-CBS. The starkest performance difference is between $c = 1$ and $c = 2$. The least performance difference is between $c = 3$ and $c = 4$. The similar picture can be seen in for the number of clauses.

5.3   Results on Large Maps

Results for large game maps are shown in Figs. 4 and 5. A different picture can be seen here. Adding capacities does not cause any significant simplification except the brc202d map which consists of narrow corridors. The interpretation is that adding extra parking place via capacities may lead to simplification only when it is not available normally. Otherwise generalized capacity constraints lead to harder instances.

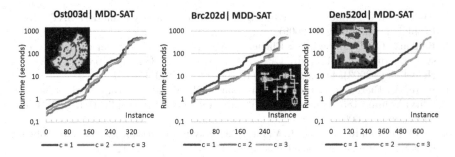

Fig. 4. Sorted runtimes of MDD-SAT on ost003d, brc202d, and den520d maps.

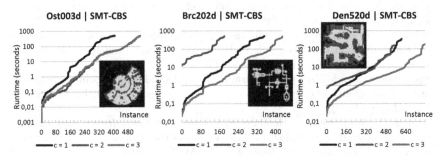

Fig. 5. Sorted runtimes of MDD-SAT on ost003d, brc202d, and den520d maps.

6   Discussion and Conclusion

We introduced multi-agent path finding problem with vertex capacity constraints. We modified two existing state-of-the-art SAT-based optimal MAPF solvers to reflect vertex capacities, the MDD-SAT solver using the *eager* encoding and the SMT-CBS solver using the *lazy* encoding.

In both solvers we observed that adding an extra room by increasing the capacity of vertices dramatically reduces the difficulty of instances. However adding further capacity has less significant effect. In large maps using higher capacities even lead to performance degradation which we attribute to more complex constraints.

In the future work we would like to apply the MAPF formulation with capacities in the real-life multi-agent problems being solved by hierarchical approaches.

Acknowledgements. This research has been supported by GAČR - the Czech Science Foundation, grant registration number 19-17966S.

References

1. Audemard, G., Lagniez, J.-M., Simon, L.: Improving glucose for incremental SAT solving with assumptions: application to MUS extraction. In: Järvisalo, M., Van Gelder, A. (eds.) SAT 2013. LNCS, vol. 7962, pp. 309–317. Springer, Heidelberg (2013). https://doi.org/10.1007/978-3-642-39071-5_23

2. Audemard, G., Simon, L.: Predicting learnt clauses quality in modern SAT solvers. In: IJCAI, pp. 399–404 (2009)
3. Bailleux, O., Boufkhad, Y.: Efficient CNF encoding of Boolean cardinality constraints. In: Rossi, F. (ed.) CP 2003. LNCS, vol. 2833, pp. 108–122. Springer, Heidelberg (2003). https://doi.org/10.1007/978-3-540-45193-8_8
4. Biere, A., Biere, A., Heule, M., van Maaren, H., Walsh, T.: Handbook of Satisfiability: Volume 185 Frontiers in Artificial Intelligence and Applications. IOS Press, Amsterdam (2009)
5. Bofill, M., Palahí, M., Suy, J., Villaret, M.: Solving constraint satisfaction problems with SAT modulo theories. Constraints $17(3)$, 273–303 (2012)
6. Boyarski, E., et al.: ICBS: improved conflict-based search algorithm for multi-agent pathfinding. In: IJCAI, pp. 740–746 (2015)
7. Dresner, K., Stone, P.: A multiagent approach to autonomous intersection management. JAIR 31, 591–656 (2008)
8. Hönig, W., et al.: Summary: multi-agent path finding with kinematic constraints. In: Proceedings of the Twenty-Sixth International Joint Conference on Artificial Intelligence, IJCAI 2017, pp. 4869–4873 (2017)
9. Kornhauser, D., Miller, G.L., Spirakis, P.G.: Coordinating pebble motion on graphs, the diameter of permutation groups, and applications. In: FOCS 1984, pp. 241–250 (1984)
10. Kumar, K., Romanski, J., Hentenryck, P.V.: Optimizing infrastructure enhancements for evacuation planning. In: Proceedings of the Thirtieth AAAI Conference on Artificial Intelligence, pp. 3864–3870. AAAI Press (2016)
11. Li, J., Surynek, P., Felner, A., Ma, H., Koenig, S.: Multi-agent path finding for large agents. In: AAAI, pp. 7627–7634. AAAI Press (2019)
12. Liu, S., Mohta, K., Atanasov, N., Kumar, V.: Towards search-based motion planning for micro aerial vehicles. CoRR abs/1810.03071 (2018). http://arxiv.org/abs/1810.03071
13. Ma, H., et al.: Overview: generalizations of multi-agent path finding to real-world scenarios. CoRR abs/1702.05515 (2017). http://arxiv.org/abs/1702.05515
14. Ma, H., Wagner, G., Felner, A., Li, J., Kumar, T.K.S., Koenig, S.: Multi-agent path finding with deadlines. In: Proceedings of the Twenty-Seventh International Joint Conference on Artificial Intelligence, IJCAI 2018, 13–19 July 2018, Stockholm, Sweden, pp. 417–423 (2018)
15. Nieuwenhuis, R.: SAT modulo theories: getting the best of SAT and global constraint filtering. In: Cohen, D. (ed.) CP 2010. LNCS, vol. 6308, pp. 1–2. Springer, Heidelberg (2010). https://doi.org/10.1007/978-3-642-15396-9_1
16. Nieuwenhuis, R., Oliveras, A., Tinelli, C.: Solving SAT and SAT modulo theories: from an abstract Davis-Putnam-Logemann-Loveland procedure to DPLL(T). J. ACM $53(6)$, 937–977 (2006)
17. Ratner, D., Warmuth, M.K.: Finding a shortest solution for the $N \times N$ extension of the 15-puzzle is intractable. In: AAAI, pp. 168–172 (1986)
18. Ryan, M.R.K.: Exploiting subgraph structure in multi-robot path planning. J. Artif. Intell. Res. (JAIR) 31, 497–542 (2008)
19. Sharon, G., Stern, R., Felner, A., Sturtevant, N.: Conflict-based search for optimal multi-agent pathfinding. Artif. Intell. 219, 40–66 (2015)
20. Sharon, G., Stern, R., Goldenberg, M., Felner, A.: The increasing cost tree search for optimal multi-agent pathfinding. Artif. Intell. 195, 470–495 (2013)
21. Sharon, G., Stern, R., Felner, A., Sturtevant, N.R.: Conflict-based search for optimal multi-agent path finding. In: AAAI (2012)

22. Silva, J., Lynce, I.: Towards robust CNF encodings of cardinality constraints. In: CP, pp. 483–497 (2007)
23. Silver, D.: Cooperative pathfinding. In: AIIDE, pp. 117–122 (2005)
24. Sinz, C.: Towards an optimal CNF encoding of Boolean cardinality constraints. In: van Beek, P. (ed.) CP 2005. LNCS, vol. 3709, pp. 827–831. Springer, Heidelberg (2005). https://doi.org/10.1007/11564751_73
25. Standley, T.: Finding optimal solutions to cooperative pathfinding problems. In: AAAI, pp. 173–178 (2010)
26. Sturtevant, N.R.: Benchmarks for grid-based pathfinding. Comput. Intell. AI Games 4(2), 144–148 (2012)
27. Surynek, P.: A novel approach to path planning for multiple robots in bi-connected graphs. In: ICRA 2009, pp. 3613–3619 (2009)
28. Surynek, P.: Time-expanded graph-based propositional encodings for makespan-optimal solving of cooperative path finding problems. Ann. Math. Artif. Intell. 81(3–4), 329–375 (2017)
29. Surynek, P.: Lazy modeling of variants of token swapping problem and multi-agent path finding through combination of satisfiability modulo theories and conflict-based search. CoRR abs/1809.05959 (2018). http://arxiv.org/abs/1809.05959
30. Surynek, P.: Unifying search-based and compilation-based approaches to multi-agent path finding through satisfiability modulo theories. In: Proceedings of the 28th International Joint Conference on Artificial Intelligence, IJCAI 2019, pp. 1177–1183. ijcai.org (2019)
31. Surynek, P., Felner, A., Stern, R., Boyarski, E.: Efficient SAT approach to multi-agent path finding under the sum of costs objective. In: ECAI, pp. 810–818 (2016)
32. Wang, K., Botea, A.: MAPP: a scalable multi-agent path planning algorithm with tractability and completeness guarantees. JAIR 42, 55–90 (2011)

Evaluating Robustness of an Acting Framework over Temporally Uncertain Domains

Alessandro Umbrico[1(✉)], Amedeo Cesta[1], Marta Cialdea Mayer[2], and Andrea Orlandini[1]

[1] Istituto di Scienze e Tecnologie della Cognizione,
Consiglio Nazionale delle Ricerche, Rome, Italy
alessandro.umbrico@istc.cnr.it
[2] Dipartimento di Ingegneria, Università degli Studi Roma Tre, Rome, Italy

Abstract. The ultimate goal of automated planning is the execution of plans by an artificial agent in the environment. When interactions and collaboration with humans are considered, robust plan execution requires even more highly flexible and adaptable control capabilities in artificial agents. Therefore, plan-based controllers should effectively deal with exogenous events and environment dynamics in order to perform Planning and Acting in an efficient and effective way. The general approach pursued here conforms to the general idea that Acting is not merely executing plans but it entails a more complex process in which dynamic knowledge processing and plan adaptation are required. To this aim, this paper focuses on Human-Robot Collaboration (HRC) and the timeline-based approach which is known to be well suited to robustly deal with uncontrollable dynamics. This paper presents and discusses new interesting results obtained by leveraging the acting capabilities of a novel timeline-based Planning and Acting framework called PLATINUm in a realistic HRC scenario. On the one hand, results show how the variability of the environment can negatively impact the performance and reliability of Acting systems. On the other hand, they show how a proper management of temporal uncertainty strongly improve the Actin reliability.

Keywords: Planning and Scheduling · Execution · Temporal uncertainty · Plan-based controller

1 Introduction

The design of autonomous agents, e.g. robots, whose behavior must be planned to act in an effective (and intelligent) way, dealing with a variety of environments and with a diversity of (possibly not fully controllable) tasks/events, entails a set of deliberative skills. Among others, Planning and Acting play a crucial role [9,13,14]: Planning is the process of synthesizing a sequence of actions that, if correctly executed, achieves a desired objective; Acting is the implementation

© Springer Nature Switzerland AG 2019
M. Alviano et al. (Eds.): AI*IA 2019, LNAI 11946, pp. 250–263, 2019.
https://doi.org/10.1007/978-3-030-35166-3_18

of an on-line closed-loop feedback function (through sensors stimulus and to actuators commands) to refine and control the achievement of planned actions. Thus, reliable autonomous agents need a tight integration of Planning and Acting technologies to realize highly flexible and reactive control behaviors.

Usually, plan-based control architectures integrate deliberative and execution processes relying on different representation formalisms/models and often pursuing different approaches. Imperative approaches exploits, e.g., STRIPS operators combined to procedural languages like, for instance, PRS [12] or RAP [8]. Stochastic approaches leverage learning to build control after experiences or training, e.g., by means of Hierarchical MDP [10]. More classical plan-based solutions pursue a temporal approach implemented in planning frameworks such as, e.g., IxTeT-eXeC [15], IDEA [20], T-REX [22], APSI [3] with ad-hoc executive sub-modules or using state machine encodings like, e.g., PLEXIL [27].

A current limit of the above mentioned approaches is the use of intrinsically different technologies and formalisms to realize Planning and Acting features. Moreover, such decoupled approaches often entail hand-written encodings and/or the use of different formalisms and representations of control problems. As a consequence, Planning and Acting processes cannot completely share crucial *knowledge* that may be useful for dynamically adapting the agent's behaviors to the actual *acting context*. Indeed, planners usually synthesize action plans without taking into full consideration execution perspectives and leading to the execution of too abstract or brittle plans. Such plans are often not suitable for "absorbing" all the possible (uncontrollable) dynamics of the environment causing a high number of *replanning attempts* and, consequently, affecting the general performance of acting systems. On the contrary, the use of shared formalisms can foster a tight integration of Planning and Acting significantly improving the reliability and flexibility of plan-based control architectures. The capability of uniformly modeling uncontrollable dynamics of the environment and leveraging this information at planning time can lead to the synthesis of plans with some desirable execution property like e.g., *strong* or *dynamic controllability* [17,28].

This paper uses a Planning and Acting approach that relies on a *uniform representation* of control problems within tightly coupled internal deliberative and executive processes. Such a uniform representation leverages the timeline-based approach, a temporal planning paradigm introduced by [19] and successfully applied in many real-world scenarios [1,5,6]. The framework fully complies with the formal characterization given in [7] that provides a comprehensive definition of timeline-based planning and execution with *temporal uncertainty*. This proposal is operationalized in a set of extended features for a Planning and Acting software, called PLATINUM [24,25] that extends previous work in timeline-based planning, i.e., APSI-TRF [2] and EPSL [26], by introducing a number of novel features and capabilities: (i) *planning capabilities* to synthesize plans ensuring *pseudo-controllability* [17] in order to deal with *temporal uncertainty*; (ii) *controllability-aware execution capabilities* to dynamically adapt the execution of timeline-based plans according to controllability properties of the domain; (iii) *acting capabilities* to integrate planning and execution within a closed-loop control process that synthesizes and executes timelines, and perform re-planning when exogenous events introduce discrepancies between the observed state of the environment and the outcome expected by the plan under execution.

An experimental assessment of new Planning and Acting capabilities in PLATINUM has been performed by considering a Human-Robot Collaboration (HRC) in a typical collaborative assembly industrial scenario. The results show that a tight integration of planning and execution together with a proper management of temporal uncertainty are crucial to realize robust *acting behaviors* capable of executing complex plans in different contexts and facing uncontrollable dynamics of the environment.

2   Challenges in Human-Robot Collaboration

Human-Robot Collaboration (HRC) constitutes a challenging scenario in which highly flexible control is needed and uncontrollable dynamics of the environment plays a crucial role. In recent years, the continuous improvements of robotic technologies in terms of reliability, efficiency and safety are pushing the diffusion of robots in an increasing number of common situations. In such situations autonomous robotic agents must usually deal with "human agents" that behave in different, unpredictable and autonomous ways. This is especially true in industrial manufacturing environments where the introduction of collaborative robots (also known as *cobots*) are being deployed in advanced manufacturing systems to tightly collaborate with human operators and carry out together different production processes.

Cobots are supposed to autonomously operate in a fenceless work cells and collaborate with human operators in different ways according to the specific production needs. There are a number of (research) challenges that cobots and underlying control technologies must properly face to be effective. Some relevant issues raised by HRC with respect to *autonomy* are the following:

- Different kind of decisions involving various tasks as well as different types of collaborations between the human and the robot are considered;
- Collaboration, task assignment and interactions between robot and human operator may change according to specific capabilities and skills of the worker;
- Adaptability and flexibility are crucial to allow a robot to robustly deal with quick changes and unpredictable/uncontrollable behaviors of the worker during process execution;
- The robot must make decisions and perform operations always guaranteeing human workers *safety*.

To address the above issues, cobots must be endowed with a number of *cognitive capabilities*. Figure 1(a)–(b) and Fig. 2(a)–(b) show these capabilities and the features considered to achieve an effective collaboration.

Figure 1(a)–(b) characterize the representation capabilities a cobot needs to *know* the structure/organization of a production process and the possible interactions with the working environment. A complete description of production

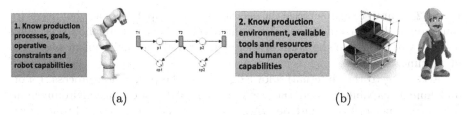

Fig. 1. Cobots need complete knowledge about production contexts: (a) Complete knowledge about the the structure of production processes, operational constraints and capabilities; (b) Complete knowledge about the structure of the environment, available resources and knowledge about the capabilities of human operators.

processes is necessary to know the sequences of tasks that can be performed to achieve production objectives. This knowledge characterizes the capabilities of a robot and defines the tasks it can actually support. Similarly, it characterizes the capabilities of the human operator and therefore ti defines the tasks he/she can actually carry out. Depending on the specific needs of a production process, some tasks can be performed either by the human and the robot. Other tasks instead may require a strict collaboration and cooperation.

Also, this knowledge characterizes operational constraints in terms of valid sequencing of tasks and resource availability constraints that must be satisfied to perform tasks and correctly carry out the related production processes. Typically indeed tasks composing a production process may rely on the availability of some tool like e.g., a screwdriver. If only one (shared) screwdriver is available within the working environment then, the tasks the human and the robot perform must be properly organized (*task allocation*) to minimize *idle times* due to "resource synchronization".

Fig. 2. Cobots need flexible control process and policies to robustly carry out production processes: (a) Flexible control processes enable dynamic allocation of tasks according to human and robot capabilities and production needs as well; (b) Flexible control policies allow cobots to dynamically adapt their behaviors to the observed behaviors of the workers, limiting the impact on the efficiency of the production.

Figure 2 (a) and (b) characterize the decision making capabilities a cobot needs to (autonomously) make decisions about the specific "shape of collaboration" and adapt its behaviors to the state of the operator and the environment observed at runtime.

According to the (internal) knowledge about the production process, robot and human capabilities and the configuration of the working environment a suited sequence of tasks must be synthesized and allocated/assigned to the two *actors*. Two levels of decision: (i) decide the tasks needed to carry out the requested production process (*process synthesis*); (ii) decide who is in charge of execution which tasks (*task allocation*). Namely, it is necessary to decide the actor (i.e., the robot or the worker) responsible for the execution of the tasks synthesized to realize the collaborative process.

Finally, uncontrollable behaviors of a human operator can affect the behaviors of a robot which must dynamically adapt task execution to observations coming from the environment to robustly complete its tasks. The behavior of the worker must be continuously observed to dynamically adapt the behavior of the robot when necessary and support safety and achieve a flexible collaboration.

3   Towards Flexible Control

Automated Planning and Scheduling technologies can play a key role to increase the flexibility and the adaptability of classical robot controllers and therefore achieve a more reliable and effective collaboration with human operators. A tight integration of planning and execution taking into account the control problem in a uniform way sharing control information (i.e., acting) is crucial to achieve the level of flexibility and reliability needed in HRC and similar scenarios [14,23]. The *human* represents an *uncontrollable* element of the environment whose behaviors can neither be controlled nor predicted with accuracy (e.g., the expected duration of task execution). Therefore, it is necessary to make decisions that take into account the uncontrollable dynamics of the environment (see the *controllability problem* [18,28]).

Our objective is to synthesize plans that "encapsulate" control knowledge enabling a flexible and robust execution and limiting the need for replanning. To this aim we pursue a timeline-based planning formalism which takes into account *temporal uncertainty* at both planning and execution level.

A first step towards this objective was the definition of the planning and execution problem with timeline taking into account controllability information in the shape of temporal uncertainty [7]. Then, we developed PLATINUM an open-source planning and execution framework[1] which complies with the proposed formalization [24]. PLATINUM has been successfully applied in realistic HRC scenarios [21] withinFourByThree[2], an H2020 project. It relies on the timeline-based approach pursuing a uniform representation of the control problem and the related causal, temporal and controllability features of the planning

---

[1] https://github.com/pstlab/PLATINUm.git.
[2] http://fourbythree.eu.

and execution problem (i.e., acting problem). The use of shared control information concerning the possible (temporal) dynamics of the environment enables a higher level of flexibility of the resulting acting processes.

3.1 Deliberating Pseudo-controllable Plans

Following the formal account of timelines given in [7], a plan is a set of *flexible timelines* enriched with a set of temporal relations representing temporal constraints that must be fulfilled. A timeline models the possible temporal behaviors of a domain features to control by specifying a sequence of *tokens* whose start and end points are temporal intervals. Tokens model the states or actions the associated domain feature assume or perform over time respectively.

Tokens can be *controllable* (the controller can decide both their start and end time), *partially controllable* (the controller can schedule their start time, but their exact duration is outside the control of the system), or *uncontrollable* (the controller can only observe their execution).

On top of this formalism, the deliberative process implemented by PLATINUM consists in a general partial-plan refinement procedure. It starts from an initial set of partially constrained timelines and iteratively refines them by detecting and solving flaws. PLATINUM extends this general refinement procedure by taking into account also *temporal uncertainty*.

The deliberative process synthesizes *pseudo-controllable* plans: it analyzes the duration bounds of uncontrollable tokens of the plan to check that they have not been squeezed with respect to the domain specification of the associated values. In such a case, the solving procedure can carry on with the search, otherwise backtracking is performed. Pseudo-controllability is a necessary but not sufficient condition for dynamic controllability [17,28]. It is interesting to analyze this property during plan synthesis because non pseudo-controllable plans must be discarded, as their execution cannot be robust. The reader can refer to previous works [24,25] for further details about the types of managed flaws and the related reasoning capabilities.

3.2 Controllability Aware Execution

The execution process implemented by PLATINUM is organized as a sequence of *control cycles* that "discretize" the temporal axis in a number of units called *ticks*. The *control frequency* of the executive determines the granularity of these ticks and the *reactivity* of the controller. During each tick, the system performs a number of operations in two consecutive phases. A *synchronization phase* is in charge of processing the *execution feedback* received until the current tick, and verifying whether the timelines of the plan comply with the observed status of the environment. A *dispatching phase* is in charge of selecting which token to execute according to the current plan status. Moreover, the actual start time of these tokens is scheduled according to the related temporal bounds. Dispatching operations are performed only if the synchronization phase is successfully completed. Otherwise a failure signal is triggered.

The synchronization and dispatching phases are supported by a data structure, called *Execution Dependency Graph* (EDG) which encodes dependencies among tokens. Such dependencies are extracted from the set of temporal relations contained in the timeline-based plan and are crucial to manage plan execution at runtime. Let us consider as an example a partially controllable token A of a timeline FTL_A and a controllable token B of another timeline FTL_B, such that the temporal relation "A during$_{[0,10][0,10]}$ B" must hold. This temporal relation requires in particular that the execution of token B ends within a minimum of 0 and a maximum of 10 time units after the complete execution of token A. According to the timelines in the plan, the end time of the token A must be scheduled within the interval $[5, 23]$ while the end time of B within the interval $[5, 31]$. Now, let us consider the case in which the current execution time is 8 and no feedback/observation about the end of token A has been received yet. In order not to violate the temporal relations of the plan, the executive must *decide* to postpone the end of the execution of B (a controllable token). An EDG encodes information that allows the executive to make such decisions at runtime.

3.3 The Execution Dependency Graph

An EDG is a directed labeled graph built from the temporal relations of a timeline-based plan. Nodes represent tokens and edges represent *execution dependencies* between tokens. An edge connecting a node A to a node B denotes an execution dependency of A with respect to B. Each edge is labeled with '*sx*' to denote a *start execution dependency* and with '*ex*' to denote a *end execution dependency*. Moreover, edge labels contain the *execution state* of the target token enabling the dependency. For example, an edge of the form $\langle A, B, sx, in\_execution \rangle$ encodes a dependency stating that: "The execution of token A can start if and only if token B is currently in execution". The *during* relations of the example above is encoded with two execution conditions and therefore with two distinct edges into the EDG. A start execution condition asserts that A can start its execution if and only if the execution of B is already started. This dependency is represented as a directed edge labeled with $\langle "sx", in\_execution \rangle$ connecting node A to node B. Similarly, an end execution condition asserts that B (controllable) can end its execution if and only if the execution of A is already ended. This dependency is represented as a directed edge labeled with $\langle "ex", executed \rangle$ connecting node B to node A. Algorithm 1 shows the procedure building an EDG from the analysis of the temporal relations of a timeline-based plan Π.

4   Assessment of the Acting Capabilities

The contribution of this work consists in an extensive assessment of the acting capability of PLATINUm. Considering our previous works, we have developed a deliberative control architecture which tightly integrates planning and execution

Algorithm 1. The execution dependency graph building procedure

1: **function** BUILDEXECUTIONDEPENDENCYGRAPH(Π)
2:     EDG $\leftarrow \emptyset$
3:     // initialize the set of nodes associated to the tokens of the timelines
4:     $\mathcal{FTL} \leftarrow GetTimelines\,(\Pi)$
5:     **for** $t_i \in \mathcal{FTL}$ **do**
6:         // set the default execution status *waiting*
7:         $n_{t_i} \leftarrow CreateNode\,(t_i, waiting)$
8:         EDG $\leftarrow AddNode\,(n_{t_i})$
9:     // initialize the set of edges associated to the temporal relations of the plan
10:    $\mathcal{R} \leftarrow GetRelations\,(\Pi)$
11:    **for** $r \in \mathcal{R}$ **do**
12:        // set the edges concerning start and end conditions of tokens
13:        $\{..., (n_{h,i}, n_{h,j}, c_{h,k})\,, ...\} \leftarrow GetStartConditions\,(r)$
14:        EDG $\leftarrow addStartConditions\,(\{..., (n_{h,i}, n_{h,j}, c_{h,k})\,, ...\})$
15:        $\{..., (n_{h,i}, n_{h,j}, c_{h,k})\,, ...\} \leftarrow GetEndConditions\,(r)$
16:        EDG $\leftarrow addEndConditions\,(\{..., (n_{h,i}, n_{h,j}, c_{h,k})\,, ...\})$
17:    **return** EDG

capabilities of PLATINUM. Also, we have developed a simulation environment to stress PLATINUM in different HRC scenarios of growing difficulty in terms of complexity of the addressed problem (e.g., number of tasks to perform) and *uncertainty* about the uncontrollable dynamics of the environment (temporal uncertainty about possible behaviors of the human).

We have here considered a typical HRC scenario consisting of an industrial robotic arm and a human operator sharing a fenceless working environment and interacting with different modalities [11]. Specifically, a realistic assembly/disassembly process, inspired by the ALFA Pilot of FOURBYTHREE, has been considered [4,16]. The original assembly/disassembly process considered during the project focused on the preparation of a die for wax injection and extraction of the pattern from the die. Although it was only a part of the complete industrial process, the underlying HRC coordination problem was (and still is) interesting with respect to our research objectives. Indeed, it represents a labour demanding operation for the human with a significant impact on the final cost of the product. Therefore the introduction of a *cobot* can improve either the working conditions of human operators and the efficiency of the process.

To give an intuition of the HRC problem, the process consists of the following three macro-tasks: (i) mount the die (assembly); (ii) inject the wax pattern; (iii) open the die and remove the wax pattern (disassembly). Focusing on the disassembly part of the process, once the injection process has finished, the die is put on the workbench by the worker who starts unscrewing bolts together with the robot. When all bolts have been unscrewed, the worker removes the top-cover of the die. Then, the worker turns the die to start removing the bottom-cover. The human and the robot must collaborate to perform such a disassembly process by suitably handling different parts of the die and screwing/unscrewing different bolts.

Hence timeline-based planning problems are defined by considering two actors (or agents) that interact over time: a *human* and a *robot*. The human is considered as an uncontrollable agent, so that all the values in human-specific state variables are uncontrollable. On the contrary, the robot is a controllable agent and the operations it can perform may be either controllable or partially controllable. For instance, while unscrewing operations carried out by the robot are controllable, its motion operations are not, as the duration of the execution of a trajectory can vary for safety reasons (the speed of a motion can decrease or be even set to zero to avoid collisions when the human is too close to the robot).

Tasks are hierarchically organized into high-level tasks, such as, e.g., preparing the piece (i.e., the metal die for wax part injection to disassemble), removing the cover of the piece, etc.), and primitive ones (e.g., unscrewing a given bolt). Relationships among higher-level and lower-level tasks are encoded through a dedicated set of synchronization rules[3] Another set of synchronization rules describes the allowed collaborations between the human and the robot. They specify, for each task, which agent can be assigned with the task (i.e., to the human, to the robot or to both of them). Such rules can concern either high-level or primitive tasks, to support different levels of granularity.

4.1   Experimental Design

Two sets of experiments have been considered to assess the deliberative capabilities and the runtime acting capabilities of the framework, respectively.

To evaluate the deliberative capabilities, the experiments have been organized by defining a number of problem specifications varying the following parameters: (i) the number of *total tasks* the human and the robot must perform; (ii) the *percentage* of tasks that can be assigned either to the human or to the robot; (iii) the *temporal uncertainty* of the actual duration of uncontrollable operations (by human) and partially-controllable operations (by robot).

The number of total tasks varies within a minimum of 10 and a maximum of 30. For each number of tasks, the percentage of tasks that can be assigned to the robot or the human vary from a minimum of 20% to a maximum of 100%. For example a percentage of 60% over a number of 10 tasks means that the 6 of the 10 tasks can be assigned to the human or to the robot while the rest of the tasks are pre-allocated to the human. Thus, it is up to the planner to decide who (between the human and the robot) performs 6 of the 10 tasks of the process. A higher percentage implies a higher number of choices and therefore a more challenging planning problem with higher number of possible collaborative solution plans.

To assess the runtime acting capabilities, experiments have been organized by taking into account plans synthesized with a fixed number of tasks (10), a

---

[3] A synchronization rule is a rule expressing causal/temporal dependencies among tokens on timelines that must hold.

fixed percentage of assignment choices (60%) and a variable amount of *temporal uncertainty*. The objective is to evaluate the capacity of robustly dealing with planning and acting in different situations (i.e., *facing* different uncontrollable dynamics of the environment in a robust way). Thus, the developed simulator randomly generates exogenous events during plan execution to stress acting capabilities in different situations.

A number of experiments have been defined by varying *temporal uncertainty* and *platform uncertainty*. The latter represents the actual uncertainty of the simulated environment. The simulator receives execution requests and randomly triggers feedback to the acting process. It determines the *temporal window* within which random feedback is triggered (values span from 5 to 30 time units).

4.2 Results

The results concerning the assessment of the deliberative capabilities of the framework show that PLATINUM can efficiently solve problems of growing complexity in terms of number of goals (i.e., the number of *total tasks*) and number of task allocation choices (i.e., the *percentage* of tasks to assign).

In the worst case indeed the planner takes up to 140 s to synthesize plans. Namely, it takes 140 s to synthesize plans that implement a collaborative process composed by 30 high-level tasks and decide the assignment of all these tasks. This is a reasonable time considering that the estimated minimum execution time of a whole collaborative process with 30 tasks is about 500 s. Also, the experiments show that an increasing value of temporal uncertainty does not impact on the solving performance of the framework.

Efficiency is not the only aspect to consider in application scenarios like HRC. The *quality* of the synthesized plans is equally important in this kind of scenarios. It is crucial to synthesize plans that enable a feasible and effective collaborations between humans and robots. A planning process synthesizing plans where tasks are assigned only to the robot would not be effective in real world applications, regardless its efficiency. A tradeoff between deliberation time and quality of generated plans must be found to synthesize effective plans. To this aim PLATINUM has been enriched with a *load balancing* search strategy to achieve an as much as possible equal *work load* distribution between the human and the robot and a low cycle time of the production process as well (i.e., low makespan).

Figure 3 shows the obtained results by aggregating the makespan of the plans and the number of tasks assigned to the human worker and the robot. It can be observed that a higher percentage of task assignment (i.e., higher number of alternative collaborative plans) leads to the synthesis of plans that achieve a better makespan and a better task distribution. Also, the chart shows that the total makespan of the collaborative process decreases when the number of tasks that can be assigned to the human and the robot increases. Namely, increasing the number of planning choices, the framework can generate plans with a better distribution of the work load between the human and the robot and therefore a lower makespan (i.e., a more efficient collaborative process).

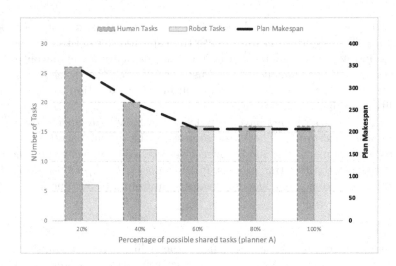

Fig. 3. Makespan and task distribution of the plans in different configurations

Concerning the assessment of the runtime capabilities of PLATINUM, the obtained results show the capability of integrating planning and acting using a common representation of the problem. Although with different performances, all the tested acting configurations were capable of completing plan execution. In particular, the results show that the use of a shared representation and a proper model of the uncontrollable dynamics of the environment can strongly improve the reliability of the acting process.

Indeed, PLATINUM was capable of completing the execution of (pseudo-controllable) plans without *replanning* in all the configurations that do not *underestimate* the uncertainty of the environment (i.e., all the configurations with *model uncertainty* greater than or equal to the *platform uncertainty*).

Figure 4 shows the total planning time and the planning sessions of the different executions with a growing variability of the platform simulator. The figure shows the behavior of the agent using different models of temporal uncertainty. Except for the first planning session which is the one needed to generate the plan, each (re)planning session represents an exogenous event causing an execution failure. The results show that the pseudo-controllable plans synthesized with a temporal uncertainty set to 30 (see *modelU30* in Fig. 4) enable the executive to "consistently" manage the (random and uncontrollable) dynamics of the platform.

It is worth underscoring that the case with temporal uncertainty set to 10 (*modelU10* in Fig. 4) is the acting configuration achieving the worst performance in terms of total acting time and therefore the highest number of planning sessions (5, total planning time about 70 s). The performance of this configuration gets worst as soon as the variability of the platform becomes greater than the modeled temporal uncertainty. This is a reasonable and expected result since an under-estimation of uncertainty would prevent the agent to properly manage possible concrete situations. The higher the distance between the model and the behavior of the system, the higher the probability that the system looses control. Therefore an *adequate model* of the temporal uncertainty is crucial to realize *reliable acting agents*.

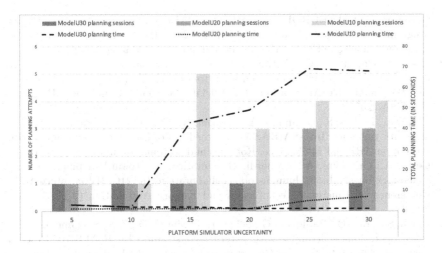

Fig. 4. Total planning time and number of replanning attempts

5   Conclusions

This paper presents an assessment of the timeline-based planning and acting framework called PLATINUM over a number of domains with an increasing amount of *temporal uncertainty*. The aim of the work is to show the capability of the framework in dealing with the uncontrollable dynamics of an environment at both planning and execution level. The evaluation has focused on a realistic Human-Robot Collaboration scenario where an industrial robot cooperates with a human operator (uncontrollable) and together they carry out a collaborative process in a reliable and efficient way. The results show that PLATINUM-based acting agents can synthesize pseudo-controllable plans and execute them through a flexible and reliable management of exogenous events and uncontrollable dynamics of the environment. Then, the pursued acting approach is well-suited to address challenging control problems where uncontrollable temporal dynamics plays a key role and a reliable acting process is strongly necessary.

In the immediate future, we plan to extend the general timeline-based formalism, so that the particular features of HRC problems could be treated in a specific and immediate way. In fact, it would be useful to define a syntactic extension of the general formalism allowing the designer to use, for example, abbreviations for task assignment, that would be automatically "compiled" into the pre-existing kernel language.

Acknowledgments. CNR authors are partially supported by EU under the H2020 SHAREWORK project (GA No. 820807).

References

1. Barreiro, J., et al.: EUROPA: a platform for AI planning, scheduling, constraint programming, and optimization. In: ICKEPS 2012: the 4th International Competition on Knowledge Engineering for Planning and Scheduling (2012)
2. Cesta, A., Cortellessa, G., Fratini, S., Oddi, A.: Developing an end-to-end planning application from a timeline representation framework. In: IAAI-09. Proceedings of the 21st Innovative Application of Artificial Intelligence Conference, Pasadena, CA, USA (2009)
3. Cesta, A., Fratini, S., Orlandini, A., Rasconi, R.: Continuous planning and execution with timelines. In: i-SAIRAS-12. Proceedings of the 11th International Symposium on Artificial Intelligence, Robotics and Automation in Space (2012)
4. Cesta, A., Orlandini, A., Bernardi, G., Umbrico, A.: Towards a planning-based framework for symbiotic human-robot collaboration. In: 21th IEEE International Conference on Emerging Technologies and Factory Automation (ETFA). IEEE (2016)
5. Chien, S., Tran, D., Rabideau, G., Schaffer, S., Mandl, D., Frye, S.: Timeline-based space operations scheduling with external constraints. In: ICAPS-10. Proceedings of the 20th International Conference on Automated Planning and Scheduling (2010)
6. Chrpa, L., Pinto, J., Ribeiro, M.A., Py, F., Sousa, J., Rajan, K.: On mixed-initiative planning and control for autonomous underwater vehicles. In: 2015 IEEE/RSJ International Conference on Intelligent Robots and Systems (IROS), pp. 1685–1690, September 2015
7. Cialdea Mayer, M., Orlandini, A., Umbrico, A.: Planning and execution with flexible timelines: a formal account. Acta Inf. **53**(6–8), 649–680 (2016)
8. Firby, R.J.: An investigation into reactive planning in complex domains. In: Proceedings of the 6th National Conference on Artificial Intelligence, Seattle, WA, USA, July 1987, pp. 202–206 (1987)
9. Ghallab, M., Nau, D.S., Traverso, P.: The actor's view of automated planning and acting: a position paper. Artif. Intell. **208**, 1–17 (2014)
10. Hauskrecht, M., Meuleau, N., Kaelbling, L.P., Dean, T.L., Boutilier, C.: Hierarchical solution of Markov decision processes using macro-actions. In: UAI 1998: Proceedings of the Fourteenth Conference on Uncertainty in Artificial Intelligence, University of Wisconsin Business School, Madison, Wisconsin, USA, 24–26 July 1998, pp. 220–229 (1998)
11. Helms, E., Schraft, R.D., Hagele, M.: rob@work: robot assistant in industrial environments. In: Proceedings. 11th IEEE International Workshop on Robot and Human Interactive Communication, pp. 399–404 (2002)
12. Ingrand, F.F., Chatila, R., Alami, R., Robert, F.: PRS: a high level supervision and control language for autonomous mobile robots. In: Proceedings of IEEE International Conference on Robotics and Automation, vol. 1, pp. 43–49 (1996)
13. Ingrand, F., Ghallab, M.: Robotics and artificial intelligence: a perspective on deliberation functions. AI Commun. **27**(1), 63–80 (2014)
14. Ingrand, F., Ghallab, M.: Deliberation for autonomous robots: a survey. Artif. Intell. **247**, 10–44 (2017)

15. Lemai, S., Ingrand, F.: Interleaving temporal planning and execution in robotics domains. In: AAAI 2004, pp. 617–622 (2004)
16. Maurtua, I., et al.: FourByThree: imagine humans and robots working hand in hand. In: 2016 IEEE 21st International Conference on Emerging Technologies and Factory Automation (ETFA), pp. 1–8, September 2016
17. Morris, P.H., Muscettola, N.: Temporal dynamic controllability revisited. Proc. AAAI **2005**, 1193–1198 (2005)
18. Morris, P.H., Muscettola, N., Vidal, T.: Dynamic control of plans with temporal uncertainty. In: International Joint Conference on Artificial Intelligence (IJCAI), pp. 494–502 (2001)
19. Muscettola, N.: HSTS: integrating planning and scheduling. In: Zweben, M., Fox, M.S. (eds.) Intelligent Scheduling. Morgan Kauffmann, Burlington (1994)
20. Muscettola, N., Dorais, G.A., Fry, C., Levinson, R., Plaunt, C.: Idea: planning at the core of autonomous reactive agents. In: Proceedings of NASA Workshop on Planning and Scheduling for Space (2002)
21. Pellegrinelli, S., Orlandini, A., Pedrocchi, N., Umbrico, A., Tolio, T.: Motion planning and scheduling for human and industrial-robot collaboration. CIRP Ann. - Manuf. Technol. **66**, 1–4 (2017)
22. Py, F., Rajan, K., McGann, C.: A systematic agent framework for situated autonomous systems. In: AAMAS, pp. 583–590 (2010)
23. Rajan, K., Saffiotti, A.: Towards a science of integrated AI and robotics. Artif. Intell. **247**, 1–9 (2017)
24. Umbrico, A., Cesta, A., Cialdea Mayer, M., Orlandini, A.: PLATINUm: a new framework for planning and acting. In: Esposito, F., Basili, R., Ferilli, S., Lisi, F.A. (eds.) AI*IA 2017. LNCS, vol. 10640, pp. 498–512. Springer International Publishing, Cham (2017). https://doi.org/10.1007/978-3-319-70169-1_37
25. Umbrico, A., Cesta, A., Mayer, M.C., Orlandini, A.: Integrating resource management and timeline-based planning. In: Twenty-Eighth International Conference on Automated Planning and Scheduling (2018)
26. Umbrico, A., Orlandini, A., Mayer, M.C.: Enriching a temporal planner with resources and a hierarchy-based heuristic. In: Gavanelli, M., Lamma, E., Riguzzi, F. (eds.) AI*IA 2015. LNCS (LNAI), vol. 9336, pp. 410–423. Springer, Cham (2015). https://doi.org/10.1007/978-3-319-24309-2_31
27. Verma, V., Jonsson, A., Pasareanu, C., Iatauro, M.: Universal-executive and PLEXIL: engine and language for robust spacecraft control and operations. In: Space 2006. American Institute of Aeronautics and Astronautics (2006)
28. Vidal, T., Fargier, H.: Handling contingency in temporal constraint networks: from consistency to controllabilities. JETAI **11**(1), 23–45 (1999)

On the Configuration of SAT Formulae

Mauro Vallati[1(✉)] and Marco Maratea[2]

[1] School of Computing and Engineering,
University of Huddersfield, Huddersfield, UK
m.vallati@hud.ac.uk
[2] DIBRIS, University of Genova, Genova, Italy
marco.maratea@dibris.unige.it

Abstract. It is well-known that the order in which clauses and literals are listed in a SAT formulae can have a strong impact on solvers' performance.

In this work we investigate how the performance of SAT solvers can be *improved* by a specifically-designed SAT formulae configuration. We introduce a fully automated approach for this configuration task, that considers a number of criteria for optimising the order in which clauses and, within clauses, literals, are listed in a formula expressed using the Conjunctive Normal Form.

Our experimental analysis, involving three state-of-the-art SAT solvers and six different benchmark sets, shows that the configurations identified by the proposed approach can have a significant positive impact on solvers' performance.

Keywords: SATisfiability · Knowledge configuration · Performance improvement

1 Introduction

The propositional satisfiability problem (SAT) is one of the most prominent problems in Artificial Intelligence (AI), and it is exploited in a wide range of real-world applications. Well-known examples include hardware and software verification [22], test-case generation [5], automated planning [23], and scheduling [7]. Nowadays, thanks also to the SAT competitions and SAT challenges,[1] there is a large-yet-growing number of ready-to-use SAT solvers that can be used in applications.

By exploiting algorithm configuration techniques, SAT solvers' behaviour can be adjusted to perform well for a specific type of instances [8,17,24], allowing them to be optimised for the actual problems at hand. To support this type of customisation, most state-of-the-art solvers expose a large number of parameters whose settings can significantly modify many parts of the solver, like the heuristic and search techniques. Furthermore, in areas of AI such as automated planning

---

[1] http://www.satcompetition.org.

© Springer Nature Switzerland AG 2019
M. Alviano et al. (Eds.): AI*IA 2019, LNAI 11946, pp. 264–277, 2019.
https://doi.org/10.1007/978-3-030-35166-3_19

[25,26] or abstract argumentation [6], it has been demonstrated that also the configuration of the knowledge models, i.e. the symbolic representation of the problem that is provided as input to automated reasoners, can lead to significant performance improvements of general domain-independent solvers. Intuitively, such results can be due to the fact that the way in which a model is represented: (i) implicitly carries some knowledge about the problem, and such knowledge can positively impact the behaviour of solvers; and (ii) can early guide the search approach towards promising areas of the search space, by ordering the way in which options are considered. It may be argued that the first aspect can be more relevant in "complex" models, such as those needed in automated planning, while the second aspect can be prominent in the case of less-structured models.

In the SAT field, it is well-known that the ordering of clauses and literals in SAT formulae can have a strong impact on the performance of solvers, and random shuffling has been routinely implemented in international competitions as a technique for avoiding some potential biases. In this context, we propose instead to exploit the impact that orderings can have on SAT solvers in order to improve performance. Here we introduce an approach for performing the automated configuration of SAT formulae expressed using the Conjunctive Normal Form (CNF). The configuration aims at identifying an ordering of clauses and, within clauses, the involved literals, of a CNF from a specific type of instances that allows to *improve* the performance of a given SAT solver. In this sense, the proposed approach exploits the fact that the ordering of elements in SAT formulae has an impact on solvers, to improve performance and reduce –at least in part– the *accidental complexity* of formulae. Accidental complexity refers to cases where instances are made harder to be solved due to the way in which they have been encoded [4].

Notably, due to the fact that the configuration has to be performed online when a new CNF is provided to the solver, it has to rely on characteristics of the CNF that are computationally cheap to extract. Through comprehensive experiments, using three state-of-the-art SAT solvers and six different benchmark sets, we demonstrate that the proposed approach for performing CNF configuration can lead to significant benefits in terms of SAT solvers' performance, and can provide valuable information for the encoding of CNFs and for further improvements of SAT solvers.

This paper is organised as follows. Firstly, we provide the relevant background on the DIMACS format, used for representing CNFs. Then, we describe the proposed approach for the automated configuration of SAT formulae. After that, we show the results of our large experimental analysis. Finally, conclusions are given.

2 SAT Formulae

In this work we focus on SAT formulae represented using Conjunctive Normal Form (CNF) and following the DIMACS format. The DIMACS format is the standard format supported by SAT solvers, and used in SAT competitions and challenges.[2]

A CNF formula is a conjunction of clauses, where a clause is a disjunction of literals. Literals can be assigned a boolean value.

```
p cnf 5 3
1 -3 0
2 3 -1 -4 0
-5 -4 0
```

Fig. 1. An example CNF encoded in the DIMACS format.

Figure 1 gives an example of a formula, presented in the DIMACS format, including five literals and three clauses. The line starting by p gives information about the formula: the instance is in the CNF, and the number of literals and clauses, respectively, are provided. In the DIMACS format a literal is uniquely identified by a number. After the initial descriptive line, clauses are listed. Each clause is a sequence of distinct non-null numbers ending with 0 on the same line. Positive numbers denote the corresponding literals. Negative numbers denote the negations of the corresponding literals. In the computation performed by modern SAT solvers, the formula is satisfied when all the literals have been assigned, and all the clauses are true at the same time. For the given example, a valid solution would be 1 2 3 -4 5, corresponding to an assignment where all variables are True, except 4.

3   Configuration of SAT Formulae

In a SAT formula, clauses are usually not ordered following a principled app-roach, but they are ordered according to the way in which the randomised gener-ator has been coded, following the way in which information from the application domain has been collected, or deliberately shuffled to prevent potential biases. This is also generally true for the order in which literals of a given clause are presented in the formula.

Here we focus on the following question: *given the set of clauses and, for each clause, the set of corresponding literals, in which order should they be listed to maximise the performance of a given solver?* The underlying hypothesis is that the order in which clauses and literals are listed can be tuned to highlights elements that are important for satisfying, or demonstrating the unsatisfiability, of the considered SAT instance by the considered SAT solver.

---

[2] http://www.satcompetition.org.

3.1 Automated Configuration of SAT Formulae

In this work we use the state-of-the-art SMAC [13] configuration approach for identifying a configuration of CNF formulae, encoded using the DIMACS format, that aims at improving the PAR10 performance of a given SAT solver. PAR10 is the average runtime where unsolved instances count as 10× cutoff time. PAR10 is a metric commonly exploited in machine learning and algorithm configuration techniques, as it allows to consider coverage and runtime at the same time.

SMAC uses predictive models of performance [18] to guide its search for good configurations. More precisely, it uses previously observed ⟨configuration, performance⟩ pairs ⟨$c, f(c)$⟩ and supervised machine learning (random forests [3]) to learn a function

$$\hat{f} : \mathcal{C} \to \mathbb{R} \tag{1}$$

that predicts the performance of arbitrary parameter configurations (including those not yet evaluated). The performance data to fit these models is collected sequentially. In a nutshell, after an initialisation phase, SMAC iterates the following three steps: (1) use the performance measurements observed so far to fit a random forest model $\hat{f}$; (2) use $\hat{f}$ to select a promising configuration $c \in \mathcal{C}$ to evaluate next, trading off exploration in new parts of the configuration space and exploitation in parts of the space known to perform well; and (3) run c on one or more benchmark instances and compare its performance to the best configuration observed so far.

The CNF configuration has to be performed online: as soon as a new formula is provided as input, the formula has to be configured before being presented to the solver. In a nutshell, given a set of parameters that can be used to modify the ordering of some aspect of the CNF formula, and given the value assigned to each parameter, the online configuration is performed by re-ordering clauses and literals accordingly. Notably, the value of each parameter has to be provided, and can be identified via an appropriate off-line learning step.

Given the depicted online scenario, we are restricted to information about the CNF that can be quickly gathered and that are computationally cheap to extract. Furthermore, the configuration must consider only general aspects that are common to any CNF. As it is apparent, the use of a computationally expensive configuration of a single CNF, that considers elements that are specific to the given CNF, would nullify the potential performance improvement, by drastically reducing the time available for the solver to find a solution (or to demonstrate unsatisfiability).

In this work, we consider the possibility to order *clauses* according to the following criteria:

- (1) the number of literals of the clause;
- (2) the fact that the clause is binary;
- (3) the fact that the clause is ternary;
- (4) the number of positive literals of the clause;
- (5) the number of negative literals of the clause;

- (6) the fact that the clause is binary, and both literals are negative;
- (7) the fact that the clause has only one negative literal.

Literals can be listed in clauses according to:

- (*i*) the number of clauses in which the literal appears;
- (*ii*) the average size of the clauses in which the literal is involved;
- (*iii*) the number of binary clauses in which the literal in involved;
- (*iv*) the number of ternary clauses in which the literal is involved;
- (*v*) the number of times the literal appears in clauses as positive;
- (*vi*) the number of times the literal appears in clauses as negative;
- (*vii*) the number of times the literal is involved in clauses where all literals are positive;
- (*viii*) the number of times the literal is involved in clauses where all literals are negative.

The set of proposed ordering criteria is aimed at being as inclusive as possible, so that different characterising aspects of clauses and literals can be taken into account, at the same time, for the configuration process.

It is easy to notice that many of the introduced criteria focus on aspects of binary and ternary clauses. This is due to their importance in the search process. For instance, binary clauses are responsible, to a great degree, of unit propagation. There are also criteria that aims at identifying potentially relevant aspects. For instance, criterion 7 aims at identifying clauses that may be representing implication relations between literals.

There are different ways for encoding the identified degrees of freedom in CNFs as parameters. This is due to the fact that orders are not natively supported by general configuration techniques [13, 19]. Results presented by Vallati et al. [25] suggest that purely categorical parametrisations are not indicated for the configuration of models, as they tend to fragment the configuration space and to introduce discontinuities. Those combined aspects make the exploration of the configuration space particularly challenging for learning approaches. For this reason, here we generate 7 continuous parameters for configuring the order of clauses, and 8 continuous parameters for configuring the order of literals in clauses. Each parameter corresponds to one of the aforementioned criteria, and they have to be combined to generate different possible orderings of clauses and literals in CNFs. Each continuous parameter has associated a real value in the interval $[-10.0, +10.0]$ which represents (in absolute value) the *weight* given to the corresponding ordering criterion. Two additional categorical selectors are also included. One which allows to activate or de-active the ordering of literals in the clauses, and the second that allows to order clauses according to the ordering (direct or inverse) followed by the involved literals. Thus, the configuration space is $\mathcal{C} = [-10.0, +10.0]^{15} \times 2 \times 3$, where 2 are the possible values of the parameter on ordering of literals in clauses, and 3 are the possible values of the categorical parameter describing whether the order of clauses should follow the order of involved literals. An ordering σ instantiates each of the 17 parameters, and can be used on any CNF. Given a CNF and an ordering σ, the corresponding configuration of the formula is obtained as follows. For each literal, an ordering score $o_l(v)$ is defined as:

$$o_l(l) = \sum_{c \in C} (value(p, c) \times weight(c)) \tag{2}$$

where c is a continuous ordering criterion in the set C of the 8 available continuous parameters for configuring literals' order, $value(p, c)$ is the numerical value of the corresponding aspect for the literal v, and $weight(c)$ is the weight assigned to the corresponding continuous parameter by the configuration technique. If the 16th parameter is set to ignore the order of literals in clauses, then literals are ordered as in the provided initial CNF. Otherwise, for every clause, the involved literals are ordered following the score $o_l(v)$. Ties are broken following the order in the original CNF configuration. As it is apparent from Eq. (2), a positive (negative) value of $weight(c)$ can be used to indicate that the aspect corresponding to the parameter c is important for the SAT solver, and that literals with that aspect should be listed early (late) in the clause to improve performance.

Similarly to what is presented in Eq. (2) for literals, clauses are ordered according to a corresponding score $o_C(d)$ –where C is the set of clauses ordering criteria–, unless clauses are forced to follow the order of literals via the appropriate parameter. In that case, clauses are ordered according to the sum of the $o_l(v)$ scores of the set of literals that appear in the clause $L(d)$, as shown in Eq. (3).

$$o_C(d) = \sum_{v \in L(d)} o_l(v) \tag{3}$$

```
p cnf 5 3
1 -3 0
2 3 -1 -4 0
-5 -4 0
```

```
p cnf 5 3
3 -1 -4 2 0
-4 -5 0
1 -3 0
```

Fig. 2. The example CNF formula non configured (top), and the configured version (bottom). Configuration has been done by listing clauses according to their length and the number of negative literals. Literals are listed following the number of clauses they are involved.

Example 1. Let us consider the CNF presented, using the DIMACS format, in Fig. 2 (top). Suppose that we are interested in listing clauses according to their length (criterion 1) and to the number of involved negative literals (criterion 5). Similarly, we are interested in listing the literals of a clause according to the number of clauses in which they appear (criterion i). This can be done by leaving all the parameters to the default value 0.0, but the ones controlling the mentioned criteria to 10.0. Considering only criteria 1 and 5, the clause 2 3 -1 -4 0 has a $o_C(d)$ score of $(4 + 2) \times 10.0 = 60.0$: it involves 4 literals, and 2 literals are negative. According to the same criteria, clause 1 -3 0 has a score of $(2 + 1) \times 10.0 = 30.0$. In a similar way, but considering the corresponding criterion, the score of literals can be calculated, and literals are then ordered accordingly in each clause. Of course, the first line of the considered CNF formula is unmodified, as the DIMACS format require it to be the first, and to present information in a given order.   □

The way in which the considered ordering criteria are combined, via Eqs. (2) and (3), gives a high degree of freedom for encoding and testing different configurations. Very specific aspects can be prioritised: for instance, it would be possible to present first clauses that are binary, and where both literals are positive, by penalising criterion 5 and giving a high positive weight to criterion 2. Furthermore, additional criteria can be added, with no need to modify or update the overall configuration framework.

4   Experimental Analysis

Our experimental analysis aims to evaluate the impact of the proposed automated approach for performing CNF configuration, on state-of-the-art SAT solvers' performance.

We selected 3 SAT solvers, based on their performance in recent SAT competitions and in their widespread use: Cadical version sc17 [2], Glucose 4.0 [1], and Lingeling version bbc [2]. For each solver, a benchmark-set specific configuration was generated using SMAC 2.08. A Python 2.7 script is used as a wrapper for extracting information from a given formula and, according to the parameters' value, reconfigure it and provide it as input for the SAT solver.

In designing our experimental analysis, we followed the Configurable SAT Solver Challenge (CSSC) [17]. The competition aimed at evaluating to which extent SAT solvers' performance can be improved by algorithm configuration for solving instances from a given class of benchmarks. In that, the CSSC goals are similar to the goals of this experimental analysis –i.e., assessing how performance can be improved via configuration–, thus their experimental settings are deemed to be appropriate for our analysis. However, CSSC focused on the configuration of SAT solvers' behaviour by modifying exposed parameters of solvers. In this work we do not directly manipulate the behaviour of SAT solvers via exposed parameters, but we focus on the impact that the configuration of a CNF formula can have on solvers.

Following CSSC settings, a cutoff of 5 CPU-time minutes, and a memory limit of 4 GB of RAM, has been set for each solver run on both training and testing instances. This is due to the fact that many solvers have runtime distributions with long tails [12], and that practitioners often use many instances and relatively short runtimes to benchmark solvers for a new application domain [17]. There is also evidence that rankings of solvers in SAT competitions would remain similar if shorter runtimes are enforced [14].

We chose benchmark sets from the CSSC 2014 edition [17], and the benchmarks used in the Agile track of the 2016 SAT competition.[3] These two competitions provide benchmarks that can highlight the importance of configuration (CSSC) –even though a different type of configuration than the one considered in this paper–, and that include instances that have to be solved quickly (Agile). In particular, CSSC benchmarks can allow us to compare the impact of the proposed CNF configuration with regards to the solvers' configuration.

Selected CSSC 2014 benchmark sets include: Circuit Fuzz (Industrial track), 3cnf, K3 (Random SAT+UNSAT Track), and Queens and Low Autocorrelation Binary Sequence (Crafted track).[4] Benchmark sets were selected in order to cover most of the tracks considered in CSSC, and by checking that at least 20% of the instances were solvable by considered solvers, when run on the default CNFs. Benchmarks were randomly divided into training and testing instances, aiming at having between 150–300 instances for testing purposes, and a similar amount of benchmarks for training. The size of each testing set is shown in Table 1.

Experiments were run on a machine equipped with Intel Xeon 2.50 Ghz processors. Each configuration process, i.e. for each pair SAT solver - benchmark set, has been given a budget of 5 sequential CPU-time days, and run on a dedicated processor.

Table 1. Results of the selected solvers on the considered benchmark sets. Between brackets, the number of considered testing instances. For each solver and benchmark, we show the number of test set timeouts achieved when running on the default and on the configured CNFs. Bold indicates the best result.

	Cadical	Glucose	Lingeling
	# timeouts: default $\rightarrow$ configured		
K3 (150)	89 $\rightarrow$ **84**	72 $\rightarrow$ **69**	76 $\rightarrow$ **75**
3cnf (250)	219 $\rightarrow$ **216**	134 $\rightarrow$ **131**	213 $\rightarrow$ **210**
Queens (150)	10 $\rightarrow$ **9**	26 $\rightarrow$ **25**	24 $\rightarrow$ **23**
Low Autocorrelation (300)	118 $\rightarrow$ **116**	115 $\rightarrow$ **109**	123 $\rightarrow$ **120**
Circuit Fuzz (185)	19 $\rightarrow$ **17**	9 $\rightarrow$ 9	12 $\rightarrow$ **10**
Agile16 (250)	31 $\rightarrow$ **29**	24 $\rightarrow$ **19**	55 $\rightarrow$ **48**
Total	486 $\rightarrow$ **471**	380 $\rightarrow$ **362**	503 $\rightarrow$ **486**

---

[3] https://baldur.iti.kit.edu/sat-competition-2016/.
[4] http://aclib.net/cssc2014/benchmarks.html.

Table 1 summarises the results of the selected SAT solvers on the considered benchmark sets. Results are presented in terms of the number of timeouts on testing instances, achieved by solvers run using either the default or the configured CNFs. Indeed, all of the considered solvers benefited from the configuration of the CNFs. Improvements vary according to the benchmark sets: the Agile16 set is, in general, the set where the solvers gained more by the use of configured CNFs. Remarkably, the improvements observed in Table 1 are comparable to those achieved in CSSC 2013 and 2014, that were achieved by configuring the solvers' behaviour [17]. In fact, these results may confirm our intuition that the way in which clauses and literals are ordered has an impact on the way in which solvers explore the search space. Listing "important" clauses earlier may lead the solver to tackle complex situations early in the search process, making it then easier to find a solution. In that, it may be argued that a solver's behaviour can be controlled internally, by modifying its exposed parameters, and externally by ordering the CNF in a suitable way.

Interestingly, the overall results (last row of Table 1) indicate that the CNF configuration does not affect all the solvers in a similar way, and that can potentially lead to rank inversions in competitions or comparisons. This is the case of Lingeling (on configured) and Cadical on default. This may suggest that current competitions could benefit by exploiting a solver-specific configuration, in order to mitigate any implicit bias due to the particular CNF configuration exploited. Randomly listing clauses and variables may of course remove some bias, but it can also be the case that different biases are introduced. In that sense, allowing solvers to be provided with a specifically-configured CNF may lead to a better comparison of performance. Finally, it is worth noting that the way in which the CNFs are configured varies significantly between solvers, as well as according to the benchmark set. In other words, there is not a single ordering that allows to maximise the performance of all the SAT solvers at once.

Table 2. Results of the selected solvers on the considered benchmark sets. For each solver and benchmark, we show the IPC score achieved when running on the default and on the configured CNFs. Bold indicates the best result. Results of different solvers can not be directly compared.

	Cadical	Glucose	Lingeling
	IPC score: default → configured		
K3	56.7 → **59.9**	71.3 → **76.3**	67.8 → **68.6**
3cnf	27.3 → **31.6**	106.6 → **107.0**	33.6 → **35.9**
Queens	136.5 → **137.6**	119.3 → **121.1**	120.6 → **122.9**
Low Autocorrelation	171.8 → **173.4**	177.2 → **183.7**	171.0 → **175.3**
Circuit Fuzz	156.3 → **160.8**	175.2 → **175.3**	161.3 → **164.3**
Agile16	208.1 → **211.3**	209.1 → **215.9**	188.6 → **196.6**
Total	756.7 → **774.6**	858.7 → **879.3**	742.9 → **763.6**

To better understand the impact of configuring CNFs on the runtime of solvers, Table 2 compares performance in terms of IPC score variations. The IPC score provides a trade-off between runtime and coverage, and is used in the International Planning Competition for comparing planners' performance.

For a solver $\mathcal{R}$ and a SAT instance p, $Score(\mathcal{R}, p)$ is defined as:

$$Score(\mathcal{R}, p) = \begin{cases} 0 & if\ p\ is\ unsolved \\ \frac{1}{1+\log_{10}(\frac{T_p(\mathcal{R})}{T_p^*})} & otherwise \end{cases}$$

where T_p^* is the minimum amount of time required by any compared system to solve the instance, and $T_p(\mathcal{R})$ denotes the CPU time required by $\mathcal{R}$ to solve the instance p. Higher values of the score indicate better performance.

In Table 2 the performance of a solver run on the default and configured formulae are compared. Results indicate that the configuration provides, for most of the benchmark sets, a noticeable improvement also in terms of IPC score.

To shed some light on the most relevant aspects of the SAT formula configuration, we assessed the importance of parameters in the considered configurations using the fANOVA tool [15]. We observed that in most of the cases, improvements are mainly due to the effect of the correct configuration of a single criterion, rather then to the interaction of two or more criteria together. In terms of clauses, parameters controlling the weight of criteria 4 and 5 are deemed to be the most important: in other words, the number of positive (or negative) literals that are involved in a clause are a very important aspect for the performance of SAT solvers. The solver that can gain the most by ordering the clauses is Lingeling. In particular, this solver shows best performance when clauses with a large number of negative literals are listed early.

Parameters related to criteria ii, vi, and $viii$ have shown to have a significant impact with regards to the literals' ordering in clauses. For Glucose and Cadical, criterion ii –i.e. the average size of the clauses in which the literal is involved– is the most important single criterion that has to be correctly configured. However, it is a bit hard to derive some general rules, as their impact on orderings vary significantly with regards to the solver and the benchmark. In a nutshell, they are important, but the best way to present the literals varies.

Generally speaking, also in the light of the criteria that are most important for clauses, the ordering of literals appears to be the most important in a CNF formulae: this is also because, in many cases, clauses are ordered according to the (separately-calculated) weight of the involved literals. This behaviour can be due to the way in which data structures are generated by solvers: usually literals are the main element –that is also the focus of heuristic search used by SAT solvers. Instead, clauses from the CNF tend to have a less marked importance during the exploration of the search space, as they are related to literals mostly via lists, and are exploited only for checking satisfiability and performing unit propagation. Clauses learnt during the search process are not included in our analysis, as they are not part of the CNF formula–but are generated online by the solver.

Finally, we want to test if there is a single general configuration that improves the performance of a solver on any formula, despite of the benchmark and underlying structure. Therefore, we trained each of the considered solvers on a training set composed by an equal proportion of instances from each of the 6 benchmark sets. As for previous configurations, we gave 5 days of sequential CPU-time for each learning process, and obtained configurations have been tested on an independent testing set that includes instances from all the benchmark sets. Results are presented in Table 3.

Table 3. Results achieved by the selected solvers on the general testing set. For each solver, we show the PAR10, number of test set timeouts, and IPC score achieved when running on the default and on the CNFs configured using the general configuration. Bold indicates the best result.

Solver	Performance: default → configured	
	# timeouts	IPC score
Cadical	101 → **98**	**172.7** → 172.5
Glucose	80 → **78**	207.5 → **211.2**
Lingeling	109 → **108**	190.7 → **191.7**

Results on the independent testing set indicate that this sort of configuration has a very limited impact on solvers' performance. This seems to confirm our previous intuition that solvers require differently configured formulae according to the underlying structure of the benchmark: it is therefore the case that structurally different sets of instances require a very different configuration. Intuitively, this seems to point to the fact that, in different structures, the characteristics that identify challenging elements to deal with, vary. Solvers, when dealing with different sets of benchmarks, are then sensitive to different aspects of the CNF formulae, that should be appropriately highlighted and configured. On the one hand, this result may be not fully satisfying, as it suggests that there is not a quick way to improve the performance of SAT solvers. On the other hand, the results of the other experiments indicate that, for real-world applications of SAT where instances share some underlying structure, there is the possibility to furtherly improve the SAT solving process by identifying a specific configuration for the solver at hand.

5   Conclusions

Previous work in the area of algorithm configuration for SAT focused on modifying the exposed parameters of SAT solvers in order to affect their behaviour. Well-known examples include the use of ParamILS for configuring SAPS and

SPEAR [16] or of ReACTR for configuring LingeLing [9], as well as the dedicated design and development of highly modular and configurable SAT solvers such as SATenstein [20] that can then be tuned for a specific set of benchmarks. Algorithm configuration has also been used as a technique for selecting and combining different SAT solvers into portfolios [21], and for creating suitable SAT solvers that would complement the performance of a given portfolio [28].

In this paper we proposed an approach for exploiting the fact that the order in which literals and clauses are listed in CNF formulae can strongly affect the performance of SAT solvers. The proposed approach allows to perform the automated configuration of formulae. We considered as configurable the order in which clauses are listed and the order in which literals are listed in the clauses. In our experimental analysis we configured formulae for improving the PAR10 performance of solvers, i.e. a tradeoff between runtime and coverage. The performed analysis, aimed at investigating how the configuration of CNF formulae affects the performance of state-of-the-art SAT solvers: (i) demonstrates that the automated configuration has a significant impact on solvers' performance; (ii) indicates that the configuration should be performed on specific set of benchmarks for a given solver; and (iii) highlights important aspects of formulae, that have a potentially strong impact on the performance of solvers.

It should be noted that different metrics can be used to configure CNF formulae. In this work we focused on the PAR10 value, but metrics with a stronger focus on runtime, coverage, or even "quality" of generated solutions can be straightforwardly considered in the introduced framework. Similarly, additional criteria to control the ordering of clauses and literals can be included.

We see several avenues for future work. We plan to evaluate the impact of configuration on weighted max SAT, where the weight of the clauses can provide another important information to the configuration process. We are also interested in evaluating if ordering clauses (and literals) that are learnt during the search process of a SAT solver, or if taking into account backdoors [10,11,27], can be beneficial for improving performance. Finally, we plan to incorporate the reordering of clauses and literals into existing approaches for configuring portfolios of SAT solvers, such as SATenstein, in order to further improve performance, and to investigate the concurrent configuration of formulae and solvers.

References

1. Audemard, G., Lagniez, J.-M., Simon, L.: Improving glucose for incremental SAT solving with assumptions: application to MUS extraction. In: Järvisalo, M., Van Gelder, A. (eds.) SAT 2013. LNCS, vol. 7962, pp. 309–317. Springer, Heidelberg (2013). https://doi.org/10.1007/978-3-642-39071-5_23
2. Biere, A.: CaDiCaL, Lingeling, Plingeling, Treengeling and YalSAT entering the sat competition 2017. In: SAT competition 2017, Solver and Benchmark Descriptions (2017)
3. Breiman, L.: Random forests. Mach. Learn. 45(1), 5–32 (2001)
4. Brooks, F.P.: No silver bullet: essence and accidents of software engineering. IEEE Computer 20, 10–19 (1987)

5. Cadar, C., Dunbar, D., Engler, D.: KLEE: unassisted and automatic generation of high-coverage tests for complex systems programs. In: Proceedings of the 8th USENIX Conference on Operating Systems Design and Implementation, pp. 209–224 (2008)

6. Cerutti, F., Vallati, M., Giacomin, M.: On the impact of configuration on abstract argumentation automated reasoning. Int. J. Approx. Reason. **92**, 120–138 (2018)

7. Crawford, J., Baker, A.: Experimental results on the application of satisfiability algorithms to scheduling problems. In: Proceedings of the International Conference of the Association for the Advancement of Artificial Intelligence (AAAI), pp. 1092–1097 (1994)

8. Falkner, S., Lindauer, M., Hutter, F.: SpySMAC: automated configuration and performance analysis of SAT solvers. In: Heule, M., Weaver, S. (eds.) SAT 2015. LNCS, vol. 9340, pp. 215–222. Springer, Cham (2015). https://doi.org/10.1007/978-3-319-24318-4_16

9. Fitzgerald, T., Malitsky, Y., O'Sullivan, B.: ReACTR: realtime algorithm configuration through tournament rankings. In: Proceedings of the Twenty-Fourth International Joint Conference on Artificial Intelligence, IJCAI, pp. 304–310 (2015)

10. Giunchiglia, E., Maratea, M., Tacchella, A.: Dependent and independent variables in propositional satisfiability. In: Flesca, S., Greco, S., Ianni, G., Leone, N. (eds.) JELIA 2002. LNCS (LNAI), vol. 2424, pp. 296–307. Springer, Heidelberg (2002). https://doi.org/10.1007/3-540-45757-7_25

11. Giunchiglia, E., Maratea, M., Tacchella, A.: (In)Effectiveness of look-ahead techniques in a modern SAT solver. In: Rossi, F. (ed.) CP 2003. LNCS, vol. 2833, pp. 842–846. Springer, Heidelberg (2003). https://doi.org/10.1007/978-3-540-45193-8_64

12. Gomes, C.P., Selman, B., Crato, N., Kautz, H.: Heavy-tailed phenomena in satisfiability and constraint satisfaction problems. J. Autom. Reason. **24**(1), 67–100 (2000)

13. Hutter, F., Hoos, H.H., Leyton-Brown, K.: Sequential model-based optimization for general algorithm configuration. In: Coello, C.A.C. (ed.) LION 2011. LNCS, vol. 6683, pp. 507–523. Springer, Heidelberg (2011). https://doi.org/10.1007/978-3-642-25566-3_40

14. Hutter, F., Hoos, H.H., Leyton-Brown, K.: Tradeoffs in the empirical evaluation of competing algorithm designs. Ann. Math. Artif. Intell. **60**(1), 65–89 (2010)

15. Hutter, F., Hoos, H.H., Leyton-Brown, K.: An efficient approach for assessing hyperparameter importance. In: Proceedings of the 31st International Conference on Machine Learning, pp. 754–762 (2014)

16. Hutter, F., Hoos, H.H., Leyton-Brown, K., Stützle, T.: ParamILS: an automatic algorithm configuration framework. J. Artif. Intell. Res. **36**, 267–306 (2009)

17. Hutter, F., Lindauer, M., Balint, A., Bayless, S., Hoos, H.H., Leyton-Brown, K.: The configurable SAT solver challenge (CSSC). Artif. Intell. **243**, 1–25 (2017)

18. Hutter, F., Xu, L., Hoos, H.H., Leyton-Brown, K.: Algorithm runtime prediction: methods & evaluation. Artif. Intell. **206**, 79–111 (2014)

19. Kadioglu, S., Malitsky, Y., Sellmann, M., Tierney, K.: ISAC-instance-specific algorithm configuration. In: Proceedings of the 9th European Conference on Artificial Intelligence ECAI, pp. 751–756 (2010)

20. KhudaBukhsh, A.R., Xu, L., Hoos, H.H., Leyton-Brown, K.: SATenstein: automatically building local search SAT solvers from components. Artif. Intell. **232**, 20–42 (2016)

21. Lindauer, M., Hoos, H., Hutter, F., Leyton-Brown, K.: Selection and configuration of parallel portfolios. In: Hamadi, Y., Sais, L. (eds.) Handbook of Parallel Constraint Reasoning, pp. 583–615. Springer, Cham (2018). https://doi.org/10.1007/978-3-319-63516-3_15

22. Prasad, M.R., Biere, A., Gupta, A.: A survey of recent advances in sat-based formal verification. Int. J. Softw. Tools Technol. Transf. **7**(2), 156–173 (2005)

23. Rintanen, J.: Engineering efficient planners with SAT. In: European Conference on Artificial Intelligence ECAI, pp. 684–689 (2012)

24. Tompkins, D.A.D., Balint, A., Hoos, H.H.: Captain Jack: new variable selection heuristics in local search for SAT. In: Sakallah, K.A., Simon, L. (eds.) SAT 2011. LNCS, vol. 6695, pp. 302–316. Springer, Heidelberg (2011). https://doi.org/10.1007/978-3-642-21581-0_24

25. Vallati, M., Hutter, F., Chrpa, L., McCluskey, T.: On the effective configuration of planning domain models. In: Proceedings of the International Joint Conference on Artificial Intelligence (IJCAI), pp. 1704–1711 (2015)

26. Vallati, M., Serina, I.: A general approach for configuring PDDL problem models. In: Proceedings of the International Conference on Automated Planning & Scheduling (ICAPS) (2018)

27. Williams, R., Gomes, C.P., Selman, B.: Backdoors to typical case complexity. In: Proceedings of the Eighteenth International Joint Conference on Artificial Intelligence, Acapulco, Mexico, 9–15 August 2003, pp. 1173–1178. Morgan Kaufmann (2003)

28. Xu, L., Hoos, H.H., Leyton-Brown, K.: Hydra: automatically configuring algorithms for portfolio-based selection. In: Proceedings of the Twenty-Fourth AAAI Conference on Artificial Intelligence, AAAI (2010)

Machine Learning for AI

Performance-Driven Handwriting Task Selection for Parkinson's Disease Classification

Maria Teresa Angelillo[1], Donato Impedovo[2], Giuseppe Pirlo[2], and Gennaro Vessio[2(✉)]

[1] Department of Psychology, Catholic University of Milan, Milan, Italy
mtangelillo@gmail.com
[2] Department of Computer Science, University of Bari, Bari, Italy
{donato.impedovo,giuseppe.pirlo,gennaro.vessio}@uniba.it

Abstract. Diagnosing and monitoring Parkinson's disease (PD) is a topic of current research in many fields, including AI. The innovative challenge is to develop a low-cost, non-invasive tool to support clinicians at the point of care. In particular, since handwriting difficulties in PD patients are well-known, changes in handwriting have emerged as a powerful discriminant factor for PD assessment. A crucial step in designing a decision support system based on handwriting concerns the choice of the most appropriate handwriting tasks to be administered for data acquisition. When data are collected, traditional approaches assume that different tasks, although not with the same impact, are all important for classification. However, not all tasks are likely to be useful for diagnosis, and the inclusion of these tasks may be detrimental to prediction accuracy. This work investigates the potential of an optimal subset of tasks for a more accurate PD classification. The evaluation is carried out by adopting a performance-driven multi-expert approach on different handwriting tasks performed by the same subjects. The multi-expert system is based on similar or conceptually different classifiers trained on features related to the dynamics of the handwriting process. The proposed approach improves baseline results on the PaHaW data set.

Keywords: e-Health · Parkinson's disease · Handwriting analysis

1 Introduction

Parkinson's disease (PD) is one of the most common neurodegenerative disorders: it is characterized by the degeneration of the dopaminergic nigrostriatal neurons of the basal ganglia resulting in a progressive cognitive, functional and behavioral decline. More specifically, akinesia, bradykinesia, rigidity and tremor are typically observed [7]. Currently, there is no cure and the gradual decline

This work was supported by the Italian Ministry of Education, University and Research within the PRIN2015-HAND Project under grant H96J16000820001.

© Springer Nature Switzerland AG 2019
M. Alviano et al. (Eds.): AI*IA 2019, LNAI 11946, pp. 281–293, 2019.
https://doi.org/10.1007/978-3-030-35166-3_20

of the patient can only be somehow managed during the disease progression. However, an early diagnosis of PD would be crucial in the perspective of the proper medical treatment to be administered and for evaluating the effects of new drug treatments.

To this end, a growing research interest has arisen, in the last years, towards computer aided diagnosis systems. Intelligent systems, in fact, are appropriate to detect subtle changes in disease symptoms which may be difficult (if not impossible) to be observed by the human expert, e.g. [3,16]. In this context, handwriting analysis can play a special role. Handwriting, in fact, is a complex activity entailing cognitive, kinesthetic and perceptual-motor components, whose changes are promising as a *biomarker* for the evaluation of PD [5]. Some works provided evidence that the automatic discrimination between unhealthy and healthy people can be accomplished on the basis of simple and easy-to-perform handwriting tasks [1,12]. Developing a handwriting-based decision support system is desirable, as it can provide a complementary approach to the pathology evaluation carried out by human experts that is non-invasive and very low-cost.

Within this direction, on-line (*dynamic*) systems can be adopted based on the use of a digitizing tablet. A very important acquisition step deals with the handwriting/hand-drawing tasks to be administered to capture the time series raw data. Several tasks have been proposed and investigated, ranging from drawing an Archimedes spiral, e.g. [20], to writing simple words or longer sentences, e.g. [9]. In general, the most employed approach to studying the potentialities of handwriting tasks involves combining the features coming from different tasks into a unique high dimensional feature vector and then feeding this vector into a traditional machine learning algorithm, e.g. [8]. Alternatively, some recent studies proposed to combine these features into ensembles of classifiers (a *multi-expert* system), each built on top of the feature space of every task, e.g. [17,19].

These approaches are effective, especially when combined with feature selection strategies; however, they may suffer from two major limitations. First, high dimensional feature spaces could cause overfitting, thus leading to an accuracy degradation when the system is deployed in a real scenario. Second, some tasks may be less useful than others and their presence may introduce additional bias in the data. In other words, the *task selection* is crucial, as selecting the best subset of tasks may strongly influence the potential of the acquired data.

In this work, the predictive potential of an optimal subset of tasks for an automatized PD diagnosis is investigated. First, several features exploiting the dynamics of the handwriting process are extracted from the raw data of different tasks. Then, the predictive potential of each task is evaluated individually. Finally, the best tasks, i.e. those with the highest prediction accuracy, are fed into an ensemble of classifiers, whose predictions are obtained via majority voting. Experiments were performed on the freely available PaHaW data set [9], as it includes several tasks performed by the same subjects.

2 Materials

The "Parkinson's disease handwriting database" (PaHaW) collects the data of 37 PD patients and 38 age and gender-matched healthy control (HC) subjects [9]. Participants were enrolled at the First Department of Neurology, Masaryk University and at the St. Anne's University Hospital, Brno, Czech Republic. All participants were right-handed, had completed at least ten years of education, and reported Czech as their native language. No significant differences related to age or gender were found between the PD and HC group. None of the subjects had a history or presence of any psychiatric symptoms or disease affecting the central nervous system, except for PD in the PD group. PD patients were examined only in their ON-state while on dopaminergic medication and, prior to acquisition, they were evaluated by a clinical neurologist. Also the HC group was examined by a clinician to make sure that there was no movement disorder or injury that could have significantly affected handwriting.

Subjects were requested to complete eight handwriting tasks in accordance with a pre-filled template:

1. Drawing an Archimedes spiral;
2. Writing in cursive the letter l;
3. The bigram le;
4. The trigram les;
5. Writing in cursive the word *lektorka* ("female teacher" in Czech);
6. *porovnat* ("to compare");
7. *nepopadnout* ("to not catch");
8. Writing in cursive the sentence *Tramvaj dnes už nepojede* ("The tram won't go today").

Note that since not all participants performed each task, we considered only those who succeeded in completing all tasks, i.e. 36 PD and 36 HC.

The handwriting signals were recorded by a Wacom Intuos digitizing tablet overlaid with a blank sheet of paper. The raw data acquired include the x- and y-coordinates of the pen tip, their time stamps, the pen inclination, i.e. azimuth and altitude, and the pen pressure. The button status is also available, which is a binary variable evaluating 0 for pen-ups ("in-air movement") and 1 for pen-downs ("on-surface movement").

Sample images of healthy and Parkinsonian writing are depicted in Fig. 1.

3 Methods

In order to fairly evaluate the effectiveness of the proposed method, we replicated the experiment in [8], as it provides baseline performance, on the same data set, obtained with the fusion of dynamic features from all tasks. The experimental methodology includes several steps which are described in the following subsections.

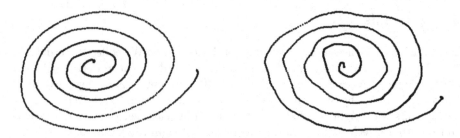

Fig. 1. Sample drawings of an Archimedes spiral performed by a healthy adult (on the left) and a PD patient (on the right). Data do not belong to PaHaW, but they have been acquired within the HAND project.

3.1 Feature Extraction

The overall set of features is summarized in Table 1. Note that the feature calculation stage resulted in either a single value or a vector feature. For all the resulting vector features the following basic statistical measures were computed: mean; median; standard deviation; 1st percentile; 99th percentile; 99th percentile – 1st percentile, which is an outlier robust range.

The horizontal and vertical components of handwriting, as recorded by the tablet, were segmented into on-surface and in-air strokes in accordance with the button status. A *stroke* corresponds to a single trait of the handwritten pattern which is connected and continuous, i.e. between two consecutive pen-lifts. By using the Cartesian coordinates of the sampled points and their time stamps, several features were then calculated for both on-surface and in-air strokes.

Kinematic features include: number of strokes; tangential, horizontal and vertical displacement, velocity, acceleration and jerk; number of changes of velocity/acceleration (NCV/NCA); NCA and NCV relative to writing duration. Displacement corresponds to the straight-line distance between two consecutive sampled points: it provides a good approximation of the pen trajectory. From displacement, velocity, acceleration and jerk can be straightforwardly calculated as the first, second and third derivative of displacement, respectively. Analogously, displacement, velocity, acceleration and jerk can be calculated with respect to both the horizontal and vertical direction. NCV and NCA are the mean number of local extrema of tangential velocity and acceleration, respectively.

Spatio-temporal features include: stroke size and duration; speed and stroke speed; stroke height and width; on-surface and in-air time; total time; normalized on-surface and in-air time; in-air/on-surface ratio.

In order to make use of the pressure signal, the following measures were also calculated: mean pressure; number of changes of pressure (NCP); relative NCP. NCP was proposed in [9] and its meaning is analogous to the concept of NCV/NCA, explained above.

The following features were also computed for both the on-surface and in-air horizontal and vertical components of handwriting: Shannon and Rényi (second and third order) entropy; signal-to-noise ratio (SNR) and empirical mode

Table 1. Features. Unless otherwise specified, they are intended both on-surface and in-air. Abbreviations: s = scalar value; v = vector of elements.

Feature	s/v	Description
Stroke number	s	Number of strokes
Displacement	v	Tangential trajectory during handwriting
Velocity	v	Rate of change of displacement with respect to time
Acceleration	v	Rate of change of velocity with respect to time
Jerk	v	Rate of change of acceleration with respect to time
Hor./ver. displacement	v	Displacement in the horizontal/vertical direction
Hor./ver. velocity	v	Velocity in the horizontal/vertical direction
Hor./ver. acceleration	v	Acceleration in the horizontal/vertical direction
Horizontal/vertical jerk	v	Jerk in the horizontal/vertical direction
NCV	s	Mean number of local extrema of velocity
NCA	s	Mean number of local extrema of acceleration
Relative NCV	s	NCV relative to writing duration
Relative NCA	s	NCA relative to writing duration
Stroke size	v	Path lenth of each stroke
Stroke duration	v	Movement time per stroke
Speed	s	Trajectory during writing divided by writing duration
Stroke speed	v	Trajectory during stroke divided by stroke duration
Stroke height	v	Height of each stroke
Stroke width	v	Width of each stroke
On-surface time	s	Overall time spent on-surface
In-air time	s	Overall time spent in-air
Total time	s	On-surface time plus in-air time
Norm. on-surface time	s	On-surface time normalized by total time
Normalized in-air time	s	In-air time normalized by total time
In-air/on-surface ratio	s	Ratio of time spent in-air/on-surface
Mean pressure	v	Average pressure over all strokes
NCP	s	Mean number of local extrema of pressure
Relative NCP	s	NCP relative to writing duration
Horizontal/vertical Shannon entropy	v	Shannon entropy of the horizontal/vertical component of the pen position
Horizontal/vertical Rényi entropy	v	Second and third order order Rényi entropy of the horizontal/vertical component of the pen position
Horizontal/vertical SNR	v	SNR of the horizontal/vertical component of the pen position
Horizontal/vertical intrinsic Shannon entropy	s	Shannon entropy of the first and second IMF of the EMD of the horizontal/vertical component of the pen position
Horizontal/vertical intrinsic Rényi entropy	s	Second and third order Rényi entropy of the first and second IMF of the EMD of the horizontal/vertical component of the pen position
Horizontal/vertical intrinsic SNR	s	SNR of the first and second IMF of the EMD of the horizontal/vertical component of the pen position

decomposition (EMD). EMD iteratively decomposes the signal into so-called intrinsic mode functions (IMFs), which are functions that satisfy two requirements: (1) the number of extrema and the number of zero crossings are either equal or differ at most by one; and (2) the mean of their upper and lower envelopes equals zero. In this paper, Shannon and Rényi entropy and SNR were applied to only the first and second IMF resulting from the decomposition. These measures were intended to provide information about the randomness and irregularity of fine movements due to PD.

All features were normalized before classification so as to have zero mean and unit variance.

3.2   Model Fitting

A set of different classifiers was adopted and evaluated: Support Vector Machines (SVMs) both with radial basis function and linear kernel, Logistic Regression (LR), Linear Discriminant Analysis (LDA) and AdaBoost (ADA). These are state-of-the-art models tailored to the small data set here adopted. A brief description of each algorithm is provided in the following. It is worth to note that, for all of them, the `scikit-learn` implementation was used [18].

Support Vector Machines. The main idea behind SVMs is to find a separating hyperplane with the largest minimal distance, i.e. a *margin*, from the closest data points of either classes. New examples are then predicted to belong to a class based on which side of the hyperplane they fall [11]. The margin of the hyperplane is chosen so as to correctly separate most of the training examples, while misclassifying some of them. In this work, a linear as well as a radial basis function (RBF) kernel were considered. The bias-variance trade-off of the algorithm depends on the fine tuning of the penalty parameter C and the kernel coefficient γ in the case of RBF kernel. We set C to 1 and γ to $\frac{1}{n}$, where n is the number of features. These values are commonly found in the literature.

Logistic Regression. LR is a *discriminative* algorithm which relies on the sigmoid function to model the posterior probability of each subject to belonging to a class: $p(y \mid x) = sigm(w^T x)$. The w coefficients can be estimated, based on the available data, by maximizing the likelihood function [11]. If the output probability is thresholded at 0.5, the following decision rule can be induced: predict class 1 if $p(y \mid x) > 0.5$; class 2 otherwise. In particular, we used the dual formulation with L2 regularization: applying the regularization term helps avoid overfitting.

Linear Discriminant Analysis. LDA is a *generative* algorithm which directly models the class conditional distribution $p(x \mid y)$ for each class k [11]. Predictions can then be obtained by applying the Bayes theorem and by outputting the class for which the estimated posterior probability is the highest. Estimating the class conditional distribution is done by assuming a multivariate Gaussian form and a covariance matrix common to all K classes. In the present study, since the number of training examples was small compared to the number of features, for a better estimation of the covariance matrix the automatic shrinkage using the Ledoit-Wolf lemma was employed [15].

AdaBoost. ADA relies on the *boosting* technique: a sequence of "base learners" is trained on the entire data set; then additional copies of the classifier are trained on the same data but with the weights of the incorrectly classified examples iteratively updated [11]. The predictions from all the weak learners are combined through a weighted majority vote to produce the final prediction. In the present paper, 500 decision trees were used as base learners.

Ensemble. In order to explore an optimal subset of tasks for PD classification, the *Voting* classifier was adopted: the individual classifiers are combined by using a voting scheme to predict the class labels; in this way, the individual weaknesses of each single classifier are balanced and mitigated. Combining the predictions generated by different classifiers is likely to provide better predictions, due to the diversification. Note that we used a majority voting scheme: the final class label for a test example is the mode of the class labels predicted by each individual classifier in the ensemble. In particular, our aim was to carry out a performance-driven task selection, i.e. a selection of the best tasks based only on their individual performance. To this end, each classification model was trained on each task individually and the performance obtained were evaluated. This served to explore the most discriminant tasks among the eight originally proposed. Then, the three best tasks, i.e. those with the highest prediction accuracy, were pooled together in an ensemble scheme whose predictions were finally obtained via majority voting. Note that we evaluated both the ensemble obtained by combining similar models and that obtained by combining different models.

3.3   Validation

For a fair comparison with [8], the classification performance was validated through a 10-fold cross-validation. The set of examples was divided into ten folds: one fold was treated as test set; the remaining folds formed the training set. The splitting was *stratified* by participant groups. The entire procedure was repeated ten times, until each fold was used as test set once.

3.4   Feature Selection

In order to reduce the dimensionality of the feature space, a feature selection technique was applied before classification. As in [8], the discriminating power of each feature was evaluated by considering its accuracy in separating PD from HC when used as a single input feature to a linear SVM classifier. All features were then ranked in accordance with this score and only the n features providing the highest score were retained for the final model fitting. Since feature selection had to be performed on different feature spaces, one for each task, we chose to not fix n, but to establish a dynamic threshold depending on the ranking of features for each specific task.

It is worth to note that supervised feature selection strategies should be part of the model selection process [11]; in other words, they should be *nested* within the cross-validation iterations, so that the most discriminating features are chosen based only on the training set, blindly to the test set. Relying on an a priori selection of features on the entire data set inadvertently introduces a bias in the classification model which may lead to overoptimistic results.

4   Experimental Results

4.1   Combining All Tasks

For a fair comparison, we preliminarily replicated the experiment in [8], in which the features coming from each task were combined into a unique high dimensional feature vector. It is worth to note that our replica did not include copying the Archimedes spiral, as the task was not considered in [8].

Table 2 reports the results obtained. In this table, as well as in the following tables, only the best mean accuracy, averaged over all the cross-validation iterations, is reported. Our replication of [8] achieved comparable results, i.e. an accuracy of 88.33% instead of 88.13%. This difference appears to be marginal and may have been due to implementation settings. Nevertheless, data may have been overfitted because of the adoption of a non-nested feature selection. Indeed, by applying a nested approach, a performance decrease can be observed, as an accuracy of 74.58% was obtained.

Table 2. Classification performance with the combination of features from all tasks.

Classification scheme	Accuracy
Drotár et al. [8]	88.13%
Present replica of [8]	88.33%
Present replica of [8], with *nested* feature selection	74.58%

4.2   Individual Tasks

In order to evaluate the predictive potential of each task individually, a classification model was considered for each of them. The results obtained are reported in Table 3. It is worth to note that the classification models employed did not completely agree about the selection of the most discriminating tasks. Nevertheless, it can be observed that the tasks achieving an accuracy higher than or equal to 75% were: writing in cursive the letter l (task 2); the bigram le (task 3) and the word *porovnat* (task 6); and writing the entire sentence (8). Surprisingly, task 3 was able to achieve a very high accuracy alone, outperforming the performance obtained by the combination of features from all tasks. This indicated that the multi-expert approach would had a good chance to improve performance.

The results obtained were expected. Writing non-sense words like *lelele* have been extensively studied in the literature, e.g. [21], showing the impairment of PD patients in fine motor control during loop-like movements. In addition, the importance of the sentence task, already observed in [8], was confirmed: writing

Table 3. Individual task performance with non-nested feature selection. In bold the best three tasks for each classifier. In italic the best three results over all tasks.

Task	SVM$_{RBF}$	SVM$_{lin}$	LR	LDA	ADA
Spiral	51.25%	61.25%	52.50%	53.33%	49.58%
lll	61.67%	*82.08%*	**77.08%**	**70.41%**	**67.91%**
le le le	**70.00%**	*89.16%*	81.25%	81.67%	69.58%
les les les	60.83%	69.16%	61.67%	54.16%	53.75%
lektorka	56.67%	74.58%	**73.33%**	**72.08%**	60.41%
porovnat	**62.50%**	*79.58%*	69.16%	61.25%	67.91%
nepopadnout	47.91%	69.58%	57.91%	52.50%	64.16%
Sentence	**71.67%**	75.83%	70.41%	68.50%	**75.00%**

Table 4. Individual task performance with nested feature selection. In bold the best three tasks for each classifier. In italic the best three results over all tasks.

Task	SVM$_{RBF}$	SVM$_{lin}$	LR	LDA	ADA
Spiral	53.75%	49.16%	52.08%	51.67%	46.67%
lll	59.16%	**61.25%**	**63.75%**	**62.91%**	*67.08%*
le le le	**67.08%**	**70.41%**	*72.50%*	69.58%	*72.50%*
les les les	57.91%	39.58%	45.41%	46.25%	53.33%
lektorka	52.91%	49.16%	54.58%	54.16%	53.33%
porovnat	**60.83%**	53.75%	53.33%	57.50%	63.75%
nepopadnout	53.33%	53.33%	55.41%	53.75%	61.67%
Sentence	**68.33%**	**67.91%**	69.16%	*70.41%*	67.91%

a long sentence, in fact, probably requires more cognitive effort, particularly a high degree of simultaneous processing, and thus escalates the effects of disease on handwriting. Producing loop-like movements and writing a sentence offer the possibility to better evaluate the motor-planning activity between a character or a word and the following one. In general, a hesitation or pause between two characters or words could point out the necessity to re-plan the writing activity, while fluid writing can reveal the presence of an anticipated motor planning. Parkinsonian patients are known to write in a more segmented fashion, showing difficulties in anticipating the forthcoming movement [2].

Conversely, very poor performance were obtained by the spiral task, confirming the findings already reported in [9]. This may have been due to the use of measures only tailored to handwriting and not to hand-drawing.

More in general, it can be noted that the performance of linear SVM were higher than those of SVM with RBF kernel, indicating that the two classes are better separated by a linear decision boundary. This is confirmed considering that similar performance were achieved by LR and LDA.

Table 5. Ensemble of tasks performance with non-nested feature selection. In bold the best result. In parentheses the best three tasks.

Ensemble	SVM$_{RBF}$	SVM$_{lin}$	LR	LDA	ADA	Overall
All tasks	61.67%	88.75%	79.17%	74.58%	79.17%	88.75%
Best tasks	69.17% (3, 6, 8)	**91.67%** (2, 3, 6)	85.83% (2, 3, 5)	80.42% (2, 3, 5)	74.17% (2, 3, 8)	**91.67%** (2, 3, 6)

Table 6. Ensemble of tasks performance with nested feature selection. In bold the best result. In parentheses the best three tasks.

Ensemble	SVM$_{RBF}$	SVM$_{lin}$	LR	LDA	ADA	Overall
All tasks	66.25%	60.83%	61.67%	62.92%	72.92%	76.25%
Best tasks	68.33% (3, 6, 8)	75.42% (2, 3, 8)	77.92% (2, 3, 8)	78.75% (2, 3, 8)	76.67% (2, 3, 8)	**79.17%** (2, 3, 8)

Similar findings are reported in Table 4, which concerns the results obtained by adopting the nested approach. As expected, an overall performance degradation was obtained. However, the predictive potential of task 2, 3 and 8 was confirmed and strengthened. Nesting feature selection within cross-validation, in fact, provides not only more reliable results but also a more robust evaluation of the performance against single randomized splittings.

4.3   Ensemble of Tasks

Table 5 shows the results obtained with the ensemble of classifiers. In the table, both the ensemble obtained by all tasks and that obtained by considering only the best three tasks, i.e. those with the highest prediction accuracy, are shown. Note that the performance achieved by the overall ensemble, i.e. by considering different classifiers, here coincide with the ensemble of linear SVM models, as they outperformed the other models over all tasks. As expected, the ensemble of the best three tasks improved the classification accuracy achieved by combining all tasks (Table 2), i.e. 91.67% vs. 88.33%.

By looking at Table 6, where the accuracy obtained by using a nested feature selection is reported, again an overall performance deterioration can be observed. Nevertheless, the proposed approach showed its usefulness, as an improvement against the combination of features from all tasks (Table 2) was obtained, i.e. 79.17% vs. 74.58%.

5   Conclusion

Parkinson's disease causes impairments in previously learned motor skills, such as handwriting. This suggests that handwriting analysis can be a powerful tool to develop intelligent systems for disease diagnosis and monitoring. Handwriting difficulties in Parkinsonian patients have been documented for a long time, however only recently a growing interest and new insights have arisen from an artificial intelligence perspective. A handwriting-based decision support system has the potential to assist clinicians at the point of care, providing a novel diagnostic tool while reducing the expenditure of public health. Moreover, it can be used to quantify aspects of the motor system and its disorders to better understand the mechanisms underlying PD, e.g. the difficulties in coordinating the components of a motor sequence movement. Finally, it can help study the effects of medication on handwriting with the aim to monitor the responsiveness of the patient to therapy. More in general, handwriting can provide a simple, user-friendly and easy-to-use instrument to support the daily clinical trials. Of course, handwriting-based intelligent systems are not expected to replace standard techniques or even doctors, but to provide additional evidence to further support the clinical assessment.

In particular, when designing such systems, special attention should be paid on the acquisition protocol, as the task selection strongly influences the potential of the acquired data. In this study, an optimal subset of tasks was investigated, by applying a performance-driven multi-expert approach on features calculated from the freely available PaHaW data set. The results obtained are encouraging, as they improved the baseline results obtained by combining the features coming from all tasks into a unique high dimensional feature vector. Note that the problem of task selection is important not only for boosting performance, but also for making data acquisition faster and easier. In fact, in a future perspective, the idea of using an ensemble learning approach could reduce the efforts in diagnosis and monitoring PD by optimizing the number of tasks to be performed by patients, and consequently reducing their frustration and allowing a less time-consuming process.

As expected, writing in cursive *lll*, *le le le* and an entire sentence were among the best tasks in terms of performance achieved. Our findings provide further evidence that these tasks are valuable biomarkers for an automatized PD diagnosis. Furthermore, in this work we showed the detrimental effect on the predictive accuracy caused by inadvertently introducing a feature selection bias within the classification workflow.

It is worth remarking that, compared to other automatic tools based on speech, e.g. [4], a lower prediction accuracy has been observed here. From the prediction point of view, few studies have been carried out focusing on handwriting analysis for PD diagnosis from a machine learning perspective. Therefore, the potentialities of this approach, as well as its limitations, have yet to be investigated in depth. On the other hand, from the inference point of view, the information related to handwriting may complement the information coming from speech, as well as other biometric traits, providing different findings which may support novel clinical insights and a better understanding of the pathology. Tablet technology, in fact, enables the implementation of a multi-modal interaction systems in which not only the input provided by the pen, but also speech and visual input can be acquired. Handwriting can thus be coupled to speech analysis based, for example, on NLP automatic assessment [10,14].

Some open issues demand further research. The major limitation of the present study is the small cardinality of the data set adopted, which makes the results obtained less reliable for a real-world scenario. Developing a large benchmark data set is one of the major open problems in the pattern recognition community for this research [5]. This holds not only for Parkinson's disease but for other neurodegenerative disorders as well [13]. Secondly, it must be underlined that the findings reported in the present paper rely on a dynamic analysis of the handwriting tasks taken into account, i.e. on the characteristics of the handwriting process while handwriting occurs. An alternative approach consists in studying the static images of handwriting, eventually reconstructed from the dynamic information given by the tablet. How to profitably combine static and dynamic features to improve classification performance needs further investigation: very promising results have been recently reported [6].

References

1. Angelillo, M.T., Balducci, F., Impedovo, D., Pirlo, G., Vessio, G.: Attentional pattern classification for automatic dementia detection. IEEE Access **7**, 57706–57716 (2019)
2. Bidet-Ildei, C., Pollak, P., Kandel, S., Fraix, V., Orliaguet, J.P.: Handwriting in patients with Parkinson disease: effect of L-dopa and stimulation of the sub-thalamic nucleus on motor anticipation. Human Mov. Sci. **30**(4), 783–791 (2011)
3. Casalino, G., Castellano, G., Pasquadibisceglie, V., Zaza, G.: Contact-less real-time monitoring of cardiovascular risk using video imaging and fuzzy inference rules. Information **10**(1), 9 (2019)
4. Chen, H.L., et al.: An efficient diagnosis system for detection of Parkinson's disease using fuzzy k-nearest neighbor approach. Exp. Syst. Appl. **40**(1), 263–271 (2013)
5. De Stefano, C., Fontanella, F., Impedovo, D., Pirlo, G., di Freca, A.S.: Handwriting analysis to support neurodegenerative diseases diagnosis: a review. Pattern Recogn. Lett. **121**, 37–45 (2019)
6. Diaz, M., Ferrer, M.A., Impedovo, D., Pirlo, G., Vessio, G.: Dynamically enhanced static handwriting representation for Parkinson's disease detection. Pattern Recogn. Lett. **128**, 204–210 (2019)
7. Dickson, D.W.: Neuropathology of Parkinson disease. Parkinsonism Relat. Disord. **46**, S30–S33 (2018)
8. Drotár, P., Mekyska, J., Rektorová, I., Masarová, L., Smékal, Z., Faundez-Zanuy, M.: Decision support framework for Parkinson's disease based on novel handwriting markers. IEEE Trans. Neural Syst. Rehabil. Eng. **23**(3), 508–516 (2015)
9. Drotár, P., Mekyska, J., Rektorová, I., Masarová, L., Smékal, Z., Faundez-Zanuy, M.: Evaluation of handwriting kinematics and pressure for differential diagnosis of Parkinson's disease. Artif. Intell. Med. **67**, 39–46 (2016)
10. Fraser, K.C., Hirst, G.: Detecting semantic changes in Alzheimer's disease with vector space models. In: Proceedings of LREC 2016 Workshop, no. 128 (2016)
11. Hastie, T., Tibshirani, R., Friedman, J.: The Elements of Statistical Learning: Data mining, Inference, and Prediction. Springer, Heidelberg (2009). https://doi.org/10.1007/978-0-387-84858-7
12. Impedovo, D., Pirlo, G., Vessio, G.: Dynamic handwriting analysis for supporting earlier Parkinson's disease diagnosis. Information **9**(10), 247 (2018)

13. Impedovo, D., Pirlo, G., Vessio, G., Angelillo, M.T.: A handwriting-based protocol for assessing neurodegenerative dementia. Cogn. Comput. **11**(4), 1–11 (2019)
14. Jessiman, L., Murray, G., Braley, M.: Language-based automatic assessment of cognitive and communicative functions related to Parkinson's disease. In: Proceedings of the First International Workshop on Language Cognition and Computational Models, pp. 63–74 (2018)
15. Ledoit, O., Wolf, M.: Honey, I shrunk the sample covariance matrix. UPF economics and business working paper (691) (2003)
16. Lella, E., Amoroso, N., Lombardi, A., Maggipinto, T., Tangaro, S., Bellotti, R.: Communicability disruption in Alzheimer's disease connectivity networks. J. Complex Netw. **7**(1), 83–100 (2018)
17. Moetesum, M., Siddiqi, I., Vincent, N., Cloppet, F.: Assessing visual attributes of handwriting for prediction of neurological disorders-a case study on Parkinson's disease. Pattern Recogn. Lett. **121**, 19–27 (2019)
18. Pedregosa, F., et al.: Scikit-learn: machine learning in Python. J. Mach. Learn. Res. **12**(Oct), 2825–2830 (2011)
19. Pereira, C.R.: Handwritten dynamics assessment through convolutional neural networks: An application to Parkinson's disease identification. Artif. Intell. Med. **87**, 67–77 (2018)
20. San Luciano, M., et al.: Digitized spiral drawing: a possible biomarker for early Parkinson's disease. PloS One **11**(10), e0162799 (2016)
21. Van Gemmert, A.W., Teulings, H.L., Stelmach, G.E.: Parkinsonian patients reduce their stroke size with increased processing demands. Brain Cogn. **47**(3), 504–512 (2001)

A Non-negative Factorization Approach to Node Pooling in Graph Convolutional Neural Networks

Davide Bacciu[(✉)] and Luigi Di Sotto

Dipartimento di Informatica, Università di Pisa, Largo B. Pontecorvo, 3, Pisa, Italy
bacciu@di.unipi.it, l.disotto@gmail.com

Abstract. The paper discusses a pooling mechanism to induce subsampling in graph structured data and introduces it as a component of a graph convolutional neural network. The pooling mechanism builds on the Non-Negative Matrix Factorization (NMF) of a matrix representing node adjacency and node similarity as adaptively obtained through the vertices embedding learned by the model. Such mechanism is applied to obtain an incrementally coarser graph where nodes are adaptively pooled into communities based on the outcomes of the non-negative factorization. The empirical analysis on graph classification benchmarks shows how such coarsening process yields significant improvements in the predictive performance of the model with respect to its non-pooled counterpart.

Keywords: Graph Convolutional Neural Networks · Differentiable graph pooling · Non-Negative Matrix Factorization

1 Introduction

Nowadays many real-world phenomena are modeled as interacting objects possibly living into high-dimensional manifolds with added topological structure. Examples can be found in genomics with protein-protein interaction networks, fake news discovery in social networks, functional networks in neuroscience. Graphs are the natural mathematical model for such data with underlying non-Euclidean nature. Current Euclidean Convolutional Neural Networks have built their success leveraging on the statistical properties of stationarity, locality and compositionality of flat domains. Rendering convolutional neural networks able also to learn over non-Euclidean domains is not that straightforward in that is required a re-designing of the computational model for adaptively learning graph embeddings. Over flat domains, i.e. grid-like structures, convolutional filters are compactly supported because of the grid regularity and the availability of consistent node ordering across different samples. This makes it possible to learn filters of fixed size and independent of the input signal dimension leveraging, to this end, weight sharing techniques. Furthermore, a set of symmetric functions

© Springer Nature Switzerland AG 2019
M. Alviano et al. (Eds.): AI*IA 2019, LNAI 11946, pp. 294–306, 2019.
https://doi.org/10.1007/978-3-030-35166-3_21

is also applied for sub-sampling purposes to fully exploit the multi-scale nature of the grids. The same does not apply to domains with highly varying topologies where learnt filters (non-Toeplitz operators) may be too representative of the considered domain, since they highly depend on the eigen-basis of the filter operator and they may thus fail to model sharp changes in the graph signal. State-of-the-art Graph Convolutional Networks (GCNs) [11,17] try to overcome the above difficulties with convolutions based on k-order Chebyshev polynomials, introducing the interesting duality of implicitly learning the graph spectrum by simply acting on the spatial representation. GCNs efficiently avoid the computational burden of performing a spectral decomposition of the graph, yielding to learned filters that are independent of the number of nodes in the graph. When considering graph classification tasks, we lack a principled multi-resolution operator providing coarser and more abstract representations of the input data as we go deeper in the network. Standard approaches to graph pooling employ symmetric functions such as max, summation or average along features axes of the graph embeddings. In [29], it is given an account of the discriminative power of these different coarsening operators. In the present work, we introduce a simple pooling operator for graphs that builds on the Non-Negative Matrix Factorization (NMF) methods to leverage on the community structure underlying graph structured data to induce subsampling, or equivalently, a multiscale view of the input graph in order to capture long-range interactions as we go deeper in Graph Convolutional Networks (GCNs). That would be of practical interest especially in the context of graph classification or regression tasks where the whole graph is fed into downstream learning systems as a single signature vector. Such mechanism is thus applied to incrementally obtain coarser graphs where nodes are pooled into communities based on the soft assignments output of the NMF of the graph adjacency matrix and Gram matrix of learned graph embeddings. Results on graph classification tasks show how jointly using such a coarsening operator with GCNs translate into improved predictive performances.

2   Background

In the following we introduce some basic notation used throughout the paper, then we briefly introduce the necessary background to understand state-of-the-art Graph Convolutional Neural Networks (GCNs). We mainly refer to spectral graph theory as introduced in [4,7,9].

2.1   Basic Notation

A graph G is a tuple $G = (\mathcal{V}, \mathcal{E})$, where $\mathcal{V}$ is the set of vertices of the graph and $\mathcal{E}$ is the set of edges connecting vertices, i.e. $\mathcal{E} \subseteq \mathcal{V} \times \mathcal{V}$. Let $\mathcal{N}(i)$ be the set of neighbours of a node $i \in \mathcal{V}$. And let $A \in \mathbb{R}^{n \times n}$, with $n = |\mathcal{V}|$, be the adjacency matrix such that

$$A_{i,j} = \begin{cases} a_{i,j} > 0 \text{ if } (i,j) \in \mathcal{E} \\ 0 \qquad \text{otherwise.} \end{cases}$$

Note that in the above formulation we consider undirected graphs, i.e. such that $(i, j) \in \mathcal{E}$ and $(j, i) \in \mathcal{E}$. Thus, matrix A is such that $A = A^T$. In the present work, without loss of generality, we generalize to undirected graphs

We also indicate with $X \in \mathbb{R}^{n \times d}$ as the matrix of the n signals $x_i \in \mathbb{R}^d$ associated to each node $i \in \mathcal{V}$.

2.2   Graph Convolution via Polynomial Filters

Spectral Construction. A first approach to representation learning on graphs is to explicitly learn the graph spectrum. In matrix notation, we can express the generalized convolution over graphs as follows [7]

$$LX = U \Lambda U^T X \tag{1}$$

where L is the combinatorial graph Laplacian, $L = D - A$, with D the degree matrix such that $D_{ii} = \sum_j a_{ij}$, where $U \in \mathbb{R}^{n \times k}$ is an orthonormal basis generalizing the Fourier basis, and where Λ is a diagonal matrix being the spectral representation of the filter [4,9]. Matrices U and Λ are the solution to the generalized eigenvalue problem $LU = U \Lambda$ [4,9]. With such an approach there are multiple problems: (a) the eigendecomposition in (1), and its application (filtering), require non-trivial computational time; (b) the corresponding filters are non-localized [11]; (c) filter size is $O(n)$, hence introducing a direct link between the parameters and the n nodes in the graph (no weight sharing).

Spatial Construction. In [11], it is proposed an alternative approach to explicit learning of the graph spectrum, by showing how it can be learned implicitly through a polynomial expansion of the diagonal operator Λ. Formally,

$$g_\theta (\Lambda) = \sum_{k=0}^{K-1} \theta_k \Lambda^k \tag{2}$$

where $\theta \in \mathbb{R}^K$ is the vector of polynomial coefficients. In [11] is pointed out that spectral filters represented as K-order polynomials are exactly K-localized and that weight sharing is thus made possible, since filters have size $O(K)$. Graph CNN (GCNN), also known as ChebNet [11], exploited the previous observation by employing Chebyshev polynomials for approximating filtering operation (1). Chebyshev polynomials are recursively defined using the recurrence relation

$$\begin{aligned} T_j(\lambda) &= 2\lambda T_{j-1}(\lambda) - T_{j-2}(\lambda); \\ T_0(\lambda) &= 1; \\ T_1(\lambda) &= \lambda. \end{aligned} \tag{3}$$

Also, polynomials recursively generated by (3) form an orthonormal basis in $[-1, 1]$ [7,11]. A filter can thus be represented as a polynomial of the form

$$
\begin{aligned}
g_\theta(\hat{L}) &= \sum_{k=0}^{K-1} \theta_k U T_k(\hat{\Lambda}) U^T \\
&= \sum_{k=0}^{K-1} \theta_k T_k(\hat{L}),
\end{aligned}
\tag{4}
$$

where $\hat{L} = 2\Lambda/\lambda_{\max} - I_n$ and $\hat{\Lambda} = 2\Lambda/\lambda_{\max} - I_n$ indicate a rescaling of the Laplacian eigenvalues to $[-1, 1]$. The filtering operation in (1) can be rewritten, for one-dimensional input graph signals, as $\hat{x} = g_\theta(\hat{L})x \in \mathbb{R}^n$, where the k-th polynomial $\hat{x}_k = T_k(\hat{L})x$ can be computed using the recurrence relation in (3) now defined as $\hat{x} = 2\hat{L}x_{k-1} - \hat{x}_{k-2}$ with $\hat{x}_0 = x$ and $\hat{x}_1 = \hat{L}x$. More generally, taking into account multi-dimensionality of input data, we have a convolutional layer as follows

$$
\hat{X} = \sigma \left(\sum_{k=0}^{K-1} T_k(\Delta) X \Theta_k \right)
\tag{5}
$$

with σ a non-linear activation, and $\Theta \in \mathbb{R}^{d_{in} \times d_{out}}$ the matrix of learnable parameters, with d_{in} number of input features and d_{out} number of neurons. A widely used convolutional layer over graphs are GCNs by [17] that are layers of the form of (5) with $K = 2$, namely

$$
\hat{X} = ReLU \left(\hat{A} X \Theta \right).
\tag{6}
$$

The Θ term, the matrix of polynomial coefficients to be learned, stems from (5) by imposing $\Theta_0 = -\Theta_1$, and with $\hat{A} = A + I$, and non-linearity being the ReLU function [17]. Thus, the main idea is to generate a representation for a node $i \in \mathcal{V}$ by aggregating its own features $x_i \in \mathbb{R}^d$ and its neighbors' features $x_j \in \mathbb{R}^d$, where $j \in \mathcal{N}(i)$. Note that, apart from the formulation meant to highlight the symmetry with convolutions on image data, the GCN model is not substantially different from the contextual approach to graph processing put forward by [22] a decade before GCN, and recently extended to a probabilistic formulation [3] by leveraging an hidden tree Markov model [1] with relaxed causality assumptions and a fingerprinting approach to structure embedding [2].

2.3   Node Pooling in Graph CNNs

A first attempt to formalize graph pooling can be found in [9], a simple framework for multiresolution clustering of a graph is given based on a naive agglomerative method. There are some recent works proposing pooling mechanisms for graph coarsening in Deep GCNs, in [10] a subset of the nodes are dropped based on a learnable projection vector where at each layer only the top-k interesting nodes are retained. In [15], it is employed a rough node sampling and a differentiable approach through a LSTM model for learning aggregated node embeddings, though it may render difficult satisfying invariance with respect to node ordering. Interestingly, in [5] it is applied a simple and well known method from Graph Theory for node decimation based on the largest eigenvector u_{max} of the graph Laplacian matrix. They further employ a more sophisticated procedure to reduce Laplacian matrix using the sparsified Kron reduction. Another relevant differentiable approach is that put forward by DiffPool [31], where the model learns soft assignments to pool similar activating patterns into the same cluster, though the idea of learning hiearchical soft-clustering of graphs via adjacency matrix decomposition using a symmetric variant of NMF can be dated back to [32]. In DiffPool, the learned soft assignment matrix is applied as a linear reduction operator on the adjacency matrix and the input signal matrix, and the coarsened graph is thus further convolved with GCNs.

3   NMFPool: Node Pooling by Non-Negative Matrix Factorization

In the following section we introduce our model, NMFPool, a principled Pooling operator enabling deep graph CNNs develop multi-resolution representations of input graphs. NMFPool leverages community structure underlying graphs to pool similar nodes to progressively gain coarser views of a graph. To that end we take inspiration from [32] in which latent community structure of graph data is made explicit via adjacency matrix decomposition using Symmetric NMF (SNMF). NMFPool is grounded on that idea, building, instead, on a general non-symmetrical NMF of the adjacency matrix without constraining solutions to be stochastic. Before going further into details of our approach, we first introduce the formal definition of the NMF problem, then we give an intuitive interpretation of its solutions to clarify why NMF would help solve the graph pooling problem on graphs. At the end we will show how to use product factors of NMF as linear operators to aggregate topology and content information associated to graphs. NMF is a popular technique for extracting salient features in data by extracting a latent space representation of the original information. Throughout the paper we refer to the original idea of NMF [19] though it has been extensively studied in numerical linear algebra in the last years by many authors and for a variety of applications. Formally, the NMF problem can be stated as follows:

Definition 1. *Given a non-negative matrix $A \in \mathbb{R}_+^{n \times m}$, find non-negative matrix factors $W \in \mathbb{R}_+^{n \times k}$ and $H \in \mathbb{R}_+^{k \times m}$, with $k < \min(m, n)$, such that*

$$A \approx WH \tag{7}$$

If we see matrix A as having m multivariate objects column-stacked, the straightforward interpretation of (7) is as follows

$$a_j \approx W h_j, \tag{8}$$

with a_j and h_j corresponding to j-th columns of A and H. The approximation (8) entails that each multi-variate object is a linear combination of columns of W weighted by coefficients in h_j. Thus W is referred to as the basis matrix or equivalently the cluster centroids matrix if we intend to interpret NMF as a clustering method. Matrix H can be seen, instead, as a low-dimensional representation of the input data making thus NMF also useful for dimensionality reduction. Latent representation, in the clustering perspective, may indicate whether a sample object belongs to a cluster. For example, we could constrain each data-point to belong to a single cluster at a time: namely, each data-point is assigned to the closest cluster $x_j \approx u_j$. We generally look for non-trivial encodings to explain community evolution in graphs. Thus, the problem could be relaxed to a soft-clustering problem in that each data-point can belong to k overlapping clusters [28]. Formulation (7) requires to define a metric to measure the quality of the approximation, and Kullback-Leibler (KL-) divergence or the more common Frobenius norm (F-norm) are common choices. Many techniques from numerical linear algebra can be used to minimize problem (7) whatever the cost function we use, although its inherently non-convex nature does not give any guarantee on global minimum [13]. In [19] were first proposed multiplicative and additive update rules that ensure monotone descrease under KL- or F-norm.

Thus, our proposed solution can be summarized into two main steps. First, we encode the input adjacency matrix to learn soft-assignments of nodes, and that could accomplished via exact NMF of the adjacency matrix. Second, we apply soft-assignments as linear operators to coarse adjacency matrix and node embeddings. To this end, we refer to algebraic operations seen in [32] for decomposing adjacency matrices and we extend it using equations widely used for graph coarsening [31], for they take into account embedding matrix reduction and nodes connectivity strength. For a complete picture, consider ℓ NMFPool layers interleaved with at least $\ell + 1$ stacked Graph Convolutions (GCs) as illustrated in Fig. 1, where the graph convolutions are computed according to (6). Then, let $Z^{(i)} \in \mathbb{R}^{n_i \times d}$ be the output of i-th GC, namely the convolved node embeddings at layer i-th, defined as

$$Z^{(i)} = \text{ReLU}\left(A^{(i)} Z^{(i-1)} \Theta^{(i)}\right) \tag{9}$$

with adjacency matrix $A^{(i)} \in \mathbb{R}^{n_i \times n_i}$, with n_i number of nodes at previous layer, and $\Theta^{(i)} \in \mathbb{R}^{d \times d}$ matrix of weights. Observe that we are assuming, without loss of generality, each GC layer (9) as having the same number of neurons. Observe also that $Z^{(0)} = X \in \mathbb{R}^{n \times d}$, namely the initial node labels, and the initial adjacency matrix is set to $A^{(0)} = \hat{D}^{-1/2} \hat{A} \hat{D}^{-1/2}$, i.e. the normalized adjacency matrix with $\hat{A} = A + I$, $A \in \mathbb{R}^{n \times n}$, and $\hat{D}$ is a diagonal matrix of node degrees [17].

The i-th NMFPool layer solves the problem in (7), i.e. the decomposition of the symmetric and positive $A^{(i)}$, by minimizing the following loss

$$||A^{(i)} - W^{(i)} H^{(i)}||_F \tag{10}$$

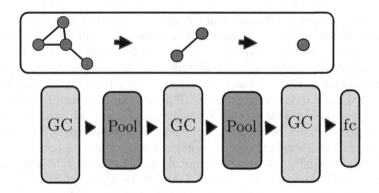

Fig. 1. High level architecture of a 3-layers GCN interleaved with 2 NMF pooling layers.

with $W^{(i)} \in \mathbb{R}_+^{n_i \times k_i}$ and $H^{(i)} \in \mathbb{R}_+^{k_i \times n_i}$, and k_i number of overlapping communities to pool the n_i nodes into, and $\|.\|_F$ the Frobenius norm. Observe that k_i's are hyper-parameters to control graph coarsening scale. The algorithm to minimize (10) depends on the underlying NMF implementation. Then NMFPool applies the encoding $H^{(i)}$ to coarsen graph topology and its content as follows

$$Z^{(i+1)} = H^{(i)T} Z^{(i)} \in \mathbb{R}^{k_i \times d} \tag{11}$$

$$A^{(i+1)} = H^{(i)T} A^{(i)} H^{(i)} \in \mathbb{R}^{k_i \times k_i}. \tag{12}$$

A graphical interpretation of the inner workings of the NMFPool layer is provided in Fig. 2, highlighting the interpretation of pooling as a matrix decomposition operator. It is crucial to point out that NMFPool layers are independent of the number of nodes in the graph, which is essential to deal with graphs with varying topologies.

4   Experiments

We assess the effectiveness of using the exact NMF of the adjacency matrix A as a pooling mechanism in graph convolutional neural networks. To this end, we consider five popular graph classification benchmarks and we further compare the performance of our approach, referred to as NMFPool in the following, with that of DiffPool, with the goal of showing how a simple and general method may easily compare to differentiable and parameterized pooling operators such as DiffPool. Results were gathered on graph classification tasks for solving biological problems on the ENZYMES [6,25], NCI1 [27], PROTEINS [6,12], and D&D [12,26] datasets and the scientific collaboration dataset COLLAB [30]. In Table 1 are summarized statistics on benchmark datasets.

In our experiments, the baseline graph convolution is the vanilla layer in (6). For both models, we employed the interleaving of pooling and convolutional

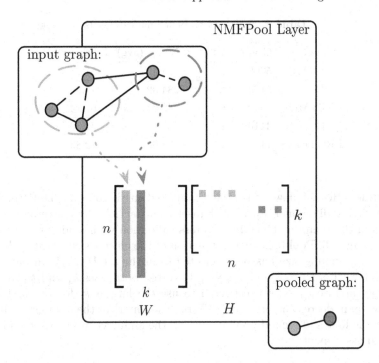

Fig. 2. The NMFPool layer. Orange circles represent nodes of input graph, and solid lines the edges. Dashed lines are the predicted edges in between nodes pooled together. Colored dashed circles represent discovered communities. (Color figure online)

layers depicted in the architecture in Fig. 1, varying the number of pooling-convolution layer pairs to assess the effect of network depth on task performance. Note that the number of layers in the convolutional architecture influences the context spreading across the nodes in the graph. Implementation of NMFPool and Diffpool is based on the Pytorch Geometric library [14], complemented by the NMF implementation available in the Scikit library. Models configurations were run on a multi-core architecture equipped with 4 NUMA nodes each with 18 cores (Intel(R) Xeon(R) Gold 6140M @ 2.30 GHz) capable of running 2 threads each for a total of 144 processing units available. We had access also to 4 Tesla V100 GPUs accelerators.

Model selection was performed for exploring a variety of configurations using stratified 3-fold cross validation. Following standard practice in graph convolution neural networks, learning rate was set with an initial value of 0.1 and then decreased by a factor of 0.1 whenever validation error did not show any improvement after 10 epochs wait. The number of neurons is the same for each graph convolutional layer and it has been selected in $\{16, 32, 64, 128\}$ as part of the cross-validation procedure. When applying the pooling operator both NMFPool and Diffpool require to define the number of communities k, similarly to how the pooling operator on images requires the definition of the pooling windows size

Table 1. Statistics on benchmark datasets.

Dataset	Graphs	Classes	Nodes (avg)	Edges (avg)
COLLAB	5000	3	74.49	2457.78
D&D	1178	2	284.32	715.66
ENZYMES	600	6	32.63	62.14
NCI1	4110	2	29.87	32.30
PROTEINS	1113	2	39.06	72.82

(and stride). Here, following the idea indicated in the original DiffPool paper [31], we choose different k for each dataset as a fraction of the average number of nodes in the samples. Thus during cross-validation we intended to study how NMFPool and DiffPool behave as a function of the cluster sizes k_i at each layer. To this end, pooling size has been selected from the set $\{k_1, k_2\}$. In particular, for models with a single pooling layer, we tested both sizes k_1 and k_2. Instead, for deeper architectures, we restricted to use the largest k_i for the first layer, following up in decreasing order of k_i. Table 2 summarizes the number of clusters used for the first and second pooling layer in the architectures considered in this empirical assessment.

Table 2. k_1 is computed using formula $k_1 = \lfloor n_{avg} \cdot p \rfloor$ with p varying in [21%–25%], and n_{avg} average number of nodes (see Table 1). Then $k_2 = k_1/2$. Fractions are chosen depending on the size of task at hand and to previous empirical observation. Except for the D&D dataset where $p = 5\%, 1\%$, being the bigger dataset we needed a good compromise between abstraction capability and computational time.

Dataset	k_1	k_2	p
COLLAB	16	8	22%
D&D	14	2	5%–1%
ENZYMES	8	4	25%
NCI1	6	3	24%
PROTEINS	8	4	21%

The outcome of the empirical assessment is summarized in Table 3, where it is reported the mean classification accuracy of the different models averaged on the dataset folds. Table 3 reports results for a vanilla GCN (no pooling) and a varying number of graph convolution layers: results show how at most two layers are sufficient to guarantee good performances, while three layers are only required for the COLLAB dataset and a single layer network obtains the best performance on the NCI1 dataset. In the experiments we thus decided to employ at most three GCN layers, namely at most two NMF and DiffPool pooling layers. It is still evident how adding more convolutional and pooling layers does not always result into better performances. The analysis of the results for NMFPool shows how the addition of the simple NMF pooling allows a consistent increase of the classification accuracy with respect to the non-pooled model for all the benchmark datasets. Note how a single pooling layer is sufficient, on most datasets, to obtain the best results, confirming the fact that pooling allows to effectively fasten the process of context spreading between the nodes. When compared to DiffPool, our approach achieves accuracies which are only marginally lower than DiffPool on few datasets. This despite the fact that DiffPool employs a solution performing an task-specific parameterized decomposition of the graph, while our solution simply looks for quasi-symmetrical product matrices by knowing nothing of the underlying task.

Table 3. Mean and standard deviation (in brackets) of graph classification accuracies on the different benchmarks, for the vanilla GCN with ℓ convolutional layers (ℓ-GC), for NMFPool and DiffPool with ℓ_p pooling layers and $\ell_p + 1$ convolutional layers (i.e. ℓ_{p_1}-NMFPool and ℓ_{p_2}-DiffPool, respectively).

Model	ENZYMES	NCI1	PROTEINS	D&D	COLLAB
1-GC	0.222 (0.023)	0.625 (0.014)	0.713 (0.019)	0.681 (0.045)	0.671 (0.007)
2-GCs	0.228 (0.023)	0.620 (0.057)	0.720 (0.034)	0.704 (0.048)	0.678 (0.007)
3-GCs	0.182 (0.022)	0.628 (0.031)	0.688 (0.024)	0.692 (0.032)	0.681 (0.002)
1-NMFPool	0.241 (0.039)	0.662 (0.026)	0.721 (0.031)	0.760 (0.015)	0.650 (0.004)
2-NMFPool	0.175 (0.023)	0.655 (0.013)	0.724 (0.020)	0.753 (0.010)	0.658 (0.002)
1-DiffPool	0.259 (0.069)	0.661 (0.017)	0.743 (0.011)	0.770 (0.007)	0.659 (0.005)
2-DiffPool	0.239 (0.064)	0.632 (0.017)	0.744 (0.026)	0.761 (0.003)	0.667 (0.022)

5 Conclusions

We introduced a pooling mechanism based on the NMF of the adjacency matrix of the graph, discussing how this approach can be used to yield a hierarchical soft-clustering of the nodes and to induce a coarsening of the graph structure. We have empirically assessed our NMPool approach with the task-specific adaptive pooling mechanism put forward by the DiffPool model on a number of state-of-the-art graph classification benchmarks. We argue that our approach can yield to potentially more general and scalable pooling mechanisms than DiffPool, allowing to choose weather the pooling mechanism has to consider the node embeddings computed by the model and the task-related information when performing the decomposition (as in DiffPool), but also allowing to directly decompose the graph structure a-priori with no knowledge of the node embeddings adaptively computed by the convolutional layer. This latter aspect, in particular, allows to pre-compute the graph decomposition and results in a multiresolution representation of the graph structure which does not change with the particular task at hand.

Future works will consider the use of symmetric and optimized NMF variants to increase prediction performances. It also would be of particular interest to improve the quality and quantity of information NMFPool retains into the encoding matrix. NMFPool could evolve out of its general purpose form, for example, making it a generative end-to-end differentiable layer using probabilistic approaches. See [8] for an attempt to solve NMF using probabilistic models. We could refer to the popular probabilistic generative model of the Variational Auto-Encoders (VAEs) [16,24] possibly extended to graphs [18]. The underlying hierarchical structure of graph data may also be taken into account by imposing latent encoding to match priors referring to hyperbolic spaces [20]. Interestingly, latent matrix encoding may not be forced to match overimposed priors, for they could make the model too biased over particular graph geometries. Instead, such priors could be directly learned from relational data using adversarial approaches [21] extended also to graph auto-encoders [23]. Another interesting feature would be to make NMFPool independent of hyper-parameter k.

Acknowledgments. This work has been supported by the Italian Ministry of Education, University, and Research (MIUR) under project SIR 2014 LIST-IT (grant n. RBSI14STDE).

References

1. Bacciu, D., Micheli, A., Sperduti, A.: Compositional generative mapping for tree-structured data - part II: topographic projection model. IEEE Trans. Neural Netw. Learn. Syst. **24**(2), 231–247 (2013)
2. Bacciu, D., Micheli, A., Sperduti, A.: Generative kernels for tree-structured data. IEEE Trans. Neural Netw. Learn. Syst. **29**(10), 4932–4946 (2018)
3. Bacciu, D., Errica, F., Micheli, A.: Contextual graph Markov model: a deep and generative approach to graph processing. In: Dy, J., Krause, A. (eds.) Proceedings of the 35th International Conference on Machine Learning, vol. 80, pp. 294–303. Proceedings of Machine Learning Research, PMLR, Stockholmsmässan, Stockholm (2018)
4. Belkin, M., Niyogi, P.: Laplacian eigenmaps and spectral techniques for embedding and clustering. In: Proceedings of the 14th International Conference on Neural Information Processing Systems: Natural and Synthetic, NIPS 2001, pp. 585–591. MIT Press, Cambridge (2001)
5. Bianchi, F.M., Grattarola, D., Livi, L., Alippi, C.: Graph neural networks with convolutional ARMA filters. CoRR abs/1901.01343 (2019)
6. Borgwardt, K.M., Ong, C.S., Schonauer, S., Vishwanathan, S.V.N., Smola, A.J., Kriegel, H.P.: Protein function prediction via graph kernels. Bioinformatics **21**(Suppl 1), i47–i56 (2005)
7. Bronstein, M.M., Bruna, J., LeCun, Y., Szlam, A., Vandergheynst, P.: Geometric deep learning: going beyond euclidean data. CoRR abs/1611.08097 (2016)
8. Brouwer, T., Frellsen, J., Liò, P.: Fast Bayesian non-negative matrix factorisation and tri-factorisation. In: NIPS 2016 : Advances in Approximate Bayesian Inference Workshop, 09 December 2016 (2016)
9. Bruna, J., Zaremba, W., Szlam, A., Lecun, Y.: Spectral networks and locally connected networks on graphs. In: International Conference on Learning Representations (ICLR 2014), CBLS, April 2014 (2014)

10. Cangea, C., Veličković, P., Jovanović, N., Kipf, T., Liò, P.: Towards sparse hierarchical graph classifiers. arXiv e-prints arXiv:1811.01287, November 2018
11. Defferrard, M., Bresson, X., Vandergheynst, P.: Convolutional neural networks on graphs with fast localized spectral filtering. CoRR abs/1606.09375 (2016)
12. Dobson, P.D., Doig, A.J.: Distinguishing enzyme structures from non-enzymes without alignments. J. Mol. Biol. **330**(4), 771–783 (2003)
13. Favati, P., Lotti, G., Menchi, O., Romani, F.: Adaptive computation of the symmetric nonnegative matrix factorization (NMF). arXiv e-prints arXiv:1903.01321, March 2019
14. Fey, M., Lenssen, J.E.: Fast graph representation learning with PyTorch geometric. CoRR abs/1903.02428 (2019)
15. Hamilton, W.L., Ying, R., Leskovec, J.: Inductive representation learning on large graphs. CoRR abs/1706.02216 (2017)
16. Kingma, D.P., Welling, M.: Auto-encoding variational bayes. arXiv e-prints arXiv:1312.6114, December 2013
17. Kipf, T.N., Welling, M.: Semi-supervised classification with graph convolutional networks. CoRR abs/1609.02907 (2016)
18. Kipf, T.N., Welling, M.: Variational graph auto-encoders. arXiv e-prints arXiv:1611.07308, November 2016
19. Lee, D.D., Seung, H.S.: Algorithms for non-negative matrix factorization. In: Leen, T.K., Dietterich, T.G., Tresp, V. (eds.) Advances in Neural Information Processing Systems, vol. 13, pp. 556–562. MIT Press (2001)
20. Mathieu, E., Le Lan, C., Maddison, C.J., Tomioka, R., Whye Teh, Y.: Hierarchical representations with Poincaré Variational auto-encoders. arXiv e-prints arXiv:1901.06033, January 2019
21. Mescheder, L.M., Nowozin, S., Geiger, A.: Adversarial variational bayes: unifying variational autoencoders and generative adversarial networks. CoRR abs/1701.04722 (2017)
22. Micheli, A.: Neural network for graphs: a contextual constructive approach. IEEE Trans. Neural Netw. **20**(3), 498–511 (2009)
23. Pan, S., Hu, R., Long, G., Jiang, J., Yao, L., Zhang, C.: Adversarially regularized graph autoencoder. CoRR abs/1802.04407 (2018)
24. Rezende, D.J., Mohamed, S., Wierstra, D.: Stochastic backpropagation and approximate inference in deep generative models. In: Xing, E.P., Jebara, T. (eds.) Proceedings of the 31st International Conference on Machine Learning, vol. 32, pp. 1278–1286. Proceedings of Machine Learning Research, PMLR, Bejing, 22–24 June 2014
25. Schomburg, I., et al.: BRENDA, the enzyme database: updates and major new developments. Nucleic Acids Res. **32**, D431–D433 (2004). https://doi.org/10.1093/nar/gkh081
26. Shervashidze, N., Schweitzer, P., van Leeuwen, E.J., Mehlhorn, K., Borgwardt, K.M.: Weisfeiler-lehman graph kernels. J. Mach. Learn. Res. **12**, 2539–2561 (2011)
27. Wale, N., Watson, I.A., Karypis, G.: Comparison of descriptor spaces for chemical compound retrieval and classification. Knowl. Inf. Syst. **14**(3), 347–375 (2008). https://doi.org/10.1007/s10115-007-0103-5
28. Watt, J., Borhani, R., Katsaggelos, A.K.: Machine Learning Refined: Foundations, Algorithms, and Applicationsa, 1st edn. Cambridge University Press, New York (2016)
29. Xu, K., Hu, W., Leskovec, J., Jegelka, S.: How powerful are graph neural networks? CoRR abs/1810.00826 (2018)

30. Yanardag, P., Vishwanathan, S.: Deep graph kernels. In: Proceedings of the 21th ACM SIGKDD International Conference on Knowledge Discovery and Data Mining, KDD 2015, pp. 1365–1374. ACM, New York (2015). https://doi.org/10.1145/2783258.2783417

31. Ying, Z., You, J., Morris, C., Ren, X., Hamilton, W., Leskovec, J.: Hierarchical graph representation learning with differentiable pooling. In: Bengio, S., Wallach, H., Larochelle, H., Grauman, K., Cesa-Bianchi, N., Garnett, R. (eds.) Advances in Neural Information Processing Systems, vol. 31, pp. 4804–4814. Curran Associates, Inc. (2018)

32. Yu, K., Yu, S., Tresp, V.: Soft clustering on graphs. In: Weiss, Y., Schölkopf, B., Platt, J.C. (eds.) Advances in Neural Information Processing Systems, vol. 18, pp. 1553–1560. MIT Press (2006). http://papers.nips.cc/paper/2948-soft-clustering-on-graphs.pdf

Winograd Convolution for DNNs: Beyond Linear Polynomials

Barbara Barabasz[✉] and David Gregg

School of Computer Science and Statistics, Trinity College Dublin, Dublin 2, Ireland
{barabasb,dgregg}@tcd.ie

Abstract. Winograd convolution is widely used in deep neural networks (DNNs). Existing work for DNNs considers only the subset Winograd algorithms that are equivalent to Toom-Cook convolution. We investigate a wider range of Winograd algorithms for DNNs and show that these additional algorithms can significantly improve floating point (FP) accuracy in many cases. We present results for three FP formats: $fp32$, $fp16$ and $bf16$ (a truncated form of $fp32$) using 2000 inputs from the ImageNet dataset. We found that in $fp16$ this approach gives us up to 6.5 times better image recognition accuracy in one important case while maintaining the same number of elementwise multiplication operations in the innermost loop. In $bf16$ the convolution can be computed using 5% fewer innermost loop multiplications than with currently used Winograd algorithms while keeping the accuracy of image recognition the same as for direct convolution method.

Keywords: DNN · Convolution · Winograd convolution · Accuracy · Floating point

1 Motivation

In DNNs, and especially in Convolutional Neural Networks (CNNs), a huge amount of time is spent computing convolution. The simple *direct* algorithm has a complexity of $O(m^2)$. In contrast, *fast* convolution algorithms, such as FFT, Toom-Cook, and Winograd convolution require fewer operations.

The family of Winograd algorithms is based on (1) transforming tiles of the input and kernel into a modulo polynomials domain (the *Winograd domain*), where (2) convolution becomes the *elementwise multiplication* (Hadamard product) with complexity $O(m)$, and (3) transforming the result back to the original domain. Winograd's method is not a convolution algorithm itself; instead it generates fast convolution algorithms that operate on fixed-sized tiles of input, kernel and output.

Winograd's can be used to generate a wide variety of convolution algorithms with different trade-offs. It requires a set of polynomials as input to generate the convolution algorithm. These polynomials can be linear (*degree* = 1) or superlinear (*degree* > 1).

© Springer Nature Switzerland AG 2019
M. Alviano et al. (Eds.): AI*IA 2019, LNAI 11946, pp. 307–320, 2019.
https://doi.org/10.1007/978-3-030-35166-3_22

If only linear polynomials are used as inputs, Winograd's method becomes much simpler, and the resulting algorithms are guaranteed to need only the theoretically minimum number of operations for the elementwise multiplication. The set of Winograd algorithms generated using only linear polynomials is also equivalent to the set of algorithms that can be generated using the Toom-Cook method [12]. Toom-Cook is much simpler than the Winograd method, and as a result it is used to generate the algorithms used in many implementations of "Winograd" convolution.

The selected tile size is critical to the performance of Winograd convolution. A larger tile size increases the number of elementwise multiplication operations needed for that tile, but also computes more results per tile. Taking account of extra operations needed at the boundary of each tile, larger tiles reduce the number of elementwise multiplication operations per computed output point. However, the floating point error also grows exponentially with the tile size [1], so existing implementations of Winograd for DNNs typically use a small tile size[1]. In this paper we investigate the effect of higher-order polynomials on the accuracy of Winograd convolution for DNNs. Our experiments show that using order-2 polynomials can dramatically reduce the measured floating point error as compared to linear polynomials. However, higher order polynomials also increase the required number of multiplications in Hadamard product. This paper addresses the question: Is there a benefit in using the Winograd method with super-linear polynomials for DNNs, as compared to the simpler Toom-Cook method?

We make the following contributions:

- We demonstrate how the Winograd algorithm with higher-order polynomials can be adapted to DNN convolution
- We present experimental results for one and two dimensional Winograd convolution, with kernels of the size 3 (1D) or 3×3 (2D), and find that higher-order polynomials can significantly reduce the FP error.
- We show how using higher-order polynomials offer similar trade-offs between *elementwise multiplications* and FP accuracy, as compared with adjusting the block size.
- We experimentally identify cases where using higher-order polynomials can improve recognition without increasing *elementwise multiplications* when using half precision ($fp16$), and where we can improve the performance keeping the accuracy of image recognition in bfloat16 precision ($bf16$).

2   Related Work

In the DNN research literature the term "Winograd convolution algorithm" is used for both Winograd and Toom-Cook convolution, and in practice the Toom-Cook algorithm is used to generate the convolution matrices. The general Winograd algorithm described in this paper is not explored a lot in literature. We

---

[1] https://intel.github.io/mkl-dnn/winograd_convolution.html

can find a description of the approach in Winograd [12], but not for the multi-channel multiple kernel convolution used for DNNs. A simple example how to construct matrices is presented in [3]. A more general and detailed description can be found in [9]. Selesnick and Burrus [7] considered cyclic convolution methods using cyclotomic polynomials in their theoretical work.

Meng and Brothers in [6] apply the idea of using complex points i and $-i$ (root points of polynomial $a^2 + 1$) for quantization network. We present a general definition of the method and present floating point accuracy for a couple of different versions of the algorithm.

There is some work done on the improvement of the FP accuracy of Winograd (Toom-Cook) convolution for DNNs. Vincent et al. [11] present the result for one set of matrices, that scaling matrices G and A^T give the more accurate results. Scaling improves the conditioning of used matrices but it is not necessarily always equivalent to decrease the floating point error of computation, particularly for the small size of matrices used in DNNs.

There are also a couple of methods that allow to increasing the accuracy of dot product computations for matrices transformation, such as more accurate summation algorithms, Strassen matrix multiplication [13], etc. However, they require more operations for the transforms, for sorting elements, or for compensated summation, and/or make the implementation more complicated. In contrast, our approach does not require additional operations for the transformations. All of those methods for improving FP accuracy could also be used together with the presented method to reduce floating point error even more. These include pairwise summation over channels, Huffman based summation method and mixed precision computations proposed in [1].

3   Toom-Cook Versus Winograd Algorithm

3.1   Winograd Algorithm Definition

Convolution can be expressed as polynomial multiplication. Mapping the elements of kernel vector h and input vector x to coefficients of polynomials $h(a)$ and $x(a)$ respectively, the elements of output vector s (convolution of h and x) are equal to the coefficients of polynomial $s(a) = h(a)x(a)$. The Winograd family of algorithms for convolution is based on Chinese Reminder Theorem (CRT) for polynomials [2]. It says that for polynomial $M(a)$ in ring of polynomials over a field $\mathbb{F}$, $M(a) = m_1(a) \ldots m_\ell(a)$ where $m_i(a)$ are irreducible and pairwise coprime there exists $s(a)$ such as $deg(s(a)) < deg(M(a))$ the unique solution of systems of congruences: $s(a) = s_i(a) \bmod m_i(a)$ and

$$s(a) = \sum_i s_i(a) N_i(a) M_i(a) \bmod M(a) \tag{1}$$

where $N_i(a)M_i(a) + n_i(a)m_i(a) = 1$ and $M_i(a) = M(a)/m_i(a)$.

To compute the result of the convolution - the coefficients of the product of polynomials $h(a)$ and $x(a)$ - we put $s_i(a) = h_i(a)x_i(a) \bmod m_i(a)$,

$h_i(a) = h(a) \ mod \ m_i(a)$ and $x_i = x(a) \ mod \ m_i(a)$. Operations modulo $m_i(a)$ are equal to finding the remainder from division by $m_i(a)$; so if we assume that all polynomials $m_i(a)$ are of the first degree then the results in modulo $m_i(a)$ arithmetic are all constant polynomials (scalars): $h_i(a) = h(a) \ mod \ m_i(a) = r_h$, $x_i(a) = x(a) \ mod \ m_i(a) = r_x$. Then we can perform the computations of $s_i(a) = h_i(a)x_i(a) \ mod \ m_i(a)$ for $i = 1,\ldots,\ell$ as single multiplication: $s_i(a) = r_h r_x$. These operations for all $i = 1,\ldots,\ell$ are represented by Hadamard product of two vectors consist of elements $h_1(a),\ldots,h_\ell(a)$ and $x_1(a),\ldots,x_\ell(a)$ (see Fig. 1).

The commonly used DNN two-dimensional Winograd convolution algorithm [5] uses the Matrix Exchange Theorem [3] and expresses the computations formula for in the following form:

$$A^T(GHG^T \odot B^T XB)A \qquad (2)$$

Where matrices H and X represents kernel and input values.

In this paper we use the modified version of the Winograd algorithm with polynomial $M(a)$ of degree equal to $deg(s(a))$ and pseudo-point ∞. The exact algorithm to compute matrix elements and a more detailed theoretical description of the method can be found in [1,3,9].

To the best of our knowledge all Winograd algorithms used in DNNs require that all $m_i(a)$ are of the first degree (i.e linear). All such algorithms derived using Winograd's method with linear polynomials can also be found using the Toom-Cook method [4,10]. Toom-Cook was analyzed and applied to signal processing problems by S. Winograd in the 1980s. Winograd also proved that Toom-Cook guarantees that the generated convolution algorithm will use the theoretically minimum possible number of *elementwise multiplications* needed to compute convolution of size $n_o \times n_o$ with a kernel of size $n_h \times n_h$. We denote these algorithms as $F(n_o \times n_o, n_h \times n_h))$ [12].

If we use polynomial $m_i(a)$ of degree $d > 1$, then the results of $h_i(a) = h(a) \ mod \ m_i(a)$ and $x_i(a) = x(a) \ mod \ m_i(a)$ are polynomials not scalars (see Fig. 2). Thus to compute $s_i(a)$ we need to multiply two polynomials $h_i(a)$, $x_i(a)$ rather than using simple scalar multiplication. However, to solve this subproblem (i.e. computing the coefficients of the product of two polynomials $h_i(a)$ and $x_i(a)$) we can apply any suitable algorithm, including the Toom-Cook algorithm $F_{T-C}(d \times d, d \times d)$. All polynomials $m_i(a)$ used in the Winograd algorithm have to be pairwise coprime, and similarly all polynomials used in the Toom-Cook algorithm to solve the sub-problem also need to be pairwise coprime. But polynomials in the two different groups do not need to be coprime. This means that we can use the same polynomials of the first degree (*points*) in both algorithms. In the Fig. 2 we can have $q_i = p_j$. Some *points* offer superior floating point accuracy, such as 0, -1 and 1 (polynomials a, $a+1$ and $a-1$) [1].

The approach with polynomials, $m_i(a)$ of degree $d > 1$ requires two steps of transformations (see Fig. 2). Firstly, we transform input/kernel into the "Polynomials Winograd domain". That means to transform input/kernel into polynomials of the degree greater than zero. We then transform both those polynomials

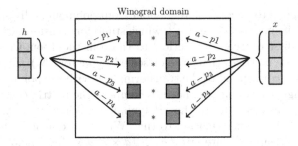

Fig. 1. Transformation of the kernel (using matrix G) and input (using matrix B^T) in one-dimensional Toom-Cook convolution algorithm $F_{T-C}(2 \times 2, 3 \times 3)$ with four root points p_1, p_2, p_3 and p_4 (polynomials $a = p_1$, $a - p_2$, $a - p_3$ and $a - p_4$).

into scalars in the "Winograd domain". To perform the second transformation we use the Toom-Cook algorithm. Similarly, after computing Hadamard product we first transform the result into "Polynomials Winograd domain" and after this into the original domain. Each of these transforms can be represented by a matrix which multiplied by the input/kernel/output to compute the transformation. We can merge the matrices for these two stages of transformation into a single transformation, allowing us to create three matrices G^W, B^W and A^W applied to the kernel, input and result of the Hadamard product respectively. For the clarity, we denote matrices constructed for Toom-Cook algorithm as $G^{(T-C)}$, $A^{(T-C)}$ and $B^{(T-C)}$.

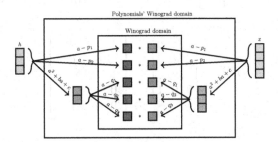

Fig. 2. Transformation of kernel (matrix G) and input (matrix B^T) in 1 dimensional Winograd convolution algorithm $F_W(2 \times 2, 3 \times 3)$ with polynomials $a - p_1$, $a - p_2$, $a^2 + ba + c$. The subproblem is solved with Toom-Cook algorithm $F_{T-C}(2 \times 2, 2 \times 2)$ (input $n = 3$) and points q_1, q_2, q_3 (polynomials $a - q_1$, $a - q_2$, $a - q_3$).

3.2   Constructing the Transform Matrices

Matrices G^W and A^W: We use the function $\text{vec}(m(a))$ to map the polynomial $m(a) = m_1 + m_2 a + \ldots + m_n a^{n-1}$ to the vector: $\text{vec}(m(a)) = \begin{bmatrix} m_1 \cdots m_n \end{bmatrix}^T$

We use $R_{m(a)}[p(a)]$ to denote the remainder from polynomial division of $p(a)$ by $m(a)$. Rows of the matrix G^W and A^W which stand for transformation with polynomials of the first degree are identical to those in the Toom-Cook algorithm. (Note that we use matrices that are not scaled by factors N_i). To construct the submatrices that correspond to the transformation with the polynomial $m_i(a)$ of the degree d higher than one, we have to compose the matrix G with G', where G' represents transformation to the "Polynomials' Winograd domain" and the G matrix stands for transformation to the "Winograd domain" and is equal to matrix $G^{(T-C)}$ of appropriate size $(F_{T-C}(d \times d, d \times d))$. Analogously, matrix $A^W = A^{(T-C)}A'$—where $A^{(T-C)}$ is generated by the Toom-Cook algorithm $F_{T-C}(d \times d, d \times d)$—and A' stands for transformation into the "Polynomials' Winograd domain" with polynomial $m_i(a)$ of the degree higher than 1. The last rows A_ℓ and G_ℓ represent the pseudo point ∞ needed to construct the modified version of the algorithm [1,3]. Below we present an example of the construction of matrices A^W and G^W for kernel of size 3×3 and output of size 2×2, choosing polynomials $m_1(a) = a$ and $m_2(a) = a^2 + ba + c$. To solve the subproblem $F_{T-C}(2 \times 2, 2 \times 2)$ we use Toom-Cook algorithm with points 0, 1.

$$G_2 = G^{(T-C)}G' = \begin{bmatrix} -1 & 0 \\ 1 & 1 \\ 0 & 1 \end{bmatrix} \begin{bmatrix} 1 & 0 & -c \\ 0 & 1 & -b \end{bmatrix} = \begin{bmatrix} -1 & 0 & c \\ 1 & 1 & -b-c \\ 0 & 1 & -b \end{bmatrix}$$

$$A_2 = A^{(T-C)}A' = \begin{bmatrix} 1 & 0 \\ 1 & 1 \\ 0 & 1 \end{bmatrix} \begin{bmatrix} 1 & 0 & -c & bc \\ 0 & 1 & -b & b^2 - c \end{bmatrix} = \begin{bmatrix} 1 & 0 & -c & bc \\ 1 & 1 & -b-c & bc + b^2 - c \\ 0 & 1 & -b & b^2 - c \end{bmatrix}$$

$$G^W = \begin{bmatrix} G_1 \\ G_2 \\ 0 & 0 & 1 \end{bmatrix} = \begin{bmatrix} 1 & 0 & 0 \\ -1 & 0 & c \\ 1 & 1 & -b-c \\ 0 & 1 & -b \\ 0 & 0 & 1 \end{bmatrix}$$

$$A^W = \begin{bmatrix} A_1 \\ A_2 \\ 0 & 0 & 0 & 1 \end{bmatrix} = \begin{bmatrix} 1 & 0 & 0 & 0 \\ 1 & 0 & -c & bc \\ 1 & 1 & -b-c & bc + b^2 - c \\ 0 & 1 & -b & b^2 - c \\ 0 & 0 & 0 & 1 \end{bmatrix}$$

The exact algorithms to compute matrices G^W and B^W are presented in Algorithm 1.

Matrix B^W. First we construct auxiliary matrix C that includes blocks C_i for $i = 1, \cdots, \ell$, where ℓ is the number of the polynomials $m_i(a)$. The C matrix represents transformation from the "Polynomials' Winograd domain" into the "Winograd domain". The rows stand by transformation with polynomials $m_i(a)$

Algorithm 1. Construction of matrix G^W and A^W to transform kernel and result of Hadamard product in a Winograd convolution algorithm

---

Input: n_o — size of output, n_h — size of kernel, G^{T-C}, A^{T-C} matrix G and A
      for $F_{T-C}(d \times d, d \times d)$, $\{m_1(a), \cdots, m_\ell(a)\}$ set of ℓ irreducible and
      pairwise coprime polynomials such as $\sum_i deg(m_i(a)) = n_h + n_o - 2$
Output: Matrices G^W and A^W for Winograd convolution

1   $n = n_h + n_o - 2$
2   **for** $i = 1$ *to* ℓ **do**
3      $d = deg(m_i(a))$
4   **if** $d == 1$ **then**
5          $p_i = root(m_i(a))$
6          $G_i = \begin{bmatrix} p_i^0 & \cdots & p_i^{n_h-1} \end{bmatrix}$, $A_i = \begin{bmatrix} p_i^0 & \cdots & p_i^{n_o-1} \end{bmatrix}$
7   **if** $d > 1$ **then**
8          $G' = \begin{bmatrix} vec(R_{m_i(a)}[a^0]) & \cdots & vec(R_{m_i(a)}[a^{n_h-1}]) \end{bmatrix}$
9          $A' = \begin{bmatrix} vec(R_{m_i(a)}[a^0]) & \cdots & vec(R_{m_i(a)}[a^{n_o-1}]) \end{bmatrix}$
10     $G_i = G^{(T-C)}G'$, $A_i = A^{(T-C)}A'$
11   $G_{\ell+1} = \begin{bmatrix} 0 & \cdots & 0 & 1 \end{bmatrix}$, $A_{\ell+1} = \begin{bmatrix} 0 & \cdots & 0 & 1 \end{bmatrix}$

12   $G^W = \begin{bmatrix} G_1 \\ \vdots \\ G_\ell \\ G_{\ell+1} \end{bmatrix}$ $A^W = \begin{bmatrix} A_1 \\ \vdots \\ A_\ell \\ A_{\ell+1} \end{bmatrix}$

---

of the first degree are equal to identity matrix. Blocks stand for transformation with polynomial $m_i(a)$ of degree greater than 1 represents transformation with matrix $B^{(T-C)}$, generated for subproblem with $F_{T-C}(d \times d, d \times d)$. A second matrix E includes the rest of operations, that is modulo $M(a)$ (remainder) from product of polynomials $M_i(a)$ and the polynomial obtained from extended Euclidean algorithm $N_i(a)$ (see formula 1). Additional zeros in rows of matrix E and column with coefficients of the polynomial $M_i(a)$ implement the modified version of the Winograd algorithm.

We present an example of constructing matrix B^W for kernels of the size 3×3 and outputs of size 2×2, choosing polynomials: $m_1(a) = a$ and $m_2(a) = a^2 + ba + c$ (as in previous subsection). Matrix $B^{(T-C)}$ is generated by the Toom-Cook algorithm $F_{T-C}(2 \times 2, 2 \times 2)$ with points $0, 1$.

$$B^{(T-C)} = \begin{bmatrix} -1 & 0 & 0 \\ 1 & 1 & -1 \\ 0 & 0 & 1 \end{bmatrix} \quad C_2 = \begin{bmatrix} -1 & 0 & -c \\ 1 & 1 & -b-1 \end{bmatrix} \quad C = \begin{bmatrix} 1 & 0 & 0 & 0 \\ 0 & -1 & 0 & -c \\ 0 & 1 & 1 & -b-1 \end{bmatrix}$$

Next, we construct the blocks of matrix E. The polynomials get from extended Euclidean algorithm [2] are: $N_1 = 1$, $N_2 = -a$.

Algorithm 2. Construction of matrix B to transform the input in the Winograd convolution algorithm

---

Input: n_o - size of output, n_h - size of kernel, $\{m_1(a), \cdots, m_{\ell(a)}\}$ set of ℓ irreducible and pairwise coprime polynomials such as
$$\sum_i deg(m_i(a)) = n_h + n_o - 2$$
Output: Matrix B^W for Winograd convolution

1 $n = n_h + n_o - 2$
2 $M(a) = \prod_i m_i(a)$
3 $M_i(a) = M(a)/m_i(a)$
4 **for** $i = 1$ *to* ℓ **do**
5      $d = deg(m_i(a))$
6   **if** $d == 1$ **then**
7          $C_i = [1]$
8   **if** $d > 1$ **then**
9          $B^{(T-C)}$ matrix B for $F_{T-C}(d \times d, d \times d)$
10   **for** $j = 1$ *to* $2d - 1$ **do**
11             $b_j(a) = B^{(T-C)}_{1,j} + B^{(T-C)}_{2,j}a + \cdots + B^{(T-C)}_{2d-1,j}a^{2d-2}$
12         $C_i = \left[vec(R_{m_i(a)}[b_1(a)] \cdots vec(R_{m_i(a)}[b_{2d-1}(a)])\right]$

13 $C = \begin{bmatrix} C_1 & & \\ & \ddots & \\ & & C_\ell \end{bmatrix}$

14 **for** $i = 1$ *to* ℓ **do**
15      $N_i(a)$ — polynomial obtained from extended Euclidean algorithm for polynomials $m_i(a)$ and $M_i(a)$
16      $E_i = \left[vec(R_{M(a)}[a^0 N_i(a)M_i(a)]) \cdots vec(R_{M(a)}[a^{d-1} N_i(a)M_i(a)])\right]$

17 $E = \begin{bmatrix} E_1 & \cdots & E_\ell \\ 0 & \cdots & 0 \end{bmatrix}$

18 $B^W = [EC \; vec(M(a))]$

$$E_1 = \begin{bmatrix} 1 \\ b \\ c \end{bmatrix} \quad E_2 = \begin{bmatrix} 0 & 0 \\ 0 & c \\ -1 & b \end{bmatrix} \quad E = \begin{bmatrix} 1 & 0 & 0 \\ b & 0 & c \\ c & -1 & b \\ 0 & 0 & 0 \end{bmatrix}$$

$$EC = \begin{bmatrix} 1 & 0 & 0 \\ b & 0 & c \\ c & -1 & b \\ 0 & 0 & 0 \end{bmatrix} \begin{bmatrix} 1 & 0 & 0 & 0 \\ 0 & -1 & 0 & -c \\ 0 & 1 & 1 & -b-1 \end{bmatrix} = \begin{bmatrix} 1 & 0 & 0 & 0 \\ b & c & c & -c(b+1) \\ c & b+1 & b & c-b(b+1) \\ 0 & 0 & 0 & 0 \end{bmatrix}$$

$$
B^W = \begin{bmatrix}
1 & 0 & 0 & 0 & 0 \\
b & c & c & -c(b+1) & c \\
c\,b+1 & b\,c & -b(b+1) & b \\
0 & 0 & 0 & 0 & 1
\end{bmatrix}
$$

3.3 Optimality of Winograd Algorithm

Toom-Cook algorithms for 2 dimensional convolution have an optimal number of multiplications $n = (n_h + n_o - 1)^2$ for fixed n_h and n_o. While computing convolution in DNNs, we break our input into the pieces of the size equal to algorithm input tile. This results in overlap of input tiles at boundaries. The exact number of overlapping input values for whole input depends on the kernel and input/output sizes (see description in [5]). We express the performance of the algorithm as the ratio of the number of multiplications per single output point. Thus, Toom-Cook algorithm $F_{T-C}(2 \times 2, 3 \times 3)$ requires 16 multiplications to compute 4 output points, so we have ratio equal to 4. For algorithm $F_{T-C}(4 \times 4, 3 \times 3)$, the *ratio* = 2.25. For Toom-Cook convolution with a fixed kernel size the *ratio* decreases with tile size. The bigger input/output tile, the fewer elementwise multiplications are needed. The elementwise multiplication dominates the execution time of DNN convolution, so reductions in these multiply operations translate to reduced execution time. Unfortunately, with increasing the input/output size the floating point error of the computations increase exponentially [1].

When we apply Toom-Cook algorithm $F_{T-C}(n_o \times n_o, n_h \times n_h)$ the *ratio* is equal to $(n_h + n_o - 1)^2/n_o^2$. In the Winograd method, as we can see from matrix construction, introducing polynomials $m_i(a)$ of the degree greater than 1 results in larger matrix sizes, which means the bigger number of multiplications. Every Toom-Cook algorithm $F_{T-C}(d \times d, d \times d)$ used to solve subproblem in Winograd algorithm requires $2d - 1$ polynomials of the first degree. The bigger number and higher degree polynomials we use the more multiplications per output point are required. To compute $F(2 \times 2, 3 \times 3)$ we can use:

- 4 polynomials of the first degree with *ratio* = $16/4 = 4$ (Toom-Cook algorithm)
- 2 polynomials of the first degree and 1 of the second degree with *ratio* = $(2 + 3)^2/4 = 6.25$
- 1 polynomial of the first degree and 1 of the third degree with *ratio* = $(1 + 5)^2/4 = 9$
- 2 polynomials of the second degree with *ratio* = $(2 * 3)^2/4 = 9$
- 1 polynomial of the fourth degree with *ratio* = $7^2/4 = 12.25$

We can notice that in above example using the polynomial $m_i(a)$ of the 4th degree do not change input (mapped to the polynomial of the 3rd degree) and kernel (mapped to the polynomial of the 2nd degree) pending transformations, so this case only introduce additional multiplications into convolution computations. Analogously using polynomial $m_i(a)$ of the 3rd degree does not change the kernel. The Winograd method for fixed kernel and output size allows us to construct algorithms with different *ratio*s, while the Toom-Cook method has a constant *ratio* for given n_h and n_o. Thus, for a fixed kernel size, we can construct sets of Winograd matrices with the same *ratio* but other output/input size. For example for $F_{T-C}(4 \times 4, 3 \times 3)$ *ratio* $= 36/16 = 2.25$ and $F_W(6 \times 6, 3 \times 3)$, with 6 polynomials of the first degree, and one polynomial of the second degree, we have the same *ratio* $= 81/36 = 2.25$ see Table 1. Given these choices with the same computational *ratio*, we can investigate the floating point error of such algorithms and use the more accurate one.

Table 1. Number of multiplications for single output point in 2 dimensional Winograd convolution algorithm for kernel 3×3 and outputs: 2×2, 4×4 and 6×6, for each number of the polynomials of the first and second degree used in CRT. In orange is Toom-Cook algorithm with all polynomials of the first degree.

Output size	2×2			4×4				6×6				
No of $m_i(a)$ of degree 1	**4**	2	0	**6**	4	2	0	**8**	6	4	2	0
No of $m_i(a)$ of degree 2	**0**	1	2	**0**	1	2	3	**0**	1	2	3	4
Ratio	**4**	6.25	9	**2.25**	3.06	4	5.06	**1.78**	2.25	2.78	3.36	4

4 Tests Results

4.1 Random Data

We tested the accuracy of the Winograd convolution algorithm for the kernel of the size 3 (1D) and 3×3 (2D). We studied a range of output tile sizes from 2–8 (1D) and 2×2–8×8 (2D). We run our initial experiments over 5000 loops where kernel and input values were chosen randomly from range $(-1, 1)$ with a normal distribution. We computed the Euclidean error of Winograd convolution performed in $fp32$ and compared it with the direct convolution in $fp64$.

We investigated Winograd convolution algorithm with the most promising configurations of polynomials of the first and second degree (as we use the kernel of size 3 or 3×3). The best results for each computation *ratio* and polynomial degree configuration are presented in Fig. 3. We construct the first degree polynomials using known good root points: $0, -1, 1, -1/2, 2, 1/2, -2, -1/4, 4$ [1]. As second degree polynomials, we considered those with the coefficients equal to $0, -1$ and 1, coprime with the polynomials of the first degree. That is: $a^2 + 1$, $a^2 + a + 1$ and $a^2 - a + 1$. To solve the subproblem for the polynomial of degree greater than 1, we use Toom-Cook convolution algorithm $F_{T-C}(2 \times 2, 2 \times 2)$ and root points $0, -1$ and ∞. In our tests, we noticed that in some cases (up to *ratio* around 1.9 for $1D$ and 3.5 for $2D$) the Winograd algorithm with one polynomial of the second degree gives a smaller floating point error than Toom-Cook, see Fig. 3). When we use only one polynomial of the second degree we found that $a^2 + 1$ works the best as it provides only two coefficients, not three.

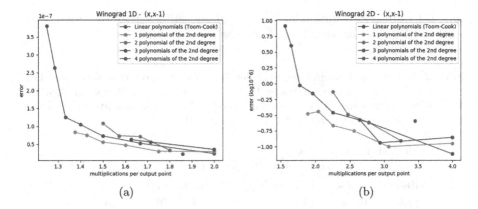

Fig. 3. Euclidean error of Winograd convolution in $fp32$ comparing to the direct method computed in $fp64$

4.2 Experiments with Real Data ImageNet on VGG16

We next run experiments for the vgg16 CNN [8] (using pretrained model from Tensorflow Slim) with thirteen 2D convolution layers, with kernel size 3×3. As inputs we use 2000 images from the ImageNet validation set. The computations were done in $fp32$. We also simulated $fp16$ and $bf16$ by performing the operations in single precision and casting the results to the lower precision.

We tested the Toom-Cook algorithms with outputs 4×4, 6×6 and 8×8. This means the *ratio* of multiplications per single output point equals 2.25, 1.78 and 1.56 respectively (see Table 1). For comparison we choose the Winograd algorithm with one polynomial of the second degree for even output sizes, from 6×6 up to 12×12. The *ratio* of multiplications per single output point are equal to 2.25, 1.89, 1.69 and 1.56 respectively. In our initial tests on random data, we have found that using the polynomial of the second degree $a^2 + 1$ works best. Polynomials of the first degree for $F_W(n_o \times n_o, 3 \times 3)$ were constructed with the root points used for $F_{T-C}((n_o - 2) \times (n_o - 2), 3 \times 3)$. For given output and kernel sizes we can construct Winograd algorithms with different computational *ratios*. In our tests, we used Winograd algorithms with only one polynomial of degree 2. We could achieve better accuracy by using more degree-2, but this would be at the cost of a worse computational *ratio*. We focus on the cases where the image recognition accuracy decreases – *ratio* equal to 2.25 in $fp16$ and *ratio* between 1.78 and 1.56 in $bf16$. We do not present the all possible results, e.g. for $F_W(12 \times 12, 3 \times 3)$ with 2 polynomials of the second degree (*ratio* = 1.78), but our results are indicative.

We looked at the percentage of image recognition (top-1) for vgg16 network with Winograd convolution layers in comparison to the same network with direct convolution using the same floating point precision. In Table 2 we present the percentage accuracy of image recognition for different FP precision. For the output sizes we consider, we do not see any changes using $fp32$. In $fp16$, all investigated Toom-Cook algorithms failed. In $bf16$ the percentage of image recognition is the same as for direct convolution for Toom-Cook algorithm with output 6×6 (*ratio* equal to 1.78), but for output size 8×8 the accuracy decreases.

Table 2. Percentage of image recognition for Toom-Cook convolution algorithm (T-C) for kernel of the size 3×3 and outputs: 4×4, 6×6 and 8×8; and Winograd algorithm (Win) with one polynomial of the second degree ($a^2 + 1$) and outputs: 6×6, 8×8, 10×10 and 12×12 in precisions $fp32$, $fp16$ and $bf16$.

Method	dir	T-C (4×4)	T-C (6×6)	T-C (8×8)	Win (6×6)	Win (8×8)	Win (10×10)	Win (12×12)
Ratio		2.25	1.78	1.56	2.25	1.89	1.69	1.56
$fp32$	70	70	70	70	70	70	70	70
$fp16$	70	10	0.05	0.05	65	0.1	0.05	0.05
$bf16$	70	70	70	68	70	70	70	62

With $fp16$, we see that using Winograd convolution instead of Toom-Cook with the same performance *ratio* (equal to 2.25), increases the recognition accuracy from 10% to 65%. The main problem we face with $fp16$ is that it cannot store the same range of values as $fp32$. Then using the same good root points (like 0, -1 and 1) more than once results in lower intermediate values, and less likelihood of overflow.

Using $bf16$, the decrease in image recognition appears for bigger input sizes than in $fp16$. The $bf16$ format allow us to represent nearly the same range of values as single precision. However, the lower number of bits results in lower accuracy of values representation and larger floating point error from operations. In our tests we can observe the impact of this for network with Toom-Cook convolution algorithm with output of the size 8×8. We have not found a configuration of polynomials that would give us the accuracy of image recognition better than 68% with the *ratio* equal to 1.56. We construct the Winograd algorithm with the accuracy of image recognition equal to 70% (the same accuracy we get using of a direct convolution algorithm) with *ratio* = 1.69.

5   Conclusions

This paper asks the question: Is there a benefit in using the Winograd method with superlinear polynomials for DNNs, as compared to the simpler Toom-Cook method (which is equivalent to Winograd with linear polynomials)? We describe the construction of Winograd transformation matrices in general case. We show that the main benefit of using superlinear polynomials is that the same good root points can be used multiple times, which improves FP accuracy. The Toom-Cook method allows a trade-off of elementwise multiplications against FP accuracy by varying the tile size. The presented Winograd method offers an larger space of trade-offs between computation and accuracy using higher order polynomials.

Thus, it allows us find an attractive one that are not available using Toom-Cook algorithm. We find that in $bf16$ precision we can construct an algorithm that maintains the same accuracy of image recognition as Toom-Cook but has better *ratio* of elementwise multiplications per single output point than Toom-Cook. In $fp16$ precision we can obtain better accuracy using Winograd convolution algorithm with one polynomial of the second degree, as compared to Toom-Cook (for the case kernel 3×3, output 4×4) with the same *ratio* of number of elementwise multiplications per output point. The presented Winograd convolution algorithm does not require additional operations in the transformation to/from the "Winograd domain", and although the Winograd method itself is complex, the generated convolution algorithm does not require a more advanced implementation.

As a future work we plan to investigate presented algorithm further. Firstly, in the context of other kernel sizes (i.e. 5×5). Secondly, for 3 dimensional kernels.

Acknowledgements. This work was supported by Science Foundation Ireland grant 12/IA/1381. We also extend our thanks to Andrew Mundy from Arm ML Research Lab for his contribution.

References

1. Barabasz, B., Anderson, A., Soodhalter, K.M., Gregg, D.: Error analysis and improving the accuracy of winograd convolution for DNNs. CoRR abs/1803.10986 (2018). http://arxiv.org/abs/1803.10986
2. Biggs, N.L.: Discrete Mathematics, 2nd edn. Oxford University Press, New York (2002)
3. Blahut, R.E.: Fast Algorithms for Signal Processing. Cambridge University Press, New York (2010)
4. Cook, S.A.: On the minimum computation time of functions. Ph.D. thesis, Harvard University, Cambridge, Massachusetts (1966)
5. Lavin, A., Gray, S.: Fast algorithms for convolutional neural networks. In: 2016 IEEE Conference on Computer Vision and Pattern Recognition (CVPR), pp. 4013–4021. IEEE, Las Vegas (2016)
6. Meng, L., Brothers, J.: Efficient winograd convolution via integer arithmetic. CoRR abs/1901.01965 (2019)
7. Selesnick, I.W., Burrus, C.S.: Extending winograd's small convolution algorithm to longer lengths. In: 1994 IEEE International Symposium on Circuits and Systems, ISCAS 1994, London, England, UK, 30 May–2 June 1994, pp. 449–452 (1994)
8. Simonyan, K., Zisserman, A.: Very deep convolutional networks for large-scale image recognition. In: International Conference on Learning Representations (2015)
9. Tolimieri, R., An, M., Lu, C.: Algorithms For Discrete Fourier Transform and Convolution, 2nd edn. Springer, New York (1997). https://doi.org/10.1007/978-1-4757-2767-8
10. Toom, A.L.: The complexity of a scheme of functional elements realizing multiplication of integers. Sov. Math. Dokl. **3**, 714–716 (1963)

11. Vincent, K., Stephano, K., Frumkin, M., Ginsburg, B., Demouth, J.: On improving the numerical stability of winograd convolutions. In: Proceedings of the 5th International Conference on Learning Representations, Toulon, France, p. 4 (2017). https://openreview.net/forum?id=H1ZaRZVKg

12. Winograd, S.: Arithmetic Complexity Computations. SIAM Publications, Bristol (1980)

13. Zhao, Y., Wang, D., Wang, L., Liu, P.: A faster algorithm for reducing the computational complexity of convolutional neural networks. Algorithms **11**(10) (2018). https://doi.org/10.3390/a11100159, http://www.mdpi.com/1999-4893/11/10/159

A Deep Hybrid Model
for Recommendation Systems

Muhammet Çakır[✉], Şule Gündüz Öğüdücü, and Resul Tugay

Computer Engineering Department, Istanbul Technical University, Istanbul, Turkey
{cakirmuha,sgunduz,tugayr}@itu.edu.tr

Abstract. Recommendation has been a long-standing problem in many areas ranging from e-commerce to social websites. Most current studies focus only on traditional approaches such as content-based or collaborative filtering while there are relatively fewer studies in hybrid recommendation systems. With the emergence of deep learning techniques in different fields including computer vision and natural language processing, Recommendation Systems (RSs) have also become an active area of for these techniques. There are several studies that utilize ID embeddings of users and items to implement collaborative filtering with deep neural networks. However, such studies do not take advantage of other categorical or continuous features of inputs. In this paper, we propose a new deep neural network architecture which uses ID embeddings, and also auxiliary information such as features of job postings and candidates. Experimental results on a real world dataset from a job website show that the proposed method improves recommendation results over deep learning models utilizing only ID embeddings.

Keywords: Content-based filtering · Collaborative Filtering · Hybrid systems · Deep neural networks · Job Recommendation · Implicit feedback

1 Introduction

Recommendation is the problem of predicting the ratio of interaction between users and items such that a user would prefer an item to another one. It is a ubiquitous problem that appears in numerous application domains ranging from dating websites to e-commerce websites. Recommendation Systems (RSs) make web experience special to their users by recommending, what to buy (e-commerce, Amazon, Ebay), which movies to watch (Netflix), whom to follow (Twitter), which songs to listen (Spotify) etc. We mainly focus on a special type of RSs in this paper, Job Recommendation (JR), which is different than conventional RSs with various aspects. In reciprocal RSs, preferences of both users and items should be considered to find a suitable match and generate recommendations as different from traditional RSs, where items are recommended to users. In a reciprocal RS for a job recruitment web service, jobs are recommended to

© Springer Nature Switzerland AG 2019
M. Alviano et al. (Eds.): AI*IA 2019, LNAI 11946, pp. 321–335, 2019.
https://doi.org/10.1007/978-3-030-35166-3_23

applicants on one side and candidates are also recommended to recruiters on the another side. The recommendation is considered to be successful only if the preferences of users at both sides are satisfied. Moreover, there are mostly no explicit feedback for recruiters and job applicants in JR as there are ratings, likes/unlikes etc. for items in conventional RSs.

In general, recommendation lists are created based on user-item past interactions, item properties, user preferences, and some other additional data. There are three main techniques used in traditional RSs: Content Based Filtering (CBF), Collaborative Filtering (CF) and Hybrid RSs.

Content-Based Filtering: This technique creates user profiles taking which users previously interact with items into account and simply recommends items with similar contents to user profiles. The recommendation process uses properties of items as contents of users [2,3,9].

Collaborative Filtering: The CF based recommendation systems represent users' preferences as n-dimensional rating vectors where n is the number of items in the system. The key idea of CF is that similar users/items share similar interests [4,5]. CF recommends items to users based on their liked items by computing similarities between users and items. There are two categories of CF:

- **Item-based:** Calculates the similarity between the items that user rates previously and other items.
- **User-based:** Calculates the similarity between users.

Hybrid Systems: These systems combine two or more types of recommendation techniques to produce better recommendations [7,8].

More recently, Deep Learning (DL) has gained a tremendous success which takes advantage of deep neural networks using contextual, textual, and/or visual information to produce better recommendation results. DL techniques can be used with all approaches to leverage existing recommendation system. On the other hand, these approaches can also be used not only in conventional RSs but also in JR which requires a special attention to adopt. In the past few years, DL has become a major direction in many fields including machine learning [10,11] and RSs [12,13] etc. DL has been used to model users and items considering their properties as an input of deep neural network. For instance, Oord *et al.* used time-frequency representation from the audio signals as an input to the network [14]. Zhang *et al.* applied embedding using items' textual content and visual content to create semantic representation on deep network [16]. Then, He *et al.* also used another embedding technique which is called ID embedding that takes users' and items' IDs to make a good recommendation instead of using simple approach that applies an inner product on the latent features of users and items [12]. We benefit from this ID embedding approach along with explicit features of job applicants and job postings to produce better recommendations in this paper.

Matrix Factorization (MF) [18] which discovers hidden factors being the underlying reason for the user feedback is the most popular CF technique among the various approaches, and it will be expanded with ID embeddings in this work. Also, Deep Neural Networks (DNNs) [31] that is a popular CBF approach will be adopted to model auxiliary information. This paper proposes a hybrid system that utilizes both MF and DNNs; DNN joins content information into a collaborative approach with ID embeddings as the first part of the hybrid model, and the main framework combines collaborative latent features from MF, and the mixed features from DNN over the last interaction layer as the second part of the hybrid model.

The main contributions of this work are as follows:

1. We propose a hybrid model that combines features of candidates and job postings along with ID embeddings. The architecture joins the strengths of linearity of MF and non-linearity of DNN to model user × item interaction.
2. A novel approach is built for reciprocal recommendation which can be easily applied on job recruitment websites. All experiments are performed with a real-world dataset provided by one of the biggest job-recruitment website in Turkey.

The rest of the paper is organized as follows: Sect. 2 reports related work about Recommendation Systems, Sect. 3 provides preliminaries about RSs and Sect. 4 presents our proposed method and general neural network architecture. In Sect. 5, we show the experimental evaluation presenting the methodology and results. Finally, Sect. 6 provides conclusion and discusses some of possible future extensions that are special for JR.

2 Related Work

Although there are some studies that focus on CBF [9,14], the majority of the approaches are based on CF [18–20]. CF approaches mainly utilize feedbacks of users for items. Users' feedbacks can be categorized in two ways: implicit feedback [21,22] which indirectly reflects preferences of users, and explicit feedback [23] which directly indicates users' choices. While implicit feedback shows behaviours like purchasing products, clicking items, and watching videos, users' ratings and reviews for products are considered as explicit feedback [12]. It is more difficult to exploit implicit feedback since user satisfaction is not directly observable than explicit. Since explicit feedback provides directly negative inference with low ratings and unfavorable reviews.

The original MF approach [18] was proposed to model explicit feedbacks of users by mapping users and items to a latent factor space so that interactions (e.g. ratings) of users and items can be represented by a dot product of latent factors of them. Many approaches have been presented to expand MF, combination of MF and neighbor-based models [23] or extension to factorization machines [24] for generating a model using user and item features. However, users mostly interact with items through implicit feedback since explicit ratings are not present all the time for many recommendations [22]. Although there is no information such as rating, like or dislike in explicit feedback in JR, some implicit feedback information can be considered as explicit feedback. For instance, the number of job view can be taken into account as a rating that is given by the applicants to the company.

CBF is mainly based on comparisons across supporting information of users and items while CF approaches use only user-item interactions. Texts, images, and videos can be considered as a wide variety of additional information [28]. At the last few years, many research efforts have been made to improve the recommendation performance with use of auxiliary information, and deep learning techniques have gained importance to process a great amount of information. They generally adopted on DNNs for modeling auxiliary information using implicit feedback, such as content of videos [31], audible features of musics [14,15], textual explanation of items [13], and categorical-continuous features of both users and items [32]. Although many applications like music and video websites have no more personal information for users and limited amount of information such as textual description, job search websites fortunately contain many categorical and continuous features for both user and item sides to adopt DL approaches.

There have been a great number of hybrid approaches proposed as a combination of collaborative and content-based methods [33–35]. A hybrid approach can be implemented in different ways either applying separately collaborative and content-based tasks and combining their predictions or joining some content-based properties into a collaborative approach, or opposite, and lastly building a general mixed model that joins collaborative and content-based properties [40]. In this work, we will adopt on both a general fixed model and concatenating content-based properties with a collaborative approach.

Furthermore, there are no more general approaches for implementing JR task. Some studies [36,37] particularly focus on JR using a specific dataset such as modeling the interactions for user-job record, user-company, user-job title, and recommendation through graph analysis in AskStory [37], and incorporating user interactions into the recommendation task with a hierarchical graphical model in LinkedIn [36]. In contrast to these models, our proposed model aims at bringing out a framework that is available for many applications such as book, music, and movie recommendation while making better recommendation for both job seekers and recruiters in JR. Also, it may not be reasonable to make reciprocal recommendation for many real-world applications since it is pointless to recommend users to items like books, movies, and musics. However, some studies [38,39] try to build a generalized framework for generating the list of the most suitable candidates. The elements of reciprocal recommendation can be two different users having bilateral relations as traditional user × item interactions. Xia et al. bring a solution to online dating problem by finding out users' power of relationships analysing user-based and graph-based features [38]. Reciprocal recommenders, such as online dating and online recruiting, have a major challenge to satisfy the mutual preferences of two users or user × item, and graph-partitioning methods are used by representing the dataset as a bipartite graph [39]. While these works make a good job of graph analysis to find out the relationships of users, deep learning based approaches have been disregarded to process a great amount of information existing in properties of users and items, textual explanation, and video/music content.

3 Preliminaries

In this part of the paper, existing solutions for CF and CBF that inspire Hybrid Recommender System (HRS) will be mentioned. These preliminaries including Matrix Factorization (MF) that utilizes user-item IDs and Deep Neural Network (DNN) that takes advantages of user-item properties build the main structure of our model.

3.1 Matrix Factorization

MF technique is only used for CF, and allows to discover the latent features underlying the interactions between users and items. Each user and item can be associated with a real-valued vector of the latent features. Let p_u and q_i denote the latent vectors for user u and item i, respectively; MF is used to estimate an interaction $\hat{y}_{ui}$ as a dot product of p_u and q_i:

$$\hat{y}_{ui} = f(u, i | p_u, q_i) = \sum_{k=1}^{K} p_{uk} q_{ki} \qquad (1)$$

where K is a parameter that represents the dimension of the latent space, p_{uk} and q_{ki} are used for user and item latent factor matrix elements, and f is a function that maps model parameters to the predicted score, respectively. MF models the interaction of user and item latent factors, and each dimension of the latent space is independent from each other. Dimensions of the latent space are linearly combined with the same weight, so MF can be considered as a linear model of latent factors.

3.2 Deep Neural Networks

There are a variety of deep learning based approaches to implement for CF and CBF. In this part, Multi-layer perceptron (MLP) that is a type of feedforward artificial neural network will be mentioned. User and item properties are integrated by concatenating them. Interaction between user and item latent features does not exclusively occur by a vector concatenation that is unsatisfactory for CF modeling [12]. This problem is resolved by adding some hidden layers after concatenating these latent vectors. Let p_u and q_i denote the latent vectors for user u and item i, respectively; DNN model is simply formulated as

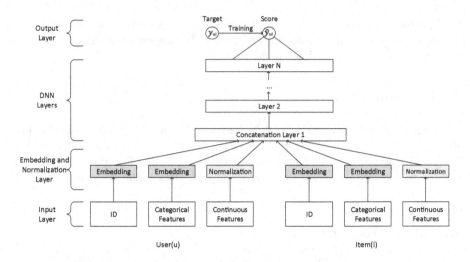

Fig. 1. General architecture of deep neural network

$$\psi_1(p_u, q_i) = o_1 = \begin{bmatrix} p_u \\ q_i \end{bmatrix}$$
$$\psi_2(o_1) = o_2 = \alpha_2(W_2^T o_1 + b_2),$$
$$\dots$$
$$\psi_N(o_{N-1}) = o_N = \alpha_L(W_N^T o_{N-1} + b_N),$$
$$\hat{y}_{ui} = \alpha_{out}(h^T o_N)$$

$$(2)$$

where W_l and b_l specify the weight matrix, bias vector, respectively. α_l is the activation function of the l-th layer of the model. Also, ψ_l represents a function that takes the output of $l - 1$-th layer as input, and produces the result of the current layer.

4   DeepHybrid Model

In this paper, a hybrid recommender system called as DeepHybrid is proposed. It uses IDs of users and items and auxiliary information of both to represent their historical interactions. Firstly, latent features of users and items are obtained using MF technique from feedback of users. Secondly, a deep learning based approach is used to get users' and items' features from both user-item IDs and user-item properties. Lastly, a hybrid model is presented which combines MF and DNN under DeepHybrid.

4.1   Features from MF

MF is the most popular approach for CF, and it maps users and items to a latent factor space for the interaction of users and items. In this work, p_u represents user properties and q_i represents item properties. Embedding vector with one-hot encoding of user (item) ID of the input layer can be seen as the latent vector of user (item) [12]. Let the user latent vector p_u be $P_T v_u^U$ and item latent vector q_i be $Q_T v_i^I$. These latent vectors are projected to the output layer as

$$\hat{y}_{ui} = \alpha_{out}(h^T(p_u \odot q_i)) \tag{3}$$

where $\odot$ defines the element-wise product of vectors, and α_{out} represents the activation function. Also, h is used as a weight vector of the output layer. In our framework, MF model will be expanded using an activation function. Unlike linear MF models, a non-linear activation function will make our MF model more meaningful.

4.2   Features from DNN

In our DNN model, auxiliary information of users and items will be added for concatenated vector that is the input of the neural network. In addition to embedding vectors obtained from one-hot encoding of user and item IDs like MF, the properties of users and items will be processed as embedding vector or normalized value. These properties can be divided into two categories as continuous and categorical features. Firstly, continuous features are real-valued numbers and normalized to [0, 1] by mapping a feature value x. The normalized value is calculated as Eq. 4 for values in the i-th quantiles.

$$n_i = \frac{i - min}{max - min} \tag{4}$$

Secondly, categorical features are embedded to n-dimensional vectors like ID embeddings depending on the number of distinct values for the stated feature. For example, age of a candidate is a continuous feature and normalized into [0, 1], and military status is considered as a categorical feature since this value is distinct, and simply divided into two categories as completed and uncompleted statuses in JRs. Figure 1 shows the architecture of DNN to process features after embedding and normalization. Let con_u, cat_u, and id_u represent continuous features, categorical features and ID embedding of users, respectively; and similar notations of con_i, cat_i, and id_i for items. User and item properties for DNN model are simply defined as

$$p_u = \begin{bmatrix} id_u \\ cat_u \\ con_u \end{bmatrix}, q_i = \begin{bmatrix} id_i \\ cat_i \\ con_i \end{bmatrix} \tag{5}$$

These properties of users and items are concatenated after embeddings and normalization. Then, the result features of these operations are processed by DNN as Eq. 2. In this manner, the model learns the interaction between p_u and q_i providing more flexibility and non-linearity than MF which only operates a dot product of user and item latent vectors.

4.3   Interaction Layer

In the interaction layer, two different mappings of latent features from categorical features, continuous features, and ID embeddings are fused in DeepHybrid as shown in Fig. 2. This model basically aims at ranking prediction as recommendation task. A top-n list is produced by the ranking network using the nearest neighbors of the candidates [28]. MF and DNN models can share the same embedding layers for processing user and item IDs, then concatenate the results of their operations. However, He *et al.* stated that MF and DNN use different embeddings, and are fused by concatenating the last layers of these models to enable more flexibility to the combined model [12].

$$
\psi^{MF} = p_u \odot q_i
$$
$$
\psi^{DNN} = \alpha_N(W_N^T(...\alpha_2(W_2^T \begin{bmatrix} p_u \\ q_i \end{bmatrix} + b_2)...)) + b_N \tag{6}
$$
$$
\hat{y}_{ui} = \alpha_{out}(h^T \begin{bmatrix} \psi^{MF} \\ \psi^{DNN} \end{bmatrix})
$$

4.4   Learning Interaction

An objective function needs to be specified to estimate model parameters. Existing solutions generally utilize a regression with squared loss. For example, rating prediction is originally a regression problem, and squared loss will exactly fit rating prediction. However, our target value y_{ui} has only two values 1 or 0 representing whether u and i have an interaction.

DeepHybrid uses the binary property of data, and y_{ui} is labeled as 1 meaning user u has positive feedback on item i, and 0 otherwise. The prediction score $\hat{y}_{ui}$ shows how user u is related to item i. In this point, our recommendation task with implicit feedback can be considered as a binary classification problem. If the probability of class-1 is high, u is more relevant to i, or vice versa. Let y_{ui} and $\hat{y}_{ui}$ denote the target and the predicted value, $\mathbf{X}$ be the interaction of users and items, respectively;

$$
L = \sum_{(u,i) \in X \cup X^-} y_{ui} \log \hat{y}_{ui} + (1 - y_{ui}) \log(1 - \hat{y}_{ui}) \tag{7}
$$

where X denotes the set of observed interactions in $\mathbf{X}$, and X^- denotes unobserved interaction. This formula is called as *log loss* (*binary cross-entropy loss*). While X represents positive instances, X^- is determined by uniformly sampling from unobserved interactions due to a lack of negative feedback. For each positive instance, a certain number of negative instances are determined.

5   Experiments

5.1   Dataset and Experimental Settings

In our experiments, we focused on Job Recommendation, and used the dataset of one of the biggest job search website in Turkey.

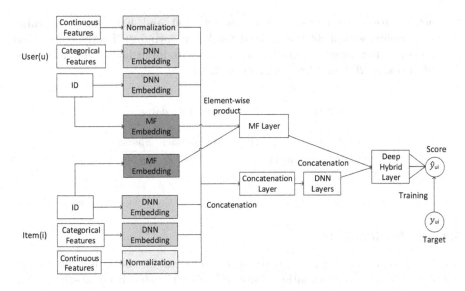

Fig. 2. DeepHybrid model

Kariyernet: Kariyernet dataset consists of many information such as which candidate applied to which job posting and some important auxiliary information of jobs and candidates. Table 1 shows the statistics of this dataset. Also, auxiliary information of users and items are provided as:

- **Candidate properties:** Firstly, age of a candidate is used as continuous feature, and normalized. Secondly, gender, military status, working status, city, department, and university are considered as categorical feature, and embedded.
- **Job posting properties:** The number of people to hire is used as continuous feature. All other features of job posting that include preferred gender, position type, position level, and educational status are taken into account as categorical feature.

Our proposed deep hybrid model was implemented on Keras using Theano backend. For all implemented models, one interaction of each user was sampled as the validation, then hyper-parameters were tuned. Negative instances were randomly selected from unobserved interactions because of lack of negative feedback. Three negative instances were allocated for each positive instance in training set. Also, model parameters were initialized with a Gaussian distribution, and optimized the binary cross entropy of Eq. 7 with mini-batch Adam [29]. For MF, the number of latent factors was chosen as 4,8,16, and 32 to obtain latent features from ID embeddings. For DNN, output dimension of embedding layer for ID embedding was selected as 16, 32, and 64. Also, normalization of continuous features naturally produces a number between 0 and 1, and categorical features were embedded to one-dimensional space. Moreover, the batch size for each iteration was tested with values 100, 200, and 400, and the learning rate was applied with 0.0001, and 0.001 for Adam optimizer. Lastly, our models showed better performance with latent factor as 16, input layer size for DNN as 64, batch size as 200, and learning rate as 0.001.

Table 1. Statistics of Kariyernet dataset

Candidates	Job postings	Applications	Sparsity
20283	16134	383434	99.99%

5.2 Evaluation Metric

Leave-one-out evaluation strategy was selected to evaluate both user recommendation and item recommendation. This evaluation that has been mostly used in other works [22,30] takes all data for training except the latest interaction of user or item as the test set. The ranking strategy generates a top-n list of items for each user. Also, m items are randomly sampled for each user as negative instances which is different from training phase. He *et al.* uses *Hit Ratio* (HR) and *Normalized Discounted Cumulative Gain* (NDCG) to evaluate the performance of top-n list [12]. This work randomly selects 99 items from unobserved items for each user in the test phase, and ranks top 10 of these items while implementing item recommendation, or the opposite for user recommendation. While NDCG is calculated by giving top items more higher score than next items, HR only accounts if the test item is available on top-10 item list.

5.3 Baseline Models and Performance Evaluation

Baselines. Baseline models were selected from the studies which utilize interactions between users and items, and calculates top-n list of items.

- **eALS (CF):** Matrix Factorization is the most popular recommendation model for CF. eALS forms a special type of MF with implicit feedback that handles all unobserved instances as negative, but gives weight to these instances depending on the popularity of items [22].
- **MF with ID Embedding (CF):** This method generalizes, and expands classical MF works. Unlike linear MF models, it takes ID embeddings of users and items, and predicts the target value using element-wise product with a nonlinear activation function like sigmoid, tanh etc. [12].
- **DNN (CBF):** This model takes only content information of users and items instead of IDs. The features are collected with the traditional taxonomy of continuous and categorical features. It embeds categorical features, normalizes continuous features, and a neural network processes these concatenated features [31].

- **NeuMF (CF):** This model is only designed for CF. It uses ID embeddings that are processed under GMF, and MLP, and then combined under an interaction layer by concatenating each other. The result is optimized by *binary cross entropy loss* [12].

Performance Evaluation. In JR systems, both jobs and candidates can be recommended to each other, and the most perfectly fit resumes can be determined for each job posting. In this work, the results were calculated for both item and user recommendation. The performance of DeepHybrid and baseline models on Kariyernet dataset is shown with HR@10 and NDCG@10 as evaluation metric in Table 2. The experiments were repeated three times, and the averages of the results were written down in terms of evaluation metrics HR and NDCG.

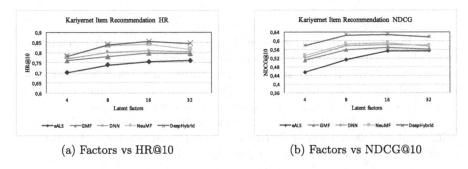

(a) Factors vs HR@10   (b) Factors vs NDCG@10

Fig. 3. Performance of HR@10 and NDCG@10 with the number of factors

In this work, DeepHybrid achieves high improvements over the state-of-the-art methods on Kariyernet dataset. Firstly, GMF and eALS use only the interaction of user and item, and GMF importantly outperforms eALS that shows that the non-linearity setting of GMF is more expressive than linear MF models like eALS. Secondly, DNN contributes on increasing HR and NDCG using only content information that is stronger learner for ranking performance. Thirdly, NeuMF made a valuable improvement on the other baseline models for both item and user recommendation since it combines the linearity and non-linearity of models, and it provides more flexibility to learn the interaction between user and item latent factors using a deep learning based approach. These three baseline models except DNN that utilizes auxiliary information use only user-item historical interaction, and are called as CF approaches. DeepHybrid achieves the best performance over all baseline models by integrating CBF and CF strategies. This model concatenates categorical and continuous features into ID embeddings, and makes latent features of users and items stronger. DeepHybrid gains approximately *%1.7* improvement over NeuMF for both item and user recommendation in terms of HR. However, the results shows that the improvement of

DeepHybrid is %6 in terms of NDCG for Kariyernet dataset, and it can be said that properties of candidates and job postings provide a strong performance for ranking on top-n list.

Table 2. Performance of DeepHybrid model

Methods	Item recommendation		User recommendation	
	HR@10	NDCG@10	HR@10	NDCG@10
eALS	0.754	0.566	0.672	0.431
GMF	0.797	0.569	0.752	0.491
DNN	0.809	0.582	0.761	0.524
NeuMF	0.841	0.591	0.779	0.543
DeepHybrid	**0.855**	**0.628**	**0.795**	**0.581**

Also, Fig. 3 shows the performance of HR@10 and NDCG@10 depending on the number of latent factors. While this factor represents the latent vector size for eALS and GMF, it is considered as the output of the last layer for other DNN based approaches. For all models, HR and NDCG evaluation metrics have lower values for latent factor 4, but they are very close to each other for 8, 16, 32. These results showed us that latent factor 16 is the most suitable one to evaluate all models since large factors cause overfitting while small factors are not sufficiently learning the model depending on the size of dataset.

6   Conclusion

In this work, we have presented DeepHybrid, a new deep learning based hybrid recommendation system to recommending candidates(items) to job postings(users). The proposed approach exploits user-item interaction for CF and auxiliary information of both users and items for CBF. DeepHybrid consists of MF and DNN coupled together by a shared common layer to predict top-n list of items. All interactions are treated as positive, and negative instances are randomly selected through lack of explicit feedback. Additionally, Kariyernet dataset was used for performance evaluation in the experiments. The proposed model finds the best candidate list for a job posting, and ranks the most suitable jobs for a candidate. Experimental results show that HR and NDCG evaluation metrics for item recommendation is higher than user recommendation due to the number of job postings and candidate application. Candidate application is a lot more than job posting. As future work, we are planning to study on processing text-based information of users and items since a great amount of information exists as a text. For example, detailed explanation of experiences and qualifications of a candidate, and explanation of a job posting might expand our latent feature space while doing JR task. Also, we are randomly selecting items to be ranked for users, and finding top-n list of these items in this work, but it is able to recommend irrelevant items to users because of random selection in a real application. Therefore, we aim at realizing candidate generation task before generating top-n list.

References

1. Barkan, O., Koenigstein, N.: Item2vec: neural item embedding for collaborative filtering. In: 2016 IEEE 26th International Workshop on Machine Learning for Signal Processing (MLSP). IEEE (2016)
2. Mooney, R.J., Roy, L.: Content-based book recommending using learning for text categorization. In: Proceedings of the Fifth ACM Conference on Digital Libraries. ACM (2000)
3. Pazzani, M.J., Billsus, D.: Content-based recommendation systems. In: Brusilovsky, P., Kobsa, A., Nejdl, W. (eds.) The Adaptive Web. LNCS, vol. 4321, pp. 325–341. Springer, Heidelberg (2007). https://doi.org/10.1007/978-3-540-72079-9_10
4. Sarwar, B.M., Karypis, G., Konstan, J.A., Riedl, J.: Item-based collaborative filtering recommendation algorithms. In: WWW 2001, pp. 285–295 (2001)
5. Schafer, J.B., Frankowski, D., Herlocker, J., Sen, S.: Collaborative filtering recommender systems. In: Brusilovsky, P., Kobsa, A., Nejdl, W. (eds.) The Adaptive Web. LNCS, vol. 4321, pp. 291–324. Springer, Heidelberg (2007). https://doi.org/10.1007/978-3-540-72079-9_9
6. Burke, R.: Knowledge-based recommender systems. Encycl. Libr. Inf. Syst. **69**, 175–186 (2000)
7. Burke, R.: Hybrid recommender systems: survey and experiments. User Model. User-Adap. Inter. **12**, 331–370 (2002)
8. Burke, R.: Hybrid web recommender systems. In: Brusilovsky, P., Kobsa, A., Nejdl, W. (eds.) The Adaptive Web. LNCS, vol. 4321, pp. 377–408. Springer, Heidelberg (2007). https://doi.org/10.1007/978-3-540-72079-9_12
9. Lops, P., de Gemmis, M., Semeraro, G.: Content-based recommender systems: state of the art and trends. In: Ricci, F., Rokach, L., Shapira, B., Kantor, P.B. (eds.) Recommender Systems Handbook, pp. 73–105. Springer, Boston, MA (2011). https://doi.org/10.1007/978-0-387-85820-3_3
10. Goodfellow, I., Bengio, Y., Courville, A.: Deep Learning. MIT press, Cambridge (2016)
11. Schmidhuber, J.: Deep learning in neural networks: an overview. Neural Netw. **61**, 85–117 (2015)
12. He, X., Liao, L., Zhang, H., Nie, L., Hu, X., Chua, T.-S.: Neural collaborative filtering. In: Proceedings of the 26th International Conference on World Wide Web, pp. 173–182. International World Wide Web Conferences Steering Committee (2017)
13. Wang, H., Wang, N., Yeung, D.-Y.: Collaborative deep learning for recommender systems. In: Proceedings of the 21th ACM SIGKDD International Conference on Knowledge Discovery and Data Mining, pp. 1235–1244. ACM (2015)
14. Van den Oord, A., Dieleman, S., Schrauwen, B.: Deep content-based music recommendation. In: Advances in Neural Information Processing Systems, pp. 2643–2651 (2013)
15. Wang, X., Wang, Y.: Improving content-based and hybrid music recommendation using deep learning. In: Proceedings of the 22nd ACM International Conference on Multimedia, pp. 627–636. ACM (2014)

16. Zhang, F., Yuan, N.J., Lian, D., Xie, X., Ma, W.-Y.: Collaborative knowledge base embedding for recommender systems. In: Proceedings of the 22nd ACM SIGKDD International Conference on Knowledge Discovery and Data Mining, pp. 353–362. ACM (2016)
17. Mikolov, T., Sutskever, I., Chen, K., Corrado, G.S., Dean, J.: Distributed representations of words and phrases and their compositionality. In: Advances in Neural Information Processing Systems, pp. 3111–3119 (2013)
18. Koren, Y., Bell, R., Volinsky, C.: Matrix factorization techniques for recommender systems. Computer **42**, 30–37 (2009)
19. Lee, D.D., Seung, H.S.: Algorithms for non-negative matrix factorization. In: Advances in Neural Information Processing Systems, pp. 556–562 (2001)
20. Mnih, A., Salakhutdinov, R.R.: Probabilistic matrix factorization. In: Advances in Neural Information Processing Systems, pp. 1257–1264 (2008)
21. Hu, Y., Koren, Y., Volinsky, C.: Collaborative filtering for implicit feedback datasets. In: ICDM, pp. 263–272. Citeseer (2008)
22. He, X., Zhang, H., Kan, M.-Y., Chua, T.-S.: Fast matrix factorization for online recommendation with implicit feedback. In: Proceedings of the 39th International ACM SIGIR Conference on Research and Development in Information Retrieval, pp. 549–558. ACM (2016)
23. Koren, Y.: Factorization meets the neighborhood: a multifaceted collaborative filtering model. In: Proceedings of the 14th ACM SIGKDD International Conference on Knowledge Discovery and Data Mining, pp. 426–434. ACM (2008)
24. Rendle, S.: Factorization machines. In: 2010 IEEE International Conference on Data Mining, pp. 995–1000. IEEE (2010)
25. Paparrizos, I., Cambazoglu, B.B., Gionis, A.: Machine learned job recommendation. In: Proceedings of the Fifth ACM Conference on Recommender Systems, pp. 325–328. ACM (2011)
26. Al-Otaibi, S.T., Ykhlef, M.: A survey of job recommender systems. Int. J. Phys. Sci. **7**, 5127–5142 (2012)
27. Pizzato, L., Rej, T., Chung, T., Koprinska, I., Kay, J.: RECON: a reciprocal recommender for online dating. In: Proceedings of the Fourth ACM Conference on Recommender Systems, pp. 207–214. ACM (2010)
28. Zhang, S., Yao, L., Sun, A., Tay, Y.: Deep learning based recommender system: a survey and new perspectives. ACM Comput. Surv. (CSUR) **52** (2019). Article no. 5
29. Kingma, D.P., Ba, J.: Adam: a method for stochastic optimization. arXiv preprint arXiv:1412.6980 (2014)
30. Rendle, S., Freudenthaler, C., Gantner, Z., Schmidt-Thieme, L.: BPR: Bayesian personalized ranking from implicit feedback. In: Proceedings of the Twenty-Fifth Conference on Uncertainty in Artificial Intelligence, pp. 452–461. AUAI Press (2009)
31. Covington, P., Adams, J., Sargin, E.: Deep neural networks for Youtube recommendations. In: Proceedings of the 10th ACM Conference on Recommender Systems, pp. 191–198. ACM (2016)
32. Cheng, H.-T., et al.: Wide & deep learning for recommender systems. In: Proceedings of the 1st Workshop on Deep Learning for Recommender Systems, pp. 7–10. ACM (2016)
33. Albadvi, A., Shahbazi, M.: A hybrid recommendation technique based on product category attributes. Expert Syst. Appl. **36**, 11480–11488 (2009)
34. Balabanović, M., Shoham, Y.: Fab: content-based, collaborative recommendation. Commun. ACM **40**, 66–72 (1997)

35. Soboroff, I., Nicholas, C.: Combining content and collaboration in text filtering. In: Proceedings of the IJCAI, pp. 86–91, sn (1999)
36. Wang, J., Kenthapadi, K., Rangadurai, K., Hardtke, D.: Dionysius: a framework for modeling hierarchical user interactions in recommender systems. arXiv preprint arXiv:1706.03849 (2017)
37. Lee, Y.-C., Hong, J., Kim, S.-W.: Job recommendation in AskStory: experiences, methods, and evaluation. In: Proceedings of the 31st Annual ACM Symposium on Applied Computing, pp. 780–786. ACM (2016)
38. Xia, P., Liu, B., Sun, Y., Chen, C.: Reciprocal recommendation system for online dating. In: Proceedings of the 2015 IEEE/ACM International Conference on Advances in Social Networks Analysis and Mining 2015, pp. 234–241. ACM (2015)
39. Li, L., Li, T.: MEET: a generalized framework for reciprocal recommender systems. In: Proceedings of the 21st ACM International Conference on Information and Knowledge Management, pp. 35–44. ACM (2012)
40. Adomavicius, G., Tuzhilin, A.: Toward the next generation of recommender systems: a survey of the state-of-the-art and possible extensions. IEEE Trans. Knowl. Data Eng. **17**, 734–749 (2005)

Kernel-Based Generative Adversarial Networks for Weakly Supervised Learning

Danilo Croce$^{(\boxtimes)}$, Giuseppe Castellucci, and Roberto Basili

Department of Enterprise Engineering, University of Roma, Tor Vergata, Rome, Italy
{croce,basili}@info.uniroma2.it, castellucci.giuseppe@gmail.com

Abstract. In recent years, Deep Learning methods have become very popular in NLP classification tasks, due to their ability to reach high performances by relying on very simple input representations. One of the drawbacks in training deep architectures is the large amount of annotated data required for effective training. One recent promising method to enable semi-supervised learning in deep architectures has been formalized within Semi-Supervised Generative Adversarial Networks (SS-GANs).

In this paper, an SS-GAN is shown to be effective in semantic processing tasks operating in low-dimensional embeddings derived by the unsupervised approximation of rich Reproducing Kernel Hilbert Spaces. Preliminary analyses over a sentence classification task show that the proposed Kernel-based GAN achieves promising results when only 1% of labeled examples are used.

Keywords: Semi-supervised learning · Kernel-based deep architectures · Generative Adversarial Network

1 Introduction

In recent years, Deep Learning methods have become very popular in many Natural Language Processing (NLP) tasks. This is mainly due to their ability to reach high performances by relying on very simple input representations, i.e., typically raw signals. As an example, recent architectures have been shown to be effective in capturing syntactic information by only observing sequences of words (e.g., LSTM as in [8]), redundant subsets of n-grams (e.g., CNNs as in [11]) up to just sequences of characters [12]. The networks learn during training the representations useful for the final decision.

One of the drawbacks in learning deep architectures is that, often, they need a huge amount of information to perform effectively. This means having large-scale annotated material to let a neural network learn the representations in its hidden layers. Unfortunately, the availability of annotated material is often scarce. This can prevent the effectiveness of deep architectures and it results in significant performance drops. A viable solution to such a problem is the adoption of semi-supervised methods [2], to improve the generalization capability of a learner

© Springer Nature Switzerland AG 2019
M. Alviano et al. (Eds.): AI*IA 2019, LNAI 11946, pp. 336–347, 2019.
https://doi.org/10.1007/978-3-030-35166-3_24

when few labeled data is available while the acquisition of unlabeled sources is possible.

One recent effective method to enable semi-supervised learning in deep architectures is formalized within the so-called Semi-Supervised Generative Adversarial Networks (SS-GANs). Generative Adversarial Networks (GANs) [9,10] are a class of neural generative models based on game theory. The goal of GANs is to train a generator network $\mathcal{G}$ in producing samples from the data distribution. The training of $\mathcal{G}$ adversarially depends on a discriminator network $\mathcal{D}$, trained to distinguish samples from the generator distribution from those characterizing real instances. $\mathcal{G}$ in turn is trained to fool $\mathcal{D}$ into accepting its outputs as being real. SS-GAN [18] has been proposed as a simple extension to GANs where $\mathcal{D}$ is devoted in both assigning a class to each example and discriminating whether it was generated by $\mathcal{G}$. SS-GANs have been shown to be very effective in semi-supervised learning in the image processing domain.

While the labeled material is used to train the classifier, the unlabeled one improves the inner representations of $\mathcal{D}$ (which must be also robust to not being fooled by $\mathcal{G}$). Results within Image Classification have been shown SS-GANs to be very effective: when exposed to a few dozens of labeled examples (but thousands of unlabeled ones), an SS-GAN is capable of obtaining a quality similar to state-of-the-art convolutional neural networks.

The usage of GANs in natural language problems has been limited so far; this is mainly due to the discrete input space typically adopted in this domain, i.e., raw words. However, in weakly supervised problems within natural language processing tasks, exploiting linguistic information can be beneficial. For example, syntactic information has been demonstrated to be useful for many language understanding tasks [17]. Recently, [4] proposed the Kernel-based Deep Architecture (KDA) that exploits an input representation of examples that is linguistically justified: they demonstrate how the syntactic information captured by a Semantic Tree Kernel can be embedded into vectors to be used as input for neural network learning.

In this paper, we investigate how to improve the robustness of deep architectures by exploiting an expressive space which encodes rich linguistic information. The aim is to improve the capability of such architectures of learning from very few annotated examples. We will exploit the information encoded by a KDA within a semi-supervised learning framework provided by an SS-GAN. In particular, a KDA, used in classification tasks involving k classes, will be extended to target an additional class, which aims at collecting examples not belonging to the input dataset, called *fake* examples. This KDA will act as a *discriminator* $\mathcal{D}$, whose aim is to separate fake examples from the real ones and, at the same time, to assign each real example to the correct class. At the same time, another network (called *generator*, $\mathcal{G}$) will be devoted to the generation of fake examples with the aim of "fooling" the discriminator, by creating examples as much similar as possible to the KDA real ones. These networks will be trained simultaneously so that the $\mathcal{G}$ is penalized when fake examples are "unmasked" by $\mathcal{D}$, while the latter will be penalized when fake examples are incorrectly assigned to one of the

k classes. In [10] this schema was shown beneficial in improving the robustness of the discriminator in the original classification task, especially when very few labeled examples are used in training, but many unlabeled examples exist.

The underlying idea is that the generalization capability of the discriminator benefits from the contribution of the labeled material to assign new instances to the target classes and from the contribution of unlabeled examples to improve the representation capability of the network within the hidden layers. The resulting architecture, namely Kernel-based Generative Adversarial Network (KGAN), enables weakly supervised learning in linguistically rich spaces. To the best of our knowledge, this is the first attempt to adopt an SS-GAN in semantic classification tasks. The experimental evaluation with respect to Question Classification shows a significant improvement in weakly supervised learning when only 1%, 2% and 5% of labeled examples are adopted.

In the remaining, Sect. 2 provides a brief introduction to SS-GAN. In Sect. 3, our approach is presented. In Sect. 4, preliminary evaluations are reported, while in Sect. 5 conclusions are derived.

2   Semi-supervised GANs

Deep neural networks are usually trained on a large amount of labeled data, which is not often available: on the contrary, unlabeled data can be easily accessed. Deep methods were initially adapted to the semi-supervised case by using concepts coming from the theory of graph-based methods [13, 21, 24].

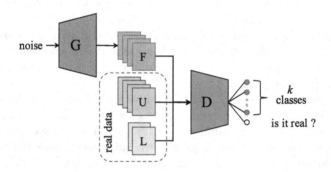

Fig. 1. SS-GAN architecture. $\mathcal{G}$ generates from noise a set of fake examples F. These along with unlabeled U and labeled L examples are used as input for the discriminator $\mathcal{D}$.

At the same time, Semi-Supervised Generative Adversarial Networks (SS-GANs) [18] support a semi-supervised setting within the GAN framework [10]. GANs are traditionally used for their generative capabilities: these are mainly devoted in generating new examples resembling so many existing distributions that a dedicated discriminator is not able at distinguishing real examples from new (i.e., fake) ones. SS-GAN has been successfully applied in semi-supervised learning problems with respect to multi-classification tasks. As shown in Fig. 1, instead of a binary classification task the discriminator $\mathcal{D}$ is trained over a $(k+1)$-class objective: true examples are classified in one of the target k classes, while the generated samples are classified into the last $k+1$ class. This $(k+1)$-class discriminator objective leads to strong empirical results in image classification since [18]. It has been also shown that the adoption of a small labeled dataset improves the effectiveness of the generative component, improving the quality of the generated images.

More formally, let $\mathcal{D}$ and $\mathcal{G}$ denote the discriminator and generator, and p_{data} and $p_{\mathcal{G}}$ denote the distribution of real data and the generated fake examples, respectively. To train a k-class classifier with a small number of labeled samples, the objective of $\mathcal{D}$ is extended as follows. It receives a data point x in input and it outputs a $(k+1)$-dimensional vector of logits $\{l_1, l_2, \ldots, l_k, l_{k+1}\})$, mapped into a probability distribution. Then,

$$p_{model}(y = k + 1|x) = \frac{exp(l_{k+1})}{\sum_{j=1}^{k+1} exp(l_j)}$$

provides the probability that x is fake, while

$$p_{model}(y = i|x, i < k + 1) = \frac{exp(l_i)}{\sum_{j=1}^{k+1} exp(l_j)}$$

provides the probability that x is real and belongs to i-th class Cat_i. $\mathcal{D}$ is expected to perform well both in the *supervised* classification task (with respect to the k-classes) and on the *unsupervised* classification task (avoiding the erroneous rejection of real examples and acceptance of fake examples generated by $\mathcal{G}$). Its loss function is thus: $L_\mathcal{D} = L_{\mathcal{D}_{sup.}} + L_{\mathcal{D}_{unsup.}}$ where:

$$L_{\mathcal{D}_{sup.}} = -\mathbb{E}_{x,y\sim p_{data}} \log\left[p_{model}(y = i|x, i < k + 1)\right]$$
$$L_{\mathcal{D}_{unsup.}} = -\mathbb{E}_{x\sim p_{data}} \log\left[1 - p_{model}(y = k + 1|x)\right]$$
$$- \mathbb{E}_{x\sim G} \log\left[p_{model}(y = k + 1|x)\right]$$

It is straightforward to observe that labeled examples are used to minimize $L_{\mathcal{D}_{sup.}}$, while the unlabeled examples are used to minimize $L_{\mathcal{D}_{unsup.}}$ thus improving its generalization capability.

At the same time, $\mathcal{G}$ is expected to generate examples that are similar to the real ones sampled from the real distribution p_{data}. The more $\mathcal{G}$ will succeed in this task, the better it will fool $\mathcal{D}$. Moreover, as suggested in [18] a good $\mathcal{G}$ should generate data approximating the statistics of real data as much as possible. In other words, the *average* example generated in a mini-batch by $\mathcal{G}$ should be as much similar as possible to the real *prototypical* one. Formally, let's $f(x)$ denote the activation on an intermediate layer of $\mathcal{D}$, this difference between such averaged inner representations should be minimized, introducing the *feature matching* loss of $\mathcal{G}$ defined as:

$$L_{G_{feature\ matching}} = \left\| \mathbb{E}_{x \sim p_{data}} f(x) - \mathbb{E}_{x \sim \mathcal{G}} f(x) \right\|_2^2$$

This, combined with the *unsupervised* loss of $\mathcal{G}$ induced by the fake examples correctly rejected:

$$L_{\mathcal{G}_{unsup.}} = -\mathbb{E}_{x\sim\mathcal{G}} \log\left[1 - p_{\text{model}}\left(y = k + 1 | x\right)\right]$$

gives rise to the final loss of $\mathcal{G}$ that is $L_\mathcal{G} = L_{\mathcal{G}_{\text{feature matching}}} + L_{\mathcal{G}_{unsup.}}$.

While in literature an SS-GAN is usually stimulated with input examples x encoding images (e.g. from the MNIST dataset), in the next section we will show that they can be easily adopted over input spaces encoding linguistic information, e.g. a low-dimensional dense space encoding tree structures derived from the dependency parse of a tree.

3   Kernel-Based GANs

In [4] it has been shown that neural networks can be trained in low-dimensional spaces which approximate a generic Reproducing Kernel Hilbert Space (RKHS) [19]. These low-dimensional approximations are derived as a reconstruction from a set of real reference training (unlabeled) examples, called *landmarks*, which can be used to compile the representation of any unseen test instance.

More formally, given an input training dataset $\mathcal{L}$, a kernel $K(o_i, o_j)$ is a similarity function over $\mathcal{L}^2$ that corresponds to a dot product in the implicit kernel space, i.e., $K(o_i, o_j) = \Phi(o_i) \cdot \Phi(o_j)$. The advantage of kernels is that the projection function $\Phi(o) = x \in \mathbb{R}^n$ is never explicitly computed [19]. In fact, this operation may be prohibitive when the dimensionality n of the underlying kernel space is extremely large, as for Tree Kernels [3]. Kernel functions are used by learning algorithms, such as Support Vector Machines [20], to operate only implicitly on instances in the kernel space, by never accessing their explicit definition.

Let us assume we apply the projection function Φ over all examples from $\mathcal{L}$ to derive representations x being the rows of the matrix X. The Gram matrix can be computed as $M = XX^\top$, with each single element corresponding to $M_{ij} = \Phi(o_i)\Phi(o_j) = K(o_i, o_j)$. The aim of the Nyström method [22] is to derive a new low-dimensional embedding $\tilde{x}$ in a l-dimensional space, with $l \ll n$ so that $\tilde{M} = \tilde{X}\tilde{X}^\top$ and $\tilde{M} \approx M$. In other words, $\tilde{M}$ is an approximation of M that is obtained by using a subset of l columns of the matrix of the available examples, called *landmarks*. Suppose we randomly sample l columns of M, and let $C \in \mathbb{R}^{|\mathcal{L}| \times l}$ be the matrix of these sampled columns. Then, we can rearrange the columns and rows of M and define $X = [X_1 \ X_2]$ such that:

$$M = XX^\top = \begin{bmatrix} W & X_1^\top X_2 \\ X_2^\top X_1 & X_2^\top X_2 \end{bmatrix}$$

$$\text{and} \quad C = \begin{bmatrix} W \\ X_2^\top X_1 \end{bmatrix} \tag{1}$$

where $W = X_1^\top X_1$, i.e., the subset of M that only considers landmarks. The Nyström approximation can be defined as:

$$M \approx \tilde{M} = CW^\dagger C^\top \tag{2}$$

where $W^\dagger$ denotes the Moore-Penrose inverse of W. The Singular Value Decomposition (SVD) is used to obtain $W^\dagger$ as follows. First, W is decomposed so that $W = USV^\top$, where U and V are both orthogonal matrices, and S is a diagonal matrix containing the (non-zero) singular values of W on its diagonal. Since W is symmetric and positive definite $W = USU^\top$. Then $W^\dagger = US^{-1}U^\top = US^{-\frac{1}{2}}S^{-\frac{1}{2}}U^\top$ and the Eq. 2 can be rewritten as

$$
\begin{aligned}
M \approx \tilde{M} &= CUS^{-\frac{1}{2}}S^{-\frac{1}{2}}U^\top C^\top \\
&= (CUS^{-\frac{1}{2}})(CUS^{-\frac{1}{2}})^\top = \tilde{X}\tilde{X}^\top
\end{aligned} \tag{3}
$$

Given an input example $o \in \mathcal{D}$, a new low-dimensional representation $\tilde{x}$ can be thus determined by considering the corresponding item of C as

$$
\tilde{x} = \Theta(o) = cUS^{-\frac{1}{2}} \tag{4}
$$

where c is the vector whose dimensions contain the evaluations of the kernel function between o and each landmark $o_j \in L$. Therefore, the method produces l-dimensional vectors. Regardless of the input examples (vectors, trees or graphs), given a valid kernel function, the Nyström method allows projecting examples in a $l-$dimensional feature space. Here, the inner product among vectors is the best approximation of the kernel function (according to the Frobenius norm) of the corresponding examples.

In [4] the above introduced Nyström representation $\tilde{x}$ of any input example o was adopted to feed a neural network architecture. We assume a labeled dataset $\mathcal{T} = \{(o,y) \mid o \in \mathcal{T},\ y \in Y\}$ being available, where o refers to a generic instance and y is its associated class. In particular, a Kernel-based Deep Architecture (KDA) is a Neural Network, for example, a Multi-Layer Perceptron (MLP), which is directly applied over input instances obtained by approximating the kernel space via the Nyström method. It means adopting a specific Nyström layer based on the Nyström embeddings of Eq. 4 to project any input instance o in a dense representation space in $\mathcal{R}^l$. The specific KDA proposed in [4] extends an MLP for classification tasks by introducing an *input layer* and a *Nyström layer* in addition to the classical sequence of non-linear *hidden layers* and the final *classification layer*, which produces the output.

The *input* layer corresponds to the input vector c, i.e., the row of the C matrix associated to an example o. Notice that, for adopting the KDA, the values of the matrix C should be all available.

The input layer is mapped to the *Nyström* layer, through the projection in Eq. 4. Notice that the embedding provides also the proper weights, defined by $US^{-\frac{1}{2}}$, so that the mapping can be expressed through the Nyström matrix $H_{Ny} = US^{-\frac{1}{2}}$: it corresponds to a pre-trained stage derived through SVD. In other words, Eq. 4 provides a static definition for H_{Ny} whose weights can be left invariant during the neural network training. Formally, the low-dimensional embedding of an input example o, is $\tilde{x} = c\,H_{Ny} = c\,US^{-\frac{1}{2}}$.

The resulting outcome $\tilde{x}$ is the input to one or more non-linear *hidden* layers. Each r-th hidden layer is realized through a matrix $H_r \in \mathbb{R}^{h_{r-1} \times h_r}$ and a bias vector $\boldsymbol{b}_r \in \mathbb{R}^{1 \times h_r}$, whereas h_r denotes the desired hidden layer dimensionality. Clearly, given that $H_{Ny} \in \mathbb{R}^{l \times l}$, $h_0 = l$. The first hidden layer, in fact, receives in input $\tilde{\boldsymbol{x}} = \boldsymbol{c} H_{Ny}$, that corresponds to $r = 0$ layer input $\boldsymbol{x}_0 = \tilde{\boldsymbol{x}}$ and its computation is formally expressed by $\boldsymbol{x}_1 = f(\boldsymbol{x}_0 H_1 + \boldsymbol{b}_1)$, where f is a non-linear activation function. The generic r-th layer is modeled as:

$$\boldsymbol{x}_r = f(\boldsymbol{x}_{r-1} H_r + \boldsymbol{b}_r) \tag{5}$$

The final layer of KDA is the *classification layer*, realized through the output matrix H_O and the output bias vector $\boldsymbol{b}_O$. Their dimensionality depends on the dimensionality of the last hidden layer (called O_{-1}) and the number $|Y|$ of different classes, i.e., $H_O \in \mathbb{R}^{h_{O-1} \times |Y|}$ and $\boldsymbol{b}_O \in \mathbb{R}^{1 \times |Y|}$, respectively. In particular, this layer computes a linear classification function with a softmax operator, so that $\hat{y} = softmax(\boldsymbol{x}_{O_{-1}} H_O + \boldsymbol{b}_O)$.

In order to avoid over-fitting, two different regularization schemes are applied. First, the dropout is applied to the input $\boldsymbol{x}_r$ of each hidden layer ($r \geq 1$) and to the input $\boldsymbol{x}_{O_{-1}}$ of the final classifier. Second, a L_2 regularization is applied to the norm of each layer[1] H_r and H_O.

Finally, the KDA is trained by optimizing a loss function made of the sum of two factors: first, the cross-entropy function between the gold classes and the predicted ones; second the L_2 regularization, whose importance is regulated by a meta-parameter λ. The final loss function is thus

$$L(y, \hat{y}) = \sum_{(o,y) \in \mathcal{L}} y \, log(\hat{y}) + \lambda \sum_{H \in \{H_r\} \cup \{H_O\}} ||H||^2$$

where $\hat{y}$ are the softmax values computed by the network and y are the true one-hot encoding values associated with the example from the labeled training dataset $\mathcal{L}$.

3.1 Kernel-Based Generative Adversarial Networks

Applying a GAN perspective on a KDA type of architecture promotes two main benefits: the semi-supervised nature of the GA approach and the expressiveness of kernel based learning. This paves the way to cost-effective and highly reliable complex NLP inference, even in poor training conditions, e.g. small labeled data sets.

A KDA can be easily extended within an adversarial learning framework, deriving the so-called **Kernel-based GAN** (KGAN) as follows. The traditional KDA is used as the discriminator, i.e., $\mathcal{D}$: the Nyström layer generates real input examples in the network, while the number of classes in the output layer will be extended to $k + 1$. At the same time, another MLP is used as Generator, i.e., $\mathcal{G}$, which receives in input random vectors and produces output (fake) examples. For simplicity, the $\mathcal{G}$ is characterized by the same number and hidden units of

---

[1] The input layer and the Nyström layer are not modified during the learning process, and they are not regularized.

the KDA (removing the classification layer). In theory, there are no restrictions on the number of hidden layers or their size. The only restriction is that the size of the last generator layer must be equal to the input space, so that the generated embeddings (the fake examples) are represented in $\mathcal{R}^l$, consistently with the adopted Nyström representation space. In such a way, fake examples are expected to resemble originals in the approximated RKHS.

A KGAN can be used over any dataset, given that a kernel function operating on the original feature space exists. Input examples can be thus projected in the l-dimensional space by using the Nyström method in order to train the overall architecture. During the training phase, the input dataset is expected to contain labeled and unlabeled examples: these are randomly extracted and grouped in mini-batches of size b to be provided to $\mathcal{D}$. Consistently with [10], at each iteration $\mathcal{G}$ will also provide b examples, which are added to the mini-batch provided to $\mathcal{D}$. After the classification of each mini-batch, the assignments provided by the discriminator with respect to the $k + 1$ target classes are used to evaluate the losses $L_{\mathcal{D}}$ and $L_{\mathcal{G}}$ (introduced in Sect. 2) so that the network parameters are adjusted, accordingly.

At classification time, only $\mathcal{D}$ is adopted and, from a computational perspective, it results in a highly scalable and efficient solution with respect to classical kernel based methods, as discussed in [4]. Overall, we expect that the expressiveness of the input kernel space, combined with the reduced number of parameters from the MLP architecture as well as with the generalization capability of the SS-GAN will embody an effective weakly-supervised paradigm. This amplifies the applicability of these neural learning methods in industrial scenarios, that are quite challenging with respect to the availability of large annotated datasets.

4   Experimental Results

In this section, we provide a set of preliminary evaluations of the KGAN approach. We are interested in assessing the impact of the semi-supervised schema, provided by the KGAN architecture, with respect to poor training conditions, i.e., where a minimal set of labeled data is available.

We replicated the experiments reported in [4] with respect to the Question Classification task. We adopted the UIUC dataset [15]: this includes a training and test set of 5, 452 and 500 questions, respectively, organized in 6 coarse-grained classes (e.g., ENTITY or HUMAN). In order to provide the input to the KGAN architecture, we generated Nyström representations of the examples by using the Compositionally Smoothed Partial Tree Kernel (CSPTK) [1]. It combines both syntactic and compositional semantic information derived from the dependency graphs of questions. Notice that in order to compute the Tree Kernel, the dependency graphs have been transformed in trees, according to [1]. In particular, explicit compositional information is used to augment a Lexically Centered Tree [5] (see Fig. 2 for an example).

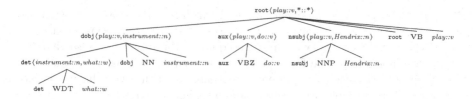

Fig. 2. Compositional Lexical Centered Tree (CLCT) of "*What instrument does Hendrix play?*". Notice that non-terminal nodes are augmented with information about relations.

Lexical vectors needed in the computation of the CSPTK are generated using a Skip-gram model[2] [16]. This kernel achieves the state-of-the-art (95% in Accuracy) over this task within a Support Vector Machine framework. It demonstrates the expressiveness of the (implicit) representation space provided by the kernel function. Notice that the representation space doesn't require any labeled example, but, it fully exploits the syntax and semantic information contained in the tree representations.

We compare the KGAN to the standard KDA defined in [4], and with the standard Kernel SVM, i.e., directly operating in the RKHS. We also compare with a well-known deep learning architecture, i.e. the Convolutional Neural Network (CNN) proposed in [11], applied over the embedding input matrix of sentences[3] for a text classification task.

KGAN has been tuned with respect to the following hyper-parameters: (i) the number of hidden layers in the discriminator among 3, 4, and 5; (ii) dropout level applied after each hidden layer among 0.95 and 0.99; (iii) whether using or not feature matching. We used a split of the training set (about 10%) to tune the hyper-parameters of each model. In our implementation, we adopted the Scaled Exponential Linear Units (SELU) as activation function [14] in each layer.

For each model, we used an increasing amount of labeled data L composed by 1%, 2%, 5%, 10%, 20%, 30%, 40%, 50% and 100% of the original dataset, as shown in Fig. 3. Notice that the KGAN used L as the portion of labeled examples. The remaining examples, i.e., U, are used without their labels, so affecting only the following losses: $L_{\mathcal{D}_{unsup.}}$ and the whole $L_{\mathcal{G}}$. We performed 5 runs shuffling the training set and reporting the average classification accuracy.

In Fig. 3, the learning curves with respect to the different portions of labeled examples are reported for each model. Notice that with only 1% of labeled examples, i.e., about 55 questions, the KGAN approach is able to provide higher performances with respect to the other supervised approaches. In fact, the KGAN obtains 64.9% in Accuracy while the Kernel SVM and the KDA obtain 58.0% and 57.8% respectively; it results in an error reduction of about 17%. Notice how the CNN (that operates mainly over the n-grams of the input texts) performs poorly in this training setting. In fact, it obtains only about 44% in Accuracy.

---

[2] For the remaining kernel parameters, the same setting of [4] is used.

[3] The word embeddings used for the CNN is the same used for the kernel computation.

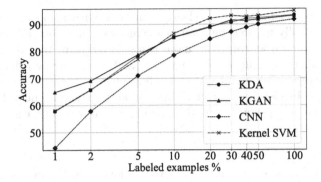

Fig. 3. Learning curve w.r.t. the QC task.

This confirms our idea that linguistically motivated information (combined with the adversarial learning) can help in reducing the amount of annotated data needed to train text classification models. The differences between the models get smaller when the size of L grows: starting about at 30–40% of the labeled examples the KGAN, KDA and Kernel SVM perform almost equally. At 100% of the examples all the model performances are very similar. In fact, the KGAN, KDA, the Kernel SVM and the CNN obtain 93.2%, 93.4%, 95.0% and 93.2%, respectively.

5   Conclusion

In this paper, the application of Generative Adversarial Networks (GAN) for semi supervised learning within semantic processing tasks is presented. The approach, namely the Kernel-based Generative Adversarial Network (KGAN), is specifically tailored to amplify the applicability of combined Kernel-based and Deep learning Architectures previously proposed as KDAs, in literature. The strict requirement of large scale annotated corpora, strongly characterizing most complex NLP inference tasks is here mitigated by the semi-supervised perspective offered bu GANs. In a KGAN approach, the specific formulation known as Semi supervised GAN (SS-GAN) has been adopted in combination with a Kernel-based Deep Architecture. This allows to bootstrap the training of an NLP classifier which directly operates in Reproducing Kernel Hilbert Spaces, in all situations when a significant amount of examples is available, but only a small subset is labeled. The resulting architecture enables to exploit both the expressiveness of semantic kernel spaces and the semi-supervised setting provided by the SS-GAN. The experimental evaluations of the KGAN in a sentence-level semantic classification task confirms the beneficial impact of an SS-GAN over a semantic processing task, i.e. Question Classification. The outcome suggests that a robust and accurate learning process is enabled within the kernel (embedding) space. Such representation space, which encodes rich syntactic information through tree kernel functions, is clearly beneficial with respect to alternative embeddings, usually tailored by shallower structures, e.g. word n-grams.

In future, we aim at targeting more tasks and explore the role of alternative kernel embeddings, in order to measure and assess the beneficial impacts. Furthermore, promising architectures for text encoding (e.g., [7]) or SS-GANs variants [6] will be clearly considered. We will also investigate neural models to *decode* the sentences generated by $\mathcal{G}$, applying neural decoders, e.g., [23].

References

1. Annesi, P., Croce, D., Basili, R.: Semantic compositionality in tree kernels. In: Proceedings of CIKM 2014. ACM (2014)
2. Chapelle, O., Schlkopf, B., Zien, A.: Semi-Supervised Learning, 1st edn. The MIT Press, Cambridge (2010)
3. Collins, M., Duffy, N.: Convolution kernels for natural language. In: Proceedings of Neural Information Processing Systems (NIPS 2001), pp. 625–632 (2001)
4. Croce, D., Filice, S., Castellucci, G., Basili, R.: Deep learning in semantic kernel spaces. In: Proceedings of the 55th Annual Meeting of the Association for Computational Linguistics (Volume 1: Long Papers), pp. 345–354. Association for Computational Linguistics (2017). https://doi.org/10.18653/v1/P17-1032, http://aclweb.org/anthology/P17-1032
5. Croce, D., Moschitti, A., Basili, R.: Structured lexical similarity via convolution kernels on dependency trees. In: Proceedings of the 2011 Conference on Empirical Methods in Natural Language Processing, pp. 1034–1046. Association for Computational Linguistics, Edinburgh, July 2011. https://www.aclweb.org/anthology/D11-1096
6. Dai, Z., Yang, Z., Yang, F., Cohen, W.W., Salakhutdinov, R.: Good semi-supervised learning that requires a bad GAN. CoRR abs/1705.09783 (2017). http://arxiv.org/abs/1705.09783
7. Devlin, J., Chang, M., Lee, K., Toutanova, K.: BERT: pre-training of deep bidirectional transformers for language understanding. CoRR abs/1810.04805 (2018). http://arxiv.org/abs/1810.04805
8. Goldberg, Y.: A primer on neural network models for natural language processing. J. Artif. Intell. Res. **57**(1), 345–420 (2016). http://dl.acm.org/citation.cfm?id=3176748.3176757
9. Goodfellow, I., et al.: Generative adversarial nets. In: Ghahramani, Z., Welling, M., Cortes, C., Lawrence, N.D., Weinberger, K.Q. (eds.) Advances in Neural Information Processing Systems, vol. 27, pp. 2672–2680. Curran Associates, Inc. (2014). http://papers.nips.cc/paper/5423-generative-adversarial-nets.pdf
10. Goodfellow, I.J.: NIPS 2016 tutorial: generative adversarial networks. CoRR abs/1701.00160 (2017). http://arxiv.org/abs/1701.00160
11. Kim, Y.: Convolutional neural networks for sentence classification. In: Proceedings of the 2014 Conference on Empirical Methods in Natural Language Processing, EMNLP 2014, Doha, Qatar, 25–29 October 2014. A meeting of SIGDAT, a Special Interest Group of the ACL, pp. 1746–1751 (2014). http://aclweb.org/anthology/D/D14/D14-1181.pdf
12. Kim, Y., Jernite, Y., Sontag, D., Rush, A.M.: Character-aware neural language models. In: Proceedings of the Thirtieth AAAI Conference on Artificial Intelligence, Phoenix, Arizona, USA, 12–17 February 2016, pp. 2741–2749 (2016). http://www.aaai.org/ocs/index.php/AAAI/AAAI16/paper/view/12489

13. Kipf, T.N., Welling, M.: Semi-supervised classification with graph convolutional networks. CoRR abs/1609.02907 (2016). http://arxiv.org/abs/1609.02907
14. Klambauer, G., Unterthiner, T., Mayr, A., Hochreiter, S.: Self-normalizing neural networks. In: Guyon, I., et al. (eds.) Advances in Neural Information Processing Systems, vol. 30, pp. 971–980. Curran Associates, Inc. (2017). http://papers.nips.cc/paper/6698-self-normalizing-neural-networks.pdf
15. Li, X., Roth, D.: Learning question classifiers: the role of semantic information. Nat. Lang. Eng. 12(3), 229–249 (2006)
16. Mikolov, T., Chen, K., Corrado, G.S., Dean, J.: Efficient estimation of word representations in vector space. CoRR abs/1301.3781 (2013)
17. Rappaport Hovav, M., Levin, B.: The syntax-semantics interface, Chap. 19, pp. 593–624. Wiley (2015). https://doi.org/10.1002/9781118882139.ch19, https://onlinelibrary.wiley.com/doi/abs/10.1002/9781118882139.ch19
18. Salimans, T., Goodfellow, I., Zaremba, W., Cheung, V., Radford, A., Chen, X.: Improved techniques for training GANs. In: Lee, D.D., Sugiyama, M., Luxburg, U.V., Guyon, I., Garnett, R. (eds.) Advances in Neural Information Processing Systems, vol. 29, pp. 2234–2242. Curran Associates, Inc. (2016). http://papers.nips.cc/paper/6125-improved-techniques-for-training-gans.pdf
19. Shawe-Taylor, J., Cristianini, N.: Kernel Methods for Pattern Analysis. Cambridge University Press, Cambridge (2004)
20. Vapnik, V.N.: Statistical Learning Theory. Wiley-Interscience, Hoboken (1998)
21. Weston, J., Ratle, F., Collobert, R.: Deep learning via semi-supervised embedding. In: Proceedings of the 25th International Conference on Machine Learning, ICML 2008, pp. 1168–1175. ACM, New York (2008). https://doi.org/10.1145/1390156.1390303, http://doi.acm.org/10.1145/1390156.1390303
22. Williams, C.K.I., Seeger, M.: Using the Nyström method to speed up kernel machines. In: Leen, T.K., Dietterich, T.G., Tresp, V. (eds.) Advances in Neural Information Processing Systems, vol. 13, pp. 682–688. MIT Press (2001)
23. Xu, K., et al.: Show, attend and tell: neural image caption generation with visual attention. CoRR abs/1502.03044 (2015). http://dblp.uni-trier.de/db/journals/corr/corr1502.html#XuBKCCSZB15
24. Yang, Z., Cohen, W.W., Salakhutdinov, R.: Revisiting semi-supervised learning with graph embeddings. In: Proceedings of the 33rd International Conference on International Conference on Machine Learning, ICML 2016, vol. 48, pp. 40–48. JMLR.org (2016). http://dl.acm.org/citation.cfm?id=3045390.3045396

Activity Prediction of Business Process Instances with Inception CNN Models

Nicola Di Mauro[1]([⊠]), Annalisa Appice[1], and Teresa M. A. Basile[2,3]

[1] Department of Computer Science, University of Bari "Aldo Moro", Bari, Italy
nicola.dimauro@uniba.it
[2] Department of Physics, University of Bari "Aldo Moro", Bari, Italy
[3] Bari Division, National Institute for Nuclear Physics (INFN), Bari, Italy

Abstract. Predicting the next activity of a running execution trace of a business process represents a challenging task in process mining. The problem has been already tackled by using different machine learning approaches. Among them, deep artificial neural networks architectures suited for sequential data, such as recurrent neural networks (RNNs), recently achieved the state of the art results. However, convolutional neural networks (CNNs) architectures can outperform RNNs on tasks for sequence modeling, such as machine translation. In this paper we investigate the use of stacked inception CNN modules for the next-activity prediction problem. The proposed neural network architecture leads to better results when compared to RNNs architectures both in terms of computational efficiency and prediction accuracy on different real-world datasets.

Keywords: Business process monitoring · Sequence prediction · Deep learning

1 Introduction

Process mining [1] refers to the analysis of executions, often called traces, of a business process. In this research area, a challenging task is represented by the learning of probabilistic predictive models [20]. When learned, these models are then exploitable on incomplete or running traces, in order to predict missing events or forecast the evolution of running traces based on patterns extracted from a historical event log. One example of these predictive models includes techniques able to predict the next activity [2,6,11,24]. This prediction ability may be considered to guarantee the higher utilization by acting proactively in anticipation.

In recent years, with the increasing popularity of deep artificial neural networks (NNs) [15] in many fields, such as image classification [18,22], automatic speech recognition [9] and natural language processing [10], growing interest has arisen in using deep learning to analyze event logs to gain accurate insights into the future of a business process.

© Springer Nature Switzerland AG 2019
M. Alviano et al. (Eds.): AI*IA 2019, LNAI 11946, pp. 348–361, 2019.
https://doi.org/10.1007/978-3-030-35166-3_25

Recurrent neural networks (RNNs) are a kind of NNs specialized to deal with sequential data using internal memory and sharing parameters across different parts of the model. The authors in [11] presented one of the first application of deep NNs, adopting RNNs with long short-term memory (LSTM) cells [16], to the problem of predicting the next process activity. In [24] the authors proposed a new LSTM architecture for the next-activity prediction problem, which gains in accuracy compared to the architecture already reported in [11].

The recent systematic study available in [23] has compared different neural networks architectures, such as generic RNNs, and specialized RNNs with LSTM and GRU units [8], designed for the next-activity prediction problem. They have proved that all the neural networks architectures outperform other classical approaches.

Techniques based on LSTM architectures, suited for predicting the sequence of future activities of an ongoing case, could be improved by leveraging the knowledge about the structure of the process execution traces as well as the *a-priori* knowledge about future development, as already proven in [12].

In order to deal with sequential data, a valid alternative to RNNs could be the use of convolutional neural networks (CNNs) [21]. The same peculiar properties of CNNs—extracting features from local input patches and allowing for representation modularity—making them excel at computer vision could be also effective for sequence processing, where time could be considered as a spatial dimension. Such one-dimensional CNNs are competitive with RNNs at a cheaper computational cost. Instead, as recently showed in [3], simple convolutional architecture outperforms canonical recurrent networks such as LSTMs across a diverse range of tasks, while demonstrating longer effective memory.

However, a classical problem with CNNs is to correctly set the kernel size. The problem has been tackled in [22] where the authors proposed an inception module that simultaneously applies many convolutions with different kernel size to the same input—an optimal local sparse structure in a convolutional network can be approximated and covered by readily available dense components.

The aim of this paper is to investigate whether the use of one-dimensional CNNs could be competitive to RNNs for the next activity prediction problem. To this purpose we define an inception architecture for sequential data where inception modules of one-dimensional convolutions are stacked on top of each other. The proposed model, like other machine learning algorithms, is able to return the probability distribution over all the possible activities for the next event given an incomplete/running trace. The empirical evaluation, performed on real-world event logs, proves the effectiveness of the proposed neural network architecture both in term of prediction accuracy and computational cost.

Other approaches, such as that proposed in [20], deal with the problem of predicting the *time-to-completion* of running business process instances. Even if our proposed method can be extended to deal with this regression task, here we focus on the next activity prediction problem.

The background definitions are reported in the following section, while the formulated inception architecture is described in Sect. 3. The findings in the evaluation of the proposed architecture are discussed in Sect. 4. Finally, Sect. 5 refocuses on the purpose of the research and draws the conclusions.

2   Next Activity Prediction Problem

In this section we provide some background definitions regarding the next-activity prediction problem.

2.1   Background

Process mining techniques aim to extract useful information from event logs, assuming that each event of a business process refers to an activity of a particular case—process trace. Further information may be linked to a specific event, such as the timestamp and other attributes. Here we define some useful process mining concepts.

Let $\mathcal{A}$ be the set of all possible activities, $\mathcal{C}$ the set of case identifiers, and $\mathcal{D}_i$ the set of attributes, $1 \leq i \leq m$. Let $\mathcal{E}$ be the set of events in a trace.

Definition 1 (Event). *An* event $e_i \in \mathcal{E}$ *is as a tuple* $e_i = (a_i, c_i, t_i, d_{i1}, \ldots, d_{im})$ *where* $a_i \in \mathcal{A}$, $c_i \in \mathcal{C}$, t_i *is the timestamp, and* $d_{ij} \in \mathcal{D}_j$, $1 \leq j \leq m$, *are additional attributes.*

Given an event $e_i = (a_i, c_i, t_i, d_{i1}, \ldots, d_{im})$, it is possible to define the functions $\pi_{\mathcal{A}}(e_i) = a_i$, $\pi_{\mathcal{C}}(e_i) = c_i$, $\pi_{\mathcal{T}}(e_i) = t_i$, and $\pi_{\mathcal{D}_j}(e_i) = d_j$ for each $1 \leq j \leq m$. As in [24] the additional attributes will not be considered in the following of this paper, thus leading to events characterised by the activity, the timestamp and the case identifier.

Definition 2 (Trace). *A* trace *is a finite sequence of events* $\sigma = \langle e_1, e_2, \ldots, e_n \rangle$, *where each* $e_i \in \mathcal{E}$, $n = |\sigma|$, *and such that* $\pi_{\mathcal{T}}(e_i) \leq \pi_{\mathcal{T}}(e_{i+1})$ *and* $\pi_{\mathcal{C}}(e_i) = \pi_{\mathcal{C}}(e_{i+1})$, $\forall 1 \leq i \leq n - 1$.

Given the trace $\sigma = \langle e_1, e_2, \ldots, e_n \rangle$, a *prefix* σ^k of σ, with $k = |\sigma^k| \leq |\sigma|$, is the trace $\sigma^k = \langle e_1, e_2, \ldots, e_k \rangle$. In particular a trace is a complete process instance—started and ended—while a prefix is an instance in execution—running trace.

Definition 3 (Event log). *An* event log *is a set of traces such that each event appears at most once in the entire log.*

Table 1 reports a part of the event log described in the *Receipt phase* dataset adopted in the following experimental evaluation.

Table 1. Two traces of the event log dataset Receipt phase.

Event	Case ID	Activity	Timestamp
e_1	10011	Confirmation of receipt	2011/10/11 13:45:40.276
e_2	10011	Check confirmation of receipt	2011/10/12 08:26:25.398
e_3	10011	Adjust confirmation of receipt	2011/11/24 15:36:51.302
e_4	10011	Check confirmation of receipt	2011/11/24 15:37:16.553
e_5	10017	Confirmation of receipt	2011/10/18 13:46:39.679
e_6	10017	Determine necessity of stop advice	2011/10/18 13:47:06.950
e_7	10017	Check confirmation of receipt	2011/10/18 13:47:26.235
e_8	10017	Adjust confirmation of receipt	2011/10/18 13:47:41.811
e_9	10017	Check confirmation of receipt	2011/10/18 13:47:57.979
e_{10}	10017	Determine necessity to stop indication	2011/10/18 13:48:15.357
e_{11}	10017	Adjust confirmation of receipt	2011/10/18 13:48:30.632
e_{12}	10017	Check confirmation of receipt	2011/10/18 13:51:01.525
e_{13}	10017	Adjust confirmation of receipt	2011/10/18 13:56:57.603

2.2 Problem Formulation

The next-activity prediction problem consists in predicting the activity of a running trace. In our setting, the input consists of an event log—a set of traces with the attributes of their corresponding events.

Given an event log $\mathcal{L} = \{\sigma_i\}_{i=1}^{N}$ consisting of N traces, the online next-activity prediction scenario could be simulated in the following way.

A dataset $\mathcal{S} = \{(s_i, a_i)\}_{i=1}^{M}$, with $M > N$, is constructed from $\mathcal{L}$, where s_i is a sequence of events corresponding to a prefix σ_j^k of a trace $\sigma_j \in \mathcal{L}$, with $k \in \mathbb{N}^+$, and where a_i is the activity of the $(k+1)$-th event of the trace σ_j. More formally, let $\sigma = \langle e_1, e_2, \ldots, e_n \rangle$ be a trace, and $\Pi_A(\sigma, k) = \pi_A(e_k)$ the function returning the activity of the k-th event of σ, then:

$$\mathcal{S} = \{(s_i, a_i)\}_{i=1}^{M} = \bigcup_{j=1}^{N} \left\{ (\sigma_j^{k_j}, \Pi_A(\sigma_j, k_j + 1)) \right\}_{k_j=1}^{|\sigma_j|-1}.$$

In particular, $\mathcal{S}$ is the dataset of all the prefixes of all the traces in $\mathcal{L}$ labelled with their next-activity in their corresponding trace.

2.3 Recurrent Neural Networks

Deep feed-forward neural networks, also called multi-layer perceptrons (MLPs), are layered deep NNs defining a mapping $\mathbf{y} = f(\mathbf{x}; \boldsymbol{\theta})$ from an input $\mathbf{x}$ space to an output $\mathbf{y}$ space—computing an higher level representation of the input—with parameters value $\boldsymbol{\theta}$ that result in the best function generating data approximation [15].

In a MLP each neuron of a layer is connected to all the neurons of the next layer without cycles. There are an input layer, an output layer, an many hidden layers. Learning deep neural networks requires computing the gradients of complicated functions, efficiently computed using the back-propagation algorithm.

Recurrent neural networks (RNNs) are NNs specialised for processing sequential data, processing all the symbols of the sequence and updating an internal fixed-length memory state $\mathbf{s}$ with the same transition matrix at each time step. Most recurrent networks are able to process sequences of variable length. The idea in RNNs is to have feedback connections thus proving a *parameters sharing* across different parts of the model.

Let $\mathbf{x}_t$ and $\mathbf{h}_t$ be, respectively, the input and the hidden state—the memory of the network—at time step t. In a RNN, the hidden state $\mathbf{h}_t$ is updated using the previous hidden state and the current input at each time step:

$$\mathbf{h}_t = f(\mathbf{U}\mathbf{x}_t + \mathbf{W}\mathbf{h}_{t-1} + \mathbf{b}),$$

where f is usually a non-linear function, such as tanh, and the parameters are the bias vector $\mathbf{b}$ along with the weight matrices $\mathbf{U}$ and $\mathbf{W}$. Then, the output $\mathbf{o}_t$ at time t is computed as a function of the hidden state,

$$\mathbf{o}_t = f(\mathbf{V}\mathbf{h}_t + \mathbf{c}),$$

where $\mathbf{c}$ is the bias vector and $\mathbf{V}$ the weight matrix.

The most effective sequence models used in practical applications are called gated RNNs, including long short-term memory (LSTM) and networks based on the gated recurrent unit. A LSTM [16] is a special RNN architecture better suited for capturing long-term dependencies than vanilla RNNs. The core idea in LSTM is to introduce a cell state $\mathbf{C}_t$, more complex than the memory cell $\mathbf{h}_t$ in vanilla RNNs, where information is added or removed by gated structures, composed of a sigmoid neural network layer and a multiplication operation.

The LSTM model can be described by the following equations, where σ is the sigmoid function, and the operator $*$ denotes the Hadamard product—elementwise product:

$$\mathbf{f}_t = \sigma(\mathbf{W}_f\mathbf{x}_t + \mathbf{V}_f\mathbf{h}_{t-1} + \mathbf{b}_f), \tag{1}$$

$$\mathbf{i}_t = \sigma(\mathbf{W}_i\mathbf{x}_t + \mathbf{V}_i\mathbf{h}_{t-1} + \mathbf{b}_i), \tag{2}$$

$$\mathbf{o}_t = \sigma(\mathbf{W}_o\mathbf{x}_t + \mathbf{V}_o\mathbf{h}_{t-1} + \mathbf{b}_o), \tag{3}$$

$$\mathbf{C}_t = \mathbf{f}_t * \mathbf{C}_{t-1} + \mathbf{i}_t * \tanh(\mathbf{W}_c\mathbf{x}_t + \mathbf{V}_c\mathbf{h}_{t-1} + \mathbf{b}_c), \tag{4}$$

$$\mathbf{h}_t = \mathbf{o}_t * \tanh(\mathbf{C}_t). \tag{5}$$

The first sigmoid layer $\mathbf{f}_t$ in Eq. 1—*forget gate*—operates on $\mathbf{h}_{t-1}$ and $\mathbf{x}_t$ and output numbers between 0 and 1 for each element in the cell state—deciding the information to throw away from the cell. Then, the sigmoid layer $\mathbf{i}_t$ in Eq. 2—*input gate*—decides the value to be updated, and the tanh layer in Eq. 4 proposes a vector of new candidate values to be added to the state. In Eq. 4 the new cell state $\mathbf{C}_t$ is obtained by forgetting some information and adding new scaled information. The new value for $\mathbf{h}_t$ is computed in Eq. 5 by firstly deciding what part of the cell state to output as computed in Eq. 3—*output gate*.

As we can see from the above equations, learning a LSTM architecture is time consuming since it requires to learn many parameters—eight weight matrices $\mathbf{W}_f, \mathbf{W}_i, \mathbf{W}_o, \mathbf{W}_c$ and four bias vectors $\mathbf{b}_f, \mathbf{b}_i, \mathbf{b}_o, \mathbf{b}_c$.

3   The Proposed Inception Networks

Instead of using RNNs for the next-activity prediction problem, in this section we show how to use CNNs to tackle the same problem.

3.1   Convolutional Neural Networks

Convolutional neural networks [19] (CNNs) are a specialized kind of NNs for processing grid-like topology data, such as time-series data—one dimensional grid taking samples at regular time intervals—and image data—two dimensional grid of pixels. A convolutional layer convolves a kernel with the input in order to obtain a feature map. Often many different kernels for the same input are used, leading to many different feature maps. Different layers may have different kernel sizes. Between stacked convolutional layers, pooling layers—max or mean—are often inserted, greatly reducing the number of inputs thus speeding up the training process and reducing the number of parameters.

Convolutions are used over more than one axis at a time. For instance, if we have a two-dimensional input, we also want to use a two-dimensional kernel.

Given a two-dimensional input $\mathbf{X}$, the k-th feature map at location (i, j) in a given convolutional l-th layer is determined by the weight matrix $\mathbf{W}_k^l$ and the bias vector $\mathbf{b}_k^l$ with a non-linear activation function, such as the sigmoid function, as:

$$h_{i,j,k}^l = \sigma(\mathbf{W}_k^l * \mathbf{x}_{i,j}^l + \mathbf{b}_k^l),$$

where $\mathbf{x}_{i,j}^l$ is the input patch centered at location (i, j) of the l-th layer. The kernel $\mathbf{W}_k^l$ is shared for each possible location (i, j), thus reducing the model complexity and making the network easier to train. The same process applies on a one-dimensional input using the convolutions on a single axis.

A pooling layer placed after a convolutional layer aims to achieve *shift-invariance* by reducing the resolution of the feature map $\mathbf{h}_{:,:,k}^l$ as:

$$y_{i,j,k}^l = \mathrm{pool}(h_{m,n,k}^l), \forall (m, n) \in \mathcal{R}_{ij},$$

where $\mathcal{R}_{ij}$ is a local neighbourhood around location (i, j).

3.2   Inception Networks

The Inception module, introduced in [22] as a building block for the GoogLeNet architecture, was an important milestone in the development of CNNs based classifiers. Since salient parts in images and sequences can have extremely large variation in size, choosing the right kernel size for the convolution operation becomes difficult—large, respectively small, kernels are suited for globally, respectively locally, distributed information. The proposed solution is to have a convolutional layer with kernels with multiple sizes operating—an inception module. The network essentially would get a bit wider rather than deeper.

Figure 1a reports a naïve inception module for sequential data with three convolutions having kernel size 1, 2, and 3 respectively, plus an alternative parallel max-pooling path of size 3. The output of the module is the simple concatenation of the convolutions and pooling.

As these inception modules are stacked on top of each other (see Fig. 1b), their output correlation statistics are bound to vary [22].

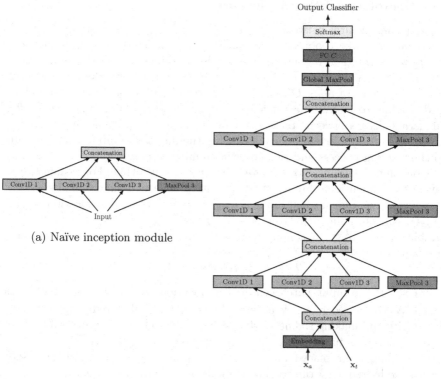

(a) Naïve inception module

(b) The overall architecture.

Fig. 1. The proposed inception architecture: (a) depicts the naïve inception module, while (b) is the stacking of three inception modules. Green boxes indicate the one-dimensional convolutions over the sequence, while red boxes indicate the pooling operations. (Color figure online)

3.3   Feature Representation

We recall that having an event log $\mathcal{L}$ we can obtain a dataset $\mathcal{S} = \{(s_i, a_i)\}_{i=1}^{M}$, as described in Sect. 2.2, consisting of all the prefixes s_i of all the traces in $\mathcal{L}$, labelled with their next-activity a_i in their corresponding trace.

However, since $\mathcal{S}$ consists of prefixes and activities denoted with categorical values, they should be converted into a numerical representation $\mathbf{x} \in \mathbb{R}^l$, with a given $l \in \mathbb{N}^+$, in order to be processed by our NN architecture.

For each sample $(s_i, a_i) = (\langle e_{i1}, e_{i2} \ldots, e_{ik_i} \rangle, a_i) \in \mathcal{S}$, we can construct its corresponding numerical representation, denoted as $((\mathbf{x}_{\mathsf{act}}^i, \mathbf{x}_{\mathsf{t}}^i), y^i)$, in the following way.

The vector $\mathbf{x}_{\mathsf{act}}^i \in \mathbb{N}^k$ corresponds to the numerical representation of the activities sequence in s_i. Let $f_c : \mathcal{A} \to [1, 2, \ldots, C]$, being $C = |\mathcal{A}|$ the cardinality of the activity-vocabulary—the number of classes—be a function assigning a numerical value to each activity, then $\mathbf{x}_{\mathsf{act}}^i = (x_{a1}^i, x_{a2}^i, \ldots, x_{ak_i}^i)$ is the vector where each $x_j^i = f_c(\pi_A(e_{ij}))$, $1 \leq j \leq k_i$. In the same way we can encode the label as $y^i = f_c(a_i)$. As usual in deep learning, in order to use losses such as the categorical cross-entropy, the class vector $\mathbf{y}$ should be converted to a binary class matrix $\mathbf{Y}$, i.e., each row $\mathbf{y}_i \in \mathbf{Y}$ is the one-hot encoding of the label y_i.

The vector $\mathbf{x}_{\mathsf{t}}^i = (x_{t1}^i, x_{t2}^i, \ldots, x_{tk_i}^i) \in \mathbb{R}^k$ is the numerical representation of the temporal information of the activities. In particular, for each event $e_{ij} \in s_i$, $1 \leq j \leq k_i$, $x_{tj}^i = \pi_T(e_{ij}) - \pi_T(e_{i(j-1)})$ represents the time difference from the previous event—it is zero for the first event in the sequence.

Example 1 (Feature representation). Let $s = (e_5, e_6, e_7, e_8)$ be a prefix, as reported in Table 1, consisting of 4 activities. Let f_c be defined with the mappings { "Confirmation of receipt" $\to 0$, "Determine necessity of stop advice" $\to 1$, "Check confirmation of receipt" $\to 2$, "Adjust confirmation of receipt" $\to 3, \ldots$}, then $\mathbf{x}_{\mathsf{act}} = (0, 1, 2, 3)$ and $\mathbf{x}_{\mathsf{t}} = (0.0, 27.271, 19.285, 15.576)$.

Thus, given the dataset $\mathcal{S} = \{(s_i, a_i)\}_{i=1}^{M}$ in a categorical representation we obtained its numerical representation $\mathcal{D} = (\mathbf{X}, \mathbf{y}) = \{(\mathbf{x}_{\mathsf{act}}^i, \mathbf{x}_{\mathsf{t}}^i), y^i\}_{i=1}^{M}$. Since all the sequences in $\mathcal{S}$ could not have the same length, then all the obtained sequences $\mathbf{x}_{\mathsf{act}}^i$ and $\mathbf{x}_{\mathsf{t}}^i$ have been pre-padded with the value 0.0 to the same length $\max_{i=1,\ldots M} |\mathbf{x}_{\mathsf{act}}^i|$ before to feed them to the NN architectures.

3.4   Architecture Details

Given the training dataset $\mathcal{D} = \{(\mathbf{x}_{\mathsf{act}}^i, \mathbf{x}_{\mathsf{t}}^i), y^i\}_{i=1}^{M}$, the NN architectures have two inputs $\mathbf{x}_{\mathsf{act}}^i \in \mathbb{N}^k$ and $\mathbf{x}_{\mathsf{t}}^i \in \mathbb{R}^k$. Categorical values in $\mathbf{x}_{\mathsf{act}}$ should be represented using a one-hot-encoding approach, as done in [23], that however could lead to large sparse vectors. Inspired by the neural language modeling works [4]—each word is mapped to a fixed size vector in $\mathbb{R}^d$, i.e., an *embedding*—$\mathbf{x}_{\mathsf{act}}^i$ is the input to an embedding layer—jointly learned with the model—with size equal to $d = \lceil C/2 \rceil$. While $\mathbf{x}_{\mathsf{t}}^i$ is simply concatenated to the output of the embedding layer whose values are in $\mathbb{R}^{k \times d}$, leading to a final input representation in $\mathbb{R}^{k \times d+1}$.

Then many inception modules, whose basic structure is reported in Fig. 1a, are stacked in order to learn increasingly complex patterns.

Each inception module applies three one-dimensional convolutional layers on the same input with different kernel sizes—resp., 1, 2, and 3. A max-pooling layer is applied on the same input. Finally, both the convolutional and pooling layer outputs are concatenated to obtain the inception output.

The last inception output in the stack is the input to a global max pooling layer, whose output is used by a final fully connected layer outputting the classification probabilities. The output probabilities have been computed using the *softmax* activation function:

$$p_i = \frac{\exp(e_i)}{\sum_{j=1}^{C} \exp(e_j)}.$$

The non-linear activation function we chose to use is the Rectifier Linear Unit (ReLU) [14] computing $\max(0, x)$. The ReLU activation function limits the gradient vanishing problem as its derivative is always one when x is positive. Let Θ denote the parameters of the network, the optimum parameters have been obtained by minimizing the mean-squared-error loss function:

$$\mathcal{L} = \frac{1}{M} \sum_{i=1}^{M} \ell_{\mathsf{mse}}(\Theta; \mathbf{y}_i, \mathbf{p}_i).$$

4   Experimental Evaluation

Here we present the empirical results of our proposed neural network architecture when compared to LSTM models. For LSTM architectures the same implementation adopted in [23] has been used[1]. However, for a fair comparison the original code for LSTM architectures have been slightly modified in the following way. In [23] the architecture takes as input the activities $\mathbf{x}_{\mathsf{act}}$ only. Here the input has been extended to consider both $\mathbf{x}_{\mathsf{act}}$ and $\mathbf{x}_{\mathsf{t}}$. Furthermore, in [23] the categorical values in $\mathbf{x}_{\mathsf{act}}$ have been one-hot-encoded, while here the previous embedding approach has been adopted.

4.1   Experimental Setup

We evaluated the performance of our proposed approach in predicting the next activity on three event logs. For each log, we used a 3-fold cross validation approach. The performance measures we adopted to assess the model performance are the Brier score [7] and the accuracy. In particular, the brier score can be interpreted as a measure of the calibration of a set of probabilistic predictions, measuring error of the predicted likelihoods over all symbols—the lower the Brier score is for a set of predictions, the better the predictions are calibrated.

The adopted logs—Table 3 reports statistics in terms of number of classes, traces, and resulting sequences—are the following:

---

[1] The original code used in [23] is available at https://github.com/TaXxER/rnnalpha.

– *Receipt phase*[2]: this log originates from the CoSeLoG project executed under NWO project number 638.001.211. It contains the records of the execution of the receiving phase of the building permit application process in an anonymous municipality in the Netherlands;
– *bpi12*[3]: this log describes a loan application process. It has been pre-processed as reported in [24];
– *helpdesk*[4]: this log contains events from a ticketing management process of the help desk of an Italian software company.

Table 2. Hyperparameter search space for our method and LSTM adopted for the TPE procedure.

OUR		LSTM	
layers	$\{1, 2, 3\}$	layers	$\{1, 2, 3\}$
batch_size	$\{2^9, 2^{10}\}$	batch_size	$\{2^9, 2^{10}\}$
learning_rate	$[0.00001, 0.01]$	dropout	$[0, 0.5]$
		layer_size	$[10, 150]$
		learning_rate	$[0.00001, 0.01]$
		l_1	$[0.00001, 0.01]$
		l_2	$[0.00001, 0.01]$

For both our method and LSTM we conducted an hyper-parameter optimization by using the 20% of the training set as a validation set. We chose the configuration of the parameter that achieved the best validation loss. The hyperparameters and their corresponding possible values are reported in Table 2. We employed the hyper-parameter optimization tree-structured Parzen estimator (TPE) as proposed in [5].

The weights are initialized following the Xavier scheme [13]. For all deep learning approaches, the weights of the neural networks have been optimized using Adam [17] minimizing the mean squared error, a variant of the stochastic gradient descent. An early stopping approach has been used for regularization— the training phase is stopped when there is no improvement of the loss on the validation set for 20 consecutive epochs. A limit on the number of epochs has been set to 200. The epoch with best validation loss was selected and the corresponding model was evaluated on the test set.

Both our proposed approach and the LSTM architecture have been implemented in Python using the Keras[5] and Tensorflow[6] libraries[7].

---

[2] https://doi.org/10.4121/uuid:a07386a5-7be3-4367-9535-70bc9e77dbe6.
[3] https://doi.org/10.4121/uuid:a07386a5-7be3-4367-9535-70bc9e77dbe6.
[4] https://doi.org/10.17632/39bp3vv62t.1
[5] https://keras.io/.
[6] https://www.tensorflow.org/.
[7] Source code available at https://github.com/nicoladimauro/nnpm.

All the experiments have been executed on a single GeForce GTX TITAN X GPU—execution time are reported in Table 5.

Table 3. Dataset statistics.

	Classes	Cases	Sequences
Receipt phase	26	1434	7143
helpdesk	8	3804	9906
bpi12	22	13087	151419

4.2   Results

As we can see from Table 4, our proposed approach outperform the LSTM one both in terms of Brier score and accuracy on all the adopted datasets. The first column in Table 4 reports the accuracy of a random predictor, guessing a label with uniform probability. The value of the Brier score are very low, corresponding to a low error of the predicted likelihoods over the symbols. This is confirmed from the accuracy scores that are always greater than those obtained using LSTM architectures. Specifically, our proposed approach obtain, when compared to the LSTM model based one, an increase of the accuracy of 12.17% on average (34.41% on *Receipt phase*, 2.34% on *helpdesk*, and 3.95% on *bpi12*). Even the Brier score is always improved on each considered dataset, decreasing of 15.38% on average (44.44% on *Receipt phase*, 4.4% on *helpdesk*, and 7.14% on *bpi12*).

Table 4. The Brier score and the classification accuracy (mean ± standard deviation on three folds) for our proposed network and LSTM on all the event logs.

	Brier score			Accuracy	
	RAND	OUR	LSTM	OUR	LSTM
Receipt	0.037 ± 0	0.010 ± 0.000	0.018 ± 0.012	0.832 ± 0.005	0.619 ± 0.365
helpdesk	0.109 ± 0	0.043 ± 0.001	0.045 ± 0.002	0.785 ± 0.005	0.767 ± 0.015
bpi12	0.043 ± 0	0.013 ± 0.000	0.014 ± 0.002	0.789 ± 0.001	0.759 ± 0.029
Average		0.022	0.026	0.802	0.715

Another interesting aspect of our proposed solution, as expected when compared to recurrent networks, regards the computational time for learning the network parameters. Indeed, it is well known that RNNs are slow to be learnt.

As we can see from Table 5, even if on some datasets, such as *helpdesk* and *bpi12*, the number of parameters of our best architecture is greater than that of the LSTM based one, the time spent in seconds to optimize them is always smaller than that used to optimize the LSTM parameters—2 times faster on average.

We can conclude from this experimental evaluation that our proposed neural network architecture is more accurate, both in term of calibrated predictions and accuracy, and more efficient than LSTM in predicting the next-activity of a running execution trace of a business process.

Table 5. The number of parameters and learning time spent in seconds (mean on three folds) of our proposed network and LSTM on all the event logs.

	# parameters		Time	
	OUR	LSTM	OUR	LSTM
Receipt phase	14.2 k	39.4 k	10.7	19.2
helpdesk	35.5 k	22.0 k	17.6	25.3
bpi12	48.4 k	36.4 k	265.1	604.7
Average			97.8	216.4

5   Conclusion

Predicting the next activity of a running execution trace of a business process represents a challenging task in process mining [20]. The problem has been successfully tackled using recurrent neural networks providing state-of-the-art results [23]. However, recurrent networks are time consuming and in many cases they have been outperformed by convolutional network when dealing with sequential data, as reported in [3].

In this paper we proposed a deep neural network model based on convolutional neural networks to tackle the problem of next-activity prediction. In particular, we proposed an inception architecture, similar to that used for computer vision, but adapted for sequential data. When compared to a LSTM recurrent neural network on different real-world dataset, the results of the proposed approach prove its validity both in terms of accuracy and computational complexity.

A possible extension of the proposed approach should be to predict at the same time both the next-activity and the its execution time as already done in [24]. Extensions of the naïve inception module to more complex ones are also possible to be investigated.

Acknowlegments. This research is partially funded by the *Knowledge Community for Efficient Training through Virtual Technologies* Italian project (KOMETA, code 2B1MMF1), under the program POR Puglia FESR-FSE 2014–2020 - Asse prioritario 1 - Ricerca, sviluppo tecnologico, innovazione - SubAzione 1.4.b - BANDO INNOLABS supported by Regione Puglia, as well as by the *Electronic Shopping & Home delivery of Edible goods with Low environmental Footprint* Italian project (ESHELF), under the Apulian INNONETWORK programme.

References

1. van der Aalst, W.M.P.: Process Mining - Data Science in Action, 2nd edn. Springer, Heidelberg (2016). https://doi.org/10.1007/978-3-662-49851-4
2. Appice, A., Mauro, N.D., Malerba, D.: Leveraging shallow machine learning to predict business process behavior. In: SCC, pp. 184–188 (2019)
3. Bai, S., Kolter, J.Z., Koltun, V.: Convolutional sequence modeling revisited. In: ICLR (2018)
4. Bengio, Y., Ducharme, R., Vincent, P., Janvin, C.: A neural probabilistic language model. JMLR **3**, 1137–1155 (2003)
5. Bergstra, J., Bardenet, R., Bengio, Y., Kégl, B.: Algorithms for hyper-parameter optimization. In: NIPS, pp. 2546–2554 (2011)
6. Breuker, D., Matzner, M., Delfmann, P., Becker, J.: Comprehensible predictive models for business processes. J. MIS Q. **40**, 1009–1034 (2016)
7. Brier, G.W.: Verification of forecasts expressed in terms of probability. Mon. Weather Rev. **78**(1), 1–3 (1950)
8. Cho, K., et al.: Learning phrase representations using RNN encoder–decoder for statistical machine translation. In: EMNLP, pp. 1724–1734 (2014)
9. Chorowski, J.K., Bahdanau, D., Serdyuk, D., Cho, K., Bengio, Y.: Attention-based models for speech recognition. In: NIPS, pp. 577–585 (2015)
10. Devlin, J., Chang, M., Lee, K., Toutanova, K.: BERT: pre-training of deep bidirectional transformers for language understanding. CoRR abs/1810.04805 (2018)
11. Evermann, J., Rehse, J.-R., Fettke, P.: A deep learning approach for predicting process behaviour at runtime. In: Dumas, M., Fantinato, M. (eds.) BPM 2016. LNBIP, vol. 281, pp. 327–338. Springer, Cham (2017). https://doi.org/10.1007/978-3-319-58457-7_24
12. Di Francescomarino, C., Ghidini, C., Maggi, F.M., Petrucci, G., Yeshchenko, A.: An eye into the future: leveraging a-priori knowledge in predictive business process monitoring. In: Carmona, J., Engels, G., Kumar, A. (eds.) BPM 2017. LNCS, vol. 10445, pp. 252–268. Springer, Cham (2017). https://doi.org/10.1007/978-3-319-65000-5_15
13. Glorot, X., Bengio, Y.: Understanding the difficulty of training deep feedforward neural networks. In: AISTATS, pp. 249–256 (2010)
14. Glorot, X., Bordes, A., Bengio, Y.: Deep sparse rectifier neural networks. In: AISTATS, vol. 15, pp. 315–323. PMLR (2011)
15. Goodfellow, I., Bengio, Y., Courville, A.: Deep Learning. MIT Press, Cambridge (2016)
16. Hochreiter, S., Schmidhuber, J.: Long short-term memory. Neural Comput. **9**(8), 1735–1780 (1997)
17. Kingma, D., Ba, J.: Adam: a method for stochastic optimization. In: ICLR (2014)
18. Krizhevsky, A., Sutskever, I., Hinton, G.E.: ImageNet classification with deep convolutional neural networks. CACM **60**(6), 84–90 (2017)
19. LeCun, Y., Haffner, P., Bottou, L., Bengio, Y.: Object recognition with gradient-based learning. In: Shape, Contour and Grouping in Computer Vision. LNCS, vol. 1681, pp. 319–345. Springer, Heidelberg (1999). https://doi.org/10.1007/3-540-46805-6_19
20. Polato, M., Sperduti, A., Burattin, A., de Leoni, M.: Time and activity sequence prediction of business process instances. Computing **100**(9), 1005–1031 (2018)
21. Schmidhuber, J.: Deep learning in neural networks: an overview. Neural Netw. **61**, 85–117 (2015)

22. Szegedy, C., et al.: Going deeper with convolutions. In: CVPR (2015)
23. Tax, N., Teinemaa, I., van Zelst, S.J.: An interdisciplinary comparison of sequence modeling methods for next-element prediction. CoRR abs/1811.00062 (2018)
24. Tax, N., Verenich, I., La Rosa, M., Dumas, M.: Predictive business process monitoring with LSTM neural networks. In: Dubois, E., Pohl, K. (eds.) CAiSE 2017. LNCS, vol. 10253, pp. 477–492. Springer, Cham (2017). https://doi.org/10.1007/978-3-319-59536-8_30

Question Classification with Untrained Recurrent Embeddings

Daniele Di Sarli⊕, Claudio Gallicchio⊕, and Alessio Micheli⁽⊠⁾⊕

Department of Computer Science, University of Pisa, Pisa, Italy
daniele.disarli@gmail.com, {gallicch,micheli}@di.unipi.it

Abstract. Recurrent Neural Networks (RNNs) are at the foundation of many state-of-the-art results in text classification. However, to be effective in practical applications, they often require the use of sophisticated architectures and training techniques, such as gating mechanisms and pre-training by autoencoders or language modeling, with typically high computational cost. In this work, we show that such techniques could actually be not always necessary. In fact, our experimental results on a Question Classification task indicate that using state-of-the-art Reservoir Computing approaches for RNN design, it is possible to achieve competitive or comparable accuracy with a considerable advantage in terms of required training times.

Keywords: Text classification · Recurrent Neural Networks · Echo State Networks

1   Introduction

Recurrent Neural Networks (RNNs) have long been the de-facto standard neural architectures for many Natural Language Processing tasks [1,8,23,29], mainly because they allow to model the input and output text as a sequence of words or characters. Unfortunately, during training vanilla implementations of RNNs suffer from the well-known problems of gradient vanishing and gradient explosion, which make these networks difficult to train in the presence of long-term dependencies within the input [2].

Some approaches have gained popularity for their ability to avoid or alleviate the problems associated with the gradient propagation during training. For example, gated architectures like Long Short-Term Memory (LSTM) [15] and Gated Recurrent Unit (GRU) [8] are based on the idea of *gating mechanisms* that selectively remember and forget by regulating the flow of information through each time step, helping to alleviate the vanishing of the gradient. Recently, the development of the Transformer architecture [34] made it possible to more easily perform training by not using any recurrent network within the model and employing self-attention mechanisms instead. Increasingly often, transfer learning is used to train a task-independent language model on a large

ⓒ Springer Nature Switzerland AG 2019
M. Alviano et al. (Eds.): AI*IA 2019, LNAI 11946, pp. 362–375, 2019.
https://doi.org/10.1007/978-3-030-35166-3_26

variety of text corpora (for example by employing an autoencoder or a classifier with a next-step prediction task) and then fine-tune it to the task at hand.

These techniques can lead to a significant increase of cost in terms of training time due to their considerable use of computational resources, with different kinds of repercussions such as economic availability, financial costs, and environmental impact. Currently, training a single Transformer model has been estimated to produce about $87\,kg$ of CO_2 on commonly used hardware and cloud computing services, with a financial cost in US dollars between \$289 and \$981 [33]. Do these high cost techniques provide an equally significant improvement in predictive performance? In this paper, we try to address this question by proposing an approach based on RNNs from the class of Reservoir Computing (RC) [26,35], and comparing it with current state-of-the-art results in the literature. In particular we propose the use of Echo State Networks (ESNs) [16,17], a recurrent RC model, to produce by means of randomly initialized and untrained weights an embedding for the input text, which can then be used for classification tasks. While the network is largely untrained, we use advances in the architectural setup of ESNs and we explore the impact of an attention mechanism in this context. Unlike the commonly used approaches, thanks to the fact that the recurrent part of our model is completely untrained, we are able to achieve a strikingly fast training process. We then experimentally assess the feasibility and the performance of our approach with a focused analysis on a Question Classification task.

We briefly introduce the characteristics and advantages of the ESN model in Sect. 2, where we also address advances on recurrent connections shaping. In Sect. 3 we present the proposed models, which we then validate on a Question Classification dataset, described in Sect. 4. Our experiments and methodology are reported in Sect. 5, while a discussion of the results is presented in Sect. 6. Finally, in Sect. 7 we draw the conclusions of this study.

2 Echo State Networks

The framework of RNNs offers a useful and effective method for modeling sequences. In what follows, we use T to denote the length of a generic input sequence. Whenever a specific sequence i is considered, its length is denoted by T_i. Moreover, we use N_U, N_R and N_Y respectively to denote the size of the input layer, the number of hidden recurrent units (i.e. the size of the state embedding), and the number of output units in the RNN model. Given an input sequence composed of vectors $u(1), \ldots, u(T) \in \mathbb{R}^{N_U}$, a generic RNN scans the input left-to-right and computes a sequence of states $x(1), \ldots, x(T) \in \mathbb{R}^{N_R}$ having the same length T. From these states, an output (in the form of a sequence or of a single element) is then computed. RNNs are usually trained by gradient descent algorithms, which are subject to the problems associated with the gradient, as briefly discussed in Sect. 1, and can be costly to run.

On the other hand, radically different approaches like ESNs [16,17], from the RC paradigm, are based on the stable initialization of the recurrent dynamics so that the training of the parameters in the recurrent part of the network can be avoided altogether. The state of the network at each time step is computed by an untrained dynamical system with randomly initialized parameters called "reservoir", and the output is typically extracted from the state of the reservoir by means of simple linear regression techniques (even though more complex approaches can be used) [26]: ESNs are thus an efficient approach to modeling and training RNNs.

The state dynamics of an ESN at a particular time step t, in the case of leaky-integrator neurons [18] and hyperbolic tangent activation functions, are ruled by the following equation:

$$x(t) = (1 - a)\, x(t - 1) + a \tanh \left(W_{in} u(t) + \hat{W} x(t - 1) \right), \tag{1}$$

where $x(0) = 0$, $W_{in} \in \mathbb{R}^{N_R \times N_U}$ is the input-to-reservoir weight matrix, and $\hat{W} \in \mathbb{R}^{N_R \times N_R}$ is the recurrent reservoir-to-reservoir weight matrix. The scalar value $a \in \mathbb{R}$ is the *leaking rate*, under the constraint that $0 < a \leq 1$. For simplicity of notation, here and in the rest of this paper the bias term is omitted.

The key difference between an ESN and a vanilla RNN is in the fact that in the ESN the values in the weight matrices W_{in} and $\hat{W}$ are not trained, instead they are initialized on the basis of stability constraints. These are given by the global asymptotic stability property known as the Echo State Property [16, 26, 36], and, under a practical perspective, they entail the control of algebraic properties of the recurrent weight matrix of the dynamical reservoir. Specifically, the weight values in $\hat{W}$ are randomly initialized and then re-scaled to control the value of the spectral radius $\rho = \rho(\hat{W})$ (i.e. its largest eigenvalue in absolute value). Similarly, the values in W_{in} are randomly chosen from a uniform distribution on $[-\omega, \omega]$, where $\omega \in \mathbb{R}^+$ acts as input scaling. The values of ρ and ω are hyperparameters that are chosen by model selection. Moreover, both W_{in} and $\hat{W}$ in Eq. 1 can be sparse matrices, since this causes a drop in the state transition computational cost, typically without any associated loss in terms of predictive performance [11].

After the input sequence has been fed in, the states produced by the ESN can be used to compute the output. Given the typical high dimensionality of the reservoir, it can be sufficient to use a simple linear layer ("readout") to perform the classification. In that case, the output $y(t) \in \mathbb{R}^{N_Y}$ for a generic state $x(t)$ is simply:

$$y(t) = W_{out} x(t), \tag{2}$$

where $W_{out} \in \mathbb{R}^{N_Y \times N_R}$ is the matrix containing the output weights, which are the only free parameters that are adjusted on a training set. Given the formulation in Eq. 2, training reduces to solving the following least squares problem:

$$\min_{W_{out}} \| W_{out} X - Y_{tg} \|_2^2. \tag{3}$$

In Eq. 3 we use $X \in \mathbb{R}^{N_R \times N_{train}}$ to denote the state matrix, i.e. the column-wise concatenation of the N_{train} states produced by the ESN that need to be

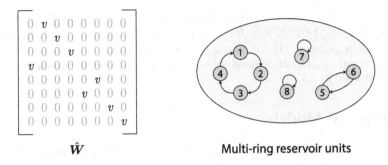

$$\hat{W} \qquad\qquad \text{Multi-ring reservoir units}$$

Fig. 1. On the left, an example of a recurrent matrix $\hat{W}$ generated as per Eq. 5. On the right, a representation of the corresponding multi-ring reservoir.

classified, and $Y_{tg} \in \mathbb{R}^{N_Y \times N_{train}}$ to indicate the column-wise concatenation of the target vectors. The parameters of the linear readout, i.e. the weight values in W_{out}, can then be computed in closed-form by exploiting direct methods, such as ridge regression [26], as follows:

$$W_{out} = Y_{tg}X^T(XX^T + \lambda_r I)^{-1}, \qquad (4)$$

where I is the identity matrix, and $\lambda_r \in \mathbb{R}^+$ is the regularization parameter.

2.1 Multi-ring Reservoir Topology

For the recurrent part, the networks that we are proposing adopt an ESN that follows the same dynamics as in Eq. 1. The only difference is that the matrix $\hat{W}$ is constructed in order to implement a constrained topology [6, 32]. In particular, we take

$$\hat{W} = vP, \qquad (5)$$

where $P \in \{0,1\}^{N_R \times N_R}$ is a randomly generated permutation matrix and $v \in \mathbb{R}^+$ is a scalar that determines the spectral radius of $\hat{W}$, i.e. $\rho(\hat{W}) = v$. This follows from the fact that since P is a permutation matrix it is also orthogonal, i.e. for any vector w:

$$\|vPw\| = v\|w\|. \qquad (6)$$

If w is an eigenvector of matrix vP with associated eigenvalue λ, i.e. $vPw = \lambda w$, then it follows that

$$\|vPw\| = |\lambda|\|w\|. \qquad (7)$$

From (6) and (7) we conclude that $|\lambda| = v$ for all eigenvalues, hence $\rho(vP) = v$. For this reason, in the following we will consider $\rho = v$, whose value is to be selected by hyperparameter search.

The "multi-ring" layout that emerges from this configuration (see Fig. 1) has many advantages, the most important one being that it allows building large reservoirs with minimal state transition cost. In fact, the matrix-vector multiplication $\hat{W}x(t - 1)$ in Eq. 1 can be implemented in linear time in the case of a multi-ring reservoir. Moreover, the space requirements for matrix $\hat{W}$ shrink from $O(N_R^2)$ to $O(N_R)$. Even further, the time required for initializing the network is reduced since it is not necessary to compute the spectral radius of $\hat{W}$ to rescale it, but it is possible to cheaply initialize the matrix with the desired value of ρ.

3   Proposed Models

Our proposed models implement a bidirectional recurrent architecture [5,30]: we use two separate networks to scan the input from left to right and from right to left. In the following sections we present the variants of the models that we designed, all of which adopt an ESN for the recurrent module but use different implementations for the readout. Specifically, the first model uses a simpler readout component and is described in Sect. 3.1. The second model, which includes a self-attention mechanism, is presented in Sect. 3.2.

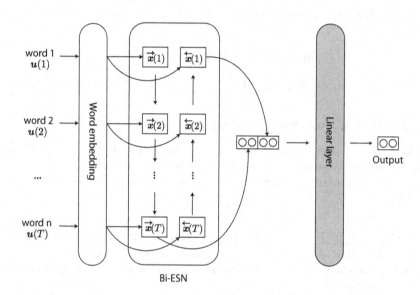

Fig. 2. Representation of the Bi-ESN model. Input words are transformed to vectors via pretrained word embeddings, then they are fed through a bidirectional leaky ESN. The final states are then concatenated for each direction, and fed to a linear classifier. The only parts of the model that undergo training are represented by a shaded background: in this case, only the final linear layer.

3.1   Bi-ESN

With our simplest model, Bi-ESN, we introduce in the literature the use of a bidirectional orthogonal (multi-ring) architecture for the reservoir of a leaky

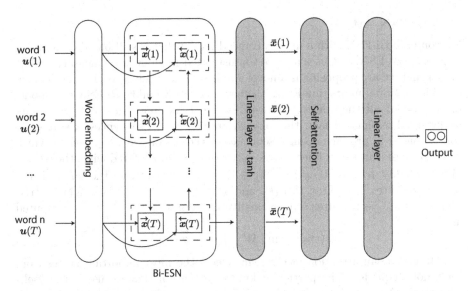

Fig. 3. Representation of the Bi-ESN-Att model. Input words are transformed to vectors via pretrained word embeddings, then they are fed through a bidirectional leaky ESN. All states from each direction are then concatenated (dashed rectangles) and fed one by one to a linear layer that performs dimensionality reduction. After that, the self-attention mechanism selects the most important states, which are summed together and fed to a linear classifier. The only parts of the model that undergo training are represented by a shaded background.

ESN, in order to produce a fixed size untrained embedding of the input text as illustrated in Fig. 2. The embedding is created by running the input through the bidirectional ESN and then taking the concatenation of the last forward and backward states, resulting in a single vector of size $2N_R$. This vector is then processed by a simple linear layer.

Let us denote with $\overrightarrow{x}(t), \overleftarrow{x}(t) \in \mathbb{R}^{N_R}$ respectively the forward and backward state associated to $u(t)$. If $\overrightarrow{x}_n(t)$ is a forward state for the n-th training example (and similarly for $\overleftarrow{x}_n(t)$), then in order to train the Bi-ESN with ridge regression we apply the same formulation as in Eq. 4, where in this case the state matrix contains the concatenation of forward and backward states, i.e. $X \in \mathbb{R}^{2N_R \times N_{train}}$, given by:

$$X = \begin{bmatrix} \overrightarrow{x}_1(T_1) & \overrightarrow{x}_2(T_2) & \dots & \overrightarrow{x}_{N_{train}}(T_{N_{train}}) \\ \overleftarrow{x}_1(1) & \overleftarrow{x}_2(1) & \dots & \overleftarrow{x}_{N_{train}}(1) \end{bmatrix} \tag{8}$$

with $T_1, T_2, \dots, T_{N_{train}}$ representing the lengths of the training input sequences.

3.2 Bi-ESN-Att

We compare Bi-ESN with a more advanced model that is still based on a multi-ring leaky Bi-ESN, but uses a more sophisticated readout implementation. The model that we are proposing is a novel application of a self-attention mechanism to a bidirectional multi-ring ESN. As shown in Fig. 3, unlike Bi-ESN this model makes use of all the states produced by the ESN, both in the forward and backward direction. In fact, the forward and backward sequences of states are concatenated to produce a single sequence of vectors of size $2N_R$, each of which goes through the same linear layer with the purpose of reducing the vector dimensionality to N_D. If $\overrightarrow{x}(t), \overleftarrow{x}(t) \in \mathbb{R}^{N_R}$ are respectively the forward and backward states associated to $u(t)$, and $W_{dr} \in \mathbb{R}^{N_D \times 2N_R}$ is a weight matrix, then the state vector after dimensionality reduction, $\bar{x}(t) \in \mathbb{R}^{N_D}$, is computed as:

$$\bar{x}(t) = \tanh\left(W_{dr}\left[\overrightarrow{x}(t), \overleftarrow{x}(t)\right]\right). \tag{9}$$

After that, an attention mechanism selects the most important states from the whole sequence. The particular kind of attention that we use is the "self-attention" [25], which unlike other techniques (see for instance [1]) does not require any additional information other than the sequence itself. Intuitively, in its simplest form the attention mechanism works by assigning a score to each of the states produced by the ESN, based on the relevance that they have in relation to the task. These scores are then used to compute a weighted sum of the state vectors, which leads to a fixed size representation for the whole sentence focused on the most important features. Let T be the length of the input sequence, let $r \in \mathbb{R}$ be the number of parts in the sentence on which the attention mechanism is allowed to focus, and let $d_a \in \mathbb{R}$ represent the number of hidden units for computing the scores. Then, if $W_{s1} \in \mathbb{R}^{d_a \times N_D}$ and $W_{s2} \in \mathbb{R}^{r \times d_a}$ are weight matrices, the self-attention scores $A \in \mathbb{R}^{r \times T}$ are computed as:

$$\bar{X} = \begin{bmatrix} \bar{x}(1)^T \\ \bar{x}(2)^T \\ \vdots \\ \bar{x}(T)^T \end{bmatrix} \in \mathbb{R}^{T \times N_D}$$

$$A = \text{softmax}\left(W_{s2}\tanh\left(W_{s1}\bar{X}^T\right)\right). \tag{10}$$

As can be noticed from Eq. 10, none of the weight matrices depend on the length of the sequence. The attention scores are then used to extract a fixed-size weighted sum of the most important states into a matrix $M \in \mathbb{R}^{r \times N_D}$:

$$M = A\bar{X}. \tag{11}$$

As for hyperparameters r and d_a, we simply take $r = 1$ and $d_a = N_D$. In this case, M reduces to a vector of size N_D that we then classify using a linear layer.

Note that all free parameters of the model can be trained end-to-end by gradient descent. Since unlike what happens in standard RNNs here the gradient only flows through a short path, we do not incur in the issue of gradient vanishing.

4   TREC Dataset

The TREC dataset for Question Classification[1] [24] is a commonly used benchmark for Natural Language Processing which deals with the classification of a number of sentences, written in English, into one of 6 classes about their topic (i.e. whether they ask about a person, a location, a number, a human being, a description or an entity).

The dataset has been split in three folds: training, validation and test. The test fold is directly provided by the authors of the dataset [24] and is composed of 500 labeled questions. We divided the training data, composed of 5452 labeled questions, by the commonly used "80/20 rule", where 80% of the instances (chosen at random) are used for training and the other 20% for validation. This yields a training set of 4362 questions and a validation set of 1090 questions, with similar class distributions between the two sets (we did not perform an explicit stratification).

The questions are tokenized and each word is then represented by a pretrained FastText embedding vector for the English language, with 300 dimensions [14]. In case of words without a corresponding embedding, a random vector of the same shape is used. This vector is different for each missing word. While the NLP community is pushing towards context-sensitive word embeddings, in the current setting we chose FastText for its relative efficiency.

5   Experiments

We performed all our experiments[2] on a single NVIDIA Tesla V100 with 16 GB of memory, and we developed our models by using the PyTorch framework [27] which provides automatic differentiation. In addition to the Bi-ESN and Bi-ESN-Att that we have described in Sect. 3, we also implemented a standard bidirectional GRU (Bi-GRU) that we use for comparison purposes on the analysis of accuracy and efficiency.

After hyperparameter tuning on the validation set, our models have been retrained on the whole training and validation data to get a final estimate of the performance. In addition, all measurements of the test performance have been performed by repeating the process 10 times, with different random initializations each time, and averaging the results.

The simple linear readout allowed us to train Bi-ESN by ridge regression, while all other models were trained by mini-batched gradient descent using the Adam algorithm [21] and cross entropy as loss function. This led to a very short training time for Bi-ESN, which allowed us to cheaply compute also an ensemble out of the predictions of 10 identical networks with different random initializations (we simply average the output scores and then take as final prediction the class corresponding to the highest averaged score). As before, also for the

---

[1] http://cogcomp.org/Data/QA/QC/.

[2] Source code for reproducing the experiments is available at https://github.com/danieleds/qc_with_untrained_recurrent_embeddings.

ensemble we repeat the training process 10 times in order to compute a mean accuracy and standard deviation, for a total of $10 \times 10 = 100$ repetitions.

For model selection of Bi-ESN and Bi-ESN-Att, we chose the number of recurrent units N_R within $[500, 10000]$. The values for ω and ρ have been selected in $[e^{-7}, e^4]$, while the connectivity ratio of the input-to-reservoir matrix and leaking rate have been chosen in $(0, 1)$. The ESN hyperparameters have been chosen separately for the forward and backward direction. For Bi-ESN-Att, the number of units N_D has been selected in $\{128, 256, 512\}$. Regarding the optimization algorithm, we chose a learning rate in $[e^{-9}, e^{-3}]$ and an early stopping strategy with a maximum of 500 epochs, while for regularization we used dropout and a weight decay strength in $[e^{-9}, 1]$. In the case of Bi-ESN, which is instead trained by ridge regression, we simply choose the regularization parameter λ_r within $[10^{-6}, 10^6]$. For searching within the hyperparameter space we used a combination of random search [4], simulated annealing [22] and tree-structured Parzen estimator [3]: at each iteration, we randomly choose one of these three algorithms to select the next point in the hyperparameter space.

6   Results

The results of our experiments are reported in Table 1. For comparison, we also report the performance achieved by state-of-the-art models in the literature.

The first important observation that can be drawn from Table 1 is that all our proposed models which are based on an ESN, and that are thus exploiting a completely untrained recurrent dynamics, are able to compete against a fully trained Bi-GRU. In the case of the ensemble model, the accuracy is even matched. The remarkable fact is that this comes with an extremely lower training cost for the Bi-ESN which has turned out to be at least 70 times more efficient than Bi-GRU. In fact even the ensemble model, which requires the training of 10 differently initialized classifiers, is still highly competitive against the Bi-GRU in terms of training time (and could trivially be further improved by applying parallelization between the different instances).

Adding an attention mechanism on top of the ESN as we did with Bi-ESN-Att led to a gain in predictive performance with respect to Bi-ESN, but this gain was rather limited. This may be due to the relative simplicity of the TREC dataset, which exhibits short sentences with a relatively simple structure. In fact, many sentences start with "Who is", "How many", "Where is", "When did", and so on. The bidirectional architecture (and in particular the backward direction), then, seems sufficient to capture these important features in the data, as illustrated in Fig. 4. Still, Bi-ESN-Att is more efficient than a simple Bi-GRU, requiring just one-seventh of the time to get trained.

Regarding the reported literature results it is worth noticing that, regarding the SVM [31] and KDA [9], the authors do not specify how model selection was performed, so it is difficult to provide a uniform comparison of the generalization capability of these models when compared to our own. Also, among the different results shown for different configurations of the approaches, we have reported

Table 1. Results on the TREC dataset. Asterisks indicate those models for which the methodology for model selection was not specified (see the text for details).

Our implementations

Model	Accuracy	Training time
Bi-GRU	93.8 ± 0.4	450s ± 40
Bi-ESN	93.3 ± 0.6	6s ± 1
Bi-ESN, ensemble	93.8 ± 0.2	62s ± 17
Bi-ESN-Att	93.5 ± 0.9	65s ± 8

Previous literature

Model	Accuracy
SVM [31]	95.0 *
Paragraph Vector [37]	91.8
Ada-CNN [37]	92.4
CNN-non-static [20]	93.6
CNN-multichannel [20]	92.2
DCNN [19]	93.0
KDA [9]	94.3 *
LSTM [38]	93.2
Bi-LSTM [38]	93.0
C-LSTM [38]	94.6
U_T [7]	93.2
CNN_{rnd} [7]	97.9
$U_T + CNN_{w2v}$ [7]	98.7

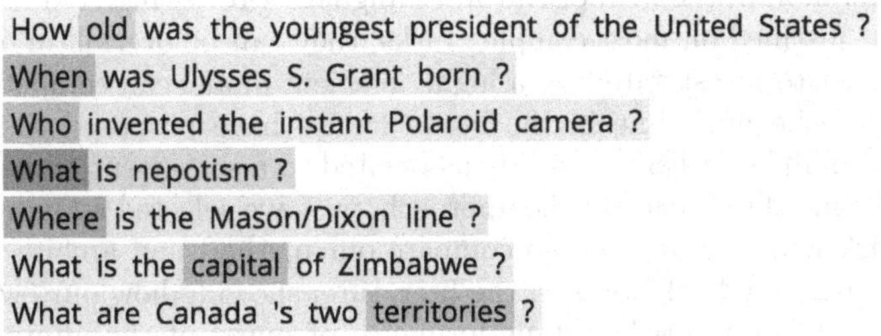

How old was the youngest president of the United States ?
When was Ulysses S. Grant born ?
Who invented the instant Polaroid camera ?
What is nepotism ?
Where is the Mason/Dixon line ?
What is the capital of Zimbabwe ?
What are Canada 's two territories ?

Fig. 4. Visualization of the intensity of the attention scores assigned by Bi-ESN-Att to some of the sentences in the dataset. As you can see, it is common for the network to focus mainly on the first word of the sentence since it carries the most important information for the task. This specific region of focus is implicitly provided by any bidirectional architecture without the need of self-attention.

the best on the test set as highlighted by the authors. Moreover, the SVM uses as features 60 highly engineered hand-coded rules, which could directly harm generalization when applied to other datasets. The CNN_{rnd} from [7] should have an architecture identical to the one previously introduced in [20], but the authors do not provide an explanation for the extremely high increase in accuracy with respect to the original paper. Finally, models U_T and $U_T + CNN_{w2v}$ make use of sentence embedding transfer learning, with weights trained on unrelated tasks on large text corpora, while we only make use of the examples within the TREC dataset and limit our use of transfer learning just to pre-trained word embeddings.

In light of the above considerations we can see how, with no more than 65 s of training time, our proposed models are able to approach or match the predictive performance of many of the models in the literature, with a few above-mentioned exceptions which could be attributed to a different model selection strategy or to the heavy use of transfer learning. A notable observation is how our Bi-ESN, with only 6 s of training time, is able to match (and slightly surpass) a fully trained Bi-LSTM, which is an architectural superset of our Bi-GRU for which we can thus estimate a supposedly similar (or worse) training time of around 7.5 min.

We were not able to reach the high accuracy of U_T+CNN$_{w2v}$ [7], however we want to highlight the fact that U_T and U_T+CNN$_{w2v}$ have more than 200M parameters. In comparison, our largest model (Bi-ESN-Att) has just 1.6M trainable parameters and, despite that, all our proposed models are able to compete with U_T, which uses the encoder of a transformer and is pre-trained with data from Wikipedia, web news, web question-answer pages and other sources.

7 Conclusion

Sophisticated architectures requiring high amounts of computational resources are not uncommon in the field of Natural Language Processing. While definitely effective and justified on most complex tasks, they can be overkill in other situations. In order to investigate how a highly efficient model can compete in these situations, for the first time in the literature we have proposed the use of a bidirectional multi-ring ESN, possibly associated to a self-attention mechanism.

To determine the efficacy of the approach, we have selected a Question Classification task which allowed us to compare our method and architecture with those of different kinds of works in the literature, showing how our own is comparable with the state-of-the-art performance of many of the alternatives. In the cases where a direct comparison has been possible, this showed the extreme efficiency of the proposed models.

In particular, we have demonstrated how a Bi-ESN shows basically the same accuracy of another recurrent model, Bi-GRU, while however presenting notable computational advantages, namely (1) not requiring any gating mechanism, and (2) keeping the input and recurrent weights untrained. In other words, the largest percentage of computational time used for training a GRU is actually unnecessary and detrimental. This can only get worse with other gated models, like LSTMs, for which to the same state size corresponds a higher number of parameters that need to be trained.

In addition, we showed how our Bi-ESN model is still able to compete against the more advanced attention mechanism of Bi-ESN-Att, which we showed to determine an improvement in accuracy that however, at least on this dataset, is quite limited. Still, the use of Bi-ESN-Att can be of interest even on this kind of dataset when looking for a more interpretable (and very efficient) model.

While within the limits of an analysis which has been focused on a Question Classification task, our results show the potential of Reservoir Computing methods and of their possible evolution. This potential is especially tangible with respect to the extreme efficiency of these methods, which is increasingly important in Natural Language Processing contexts that are often characterized by considerable amounts of data.

As future works, we plan to extend our analysis to more complex tasks in which an attention mechanism can have a higher impact. Moreover, we would like to assess the role of multiple recurrent layers as in DeepESN [12,13], which could provide richer information at different time scales, and of kernels [9], which could help extract more interesting features from the data. Finally, given the recently proven effectiveness of large language models for transfer learning [10,28], it would be interesting to explore how Reservoir Computing approaches can reduce the huge amount of time required to train these models, both in the case of training the language model itself, and in the case of training the task-dependent network.

References

1. Bahdanau, D., Cho, K., Bengio, Y.: Neural machine translation by jointly learning to align and translate. In: 3rd International Conference on Learning Representations, ICLR 2015, Conference Track Proceedings (2015). http://arxiv.org/abs/1409.0473
2. Bengio, Y., Simard, P.Y., Frasconi, P.: Learning long-term dependencies with gradient descent is difficult. IEEE Trans. Neural Netw. 5(2), 157–166 (1994)
3. Bergstra, J., Bardenet, R., Bengio, Y., Kégl, B.: Algorithms for hyper-parameter optimization. In: Advances in Neural Information Processing Systems 24: 25th Annual Conference on Neural Information Processing Systems 2011. Proceedings of a Meeting Held at Granada, Spain, 12–14 December 2011, pp. 2546–2554 (2011)
4. Bergstra, J., Bengio, Y.: Random search for hyper-parameter optimization. J. Mach. Learn. Res. 13, 281–305 (2012)
5. Bianchi, F.M., Scardapane, S., Løkse, S., Jenssen, R.: Bidirectional deep-readout echo state networks. In: 26th European Symposium on Artificial Neural Networks, ESANN 2018 (2018)
6. Boedecker, J., Obst, O., Mayer, N.M., Asada, M.: Studies on reservoir initialization and dynamics shaping in echo state networks. In: Proceedings of the 17th European Symposium on Artificial Neural Networks (ESANN), pp. 227–232. d-side publi (2009)
7. Cer, D., et al.: Universal sentence encoder for English. In: Proceedings of the 2018 Conference on Empirical Methods in Natural Language Processing, EMNLP 2018: System Demonstrations, pp. 169–174. Association for Computational Linguistics (2018)
8. Cho, K., et al.: Learning phrase representations using RNN encoder-decoder for statistical machine translation. In: Proceedings of the 2014 Conference on Empirical Methods in Natural Language Processing, EMNLP 2014, pp. 1724–1734. ACL (2014)

9. Croce, D., Filice, S., Basili, R.: On the impact of linguistic information in kernel-based deep architectures. In: Esposito, F., Basili, R., Ferilli, S., Lisi, F. (eds.) AI*IA 2017. LNCS, vol. 10640, pp. 359–371. Springer, Cham (2017). https://doi.org/10.1007/978-3-319-70169-1_27

10. Devlin, J., Chang, M., Lee, K., Toutanova, K.: BERT: pre-training of deep bidirectional transformers for language understanding. CoRR abs/1810.04805 (2018). http://arxiv.org/abs/1810.04805

11. Gallicchio, C., Micheli, A.: Architectural and Markovian factors of echo state networks. Neural Netw. 24(5), 440–456 (2011)

12. Gallicchio, C., Micheli, A.: Deep reservoir computing: a critical analysis. In: 24th European Symposium on Artificial Neural Networks, ESANN 2016 (2016)

13. Gallicchio, C., Micheli, A., Pedrelli, L.: Deep reservoir computing: a critical experimental analysis. Neurocomputing 268, 87–99 (2017)

14. Grave, E., Bojanowski, P., Gupta, P., Joulin, A., Mikolov, T.: Learning word vectors for 157 languages. In: Proceedings of the International Conference on Language Resources and Evaluation (LREC 2018) (2018)

15. Hochreiter, S., Schmidhuber, J.: Long short-term memory. Neural Comput. 9(8), 1735–1780 (1997)

16. Jaeger, H.: The "echo state" approach to analysing and training recurrent neural networks - with an erratum note. Technical report. German National Research Center for Information Technology GMD, Bonn, Germany (2001)

17. Jaeger, H., Haas, H.: Harnessing nonlinearity: predicting chaotic systems and saving energy in wireless communication. Science 304(5667), 78–80 (2004)

18. Jaeger, H., Lukosevicius, M., Popovici, D., Siewert, U.: Optimization and applications of echo state networks with leaky-integrator neurons. Neural Netw. 20(3), 335–352 (2007). https://doi.org/10.1016/j.neunet.2007.04.016

19. Kalchbrenner, N., Grefenstette, E., Blunsom, P.: A convolutional neural network for modelling sentences. In: Proceedings of the 52nd Annual Meeting of the Association for Computational Linguistics, ACL 2014, Volume 1: Long Papers, pp. 655–665. The Association for Computer Linguistics (2014)

20. Kim, Y.: Convolutional neural networks for sentence classification. In: Proceedings of the 2014 Conference on Empirical Methods in Natural Language Processing, EMNLP 2014, pp. 1746–1751. ACL (2014)

21. Kingma, D.P., Ba, J.: Adam: a method for stochastic optimization. In: 3rd International Conference on Learning Representations, ICLR 2015, Conference Track Proceedings (2015)

22. Kirkpatrick, S., Gelatt, D., Vecchi, M.P.: Optimization by simulated annealing. Science 220(4598), 671–680 (1983)

23. Lei, Z., Yang, Y., Yang, M., Liu, Y.: A multi-sentiment-resource enhanced attention network for sentiment classification. In: Proceedings of the 56th Annual Meeting of the Association for Computational Linguistics, ACL 2018, Volume 2: Short Papers, pp. 758–763. Association for Computational Linguistics (2018)

24. Li, X., Roth, D.: Learning question classifiers. In: 19th International Conference on Computational Linguistics, COLING 2002 (2002)

25. Lin, Z., et al.: A structured self-attentive sentence embedding. In: 5th International Conference on Learning Representations, ICLR 2017, Conference Track Proceedings (2017)

26. Lukosevicius, M., Jaeger, H.: Reservoir computing approaches to recurrent neural network training. Comput. Sci. Rev. 3(3), 127–149 (2009)

27. Paszke, A., et al.: Automatic differentiation in PyTorch (2017). https://openreview.net/forum?id=BJJsrmfCZ

28. Radford, A., Wu, J., Child, R., Luan, D., Amodei, D., Sutskever, I.: Language models are unsupervised multitask learners (2019). https://d4mucfpksywv.cloudfront.net/better-language-models/language-models.pdf
29. Sachan, D.S., Zaheer, M., Salakhutdinov, R.: Revisiting LSTM networks for semi-supervised text classification via mixed objective function. In: AAAI 2019 (2019)
30. Schuster, M., Paliwal, K.K.: Bidirectional recurrent neural networks. IEEE Trans. Signal Process. **45**(11), 2673–2681 (1997)
31. da Silva, J.P.C.G., Coheur, L., Mendes, A.C., Wichert, A.: From symbolic to sub-symbolic information in question classification. Artif. Intell. Rev. **35**(2), 137–154 (2011)
32. Strauss, T., Wustlich, W., Labahn, R.: Design strategies for weight matrices of echo state networks. Neural Comput. **24**(12), 3246–3276 (2012)
33. Strubell, E., Ganesh, A., McCallum, A.: Energy and policy considerations for deep learning in NLP. In: ACL, no. 1, pp. 3645–3650. Association for Computational Linguistics (2019)
34. Vaswani, A., et al.: Attention is all you need. In: Advances in Neural Information Processing Systems 30: Annual Conference on Neural Information Processing Systems, pp. 6000–6010 (2017)
35. Verstraeten, D., Schrauwen, B., D'Haene, M., Stroobandt, D.: An experimental unification of reservoir computing methods. Neural Netw. **20**(3), 391–403 (2007)
36. Yildiz, I.B., Jaeger, H., Kiebel, S.J.: Re-visiting the echo state property. Neural Netw. **35**, 1–9 (2012)
37. Zhao, H., Lu, Z., Poupart, P.: Self-adaptive hierarchical sentence model. In: Proceedings of the Twenty-Fourth International Joint Conference on Artificial Intelligence, IJCAI 2015, pp. 4069–4076. AAAI Press (2015)
38. Zhou, C., Sun, C., Liu, Z., Lau, F.C.M.: A C-LSTM neural network for text classification. CoRR abs/1511.08630 (2015). http://arxiv.org/abs/1511.08630

Prediction of Decline in Activities of Daily Living Through Deep Artificial Neural Networks and Domain Adaptation

Lorenzo Donati[ID], Daniele Fongo[ID], Luca Cattelani[✉][ID],
and Federico Chesani[ID]

Department of Computer Science and Engineering, University of Bologna,
Bologna, Italy
luca.cattelani@unibo.it

Abstract. In order to improve information available at the clinical level and to better focus resources for preventive interventions, it is paramount to estimate the general exposure to risk of adverse health events, commonly referred as frailty. This study compares the performance of shallow and deep multilayer perceptrons (sMLP and dMLP), and of long short-term memories (LSTM), on the prediction of a subject decline in activities of daily living, with and without a previous autoencoder based domain adaptation from an external dataset. Samples originates from two large epidemiological datasets: the English Longitudinal Study of Ageing (ELSA) and The Irish Longitudinal Study on Ageing, with 107879 and 15710 eligible samples, respectively. Deep networks performed better than shallow ones, while dMLP and LSTM performance were similar. Domain adaptation improved predictive ability in all comparisons. On the bigger ELSA dataset, sMLP attains a Brier score of 0.32 without domain adaptation, and 0.15 with domain adaptation, while dMLP attains 0.20 and 0.11, respectively. Thus, experimental results support the use of deep architectures in the prediction of functional decline, and of domain adaptation when data from another similar domain is available. These results may help improving the state of the art in predictive models for clinical practice and population screening.

Keywords: Artificial neural networks · Deep learning · Domain adaptation · Frailty · Risk assessment · Transfer learning

1 Introduction

Many persons, due to age but also other factors, are subject to a generally increased risk of adverse health events. This state of increased risk is commonly called frailty [15,39]. Frailty leads to an increased risk of various adverse outcomes, like functional decline, loss of self sufficiency, and death [9,11,34].

Differently from other measures that capture the present state of a person [10,24,25], frailty measures expectation for future states. Lacking a consensus

© Springer Nature Switzerland AG 2019
M. Alviano et al. (Eds.): AI*IA 2019, LNAI 11946, pp. 376–391, 2019.
https://doi.org/10.1007/978-3-030-35166-3_27

on an exact outcome to predict, on the temporal aspects of the prediction, and on the importance of the various observables, numerous frailty definitions and measures have been proposed [7,17,35].

Frailty measures may be adopted in clinical practice, and the predictive validity of some of them have been analyzed [14]. After identifying the most frail persons, an intervention program to reduce their risk exposure can be deployed. Various programs have been tested, mostly, but not exclusively, based on physical exercise [45,51,56].

It can be argued that dichotomizing the population in frail and not frail individuals may be too coarse grained for most applications, and it can be more effective to see frailty as a scalar index, or even as a composition of scalar indexes, one for each aspect of interest. In this work, frailty indicators have been tested as predictors of the specific outcome of developing an ADL (activity of daily living) or IADL (instrumental activity of daily living) disability [23,52].

Together with classical statistical models, we assist to an increasing application of machine learning techniques in the health domain [48]. In recent years there has been an explosion of artificial neural networks (ANNs) [43] and deep learning (DL) [33] applications in many fields. The most common form of "deep neural network" (DNN) is the multilayer perceptron (MLP), where connections between units do not form cycles (feedforward ANN). When inputs are sequences of observations, recurrent neural networks (RNNs) may be leveraged to capture the dynamics of the sequences via cycles in the network of nodes [4,36,37]. A particularly widespread and successful RNNs is the long short-term memory (LSTM) for its ability to learn relationships across long sequences of observations [26]. ANN, RNN, and DL have been applied profusely and with clear benefits to the health domain [38,40,46,47], that is the focus of this work.

Many recent DL results are produced by the combination of supervised learning and unsupervised learning [3,5]. Typically, unsupervised pre-training is exploited to extract effective high-level features that are then used as input by the supervised training [19]. One of the most used techniques in unsupervised pre-training is the autoencoder [53].

Sometimes there is a target domain with no/few labelled samples, and a similar domain with many labelled samples. The domain adaptation problem, also often called transfer learning, concerns exploiting the existing labelled data from a domain, called source domain, to learn useful knowledge to be adapted/transferred to a target domain [1,57]. Domain adaptation for deep learning has been studied mostly for visual applications [13,41,55], but also for other domains, like speech [16], sentiment classification [22], or health [44].

Starting from two well established north-European epidemiological datasets, namely the English Longitudinal Study of Ageing (ELSA) [27,50] and The Irish Longitudinal Study on Ageing (TILDA) [28,29,58], we trained various configurations of DNNs in estimating the risk for young-old community dwelling persons of suffering a functional decline with respect to ADL and IADL. We used unsupervised pre-training by autoencoders followed by supervised training by neural networks, both MLP and LSTM, and performed domain adaptation from one dataset to the other. To the best of our knowledge, this is the first application of DNN with domain adaptation to epidemiological datasets in order to estimate the risk of decline in ADL and IADL. Being this a complex and possibly time-dependent domain, the final intent of this project was to test the following issues.

- Measure the effectiveness of an ANN classifier when used to predict decline in ADL and IADL.
- Verify if the long-time dependencies in the datasets are meaningful for the prediction, by comparing MLP and RNN approaches.
- Measure the effectiveness of using an autoencoder to perform a knowledge transfer between different datasets.

We compared the use of shallow vs. deep networks, MLP vs. LSTM, unsupervised pre-training with autoencoders vs. no pre-training. In Sect. 2 we describe the datasets, the operationalization of the outcome, the preprocessing steps, including the feature selection, the algorithms and hyperparameters of the various ANNs tested, and the quality measures collected. In Sect. 3 we list the hyperparameters that produced the best results for each type of ANN and quality measure. The best results for each net are also depicted. These are discussed in Sect. 4, and some conclusions are drawn in Sect. 5.

2   Methods

2.1   Domain and Outcome

The project, whose details are more thoroughly reported by Donati [18] and Fongo [20] in their Master theses, analyses the data of two longitudinal studies on ageing-related parameters in order to predict the functional decline of young-old patients.

The two datasets are collected respectively by ELSA [27] and TILDA [28,58]. The datasets are divided in waves, each one representing the biennial report on health, economic, and social information for every subject of the study. The data are acquired through periodical questionnaires and medical tests. The available data spans over a wide variety of semantic meanings, e.g. the subject's weight, the reaction time to specific stimuli measured in seconds, the amount of debts or assets divided in economic categories, the education of the subject, etc. For the ELSA dataset, we also have access to the relative values for the subject's spouse, if available.

The ELSA dataset is made of 107,879 records spread over 6 waves, and collects 570 different metrics. The data are all represented as numeric values, mapping eventual categorical metrics onto an integer variable.

Since the TILDA study is more recent, the relative dataset is made of only 15,710 records divided in 2 waves, but collects over 1600 metrics. Furthermore, the data are represented either as numeric values or categorical strings.

The measured outcome is the worsening of the functional status of the subjects. As a proxy value we used the sum of ADLs and IADLs [49] scores, reported by both the datasets. ADLs and IADLs represent the amount of self-care activities that a person has to manage in order to be fully independent, therefore we used the drop of their summed score between two consecutive waves as a measure of functional decline.

We decided not to define custom features to treat the death of the subjects in order to leave the network unbiased. Furthermore, we only had access to the time of death for one of the two datasets, and even in that case we had no way to distinguish between an accidental death and a natural death. As a result, the networks did not distinguish between a subject leaving the trial or dying, as in both case the functional status just stops updating like every other variables.

2.2 Preprocessing

During the pre-processing phase we converted at first every error value, representing different types of invalid or missing data, to a single error value.

Then, we automatically selected the most significant fields of each dataset through an implementation of the Minimum Redundancy Maximum Relevance (mRMR) algorithm based on a study by Berrendero [6]. The mRMR algorithms guarantee the correctness of the selection by ranking the fields in order of relevance with respect to the target field (i.e. the functional status in our case) and then choosing the subset with the least redundancy among one another. In particular, to measure both the relevance and the redundancy we used the correlation coefficient for the numerical data and the mutual information for the categorical data.

In the final step of the pre-processing we normalized the numerical variables through feature scaling and projected the categorical variables onto one-hot vectors. The input layer of the neural networks was made by concatenating all the processed fields in a single vector of 321 floating point nodes.

2.3 Development

To predict the functional decline of the subjects we tried several approaches, using multiple neural network classifiers and even introducing a Stacked Denoising Autoencoder (SDAE) [54]. The SDAE is a particular neural network trained through unsupervised learning that is able to extract high-level features from the raw data. In this project we used the SDAE to perform a knowledge transfer between the two reference datasets by training thoroughly the network on a source dataset and then use the trained network on a different target dataset. In order to compare the performance of the three different implemented classifiers and also measure the knowledge transfer provided by the Stacked Denoising Autoencoder, we defined two parallel data flows.

In the first one, the classifiers are trained on the raw data of the two datasets, while in the second path the SDAE is trained to extract high-level features from the raw data and then the classifiers are trained on the encoded data to verify the eventual improvement in the quality of the classification granted by the knowledge transfer.

The SDAE was made by nesting up to three Denoising Autoencoders with Masking noise one within the other, and it was trained using unsupervised learning in order to reproduce at each layer the uncorrupted signal of the outer layer.

We tried three different approaches to the classification through neural networks.

The baseline classifier is a shallow Multilayer Perceptron (sMLP) with only one hidden layer. This is one of the simplest neural networks and it serves as a comparison for more complex networks that are slower to train but could bear more accurate results.

We also implemented a deep Multilayer Perceptron (dMLP) with up to three hidden layers in order to verify if the functional decline can be predicted using only the last (most recent) observation of the subjects.

Conversely, to test the hypothesis of the time-dependence we introduced a LSTM classifier that analyses the whole timeline of a patient in order to perform a more accurate prediction.

All the classifiers output a probability of functional decline and were trained using a cost-sensitive backpropagation algorithm (or backpropagation through time for the LSTM) applied to the Kullback–Leibler divergence loss function [31]. Furthermore, we trained all the three classifiers and the SDAE with a stochastic gradient descent (SGD) algorithm, and in order to reduce overfitting we used an implementation of the early-stop algorithm with look-ahead proposed by Prechelt [42]. These choices were made to reflect the state-of-the-art in deep neural network technology and are de facto standards in most of the current implementations [2,33,59].

2.4   Validation

In order to validate the hyperparameters of each neural network, we divided the datasets into a training set, a validation set, and a test set (respectively 70%, 20%, and 10% of the original datasets) using a holdout process and granting the integrity of the timelines.

At first we trained the classifiers on the raw data (not encoded by the SDAE) and we validated their hyperparameters through a grid search from a pool of possible values. Since the loss function used during the training was itself one of the hyperparameters, in the validation phase we relied on four external metrics to measure the quality of the classification: the Accuracy of the prediction, the Cohen's Kappa [12], the Brier Score [8], and the Area Under the ROC Curve (AUC) [32]. We decided to use both the Brier Score and the Cohen's Kappa because the former represents a cost function for predicting the wrong outcome, while the latter is a robust measure of inter-rater reliability which takes into account the possibility of the agreement occurring by chance.

After the validation of the classifiers, we trained the SDAE in a two-phases process. At first we performed a greedy layer-wise pre-training with data stochastically acquired from both the datasets, then we fine-tuned the network through deep-learning using data from only one of the datasets and we validated it on the data of the other dataset in order to measure the knowledge transfer from the first to the second dataset provided by the SDAE.

The validation of the SDAE was performed on a pool of possible hyperparameters through a grid-search. Furthermore, the SDAE's hyperparameters were validated to maximize the quality of the classification done by the four downstream classifiers as measured by the four aforementioned metrics.

For the neural networks we explored an extensive set of hyperparameters: two optimization functions using either Stochastic Gradient Descent or Stochastic Adam [30], a batch size in {32, 64, 128, 256}, an initial learning rate in {0.1, 0.01, 0.001}, a learning rate decay either fractional ($\frac{1}{1+t}$) or exponential (α^t, with $\alpha = 0.99$), an activation function of the hidden layers using either softplus, ReLU, logistic function, or hyperbolic tangent, a weight initialization using either a Gaussian or Xavier initializer [21], and an optional Gaussian noise (standard deviation equal to 0.05) on the input layer of the classifiers. We also explored several state sizes for the hidden layers depending on the network. The elements between square brackets represent a single network with multiple layers having each one a number of nodes equal to the corresponding value (e.g. [100, 50] is a two-layers network with 100 nodes in the first layer and 50 in the second). Regarding the SDAE, the notation refers to the encoding network, with the decoding network being reversed.

- LSTM: {50, 100, 200, 300}
- dMLP: {[100, 50], [200, 100], [200, 100, 50], [300, 200, 100], [150, 150], [300, 300], [150, 150, 150], [300, 300, 300]}
- sMLP: {100, 200, 300, 400, 500, 600, 700, 800}
- SDAE: {100, 300, 500, [150, 75, 25], [300, 150, 50], [100, 100, 100], [300, 300, 300]}

Finally, for the SDAE we also tested two different loss function using either the root-mean-square error (RMSE) or the cross-entropy (CE), and a masking noise on the input layer in 0.3, 0.6, 0.9. For the inner Denoising Autoencoders we always used a Gaussian noise instead during the greedy layer-wise pre-training.

3   Results

3.1   Optimal Hyperparameters

After the validation phase we found out that most of the hyperparameters had the same optimal value across all the networks, namely the Adam optimizer, the batch size equal to 128 items, the exponential learning rate decay, the hyperbolic tangent activation function, and the Xavier initializer. Furthermore, the added Gaussian noise always improved the robustness and ultimately the quality of the classification.

For the LSTM the best learning rate was 0.001 and the best state size was 200. The dMLP got optimal results with learning rate equal to 0.001 and state size equal to [300, 300, 300]. The sMLP preferred a bigger initial learning rate of 0.01 and a state size of 400 nodes.

For the SDAE we found different optimal learning rates, loss functions, input masking noises and state sizes, depending on three factors: the direction of the knowledge transfer between the two datasets (ELSA to TILDA or TILDA to ELSA, EtoT and TtoE from now on), the downstream classifier (LSTM, dMLP or sMLP), and the metric used to measure the quality of the classification (Accuracy, Cohen's Kappa, Brier Score, or AUC). The detailed optimal hyperparameters for the SDAE are reported in the Tables 1, 2 and 3, but in most cases for the knowledge transfer in direction EtoT it was preferred a learning rate of 0.01, the RMSE loss function, a 30% masking noise and a state size equal to 300 nodes, while in direction TtoE we found better performance with a learning rate equal to 0.001, the cross-entropy loss function, a masking noise between 30% and 60%, and a state size of [300, 300, 300].

Table 1. Best SDAE hyperparameters w.r.t. sMLP classification

		Loss	LR	Noise	Size
EtoT	Accuracy	RMSE	0.01	0.3	300
	Kappa				
	Brier				
	AUC	CE	0.001		[300, 300, 300]
TtoE	Accuracy	CE	0.001	0.3	[300, 300, 300]
	Kappa				
	Brier				
	AUC				

Table 2. Best SDAE hyperparameters w.r.t. dMLP classification

		Loss	LR	Noise	Size
EtoT	Accuracy	RMSE	0.01	0.3	300
	Kappa				
	Brier				100
	AUC			0.6	300
TtoE	Accuracy	RMSE	0.001	0.3	100
	Kappa				
	Brier			0.6	[300, 300, 300]
	AUC	CE		0.3	

Table 3. Best SDAE hyperparameters w.r.t. LSTM classification

		Loss	LR	Noise	Size
EtoT	Accuracy	RMSE	0.01	0.3	300
	Kappa				
	Brier	CE			500
	AUC	RMSE			
TtoE	Accuracy	CE	0.001	0.6	[300, 300, 300]
	Kappa				
	Brier				
	AUC				

3.2 Metrics

As shown in Fig. 1, the accuracy of the classifiers on the raw Tilda's test set spanned from a minimum of 73% to a maximum of 85%, while on the raw Elsa's test set the accuracy was as low as 45% and at best equal to 72%. When the same test was performed on Tilda's data encoded with a SDAE that was previously fine-tuned on Elsa's dataset (EtoT) the accuracy reached 90% or more for every classifier. Vice versa, the accuracy on the encoded Elsa's test set (TtoE) spanned between 80% and 89%, with a maximum increase of +35% points relative to the shallow MLP.

The Cohen's Kappa, as shown in Fig. 2, saw an average increase of +0.25 points when measured on the encoded Tilda test sets compared to the raw data, and an average increase of +0,37 points thanks to the encoding of Elsa's test set.

The Brier score reported in Fig. 3 was almost always halved by the application of the SDAE encoding on the two test sets.

Finally, the AUC reported in Fig. 4 shows an average improvement of 0.10 and 0.15 points on Tilda and Elsa's test sets respectively thanks to the application of the SDAE.

4 Discussion

Since most of the optimal hyperparameters are shared between all the classifiers and even the SDAE, it may be possible that they are better suited to encapsulate some of the inner characteristics of the problem we are trying to solve. For example, the batch size could be correlated with the size of the datasets and their specific inner variance, while the hyperbolic tangent may compute at best over the nuances of the signal carried by the normalized input vector.

Regarding the SDAE's hyperparameters, we can observe a clear divergence between the two directions of the knowledge transfer. EtoT transfer generally works better when performed by a shallower SDAE with a learning rate equal to 0.01, while TtoE prefers a deeper SDAE with a slower learning rate. This

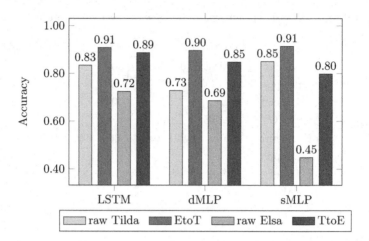

Fig. 1. Accuracy of the three probabilistic classifiers on ELSA and TILDA test sets, both before and after SDAE encoding. The higher, the better.

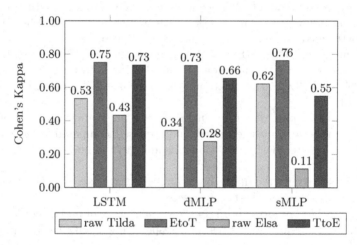

Fig. 2. Cohen's Kappa of the three probabilistic classifiers on ELSA and TILDA test sets, both before and after SDAE encoding. The higher, the better.

property reflects the underlying characteristics of the two datasets. In fact, being Tilda smaller in size and more consistent while also having less invalid or missing values or records, it's easier to extract patterns and knowledge from the more complex Elsa dataset and then transfer them into the simpler one, thus causing a optimal network that is smaller and faster. On the contrary, acquiring enough knowledge from a simple environment in order to extract significant features from a complex environment is far more difficult and requires a bigger network and a slower albeit more accurate training.

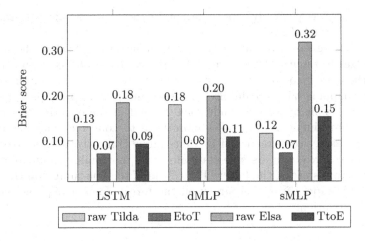

Fig. 3. Brier score of the three probabilistic classifiers on ELSA and TILDA test sets, both before and after SDAE encoding. The lower, the better.

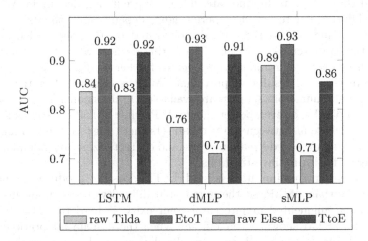

Fig. 4. AUC of the three probabilistic classifiers on ELSA and TILDA test sets, both before and after SDAE encoding. The higher, the better.

Analysing the results provided by the four metrics, we can notice that both deep classifiers are more consistent across all the experiments when compared to the sMLP. The LSTM performed especially well compared to every other classifier when applied on the raw data of both datasets. This phenomenon is particularly evident when looking at the raw Elsa data, since that dataset has 6 waves and thus it contains more temporal information compared to Tilda.

On a further analysis, regardless of the initial performance on the raw data, after the encoding performed by the SDAE all the neural network classifiers reached similar values for almost all the metrics, meaning that the domain adaptation process was probably more relevant to the final classification than the choice of the actual classifier.

It can be argued that during the pre-training of the SDAE, the network acknowledges too much of the target dataset (although limited to its training set) and therefore it could learn to use different neurons depending on the dataset instead of mapping one domain into the other and performing a proper knowledge transfer. This hypothesis finds some ground in the experimental results, since the pre-training usually takes more time to converge than fine-tuning. However the faster convergence of the fine-tuning is mostly attributable to the network being already in a stable state after the pre-training, compared to the random starting state of the latter. The effects of the fine-tuning on the source domain with respect to the accuracy on the target domain requires therefore further investigation.

5   Conclusion

We found that ANNs techniques are viable for predicting decline in ADL and IADL, exhibiting fair to excellent performance depending on the data and the specific technique. We statistically demonstrated on two big epidemiological datasets the effectiveness of a tool in predicting decline, while its potential use and benefits in real environments are open to further studies.

The experimental results support that dMLP is clearly better than sMLP when sufficiently numerous samples are available. On the smaller TILDA dataset, sMLP is comparable or even better than dMLP, while dMLP is clearly better on ELSA. Somewhere in-between the two datasets there must be the turning point between the shallow and deep approaches, and characterizing this boundary may be of interest for future investigations.

When the domain adaptation is used, LSTM does not produce significantly better results than dMLP, so the augmented difficulty in providing historical data, and the augmented architectural complexity, is hard to justify. On the opposite the LSTM shows better efficacy when the domain adaptation is not used. It is arguable how much these results depend on the peculiarities of the datasets, having TILDA just 2 waves, and the general availability of long temporal chains of observations. These results are not conclusive and the relative performance of LSTM for the prediction of functional decline remains to be further investigated.

We demonstrated that domain adaptation can be a concrete tool when working with epidemiological data. Specifically, using an unsupervised pretraining phase on both source and target datasets with a SDAE, and then a supervised training only on source data, we obtained excellent results on the target dataset in all examined cases, without requiring labeled data from it. An open question is if the ability of SDAEs to extract common features from two epidemiological datasets may be pushed forward to reach a methodology for the full automation of dataset alignment, to merge two or more datasets into a common one without the time-consuming human micromanagement.

Acknowledgment. The data relative to ELSA were made available through the United Kingdom Data Archive - www.data-archive.ac.uk. ELSA was developed by a team of researchers based at the NatCen Social Research, University College London and the Institute for Fiscal Studies. The data were collected by NatCen Social Research. The funding is provided by the National Institute of Aging in the United States, and a consortium of United Kingdom government departments coordinated by the Office for National Statistics.

TILDA is an interinstitutional initiative led by Trinity College Dublin. TILDA data have been co-funded by the Government of Ireland through the Office of the Minister for Health and Children, by Atlantic Philanthropies, and by Irish Life; have been collected under the Statistics Act, 1993, of the Central Statistics Office. The project has been designed and implemented by the TILDA study team, Department of Health and Children. Copyright and all other intellectual property rights relating to the data are vested in TILDA. Ethical approval for each wave of data collection is granted by the Trinity College Research Ethics Committee. TILDA data is accessible for free from the following sites: Irish Social Science Data Archive at University College Dublin http://www. ucd.ie/issda/data/tilda/; Interuniversity Consortium for Political and Social Research at the University of Michigan (http://www.icpsr.umich.edu/icpsrweb/ICPSR/studies/ 34315).

The original data creators, depositors or copyright holders, the funders of the data collections and the archives of the datasets bear no responsibility for their further analysis or interpretation presented here.

Conflict of Interest. All authors declare no competing interests and to be aware of the submission of this manuscript.

References

1. Bengio, Y.: Deep learning of representations for unsupervised and transfer learning. In: JMLR Workshop Conference Proceedings, vol. 7, pp. 1–20 (2011). https://doi. org/10.1109/IJCNN.2011.6033302
2. Bengio, Y.: Practical recommendations for gradient-based training of deep architectures. CoRR abs/1206.5533 (2012). http://arxiv.org/abs/1206.5533
3. Bengio, Y.: Deep learning of representations: looking forward. In: Dediu, A.-H., Martín-Vide, C., Mitkov, R., Truthe, B. (eds.) SLSP 2013. LNCS, vol. 7978, pp. 1–37. Springer, Heidelberg (2013). https://doi.org/10.1007/978-3-642-39593-2_1
4. Bengio, Y., Boulanger-Lewandowski, N., Pascanu, R.: Advances in optimizing recurrent networks. In: 2013 IEEE International Conference on Acoustics, Speech and Signal Processing, pp. 8624–8628. IEEE (2013)
5. Bengio, Y., Courville, A., Vincent, P.: Representation learning: a review and new perspectives. IEEE Trans. Pattern Anal. Mach. Intell. **35**(8), 1798–1828 (2013). https://doi.org/10.1109/TPAMI.2013.50, http://www.ncbi.nlm.nih.gov/ pubmed/23787338
6. Berrendero, J.R., Cuevas, A., Torrecilla, J.L.: The mRMR variable selection method: a comparative study for functional data. J. Stat. Comput. Simul. **86**(5), 891–907 (2016). https://doi.org/10.1080/00949655.2015.1042378
7. Bouillon, K., et al.: Measures of frailty in population-based studies: an overview. BMC Geriatr. **13**(1), 64 (2013). https://doi.org/10.1186/1471-2318-13-64

8. Brier, G.W.: Verification of forecasts expressed in terms of probability. Mon. Weather Rev. **78**, 1 (1950). https://doi.org/10.1175/1520-0493(1950)078⟨0001: VOFEIT⟩2.0.CO;2

9. Buckinx, F., Rolland, Y., Reginster, J.Y., Ricour, C., Petermans, J., Bruyère, O.: Burden of frailty in the elderly population: perspectives for a public health challenge. Arch. Public Health **73**(1), 19 (2015). https://doi.org/10.1186/s13690-015-0068-x

10. Buz, J., Cortés-Rodríguez, M.: Measurement of the severity of disability in community-dwelling adults and older adults: interval-level measures for accurate comparisons in large survey data sets. BMJ Open **6**(9), e011842 (2016). https://doi.org/10.1136/bmjopen-2016-011842, https://bmjopen. bmj.com/content/6/9/e011842

11. Chang, S.F., Lin, P.L.: Frail phenotype and mortality prediction: a systematic review and meta-analysis of prospective cohort studies. Int. J. Nurs. Stud. **52**(8), 1362–1374 (2015). https://doi.org/10.1016/j.ijnurstu.2015.04.005

12. Cohen, J.: A coefficient of agreement for nominal scales. Educ. Psychol. Meas. **20**(1), 37–46 (1960). https://doi.org/10.1177/001316446002000104

13. Csurka, G.: Domain adaptation for visual applications: a comprehensive survey, pp. 1–46. CoRR abs/1702.05374 (2017). http://arxiv.org/abs/1702.05374

14. Daniels, R., Van Rossum, E., Beurskens, A., Van Den Heuvel, W., De Witte, L.: The predictive validity of three self-report screening instruments for identifying frail older people in the community. BMC Public Health **12**(1), 69 (2012). https://doi.org/10.1186/1471-2458-12-69

15. De Lepeleire, J., Iliffe, S., Mann, E., Degryse, J.M.: Frailty: an emerging concept for general practice. Br. J. Gen. Pract. **59**(562), 364–369 (2009). https://doi.org/10.3399/bjgp09X420653

16. Deng, J., Zhang, Z., Eyben, F., Schuller, B.: Autoencoder-based unsupervised domain adaptation for speech emotion recognition. IEEE Signal Process. Lett. **21**(9), 1068–1072 (2014). https://doi.org/10.1109/LSP.2014.2324759

17. Dent, E., Kowal, P., Hoogendijk, E.O.: Frailty measurement in research and clinical practice: a review. Eur. J. Intern. Med. **31**, 3–10 (2016). https://doi.org/10.1016/j.ejim.2016.03.007

18. Donati, L.: Domain adaptation through deep neural networks for health informatics (2017)

19. Erhan, D., Courville, A., Vincent, P.: Why does unsupervised pre-training help deep learning? J. Mach. Learn. Res. **11**, 625–660 (2010). https://doi.org/10.1145/1756006.1756025, http://portal.acm.org/citation.cfm?id=1756025

20. Fongo, D.: Previsione del declino funzionale tramite l'utilizzo di reti neurali ricorrenti (2017)

21. Glorot, X., Bengio, Y.: Understanding the difficulty of training deep feedforward neural networks. In: Teh, Y.W., Titterington, M. (eds.) Proceedings of the Thirteenth International Conference on Artificial Intelligence and Statistics. Proceedings of Machine Learning Research, vol. 9, pp. 249–256. PMLR, Chia Laguna Resort, Sardinia, Italy, 13–15 May 2010. http://proceedings.mlr.press/v9/glorot10a.html

22. Glorot, X., Bordes, A., Bengio, Y.: Domain adaptation for large-scale sentiment classification: a deep learning approach. In: Proceedings of the 28th International Conference on Machine Learning, no. 1, pp. 513–520 (2011). http://www.icml-2011.org/papers/342_icmlpaper.pdf

23. Gobbens, R.J.J., Van Assen, M.A.L.M.: The prediction of ADL and IADL disability using six physical indicators of frailty: a longitudinal study in the Netherlands. Curr. Gerontol. Geriatr. Res. **2014** (2014). https://doi.org/10.1155/2014/358137
24. Haley, S.M., et al.: Late life function and disability instrument: I. Development and evaluation of the disability component. J. Gerontol. A Biol. Sci. Med. Sci. **57**(4), M209–M216 (2002)
25. Haley, S.M., et al.: Late life function and disability instrument: II. Development and evaluation of the function component. J. Gerontol. A Biol. Sci. Med. Sci. **57**(4), M217–M222 (2002). https://doi.org/10.1093/gerona/57.4.M217
26. Hochreiter, S., Schmidhuber, J.: Long short-term memory. Neural Comput. **9**(8), 1–32 (1997). https://doi.org/10.1144/GSL.MEM.1999.018.01.02
27. Banks, J., Batty, G.D., Nazroo, J., Steptoe, A.: The dynamics of ageing: evidence from the English Longitudinal Study of Ageing 2002–15 (Wave 7). The Institute for Fiscal Studies (2016)
28. Kenny, R.A.: The Irish longitudinal study on ageing (TILDA) 2009–2011 (2014). https://doi.org/10.3886/ICPSR34315.v1
29. Kenny, R.A., et al.: The design of the Irish longitudinal study on ageing. Lifelong Learn. (2010)
30. Kingma, D.P., Ba, J.: Adam: a method for stochastic optimization. CoRR abs/1412.6980 (2014). http://arxiv.org/abs/1412.6980
31. Kullback, S., Leibler, R.A.: On information and sufficiency. Ann. Math. Stat. **22**(1), 79–86 (1951)
32. Kumar, R., Indrayan, A.: Receiver operating characteristic (ROC) curve for medical researchers. Indian Pediatr. **48**(4), 277–287 (2011). https://doi.org/10.1007/s13312-011-0055-4
33. Lecun, Y., Bengio, Y., Hinton, G.: Deep learning. Nature **521**(7553), 436–444 (2015). https://doi.org/10.1038/nature14539
34. Lee, L., Heckman, G., Molnar, F.J.: Frailty: identifying elderly patients at high risk of poor outcomes. Can. Fam. physician Mèdecin Fam. Can. **61**(3), 227–231 (2015). http://www.cfp.ca/content/61/3/227
35. Lee, L., Patel, T., Hillier, L.M., Maulkhan, N., Slonim, K., Costa, A.: Identifying frailty in primary care: a systematic review. Geriatr. Gerontol. Int. **17**(10), 1358–1377 (2017). https://doi.org/10.1111/ggi.12955
36. Lipton, Z.C., Berkowitz, J., Elkan, C.: A critical review of recurrent neural networks for sequence learning. arXiv preprint, pp. 1–38 (2015). https://doi.org/10.1145/2647868.2654889, http://arxiv.org/abs/1506.00019
37. Lipton, Z.C., Kale, D.C., Elkan, C., Wetzell, R.: Learning to diagnose with LSTM recurrent neural networks. In: ICLR, pp. 1–18 (2015). http://arxiv.org/abs/1511.03677
38. Lisboa, P.: A review of evidence of health benefit from artificial neural networks in medical intervention. Neural Netw. **15**(1), 11–39 (2002). https://doi.org/10.1016/S0893-6080(01)00111-3
39. Markle-Reid, M., Browne, G.: Conceptualizations of frailty in relation to older adults. J. Adv. Nurs. **44**(1), 58–68 (2003). https://doi.org/10.1046/j.1365-2648.2003.02767.x
40. Miotto, R., Wang, F., Wang, S., Jiang, X., Dudley, J.T.: Deep learning for healthcare: review, opportunities and challenges. Brief. Bioinform. (February) 1–11 (2017). https://doi.org/10.1093/bib/bbx044
41. Patel, V.M., Gopalan, R., Li, R., Chellappa, R.: Visual domain adaptation: a survey of recent advances. IEEE Signal Process. Mag. **32**(3), 53–69 (2015). https://doi.org/10.1109/MSP.2014.2347059

42. Prechelt, L.: Early stopping—but when? In: Montavon, G., Orr, G.B., Müller, K.-R. (eds.) Neural Networks: Tricks of the Trade. LNCS, vol. 7700, pp. 53–67. Springer, Heidelberg (2012). https://doi.org/10.1007/978-3-642-35289-8_5

43. Prieto, A., et al.: Neural networks: an overview of early research, current frameworks and new challenges. Neurocomputing **214**, 242–268 (2016). https://doi.org/10.1016/j.neucom.2016.06.014

44. Purushotham, S., Carvalho, W., Nilanon, T., Liu, Y.: Variational adversarial deep domain adaptation for health care time series analysis. In: 29th Conference on Neural Information Processing System (NIPS) (2016). https://wcarvalho.github.io/files/nips_2016/VADA_main.pdf

45. Puts, M.T., et al.: Interventions to prevent or reduce the level of frailty in community-dwelling older adults: a scoping review of the literature and international policies. Age Ageing **46**(3), 383–392 (2017). https://doi.org/10.1093/ageing/afw247

46. Ravi, D., et al.: Deep learning for health informatics. IEEE J. Biomed. Health Inform. **21**(1), 1 (2016). https://doi.org/10.1109/JBHI.2016.2636665, http://ieeexplore.ieee.org/document/7801947/

47. Robert, C., Arreto, C.D., Azerad, J., Gaudy, J.F.: Bibliometric overview of the utilization of artificial neural networks in medicine and biology. Scientometrics **59**(1), 117–130 (2004). https://doi.org/10.1023/B:SCIE.0000013302.59845.34

48. Song, X., Mitnitski, A., Cox, J., Rockwood, K.: Comparison of machine learning techniques with classical statistical models in predicting health outcomes. Medinfo **11**, 736–740 (2004)

49. Spector, W.D., Fleishman, J.: Combining activities of daily living with instrumental activities of daily living to measure functional disability. J. Gerontol. Ser. B Psychol. Sci. Soc. Sci. **53**(1), S46–S57 (1998)

50. Steptoe, A., Breeze, E., Banks, J., Nazroo, J.: Cohort profile: the English longitudinal study of ageing. Int. J. Epidemiol. **42**(6), 1640–1648 (2013). https://doi.org/10.1093/ije/dys168

51. Tak, E., Kuiper, R., Chorus, A., Hopman-Rock, M.: Prevention of onset and progression of basic ADL disability by physical activity in community dwelling older adults: a meta-analysis. Ageing Res. Rev. **12**(1), 329–338 (2013). https://doi.org/10.1016/j.arr.2012.10.001

52. Vermeulen, J., Neyens, J.C., Van Rossum, E., Spreeuwenberg, M.D., De Witte, L.P.: Predicting ADL disability in community-dwelling elderly people using physical frailty indicators: a systematic review. BMC Geriatr. **11**, 33 (2011). https://doi.org/10.1186/1471-2318-11-33

53. Vincent, P., Larochelle, H., Bengio, Y., Manzagol, P.A.: Extracting and composing robust features with denoising autoencoders. In: Proceedings of 25th International Conference on Machine Learning, ICML 2008, pp. 1096–1103 (2008). https://doi.org/10.1145/1390156.1390294, http://portal.acm.org/citation.cfm?doid=1390156.1390294

54. Vincent, P., Larochelle, H., Bengio, Y., Manzagol, P.A.: Extracting and composing robust features with denoising autoencoders. In: Proceedings of the 25th International Conference on Machine Learning, ICML 2008, pp. 1096–1103. ACM, New York (2008). https://doi.org/10.1145/1390156.1390294

55. Wang, M., Deng, W.: Deep visual domain adaptation: a survey. arXiv preprint (2018). http://arxiv.org/abs/1802.03601

56. Weber, M., et al.: Feasibility and effectiveness of intervention programmes integrating functional exercise into daily life of older adults: a systematic review. Gerontology 64, 172–187 (2017). https://doi.org/10.1159/000479965, http://www.ncbi.nlm.nih.gov/pubmed/28910814

57. Weiss, K., Khoshgoftaar, T.M., Wang, D.D.: A survey of transfer learning. J. Big Data 3, 9 (2016). https://doi.org/10.1186/s40537-016-0043-6

58. Whelan, B.J., Savva, G.M.: Design and methodology of the Irish longitudinal study on ageing. J. Am. Geriatr. Soc. 61, S265–S268 (2013). https://doi.org/10.1111/jgs.12199

59. Zhou, Z.H., Liu, X.Y.: Training cost-sensitive neural networks with methods addressing the class imbalance problem. IEEE Trans. Knowl. Data Eng. 18(1), 63–77 (2006). https://doi.org/10.1109/TKDE.2006.17

Capturing Frame-Like Object Descriptors in Human Augmented Mapping

Mohamadreza Faridghasemnia[1]([✉]), Andrea Vanzo[2], and Daniele Nardi[1]

[1] Department of Computer, Control and Management Engineering "Antonio Ruberti", Sapienza University of Rome, Rome, Italy
`m.farid@ieee.org`
[2] Mathematical and Computer Science School,
Heriot-Watt University, Edinburgh, UK

Abstract. The model of an environment plays a crucial role in autonomous mobile robots, by providing them with the necessary task-relevant information. As robots become more intelligent, they need a richer and more expressive environment model. This model is a map that contains a structured description of the environment that can be used as the robot's knowledge for several tasks, such as planning and reasoning. In this work, we propose a framework that allows to capture important environment descriptors, such as functionality and ownership of the robot's surrounding objects, through verbal interaction. Specifically, we propose a corpus of verbal descriptions annotated with frame-like structures. We use the proposed dataset to train two multi-task neural architectures. We compare the two architectures through an experimental evaluation, discussing the design choices. Finally, we describe the creation of a simple interactive interface with our system, implemented through the trained model. The novelties of this work are: (i) the definition of a new problem, i.e., addressing different object descriptors, that plays a crucial role for the robot's tasks accomplishment; (ii) a specialized corpus to support the creation of rich Semantic Maps; (iii) the design of different neural architectures, and their experimental evaluation over the proposed dataset; (iv) a simple interface for the actual usage of the proposed resources.

Keywords: Natural Language understanding · Semantic mapping · Human robot interaction · Neural networks · Semantic mapping corpus · Corpus annotator

1 Introduction

Robot's internal knowledge of the operational environment is usually encoded in the form of a structured map. The problem of how to represent and build this map is one of the attractive fields in robotics [6]. This map is called Semantic Map [14] and plays a key role in robotics. Indeed, a Semantic Mapping is an

© Springer Nature Switzerland AG 2019
M. Alviano et al. (Eds.): AI*IA 2019, LNAI 11946, pp. 392–404, 2019.
https://doi.org/10.1007/978-3-030-35166-3_28

essential component for robot tasks accomplishment, since it holds the information needed to perform a task. Consider, for example, a user that instructs the robot to *"bring the book"*. In this task, if the robot relies solely on a metric map, it can only detect the geometrical information of places (e.g. walls), without having access to information about what is a *"book"*, and where it is located. These essential pieces of information are held in a Semantic Map. Hence, Semantic Maps allow the robot to successfully execute the user command. By the growing role of robotics in different applications and heterogeneous environments, building and representing this map has become more and more complex. In each different scenario, robots need a specific Semantic Map that holds all the knowledge needed for performing application-relevant tasks.

As the growing intelligence of robots, their internal representation should be enriched with supplementary information. For example, information about the restrictions of a place is necessary for trajectory planning; objects' affordances are important for the successful accomplishment of a task, since some objects might be non-functional for the task itself. Such knowledge can be acquired through different modalities. One might rely on the post-processing of sensors' raw data; knowledge bases could be manually engineered by a domain expert. Another way of acquiring the required knowledge is by relying on Natural Language interactions. Natural Language feedbacks shared between robot and user allow to (i) enrich the Semantic Map with new supplementary information, (ii) remove uncertainties of other input modalities, (iii) check the consistency of the knowledge base, and (iv) disambiguate potentially ambiguous commands. However, understanding Natural Language is a complex task to be performed automatically. For example, when a user utters *"this is titanic"*, different interpretations can be obtained depending on different features of the language, such as allusion, time, context, place, etc. This sentence in the context of movie-store, can be interpreted as pointing to a movie. Conversely, the user might want to specify the size of an object, with *"titanic"* used as an adjectival modifier of the targeted (implicit) object.

In this work, we propose a novel system for understanding linguistic expressions in the context of Semantic Mapping. To the best of our knowledge, this is the first work addressing semantic mapping with more than position descriptors. Specifically, while state of the art systems are capable of understanding only category and position of objects, we focus here on seven important descriptors that can be captured through dialogic interaction, such as functionality and ownership of objects/places. To this aim, a corpus of sentences for the scenario of Semantic Mapping of domestic environments is created, and sentences are annotated according to Frame Semantics theory [5]. The annotation process is performed with a sentence annotator specifically designed for this work. Then, the dataset is used for training two neural architectures. Both models are based on Long Short-Term Memory (LSTM) networks [7]; while the former is based on the ordinary pipeline architecture, the latter inherits its architecture from hierarchical classifiers. The two architectures are evaluated and compared in our scenario. Then, we show a qualitative analysis, by presenting some parsed sentences; finally, the design of a simple interaction with our proposed system is described.

Section 2 discusses the relevant literature. In Sect. 3 we propose SEmantic MApping Corpus (SeMaC) and its annotation process, describing its novelties. In Sect. 4, two different neural architectures are adapted for our task. Section 5 presents experimental results and a comparison of the two neural models, and discusses some showcased examples. Moreover, a further investigation of the proposed system in a different context is performed to assess the generalization capability of the proposed system. In Sect. 6, the creation of the simple interface for interaction to our system is described in detail. Section 7 draws the conclusions and some ideas for future works.

2   Related Work

Our work concerns the design and implementation of a framework for understanding Natural Language interaction in the context of Semantic Mapping. In this section, we review some of the state of the art, according to each part of our framework; namely, approaches for language understanding, datasets, and Natural Language interaction in Semantic Mapping.

Several approaches have been proposed to tackle the problem of language understanding in robotics, such as [10] and [3], where they focused on Robot Control Language (RCL) and tried to parse any sentence in their context into RCL grammar tree. The work presented in [8] introduces Spatial Description Clauses (SDC), where each SDC represents a linguistic aspect of a command that can be mapped to a real-world entity. Such approaches need a parser to assign the role of each word in a sentence with respect to a predefined grammar, and their approach is prone to failure if a sentence with the same intent, but with an unseen grammar is given. Such approaches can understand the shallow meaning of a sentence, but do not capture the meaning of complex linguistic expressions.

There are various works in the field of NLU's dataset, such as [9], where they focused on collecting movie subtitles. Movie's dialogs are very close to daily human conversations, but this dataset contains different contexts, and it is not annotated. The dataset proposed in [2], focuses on extracting semantics structures, domain concepts and other linguistic features from sentences, using frame semantics theory. Their dataset contains dialogs between human-human and human-machine; each sentence is annotated with dialog intent and frame semantic elements. Human-Robot Interaction Corpus (HuRIC) is another dataset for human-robot interaction in Natural Language [1]. This corpus is oriented to the commands to service robots in a home, which is annotated with lemmas, part-of-speech, frame semantics. There are many other datasets published, but all of them are either context-free or context-sensitive to their context of interest. For our objective, we developed a new specialized dataset.

There are many works in Natural Language interaction in the context of Semantic Mapping. The work proposed in [15] use Natural Language for semantic attribute acquisition, such as the category of objects inferred from a visual classifier. In another work, [11], the authors use Natural Language for removing uncertainties of position and category of objects, using a shallow language understanding module. In [16], they propose another framework for learning a human-centric model of the environment from Natural Language descriptions, focusing on spatial relationships between objects and location inherited from the dialog. Although all the presented approaches are capable of understanding a language, none of them addresses any semantic attributes other than position and category of objects.

3   Dataset

In this section, we present the new SEmantic MApping Corpus (SeMaC), and its corpus annotator, and discuss their novelties.

The proposed corpus is specialized for the scenario of Semantic Mapping in the range of domestic robots, and its annotator is designed for annotating sentences according to frame-like structures.

3.1   Corpus

Although a variety of corpora are already available, a corpus specialized for Semantic Mapping is still missing. Such a corpus should contain all linguistic expressions that humans use in their daily conversation. For this work, we created a Semantic Mapping Corpus (SeMaC) which contains 590 sentences, sampled from movies subtitles. These sentences are randomly found in a dataset released by [9], where contexts are aligned to the context of Semantic Mapping by a slight modification in verbs and objects. This approach lets our corpus hold different linguistic expressions, such as formal, informal and slang expressions, in the context of Semantic Mapping. SeMaC is annotated using frame-like structures, with SeMaC data annotator. SeMaC collects seven different semantic information, summarized in the following.

- *Ownership.* This class contains 90 sentences dedicated to assigning ownership of objects. Sentences as *"this book belongs to me"* and *"this chair is a property of her"* indicate the owner of an object, where such information cannot be obtained from any other input modalities of a Semantic Mapping system, other than Natural Language interaction with the user.
- *Functionality.* This class contains 80 sentences describing the functionality status of objects. For example, *"this chair is broken"* or *"this television is not fixed yet"* indicate whether an object can be used or it is broken. This information plays a crucial role in the planning of a robot, where the robot should ignore non-functional objects. This information can be obtained only through Natural Language interaction with the user.
- *Restrictions.* 90 sentences in this class assign any restriction that might be applied to actions or objects. For example, *"you can not enter the room"* or *"you do not have to touch my book"* give information about restrictions

applied to objects or actions, to the robot or the robot's master. As well as the previous one, this information can only be obtained only through Natural Language interaction with the user.

- *Weight.* 80 sentences in this class describe the weight of objects. For example, through *"this book is not heavy, around 500 grams"*, or *"this object is like feather"*, the user can give information about the weight of an object. This information can be obtained through a knowledge base. However, information coming from a knowledge base is valid for all objects in a category; conversely, the proposed system allows the user to assign this property to each object and overwrite/update the pre-existing beliefs.
- *Size.* 90 sentences in this class describe the size of objects. For example, *"this refrigerator is very big"* or *"our office is vast"* express the size of an object or an environment. This information might be used alongside the robot's perception for objects, where robot's perception is not sure about the size of an entity, interaction through Natural Language can confirm it.
- *Labeling.* 80 sentences in this class assign a category or a name to the objects. For example, *"this object is a book"* or *"I am Farid"* can assign the category or name to the real-world entities. Assigning a category to an object through Natural Language can assure the robot about the type of an object, while the robot has low confidence in its perception. Assigning a name to an object in a category is an important piece of information for the robot that can be used for understanding referential expressions.
- *Position.* 80 sentences in this class describe the objects' position. Sentences such as *"the book is on the desk"* or *"we are in the kitchen"* express the relative or absolute position of real-world entities.

It is worth to note that, the first five aforementioned classes give crucial properties in robot planning, where they solely can be obtained through Natural Language interaction with the user. Table 1 provides some statistics of the corpus, including the number of sentences in SeMaC, the number of unique words that appeared in SeMaC, the average number of words in each sentence, the average number of words that have frame type label, and the average number of words that have frame elements label.

Table 1. Statistics of SeMaC.

Number of sentences	590
Vocabulary size	557
The average length of sentences	5.21
The average length of frames per sentence	4.53
The average number of frame elements per sentence	3.31

3.2 Corpus Annotator

For annotating SeMaC, we design a corpus annotator that allows us to make the annotation process faster than any other corpus annotator. SeMaC corpus annotator is designed to work with Microsoft Word document, by using format painter. For a better understanding of this annotator, we make the following example. Let us suppose we have a Word (.docx) document and the following line has been written in that as following.

*line*1 : Location LexicalUnit Theme Being_located ¶

*line*2 : The knife is located in the kitchen ¶

The first line of this document is dedicated to defining labels, and the rest of the lines are sentences in the corpus. In this example, SeMaC annotator will capture all the words that have red font color as the label of "*Location*", and all the words that are highlighted in yellow are labeled "*Being_located*". This simple idea makes the annotation process faster and effortless. In the current version of this annotator, it can assign 5 different labels to each word, wherein this work we use two of these labels for frame types and frame elements.

4 Neural Models

In this section, we propose two neural network models for understanding the sequence of words in a sentence. Understanding Natural Language is a complex task for computers. Even though a variety of approaches already exist, such as using grammar parsers, they might obtain good results in some contexts, while bearing problems when dealing different linguistic expressions. For learning SeMaC, we adapt two different architectures of deep neural networks. These architectures are based on Long Short-Term Memory (LSTM) networks, which recently have caught significant attention due to their abilities in dealing with time series and sequences. In this work, we use pipeline and hierarchical neural network architecture, as depicted in Fig. 1. The pipeline architecture is made of two LSTM layers in sequence. These layers are both shared by the two tasks of predicting the frame types and frame elements. In the second architecture, we directly supervise each LSTM encoding with the corresponding task, to learn better representation for the given task. We assume the prediction of frame types to be easier than frame elements; hence, we shape the network as a hierarchy, letting the first block of LSTM to predict frame types, and the second block to predict frame elements. As the design of hierarchy, the first LSTM block is fed by input, and the second LSTM block is benefited from input alongside the output of the first LSTM block. The sequence of words in sentences are embedded by using NumberBatch ConceptNet [13], which is benefiting from retrofitting [4] of state of the art word embeddings and ConceptNet knowledge graph [12]. The choice of NumberBatch as word embedding is because of its knowledge graph information that has been injected to vectors by retrofitting. Information from a knowledge graph lets the system understand more complex expressions. In the next section, we compare these two models on results and identify the most promising one.

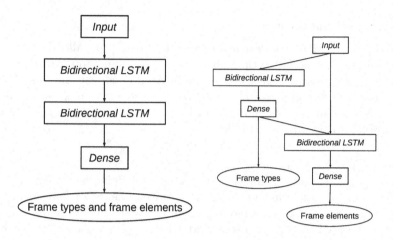

Fig. 1. Pipeline, on left, and hierarchical, on right, architectures.

5   Results

In this section we discuss the experimental results we obtained with the proposed neural models, we discuss some showcase examples, and provide an evaluation performed in a different context.

5.1   Choosing the Best Architecture

In order to identify the most suitable architectural design among hierarchical and pipeline, we train both models with 10-fold cross validation strategy, while each time we only change the dropout. This test is done with the batch size of 128 and 150 LSTM units for each LSTM block. For training, Nadam optimizer is used for training of 100 epochs without early stopping.

Then, we use nested cross-validation with grid search for finding hyperparameters. Although this experimental design is computationally heavy, it gives a fair comparison between the models. In this experiment we let the algorithm choose dropout, number of LSTM units and optimizer, as stated in Table 2; batch size is set to 128, the number of training iterations is set to 250 epochs with early stopping. In this test, we compute the micro F1 score for both frame types and frame elements and the percentage of sentences that correctly predicted all the frame.

Table 2. Hyperparameters for optimization.

Dropout	LSTM unit	Optimizer
0.3, 0.5, 0.8	100, 200, 300	rmsprop, nadam, adam

The test of dropout exploit various characteristics of SeMaC and models. As shown in Fig. 2, though more visible in hierarchical architecture, both models tend to choose a slightly high dropout for learning SeMaC, which indicates the high variation in this dataset. Moreover, we can see that the hierarchical architecture is less sensitive to changes of dropout, even though we observed that to avoid oscillations in the learning curve, we should use a rather high dropout, with early stopping for smoothing the learning curve and immunity to overfitting. Also, it can be seen that the pipeline architecture is suffering from underfitting in 100 epochs, which is probably due to the problem of gradient descent in deep networks.

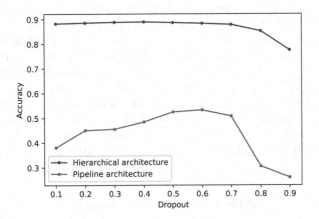

Fig. 2. Dropout test for both hierarchical (blue) and pipeline (red) architectures. (Color figure online)

The F1 score of nested cross-validation is shown in Table 3; the hierarchical architecture outperforms the pipeline architecture in both frame type and frame elements. It is worth to note that as the number of frame types is much less than the number of frame elements, it is expected that the F1 score of the frame type score becomes less than the frame elements score. This can be seen in the pipeline architecture. However, as showed in Table 3 the hierarchical architecture has a better score in frame elements, which is most likely because of the first LSTM block (frame-type classifier) which provides more information for frame-element's LSTM block. It has been observed that the number of sentences, whose both labels of each of its word are correctly predicted (exact match score) is much higher in the hierarchical architecture.

5.2 Showcase Examples

As it will be described in the next section, understanding an utterance towards making a dialog is upon the prediction of word's labels according to frame semantics theory. To this aim, we let the hierarchical architecture learn the whole

Table 3. Results of metrics for both architectures.

Metric	Hierarchical	Pipeline
F1- Frame types	0.87	0.7
F1- Frame elements	0.89	0.67
Exact match	0.73	0.40

SeMaC with the dropout of 0.6, 150 hidden units for each LSTM block and training with Nadam optimizer for 100 epochs. We used this trained model to predict some showcase examples, which do not appear in SeMaC, as shown in Tables 4, 5 and 6, where frame types, frame elements, and the confidence of the prediction are stated. We can see that the proposed system is capable of understanding different linguistic expressions, even those that are not in SeMaC. We grant the fact that the neural network prediction of sentences in the training set (SeMaC) is perfectly predicted, and here we just provide some challenging examples. In particular, none of the words *"titanic"*, *"whacking"*, and *"exclusive"* appear in SeMaC. As we can see, in these showcase examples the trained model is able to predict the correct labels. Although we noticed that in some predictions the confidence is very low, the model can still capture important information such as the object, property of the object, and the frame of the phrase.

Table 4. Prediction of showcase 1.

Lexical	Frame type	Frame element
This	Size (83)	Entity (97)
is	Size (82)	ND (-)
titanic	Size (21)	Lexical unit size (15)

Table 5. Prediction of showcase 2.

Lexical	Frame type	Frame element
Kitchen	Size (95)	Entity (98)
is	Size (94)	ND (-)
whacking	Size (91)	Lexical Unit Size (77)

5.3 A Different Context

In this subsection, we describe the results of the proposed model over sentences of a different context, to examine the generality of the proposed system. We use

Table 6. Prediction of showcase 3.

Lexical	Frame type	Frame element
Knife	Possession (87)	Possession(Object) (71)
is	Possession (64)	ND (-)
exclusive	Possession (9)	ND (-)
to	Possession (13)	ND (-)
her	Possession (96)	Owner (70)

the model trained over SeMaC for predicting sentences from annotations of MS-coco dataset, whose sentences are more complex and different from SeMaC (e.g. different verbs and objects). We choose 10 sentences per each of our classes for this prediction, as for some of our classes we were not able to find more instances. As the annotations in MS-coco are describing images, each annotation is a complex structured sentence, with multiple overlapping frames. Our proposed model achieves 0.39, 0.50 for F1 score of frame elements and frame types, respectively. Then, we prune each annotation to have a single-frame sentences. This pruning shortened the average size of sentences by 30%. F1 score of single framed sentences reaches 0.59, 0.74 for frame elements, and frame types, respectively. It is worth noting that testing sentences with multiple overlapping frame is not legit for a model that has been trained on sentences with single frame. Instead, the result with pruned sentences supports the generality of the proposed system.

6   Interactive Interface

In order to validate our approach, we implemented a simple interactive interface for our system. In this section, we describe this interface, by discussing the process of understanding a sentence, given the predicted labels, and the generation process of a back-channel. In particular, we define understanding a sentence as a process of finding the semantic frame label of each word in a sentence, and capturing the intrinsic meaning of words. Capturing the concept of words becomes more challenging if we want to deal with unseen words. For example, the robot should be able to understand *"broken"* is a lexical unit that is used for objects that are not working, while *"fixed"* causes the functionality of an object.

We use the trained model as the core of our interactive system, which can predict labels of any given sentence. Given the frame type of a sentence, we can have the intent of a sentence. This intent accompanied with frame elements, helps us to have the object and the property that the sentence is intended to assign to the object. In this work, our focus is on understanding the language, assuming the problem of grounding objects as solved. Let us make an example to show the understanding process of a property. For example, in the sentence *"the chair is out of order"*, firstly we find the semantics of *"out of order"*, which can be obtained from the semantic vectors of each word. Afterwards the semantics is compared to predefined semantics, such as functional, and broken. The cosine distance between these semantic vectors gives the meaning of the property. We improved this methodology by comparing the property with the centroid of a concept instead of a single word. We define a concept ς as a spatial region in the semantic space, where the semantic vectors of all verbal expressions are used for describing a particular concept exist.

For example, the concept of *"not working"*, contains different expressions, where all bear the same meaning. Let σ_i be the semantic representation of a word and ς_c be the centroid of a concept, where each σ_i can be used for expressing ς. The centroid of the concept can be obtained by:

$$\varsigma_c = \frac{1}{n} \sum_{i=0}^{n} \sigma_i \text{ Where } \sigma_i \text{ is an expression for } \varsigma \tag{1}$$

Through the same methodology, any property can be compared to the centroid of concepts, and the closest concept indicates the meaning of property. This approach lets the system understand arbitrary properties, even those not appeared in SeMaC. The same methodology has been used for different classes of attributes.

We use a straightforward methodology for the generation of back-channels, which is a template-based approach. In this methodology, a template is chosen from seven predefined templates, based on the most appeared frame type in the predicted frame types; thereafter, free-slots of the template are filled by using frame elements and concepts. In particular, our context for the back-channel generation can be simplified as finding an object and a property that we want to assign to it. The object can be directly concluded from frame elements, and the assigned property is obtained from frame elements and their corresponding concept. Table 7 provides examples of sentences understood by the system, with their corresponding generated back-channels.

Table 7. Five interaction between human and the proposed system.

No.	User utterance	Robot utterance
1	This is out of order	Ok, I save this as improper
2	Knife is exclusive to her	Got it! knife belongs to her
3	Kitchen is messed up	Oh, ok, I save kitchen as improper
4	This is titanic	Ok, got it, this is huge
5	Kitchen is not whacking	Oh, ok, kitchen is not huge then

7   Conclusion

In this work, a framework for Natural Language understanding specialized for Semantic Mapping is created. This framework lets a robot enrich its Semantic Map with some crucial information about its surroundings through Natural

Language interaction. In particular, the proposed framework is composed of three parts: dataset, prediction model, and interaction interface. We validate our proposed framework with some showcase examples, showing that the proposed framework is able to enrich a semantic map by seven different environment descriptors. This work can be extended towards many directions. For example, linguistic allusions, where allusion is a common expression in humans dialog, and a user-specific allusion synthesizing can consistently improve the understanding of Natural Language. Moreover, the proposed system can be extended by letting the robot ask spot questions to gather new information or to refine its uncertainty.

References

1. Bastianelli, E., Castellucci, G., Croce, D., Iocchi, L., Basili, R., Nardi, D.: Huric: a human robot interaction corpus. In: LREC, pp. 4519–4526 (2014)
2. Dinarelli, M., Quarteroni, S., Tonelli, S., Moschitti, A., Riccardi, G.: Annotating spoken dialogs: from speech segments to dialog acts and frame semantics. In: Proceedings of the 2nd Workshop on Semantic Representation of Spoken Language, pp. 34–41. Association for Computational Linguistics (2009)
3. Dukes, K.: Semantic annotation of robotic spatial commands. In: Language and Technology Conference (LTC) (2013)
4. Faruqui, M., Dodge, J., Jauhar, S.K., Dyer, C., Hovy, E., Smith, N.A.: Retrofitting word vectors to semantic lexicons. arXiv preprint arXiv:1411.4166 (2014)
5. Fillmore, C.J.: Frames and the semantics of understanding. Quad. Semantica 6(2), 222–254 (1985)
6. Galindo, C., Fernández-Madrigal, J.-A., González, J., Saffiotti, A.: Robot task planning using semantic maps. Robot. Auton. Syst. 56(11), 955–966 (2008)
7. Hochreiter, S., Schmidhuber, J.: Long short-term memory. Neural Comput. 9(8), 1735–1780 (1997)
8. Kollar, T., Tellex, S., Roy, D., Roy, N.: Grounding verbs of motion in natural language commands to robots. In: Khatib, O., Kumar, V., Sukhatme, G. (eds.) Experimental Robotics. STAR, vol. 79, pp. 31–47. Springer, Berlin (2014). https://doi.org/10.1007/978-3-642-28572-1_3
9. Lison, P., Tiedemann, J.: Opensubtitles 2016: extracting large parallel corpora from movie and tv subtitles (2016)
10. Matuszek, C., Herbst, E., Zettlemoyer, L., Fox, D.: Learning to parse natural language commands to a robot control system. In: Desai, J., Dudek, G., Khatib, O., Kumar, V. (eds.) Experimental Robotics. STAR, vol. 88, pp. 403–415. (2013). https://doi.org/10.1007/978-3-319-00065-7_28
11. Pronobis, A., Jensfelt, P.: Large-scale semantic mapping and reasoning with heterogeneous modalities. In: 2012 IEEE International Conference on Robotics and Automation (ICRA), pp. 3515–3522. IEEE (2012)
12. Speer, R., Chin, J., Havasi, C.: Conceptnet 5.5: an open multilingual graph of general knowledge. In: AAAI, pp. 4444–4451 (2017)
13. Speer, R., Lowry-Duda, J.: Conceptnet at semeval-2017 task 2: extending word embeddings with multilingual relational knowledge. arXiv preprint arXiv:1704.03560 (2017)

14. Surmann, H., Nüchter, A., Hertzberg, J.: An autonomous mobile robot with a 3D laser range finder for 3D exploration and digitalization of indoor environments. Robot. Auton. Syst. **45**(3–4), 181–198 (2003)
15. Vanzo, A., Part, J.L., Yu, Y., Nardi, D., Lemon, O.: Incrementally learning semantic attributes through dialogue interaction. In: Proceedings of the 17th International Conference on Autonomous Agents and MultiAgent Systems, pp. 865–873. International Foundation for Autonomous Agents and Multiagent Systems (2018)
16. Walter, M.R., Hemachandra, S., Homberg, B., Tellex, S., Teller, S.: Learning semantic maps from natural language descriptions. Robot. Sci. Syst. (2013)

Verification and Repair of Neural Networks: A Progress Report on Convolutional Models

Dario Guidotti[1], Francesco Leofante[1,2], Luca Pulina[3],
and Armando Tacchella[1(✉)]

[1] University of Genoa, Genoa, Italy
{dario.guidotti,francesco.leofante}@edu.unige.it,
armando.tacchella@unige.it
[2] RWTH Aachen University, Aachen, Germany
[3] University of Sassari, Sassari, Italy
lpulina@uniss.it

Abstract. Recent public calls for the development of explainable and verifiable AI led to a growing interest in formal verification and repair of machine-learned models. Despite the impressive progress that the learning community has made, models such as deep neural networks remain vulnerable to adversarial attacks, and their sheer size represents a major obstacle to formal analysis and implementation. In this paper we present our current efforts to tackle repair of deep convolutional neural networks using ideas borrowed from Transfer Learning. With results obtained on popular MNIST and CIFAR10 datasets, we show that models of deep convolutional neural networks can be transformed into simpler ones preserving their accuracy, and we discuss how formal repair through convex programming techniques could benefit from this process.

Keywords: Transfer Learning · Network repair · Convex optimization

1 Introduction

The need for the development of explainable and verifiable AI has been put forward in a number of public events, e.g., the Workshop on Explainable AI held at IJCAI 2017[1], and research programs, e.g., the DARPA program on Explainable Artificial Intelligence.[2] These "calls to arms" did not go unanswered, originating several related research streams. Among them, particularly vibrant is the one concerned with automated verification and repair of machine-learned models. Albeit the first contribution in this direction appeared about ten years ago [15], a recent extensive survey [8] cites more than 200 papers, most of which published in the last three years. In particular, there is high interest in verifying Deep

---

[1] http://home.earthlink.net/~dwaha/research/meetings/ijcai17-xai/.
[2] https://www.darpa.mil/program/explainable-artificial-intelligence.

© Springer Nature Switzerland AG 2019
M. Alviano et al. (Eds.): AI*IA 2019, LNAI 11946, pp. 405–417, 2019.
https://doi.org/10.1007/978-3-030-35166-3_29

Neural Networks (DNNs): their adoption and successful application in various domains have made them one of the most popular machine-learned models to date—see, e.g., [20] on image classification, [24] on speech recognition, and [10] for the general principles and a catalog of success stories.

Despite the impressive progress that the learning community has made in the field, it is well known—see, e.g., [5,19]—that DNNs can be vulnerable to *adversarial perturbations*, i.e., minimal changes to correctly classified input data that cause a network to respond in unexpected and incorrect ways. Independently from the accuracy of a network, the vulnerability to adversarial attacks calls for techniques to improve robustness and guarantee desired properties. Repair [6,7,15] is one such technique, whereby we seek to adjust the parameters of the network in order to formally guarantee that the network will respond correctly even in the presence of adversarial perturbations. In practice, the sheer size of these models still represents a major obstacle to formal analysis of any kind. Typical state of the art neural networks for tasks like image classification have more than a hundred millions of parameters [18], which makes off-the-shelf techniques hardly applicable.

In this paper we focus on the repair of Convolutional Neural Networks (CNNs), a type of DNN mainly used in computer vision—see [11] for a survey related to DNN architectures and their applications. In particular, we discuss our current efforts to repair CNNs using convex programming and ideas borrowed from Transfer Learning (TL) [22]. In general, TL is the simplification of learning in a new task through the transfer of knowledge from a related task that has already been learned. As posited in [17], the idea is to keep the convolutional part of the network as a learned feature extractor, and replace the final classification layer with one featuring less parameters and/or a smaller model complexity. Noticeably, the replacement may yield networks whose accuracy is comparable with the one of the original DNNs, yet more amenable to formal analysis.

More specifically, we contribute an experimental analysis based on the popular MNIST[3] and CIFAR10[4] datasets. The first step is to train CNNs on both datasets and to replace their final fully-connected layer with linear support vector machines. This step reduces by orders of magnitude the number of free parameters, e.g., from 4.7 million to 65 thousand in the case of CIFAR10, while preserving accuracy. We discover adversarial attacks on such "hybrid" models using the Fast Gradient Sign Method described in [5]. Since we replace nonlinear layers with linear ones, we are able to define a repair procedure as a convex optimization problem—as done in [7] for kernel-based learning models. The resulting problem can be solved with off-the-shelf tools—CVXOPT[5] in our case. The results we obtain are still preliminary, but show some promise as far as scaling to networks of larger size is concerned. However, the repair procedure is not yet general enough to make the networks immune to perturbations

---

[3] http://yann.lecun.com/exdb/mnist/.

[4] https://www.cs.toronto.edu/~kriz/cifar.html.

[5] https://cvxopt.org/index.html.

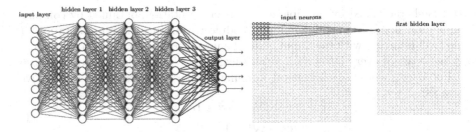

Fig. 1. Generic architecture of a fully connected DNN with 3 hidden layers (left) and graphics representation of a local receptive field (right). The images are taken from [12].

other than those considered by the repair procedure. While this might not be a strong limitation when considering real-world instead of artificial adversaries—see [4]—further investigations are needed to confirm whether our method could be effective for practical applications.

To the extent of our knowledge, this is the first time that TL is leveraged in order to repair a CNN through convex programming techniques. The idea of replacing parts of a CNN to improve its performances is not new, as it has been explored in [17] and [21], among others. However, the focus of these contributions is to improve the accuracy of the network, rather than providing models whose properties can be certified more easily than the original one. Trying to apply formal verification techniques to networks of size smaller than the original could be done following alternative paths. For instance, in [2] the authors show that it is possible to find small-sized subnetworks in CNNs which prove to be remarkably accurate on some datasets including MNIST and CIFAR10. These subnetworks could be extracted and certified considering our approach or other state-of-the-art tools like PLANET [1] or RELUPLEX [9]. Finally, the aim of obtaining networks robust to adversarial examples, but not necessarily smaller than the original ones, can be pursued using results in robust training: recent results—see, e.g., [23]—seem to open this possibility also for CNNs of considerable size.

The rest of the paper is structured as follows. In Sect. 2 we give an overview of CNNs, and on the methodology we use to simplify them inspired to TL. In Sect. 3 we introduce and analyze the baseline models, and we show the logic behind of our repair procedure. We present experimental results in Sect. 4 and we conclude the paper with some final remarks and our future research agenda in Sect. 5.

2 Preliminaries

2.1 Convolutional Neural Networks

According to [10], *representation learning* "is a set of methods that allows a machine to be fed with raw data and to automatically discover the representations needed for detection of classification". DNNs are representation learning models characterized by multiple levels of representation, obtained by composing several non-linear modules. Each module transforms the representation at one level (starting with raw input) into the next, more abstract, representation. At the heart of every DNN lie the "classical" neural network modules as shown in Fig. 1(left) whose mathematical formulation can be expressed in a recursive form as:

$$\mathbf{h}^{(1)} = \Phi^{(1)}(\mathbf{W}^{(1)} \cdot \mathbf{x} + \mathbf{b}^{(1)})$$
$$\mathbf{h}^{(i)} = \Phi^{(i)}(\mathbf{W}^{(i)} \cdot \mathbf{h}^{(i-1)} + \mathbf{b}^{(i)}) \tag{1}$$

where $\Phi^{(i)}$ is the activation function, $\mathbf{W}^{(i)} \in \mathbb{R}^{d_i \times d_{i-1}}$ is a matrix of weights and $\mathbf{b}^{(i)} \in \mathbb{R}^{d_i}$ is the vector of the biases of the i-th layer. $\mathbf{h}^{(i)} \in \mathbb{R}^{d_i}$ corresponds to the output of the i-th layer and the range of i depends on the number of layers. A module like this is said to be *fully connected*, because the weighted sum of the outputs of each neuron in level i is fed to every neuron in level $i + 1$, creating the topology shown in Fig. 1(left). CNNs are a specific kind of DNNs, typically adopted in computer vision applications, characterized by one or more *convolutional modules*. The distinctive element of such modules is that they feature connections for small, localized regions of the input vector, i.e., each neuron of the hidden layer is connected only to a small subset of the input neurons. This subset of the input neurons is called *local receptive field* of the hidden neuron. A graphical example of a local receptive is depicted in Fig. 1(right). Another important feature of convolutional modules is that all the local receptive fields share the same weights and bias reducing the overall number of weights substantially. In practice, each local receptive field is trained to detect a specific feature in the input image, i.e., distinctive elements of input portions. As a consequence, in a specific hidden layer, different sets of shared weights are used: each of these sets is trained to detect specific feature in the image. Usually each convolutional module is followed by a *pooling layer*, which simplifies the information received. For instance, each unit of a pooling layer could take a subset of neurons from the previous module and select their maximum activation—an operation called *max-pooling*. Since our experiments are about image classification, in the following we consider a CNN arrangement widely adopted for this task, i.e., a series of convolutional modules and pooling layers followed by fully connected modules. The first part of the network can be seen as an application of a (learned) kernel to the original input whereas the second part can be seen as the actual classifier. For a more detailed study on Convolutional Neural Networks we refer to [12].

2.2   Transfer Learning

As mentioned in [22], TL is "the improvement of learning in a new task through the transfer of knowledge from a related task that has already been learned". TL has been suggested in the context of deep learning applications—see, e.g., [17]— where pre-trained models are used as starting points for computer vision or natural language tasks. Since the training of DNNs requires substantial computational resources, it is often the case that reusing (parts of) pre-trained models enables applications which would not be feasible otherwise. For instance, in [17], a pre-trained convolutional module is extracted from a CNN and then applied as a feature extractor in the context of an object recognition task where the paucity of training samples would make training of the full CNN untenable. On the other hand, combining the pre-trained convolutional module with a newly trained classifier, makes for an effective combination, enabling to solve classification tasks that were not within the reach of the original CNN. TL and its applications suggest the possibility of replacing some modules of a DNN which are hardly analyzable with formal methods, with others that are more amenable to such analysis. As long as the accuracy of the resulting network, which we call *hybrid network* in the following, is close to the original DNN, one may (*i*) replace the original network with the hybrid one and (*ii*) fix the hybrid one instead of the original network, should adversarial examples be found also for the hybrid network. In particular, we build hybrid networks by collating the convolutional module of a CNN followed by a linear Support Vector Machine (lSVM), i.e., a classifier based on separating hyper-planes in which the distance of the hyper-plane from the nearest samples of both classes is maximized. In our experiments we consider multiclass lSVMs, i.e., in order to discriminate among k classes we compute k different separating hyper-planes each one discriminating among one class and the remaining $k - 1$. The input-output relation of a multiclass lSVM is defined as follows:

$$\mathbf{f}(\mathbf{x}) = \mathbf{W} \cdot \mathbf{x} + \mathbf{b}$$
$$y = argmax(\mathbf{f}(\mathbf{x})) \tag{2}$$

where $\mathbf{x} \in \mathbb{R}^d$ is the vector of the inputs, $\mathbf{b} \in \mathbb{R}^k$ is the vector of the biases, $\mathbf{W} \in \mathbb{R}^{k \times d}$ is the matrix of the weights corresponding to k lSVMs, each working to detect one of the k classes. The function $\mathbf{f}(\mathbf{x})$ is the decision function corresponding to the input $\mathbf{x}$. It contains the signed distances of the input $\mathbf{x}$ from each decision hyper-plane. From the definition of the decision function we can derive the correct class y for an input $\mathbf{x}$.

3   Repair of Hybrid Networks

3.1   Hybrid Networks

For the sake of our experiments, we have developed two CNNs and two corresponding hybrid networks for each dataset considered. Given the preliminary nature of this work the datasets considered are CIFAR10 and MNIST, two of the most famous basic datasets for image classification. The MNIST dataset contains 60000 grayscale images of handwritten digits whereas the CIFAR10 dataset contains 60000 color images in 10 different mutually exclusive classes: both datasets are divided in a training set of 50000 images and a test set of 10000 images.

The network considered for the MNIST dataset (MNIST-NN) is a CNN with 2 convolutional layers, 2 max-pooling layers and 2 fully connected layers. The convolutional layers have kernel size equal to 5×5 and stride length equal to 1, the max-pooling layers have kernel size equal to 2×2. There is a max-pooling layer after each convolutional layer. The two fully connected layers have 500 and

10 hidden neurons respectively and the inputs of the first layer are the values generated from 800 neurons of the second max-pooling layer. The total number of parameters of the network is 407330 and 99.5% of them are part of the fully connected layers.

The network developed for the CIFAR10 dataset (CIFAR10-NN) is a CNN with 6 convolutional layers, 3 max-pooling layer and 3 fully connected layers. The convolutional layers have kernel size equal to 3×3, stride length equal to 1, padding equal to 1 and present respectively 32, 64, 128, 128, 256 and 256 different kernels, the max-pooling layers has kernel size equal to 2×2. There is a max pooling layer every 2 convolutional layers. The three fully connected layers have 1024, 512 and 10 hidden neurons respectively, and the inputs of the first layer are the values generated from 4096 neurons of the third max-pooling layer. The activation functions are all ReLU. The total number of parameters is 4747904 and 99.5% of them are part of the fully connected layers. The network considered is similar to the Conv-6 network presented in [3], but our network features a first convolutional layer with 32 kernels whereas the corresponding layer of the Conv-6 network has 64 kernels.

In this work we have used PyTorch [13] for the implementation and training of all the networks. The MNIST network is trained using the SGD optimizer with learning rate equals 0.001, momentum 0.9 and train batch size 64, for 10 epochs. The CIFAR10 network is trained using the Adam optimizer with learning rate equals 0.001, weight decay $5e$–4 and train batch size 128, for 25 epochs. The hybrid networks consist of the union of the convolutional and max-pooling layers of the original networks with lSVM multiclass classifiers: in this work we have used off-of-the-shelf implementations provided by scikit-learn [14]. In particular, both for MNIST-NN and for CIFAR10-NN, we have designed corresponding *linear* hybrids. We identify the linear hybrids as MNIST-LH and CIFAR10-LH. All networks are trained using standard training parameters recommended respectively from PyTorch and scikit-learn documentation.

As a preliminary experiment we have analyzed the accuracy gap between the hybrid models and the corresponding neural networks: for CIFAR10 models our results are 85.4% (NN) and 85.6% (LH). The accuracies of the MNIST models are 97.12% (NN) and 98.72% (LH). All the accuracies were computed as the number of correctly classified images against all the images of the test sets provided by the MNIST and CIFAR10 repositories. These figures tell us that, for the MNIST dataset, hybrid models can be more accurate than the corresponding CNN. CIFAR10 is more complex than MNIST, nevertheless the results still hold.

3.2   Repair

The main idea behind our repair approach is to circumvent the repair of CNNs and attempt to repair the corresponding hybrid networks instead. To repair hybrid networks, we generate adversarial examples for them, and then we solve an optimization problem in the space of the network's parameter, with the objective to reduce as much as possible the impact of the adversaries. In order to make the optimization problem computationally feasible, we consider the convolutional modules of our hybrid models as a fixed feature map and we do not include their parameters into the optimization problem, but we concentrate on the final layers instead. In practice, this corresponds to analyzing the network in feature space, instead of input space—as done in [6,7]. Owing to this, and to the fact that fully connected layers of the CNN are substituted by lSVMs in our hybrid networks, the number of free variables for the convex optimization problem is drastically reduced. For example, in the case of the MNIST models, we managed to reduce the number of variables from 405510 to approximately 8000.

Thanks to the linearity of the lSVM considered it is possible to limit the convex optimization problem to piece-wise linearity—because of absolute values— eliminating the need of a non-linear solver or abstraction techniques to manage non-linearities. In Eq. (3) we present the mathematical definition of our optimization problem: parameters c and d are the number of possible classes and the number of feature of the adversarial example in the feature space, respectively; parameters $\gamma_{i,j}$ are the modification on the weights $w_{i,j}$ of the lSVM model; the variables δ_i are slack variable necessary to keep the problem solvable at the price of some error on the prediction of the decision function for the adversarial example of interest; finally, y_i are the correct values of the decision function of the lSVM classifier for the adversarial example and x_j are the feature of the adversarial sample of interest in the feature space. All the variable considered take real values.

$$
\begin{aligned}
min \sum_{i=1}^{c}\sum_{j=1}^{d}|\gamma_{i,j}| + \sum_{i=1}^{c}\delta_i \\
y_i - \delta_i \leq \sum_{j=1}^{d}(w_{i,j} + \gamma_{i,j})x_j \leq y_i + \delta_i \qquad \forall i = 1,...,c \\
\delta_i \geq 0 \qquad\qquad\qquad\qquad\qquad \forall i = 1,...,c
\end{aligned}
\tag{3}
$$

In this case we consider only one adversarial example, but the extension of the problem to the case in which more than one adversarial sample is considered is trivial. The cost function seeks to minimize the (absolute) variation of the weights of the lSVM, while satisfying the constraint of bringing the prediction of the decision function of the adversarial example *as close as possible* to the correct decision function. In the case of the CIFAR10 model we need a further simplification: even with the replacement of the fully connected layers the number of variables in the convex optimization problem is 40960 and the optimization procedure is not able to solve the problem. Therefore we decided to apply a feature-selection procedure on the output of the convolutional layers of our model. For each feature we consider two set of samples: the first one taken from the original inputs and the second one taken from the adversarial inputs. We compare the sets of samples using the Wilcoxon Signed Rank test against the null hypothesis that the two sets come from the same distribution. The procedure computes the p-values of the test for each feature and selects the ones which present a p-value below a given threshold: in our experiments we choose a threshold value of 0.1. The rationale of our procedure is to retain only the features which are affected significantly by the adversarial inputs and change only the corresponding weights in the SVM. After feature selection we manage to reduce the number of variables of the convex optimization problem below 6000, therefore making the problem manageable for the solver.

4 Experimental Results

We test our repair procedure on both the MNIST and CIFAR10 datasets, using the Fast Sign Gradient Method (FSGM) [5] as adversarial attack of choice. The FSGM works by using the gradients of the neural network to create an adversarial example. For an input image, the method uses the gradients of the loss with respect to the input image to create a new image that maximises the loss (*i.e.* the adversarial sample). In order to generate adversarial samples for our models we utilize FoolBox [16] which provides a number of ready-made adversarial attacks. Another advantage of FoolBox is that it accepts as model to be attacked *every* valid PyTorch model, which allows us to attack also our hybrid models without complex workarounds. In our tests, we analyze the loss of accuracy of our models corresponding to increasing magnitudes of adversarial attacks, as shown in Fig. 2. We control the magnitude of the adversarial attack using the parameter ε.

As it can be expected, the accuracies of both the MNIST and CIFAR10 models drops for increasing values of ε and in general the LH models seem to be more vulnerable to this kind of adversarial attack. Given that our aim is to repair the LH models, this is not a limitation for our approach. As it can be observed in Fig. 2 for $\varepsilon = 0.15$ the adversarial perturbation for the MNIST images is clearly recognizable even if it would not fool a human observer. For the CIFAR10 dataset we consider smaller adversarial perturbations: as it can be seen in Fig. 2, for $\varepsilon = 0.025$ the models accuracy is already below the baseline.

In our main experiment we analyzed the behavior of MNIST-LH and of its repaired version (MNIST-RLH) for $\varepsilon = [0.025, 0.05, 0.075, 0.1, 0.125, 0.15]$ and the behavior of CIFAR10-LH and of its repaired version (CIFAR10-RLH) for $\varepsilon = [.001, .005, .01, .015, 0.02, 0.025]$. More specifically, for each ε, we compute the accuracies of the LH, NN and RLH models on the following test sets: MNIST/CIFAR10 test set (Data), MNIST/CIFAR10 test sets in which all the images for which we found a corresponding adversarial example have been replaced with the adversarial example. Since the adversarial attack is model-dependent, the latter test set corresponds to three different sets computed on MNIST/CIFAR10-NN (NADV), MNIST/CIFAR10-LH (HADV) and MNIST/CIFAR10-RLH (RHADV) (Table 1).

Table 1. Synopsis of networks and related adversaries.

Network	Description	Adversaries
NN	Convolutional NN	NADV
(R)LH	(Repaired) Linear hybrid network	(R)HADV
KH	Kernel-based hybrid network	—

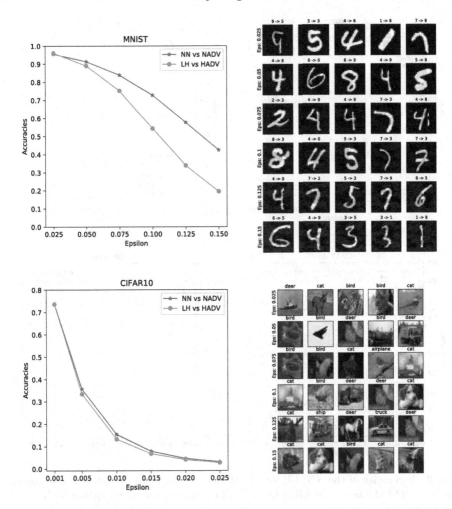

Fig. 2. Accuracies of MNIST-NN, MNIST-LH (above) and CIFAR10-NN, CIFAR10-LH (below) as ε increases (left) and graphics representation of some adversarial examples (right). The epsilons of the graphical representation for CIFAR10 do not correspond to the ones in the accuracies graph because otherwise they would be completely indiscernible to the human eye

In Fig. 3(left) it is possible to see how repair affects the accuracy of the models both with respect to adversarial samples only (ADV) and with respect to the original test set (Data). In the case of MNIST, even considering only one adversarial in the optimization problem (3), the resulting model (MNIST-RLH) manages to generalize also on other adversarial examples, e.g. it manages to classify correctly *at least* 20% of the adversarial examples. In the case of CIFAR10, even if the repaired model is more accurate than the original one with respect to the adversarial samples the improvement is not substantial; in

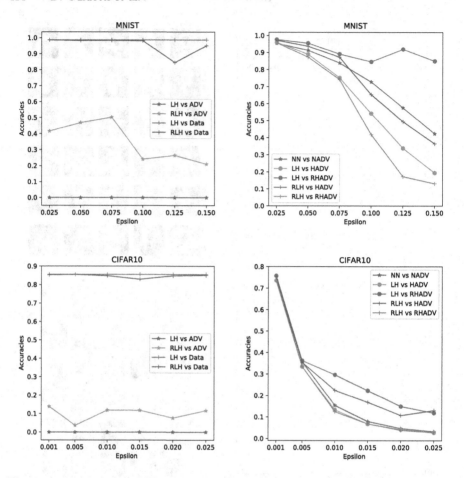

Fig. 3. Accuracies of the NN, LH and RLH models computed on different test sets of interest (MNIST above, CIFAR10 below). All the accuracies are computed for increasing values of ε.

our opinion this is due to the fact that both the model and the dataset are more complex than the ones in MNIST. In Fig. 3(right) it is also possible to see how the accuracy of the RLH models compares with the accuracies of the LH and NN ones with respect to the datasets NADV and HADV: from the images on the right it is clear that, while the repaired model is more robust to the adversarial sample computed on the non-repaired model, it has not acquired robustness against adversarial attacks in general. Moreover, it appears clear that the original model (NN) is still more robust to adversarial attacks. From the same images it is also possible to see that, as the RLH models are somewhat robust with respect to the adversarial example computed on the LH ones, so the LH models are somewhat robust with respect to the adversarial example computed on the RLH ones. This result suggests that the adversarial examples computed on the

LH and RLH models belong to different categories of adversarial examples. This phenomenon requires further investigation to be confirmed. The code for the experiments presented in this section can be found at https://gitlab.sagelab.it/dguidotti/aiia2019-code.

5   Conclusions and Future Work

The main idea presented in this paper is to study the safety of DNNs in a "modular" fashion using techniques adopted from transfer learning. In particular, we consider how the properties of CNNs change if we replace the fully connected module with lSVMs obtaining hybrid networks. Our results confirm that such replace does not impact on the accuracy in a relevant manner, while making repair of hybrid networks feasible using a relatively simple encoding in a convex optimization problem. Our experimental results on MNIST show that, even using very few adversaries, the repair procedures manage to provide a model which presents an acceptable generalization on all the adversaries computed using the original hybrid model. On the other hand, our results on CIFAR10 show a more intricate picture, one in which the repaired network can be made robust against specific adversaries but generalization is still not completely achieved. Overall, the repaired models are still vulnerable to the same adversarial attack, e.g. the repaired models developed a resistance to the adversarial *examples* of the old model, but not to the general adversarial *attack*. The different grade of resistance of the original and repaired models to the reciprocal adversarial examples appears to indicate that different categories of adversarial example may exist.

Given the results obtained from this work, our future lines of research will concentrate on understanding the properties of categories of adversarial samples in hybrid convolutional-lSVM networks and adding verification-driven kernels to our SVMs in order to obtain robust hybrid convolutional-SVM networks. Moreover, we will try to extend our work in order to repair CNNs without swapping away the fully connected modules and to explain how adversarial attacks affect the convolutional part of the networks and therefore the input in the feature space.

Acknowledgments. The research of Francesco Leofante and Luca Pulina has been funded by the Sardinian Regional Project PRO-COMFORT (POR FESR Sardegna 2014-2020 - Asse 1, Azione 1.1.3). The research of Luca Pulina has been also partially funded by the Sardinian Regional Projects PROSSIMO (POR FESR Sardegna 2014/20-ASSE I), SMART_UzER (POR FESR Sardegna 2014-2020, Asse I, Azione 1.2.2), and by the University of Sassari (research fund "Metodi per la verifica di reti neurali").

References

1. Ehlers, R.: Formal verification of piece-wise linear feed-forward neural networks. In: D'Souza, D., Narayan Kumar, K. (eds.) ATVA 2017. LNCS, vol. 10482, pp. 269–286. Springer, Cham (2017). https://doi.org/10.1007/978-3-319-68167-2_19
2. Frankle, J., Carbin, M.: The lottery ticket hypothesis: Finding sparse, trainable neural networks. arXiv preprint arXiv:1803.03635 (2018)
3. Frankle, J., Carbin, M.: The lottery ticket hypothesis: training pruned neural networks. CoRR abs/1803.03635 (2018). http://arxiv.org/abs/1803.03635
4. Gilmer, J., Adams, R.P., Goodfellow, I., Andersen, D., Dahl, G.E.: Motivating the rules of the game for adversarial example research. arXiv preprint arXiv:1807.06732 (2018)
5. Goodfellow, I.J., Shlens, J., Szegedy, C.: Explaining and harnessing adversarial examples. In: ICLR (2015)
6. Guidotti, D., Leofante, F., Castellini, C., Tacchella, A.: Repairing learned controllers with convex optimization: a case study. In: Rousseau, L.-M., Stergiou, K. (eds.) CPAIOR 2019. LNCS, vol. 11494, pp. 364–373. Springer, Cham (2019). https://doi.org/10.1007/978-3-030-19212-9_24
7. Guidotti, D., Leofante, F., Tacchella, A., Castellini, C.: Improving reliability of myocontrol using formal verification. IEEE TNSRE 27(4), 564–571 (2019)
8. Huang, X., et al.: Safety and trustworthiness of deep neural networks: a survey. arXiv preprint arXiv:1812.08342 (2018)
9. Katz, G., Barrett, C., Dill, D.L., Julian, K., Kochenderfer, M.J.: Reluplex: an efficient SMT solver for verifying deep neural networks. In: Majumdar, R., Kunčak, V. (eds.) CAV 2017. LNCS, vol. 10426, pp. 97–117. Springer, Cham (2017). https://doi.org/10.1007/978-3-319-63387-9_5
10. LeCun, Y., Bengio, Y., Hinton, G.E.: Deep learning. Nature 521(7553), 436–444 (2015)
11. Liu, W., Wang, Z., Liu, X., Zeng, N., Liu, Y., Alsaadi, F.E.: A survey of deep neural network architectures and their applications. Neurocomputing 234, 11–26 (2017)
12. Nielsen, M.A.: Neural Networks and Deep Learning, vol. 25. Determination Press, San Francisco (2015)
13. Paszke, A., et al.: Automatic differentiation in pytorch (2017)
14. Pedregosa, F., et al.: Scikit-learn: machine learning in Python. J. Mach. Learn. Res. 12, 2825–2830 (2011)
15. Pulina, L., Tacchella, A.: An abstraction-refinement approach to verification of artificial neural networks. In: Touili, T., Cook, B., Jackson, P. (eds.) CAV 2010. LNCS, vol. 6174, pp. 243–257. Springer, Heidelberg (2010). https://doi.org/10.1007/978-3-642-14295-6_24
16. Rauber, J., Brendel, W., Bethge, M.: Foolbox: a Python toolbox to benchmark the robustness of machine learning models. arXiv preprint arXiv:1707.04131 (2017). http://arxiv.org/abs/1707.04131
17. Schwarz, M., Schulz, H., Behnke, S.: RGB-D object recognition and pose estimation based on pre-trained convolutional neural network features. In: 2015 IEEE International Conference on Robotics and Automation (ICRA), pp. 1329–1335. IEEE (2015)
18. Simonyan, K., Zisserman, A.: Very deep convolutional networks for large-scale image recognition. arXiv preprint arXiv:1409.1556 (2014)
19. Szegedy, C., et al.: Intriguing properties of neural networks. In: ICLR (2014)

20. Taigman, Y., Yang, M., Ranzato, M., Wolf, L.: Deepface: closing the gap to human-level performance in face verification. In: CVPR, pp. 1701–1708 (2014)
21. Tang, Y.: Deep learning using linear support vector machines. arXiv preprint arXiv:1306.0239 (2013)
22. Torrey, L., Shavlik, J.: Transfer learning. In: Handbook of Research on Machine Learning Applications and Trends: Algorithms, Methods, and Techniques, pp. 242–264. IGI Global (2010)
23. Wong, E., Schmidt, F., Metzen, J.H., Kolter, J.Z.: Scaling provable adversarial defenses. In: Advances in Neural Information Processing Systems, pp. 8400–8409 (2018)
24. Yu, D., Hinton, G.E., Morgan, N., Chien, J., Sagayama, S.: Introduction to the special section on deep learning for speech and language processing. IEEE Trans. Audio Speech Lang. Process. **20**(1), 4–6 (2012)

Learning Activation Functions by Means of Kernel Based Neural Networks

Giuseppe Marra[1,2]([⊠]), Dario Zanca[2], Alessandro Betti[1,2], and Marco Gori[2]

[1] DINFO, University of Firenze, Florence, Italy
g.marra@unifi.it
[2] DIISM, University of Siena, Siena, Italy

Abstract. The neuron activation function plays a fundamental role in the complexity of learning. In particular, it is widely known that in recurrent networks the learning of long-term dependencies is problematic due to vanishing (or exploding) gradient and that such problem is directly related to the structure of the employed activation function. In this paper, we study the problem of learning neuron-specific activation functions through kernel-based neural networks (KBNN) and we make the following contributions. First, we give a representation theorem which indicates that the best activation function is a kernel expansion over the training set, then approximated with an opportune set of points modeling 1-D clusters. Second, we extend the idea to recurrent networks, where the expressiveness of KBNN can be an determinant factor to capture long-term dependencies. We provide experimental results on some key experiments which clearly show the effectiveness of KBNN when compared with RNN and LSTM cells.

1 Introduction

By and large, the appropriate selection of the activation function in deep architectures is regarded as an important choice for achieving challenging performance. For example, the rectifier function [7] has been playing an important role in the impressive scaling up of nowadays deep nets. Likewise, LSTM cells [8] are widely recognized as the most important ingredient to face long-term dependencies when learning by recurrent neural networks. Both choices come from insightful ideas on the actual non-linear process taking place in deep nets. At a first glance, one might wonder why such an optimal choice must be restricted to a single unit instead of extending it to the overall function to be learned. In addition, this general problem has been already been solved; its solution [5, 6, 12] is in fact at the basis of kernel machines whose limitations as shallow nets have been widely addressed (see e.g. [10, 11]). However, the optimal formulation given for the neuron non-linearity enjoys the tremendous advantage of acting on 1-D spaces. This strongly motivates the reformulation of the problem of learning in deep neural network as a one where the weights and the activation functions are jointly determined by optimization in the framework of regularization operators [14], that are used to enforce the smoothness of the solution. The idea of

© Springer Nature Switzerland AG 2019
M. Alviano et al. (Eds.): AI*IA 2019, LNAI 11946, pp. 418–430, 2019.
https://doi.org/10.1007/978-3-030-35166-3_30

learning the activation function is not entirely new. In [16], activation functions are chosen from a pre-defined set and combine this strategy with a single scaling parameter that is learned during training. It has been argued that one can think of this function as a neural network itself, so the overall architecture is still characterized by a directed acyclic graph [3]. Other approaches learn activation functions as piecewise linear [1], doubled truncated gaussian [15] or Fourier series [4]. A more recent work by [13] introduces a family of activation functions that are based on a kernel expansion at every neuron. The proposed approach is based on the nice intuition that a kernel-based representation for the neuron function is computationally efficient, yet very effective in terms of representation.

In this paper, we study the problem of learning neuron-specific activation functions through kernel-based neural networks (KBNN) and provide two main contributions.

First, we prove that, like for kernel machines, the optimal solution of the variational problem that characterizes the process of supervised learning in the framework of regularization can be expressed by a kernel expansion, so as the overall optimization is reduced to the discovery of a finite set of parameters. The risk function to be minimized contains the weights of the network connections, as well as the parameters associated with the points of the kernel expansion. Hence, the classic learning of the weights of the network takes place with the concurrent development of the optimal shape of the activation functions, one for each neuron. As a consequence, the machine architecture preserves both the strong representational power of deep networks in high dimensional spaces and the effective setting of kernel machines for the learning of the activation functions.

As a second contribution, we extend the idea to Kernel-Based Recurrent Networks (KBRN). In fact, unlike most of the activation functions used in deep networks, those that are developed during learning are not necessarily monotonic. We claim that this property has a crucial impact in their adoption in classic recurrent networks, since this properly addresses classic issues of gradient vanishing when capturing long-term dependencies and provide experimental results on some key experiments which clearly show the effectiveness of KBNN when compared with RNN and LSTM cells [8]. The intuition is that the associated iterated map can either be contractive or expansive. Hence, while in some states the contraction yields gradient vanishing, in others the expansion results in to gradient pumping, which allows the neural network to propagate information back also in case of long time dependences. The possibility of implementing contractive and expanding maps during the processing of a given sequence comes from the capabilities of KBRN to develop different activation functions for different neurons that are not necessarily monotonic. This variety of units is somewhat related to the clever solution proposed in LSTM cells, where the authors realized early that there was room for getting rid of the inherent limitation of the contractive maps deriving from sigmoidal units. Experimental results are provided for some ad hoc cases, which highlight the expressiveness of the proposed units, and for challenging benchmarks that are inspired from seminal paper [2], where the distinctive information for the classification of long sequences is only located in the first positions, while the rest contains uniformly distributed noisy information.

2   Representation and Learning

The feedforward architecture that we consider is based on a directed graph $D \sim (V, A)$, where V is the set of ordered vertices and A is the set of the oriented arcs. Given $i, j \in V$ there is connection from i to j iff $i \prec j$. Instead of assuming a uniform activation function for each vertex of D, a specific function f is attached to each vertex. We denote with I the set of input neurons, with O the set of the output neurons and with $H = V \setminus (I \cup O)$ the set of hidden neurons; the cardinality of these sets will be denoted as $|I|$, $|O|$, $|H|$ and $|V| \equiv n$. Without loss of generality we will also assume that: $I = \{1, 2, \ldots, |I|\}$, $H = \{|I|+1, |I|+2, \ldots, |I|+|H|\}$ and $O = \{|I|+|H|+1, |I|+|H|+2, \ldots |I|+|H|+|O|\}$.

The learning process is based on the training set $T_N = \{ (e^\kappa, y^\kappa) \in \mathbb{R}^{|I|} \times \mathbb{R}^{|O|} \mid \kappa = 1, \ldots N \}$. Given an input vector $z = (z_1, z_2, \ldots z_{|I|})$, the output associated with the vertices of the graph is computed as follows[1]:

$$x_i(z) = z_i(i \in I) + f_i(a_i)(i \notin I), \tag{1}$$

with $a_i = \sum_{j \in \mathrm{pa}(i)} w_{ij} x_j + b_i$, where $\mathrm{pa}(i)$ are the parents of neuron i, and $f_i \colon \Omega_\Lambda \to \mathbb{R}$ are one dimensional real functions; $\Omega_\Lambda := [-\Lambda, \Lambda]$, with Λ chosen big enough, so that Eq. (1) is always well defined. Now let $f = (f_1, f_2, \ldots, f_n)$ and define the output function of the network $F(\cdot, w, b; f) \colon \mathbb{R}^{|I|} \to \mathbb{R}^{|O|}$ by

$$F_i(z, w, b; f) := x_{i+|I|+|H|}(z), \quad i = 1, \ldots, |O|.$$

The learning problem can then be formulated as a double optimization problem defined on both the weights w, b and on the activation functions f_i. It is worth mentioning that while the optimization on the weights of the graph reflects all important issues connected with the powerful representational properties of deep nets, the optimal discovery of the activation functions are somewhat related to the framework of kernel machines. Such an optimization is defined with respect to the following objective function:

$$E(f; w, b) := \frac{1}{2} \sum_{i=1}^{n} (P f_i, P f_i)$$

$$+ \sum_{\kappa=1}^{N} V(e^\kappa, y^\kappa, F(e^\kappa, w, b; f)),$$

which accumulates the empirical risk and a regularization term [14]. Here, we indicate with $(\cdot, \cdot)$ the standard inner product of $L^2(\Omega_\Lambda)$, with P a differential operator of degree p, while V is a suitable loss function.

---

[1] We use Iverson's notation: Given a statement A, we set (A) to 1 if A is true and to 0 if A is false.

Clearly, one can optimize E by independently checking the stationarity with respect to the weights associated with the neural connections and the stationarity with respect to the activation functions. Now we show that the stationarity condition of E with respect to the functional variables f (chosen in a functional space X_p that depends on the order of differential operator P) yields a solution that is very related to classic case of kernel machines that is addressed in [14]. Let us consider a variation $v_i \in C_c^\infty(\Omega_\Lambda)$ with vanishing derivatives on the boundary[2] of Ω_Λ up to order $p - 1$ and define $\varphi_i(t) := E(f_1, \ldots, f_i + tv_i, \ldots, f_n; w, b)$. The first variation of the functional E along v_i is therefore $\varphi_i'(0)$. When using arguments already discussed in related papers [5,12,14] we can easily see that

$$\varphi_i'(0) = \int_{\Omega_\Lambda} \left(Lf_i(a) + \sum_{\kappa=1}^N \alpha_i^\kappa \delta_{a_i^\kappa}(a) \right) v_i(a)\, da,$$

where $\alpha_i^\kappa = \nabla_F V \cdot \partial_{f_i} F$ and $L = P^*P$, P^* being the adjoint operator of P. We notice in passing that the functional dependence of E on f is quite involved, since it depends on the compositions of linear combinations of the functions f_i (see Fig. 1–(a)). Hence, the given expression of the coefficients α_i^κ is rather a formal equation that, however, dictates the structure of the solution.

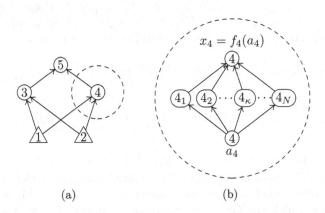

(a)   (b)

Fig. 1. (a) A simple network architecture; the output evaluated using Eq. (1) is $x_5(z_1, z_2) = f_5(w_{53}f_3(w_{31}z_1 + w_{32}z_2 + b_3) + w_{54}f_4(w_{41}z_1 + w_{42}z_2 + b_4) + b_5)$. (b) Highlight of the structure of neuron 4 (encircled in the dashed line) of (a): The activation function f_4 of the neuron is computed as an expansion over the training set. Each neuron 4_j, $j = 1, \ldots, N$ in the figure corresponds to the term $g(a_4 - a_4^j)$ in Eq. (3).

The stationarity conditions $\varphi_i'(0) = 0$ reduce to the following Euler-Lagrange (E-L) equations

$$Lf_i(a) + \sum_{\kappa=1}^N \alpha_i^\kappa \delta_{a_i^\kappa}(a) = 0, \quad i = 1 \ldots n, \tag{2}$$

----

[2] We are assuming here that the values of the functions in X_p at the boundaries together with the derivatives up to order $p - 1$ are fixed.

where a_i^κ is the value of the activation function on the κ-th example of the training set. Let g be the Green function of the operator L, and let k be the solution of $Lk = 0$. Then, we can promptly see that

$$f_i(a) = k(a) - \sum_{\kappa=1}^{N} \alpha_i^\kappa g(a - a_i^\kappa) \tag{3}$$

is the general form of the solution of Eq. (2). Whenever L has null kernel, then this solution is reduced to an expansion of the Green function over the points of the training set. For example, this happens in the case of the pseudo differential operator that originates the Gaussian as the Green function. If we choose $P = d/dx$, then $L = -d^2/dx^2$. Interestingly, the Green function of the second derivative is the rectifier $g(x) = -\frac{1}{2}(|x| + x)$ and, moreover, we have $k(x) = mx + q$. In this case

$$f_i(a) = \theta_i a + \nu_i + \frac{1}{2} \sum_{\kappa=1}^{N} \alpha_i^\kappa |a - a_i^\kappa|, \tag{4}$$

where $\theta_i = m + \frac{1}{2}\sum_{\kappa=1}^{N}\alpha_i^\kappa$, while $\nu_i = q - \frac{1}{2}\sum_{\kappa=1}^{N}\alpha_i^\kappa a_i^\kappa$. Because of the representation structure expressed by Eq. (3), the objective function of the original optimization problem collapses to a standard finite-dimensional optimization on[3]

$$\hat{E}(\alpha, w, b) := E\left(k(a) - \sum_\kappa \alpha^\kappa g(a - a^\kappa); w, b\right)$$

$$= R(\alpha) + \sum_{\kappa=1}^{N} V(e^\kappa, y^\kappa, \hat{F}(e^\kappa, w, b; \alpha));$$

here $R(\alpha)$ is the regularization term and $\hat{F}(e^\kappa, w, b; \alpha) := F(e^\kappa, w, b; k(a) - \sum_\kappa \alpha_i^\kappa g(a - a_i^\kappa))$. This collapse of dimensionality is the same which leads to the dramatic simplification that gives rise to the theory of kernel machines. Basically, in all cases in which the Green function can be interpreted as a kernel, this analysis suggests the neural architecture depicted in Fig. 1, where we can see the integration of graphical structures, typical of deep nets, with the representation in the dual space typical of kernel methods.

3   Recurrent Case and Approximation Issues

We can promptly see that the idea behind kernel-based deep networks can be extended to cyclic graphs, that is to recurrent neural networks. In that case, the analogous of Eq. (1) is:

---

[3] Here we omit the dependencies of the optimization function from the parameters that defines k.

$$h_i^{t+1} = f_i(a_i^{t+1});$$

$$a_i^{t+1} = b_i + \sum_{j \in \mathrm{pa}_{t \to t+1}(i)} w_{ij} h_j^t + \sum_{j \in \mathrm{pa}_{t+1}(i)} u_{ij} x_j^{t+1}.$$

Here we denote with x_i^t the input at step t and with h_i^t the state of the network. The set $\mathrm{pa}_{t \to t+1}(i)$ contains the vertices j that are parents of neuron i; the corresponding arcs (j, i) are associated with a delay, while $\mathrm{pa}_t(i)$ vertices j with non-delayed arcs (j, i). The extension of learning in KBNN to the case of recurrent nets (KBRN) is a straightforward consequence of classic Backpropagation Through Time.

The actual experimentation of the model described requires to deal with a number of important algorithmic issues. In particular, we need to address the typical problem associated with the kernel expansion over the entire training set, that is very expensive in computational terms. However, we can early realize that KBNNs only require to express kernel in 1-D, which dramatically simplify the kernel approximation. Hence, instead of expanding f_i over the entire training set, we can use a number of points d with $d \ll N$. This means that the expansion in Eq. (3) is approximated as follows

$$f_i(a) \approx k(a) - \sum_{k=1}^{d} \chi_i^k g(a - c_i^k), \tag{5}$$

where c_i^k and χ_i^k are the centers and parameters of the expansion, respectively. Notice that χ_i^k are replacing α_i^κ in the formulation given in Sect. 2. We consider c_i^k and χ_i^k as parameters to be learned, and integrate them in the whole optimization scheme.

In the experiments described below we use the rectifier (ReLU) as Green function $(g(x) = -\frac{1}{2}(|x| + x))$ and neglect the linear terms from both $g(x)$ and $k(x)$. We can easily see that this is compatible with typical requirements in machine learning experiments, where in many cases the expected solution is not meaningful with very large inputs. For instance, the same assumption is typically at the basis of kernel machines, where the asymptotic behavior is not typically important. The regularization term $R(\chi)$ can be inherited from the regularization operator P. For the experiments carried out in this paper we decided to choose the ℓ_1 norm[4]:

$$R(\chi) \approx \lambda_\chi \sum_{\substack{1 \le k \le d \\ 1 \le i \le n}} |\chi_i^k|,$$

with $\lambda_\chi \in \mathbb{R}$ being an hyper-parameter that measures the strength of the regularization.

In a deep architecture, when stacking multiple layers of kernel-based units, the non-monotonicity of the activation functions implies the absence of guarantees about the interval on which these functions operate, thus requiring them to

---

[4] This choice is due to the fact that we want to enforce the sparseness of χ, i.e. to use the smallest number of terms in expansion 5.

be responsive to very heterogeneous inputs. In order to face this problem and to allow kernel-based units to concentrate their representational power on limited input ranges, it is possible to apply a normalization [9] to the input of the function. In particular, given $f_i(a_i^\kappa)$, a_i^κ can be normalized as:

$$\hat{a}_i^\kappa = \gamma_i \frac{(a_i^\kappa - \mu_i)}{\sigma_i} + \beta_i;$$

where

$$\mu_i = \frac{1}{N} \sum_{\kappa=i}^{N} a_i^\kappa, \qquad \sigma_i = \frac{1}{N} \sum_{\kappa=i}^{N} (a_i^\kappa - \mu_i)^2;$$

while γ_i and β_i are additional trainable parameters.

4   Experiments

We carried out several experiments in different learning settings to investigate the effectiveness of the KBNN with emphasis on the adoption of kernel-based units in recurrent networks for capturing long-term dependences. Clearly, KBNN architectures require to choose both the graph and the activation function. As it will be clear in the reminder of this section, the interplay of these choices leads to gain remarkable properties.

4.1   The XOR Problem

We begin presenting a typical experimental set up in the classic XOR benchmark. In this experiment we chose a single unit with the Green function $g(z) = |z|$, so as $y = f(w_1 z_1 + w_2 z_2 + b)$ turns out to be

$$y = \sum_{k=1}^{d} \chi^k |w_1 z_1 + w_2 z_2 + b - c^k|$$

where w_1, w_2 and b are trainable variables and the learning of f corresponds with the discovery of both the centroids c^k and the associated weights χ^k. The simplicity of this learning task allows us to underline some interesting properties of KBNNs. We carried out experiment by selecting a number of points for the expansion of the Green function that ranges from 50 to 300. This was done purposely to assess the regularization capabilities of the model, that is very much related to what typically happens with kernel machines. In Fig. 2, we can see the neuron function f at the end of the learning process under different settings. In the different columns, we plot function f with a different numbers d of clusters, while the two rows refer to experiments carried out with and without regularization. As one could expect, the learned activation functions become more and more complex as the number of clusters increases. However, when performing regularization, the effect of the kernel-based component of the architecture plays a crucial role by smoothing the functions significantly.

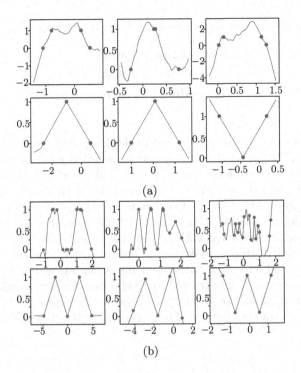

(a)

(b)

Fig. 2. XOR. The plots show the activation functions learned by the simplest KBNN which consists of one unit only for the 2-dim (2a) and 4-dim (2b) XOR. The first/second row refer to experiments with without/with regularization, whereas the three columns correspond with the chosen number of point for the expansion of the Green function $d = 50, 100, 300$.

4.2 The Charging Problem

Let us consider a dynamical system which generates a Boolean sequence according to the model

$$h_t = x_t + [h_{t-1} - 1 > 0] \cdot (h_{t-1} - 1)$$
$$y_t = [h_t > 0], \tag{6}$$

where $h_{-1} = 0$, $x = \langle x_t \rangle$ is a sequence of integers and $y = \langle y_t \rangle$ is a Boolean sequence, that is $y_t \in \{0, 1\}$. An example of sequences generated by this system is the following:

$$t = 0\,1\,2\,3\,4\,5\,6\,7\,8\,9\,10\ldots$$
$$x_t = 0\,0\,0\,4\,0\,0\,0\,0\,0\,0\,0\ldots$$
$$y_t = 0\,0\,0\,1\,1\,1\,1\,0\,0\,0\,0\ldots.$$

Notice that the system keeps memory when other 1 bit are coming, that is

$$t = 0\,1\,2\,3\,4\,5\,6\,7\,8\,9\,10\ldots$$
$$x_t = 0\,0\,0\,4\,0\,2\,0\,0\,0\,0\,0\ldots$$
$$y_t = 0\,0\,0\,1\,1\,1\,1\,1\,1\,0\,0\ldots$$

The purpose of this experiment was that of checking what are the learning capabilities of KBRN to approximate sequences generated according to Eq. 6. The intuition is that a single KBNN-neuron is capable to *charge* the state according to an input, and then to *discharge* it until the state is reset. We generated sequences $\langle x_t \rangle$ of length $L = 30$. Three random element of each sequence were set with a random number ranging from 0 to 9. We compared KBRN, RNN with sigmoidal units, and recurrent with LSTM cells, with a single hidden unit. We used a KBRN unit with $d = 20$ centers to approximate the activation function. The algorithm used for optimization used the Adam algorithm with $\lambda = 0.001$ in all cases. Each model was trained for 10000 iterations with mini-batches of size 500. Figure 3 shows the accuracy on a randomly generated test set of size 25000 during the training process. The horizontal axis is in logarithmic scale.

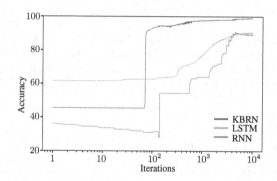

Fig. 3. Charging Problem. The plot shows the accuracy obtained by recurrent nets with classic sigmoidal unit, LSTM cell, and KBNN unit. The horizontal axis is in logarithmic scale.

4.3 Learning Long-Term Dependencies

We carried out a number of experiments aimed at investigating the capabilities of KBRN in learning tasks where we need to capture long-term dependencies. The difficulties of solving similar problems was addressed in [2] by discussions on gradient vanishing that is mostly due to the monotonicity of the activation functions. The authors also provided very effective yet simple benchmarks to claim that classic recurrent networks are unable to classify sequences where the distinguishing information is located only at the very beginning of the sequence; the rest of the sequence was supposed to be randomly generated. We defined a number of benchmarks inspired by the one given in [2], where the decision on the classification of sequence $\langle x_t \rangle$ is contained in the first L bits of a Boolean sequence of length $T \gg L$. We compared KBRN and recurrent nets with LSTM cells using an architecture where both networks were based on 20 hidden units, which makes the two models having approximately the same number of trainable parameters. We used the Adam algorithm with $\lambda = 0.001$ in all cases. Each model was trained for a maximum of $100,000$ iterations with mini-batches of size 500; for each iteration, a single weight update was performed. For the LSTM cells, we used the standard implementation provided by TensorFlow (following [17]). For KBRN we used a number of centroids $d = 100$ and the described normalization.

We generated automatically a set of benchmarks with $L = 2$ and variable length T, where the binary sequences $\langle x_t \rangle$ can be distinguished when looking simply at the first two bits, while the rest is a noisy string with uniformly random distribution. Here we report some of our experiments when choosing the first two discriminant bits according to the $\vee$, $\wedge$, $\oplus$ and $\equiv$ functions.

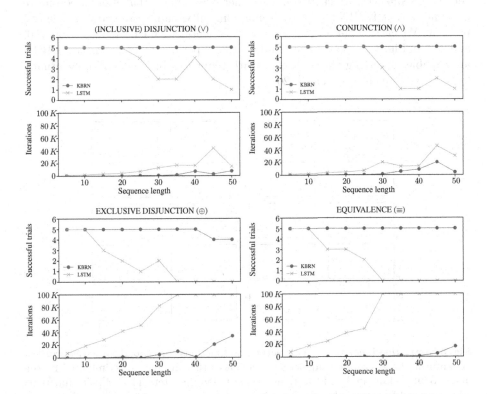

Fig. 4. Capturing Long-Term dependencies. Number of successful trials and average number of iterations for a classification problem when the $\vee$, $\wedge$, $\oplus$ and $\equiv$ functions are used to determine the target, given the first two discriminant bits.

For each Boolean function, that was supposed to be learned, and for several sequence lengths (up to 50), we performed 5 different runs, with different initialization seeds. A trial was considered successful if the model was capable of learning the function before the maximum allowed number of iterations was reached. In Fig. 4 we present the results of these experiments while in Fig. 5 we show the learned activation functions.

Each of the four quadrants of Fig. 4 is relative to a different Boolean function, and reports two different plots. The first one has the sequence length on the x-axis and the number of successful trials on the y-axis. The second plot has the sequence length on the x-axis and, on the y-axis, the average number of iterations required to solve the task. The analysis of these plots allows us to draw a couple of interesting conclusions: *(i)* KBRN architectures are capable of solving the problems in almost all cases, regardless of the sequence length, while recurrent networks with LSTM cells started to experiment difficulties for sequences longer than 30, and *(ii)*, whenever convergence is achieve, KBRN architectures converge significantly faster than LSTM.

In order to investigate with more details the capabilities of KBRN of handling very long sequences, we carried out another experiment, that was based on the benchmark that KBRN solved with more difficulty, namely the equivalence ($\equiv$) problem. We carried out a processing over sequences with length $60, 80, 100, 150,$ and 200. In Fig. 6, we report the results of this experiment. As we can see, KBRN are capable of solving the task even with sequences of length 150, eventually failing with sequences of length 200.

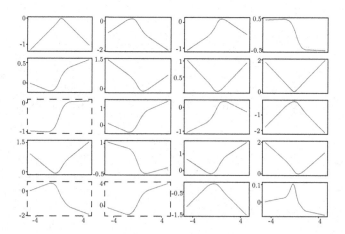

Fig. 5. Activation functions. The 20 activation functions corresponding to the problem of capturing long-term dependencies in sequences that are only discriminated by the first two bit ($\equiv$ function). All functions are plotted in the interval $[-4, 4]$. The functions with a dashed frame are the ones for which $|f'| > 1$ in some subset of $[-4, 4]$.

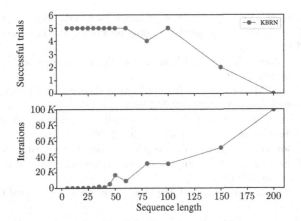

Fig. 6. Capturing Long-Term dependencies. Number of successful trials and average number of iterations when facing the $\equiv$ problem with sequences of length ranging from 5 to 200, when the distinguishing information is located in the first two bits.

5 Conclusions

In this paper we have introduced Kernel-Based Deep Neural Networks. The proposed KBDNN model is characterized by the classic primal representation of deep nets, that is enriched with the expressiveness of activation functions given by kernel expansion. The idea of learning the activation function is not entirely new. However, in this paper we have shown that the KBDNN representation turns out to be the solution of a general optimization problem, in which both the weights, that belong to a finite-dimensional space, and the activation function, that are chosen from a functional space are jointly determined. This bridges naturally the powerful representation capabilities of deep nets with the elegant and effective setting of kernel machines for the learning of the neuron functions.

A massive experimentation of KBDNN is still required to assess the actual impact of the appropriate activation function in real-world problems. However, this paper already proposes a first important conclusion which involves recurrent networks, that are based on this kind of activation function. In particular, we have provided both theoretical and experimental evidence to claim that the KBRN architecture exhibits an ideal computational structure to deal with classic problems of capturing long-term dependencies.

References

1. Agostinelli, F., Hoffman, M., Sadowski, P., Baldi, P.: Learning activation functions to improve deep neural networks. ArXiv preprint arXiv:1412.6830 (2014)
2. Bengio, Y., Frasconi, P., Simard, P.: The problem of learning long-term dependencies in recurrent networks. In: IEEE International Conference on Neural Networks, pp. 1183–1188. IEEE (1993)

3. Castelli, I., Trentin, E.: Combination of supervised and unsupervised learning for training the activation functions of neural networks. Pattern Recogn. Lett. **37**, 178–191 (2014)
4. Eisenach, C., Wang, Z., Liu, H.: Nonparametrically learning activation functions in deep neural nets (2016)
5. Girosi, F., Jones, M., Poggio, T.: Regularization theory and neural networks architectures. Neural Comput. **7**, 219–269 (1995)
6. Girosi, F., Jones, M., Poggio, T.: Regularization networks and support vector machines. Adv. Comput. Math. **13**(1), 1–50 (2000)
7. Glorot, X., Bordes, A., Bengio, Y.: Deep sparse rectifier neural networks. In: Proceedings of the Fourteenth International Conference on Artificial Intelligence and Statistics, pp. 315–323 (2011)
8. Hochreiter, S., Schmidhuber, J.: Long short-term memory. Neural Comput. **9**(8), 1735–1780 (1997)
9. Ioffe, S., Szegedy, C.: Batch normalization: accelerating deep network training by reducing internal covariate shift. In: International Conference on Machine Learning, pp. 448–456 (2015)
10. LeCun, Y., Bengio, Y., Hinton, G.E.: Deep learning. Nature **521**(7553), 436–444 (2015)
11. Mhaskar, H., Liao, Q., Poggio, T.A.: Learning real and boolean functions: when is deep better than shallow. ArXiv preprint arXiv:1603.00988 (2016)
12. Poggio, T., Girosi, F.: Networks for approximation and learning. Proc. IEEE **78**(9), 1481–1497 (1990)
13. Scardapane, S., Van Vaerenbergh, S., Totaro, S., Uncini, A.: Kafnets: kernel-based non-parametric activation functions for neural networks. arXiv preprint arXiv:1707.04035 (2017)
14. Smola, A.J., Schoelkopf, B., Mueller, K.R.: The connection between regularization operators and support vector kernels. Neural Netw. **11**, 637–649 (1998)
15. Su, Q., Liao, X., Carin, L.: A probabilistic framework for nonlinearities in stochastic neural networks. In: Advances in Neural Information Processing Systems 30, pp. 4486–4495. Curran Associates Inc. (2017)
16. Turner, A.J., Miller, J.F.: Neuroevolution: evolving heterogeneous artificial neural networks. Evol. Intell. **7**(3), 135–154 (2014)
17. Zaremba, W., Sutskever, I., Vinyals, O.: Recurrent neural network regularization. ArXiv preprint arXiv:1409.2329 (2014)

Leveraging Multi-task Learning for Biomedical Named Entity Recognition

Tahir Mehmood[1,2(✉)], Alfonso Gerevini[1], Alberto Lavelli[2], and Ivan Serina[1]

[1] University of Brescia, 25121 Brescia, Italy
{t.mehmood,alfonso.gerevini,ivan.serina}@unibs.it
[2] Fondazione Bruno Kessler, 38123 Povo, Trento, Italy
{t.mehmood,lavelli}@fbk.eu

Abstract. Biomedical named entity recognition (BioNER) is the task of categorizing biomedical entities. Due to the specific characteristics of the names of biomedical entities, such as ambiguity among different concepts or different ways of referring to the same entity, the BioNER task is usually considered more challenging compared to standard named entity recognition tasks. Recent techniques based on deep learning not only significantly reduce the hand crafted feature engineering phase but also determined relevant improvements in the BioNER task. However, such systems are still facing challenges. One of them is the limited availability of annotated text data. Multi-task learning approaches tackle this problem by training different related tasks simultaneously. This enables multi-task models to learn common features among different tasks where they share some layers. To explore the advantages of the multi-task learning, we propose a model based on convolution neural networks, long-short term memories, and conditional random fields. The model we propose shows comparable results to state-of-the-art approaches. Moreover, we present an empirical analysis considering the impact of different word input representations (word embedding, character embedding, and case embedding) on the model performance.

Keywords: Biomedical named entity recognition · Multi-task learning · Bidirectional long short-term memory

1 Introduction

Named entity recognition (NER) identifies portions of text and classifies them into predefined categories, e.g. person name, location, etc. NER is an information extraction task and is required in many applications such as question answering systems, information retrieval, co-reference resolution, machine translation, etc. [3]. Most biomedical text data are available as free, unstructured text. The increasing amount of medical texts publicly available makes it difficult for physicians to keep themselves up to date. Identifying biomedical concepts such as disease, chemical, protein, etc in the text data and labelling them with predefined categories is called biomedical named entity recognition (BioNER).

© Springer Nature Switzerland AG 2019
M. Alviano et al. (Eds.): AI*IA 2019, LNAI 11946, pp. 431–444, 2019.
https://doi.org/10.1007/978-3-030-35166-3_31

Recent advances in BioNER derive from the application of deep neural networks, which help researchers to get rid of the manual feature engineering step. Deep learning is now the state-of-the-art technique; however, the complexity of biomedical text data limits the performance of these systems.

Biomedical documents are more complex than normal texts and the names of the entities show peculiar characteristics. Long multi-word expressions *(10-ethyl-5-methyl-5,10-dideazaaminopterin)*, ambiguous words (*TNF alpha* can be used for both DNA and Protein) [8], spelling alternations (e.g., *10-Ethyl-5-methyl-5,10-dideazaaminopterin* vs. *10-EMDDA*) make the BioNER task even more challenging. BioNER is also an important preliminary task for other tasks like the extraction of relations between entities (e.g., chemical induced disease relation, drug-drug interaction, . . .).

Moreover, annotated biomedical text data are not available in large amounts. This is another reason why the performance of the BioNER systems available is not satisfactory. Manually producing such annotated text data for biomedical entities is a time consuming and expensive job. One solution to such a limitation is to use the multi-task approach where different related tasks are trained together simultaneously. Such approach has shown significant improvements in different fields [1]. In this paper, we propose a multi-task model (MTM-CNN) using convolution neural networks (CNNs), Bidirectional long-short term memories (BiLSTM), and conditional random fields (CRFs). Furthermore, we have conducted an empirical analysis of the impact of different word input representations to our model.

The rest of the paper is organized as follows; Sect. 2 gives a brief background of the multi-task learning, followed by Sect. 3 where our multi-task model (MTM-CNN) is discussed. The experimental setup is presented in Sect. 4 which is followed by the results and discussion (Sect. 5). Section 6 concludes and presents possible future research directions.

2 Multi-task Learning

In general, a deep learning model performance highly depends on the amount of annotated data and it performs better with a large amount of data. Unfortunately, in different biomedical tasks, only a limited quantity of annotated text data is available and in this case deep learning models are unable to generalize well. Moreover, manually annotating new data is a time consuming job. This issue can be reduced by using two methods: transfer learning and multi-task learning.

Transfer learning is a kind of knowledge transfer from one domain (auxiliary task) to another domain (main task). In transfer learning, the model is partially trained on an auxiliary task. The pre-trained model is then reused on the main task. This enables the model to fine tune the weights of the layers which are learned during the training on the auxiliary task. Such method helps the model to generalize well on the main task. This implies learning generalized features among auxiliary and main tasks. More specifically, this method learns and transfers shallow features from one domain to another domain [12]. Retraining on the main task can involve the addition of new layers or the freezing of some layers in the original model. The weights of those layers which are frozen are not updated during the training phase on the main task [10]. However, to decide which layers should be kept frozen or trainable is an empirical problem.

Contrary to transfer learning, multi-task learning (MTL) is an approach where different related tasks are trained simultaneously. Unlike transfer learning, multi-task learning optimizes the model under construction concurrently. In MTL approaches, some of the layers in the model are shared among different tasks while keeping some layers task-specific. Training jointly on related tasks helps the multi-task model to learn common features among different tasks by using shared layers [2]. This also helps model to generalize well for the related tasks. The task-specific layers, usually the lower layers, learn features that are more related to the current task. Training related tasks together helps the model to optimize the value of the parameters. Moreover, the MTL lowers the chances of overfitting as the model has to learn the common representation among all tasks. MTL has been widely adopted in many different domains [1, 12].

Crichton et al. [5] proposed a multi-task model (MTM) based on CNN to perform BioNER. However, they only focused on the word level features ignoring the character level ones. Although word level features give much information about the entities, character level features help to extract common sub-word structures among the same entities. Furthermore, depending solely on the word level features can lead to out-of-vocabulary problems when a specific word is not found in the pre-trained word embedding. Wang et al. [17] also performed BioNER using different multi-task models. They found that the MTM with the word level features and extraction of the character level features using BiLSTM enhances performance of the model. They concluded that the character level feature should be considered for the BioNER task.

3   Our Proposal

In this paper, we propose a multi-task model with a Convolution neural network (MTM-CNN) that uses the MTL approach as shown in Fig. 1. Our MTM-CNN model differs from the model presented by Wang et al. [17] in three ways. First, we use the orthographic-level representation of a word in our model. Many studies have exploited word's orthographic-level information for their models [6,9,15]. Providing some explicit orthographic-level information of the word to the model can enhance the model performance where deep learning models implicitly learn orthographic-level features. This can also help CRF whose output highly depends on hand-crafted features [11]. Thus, we believe that considering the orthographic-level representation of the word will help our model to extract more information about the entities. In this paper, we are referring to the explicit orthographic-level features as *case-level features* and we use the two terms interchangeably. In this work the orthographic-level (case-level) feature includes information on the structure of the word, i.e. either the word is starting with a capital letter followed by small letters or all the letters in the word are capital or contain digits, etc.

Secondly, we use CNN instead of BiLSTM, differently to the Wang et al. [17], to extract features at a character level. Many of the approaches have used CNN at a character level [4,14] due to its finer ability of feature extraction. CNN learns global level features from local level ones. This enables CNN to extract more hidden features. Thirdly, we implement stacked layers of BiLSTMs. Using stacked BiLSTMs helps hidden states of BiLSTM to learn the hidden structure of the data presented at different time stamps. This will help BiLSTM to learn features at a more abstract level.

As said earlier, we implemented two stacked BiSLTMs where the first is shared among all the tasks while the lower is task specific. In particularly, the lower layers in our proposed MTM-CNN model are task specific. Thus, for the specific task, both shared layers and layers belonging to that specific task are activated. Finally, we use CRFs for output labeling. CRFs have the ability to tag the current token by considering neighboring tags at a sentence level [9]. Yang et al. [18] performed experiments comparing CRF and Softmax and found out that CRF produces better results compared to Softmax.

An alternative training approach was adopted for the training phase. Let us suppose we have $D_1, D_2, \ldots, D_t$ training sets, related to the $T_1, T_2, \ldots, T_t$ tasks respectively. During the training phase, a training set D_i is selected randomly and both shared layers and the ones specific to the corresponding task T_i are activated. Every task has its own optimizer so during training only the one specific to the task T_i is activated and the loss function related to it is optimized. It means that the parameters of the shared layers and of the task-specific ones are changed during the training of the specific task. The optimizing parameters of the shared layers for all the tasks help the model to find common features among different tasks.

4   Experiments

We performed experiments on the 15 datasets which are also used by Crichton et al. [5] and Wang et al. [17]. The bio-entities in these datasets are Chemical, Species, Cell, Gene/Protein, Cell Component, and Disease[1]. Brief descriptions of datasets, taken from [5], are given in Table 1. Each dataset contains separate training, development, and test sets. In addition, the name of the entities and their distribution in the dataset (percentage wise) is reported in the Table 2. The values in the table represent the percentage of an individual entity, the O-outside tag is not included, contributing in the train/dev/test file. We followed the same experimental setup adopted by Wang et al.[2], using both train and development set data for training the model. Therefore, the table contains the cumulative distribution of the entities for both the training and development set.

Moreover, to represent words, we use a domain-specific pre-trained word embedding since the general one can cause a high rate of out-of-vocabulary

---

[1] The datasets can be found at the following link https://github.com/cambridgeltl/ MTL-Bioinformatics-2016.

[2] https://github.com/yuzhimanhua/Multi-BioNER.

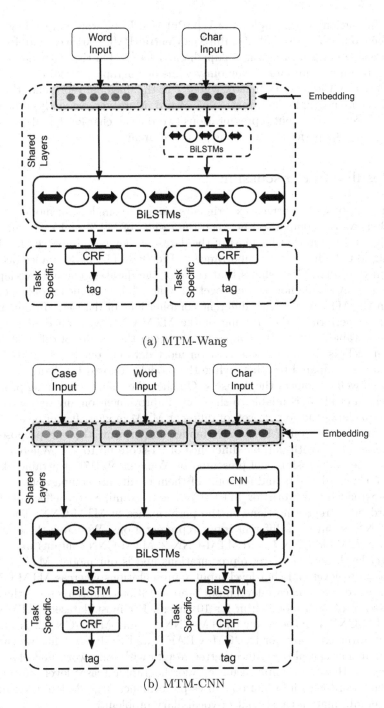

(a) MTM-Wang

(b) MTM-CNN

Fig. 1. Architecture of MTM Models. (a) The MTM model proposed by *Wang et al.* (b) The MTM-CNN model we propose

words. In particular, we employ the WikiPubMed-PMC word embedding which is trained on a large set of the PubMedCentral(PMC) articles and PubMed abstracts as well as on English Wikipedia articles [7]. On the other hand, character embedding is initialized randomly while orthographic (case) embedding is represented by the identity matrix where 1 in the diagonal represents the presence of the orthographic information of a word. Moreover, we analyse the effect of the different word input representations (word level, char level, and case level) of a word on the performance of our proposed architecture.

5   Results and Discussion

As a first step, we performed experiments using the single task model (STM). Table 3 shows the comparison between the results of MTM and its counterpart STM. It can be seen that for most of the datasets they have improved markedly by using MTM, showing its importance in BioNER. The performance decrease noted in the MTM-CNN shows that some of the datasets contain overlapping entities so they should not be used together. One solution to such problem can be to train the MTM-CNN with different combinations of datasets. In our experiments, we performed the training of the MTM-CNN with all datasets. Furthermore, Table 4 shows the comparison between the results of different state-of-the-art STMs. It can be seen that on most datasets our STM yields better performance compared to others while the model proposed by Wang et al. [17] performed well on four of the datasets. On the other hand, the model proposed by Crichton et al. [5] is unable to show any improvement on any dataset.

Table 5 shows the comparison of different MTM models. It can be seen that for all the datasets our MTM-CNN model outperforms the one proposed by Crichton et al. [5] with notable difference of F1-score up to 4%. Whereas compared to the multi-task model presented by Wang et al. [17], it attained better results for most datasets and for some of them results are comparable.

We extended our work for MTM-CNN and examined the effect of different word input representations on the performance of MTM-CNN. Therefore, MTM-CNN is run with different input representations. We name these models MTM-CNN, MTM-CNN_1, and MTM-CNN_2. MTM-CNN contains word-level, character-level, and case-level representations and is our model. MTM-CNN_1 contains word-level and char-level input representations whereas MTM-CNN_2 contains word-level and case-level input representations. Table 6 reports the average F1-score of each model (run for 10 times). For most datasets MTM-CNN and MTM-CNN_1 outperformed MTM-CNN_2 while MTM-CNN_2 is able to show improvements only for BC2GM, CRAFT, and Ex-PTM. Thus we can say that our model can also produce better results with only word and char level information. However, simply using only orthographic (case) level information along with word-level information causes performance degradation as excluding char level information causes out-of-vocabulary problem.

Finally, we also modified our MTM model by using Softmax instead of CRF to find out the impact of Softmax and CRF on our model. Table 7 shows results

Table 1. Datasets description [5].

Dataset	Contents	Entity counts
AnatEM	Anatomy NE	13,701
BC2GM	Gene/Protein NE	24,583
BC4CHEMD	Chemical NE	84,310
BC5CDR	Chemical,Disease NEs	Chemical:15,935; Disease:12,852
BioNLP09	Gene/Protein NE	14,963
BioNLP11EPI	Gene/Protein NE	15,811
BioNLP11ID	4 NEs	Gene/Protein:6551; Organism:3471 Chemical:973; Regulon-operon:87
BioNLP13CG	16 NEs	Gene/Protein:7908; Cell:3492; Chemical:2270; Organism:1715; Tissue: 587; Multi-tissue structure:857; Amino acid:135; Cellular component:569; Organism substance: 283; Organ: 421; Pathological formation:228; Immaterial anatomical entity:102; Organism subdivision:98; Anatomical system:41; Cancer:2582; Developing anatomical structure:35
BioNLP13GE	Gene/Protein NE	12,057
BioNLP13PC	4 NEs	Gene/Protein:10,891; Chemical:2487; Complex:1502; Cellular component:1013
CRAFT	6 NEs	SO:18,974; Gene/Protein:16,064; CL:5495; Taxonomy:6868; Chemical:6053; GO-CC:4180
Ex-PTM	Gene/Protein NE	4698
JNLPBA	5 NEs	Gene/Protein:35,336; DNA:10,589; Cell Type:86391; Cell Line:4330; RNA:1069
Linnaeus	Species NE	4263
NCBI-Disease	Disease NE	6881

comparison for softmax and CRF. It can be seen that using Softmax at output layer it is only able to obtain good results for the linnaeus dataset compared to the model with CRF, while for the rest of the datasets, it is unable to improve the results.

To statistically evaluate the performance of the proposed model, we applied Friedman test which is used when three or more comparisons are drawn [16,19].

Table 2. Entities percentage distribution in Training+Development and test dataset

Dataset	Entities name	Train+Dev Set	Test set
AnatEM	Anatomy	7.241	7.865
BC2GM	Gene	10.505	10.526
BC4CHEMD	Chemical	7.284	7.162
BC5CDR	Chemical	6.061	5.622
	Disease	5.971	5.740
BioNLP09	Protein	9.573	10.274
BioNLP11EPI	Protein	7.662	7.840
BioNLP11ID	Reulon-operon	0.047	0.131
	Chemical	7.036	0.700
	Organism	4.421	3.801
	Protein	4.575	4.134
BioNLP13CG	Gene_or_gene_product	9.975	9.236
	Cancer	2.423	2.896
	Amino_acid	0.088	0.123
	Simple_Chemical	2.631	2.550
	Organism	1.462	1.209
	Cell	4.464	3.987
	Tissue	0.579	0.559
	Organ	0.262	0.328
	Multi_tissue_structure	0.818	0.881
	Cellular_component	0.479	0.472
	Pathological_formation	0.191	0.241
	Immaterial_anatomical	0.075	0.078
	Organism_subdivision	0.060	0.091
	Anatomical_system	0.036	0.049
	Developing_anatomical_structure	0.018	0.040
	Organism_substance	0.197	0.238
BioNLP13GE	Protein	8.100	7.781
BioNLP13PC	Gene_or_gene_product	13.447	13.268
	Simple_chemical	3.272	3.571
	Complex	3.190	3.232
	Cellular_component	0.889	0.879
CRAFT	SO	4.330	3.860
	GGP	4.240	4.320
	Taxon	1.280	1.160
	CHEBI	1.210	1.250
	CL	1.330	1.190
	GO	0.960	0.990
Ex-PTM	Protein	7.967	7.616
JNLPBA	Protein	11.190	9.740
	DNA	5.130	2.810
	Cell_type	3.140	4.860
	Cell_line	2.780	1.470
	RNA	0.504	0.300
Linnaeus	Species	1.153	1.350
NCBI-Disease	Disease	8.220	8.356

Friedman test ranks the values in the column and uses these rank values to find the significance of the data. We found that the results produced by the proposed model and its variants are statistically significant. The total ranks for each dataset is given in the Table 8. We further performed post-hoc Namenyi test for pairwise comparison of the models [13]. Figure 2 shows the post-hoc pairwise analysis of the models where we can see that the result produced by the MTM-CNN-Softmax model is statistically significant with other models with

Table 3. STM vs MTM-CNN

Datasets	STM	MTM-CNN
AnatEM	85.89	**86.99**
BC2GM	**80.90**	80.82
BC4CHEMD	**88.60**	87.39
BC5CDR	85.66	**87.85**
BioNLP09	87.03	**88.74**
BioNLP11EPI	81.48	**84.75**
BioNLP11ID	83.21	**87.65**
BioNLP13CG	81.27	**84.25**
BioNLP13GE	73.36	**79.82**
BioNLP13PC	86.33	**88.84**
CRAFT	**83.84**	83.15
Ex-PTM	72.70	**80.95**
JNLPBA	74.48	**74.05**
linnaeus	87.38	**87.79**
NCBI-disease	84.11	**85.66**

Table 4. Single task model results comparison

Datasets	Wang et al.	Crichton et al.	STM
AnatEM	85.30	81.55	**85.89**
BC2GM	80.00	72.63	**80.90**
BC4CHEMD	**88.75**	82.95	88.60
BC5CDR	**86.96**	83.66	85.66
BioNLP09	84.22	83.90	**87.03**
BioNLP11EPI	77.67	77.72	**81.48**
BioNLP11ID	74.60	81.50	**83.21**
BioNLP13CG	**81.84**	76.74	81.27
BioNLP13GE	69.30	73.28	**73.36**
BioNLP13PC	85.46	80.61	**86.33**
CRAFT	81.20	79.55	**83.84**
Ex-PTM	67.66	68.56	**72.70**
JNLPBA	72.17	69.60	**74.48**
linnaeus	86.94	83.98	**87.38**
NCBI-disease	83.92	80.26	**84.11**

$p_{value} < 0.001$ (NS represents Not Significant). However, rest of the models are statistically not significant with each other. We further extended the analyses

Table 5. Results comparison for different multi-task models

Datasets	Wang et al.	Crichton et al.	MTM-CNN
AnatEM	86.04	82.21	**86.99**
BC2GM	78.86	73.17	**80.82**
BC4CHEMD	**88.83**	83.02	87.39
BC5CDR	**88.14**	83.90	87.85
BioNLP09	88.08	84.2	**88.74**
BioNLP11EPI	83.18	78.86	**84.75**
BioNLP11ID	83.26	81.73	**87.65**
BioNLP13CG	82.48	78.90	**84.25**
BioNLP13GE	**79.87**	78.58	79.82
BioNLP13PC	88.46	81.92	**88.84**
CRAFT	82.89	79.56	**83.15**
Ex-PTM	80.19	74.90	**80.95**
JNLPBA	72.21	70.09	**74.05**
linnaeus	**88.88**	84.04	87.79
NCBI-disease	85.54	80.37	**85.66**

Table 6. Results comparison for all MTM-CNN models

	MTM-CNN	MTM-CNN_1	MTM-CNN_2
	word, char, case	word, char	word, case
AnatEM	**86.99**	86.86	86.43
BC2GM	80.82	81.00	**81.01**
BC4CHEMD	87.39	**87.66**	87.21
BC5CDR	87.85	**88.08**	87.93
BioNLP09	**88.74**	88.67	88.64
BioNLP11EPI	84.75	**85.17**	84.66
BioNLP11ID	**87.65**	87.28	87.01
BioNLP13CG	84.25	**84.39**	84.09
BioNLP13GE	79.82	**80.44**	80.42
BioNLP13PC	88.84	**89.02**	88.59
CRAFT	83.15	83.12	**83.94**
Ex-PTM	80.95	80.83	**80.97**
JNLPBA	**74.05**	73.93	73.99
linnaeus	**87.79**	87.45	87.88
NCBI-disease	**85.66**	85.38	85.07

Table 7. Results comparison for our multi-task model with CRF and Softmax at the output layer

Datasets	MTM-CNN	MTM-CNN-Softmax
AnatEM	**86.99**	85.84
BC2GM	**80.82**	78.71
BC4CHEMD	**87.39**	84.40
BC5CDR	**87.85**	86.78
BioNLP09	**88.74**	88.00
BioNLP11EPI	**84.75**	83.29
BioNLP11ID	**87.65**	87.34
BioNLP13CG	**84.25**	82.98
BioNLP13GE	**79.82**	79.69
BioNLP13PC	**88.84**	87.79
CRAFT	**83.15**	80.98
Ex-PTM	**80.95**	79.60
JNLPBA	**74.05**	71.52
linnaeus	87.79	**88.37**
NCBI-disease	**85.66**	84.17

Table 8. Friedman test ranks for all datasets

	MTM-CNN	MTM-CNN_1	MTM-CNN_2	MTM-CNN-Softmax
AnatEM	34	32	21	13
BC2GM	28	31	31	10
BC4CHEMD	32	32	26	10
BC5CDR	26	33	31	10
BioNLP09	32.5	27.5	25	15
BioNLP11EPI	26	37	27	10
BioNLP11ID	31	24	19	26
BioNLP13CG	32	32	25	11
BioNLP13GE	21	32	26	21
BioNLP13PC	29	35.5	25.5	10
CRAFT	23.5	29	37.5	10
Ex-PTM	30	27	28	15
JNLPBA	34	28	28	10
linnaeus	24	18	27	31
NCBI-disease	36	28	22	14
Total Ranks	**439**	**446**	**399**	**216**
Avg Ranks	$\bar{r}_p$ **2.92**	$\bar{r}_q$ **2.97**	$\bar{r}_r$ **2.66**	$\bar{r}_s$ **1.44**

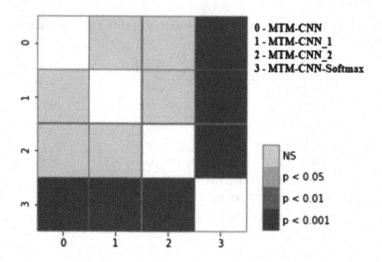

Fig. 2. Posthoc pairwise analysis with Nemenyi of FriedmanTest

of the post-hoc Namenyi test to observe the models that are statistically better from one another. Figure 3 shows the graphical representations where we can see that MTM-CNN, MTM-CNN_1, MTM-CNN_2, are statistically better than MTM-CNN-Softmax.

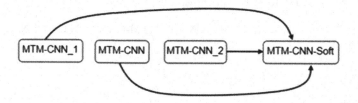

Fig. 3. Graphical representation of the Friedman test

6   Conclusion and Future Work

In this paper we showed that BioNER performance can be drastically improved by using a multi-task approach. The results depict that the multi-task approach can be a good solution when not enough data are available to perform BioNER. We also performed an empirical analysis of different input representations of word input to examine their impact to our model. For future work, we will extend it using attention mechanisms since a number of studies have shown significant advantages of attention mechanisms over traditional LSTMs. Moreover, we will also expand our multi-task model to perform the relation extraction task in which BioNER can be used as an auxiliary task while keeping the relation extraction task as the main task.

References

1. Argyriou, A., Evgeniou, T., Pontil, M.: Multi-task feature learning. In: Advances in Neural Information Processing Systems, pp. 41–48 (2007)
2. Bansal, T., Belanger, D., McCallum, A.: Ask the GRU: multi-task learning for deep text recommendations. In: Proceedings of the 10th ACM Conference on Recommender Systems, pp. 107–114. ACM (2016)
3. Chieu, H.L., Ng, H.T.: Named entity recognition: a maximum entropy approach using global information. In: Proceedings of the 19th International Conference on Computational Linguistics-Volume 1, pp. 1–7. Association for Computational Linguistics (2002)
4. Collobert, R., Weston, J., Bottou, L., Karlen, M., Kavukcuoglu, K., Kuksa, P.: Natural language processing (almost) from scratch. J. Mach. Learn. Res. **12**(Aug), 2493–2537 (2011)
5. Crichton, G., Pyysalo, S., Chiu, B., Korhonen, A.: A neural network multi-task learning approach to biomedical named entity recognition. BMC Bioinform. **18**(1), 368 (2017)
6. Dugas, F., Nichols, E.: DeepNNNER: applying BLSTM-CNNs and extended lexicons to named entity recognition in tweets. In: Proceedings of the 2nd Workshop on Noisy User-generated Text (WNUT), pp. 178–187 (2016)
7. Giorgi, J.M., Bader, G.D.: Transfer learning for biomedical named entity recognition with neural networks. Bioinformatics **34**(23), 4087–4094 (2018)
8. Gridach, M.: Character-level neural network for biomedical named entity recognition. J. Biomed. Inform. **70**, 85–91 (2017)
9. Huang, Z., Xu, W., Yu, K.: Bidirectional LSTM-CRF models for sequence tagging. CoRR abs/1508.01991 (2015). http://arxiv.org/abs/1508.01991
10. Li, Z., Hoiem, D.: Learning without forgetting. IEEE Trans. Pattern Anal. Mach. Intell. **40**(12), 2935–2947 (2018). https://doi.org/10.1109/TPAMI.2017.2773081
11. Limsopatham, N., Collier, N.: Learning orthographic features in bi-directional LSTM for biomedical named entity recognition. In: Proceedings of the Fifth Workshop on Building and Evaluating Resources for Biomedical Text Mining, BioTxtM@COLING 2016, Osaka, Japan, 12 December 2016, pp. 10–19 (2016). https://aclanthology.info/papers/W16-5102/w16-5102
12. Luong, M., Le, Q.V., Sutskever, I., Vinyals, O., Kaiser, L.: Multi-task sequence to sequence learning. In: 4th International Conference on Learning Representations, ICLR 2016, San Juan, Puerto Rico, 2–4 May 2016, Conference Track Proceedings (2016). http://arxiv.org/abs/1511.06114
13. Pohlert, T.: The pairwise multiple comparison of mean ranks package (PMCMR)
14. dos Santos, C., Guimaraes, V., Niterói, R., de Janeiro, R.: Boosting named entity recognition with neural character embeddings. In: Proceedings of NEWS 2015 The Fifth Named Entities Workshop, p. 25 (2015)
15. Segura-Bedmar, I., Suárez-Paniagua, V., Martínez, P.: Exploring word embedding for drug name recognition. In: Proceedings of the Sixth International Workshop on Health Text Mining and Information Analysis, Louhi@EMNLP 2015, Lisbon, Portugal, 17 September 2015, pp. 64–72 (2015). https://doi.org/10.18653/v1/W15-2608
16. Sheldon, M.R., Fillyaw, M.J., Thompson, W.D.: The use and interpretation of the Friedman test in the analysis of ordinal-scale data in repeated measures designs. Physiother. Res. Int. **1**(4), 221–228 (1996)

17. Wang, X., et al.: Cross-type biomedical named entity recognition with deep multi-task learning. Bioinformatics **35**(10), 1745–1752 (2019)
18. Yang, J., Liang, S., Zhang, Y.: Design challenges and misconceptions in neural sequence labeling. In: Proceedings of the 27th International Conference on Computational Linguistics, COLING 2018, Santa Fe, New Mexico, USA, 20–26 August 2018, pp. 3879–3889 (2018). https://aclanthology.info/papers/C18-1327/c18-1327
19. Zimmerman, D.W., Zumbo, B.D.: Relative power of the Wilcoxon test, the Friedman test, and repeated-measures ANOVA on ranks. J. Exp. Educ. **62**(1), 75–86 (1993)

Applying Self-interaction Attention for Extracting Drug-Drug Interactions

Luca Putelli[1,2]([envelope]), Alfonso E. Gerevini[1]([envelope]), Alberto Lavelli[2]([envelope]),
and Ivan Serina[1]([envelope])

[1] Universitá degli Studi di Brescia, Brescia, Italy
{alfonso.gerevini,ivan.serina}@unibs.it
[2] Fondazione Bruno Kessler, Trento, Italy
{l.putelli,lavelli}@fbk.eu

Abstract. Discovering the effect of the simultaneous assumption of drugs is a very important field in medical research that could improve the effectiveness of healthcare and avoid adverse drug reactions which can cause health problems to patients. Although there are several pharmacological databases containing information on drugs, this type of information is often expressed in the form of free text. Analyzing sentences in order to extract drug-drug interactions was the objective of the DDIExtraction-2013 task. Despite the fact that the challenge took place six years ago, the interest on this task is still active and several new methods based on Recurrent Neural Networks and Attention Mechanisms have been designed. In this paper, we propose a model that combines bidirectional Long Short Term Memory (LSTM) networks with the Self-Interaction Attention Mechanism. Experimental analysis shows how this model improves the classification accuracy reducing the tendency to predict the majority class resulting in false negatives, over several input configurations.

1 Introduction

Healthcare professionals constantly study the risks of taking medications. This discipline, called pharmacovigilance, focuses on side effects and adverse drug reactions (ADR) in order to minimize the risk of health issues that may affect patients. With the rise of this discipline, pharmacological databases like Drug-Bank or IUPHAR/BPS were created. Moreover, starting from 1997 the scientific literature database MedLine is free and accessible via its search engine, PubMed, providing abstracts and references concerning healthcare related topics.

In order to use these data for clinical purposes, we need to ensure the quality and the consistency of the information about ADR. With the increase of pharmacovigilance publications, keeping these databases updated and trustworthy can be a very complex and demanding issue for humans who would be required to read a huge amount of texts.

The DDIExtraction-2013 task [25] is a machine learning challenge that addresses these issues. In order to build or to control pharmacological knowledge bases, it is necessary to define a machine learning model that extracts

© Springer Nature Switzerland AG 2019
M. Alviano et al. (Eds.): AI*IA 2019, LNAI 11946, pp. 445–460, 2019.
https://doi.org/10.1007/978-3-030-35166-3_32

relations between drugs. In particular, the goal is to find and classify Drug-Drug Interactions (DDIs), i.e. potential adverse drug reactions that occur when two drugs are assumed simultaneously by a patient. DDIs have to be extracted from a corpus of free-text sentences, combining machine learning with natural language processing (NLP) techniques.

In the last few years, deep neural networks obtained great results over text data. Word embedding techniques and neural network based algorithms like Word2Vec [18] and Glove [21] are the typical way to represent words. Similarly, Recurrent Neural Networks (RNN) and Long Short Term Memory networks (LSTM) are now the state-of-the-art technology for most of natural language processing tasks like text classification or relation extraction. These techniques process the entire sequence of words, allowing the model to capture dependencies among words and keeping the context information for the whole sentence.

Since in a relation extraction task some words are more important than others, the attention mechanism scores the relevance of the words for classification purpose [10] creating a context representation vector. The main idea behind the attention mechanism [1] is that the model "pays attention" only to the parts of the input where the most relevant information is present. There are several types of attention mechanisms, like Global Attention, which considers all the words for building the context, Local Attention that relies only on a subset of words [16], or Self-Attention [27] into which multiple attention mechanisms are applied in parallel, trying to discover every connection between pair of words.

This is the main goal also of the self-interaction mechanism [34] that applies attention with a different weight vector for each word in the sequence, producing a matrix that represents the influence between all word pairs. We consider this information very meaningful, especially in a challenge like this one where we need to discover connections between pairs of words.

In this paper we show how self-interaction attention improves the results in the DDI-2013 task, in particular reducing the tendency to predict the majority class, which is the main issue for this challenge due to the strong dataset unbalance. We also compare our approach with the other state-of-the-art methods.

2 Related Work

The best performing teams in the DDI-2013 original challenge [25] used SVM [3]. In particular, in [5] the information from the global context of the sentence and the local context of the two drug mentions in order is exploited defining a new kernel. This work also deals with the skewness of the dataset with different techniques: filtering instances from the training-set, removing sentences with two drug mentions with the same name and exploiting negations.

More recently, deep learning techniques have proved to be the new state of the art. Even for this task, in the last two years several papers have applied Convolutional Neural Networks (CNN) or Recurrent Neural Networks (RNN).

2.1   CNN Approaches

Authors in [22] propose a Multichannel Convolutional Neural Network into which each sentence is represented by five stacked matrices. Given a sentence of m words and a word embedding representation of s real numbers, the matrix $M \in \mathbb{R}^{m \times s}$ constitutes a channel. This work considers five different word embedding representations and builds a five-channels input which is passed to a convolutional layer followed by a max-pooling [20, 26] layer and a last fully connected layer with softmax activation [8, Chapter 6.2.2].

In [15] is defined a single channel model with one convolutional layer with tanh activation and a max-pooling layer. The simplicity of the model is balanced by a more thorough negative filtering that excludes drug mention pairs with the same name, if one is the abbreviation, acronym or a special case (like, for example "Drug1 such as Drug2") of the other or if they appear in a coordinate structure.

2.2   RNN and Attention-Based Models

Recurrent Neural Networks (RNN) and their ability to analyze sequences of data are the main concepts contained in several works [19]. In particular, Long Short Term Memory (LSTM) units in RNN allow to keep and learn context information through sentences. Moreover, LSTM neural networks can lose important contextual information if the sequence is particularly long and complicated [23]. The main response to this issue is to develop an attention-based model [1,16], scoring the importance of sequence segments for the machine learning task. In this challenge, the attention mechanism assigns weights to the most influential words, i.e. the ones that indicate the presence or the absence of a relation between two drugs. For the DDI-2013 task, LSTM and Attention-based models obtain the best results, outperforming SVM and CNN methods. In this section we present a selection of works following this approach.

The work presented in [11] is proposed a double LSTM. The sentences are processed by two different bidirectional LSTM layers: one followed by a max-pooling layer and the other one by a custom made attention-pooling layer that assigns weights to words. The results of these two paths are concatenated and followed by a fully connected layer with softmax activation function.

The work in [32] uses a multi-path LSTM neural network. Three parallel bidirectional LSTM layers process the sentence sequence and a fourth one processes the shortest dependency path between the two candidate drugs in the dependency tree. The output of these four layers is merged and handled by another bidirectional LSTM layer and passed to a softmax classifier. In this work, the attention mechanism assigns scores to the words with respect to the two candidate drugs before the sequence is treated by the LSTM layers ("input attention").

Similarly, in [35] the attention is directly applied to word vectors, creating a "candidate-drugs-oriented" input which is processed by a single LSTM layer. This mechanism, called "drug-oriented input attention", calculates the relevance degree between each word and the two drug mentions using the scalar product as score function. Given the word w_i and the two drug mentions (with $j \in \{1, 2\}$) and their vector representation u_{w_i} and u_{d_j}, this work calculates the relevance degree α_i^j as the scalar product between u_{w_i} and u_{d_j} divided by the length of the sentence and then the softmax function is applied. α_i is defined ad the average of the contributions α_i^1 and α_i^2. The new "candidate-drugs-oriented input" is obtained as the element-wise multiplication between the original representation u_{w_i} and α_i.

The work in [30] uses a RNN with Gated Recurrent Units (GRU) [4] instead of LSTM units, followed by a traditional attention mechanism, and it exploits information contained in other sentences with a custom made sentence attention.

While self-attention [27] is quite popular for this task [6,13], to the best of our knowledge the self-interaction mechanism, which shares the main concept of discovering the influence between all word pairs, has not been tried in a relation extraction task yet.

3 Dataset Description

This dataset was released for the shared challenge SemEval 2013 - Task 9 [25] and contains annotated documents from the biomedical literature. In particular, there are two different sources: abstracts from MedLine research articles and texts from the pharmacological database DrugBank.

Every document is divided into sentences and, for each sentence, the dataset provides annotations of every drug mentioned. The task requires to classify all the possible pairs of drugs that can be found in the given sentences. If the sentence mentions only two drugs, there is only one pair but, in general, if the sentence mention n drugs, there are $\binom{n}{2}$ instances, provided with their classification value. There are five different classes: **unrelated:** the text states that there is no relation between the two drugs mentioned; **effect:** the text describes the effect of the drug-drug interaction; **advise:** the text gives a recommendation to avoid the simultaneous assumption of two drugs; **mechanism:** the text describes an anomaly of the absorption of a drug, if assumed simultaneously with another one; **int:** the text states a generic interaction between the drugs not giving further details.

4 Pre-processing

The pre-processing phase exploits the "en_core_web_sm" model of spaCy[1], a Python tool for Natural Language Processing, and it is composed by the following steps:

Tokenization and PoS tagging: each sentence is divided into tokens. If a drug name is composed by more than one token (for example, "TNF antagonist"), these tokens are merged into a single one. Each token is also labelled with a part-of-speech tag by spaCy.

---

[1] https://spacy.io.

Substitution: given a pair of drug mentions in a sentence, the corresponding tokens are replaced by the standard terms `PairDrug1` and `PairDrug2`. In the particular case when the pair is composed by two mentions of the same drug, these two drug names are replaced by `NoPair`. Every other drug mentioned in the sentence is replaced with the generic term `Drug`.

Shortest dependency path: spaCy analyzes the grammatical structure of the sentence and provides its dependency tree, with tokens as nodes and dependency relations between the words as edges. Every edge is also labelled with a dependency tag, such as `neg` for negations or `dobj` for subjects. Then, we calculate the shortest path in the dependency tree between `PairDrug1` and `PairDrug2`.

4.1   Negative Instance Filtering

The DDI-2013 dataset contains a large amount of "negative instances", i.e. instances that belong to the unrelated class. In an unbalanced dataset, machine learning algorithms are more likely to classify a new instance over the majority class, leading to poor performance for the minority classes [28]. In order to avoid that, and given that previous works on this dataset [5,11,35] have demonstrated a positive effect of reducing the number of negative instances, we have filtered out some instances from the training-set relying only on the structure of the sentence.

First of all, since the purpose of this task is to find relations between pairs of different drugs, if the two drug mentions have the same name or they differ only for the final character (for example "antidepressant" and "antidepressants") we can automatically label such instance as negative.

In addition to this case, we can filter out a candidate pair if the two drug mentions appear in coordinate structure, like in a list. For example, in the sentence "The majority of patients in RA clinical studies received one or more of the following concomitant medications with ORENCIA: *MTX, NSAIDs, corticosteroids, TNF blocking agents, azathioprine, gold, hydroxychloroquine, leflunomide, sulfasalazine,* and *anakinra*" the drug names in italic are in a coordinate structure, so we can apply the negative filtering for all the possible pairs between two drugs in this list.

While other works like [11] and [15] apply custom-made rules for this dataset, such as filtering for particular regular expressions involving the two drug mentions, our choice is to keep the pre-processing phase as general as possible, with the purpose of defining an approach that can be applied for other relation extraction tasks. In order to filter the drug mentions that appear in coordinate structures avoiding dataset oriented techniques, we exploit the dependency tree checking the shortest dependency path between the two drug mentions: if it contains only drug names or the word "and", the instance can be filtered out.

These rules are applied to both the training set and the test set. In the first case, negative instances with two drug mentions having the same name or in a coordinate structure are not considered as training examples. Instead, no negative instances are excluded from the test-set: all those instances with two drug mentions having the same name or in a coordinate structure are classified as unrelated.

4.2 Offset Features

The representation of each token (i.e. each word) in the sentence includes four features: the word itself, its PoS tag and two offset features D_1 and D_2 [31]. Given a word W in the sentence, D_1 is calculated as the distance (in terms of words) from the first drug mention. Similarly, D_2 is calculated as the distance from the second drug mention. For example, in the sentence "Intravenous PairDrug1 was shown to double the bioavailability of oral PairDrug2", the word "shown" has D_1 equals to 2 and D_2 equals to -7.

5   Model Description

In this section we present the LSTM based model, the self-attention mechanism and how it is used for relation extraction.

5.1 Embedding

In order to build the input for our neural network model, each feature has to be mapped into a vector of real numbers [14].

Each word in our corpus is represented with a vector of length 200. These vectors are obtained with a Word2Vec [18] fine-tuning. We initialized a Word2Vec model with the vectors obtained by the authors of [17] the same algorithm over PubMed abstracts and PMC texts, and trained our Word2Vec model using the DDI-2013 corpus.

PoS tags are represented with vectors of length 20. These are obtained applying the Word2Vec method to the sequence of PoS tags in our corpus.

The offset features are represented with two vectors of length 3. These vectors are obtained using an embedding layer and they are trained contextually with the entire model.

5.2 Bidirectional LSTM Layer

A Recurrent neural network is a deep learning model for processing sequential data, like natural language sentences. Its issues with vanishing gradient are avoided using LSTM cells [7,9]. Given $x_1, x_2 \ldots x_m$, h_{t-1} and c_{t-1} where m is the length of the sentence and $x_i \in \mathbb{R}^d$ is the vector obtained by concatenating the embedded features, h_{t-1} and c_{t-1} are the hidden state and the cell state of the previous LSTM cell (h_0 and c_0 are initialized as zero vectors), new hidden state and cell state values are computed as follows:

$$\hat{c}_t = \tanh(W_c[h_{t_i}, x_t] + b_c)$$
$$i_t = \sigma(W_i[h_{t_i}, x_t] + b_i)$$
$$f_t = \sigma(W_f[h_{t_i}, x_t] + b_f)$$
$$o_t = \sigma(W_o[h_{t_i}, x_t] + b_o)$$
$$c_t = i_t * \hat{c}_t + f_t * c_{t-1}$$
$$h_t = \tanh(c_t) * o_t$$

with σ being the sigmoid activation function and $*$ denoting the element wise product. $W_f, W_i, W_o, W_c \in \mathbb{R}^{(N+d) \times N}$ are weight matrices and $b_f, b_i, b_o, b_c \in \mathbb{R}^N$ are bias vectors. Weight matrices and bias vectors are randomly initialized and learned by the neural network during the training phase. N is the LSTM layer size and d is the dimension of the feature vector for each input word. The vectors in square brackets are concatenated.

Bidirectional LSTM not only computes the input sequence in the order of the sentence but also backwards [24]. Hence, we can compute h^r using the same equations described earlier but reversing the word sequence. Given h_t computed in the sentence order and h_t^r in the reversed order, the output of the t bidirectional LSTM cell h_t^b is the result of the concatenation: $h_t^b = [h_t, h_t^r]$

5.3 Sentence Representation and Attention Mechanism

The LSTM layers produce, for each word input w_i, a vector $h_i \in \mathbb{R}^n$ which is the result of computing every word from the start of the sentence to w_i. Hence, given a sentence of length m, h_m can be considered as the sentence representation produced by the LSTM layer. So, for a sentence classification task, h_m can be used as the input to a fully connected layer that provides the classification. LSTM neural networks have difficulties preserving dependencies between distant words [23] and, especially for long sentences, h_m may not be influenced by the first words or may be affected by less relevant words. The attention mechanism [1,10] deals with these problems taking into consideration each h_i, computing weights α_i for each word contribution:

$$u_i = \tanh(W_a h_i + b_a)$$
$$\alpha_i = softmax(v^T u_i) = exp(v^T u_i) / \sum_{k=1}^n exp(v^T u_k)$$

where $W_a \in \mathbb{R}^{N \times N}$, $b_a \in \mathbb{R}^N$ and $v \in \mathbb{R}^N$ are trainable parameters of attention mechanism.

The attention mechanism outputs the sentence representation, also called the *context vector*:

$$s = \sum_{i=1}^m \alpha_i h_i$$

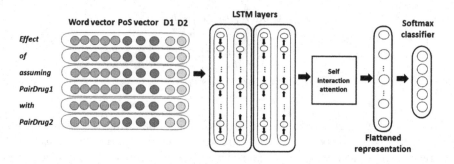

Fig. 1. Model 1

5.4   Model 1

As proposed by [34], self-interaction mechanism uses multiple v_i for each word w_i instead of using a single one. This way, we can extract the influence (called *action*) between the *action controller* w_i and the rest of the sentence, i.e. each w_k for $k \in \{1, m\}$. The action of w_i is calculated as follows:

$$s_i = \sum_{k=1}^{m} \alpha_{i,k} u_i$$
$$\alpha_{i_k} = exp(v_k^T u_i) / \sum_{j=1}^{m} exp(v_j^T u_i)$$

with u_i defined in the same way as the traditional mechanism.

In order to obtain also in this case a *context vector* representing the sentence, in [34] each s_i is aggregated into a single vector s as its average, maximum or even applying another standard attention layer. In our model we choose to avoid any pooling operations and to concatenate instead each s_i, creating a *flattened representation* [6] and passing it to the classification layer.

The model designed (see Fig. 1) and tested for the DDI-2013 Relation Extraction includes the following layers: three parallel **embedding layers**: one with pre-trained word vectors, one with pre-trained PoS tag vectors and one that calculates the embedding of the offset features; two **bidirectional LSTM layers** that process the word sequence; the **self-interaction attention mechanism**; a **fully connected layer** with 5 neurons (one for each class) and softmax activation function that provides the classification.

Our work differs from the others in these aspects: the **independent negative filtering** that uses only the dependency tree, avoids dataset-oriented techniques and can be applied for other relation extraction tasks; the **self-interaction attention mechanism** with its ability to represent the influence between each pair of words; and the **flattened representation** for avoiding any pooling operations and preserving all the information.

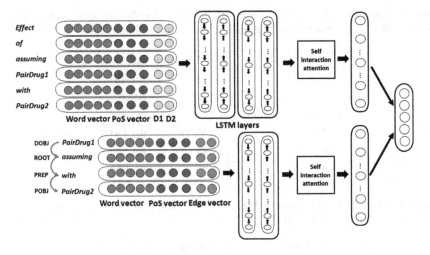

Fig. 2. Model 2

5.5 Model 2

This model is composed by two channels in parallel (see Fig. 2): the first one replicates exactly the first model, the second is composed by one LSTM layer and a subsequent self-interaction mechanism. This channel does not process the entire sequence but only the words belonging to the Shortest Dependency Path [32], alongside with PoS tags. Also, for this second model the edge labels that represent grammatical relations between words are embedded in vectors of size 10. The output of the two channels is concatenated and forms the input for the fully-connected softmax layer.

6 Results and Discussion

6.1 Experimental Settings

Our models are implemented using Keras library with Tensorflow backend. We perform a simple random hyper-parameter search [2] in order to optimize the learning phase and avoiding overfitting, using a subset of sentences as validation set. This is the configuration of the model: *LSTM layer size*: 80, *dropout*: 0.45, *recurrent dropout*: 0.48, *optimization algorithm*: Adam, *learning rate*: 0.0001. For Model 2, considering that the shortest dependency path input is shorter than the entire sentence, the size of the LSTM layer is 40.

6.2 Evaluation

We tested our two models with different input configurations: using only word vectors, word and PoS tag vectors or adding also the offset features. For the second model, we tested also the inclusion of the edge labels embedding.

Table 1. Overall recall (%) comparison with different models and input configurations. The asterisk denotes statistically significant results according to the Wilcoxon test.

Model: Input	No Attention	Attention
1: Word	64.44	**69.68***
1: Word+Tag	**65.37**	64.96
1: Word+Tag+Offset	60.67	**70.88***
2: Word	57.30	**65.78***
2: Word+Tag	58.42	**65.27***
2: Word+Tag+Edge	56.70	**62.00***

Table 2. Detailed F-Score comparison with different configurations. For each class, best F-Score is marked in bold.

	Effect		Mechanism		Advise		Int	
	No Att	Att	No Att	Att	No Att	Att	No Att	Att
1: Word	0.68	**0.70**	0.69	0.70	0.77	0.78	0.53	0.45
1: Word+Tag	0.67	0.69	0.71	0.70	0.78	0.77	**0.55**	0.43
1: Word+Tag+Offset	0.65	0.69	0.68	**0.76**	0.74	**0.78**	0.50	0.49
2: Word	0.65	0.68	0.65	0.72	0.65	0.76	0.50	0.50
2: Word+Tag	0.63	0.69	0.68	0.69	0.69	0.74	0.51	0.53
2: Word+Tag+Edge	0.65	0.66	0.67	0.71	0.66	0.70	0.49	0.45

In Table 1 we show the recall measure for each input configurations. The effect of self-interaction is also verified through Wilcoxon test [29]: for all input configurations except one, the models with self-interaction attention perform significantly better than without it with confidence of 99%. The Word+Tag configuration shows a little performance decrease, but this is not statistically significant.

Since our negative filtering avoids the application of dataset-oriented techniques for generalization purpose, self-interaction can be seen as a method for reducing the effect of the presence of a large majority class like unrelated.

In Table 2 we show the F-Score for each class of the dataset. Model 1 performs better than Model 2, despite the introduction of new information with the shortest dependency path. The best configuration includes word vectors, PoS tagging vectors and offset features as input. The overall performance of this configuration is considered also in Table 3. Both models and all the configurations obtain good results, predicting the unrelated class with a F-Score between 0.95 and 0.96.

Figure 3 shows improvements of the recall average over each input configuration produced by adding the self-interaction attention mechanism. Similar results are obtained also with Model 2. On the other hand, we can observe a slight performance worsening regarding the int class. We address this issue in Sect. 6.3.

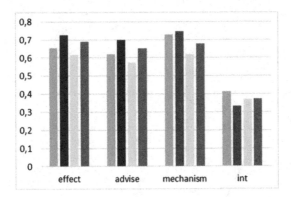

Fig. 3. Recall improvements in Model 1 and Model 2. Comparison of the average recall for each class with (in blue for Model 1, in green for Model 2) or without (in light blue for Model 1, in light green for Model 2) the self-interaction attention mechanism. (Color figure online)

In Table 3 we compare our results with other state-of-the-art methods. Our method produces better or similar results than most of the other approaches which apply dataset-oriented negative filtering techniques. In terms of F-Score, Word Attention LSTM [35] outperforms our approach and the other LSTM-based models by more than 4%. We discuss this issue in Sect. 6.4.

Table 3. Comparison with overall metrics of other state-of-the-art methods: precision (P), recall (R) and F-Score (F), ordered by F. Results higher than ours are marked in bold. Our results are obtained with the best configuration of Model 1.

Method	P(%)	R(%)	F(%)
UTurku (SVM)	73.2	49.9	59.4
FBK-irst (SVM)	64.6	65.6	65.1
Zhao SCNN	72.5	65.1	68.6
Liu CNN	75.7	64.7	69.8
Multi-Channel	76.0	65.3	70.2
Joint-LSTMs	73.4	69.7	71.5
Our method	**73.0**	**70.9**	**71.9**
GRU	**73.7**	70.8	**72.2**
SDP-LSTM	**74.1**	71.8	**72.9**
Word-Att LSTM	**78.4**	**76.2**	**77.3**

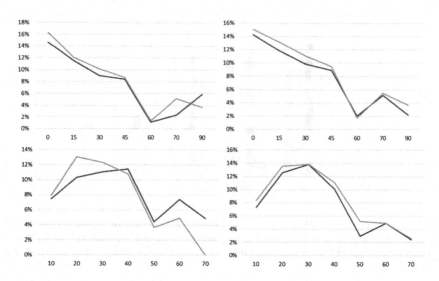

Fig. 4. On the y-axis, percentage of error respect to the x-axis representing the sentence length (top) or the distance between the drug mentions (bottom). Model 1 is on the left, Model 2 is on the right and, for all the diagrams, blue indicates the model configuration with attention, lighter blue without it (Color figure online)

6.3   Discussion and Error Analysis

In order to lay the foundation of our future work and to understand the short-comings of our approach, we have analyzed the error distribution for our best model. The main problem with our system is again the distinction between all the related classes and the negative class. While the self-interaction mechanism decreases this error by 14.6%, this distinction includes the 83.5% of all the mis-classification errors. On the contrary, the distinction for the three main related classes advise, mechanism and effect works quite well with or without the attention mechanism. Only 30 misclassifications for 861 test instances belonging to those three classes are due to this distinction task.

The int class, to which only 1.6% of all test instances belongs, presents more issues. In fact, our system tends to classify these instances as effect even more than predicting the unrelated class. We speculate that our model recognizes that these kinds of sentences present some sort of relation and it tends to classify with the most frequent related class.

We also analyze how our system works with respect to sentence length and to the distance between the two drug mentions. Figure 4 shows that our system performs worse over short or medium length sentences. The attention mechanism does not significantly change the error distribution over the length of the sentences or the distance between the drug mentions, except in Model 1 for distances between 10 and 40 or 60 and 70 words.

6.4   Drug-Oriented Attention Model

In order to understand why the approach of [35] (described, along with other works, in Sect. 2.2) outperforms our models, we have tried to replicate their model, which uses word embedding, PoS-embedding and the offset features as input. The word vectors are then subject to the drug-oriented input attention, using dot_score as score function, since it provides the best performance. The drug-oriented word vectors, concatenated with the other features, are processed by a bidirectional LSTM layer. The output h_m at the last time step of the sequence (i.e. the last word), which reflects the whole sentence, is taken by the softmax classifier.

We have replicated their architecture using our word embedding representation but we could not obtain same results or to obtain better performance with respect to our model. We have also analyzed the effect of the drug-oriented input attention: for each input configuration (only word vectors or including PoS tag vectors with or without offset features), their attention mechanism did not improve the performance.

Their paper also reports that the baseline bidirectional LSTM model, without the input attention, obtains a F-Score of 76.2%. Since this result with a quite simple architecture outperforms not only our method but also every other known approach, we speculate that the difference is due to some pre-processing techniques, which are not adequately presented in the article, or to the quality of the word embedding provided in input, which is not publicly available.

7   Conclusions and Future Work

Our experiments show that the self-interaction mechanism increases the classification accuracy, in particular avoiding false negatives and reducing the tendency of predicting the majority class, even with the use of a less thorough and more general filtering of negative instances.

However, other approaches give better results than ours. We think that their advantage is obtained by a better pre-processing phase, a more precise and dataset-oriented negative instance filtering, a more thorough hyper-parameter optimization or the inclusion of other information like the grammatical structure expressed in the dependency tree. In particular, SDP-LSTM [32] uses a parallel LSTM channel that processes the shortest dependency path, alongside with an input attention layer. Instead, our attempt to add a SDP parallel channel does not improve performance.

As future work, our objective is to analyze the effect of the input attention mechanism, understanding why our attempt to apply the drug-oriented input attention did not produce any improvement. We will also work on incorporating the information produced by the dependency parser using parallel channels or adding Graph Convolutional Layers, following the approach used in [33].

Another direction includes the exploitation of a different pre-trained language modeling. For example, BioBERT [12] obtains good results for several NLP tasks like Named Entity Recognition or Question Answering, and we plan to apply it to our task.

References

1. Bahdanau, D., Cho, K., Bengio, Y.: Neural machine translation by jointly learning to align and translate (2014). http://arxiv.org/abs/1409.0473. cite arxiv:1409.0473Comment. Accepted at ICLR 2015 as oral presentation
2. Bergstra, J., Bengio, Y.: Random search for hyper-parameter optimization. J. Mach. Learn. Res. **13**(1), 281–305 (2012). http://dl.acm.org/citation.cfm? id=2503308.2188395
3. Björne, J., Kaewphan, S., Salakoski, T.: UTurku: drug named entity recognition and drug-drug interaction extraction using SVM classification and domain knowledge. In: Second Joint Conference on Lexical and Computational Semantics (*SEM), Volume 2: Proceedings of the Seventh International Workshop on Semantic Evaluation, SemEval 2013, pp. 651–659. Association for Computational Linguistics, Atlanta, June 2013. https://www.aclweb.org/anthology/S13-2108
4. Cho, K., et al.: Learning phrase representations using RNN encoder-decoder for statistical machine translation. In: Proceedings of the 2014 Conference on Empirical Methods in Natural Language Processing (EMNLP), pp. 1724–1734. Association for Computational Linguistics, Doha, October 2014. https://doi.org/10.3115/v1/D14-1179, https://www.aclweb.org/anthology/D14-1179
5. Chowdhury, M.F.M., Lavelli, A.: FBK-irst: a multi-phase kernel based approach for drug-drug interaction detection and classification that exploits linguistic information. In: Proceedings of the 7th International Workshop on Semantic Evaluation, SemEval@NAACL-HLT 2013, Atlanta, Georgia, USA, 14–15 June 2013, pp. 351–355 (2013). http://aclweb.org/anthology/S/S13/S13-2057.pdf
6. Du, J., Han, J., Way, A., Wan, D.: Multi-level structured self-attentions for distantly supervised relation extraction. CoRR abs/1809.00699 (2018). http://arxiv.org/abs/1809.00699
7. Gers, F.A., Schmidhuber, J., Cummins, F.A.: Learning to forget: continual prediction with LSTM. Neural Comput. **12**, 2451–2471 (2000)
8. Goodfellow, I., Bengio, Y., Courville, A.: Deep Learning. MIT Press, Cambridge (2016). http://www.deeplearningbook.org
9. Hochreiter, S., Schmidhuber, J.: Long short-term memory. Neural Comput. **9**, 1735–80 (1997). https://doi.org/10.1162/neco.1997.9.8.1735
10. Kadlec, R., Schmid, M., Bajgar, O., Kleindienst, J.: Text understanding with the attention sum reader network. CoRR abs/1603.01547 (2016)
11. Kumar, S., Anand, A.: Drug-drug interaction extraction from biomedical text using long short term memory network. CoRR abs/1701.08303 (2017)
12. Lee, J., et al.: BioBERT: pre-trained biomedical language representation model for biomedical text mining. arXiv preprint arXiv:1901.08746 (2019)
13. Li, L., Guo, Y., Qian, S., Zhou, A.: An end-to-end entity and relation extraction network with multi-head attention. In: Sun, M., Liu, T., Wang, X., Liu, Z., Liu, Y. (eds.) CCL/NLP-NABD -2018. LNCS (LNAI), vol. 11221, pp. 136–146. Springer, Cham (2018). https://doi.org/10.1007/978-3-030-01716-3_12
14. Li, Y., Yang, T.: Word embedding for understanding natural language: a survey. In: Srinivasan, S. (ed.) Guide to Big Data Applications. SBD, vol. 26, pp. 83–104. Springer, Cham (2018). https://doi.org/10.1007/978-3-319-53817-4_4

15. Liu, S., Tang, B., Chen, Q., Wang, X.: Drug-drug interaction extraction via convolutional neural networks. Comput. Math. Methods Med. **2016**, 8 (2016)
16. Luong, M.T., Pham, H., Manning, C.D.: Effective approaches to attention-based neural machine translation. arXiv preprint arXiv:1508.04025 (2015)
17. McDonald, R., Brokos, G., Androutsopoulos, I.: Deep relevance ranking using enhanced document-query interactions. CoRR abs/1809.01682 (2018)
18. Mikolov, T., Sutskever, I., Chen, K., Corrado, G.S., Dean, J.: Distributed representations of words and phrases and their compositionality. In: Burges, C.J.C., Bottou, L., Welling, M., Ghahramani, Z., Weinberger, K.Q. (eds.) Advances in Neural Information Processing Systems 26, pp. 3111–3119. Curran Associates, Inc. (2013). http://papers.nips.cc/paper/5021-distributed-representations-of-words-and-phrases-and-their-compositionality.pdf
19. Tarwani, K.M., Edem, S.: Survey on recurrent neural network in natural language processing. Int. J. Eng. Trends Technol. **48**, 301–304 (2017). https://doi.org/10.14445/22315381/IJETT-V48P253
20. Nagi, J., et al.: Max-pooling convolutional neural networks for vision-based hand gesture recognition. In: 2011 IEEE International Conference on Signal and Image Processing Applications (ICSIPA), pp. 342–347, November 2011. https://doi.org/10.1109/ICSIPA.2011.6144164
21. Pennington, J., Socher, R., Manning, C.: Glove: global vectors for word representation. In: Proceedings of the 2014 conference on Empirical Methods in Natural Language Processing (EMNLP), pp. 1532–1543 (2014)
22. Quan, C., Hua, L., Sun, X., Bai, W.: Multichannel convolutional neural network for biological relation extraction. BioMed. Res. Int. **2016**, 10 (2016)
23. Raffel, C., Ellis, D.P.W.: Feed-forward networks with attention can solve some long-term memory problems. CoRR abs/1512.08756 (2015)
24. Schuster, M., Paliwal, K.K.: Bidirectional recurrent neural networks. IEEE Trans. Sig. Process. **45**(11), 2673–2681 (1997)
25. Segura-Bedmar, I., Martínez, P., Herrero-Zazo, M.: Lessons learnt from the DDIExtraction-2013 shared task. J. Biomed. Inform. **51**, 152–164 (2014)
26. Suárez-Paniagua, V., Segura-Bedmar, I.: Evaluation of pooling operations in convolutional architectures for drug-drug interaction extraction. BMC Bioinform. **19**, 209 (2018). https://doi.org/10.1186/s12859-018-2195-1
27. Vaswani, A., et al.: Attention is all you need. CoRR abs/1706.03762 (2017)
28. Weiss, G., Provost, F.: The effect of class distribution on classifier learning: an empirical study. Technical report, Department of Computer Science, Rutgers University (2001)
29. Wilcoxon, F.: Individual comparisons by ranking methods. Biom. Bull. **1**(6), 80–83 (1945). http://www.jstor.org/stable/3001968
30. Yi, Z., et al.: Drug-drug interaction extraction via recurrent neural network with multiple attention layers. In: Cong, G., Peng, W.-C., Zhang, W.E., Li, C., Sun, A. (eds.) ADMA 2017. LNCS (LNAI), vol. 10604, pp. 554–566. Springer, Cham (2017). https://doi.org/10.1007/978-3-319-69179-4_39
31. Zeng, D., Liu, K., Lai, S., Zhou, G., Zhao, J.: Relation classification via convolutional deep neural network. In: Proceedings of COLING 2014, the 25th International Conference on Computational Linguistics: Technical Papers, pp. 2335–2344. Dublin City University and Association for Computational Linguistics, Dublin, August 2014. https://www.aclweb.org/anthology/C14-1220
32. Zhang, Y., Zheng, W., Lin, H., Wang, J., Yang, Z., Dumontier, M.: Drug-drug interaction extraction via hierarchical RNNs on sequence and shortest dependency paths. Bioinformatics **34**(5), 828–835 (2018)

33. Zhang, Y., Qi, P., Manning, C.D.: Graph convolution over pruned dependency trees improves relation extraction. CoRR abs/1809.10185 (2018)
34. Zheng, J., Cai, F., Shao, T., Chen, H.: Self-interaction attention mechanism-based text representation for document classification. Appl. Sci. **8**(4), 613 (2018). https://doi.org/10.3390/app8040613. http://www.mdpi.com/2076-3417/8/4/613
35. Zheng, W., et al.: An attention-based effective neural model for drug-drug interactions extraction. BMC Bioinform. **18**, 445 (2017). https://doi.org/10.1186/s12859-017-1855-x

Learning Abstract Planning Domains and Mappings to Real World Perceptions

Luciano Serafini[✉] and Paolo Traverso

Fondazione Bruno Kessler, Trento, Italy
{serafini,traverso}@fbk.eu

Abstract. Most of the works on planning and learning, e.g., planning by (model based) reinforcement learning, are based on two main assumptions: (i) the set of states of the planning domain is fixed; (ii) the mapping between the observations from the real word and the states is implicitly assumed, and is not part of the planning domain. Consequently, the focus is on learning the transitions between states. Current approaches address neither the problem of learning new states of the planning domain, nor the problem of representing and updating the mapping between the real world perceptions and the states. In this paper, we drop such assumptions. We provide a formal framework in which (i) the agent can learn dynamically new states of the planning domain; (ii) the mapping between abstract states and the perception from the real world, represented by continuous variables, is part of the planning domain; (iii) such mapping is learned and updated along the "life" of the agent. We define and develop an algorithm that interleaves planning, acting, and learning. We provide a first experimental evaluation that shows how this novel framework can effectively learn coherent abstract planning models.

1 Introduction and Motivations

Several automated planning techniques are based on abstract representations of the world, usually called *planning domains*. A planning domain can be formalized by a finite state transition system[1], i.e., a finite set of states, actions, and a transition relation [7,8]. This abstract representation is both conceptually relevant and practically convenient, since it allows a planner to reason and generate plans at a high level of abstraction. For instance, in order to plan how to move a robot from a room to another room in a building, it may be convenient to adopt a planning domain that encodes an abstract topological map of the building, such that each state corresponds to (the fact that the robot is in) a given room, and transitions correspond to (complex) actions that move the robot from one room to an adjacent room.

While an agent can conveniently plan at the abstract level, it perceives the world and acts in it through sensors and actuators that work with data in a continuous space, typically represented with variables on real numbers. For instance,

---

[1] The transition system can be either deterministic, nondeterministic, or stochastic.

© Springer Nature Switzerland AG 2019
M. Alviano et al. (Eds.): AI*IA 2019, LNAI 11946, pp. 461–476, 2019.
https://doi.org/10.1007/978-3-030-35166-3_33

a robot does not perceive directly the fact that it is in a given room/state, instead it perceives, e.g., to be in a position of the building through sensors like odometers or the images from its camera. Similarly agent actions' effects in the environment are continuous transformations, e.g., "the robot has moved forward 5.4 m". It is part of the cognitive capability of the agent to fill the gap between these two different levels of abstractions.

Most of the works in planning and learning, see, e.g., [6,22] assume that (i) the finite set of states of the planning domain is fixed once forever at design time, and (ii) the correspondence between the abstract states and the observations (represented with continuous variables) is implicit and fixed at design time. This is the case of most of the works on planning by (model based) reinforcement learning, see, e.g., [14,19–23][2], which focus on learning and updating the transitions between states, e.g., the probabilities of action outcomes (or rewards) in an MDP framework. They support neither the learning of new states nor the updating of the mapping between the real world and the abstract model.

In many cases, however, having a fixed set of states and a fixed mapping between the perceived data and the abstract model is not adequate. There may be situations in which the agent perceives data which are not compatible with any of the states of its abstract model. For instance, a robot may end up in unknown and unexpected states of the world. Consider the simple example in which the task is to navigate in a restricted part of a building, and instead, due to some reasons, like a navigation error, or an unexpected open door, the robot ends up in a different part of the building. Similarly, along its life, an agent could also revise its mapping between its abstract model and the real sensed data. In general, the (number of) states and the mapping to perceptions may be not obvious at design time, and thus be incomplete or not adequate.

In this paper, we provide a formal framework in which the agent can learn dynamically new states of the planning domain. Moreover, the mapping between abstract states and the real world is part of the planning domain of the agent, and it is learned and updated along the "life" of the agent. Given this framework, we provide the following contributions: (i) We model agent's perception of the real world by a *perception function* that returns the likelihood of observing some continuous data being in a state of the domain. We define a criteria based on the perception function to extend the set of states. Intuitively, when the likelihood is too low for all the existing states, a new state is created; (ii) We define an algorithm that interleaves planning, acting, and learning. It is able to discover that the abstract model is not coherent with the real world. While planning and acting, the algorithm updates both the set of states and the perception function of the planning domain. The learning mechanism can be defined in several different ways, depending on whether we follow a cautious strategy, where changes are made only if there is a certain number of evidences from acting and perceiving the real world, or a more impulsive reaction to what the agent has just observed. Moreover, we define a measure of coherence between the planning domain and

---

[2] In some works (see, e.g., [1,4,17]) the two levels are collapsed, since planning is performed in a continuous space.

the real world as perceived by the agent; (iii) We provide a preliminary experimental evaluation that shows how this novel model for planing, acting, and learning lets the agent converge to a model which is increasingly coherent with the state of the world.

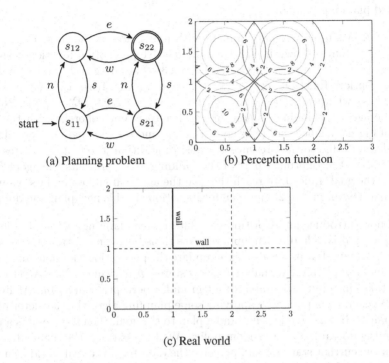

(a) Planning problem   (b) Perception function

(c) Real world

Fig. 1. (a) A planning problem on a domain composed of 4 states, corresponding to 4 rooms, no walls between them, and 4 actions n, s, w, and e (go north, south, west, and east). Transitions that don't change the state are not shown. (b) A perception function associated to the planning domain. (c) The real world: the building has 6 (and no 4) rooms, and two walls

2 Planning, Acting, and Learning

A *(deterministic) planning domain* is a triple $\mathcal{D} = \langle S, A, \gamma \rangle$, composed of a finite non empty set of states S, a finite non empty set of actions A, and a state transition function $\gamma : S \times A \rightarrow S$. A *planning problem* is a triple $\mathcal{P} = \langle \mathcal{D}, s_0, S_g \rangle$ composed of a planning domain $\mathcal{D}$, an initial state $s_0 \in S$ and a set of goal states $S_g \subseteq S$. A *plan* π for $\mathcal{D}$ is a policy, i.e., a partial function from S to A. The way in which an agent perceives the world is modeled by a *perception function*, i.e., a function $f : \mathbb{R}^n \times S \rightarrow R^+$, defined as $f(\boldsymbol{x}, s) = p(\boldsymbol{x}|s)$, where $p(\boldsymbol{x}, s)$ is a join PDF on $\mathbb{R}^n \times S$. In other words, $f(\boldsymbol{x}, s)$ is the likelihood of observing $\boldsymbol{x}$ being in a state s.

Definition 1 (Extended planning domain). *An* extended planning domain *is a pair* $\langle \mathcal{D}, f \rangle$ *where* $\mathcal{D}$ *is a planning domain and* f *a perception function on the states of* $\mathcal{D}$.

Hereafter, if not explicitly specified, with "planning domain" we will refer to extended planning domain.

Example 1. A simple planning domain with four states is shown in Fig. 1. The transition system is shown in Fig. 1(a), the relative perception function is shown in Fig. 1(b), and the real world, composed of a 3×2 building is shown in Fig. 1(c). The perception function $f(\langle x, y \rangle, s_{ij})$, shown in Fig. 1(b), is $f(\langle x, y \rangle, s) = p(\langle x, y \rangle \mid s)$ where $p(\langle x, y \rangle | s_{ij}) = \mathcal{N}(\boldsymbol{\mu} = \langle i - 0.5, j - 0.5 \rangle, \boldsymbol{\Sigma} = (\begin{smallmatrix} 1 & 0 \\ 0 & 1 \end{smallmatrix}))$. Notice that, the agent's planning domain in Fig. 1(a–b) is not coherent with the real world of Fig. 1(c), since the transitions from s_{12} and s_{21} to s_{22} are not possible in the real world, due to the presence of walls. In addition, there are no states corresponding to the rightmost part of the building. This prevents the agent from reaching the goal. Indeed, to reach the goal the agent should extend its planning domain, as shown in Fig. 2, and plan for its actions in this new planning domain.

We now introduce an algorithm that interleaves planning, acting and learning. Not only it is able to learn/update transitions between existing states of the planning domain, but it can also learn/update the perception function, and properly extend the planning domain with new states. Algorithm 1 PLANACTLEARN (PAL) takes in input a planning problem and a perception function. At line 4, $plan(\mathcal{P})$ generates a plan π by applying some planning algorithm for deterministic domains[3]. If $plan(\mathcal{P})$ does not find a plan to the goal, then it generates a plan to learn the domain, e.g., a random policy. We then execute the planned action $\pi(s_0)$ in the current state s_0, and perceive the data from the real world as a vector of real numbers $\boldsymbol{x}$ (line 6). We then determine the state s_0' that maximizes the likelihood of observing $\boldsymbol{x}$ (line 7); if such a likelihood is below the threshold $(1 - \epsilon) \cdot \max p_{init}(\cdot, \cdot)$ with $\epsilon \in [0, 1]$, and where $p_{init}(\cdot, \cdot)$ is the initialization function of the perception function, then we extend the set of states S with a new state s_{new}, and initialise its perception function $f(\cdot, s_{new})$ with $p_{init}(\cdot, \boldsymbol{x})$ (lines 9–11). Notice that, low values of ϵ, promote the easy introduction of new states, while with high values of ϵ we are cautious in creating new states. In the extreme case, i.e., with $\epsilon = 1$, we never add new states.

We then extend the sequence of transitions $\mathcal{T}$ and of observations $\mathcal{O}$, and learn the new transition function γ and the new perception function f. The functions update_trans and update_perc update the transition function γ and the perception function f, respectively, depending on the data available in $\mathcal{T}$ and $\mathcal{O}$. The update functions take into account (i) the current model, (ii) what has been observed in the past, i.e., $\mathcal{T}$ and $\mathcal{O}$, and (iii) what has been just observed, i.e., $\langle s_0, \pi(s_0), s_0' \rangle$ and $\langle s_0', \boldsymbol{x} \rangle$. The update functions can be defined in several different

---

[3] We assume that the sequential plan returned by the planning algorithm can be transformed into a policy π. Since here we plan for reachability goals, sequences of actions can be mapped into policies.

Algorithm 1. PLANACTLEARN - PAL

Require: $\mathcal{P} = \langle\langle S, A, \gamma\rangle, s_0, S_g, f\rangle$ {A planning problem with a perception function}
Require: $p_{init}(\cdot, \cdot)$ initialization for $f(\cdot, s)$
1: $\mathcal{T} \leftarrow \langle\rangle$ {The empty history of transitions}
2: $\mathcal{O} \leftarrow \langle\rangle$ {The empty history of observations}
3: **while** $s_0 \notin S_g$ **do**
4:     $\pi \leftarrow plan(\mathcal{P})$
5:     **while** $\pi(s_0)$ is defined and γ has not been changed **do**
6:         $\boldsymbol{x} \leftarrow act(\pi(s_0))$
7:         $s_0' \leftarrow \operatorname{argmax}_{s \in S} f(\boldsymbol{x}, s)$
8:         **if** $f(\boldsymbol{x}, s_0') < (1 - \epsilon) \cdot \max p_{init}(\cdot, \cdot)$ **then**
9:             $s_0' \leftarrow s_{new}$
10:             $S \leftarrow S \cup \{s_{new}\}$
11:             $f(\cdot, s_{new}) = p_{init}(\cdot, \boldsymbol{x})$
12:         **end if**
13:         $\mathcal{T} \leftarrow append(T, \langle s_0, \pi(s_0), s_0'\rangle)$ {extend the transition history with the last one}
14:         $\mathcal{O} \leftarrow append(\mathcal{O}, \langle s_0', \boldsymbol{x}\rangle)$ {extend the observation history with the last one}
15:         $\gamma \leftarrow$ update_trans$(\gamma, \mathcal{T}, s_0, \pi(s_0))$
16:         $f \leftarrow$ update_perc$(f, \mathcal{O}, s_0')$
17:         $s_0 \leftarrow s_0'$
18:     **end while**
19: **end while**

---

ways, depending on whether we follow a cautious strategy, where changes are made only if there is a certain number of evidences from acting and perceiving the real world, or a more impulsive reaction to what the agent has just observed.

Updating Transitions: update_trans decides whether and how to update the transition function. suppose that, after executing the action a from the state s_0, the agent perceives $\boldsymbol{x}$, and suppose that $s_0' = \operatorname{argmax}_s(f(\boldsymbol{x}, s))$, i.e., the most likely reached state, is different from the state predicted by the agent planning domain, i.e., $s_0' \neq \gamma(a, s_0)$, then γ may need to be revised to take into account this discrepancy. since our domain is deterministic (the transition γ must lead to a single state), if the execution of an action leads to an unexpected state, we have only two options: either change γ with the new transition or not. we propose the following transition update function that depends on α: we define $\gamma' = $ update_trans$(\gamma, \mathcal{T}, s, a)$ to be the same as γ for all $(s', a') \neq (s, a)$ and

$$\gamma'(s, a) \in \{\operatorname*{argmax}_{s' \in S} \left(\alpha \cdot 𝟙_{s' = \gamma(s,a)} + (1 - \alpha) \cdot |\{i \mid \mathcal{T}_i = \langle s, a, s'\rangle\}|\right)\} \quad (1)$$

where $𝟙_{s' = \gamma(s,a)}$ is equal to 1 if $s' = \gamma(s, a)$ and 0 otherwise, $\mathcal{T}_i$ is the i-th element of $\mathcal{T}$, and $\alpha \in [0, 1]$. Notice that, if $\alpha = 1$, we are extremely cautious, we strongly believe in our model of the world, and we never change the transition γ. Conversely, if $\alpha = 0$, we are extremely impulsive, we do not trust our model, and just one evidence makes us to change the model. In the intermediate cases,

$\alpha \in (0, 1)$, depending on the value of α, we need more or less evidence to change the planning domain.

Updating the Perception Function: The update of the perception function about a state s is based on the current perception function $f(x, s)$ and the set of observations $\mathcal{O}(s)$ about the state s. We suppose that the perception function is parametric on $\boldsymbol{\theta} = \langle \theta_1, \ldots, \theta_k \rangle$. In Example 1, $\boldsymbol{\theta} = \langle \theta_1, \theta_2 \rangle$ with $\theta_1 = \boldsymbol{\mu}$ and $\theta_2 = \boldsymbol{\Sigma}$, i.e., the mean and the covariance matrix of the normal distribution associated to any state. Given a new observation $\langle x, s \rangle$ and a set of previous observations $\mathcal{O}(s) = \langle x^{(0)}, \ldots, x^{(k)} \rangle$ about an abstract state $s \in S$, we have to update the parameters $\boldsymbol{\theta}_s$ of the perception function $f(\cdot, s)$ in order to maximize the likelihood of the entire set of observations extended with the new observation. Also in this case the agent can be more or less careful in the revision. This is expressed by a parameter $\beta \in [0, 1]$, where, the higher the value of β the more careful the agent is in the revision. If $f(x, s) = p(x \mid \boldsymbol{\theta}_s)$, we define $f' = $ update_perc$(f, \mathcal{O}, s)$ where $f'(\cdot, s')$ is equal to $f(\cdot, s')$ for all $s' \neq s$ and $f'(\cdot, s) = p(\cdot \mid \boldsymbol{\theta}')$ where:

$$\boldsymbol{\theta}' = \beta \cdot \boldsymbol{\theta}_s + (1 - \beta) \cdot \underset{\boldsymbol{\theta}''}{\operatorname{argmax}} \, \mathcal{L}(\boldsymbol{\theta}'', \mathcal{O}(s)) \tag{2}$$

where $\mathcal{L}(\boldsymbol{\theta}, x^{(1)}, \ldots, x^{(n)})$ is the likelihood of the parameters $\boldsymbol{\theta}$ for the observations $x^{(1)}, \ldots, x^{(n)}$, defined as:

$$\mathcal{L}(\boldsymbol{\theta}, x^{(1)}, \ldots, x^{(n)}) = \prod_{i=1}^{n} p(x^{(i)} \mid \boldsymbol{\theta}) \tag{3}$$

Intuitively Eq. (2) defines the parameters $\boldsymbol{\theta}'_s$ of the updated perception function for a state s as a convex combination, based on the parameter β, of the parameters of the previous perception function for s, i.e., $\boldsymbol{\theta}_s$ and the parameters $\boldsymbol{\theta}''$ that maximize the likelihood of the past and current observations about state s (Eq. (3)). An efficient procedure for incremental estimation of the second term of (2), is described in [2]. In case of Multivariate Gaussian distribution, $\boldsymbol{\theta}_s$ contains the mean $\boldsymbol{\mu}_s$ and covariance matrix $\boldsymbol{\Sigma}_s$, and the updates defined in Eq. (2) can be efficiently computed as follows:

$$\boldsymbol{\mu}'_s = \beta \cdot \boldsymbol{\mu}_s + (1 - \beta)(\boldsymbol{\mu}_s + \Delta \boldsymbol{\mu}_s)$$
$$\boldsymbol{\Sigma}'_s = \beta \cdot \boldsymbol{\Sigma}_s + (1 - \beta)(\boldsymbol{\Sigma}_s + \Delta \boldsymbol{\Sigma}_s)$$

where $\Delta \boldsymbol{\mu}_s = \frac{1}{|\mathcal{O}(s)|}(x - \boldsymbol{\mu}_s)$ and $\Delta \boldsymbol{\Sigma}_s^2 = \frac{1}{|\mathcal{O}(s)|}(x - \boldsymbol{\mu}'_s)^2 + \frac{|\mathcal{O}(s)|-1}{|\mathcal{O}(s)|}(\Delta \boldsymbol{\mu}_s^2 - 2\boldsymbol{\mu}_s \Delta \boldsymbol{\mu}_s) - \frac{1}{|\mathcal{O}(s)|}\boldsymbol{\Sigma}_s^2$. Concerning the parameter $\beta \in [0, 1]$, it plays the similar role as α in the case of the revision of the transition function. It balances the update depending on whether the agent is cautious or impulsive about the current perception function, and the new perceptions.

Example 2. Let us now describe how our algorithm works in Example 1 and how the goal is reached by creating new states and changing the model to the one described in Fig. 2.

1. Suppose that the robot is initially in the position $(0.5, 0.5)$. Since the state $s \in S$ that maximizes $f((0.5, 0.5), s)$ is s_{11} the agent believes to be in this state.
2. (line 4) According to the planning domain in Fig. 1(a), $Plan(\mathcal{P})$ can generate two plans, the one that reaches the goal passing through s_{21} and the one that passes through s_{12}. Let us suppose that it generates the former, i.e., the plan $\pi(s_{11}) = e$ and $\pi(s_{21}) = n$.
3. (line 6–7) Since $\pi(s_{11})$ is defined, we execute the action e, which moves the robot of one unit in the east direction, and returns the current position in $\boldsymbol{x}$, which will be some value close to $\langle 1.5, 0.5 \rangle$. Notice that we cannot assume that $\boldsymbol{x}$ is exactly $\langle 1.5, 0.5 \rangle$, since we have to take into consideration that sensors and actuators can be noisy. So suppose that the observed values after the execution of $\pi(s_{11})$ are $\langle 1.51, 0.49 \rangle$. Given the current f, the state s that maximizes $f(\boldsymbol{x}, s)$ is s_{21}, therefore $s'_0 = s_{21}$.
4. (lines 8, 13, 14) Suppose that the condition on line 8 is false. We then do not create a new state. We add the transition to the history and we have $\mathcal{T} = \langle\langle s_{11}, e, s_{21} \rangle\rangle$. Similarly we have $\mathcal{O} = \langle\langle s_{21}, \langle 1.51, 0.49 \rangle\rangle\rangle$.
5. (lines 15) We then update the transition function: update_trans does not produce any change, since $s_{21} = \gamma(s_{11}, e)$. Indeed in this case the transition function γ correctly predicts, at the abstract level, the effects of the execution of action e in state s_{11}.
6. (line 16) The update of the perception function will slightly move the mean $\boldsymbol{\mu}$, from $\langle 1.5, 0.5 \rangle$ in the direction of the current perception i.e., $\langle 1.51, 0.49 \rangle$ and the $\boldsymbol{\Sigma}$ will also be updated.
7. We then update s'_0 to s_{21} and go back to (lines 3, 4). Since $\pi(s_{21}) = n$, we execute the action moving one unit north from s_{21}. But the execution of this action does not have the effect that is expected by the agent, i.e., it does not reach state s_{22}. Indeed, the execution of n starting from the position $\langle 1.51, 0.49 \rangle$ would result in hitting the wall, the presence of which was not expected by the agent. Let us suppose that the execution of this action will result in the robot doing nothing, and $act(\pi(s_{21}))$ will return the value $\boldsymbol{x}$ which is the same as the previous one i.e., $\boldsymbol{x} = \langle 1.51, 0.49 \rangle$.
8. s_{21} is the state that maximizes the observed $\boldsymbol{x}$, and we proceed as before, by not generating a new state and appending the new transition to $\mathcal{T}$ such that $\mathcal{T} = \langle\langle s_{11}, e, s_{21} \rangle, \langle s_{21}, n, s_{21} \rangle\rangle$ while $\mathcal{O}$ becomes $\langle\langle s_{21}, \langle 1.51, 0.49 \rangle\rangle, \langle s_{21}, \langle 1.51, 0.49 \rangle\rangle\rangle$
9. (line 15) The transition function this time gets updated in different ways depending on the value of α. Let's compute the arguments of the argmax of Eq. (1) with $a = n$ and $s = s_{21}$;

s'	$\alpha \cdot \mathbb{K}_{s' = \gamma(s_{21}, n)} + (1 - \alpha) \cdot |\{i \mid \mathcal{T}_i = \langle s_{21}, n, s' \rangle\}|$
s_{11}	$\alpha \cdot 0 + (1 - \alpha) \cdot 0 = 0$
s_{21}	$\alpha \cdot 0 + (1 - \alpha) \cdot 1 = (1 - \alpha)$
s_{12}	$\alpha \cdot 0 + (1 - \alpha) \cdot 0 = \alpha$
s_{22}	$\alpha \cdot 1 + (1 - \alpha) \cdot 0 = 0$

If $\alpha < 1/2$, we are reasonably keen to learn from acting in the real world that the state that maximizes Eq. (1) is s_{21} and update_trans deletes $\gamma(s_{21}, n) =$

s_{22} and adds $\gamma(s_{21}, n) = s_{21}$, i.e., the agent understands that there is a wall that does not allow the robot to move north from state s_{21}. If instead $\alpha > 1/2$, then the state that maximizes (1) is s_{22} and $\gamma(s_{21}, n) = s_{22}$ will be kept. Notice that after k attempts to execute the actions n in state s_{21} without updating the transition function, in order to change the transition function it is enough to have $\alpha < \frac{k}{1+k}$. So if $\alpha \neq 1$, sooner or later the agent will update γ.

10. At this point we go back to $Plan(\mathcal{P})$ which generates the alternative plan that passes through s_{12}, and sends the robot back to state s_{11} and then to state s_{12}, in a similar way to what happened in the case of going through s_{21}.

11. At this point the planning domain of the agent is shown below. Notice that the goal is not reachable.

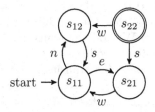

12. After having explored all the possibilities without reaching the goal, $Plan(\mathcal{P})$ generates random (exploration) plans. Suppose that it generates a plan π with $\pi(s_{21}) = e$. The observation after the execution of such a π returns $\boldsymbol{x} = \langle x, y \rangle$ close to $\langle 2.5, 0.5 \rangle$. In that position s_{21} maximises $f(\boldsymbol{x}, s)$, however the value of $f(\boldsymbol{x}, s_{21})$ is extremely low, and let us suppose it is below the threshold $(1 - \epsilon) \cdot \max p_{init}(\cdot)$. We therefore create a new state, say s_{31}.

13. $\mathcal{T}$ gets updated by adding the transition $\langle s_{21}, e, s_{31} \rangle$, and $\mathcal{O}$ by adding the pair $\langle s_{31}, \boldsymbol{x} \rangle$. The update function update_trans may create the new transition $\gamma(s_{21}, e) = s_{31}$ (if α is small enough) and update_perc will initialize the perception function $f(\cdot, s_{31})$ with $p_{init} \sim \mathcal{N}(\boldsymbol{\mu}, \boldsymbol{\Sigma})$ with $\boldsymbol{\mu} = \boldsymbol{x}$, and $\boldsymbol{\Sigma} = \left(\begin{smallmatrix} .1 & 0 \\ 0 & .1 \end{smallmatrix} \right)$.

14. The next step is similar to the previous one. Since there is no plan to the goal, $plan(\mathcal{P})$ tries to learn the domain, and state s_{32} is created, transition $\gamma(s_{31}, n)$ and the corresponding f are created. Since no plan to the goal exists yet, while trying to learn the domain, $plan(\mathcal{P})$ may add the new transitions $\gamma(s_{31}, w) = s_{21}$ and $\gamma(s_{32}, s) = s_{31}$

15. In the final step, $plan(\mathcal{P})$ learns the transition $\gamma(s_{32}, w) = s_{22}$, and finally finds the plan to the goal $\pi(s_{32}) = w$. Furthermore, the agent has updated its initial planning domain, obtaining the planning domain shown in Fig. 2. Notice that this planning domain is not completely correct, as there are no information about the execution of actions in s_{22}. This is due to the fact that, in this simple example, the agent has planned no actions in s_{22} (since it was the goal) and therefore it has not learned anything about the transitions and the perceptions functions of this node.

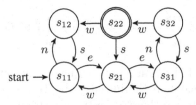

Fig. 2. The new planning domain obtained by extending the initial domain of Fig. 1, with two new states

3   Measuring the Coherence of the Model

In order to estimate the quality of the model generated by the PAL algorithm, we should define a method to measure the coherence between an abstract model with perception function and the real world.

We introduce a measure called *divergence*. Intuitively, a low divergence means that if $\gamma(a, s) = s'$, then if the agent perceives to be in s and performs a, then after the execution of a it will perceive to be in the state s'.

We suppose to have a stochastic model of the real execution of actions. Under Markovian hypothesis, every action $a \in A$ can be modeled as a conditional PDF $p_a(\boldsymbol{x}'|\boldsymbol{x})$, which expresses the probability of measuring $\boldsymbol{x}'$ after executing the action a in a state in which the agent perceives $\boldsymbol{x}$. It represents the effects of executing the action a in the real world.

To measure the quality of the abstract planning domain, we have to compare p_a with how the action a is modeled in the domain. Suppose that an agent perceives $\boldsymbol{x}$, and that the state s maximizes the likelihood of perceiving $\boldsymbol{x}$. Suppose that the action a is executed. According to its abstract model, the agent will believe to be in the state $s' = \gamma(a, s)$. After the actual execution of action a, it will perceive $\boldsymbol{x}'$ with a probability $p_a(\boldsymbol{x}'|\boldsymbol{x})$. However, according to the agent's abstract model, the probability of observing $\boldsymbol{x}'$ after the execution of a is $p(\boldsymbol{x}'|s')$. The closer the two distributions are, the more coherent the abstract representation is. To estimate how well $p(\boldsymbol{x}'|s')$ approximates the real distribution $p_a(\boldsymbol{x}'|\boldsymbol{x})$, we use the notion of *divergence*, which is the opposite notion of coherence (the lower the divergence, the higher the coherence), and we formalize it with the *KL divergence* $KL(p_a(\boldsymbol{x}'|\boldsymbol{x})||p(\boldsymbol{x}'|s'))$, defined as:

$$\int_{\boldsymbol{x}'} p_a(\boldsymbol{x}'|\boldsymbol{x}) \log \left(\frac{p_a(\boldsymbol{x}'|\boldsymbol{x})}{p(\boldsymbol{x}'|s')} \right) d\boldsymbol{x}'$$

We can therefore define the divergence measure as

$$\int_{\boldsymbol{x}} \sum_{a \in A} KL(p_a(\boldsymbol{x}'|\boldsymbol{x})||p(\boldsymbol{x}'|\gamma(a, s_{\boldsymbol{x}}))) \cdot p_A(\boldsymbol{x}) \, d\boldsymbol{x} \qquad (4)$$

where $s_{\boldsymbol{x}} = \mathrm{argmax}_{s \in S} f(\boldsymbol{x}, s))$ and $p_A(\boldsymbol{x})$ is a distribution of all the possible perceptions that can be obtained by the agent following all the possible sequences of actions, i.e.,

$$p_A(\boldsymbol{x}) = \sum_{\langle a_1 \ldots, a_n \rangle \in A^+} p_{a_n}(\boldsymbol{x}|\boldsymbol{x}^{(n-1)}) \cdot \prod_{i=1}^{n-1} p_{a_i}(\boldsymbol{x}^{(i)}|\boldsymbol{x}^{(i-1)})$$

where A^+ is the set of finite non empty sequences of actions in A and $\boldsymbol{x}^{(0)}$ is the perception of the agent in the initial state. However, computing (4) analytically is very difficult. We therefore estimate (4) by random walk sampling method. Starting from an initial observation $\boldsymbol{x}^{(0)}$ we generate N random walks $\mathbf{a}_1, \ldots, \mathbf{a}_N$, with $\mathbf{a}_i = \langle a_{i,1}, \ldots, a_{i,n_i} \rangle$ and sample $\boldsymbol{x}^{(i)}$ from $\prod_{j=1}^{n_i} p_{a_{ij}}(\boldsymbol{x}_j|\boldsymbol{x}_{j-1})$. We approximate (4) with

$$\frac{1}{N} \sum_{k=1}^{N} \sum_{a \in A} \mathrm{KL}(p_a(\boldsymbol{x}'|\boldsymbol{x}^{(k)})||p(\boldsymbol{x}'|\gamma(a, s^{(k)}))) \tag{5}$$

where $s^{(k)} = \mathrm{argmax}_{s \in S} f(\boldsymbol{x}^{(k)}, s)$ for $1 \leq k \leq n$. In our specific example, since we are working with Gaussian distributions, we have that $p_a(\boldsymbol{x}'|\boldsymbol{x}) = \mathcal{N}(\boldsymbol{\mu} = a(\boldsymbol{x}), \boldsymbol{\Sigma} = \boldsymbol{\Sigma}_a)$, where $a(\boldsymbol{x})$ is some real function that maps $\boldsymbol{x}$ in the expected value $a(\boldsymbol{x})$ after performing the action a, and $\boldsymbol{\Sigma}_a$ is the model of the noise of the sensors/actuators associated to a. For instance, in Example 1

$$e(\langle x, y \rangle) = \begin{cases} \langle x+1, y \rangle & \text{If there are no walls between} \\ & \langle x, y \rangle \text{ ad } \langle x+1, y \rangle \\ \langle x, y \rangle & \text{Otherwise} \end{cases}$$

Furthermore, the KL divergence of Multivariate Gaussians can be computed analytically.

4   Experimental Evaluation

To explain and evaluate PAL and its effects depending on different parameter settings, we propose two sets of experiments. We first run PAL on Example 1 and successively we run the algorithm on a larger artificial test case[4]. Since the paper does not focus on a specific plan generation technique, we implement our approach using a naive planner, which uses an heuristic based on the distance from the goal.

In the first experiment, the initial planning domain is shown in Fig. 1 and, for different configurations of the parameters α, β, and ϵ in $\{0.0, 0.5, 1.0\}$, we run the PAL algorithm 10 times. We measure the average number of states of the final model ($|S|$), the reduction/improvement of the divergence ("% lrn") and the percentage of achieved goals (%G). The results are reported in Table 1[5]. Consider first the effects of the parameter ϵ:

---

[4] The code is available in the additional material.

[5] The reviewer/reader interested to graphically see the computation of PAL on this simple example with different parameters can download the additional material and run the command `python PALex1.py <alpha> <beta><epsilon>`.

- $\epsilon = 1$ prevents the creation of new states. Indeed, in all cases, no new state is created, and, as expected, the learned model is not more coherent than the initial one - the percentage of learning "% lrn" ranges from a negative number (-11.7) to very low improvement (0.26). Indeed, without creating new states, PAL never understands that there are new rooms. Because of this lack of coherence, in many cases PAL does not manage to reach the goal within the given timeout (100 steps). The reason why in some cases it manages to reach the goal is simply due to the fact that, when no plan exists according to the model, then a random policy is tried, which in some cases reaches the goal by chance, due to the simple and small domain.
- $\epsilon = 0$ tends to create many new states: $|S| \in [20.2, 32.9]$. In spite of this, when $\alpha = 0$, the learning is much better than when no new states are created ("% lrn" $\in [0.49, 0.54]$) and the goal is often reached. The learning gets worse by increasing α, since we learn many new states that are however scarcely connected to the states in the initial model.
- $\epsilon = 0.5$ represents a balanced situation. The number of new learned states is the right one ($|S| \approx 6$) for all the values of the other parameters. Moreover, with $\alpha = 0$ we have the best learning of a coherent model ("% lrn" $= 0.72$)), since we allow the update of the transition function by connecting the two new states with the four initial ones. The performance of learning smoothly decreases by increasing α to 0.5, while it becomes low in the case of $\alpha = 1$, due to the fact that the new states are not connected with the old ones.

In the case $\alpha = 0$ and $\alpha = 0.5$, the parameter β, when it is low ($\beta = 0$), tends to decrease the amount of learning towards a coherent model, by producing the two worst results ("% lrn" $= -11.17$ and -4.71) in the case $\epsilon = 1$. This is because, since we cannot learn new states, with a low β we allow the perception function to move the same old states to different positions, thus creating a rather incoherent model.

Table 1. Performance of PAL on Example 1 depending on α, β, and ϵ. Results are averaged on the 10 runs.

α	β	$\epsilon = 0.0$			$\epsilon = 0.5$			$\epsilon = 1.0$		
		$|S|$	%lrn	%G	$|S|$	%lrn	%G	$|S|$	%lrn	%G
0.0	0.0	21.6	0.49	1.0	6.0	0.72	0.7	4.0	-4.71	0.1
	0.5	24.7	0.50	0.9	5.9	0.72	0.8	4.0	-0.41	0.9
	1.0	20.2	0.54	0.9	5.9	0.72	0.7	4.0	0.18	0.9
0.5	0.0	25.8	0.19	1.0	5.9	0.66	0.8	4.0	-11.17	0.2
	0.5	30.7	0.15	0.7	5.9	0.69	0.8	4.0	0.26	0.8
	1.0	32.9	0.16	0.7	6.0	0.63	0.8	4.0	0.07	0.7
1.0	0.0	25.0	0.15	0.9	5.9	0.25	0.5	4.0	0.01	0.1
	0.5	24.4	0.18	0.8	5.8	0.24	0.8	4.0	-1.26	0.8
	1.0	28.5	0.16	0.8	6.0	0.27	1.0	4.0	0.00	0.9

In the second set of experiments, we consider a 5×5 building with randomly generated walls[6] completely unknown by the agent. Differently from the previous experiments, we test the capability of PAL to create a planning domain from scratch, while it is trying to achieve 10 randomly generated goals. We initialise the agent with a model containing only two states, i.e., $S = \{s_0, s_{g_0}\}$. The mean μ_{s_0} of the initial state is set to $\langle 0.5, 0.5 \rangle$, the mean of s_{g_0} of the perception function of s_{g_0} is randomly generated. The covariance matrixes Σ_{s_0} and $\Sigma_{s_{g_0}}$ are initialized to $\left(\begin{smallmatrix} .1 & 0 \\ 0 & .1 \end{smallmatrix} \right)$. The objective of the agent is to reach the goal s_{g_0}, and successively to reach other 9 goals $s_{g_1}, \ldots, s_{g_9}$, which are also randomly generated. We run this experiment, for every combination of α, β, and ϵ in $\{0.0,\ 0.5,\ 1.0\}$. In Fig. 3 we report the divergence (in the three plots on the left of the figure) and the number of states that are generated (in the three plots on the right) depending on the time used by PAL to plan, act and learn (the x axis), and depending on the parameters α, β, and ϵ. Notice that the graphs have different scales, since with a uniform scale some of the graphs would not be readable.

If $\epsilon = 1$, PAL cannot add new states to the planning model, and therefore, planning is useless, and the agent adopts a random walk strategy. Furthermore, the divergence is computed only on a single state. The consequence is that α does not have any effect, since with a single state there is no transition to revise. Instead, the value of β has the effect of (dis)allowing the change of the perception function associated to the single state s_0. If $\beta = 1$, the perception function $f(\boldsymbol{x}, s_0)$ is not changed and, consequently, the divergence is constant (i.e., it takes its initial value ≈ 5000); with $\beta \neq 1$, instead, the perception function $f(\boldsymbol{x}, s_0)$ is updated to take into account the observations that the agent accumulates during its random walk, but after short time it converges to a constant value ≈ 13.0.

If $\epsilon = 0$, PAL tends to generate an eccessive number of states independently from α and β: We get to about 600 states in 800 s. In this case PAL learns a domain by decreasing significantly the divergence, which gets below 500 for all the values of α and β. It takes however a long time to complete the tasks, up to 800 s, because the model is uselessly accurate.

If $\epsilon = 0.5$, PAL generates a reasonable number of states. For all the values of α and β, the completion of the task requires much less time than the case of $\epsilon = 0$. The best model, i.e., the one closest to our intuition, is the one generated in the case of $\epsilon = 0.5$, $\alpha = 0.5$, and $\beta = 0$. It has indeed 25 states, each one corresponding to the 25 rooms in the building, and with transitions taking into account the walls. In this case, the divergence rapidly decreases to values below 100. Moreover, in all cases in which $\epsilon = 0.5$, we have divergences much lower than in the case $\epsilon = 0$ (please notice the different scale in the two graphs). Finally, we have lower divergences for low values of α ($\alpha = 0$ and 0.5) than in

---

[6] A picture of this world is reported in the additonal material.

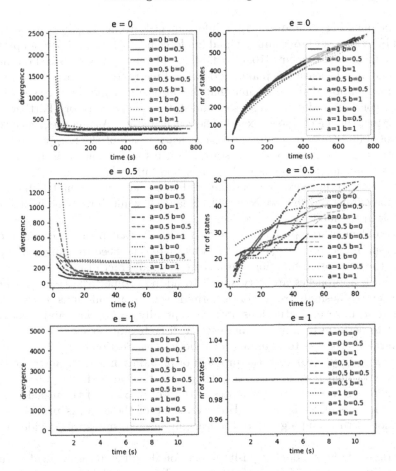

Fig. 3. Experiments with 5×5 building. a, b, and e stand for α, β, and ϵ, respectively.

the case of $\alpha = 1$, since, as usual, $\alpha = 1$ does not allow PAL to connect the new states to the old ones.

In conclusion, the experiments show that the new formal framework allows PAL (with a very simple planning algorithm) to learn the abstract model (even from scratch) and, with a reasonable set up of the parameters, to learn coherent models in reasonable time.

5   Related Work

Our approach shares some similarities with the work on planning by model based reinforcement learning (RL) [6,13,22], especially with approaches defined on abstract discrete models. In [23] planning domains are specified in the action language $\mathcal{BC}$ in a hierarchical reinforcement learning setting. In [19] hierarchical abstract machines impose constraints on reinforcement learning. [20] combines symbolic planning techniques with reinforcement learning. In [14] plans are generated by answer set programming, and reinforcement learning allows adaptation to a changing environment. [10,11] adopts a different approach based on model based planning to learn the planning domain directly from execution traces. All the works mentioned above assume that the set of states and the correspondence between continuous data from sensors and states are fixed a priori. Furthermore, after acting, the agent knows exactly the reached state. As a consequence there is no possibility to learn a new state, or to learn to adapt the mapping between perceptions in the real world and states. We, instead, allow to introduce new states at run-time, and to adapt the perception function.

Moreover, we have explicit parameters like α and β in the update_trans and update_perc functions that we can use to balance how much we trust in an initial model or in the model learned so far.

A complementary approach is pursued in works that plan directly in a continuous space, see, e.g., [1,4,17]. In this way there is no need to define a mapping such as the perception function, since there is no abstract discrete model of the world. Such approaches are very suited to address some tasks, e.g., moving a robot arm to a desired position or performing some manipulations. However, we believe that, in several situations, it is conceptually appropriate and practically efficient to perform planning in an abstract discrete state space.

Several approaches to planning for robotics (see Section 7 of [12] for a comprehensive survey) deal with the problem of planning in and learning the environment in which they operate, and they have to deal with the robot ending up in unknown and unexpected states of the world. Some of them make use of an abstract model of the world. However, none of these works provide a formalization of the mapping and of the learning mechanism as we provide in this paper.

Works on domain model acquisition focus on the different problem of learning action schema, see, e.g. [5,9,15,16,18,24]. Finally, our work has some similarities with planning in hybrid domains (see, e.g., [3]), since we deal with a discrete model and continuous data coming from sensors. However we do not plan in a hybrid domain, since our plan generation is performed in the discrete space.

6   Conclusion and Future Work

We have provided a formal framework that supports the incremental construction of an abstract planning domain by learning new states and the mapping between states and real world perceptions. We have provided a planning-acting-learning algorithm that allows an agent to learn a coherent abstract planning model while planning and acting to achieve its goals. We have provided an experimental evaluation that shows how this can be obtained with different learning modalities.

In this paper we focus on deterministic domains; in the future we plan to extend our work to nondeterministic and probabilistic planning domains, e.g., by learning probability distributions on γ. Moreover we plan to integrate in our framework a state-of-the-art on-line planner, and to run experiments on more complex and realistic domains.

References

1. Abbeel, P., Quigley, M., Ng, A.Y.: Using inaccurate models in reinforcement learning. In: Machine Learning, Proceedings of the Twenty-Third International Conference, ICML 2006, 25–29 June 2006, Pittsburgh, Pennsylvania, USA, pp. 1–8 (2006)
2. Bishop, C.M.: Pattern Recognition and Machine Learning (Information Science and Statistics). Springer, Heidelberg (2006)
3. Bogomolov, S., Magazzeni, D., Podelski, A., Wehrle, M.: Planning as model checking in hybrid domains. In: Proceedings of the Twenty-Eighth AAAI Conference on Artificial Intelligence, 27–31 July 2014, Québec City, Québec, Canada, pp. 2228–2234 (2014)
4. Co-Reyes, J.D., Liu, Y., Gupta, A., Eysenbach, B., Abbeel, P., Levine, S.: Self-consistent trajectory autoencoder: hierarchical reinforcement learning with trajectory embeddings. In: Proceedings of the 35th International Conference on Machine Learning, ICML 2018, 10–15 July 2018, Stockholmsmässan, Stockholm, Sweden, pp. 1008–1017 (2018)
5. Cresswell, S., McCluskey, T.L., West, M.M.: Acquiring planning domain models using LOCM. Knowl. Eng. Rev. **28**(2), 195–213 (2013)
6. Geffner, H., Bonet, B.: A Concise Introduction to Models and Methods for Automated Planning. Synthesis Lectures on Artificial Intelligence and Machine Learning. Morgan & Claypool Publishers, San Rafael (2013)
7. Ghallab, M., Nau, D.S., Traverso, P.: Automated Planning - Theory and Practice. Elsevier, Hoboken (2004)
8. Ghallab, M., Nau, D.S., Traverso, P.: Automated Planning and Acting. Cambridge University Press, Cambridge (2016)
9. Gregory, P., Cresswell, S.: Domain model acquisition in the presence of static relations in the LOP system. In: Proceedings of the Twenty-Fifth International Joint Conference on Artificial Intelligence, IJCAI 2016, 9–15 July 2016, New York, NY, USA, pp. 4160–4164 (2016)
10. Henaff, M., Whitney, W.F., LeCun, Y.: Model-Based Planning with Discrete and Continuous Actions. ArXiv e-prints (2017)
11. Henaff, M., Whitney, W.F., LeCun, Y.: Model-based planning in discrete action spaces. CoRR abs/1705.07177 (2017)
12. Ingrand, F., Ghallab, M.: Deliberation for autonomous robots: a survey. Artif. Intell. **247**, 10–44 (2017)
13. Kaelbling, L.P., Littman, M.L., Moore, A.W.: Reinforcement learning: a survey. J. Artif. Intell. Res. **4**, 237–285 (1996)
14. Leonetti, M., Iocchi, L., Stone, P.: A synthesis of automated planning and reinforcement learning for efficient, robust decision-making. Artif. Intell. **241**, 103–130 (2016)
15. McCluskey, T.L., Cresswell, S., Richardson, N.E., West, M.M.: Automated acquisition of action knowledge. In: ICAART 2009 - Proceedings of the International Conference on Agents and Artificial Intelligence, 19–21 January 2009, Porto, Portugal, pp. 93–100 (2009)

16. Mehta, N., Tadepalli, P., Fern, A.: Autonomous learning of action models for planning. In: Advances in Neural Information Processing Systems 24: 25th Annual Conference on Neural Information Processing Systems 2011, 12–14 December 2011, Granada, Spain, pp. 2465–2473 (2011)

17. Mnih, V., et al.: Human-level control through deep reinforcement learning. Nature **518**(7540), 529–533 (2015)

18. Mourão, K., Zettlemoyer, L.S., Petrick, R.P.A., Steedman, M.: Learning STRIPS operators from noisy and incomplete observations. In: Proceedings of the Twenty-Eighth Conference on Uncertainty in Artificial Intelligence, 14–18 August 2012, Catalina Island, CA, USA, pp. 614–623 (2012)

19. Parr, R., Russell, S.J.: Reinforcement learning with hierarchies of machines. In: Advances in Neural Information Processing Systems 10, [NIPS Conference, Denver, Colorado, USA, 1997], pp. 1043–1049 (1997)

20. Ryan, M.R.K.: Using abstract models of behaviours to automatically generate reinforcement learning hierarchies. In: Machine Learning, Proceedings of the Nineteenth International Conference (ICML 2002), University of New South Wales, 8–12 July 2002, Sydney, Australia, pp. 522–529 (2002)

21. Sutton, R.S.: Integrated architectures for learning, planning, and reacting based on approximating dynamic programming. In: Machine Learning, Proceedings of the Seventh International Conference on Machine Learning, 21–23 June 1990, Austin, Texas, USA, pp. 216–224 (1990)

22. Sutton, R.S., Barto, A.G.: Reinforcement Learning - An Introduction. Adaptive Computation and Machine Learning. MIT Press, Cambridge (1998)

23. Yang, F., Lyu, D., Liu, B., Gustafson, S.: PEORL: integrating symbolic planning and hierarchical reinforcement learning for robust decision-making. In: Proceedings of the Twenty-Seventh International Joint Conference on Artificial Intelligence, IJCAI 2018, 13–19 July 2018, Stockholm, Sweden, pp. 4860–4866 (2018)

24. Zhuo, H.H., Kambhampati, S.: Action-model acquisition from noisy plan traces. In: IJCAI 2013, Proceedings of the 23rd International Joint Conference on Artificial Intelligence, 3–9 August 2013, Beijing, China, pp. 2444–2450 (2013)

Towards Effective Device-Aware Federated Learning

Vito Walter Anelli, Yashar Deldjoo, Tommaso Di Noia,
and Antonio Ferrara$^{(\boxtimes)}$

Polytechnic University of Bari, Bari, Italy
{vito.anelli,yashar.deldjoo,tommaso.noia,antonio.ferrara}@poliba.it

Abstract. With the wealth of information produced by social networks, smartphones, medical or financial applications, speculations have been raised about the sensitivity of such data in terms of users' personal privacy and data security. To address the above issues, Federated Learning (FL) has been recently proposed as a means to leave data and computational resources distributed over a large number of nodes (clients) where a central coordinating server aggregates only locally computed updates without knowing the original data. In this work, we extend the FL framework by pushing forward the state the art in the field on several dimensions: (i) unlike the original FedAvg approach relying solely on single criteria (i.e., local dataset size), a suite of *domain-* and *client-specific criteria* constitute the basis to compute each local client's contribution, (ii) the multi-criteria contribution of each device is computed in a prioritized fashion by leveraging a *priority-aware aggregation operator* used in the field of information retrieval, and (iii) a mechanism is proposed for *online-adjustment* of the aggregation operator parameters via a local search strategy with backtracking. Extensive experiments on a publicly available dataset indicate the merits of the proposed approach compared to standard FedAvg baseline.

Keywords: Federated learning · Aggregation · Data distribution

1 Introduction and Context

The vast amount of data generated by billions of mobile and online IoT devices worldwide holds the promise of significantly improved usability and user experience in intelligent applications. This large-scale quantity of rich data has created an opportunity to greatly advance the intelligence of machine learning models by catering powerful deep neural network models. Despite this opportunity, nowadays such pervasive devices can capture a lot of data about the user, information such as what she does, what she sees and even where she goes [15]. Actually, most of these data contain sensitive information that a user may deem private. To respond to concerns about sensitivity of user data in terms of data privacy and security, in the last few years, initiatives have been made by governments

© Springer Nature Switzerland AG 2019
M. Alviano et al. (Eds.): AI*IA 2019, LNAI 11946, pp. 477–491, 2019.
https://doi.org/10.1007/978-3-030-35166-3_34

to prioritize and improve the security and privacy of user data. For instance, in 2018, General Data Protection Regulation (GDPR) was enforced by the European Union to protect users' personal privacy and data security. These issues and regulations pose a new challenge to traditional AI models where one party is involved in collecting, processing and transferring all data to other parties. As a matter of fact, it is easy to foresee the risks and responsibilities involved in storing/processing such sensitive data in the traditional *centralized* AI fashion.

Federated learning is an approach recently proposed by Google [9,10,14] with the goal to train a global machine learning model from a massive amount of data, which is *distributed* on the client devices such as personal mobile phones and/or IoT devices. It is noteworthy that FL differs from traditional distributed learning since we assume that training data (which is supposed to be sensitive) is kept on the very large set of users' private devices they were generated on (e.g., data generated from users' interaction with mobile applications). Therefore, we have to deal with data that is quantitatively unbalanced and differently distributed over devices, i.e. each device data is not a representative sample of the overall distribution. Instead, in a traditional distributed setting, data has to be collected in a centralized location and then evenly distributed over proprietary compute nodes. As a matter of fact, with FL we leverage users' computing power for training a shared ML model while preserving privacy, by actually decoupling the ability to learn a ML model from the need to centrally store private data.

In principle, a FL model is able to deal with fundamental issues related to privacy, ownership and locality of data [2]. In [14], authors introduced the *FederatedAveraging* (FedAvg) algorithm, which combines local stochastic gradient descent on each client via a central server that performs model aggregation by averaging the values of local hyperparameters. To ensure that the developments made in FL scenarios uphold to real-world assumptions, in [3] the authors introduced LEAF, a modular benchmarking framework supplying developers/researchers with a rich number of resources including open-source federated datasets, an evaluation framework, and a number of reference implementations.

Despite its potentially disruptive contribution, we argue that FedAvg exposes some major shortcomings. First, the aggregation operation in FedAvg sets the contribution of each agent proportional to each individual client's local dataset size. A wealth of qualitative measures such as the number of sample classes held by each agent, the divergence of each computed local model from the global model — which may be critical for convergence [16] —, some estimations about the agent computing and connection capabilities or about their honesty and trustworthiness are ignored. While FedAvg only uses limited knowledge about local data, we argue that the integration of the above-mentioned qualitative measures and the expert's domain knowledge is indispensable for increasing the quality of the global model.

The work at hand considerably extends the FedAvg approach [14] by building on three main assumptions:

- we can substantially improve the quality of the global model by incorporating *a set of criteria* about domain and clients, and properly assigning the contribution of individual update in the final model based on these criteria;
- the introduced criteria can be combined by using different aggregation operators; toward this goal, we assert about the potential benefits of using a *prioritized multi-criteria aggregation operator* over the identified set of criteria to define each individual's local update contribution to the federation process;
- computation of parameters for the aggregation operator (the priority order of the above-mentioned criteria) via an *online monitoring and adjustment* is an important factor for improving the quality of global model.

The remainder of the paper is structured as follows. Section 2 is devoted to introducing the proposed FL system, it first describes the standard FL model and then provides a formal description of the proposed FL approach and the key concepts behind integration of local criteria and prioritized multi-criteria aggregation operator in the proposed system. Section 3 details the experimental setup of the entire system by relying on LEAF, an open-source benchmarking framework for federated settings, which comes with a suite of datasets realistically pre-processed for FL scenarios. Section 4 presents results and discussion. Finally, Sect. 5 concludes the paper and discusses future perspectives.

2 Federated Learning and Aggregation Operator

In the following, we introduce the main elements behind the proposed approach. We start by presenting a formal description to the standard FL approach (cf. Sect. 2.1) and then we describe our proposed FL approach (cf. Sect. 2.2).

2.1 Background: Standard FL

In a FL setup, a set $\mathcal{A} = \{A_1, \ldots, A_K\}$ of agents (clients) participate to the training federation with a server S coordinating them. Each agent A_k stores its local data $\mathcal{D}_k = \{(x_1^k, y_1^k), (x_2^k, y_2^k), \ldots, (x_{|\mathcal{D}_k|}^k, y_{|\mathcal{D}_k|}^k)\}$, and never shares them with S. In our setting, x_i^k represents the data sample i of agent k and y_i^k is the corresponding label. The motivation behind a FL setup is mainly efficiency — K can be very large — and privacy [1,14]. As local training data $\mathcal{D}_k$ never leaves federating agent machines, FL models can be trained on user private (and sensitive) data, e.g., the history of her typed messages, which can be considerably different from publicly accessible datasets.

The final objective in FL is to learn a global model characterized by a parameter vector $\mathbf{w}^G \in \mathbb{R}^d$, with d being the number of parameters for the model, such that a global loss is minimized without a direct access to data across clients. The basic idea is to train the global model separately for each agent k on $\mathcal{D}_k$, such that a local loss is minimized and the agents have to share with S only the computed model parameters $\mathbf{w}^k$, which will be aggregated at the server level.

By means of a communication protocol, the agents and the global server exchange information about the parameters of the local and global model. At the t-th round of communication, the central server S broadcasts the current global model $\mathbf{w}_t^G$ to a fraction of agents $\mathcal{A}^- \subset \mathcal{A}$. Then, every agent k in $\mathcal{A}^-$ carries out some optimization steps over its local data $\mathcal{D}_k$ in order to optimize a local loss. Finally, the computed local parameter vector $\mathbf{w}_{t+1}^k$ is sent back to the central server. The central server S computes a weighted mean of the resulting local models in order to obtain an updated global model $\mathbf{w}_{t+1}^G$

$$\mathbf{w}_{t+1}^G = \sum_{k=1}^{|\mathcal{A}^-|} p_{t+1}^k \mathbf{w}_{t+1}^k. \tag{1}$$

For the sake of simplicity of discussion, throughout this work, we do not consider the time dimension and focus our attention on one time instance as given by Eq. (2)

$$\mathbf{w}^G = \sum_{k=1}^{|\mathcal{A}^-|} p^k \mathbf{w}^k, \tag{2}$$

in which $p^k \in [0,1]$ is the weight associated with agent k and $\sum_{k=1}^{|\mathcal{A}^-|} p^k = 1$.

We argue that collecting information about clients and incorporating that knowledge to compute the appropriate agent-dependent value p^k is important for computing an effective and efficient federated model. Moreover, it is worth noticing that p^k may encode and carry out some useful knowledge in the optimization of the global model with respect to relevant domain-specific dimensions.

2.2   Proposed Federated Learning Approach

As discussed at the end of the previous section, we may have different factors and/or criteria influencing the computation of p^k. Given a set of properly identified criteria about clients, it could be then possible to enhance the global model update procedure by using this information.

To connect it to the formalism presented before, let us assume $C = \{C_1, ..., C_m\}$ be a set of measurable properties (criteria) characterizing local agent k or local data $\mathcal{D}_k$. We use the term $c_i^k \in [0,1]$ to denote, for each agent k, the degree of satisfaction of criterion C_i in a specific round of communication. Hence, in the proposed FL aggregation protocol, the central server computes p^k as

$$p^k = \frac{f(c_1^k, ..., c_m^k)}{Z} = \frac{s^k}{Z}, \tag{3}$$

where f is a *local aggregation operation* over the set of properties (criteria), which represent agent k, $s^k \in \mathbb{R}$ is a numerical score evaluating the k-th agent contribution based on the m identified properties and, finally, Z is a normalization factor. In order to ensure that $\sum_{k=1}^{|\mathcal{A}^-|} p^k = 1$ where $p^k \in [0,1]$, we compute $Z = \sum_{k=1}^{|\mathcal{A}^-|} s^k$.

Example 1. Let us consider three criteria C_1, C_2, C_3 describing, e.g., three specific qualities of the local devices, their produced models or their data. Let us suppose that we have just two clients, and client 1 obtained evaluations $c_1^1 = 0.5, c_2^1 = 0.8, c_3^1 = 0.9$, while client 2 obtained $c_1^2 = 0.2, c_2^1 = 0.9, c_3^1 = 0.7$. Based on Eq. 3, overall evaluation of client 1 and 2 will be proportional and equal to $\frac{f(0.5, 0.8, 0.9)}{Z}$ and $\frac{f(0.2, 0.9, 0.7)}{Z}$ in which $Z = f(0.5, 0.8, 0.9) + f(0.2, 0.9, 0.7)$. □

In the following, we briefly discuss the identified set of criteria (together with a motivation for the selection), the selected aggregation operator f, and the online adjustment procedure.

Identification of Local Criteria. In FedAvg, the server performs aggregation to compute p^k, without knowing any information about participating clients, except for a pure quantitative measure about local dataset size. Our approach relies on the assumption that it might be much better to use multiple criteria encoding different useful knowledge about clients to obtain a more informative global model during training. This makes it possible for a domain expert to build the federated model by leveraging different any additional *domain-* and *client-specific* knowledge.

For instance, one may want to choose the criteria in such a way that the rounds of communication needed to reach a desired target accuracy are minimized. Moreover, a domain expert could ask users/clients to measure their adherence to some other target properties (e.g. their nationality, gender, age, job, behavioral characteristics, etc.), in order to build a global model emphasizing the contribution of some classes of users; in this way, the domain expert may, in principle, build a model favoring some targeted commercial purposes.

All in all, we may have a suite of criteria to reach the final global goal (in Sect. 3 we will see the example adopted in our experimental setup).

Prioritized Multi-criteria Aggregation Operator. Once local criteria evaluations have been collected, the central server aggregates them for each device in order to obtain a final score associated to that device. Over the years, a wide range of aggregation operators have been proposed in the field of information retrieval (IR) [13]. We selected some prominent ones and exploited them in our FL setup. In particular, we focused on the weighted averaging operator, the ordered weighted averaging (OWA) models [17,18], which extend the binary logic of *AND* and *OR* operators by allowing representation of intermediate quantifiers, the Choquet-based models [4,7,8], which are able to interpret positive and negative interactions between criteria, and finally the priority-based models [6]. Due to the lack of space, here we report only the approach and the experimental evaluation related to the last one, modeled in terms of a MCDM problem, because of its better performance.

The core idea of the *prioritized multi-criteria aggregation operator* proposed in [6] is to assign a priority order to the involved criteria. The main rationale behind the idea is to allow a domain expert to model circumstances where the lack of fulfillment of a higher priority criterion cannot be compensated with the fulfillment of a lower priority one [13]. As an example, we may consider the case where the domain expert may want to consider extremely important the age of an agent's user rather than its dataset size, so that even a large local dataset would be penalized if the user age criteria is not satisfied.

Formally, the prioritized multi-criteria aggregation operator $f : [0,1]^m \rightarrow [0,m]$ measures an overall *score* from a prioritized set of criteria evaluations on the local model $\mathbf{w}^k$ as in the following [6]:

$$s^k = f(c_1^k, ..., c_m^k) = \sum_{i=1}^{m} \lambda_i \cdot c_{(i)}^k$$

$$\lambda_1 = 1, \quad \lambda_i = \lambda_{i-1} \cdot c_{(i-1)}^k, \quad i \in [2,m]$$

(4)

where $c_{(i)}^k$ is the evaluation of $C_{(i)}$ for device k and the $\cdot_{(i)}$ notation indicates the indices of a sorted priority order for criteria, as specified by the domain expert, from the most important to the least important one. For each score $c_{(i)}^k$, an importance weight λ_i is computed, depending both on the specified priority order over the criteria and on the fulfillment and the weight of the immediately preceding criterion.

Example 2. Let us suppose that we are interested in evaluating device k based on three criteria C_1, C_2, C_3 and their respective evaluations are $c_1^k = 0.5, c_2^k = 0.8, c_3^k = 0.9$. Let the priority order of criteria be $C_{(1)} = C_1, C_{(2)} = C_2, C_{(3)} = C_3$, from the most important to the least important; then, $\lambda_1 = 1, \lambda_2 = \lambda_1 \cdot c_{(1)}^k = 0.5, \lambda_3 = \lambda_2 \cdot c_{(2)}^k = 0.4$. Hence, the final device score will be $s^k = (1 \cdot 0.5) + (0.5 \cdot 0.8) + (0.4 \cdot 0.9) = 1.26$. If we change the priority order to be $C_{(1)} = C_3, C_{(2)} = C_2, C_{(3)} = C_1$, we would then obtain $\lambda_1 = 1, \lambda_2 = \lambda_1 \cdot c_{(1)}^k = 0.9, \lambda_3 = \lambda_2 \cdot c_{(2)}^k = 0.72$ with a final device score of $s^k = (1 \cdot 0.9) + (0.9 \cdot 0.8) + (0.4 \cdot 0.5) = 1.82$. We see that this latter value is higher than the previous one since the most important criterion here is better fulfilled.   □

Online Adjustment. The aggregation operator we are using takes as parameter the priority order of the involved criteria and, as a consequence, one of the problem is to identify the best ordering for Eq. 4 which takes benefit of the gathered information. Although by definition this priority order could be defined by a domain expert, here we propose to choose the best one in an online fashion such that we can maximize the performances of the model at each round of communication.

Let $(C_{(1),t}, ..., C_{(m),t})$ be the last priority ordering of the criteria used to compute the local scores p_t^k (see Eqs. (3) and (4)) at time t. The sequence of steps needed to compute the updates to the global model is formalized in Algorithm 1 and commented in the following.

Lines 1–7 On each device, we locally train the last broadcasted global model $\mathbf{w}_t^G$ with the local training data, in order to compute $\mathbf{w}_{t+1}^k$; then, we measure the local scores for each of the identified criteria.

Algorithm 1. Sequence of steps executed by the server to compute the new global model with online adjustment of aggregation operator parameters. Functions *ModelUpdate*, *PropertyMeasure*, and *LocalTestAccuracy* are executed locally on the k-th device. Variable acc_t is an estimation of the global accuracy.

Require: $\mathbf{w}_t^G$, acc_t, $(C_{(1),t}, ..., C_{(m),t})$
Ensure: $\mathbf{w}_{t+1}^G$, acc_{t+1}, $(C_{(1),t+1}, ..., C_{(m),t+1})$
 1: broadcast $\mathbf{w}_t^G$ to clients in $\mathcal{A}^-$
 2: **for** each client $k \in \mathcal{A}^-$ **in parallel do**
 3:    $\mathbf{w}_{t+1}^k \leftarrow \text{ModelUpdate}(k, \mathbf{w}_t^G)$
 4:    **for** each criterion $C_i \in C$ **do**
 5:       $c_{i,t+1}^k \leftarrow \text{PropertyMeasure}(k, \mathbf{w}_{t+1}^k, C_i)$
 6:    **end for**
 7: **end for**
 8: $P \leftarrow (C_{(1),t}, ..., C_{(m),t})$
 9: **for** each client $k \in \mathcal{A}^-$ **do**
10:    $p_{t+1}^k \leftarrow f(c_{(1),t+1}^k, ..., c_{(m),t+1}^k)/Z$
11: **end for**
12: $\overline{\mathbf{w}}_{t+1}^G \leftarrow \sum_{k=1}^{|\mathcal{A}^-|} p_{t+1}^k \mathbf{w}_{t+1}^k$
13: **for** each client $k \in \mathcal{A}$ **in parallel do**
14:    $acc_{t+1}^k \leftarrow \text{LocalTestAccuracy}(k, \overline{\mathbf{w}}_{t+1}^G)$
15: **end for**
16: $acc_{t+1} \leftarrow$ weighted average of acc_{t+1}^k w.r.t. local test set size, $\forall k \in \mathcal{A}$
17: **while** $acc_{t+1} < acc_t$ **do**
18:    **if** other priority orderings are available **then**
19:       $P \leftarrow$ another priority ordering of criteria $(C_{(1)}, ..., C_{(m)})\star$
20:       repeat steps 9—16
21:    **else**
22:       $P \leftarrow$ priority ordering for which we get the maximum value for acc_{t+1}
23:       $acc_{t+1}^k \leftarrow$ accuracy of the model which performed best
24:       repeat steps 9—12
25:       **break**
26:    **end if**
27: **end while**
28: $(C_{(1),t+1}, ..., C_{(m),t+1}) \leftarrow P$
29: $\mathbf{w}_{t+1}^G \leftarrow \overline{\mathbf{w}}_{t+1}^G$

Lines 9–11 For each device, we use the priority ordering of criteria already used in the previous round of communication to compute the local score p_{t+1}^k.

Line 12 A new *candidate* global model $\overline{\mathbf{w}}_{t+1}^G$ is built by computing a weighted averaging of the local models w.r.t. the computed p_{t+1}^k.

Lines 13–15 On each device, $\overline{\mathbf{w}}_{t+1}^G$ is locally tested using the local test set.

Lines 16–29 An estimation of a global accuracy is computed weighting local accuracies w.r.t. local test set size; then, if the obtained accuracy is higher on average than the accuracy obtained with $\mathbf{w}_t^G$, then we update the global value $\mathbf{w}_{t+1}^G \leftarrow \overline{\mathbf{w}}_{t+1}^G$ and we proceed with the next round of communication; otherwise, another permutation is considered and, once a new p_{t+1}^k is computed for each device, we go back to step 3; if no other permutations are available, the candidate global model which produced the least worst test accuracy is assigned to $\mathbf{w}_{t+1}^{G}$.

The above-mentioned steps are also graphically illustrated by means of a plot in Fig. 1, where an exemplification with dummy values is presented. Training steps proceed with the same parametrization until a lower accuracy is obtained (blue point in round of communication 8); then, the previous model is restored and the other configurations are tested, until a higher accuracy is found (e.g., orange point in round 8). When a higher accuracy cannot be found, the least worst option is selected (e.g., green point in round 10).[1]

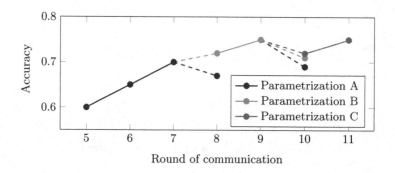

Fig. 1. An illustration of the online parameter adjustment for the aggregation operator. (Color figure online)

3 Experimental Setup

In this section we describe the experimental setup used to validate the performance of the proposed FL system.

Experimental Evaluation Framework. In order to perform the experimental validation and performance evaluation, an extensive set of experiments has been carried out by relying on LEAF [3], a modular open-source benchmarking framework for federated settings, which comes with a suite of datasets appropriately preprocessed for FL scenarios. LEAF also provides reproducible reference

---

[1] We should be reminded that the proposed adjustment algorithm may involve some communication and computational overhead due to the need of evaluating each of the candidate global models on local test data. We have not included this overhead in the count of rounds, since in the literature of FL a round of communication is defined as the entire process of model exchanging between clients and server and local model training [11]. Alternatively, we could define these extra rounds as *testing rounds*, which imply the same communication cost as a round of communication, but a significantly lower computational power. In the worst case, we would need $m!$ testing rounds for each round of communication, where m is the number of criteria.

implementations and introduces both system and statistical rigorous metrics for understanding the quality of the FL approach.

As for the metrics computation, the global model is tested on each device over the local test sets. The objective of LEAF is to capture the distribution of performance across devices by considering the 10th and 90th percentiles of the local accuracy values and by estimating a global accuracy (local accuracy values are averaged weighting them based on local test set size).

In this work, we improve the validation of the FL setting by using an approach which offers an overview of the whole training performances, instead of metrics describing a single round of communication. More specifically, *we measure the number of round of communication required to allow a certain percentage of devices, which participate to the federation process, to reach a target accuracy (e.g., 75% or 80%)*, since this measurement is able to fairly show how effective and efficient is the model across the devices.

Federated Dataset. We run our experiments using the FEMNIST dataset [3], which contains handwritten characters and digits from various writers and their true labels. Unlike the original FedAvg algorithm [14], which uses the MNIST dataset [12] artificially split by labels, the FEMNIST dataset [3], is larger and more realistically distributed. The dataset contains 805,263 examples of 62 classes of handwritten characters and digits from 3,550 writers and it is built by partitioning data in ExtendedMNIST [5] — an extended version of MNIST with letters and digits — based on writers of digits/characters. It is important to note that data in FEMNIST is inherently non-IID distributed, as the local training data can vary between clients; therefore, it is not representative of the whole population distribution. We use the described dataset to perform a digit/character classification task, although for computational limits we use a subsampled version (10% of total, 371 clients involved). Even though this training data is quite simple, in our view FEMNIST is sufficiently appropriate for our purposes, since one of the most motivating example of FL is when the training data comes from personal users' interaction with mobile applications. Actually, one could find interesting to eventually experiment our approach with different datasets, for example with a less marked user-dependence.

Convolutional Model. Similar to [14], the classification task is performed by using a convolutional neural network (CNN). The network has two convolutional layers with 5×5 filters — the first with 32 channels, the second with 64, each followed by 2×2 max pooling —, a fully connected layer with 2048 units and ReLu activation, and a final softmax output layer, with a total of 6,603,710 parameters.

Hyperparameter Settings. We set the hyperparameters for the whole set of our experiments as follows, also guided by the results obtained in [14]. As for the FedAvg client fraction parameter, in each round of communication only 10% of clients are selected to perform the computation. For what concerns the parameters of stochastic gradient decent (SGD), we set the local batch size to 10 and the number of local epochs equal to 5. This is the configuration that in the baseline makes it possible to reach the target accuracy in less rounds of communication. Moreover, we set the learning rate to $\eta = 0.01$. Finally, we set the maximum number of rounds of communication per each experiment to 1000.

Identified Local Criteria. In our experimental setting, the proposed FL system extends pure quantitative criteria in FedAvg [14] — dataset size — and leverages two new criteria. Please note that we are not stating that the proposed ones are the only possible criteria. We present them just to show how the introduction of new information may lead to a better final model. More specifically, in our experimental evaluation, we aim at both reducing the number of rounds of communication necessary to reach a target accuracy and making the global model not diverging towards local specializations and overfittings.

The criteria have been defined so that $c_i^k \in [0, 1]$ with 0 meaning bad performance and 1 good performance. Moreover, in order to make each criterion lying in the same interval scale, we normalized them such that $\sum_{k=1}^{|\mathcal{A}^-|} c_i^k = 1$.

Local Dataset Size(**base DS**). The first criterion we considered is the one already used by FedAvg [14] namely the local dataset size given by $c_1^k = |\mathcal{D}_k|/|\cup_{i \in \mathcal{A}^-} \mathcal{D}_i|$. This criterion is a *pure quantitative measure* about the local data, which will serve both as baseline in empirical validation of the results (i.e., when used in isolation) and as part of the entire identified set of criteria in the developed FL system (i.e., when used in a group).

Local Label Diversity(**Ld**). The second considered criterion is the *diversity of labels* in each local dataset, measuring the diversity of each local dataset in terms of class labels. We assert this criterion to be important since it can provide a clue on how much each device can be useful for learning to predict different labels. To quantify this criterion we use $c_2^k = \delta(\mathcal{D}_k)/\sum_{i \in \mathcal{A}^-} \delta(\mathcal{D}_i)$ where δ measures the number of different labels (classes) present over the samples of that dataset.

Local Model Divergence(**Md**). With non-IID distributions — and this is the case of our dataset — model performance dramatically gets worse [19]. Moreover, a large number of local training epochs may lead each device to move further away from the initial global model, towards the opposite of the global objective [16]. Therefore, a possible solution inspired by [16] is to limit these negative effects, by penalizing higher divergences and highlighting local models that are not very far from the received global model. We evaluate the local model divergence as $c_3^k = \varphi^k / \sum_{i \in \mathcal{A}^-} \varphi^i$ where $\varphi^i = \frac{1}{\sqrt{||\mathbf{w}^G - \mathbf{w}^i||_2 + 1}}$.

4   Results and Discussion

In order to validate the empirical performance of the proposed FL system, an extensive set of experiments has been carried out with respect to three under-study exploration dimensions in agreement with the assumptions presented in Sect. 1. The final results are shown in Table 1. Note that they are presented for reaching two distinctive desired target global accuracy of 75% and 80%.[2] Each column indicates the percentage of devices participating to the federation that is able to reach a desired target accuracy[3]. In addition, we present the results in three groups of (**Low, Mid, High**) for percentage of participating devices.

Study A: Effect of Individual Criteria. Study A contemplates answering the question: "*Are we able to introduce a set of device- and data- dependent criteria through the help of which we can train a better global model?*". The results for this study are summarized in the row **Ind** of Table 1. To answer the previous question, we considered the effect of each of the three identified criteria **base Ds, Md, Ld** *in isolation*, i.e., alternatively using only one of them. The results with respect to both desired accuracies of 75% and 80% show that the new identified criteria (**Md** and **Ld**) have an impact in the final quality of the global model, which is *comparable* (in **Low** and **Mid** cases) or *superior* with respect to the conventional **base Ds** criteria (in the case of **High**). For example, when comparing **Md** and **Ld**, one can notice the results are equal to 25.5 v.s. 27 with a marginal difference of only 6%. This is while, if we desire to satisfy a higher number of devices (**High** case) to reach a certain accuracy, the proposed criteria show a quality substantially better than the **base Ds** criteria. For example, **Ld** has a mean performance of 405 compared with 552.5 obtained **base Ds**. This is equal to an improvement of 36% with respect to existing baseline. These initial results already show how the global model can benefit from considering other criteria than just the dataset size.

Study B: Impact of Priority Order in Multi-criteria Aggregation. Study B focuses on the question: "*Are we able to exploit the potential benefits of a prioritized multi-criteria aggregation operator to build a more informative global model based on the identified criteria?*". The results for this study are summarized in row **MCA** of Table 1. To answer this research question, we performed one experiment for each individual permutation of criteria in the prioritized multi-criteria aggregation setting. Since there are 3 identified criteria, we have in total 6 permutations of criteria. For a fine-grained analysis, we provide the results obtained for *all the permutation runs*, denoted, e.g., by **Ds ≻ Ld ≻ Md**,

---

[2] We chose these values since they represent reasonable accuracy values and higher were not reached in the 1,000 allowed rounds of communication.

[3] The total number of participating devices in the federation is 371, thus 20%, as an example, indicates the round of communication required for $0.2 \times 317 = 75$ devices to reach the desired target accuracy.

Ds ≻ **Md** ≻ **Ld**. By looking at the results, we can notice that in **Low** and **Mid** categories, the best results are obtained for **Ds** ≻ **Ld** ≻ **Md** and **Ds** ≻ **Md** ≻ **Ld**. These results share a similar characteristic, which involves the fact that by considering **Ds** as the first important criterion, we can grant a smaller subset of devices the chance to reach to a desired target accuracy in faster pace/rate. This result is in agreement with individual results (see **Ind** in Table 1) in the sense that the *criterion **Ds** provides the best quality in **Low** and **Mid** study cases for both desired target accuracy of 75% and 80%*. However, when concentrating on the **High** category, one can notice **Md** ≻ **Ds** ≻ **Ld** provides the best performance. This result is a bit surprising and shows that to satisfy a higher number of devices, the criterion **Md** plays the most important role. This result is surprising from the sense that in the individual results (see **Ind** in Table 1), **Ld** has the most important performance, while in the obtained result it has the lowest priority. Interestingly, we may notice that in all these best cases, the pattern **Ds** ≻ **Ld** always occurs[4].

Study C: Impact of Online Adjustment of the Priority-Order in Multicriteria Aggregation. Finally, study C answers the question: "*Is it possible to update parameters for the aggregation operator (the priority order of the abovementioned criteria) via an online monitoring and adjustment or improving the quality of global model?*". The results for this study are summarized in row **Final** of Table 1. This study in fact is concerned with the *dynamic* behavior of our proposed FL approach, by letting the server choose at each round of communication the priority ordering maximizing the accuracy (i.e, obtain the best sub-optimal accuracy). Similar to the previous study, here we also run six experiments, related to the six possible *initializations* for the priority combinations. In Table 1 we show results related to the best run and to their mean. In this final experimental setting, we see an overall improvement in the performances of the proposes approach when we initialize the priority ordering with **Md** ≻ **Ds** ≻ **Ld**. Also in this case, the pattern **Ds** ≻ **Ld** occurs. In this final stage of our proposed approach we can notice it outperforms FL original algorithm, although we take into account the increased communication and computational requirements already discussed in Sect. 2.2.

---

[4] We remember here that a preference relation ≻ is transitive. Hence **Ds** ≻ **Md** ≻ **Ld** implies **Ds** ≻ **Ld**.

Table 1. Final results of the empirical evaluation. Each cell provides the number of rounds of communication necessary to make the percentage of devices specified in the columns reach a desired target accuracy (either 75% or 80% in our case). Runs that did not reach the target accuracy for the specified percentage of devices in the 1,000 allowed rounds are marked with —. The best results obtained in study MCA are shown in **underlined bold**, while the best results in study Final are shown in **bold**.

Study/% devices		Low			Mid			High		
		20%	30%	Mean	40%	50%	Mean	70%	75%	mean
Target accuracy 75%										
Ind	*Dataset size (base)*	*22*	*29*	*25.5*	*39*	*62*	*50.5*	*304*	*801*	*552.5*
	Model divergence	24	30	27	41	67	54	274	768	521
	Label diversity	25	32	28.5	43	70	56.5	278	532	405
MCA	Ds ≻ Ld ≻ Md	**20**	**29**	**24.5**	**39**	**60**	**49.5**	300	823	561.5
	Ds ≻ Md ≻ Ld	**20**	**29**	**24.5**	**39**	**60**	**49.5**	300	669	484.5
	Ld ≻ Ds ≻ Md	24	31	27.5	41	68	54.5	259	768	513.5
	Md ≻ Ds ≻ Ld	24	32	28	45	70	57.5	**255**	**532**	**393.5**
	Ld ≻ Md ≻ Ds	23	30	26.5	41	68	54.5	270	729	499.5
	Md ≻ Ld ≻ Ds	24	32	28	46	70	58	255	620	437.5
	Mean	22.5	30.5	26.5	41.8	66	53.9	273.17	690.1	481.6
Final	Md ≻ Ds ≻ Ld	**12**	**19**	**15.5**	**26**	**57**	**41.5**	**164**	**494**	**329**
	Mean	20.5	27.5	24	38.6	61.8	50.2	223	611.8	417.4
Target accuracy 80%										
Ind	*Dataset size (base)*	*31*	*45*	*38*	*72*	*136*	*104*	—	—	—
	Model divergence	31	46	38.5	82	151	116.5	—	—	—
	Label diversity	36	53	44.5	90	161	125.5	—	—	—
MCA	Ds ≻ Ld ≻ Md	**30**	**45**	**37.5**	**72**	**135**	**103.5**	—	—	—
	Ds ≻ Md ≻ Ld	**30**	**45**	**37.5**	**72**	**135**	**103.5**	—	—	—
	Ld ≻ Ds ≻ Md	31	46	38.5	82	149	115.5	—	—	—
	Md ≻ Ds ≻ Ld	36	53	44.5	84	161	122.5	—	—	—
	Ld ≻ Md ≻ Ds	31	46	38.5	82	151	116.5	—	—	—
	Md ≻ Ld ≻ Ds	36	53	44.5	90	161	125.5	—	—	—
	Mean	32.3	48	40.1	80.3	148.6	114.5	—	—	—
Final	Md ≻ Ds ≻ Ld	**21**	**36**	**28.5**	**61**	**133**	**97**	—	—	—
	Mean	30	43.5	36.7	78.1	142.6	110.4	—	—	—

5   Conclusions and Future Perspectives

In this work, we presented a practical protocol for effectively aggregating data by proposing a set of *device-* and *data-aware* properties (criteria) that are exploited by a central server in order to obtain a more qualitative/informative global model. Our experiments show that the standard federated learning standard, FedAvg can be substantially improved by training high-quality models using relatively few rounds of communication, by using a properly defined set of local criteria and using aggregation strategy that can exploit the information from such criteria. We want to stress here that devising such criteria is not a trivial task, and we deem necessary the knowledge of experts in the specific field or domain. Moreover, it would be arduous to find a general criterion that would meet the needs of all domains. Future perspectives for this work concern with the identification of other local criteria — both general purpose and domain-specific —, the experimentation with other aggregation operators and with other interesting datasets, as well as the extension of this federated approach to other machine learning systems, such as those in recommendation domain.

Acknowledgements. The authors wish to thank Angelo Schiavone for fruitful discussions and for helping with the implementation of the framework.

References

1. Bagdasaryan, E., Veit, A., Hua, Y., Estrin, D., Shmatikov, V.: How to backdoor federated learning. arXiv preprint arXiv:1807.00459 (2018)
2. Bonawitz, K., et al.: Towards federated learning at scale: system design. CoRR abs/1902.01046 (2019). http://arxiv.org/abs/1902.01046
3. Caldas, S., et al.: Leaf: a benchmark for federated settings. arXiv preprint arXiv:1812.01097 (2018)
4. Choquet, G.: Theory of capacities. Annales de l'Institut Fourier **5**, 131–295 (1954). https://doi.org/10.5802/aif.53
5. Cohen, G., Afshar, S., Tapson, J., van Schaik, A.: EMNIST: extending MNIST to handwritten letters. In: 2017 International Joint Conference on Neural Networks (IJCNN), pp. 2921–2926. IEEE (2017)
6. da Costa Pereira, C., Dragoni, M., Pasi, G.: Multidimensional relevance: prioritized aggregation in a personalized information retrieval setting. Inf. Process. Manag. **48**(2), 340–357 (2012). https://doi.org/10.1016/j.ipm.2011.07.001
7. Grabisch, M.: The application of fuzzy integrals in multicriteria decision making. Eur. J. Oper. Res. **89**(3), 445–456 (1996). https://doi.org/10.1016/0377-2217(95)00176-X. http://www.sciencedirect.com/science/article/pii/037722179500176X
8. Grabisch, M., Roubens, M.: Application of the Choquet integral in multicriteria decision making. In: Fuzzy Measures and Integrals, pp. 348–374 (2000)
9. Konecný, J., McMahan, B., Ramage, D.: Federated optimization: distributed optimization beyond the datacenter. CoRR abs/1511.03575 (2015). http://arxiv.org/abs/1511.03575
10. Konecný, J., McMahan, H.B., Ramage, D., Richtárik, P.: Federated optimization: distributed machine learning for on-device intelligence. CoRR abs/1610.02527 (2016). http://arxiv.org/abs/1610.02527
11. Konecný, J., McMahan, H.B., Yu, F.X., Richtárik, P., Suresh, A.T., Bacon, D.: Federated learning: strategies for improving communication efficiency. CoRR abs/1610.05492 (2016). http://arxiv.org/abs/1610.05492
12. Lecun, Y., Bottou, L., Bengio, Y., Haffner, P.: Gradient-based learning applied to document recognition. Proc. IEEE **86**(11), 2278–2324 (1998). https://doi.org/10.1109/5.726791
13. Marrara, S., Pasi, G., Viviani, M.: Aggregation operators in information retrieval. Fuzzy Sets Syst. **324**, 3–19 (2017). https://doi.org/10.1016/j.fss.2016.12.018
14. McMahan, B., Moore, E., Ramage, D., Hampson, S., Arcas, B.A.: Communication-efficient learning of deep networks from decentralized data. In: Proceedings of the 20th International Conference on Artificial Intelligence and Statistics, AISTATS

2017, Fort Lauderdale, FL, USA, 20–22 April 2017, pp. 1273–1282 (2017). http://proceedings.mlr.press/v54/mcmahan17a.html

15. Miller, K.W., Voas, J.M., Hurlburt, G.F.: BYOD: security and privacyconsiderations. IT Prof. **14**(5), 53–55 (2012). https://doi.org/10.1109/MITP.2012.93

16. Sahu, A.K., Li, T., Sanjabi, M., Zaheer, M., Talwalkar, A., Smith, V.: On the convergence of federated optimization in heterogeneous networks. arXiv preprint arXiv:1812.06127 (2018)

17. Yager, R.R.: On ordered weighted averaging aggregation operators in multicriteria decisionmaking. IEEE Trans. Syst. Man Cybern. **18**(1), 183–190 (1988). https://doi.org/10.1109/21.87068

18. Yager, R.R.: Quantifier guided aggregation using OWA operators. Int. J. Intell. Syst. **11**(1), 49–73 (1996)

19. Zhao, Y., Li, M., Lai, L., Suda, N., Civin, D., Chandra, V.: Federated learning with non-IID data. CoRR abs/1806.00582 (2018). http://arxiv.org/abs/1806.00582

AI and Humans

Manipulating an Election in Social Networks Through Edge Addition

Vincenzo Auletta, Diodato Ferraioli[(✉)], and Vincenzo Savarese

Università di Salerno, Fisciano, Italy
{auletta,dferraioli}@unisa.it, savaresevinc@gmail.com

Abstract. We investigate the effects that social influence can have on the behaviour of agents in a social network in the context of an election. In particular, we study how the structure of a social network can be manipulated in order to determine the outcome of an election.

We consider an election with m candidates and n voters, each one with her own ranking on the candidates. Voters are part of a social network and the information that each voter has about the election is limited to what her friends are voting. We consider an iterative elective process where, at each round, each voter decides her vote, based on what her neighbors voted in the previous round and her own ranking. Thus, a voter may strategically decide to vote for a candidate different from her favorite to avoid the election of a candidate she dislikes.

Following [36] we investigate how a central organization that knows rankings of all the voters and the structure of the social network can determine the outcome of the election by creating new connections among voters.

Our main result is an algorithm that, under mild conditions on the social network topology and on the voters' rankings, is able to produce a limited number of links to be added to the social network in order to make our sponsored candidate be the winner of the election. Our results can be seen as another indication that the control of social media is a great threat to our democracy since the controller has an extraordinary power in determining which information we are exposed to and can use this power to control and influence crucial decisions.

Keywords: Social networks · Election manipulation · Strategic voting

1 Introduction

The influence that social media have on our choices and our everyday life is getting more and more relevant. For example, it is quite common to choose restaurants, hotels or holiday destinations by looking at how other users rate these places on social sites as Yelp, TripAdvisor, or also Facebook. The spirit of

The work is partially supported by GNCS-INdAM and by the Italian MIUR PRIN 2017 Project ALGADIMAR "Algorithms, Games, and Digital Markets".

these services is that you can take advantage of the experience of the community in taking your decisions. However, our choices will be strictly intertwined not only to what our friends did or thought, but also on which data the social media decided to show or conceal or in which order they are presented.

In this work we address the problem of the manipulability of a social network from the point of view of the social choice theory. We consider a setting of an election with n voters (e.g., the users of a social media service) and m candidates. Voters are arranged in a graph, describing the social relationship existing among the voters. Voters are then involved in an iterative voting session [31], in which they are required to submit a vote at each time step, based on the information they received about the election, and from one step to the next one, they can revise their previous decisions, and vote for a different candidate.

Specifically, in this work, in order to understand to which extent the social media can influence our choices by deciding which information we are exposed, we consider the setting proposed in [36], in which each voter has her personal ranking on the candidates, and she is exposed to limited information about the election, consisting only of the votes expressed by her neighbors in the network (and, possibly, a poll). Voters are then assumed to behave strategically, in the sense that they decide their vote in response to what their neighbors are voting in order to optimize their personal welfare. Thus, a voter may decide to vote for a candidate that she does not prefer, as long as her vote can lead, according to her limited view of the election (restricted to her neighborhood and the poll), to an outcome that she would prefer to the current outcome.

In [36] it has been investigated to what extent a central entity that has global knowledge on the voters' rankings and the control of the social network (e.g., the social media owner or manager) may influence the outcome of the election process, by manipulating the view of the voters through the addition or the deletion of links in the social network. In particular, they focus only on the addition case, since this operation is less invasive and can be realized without arising suspects in the voters. We remark that this scenario is very relevant, since current technology would be already able to implement this kind of manipulation (e.g., Facebook's friend suggestions).

Unfortunately, the results in [36] address the issue only partially. Indeed, they design a polynomial time algorithm that, given the social network and the voters' rankings, compute a set of edges that a central designer may add to the network in order to have that a candidate w will be voted by the majority of voters. This interesting result has the drawback that the number of added links is extremely large and this makes the algorithm infeasible in real settings. However, deciding the minimum number of edges that are necessary to add in order to make the sponsored candidate win, would be hard, even in simpler settings [18].

To address these issues, in [36] it has been proposed an alternative heuristic that works in two phases: first, it *influences* a subset of voters, by adding edges to the social network in order to modify their view so that they "autonomously" decide to vote for our sponsored candidate w, and then, it *stabilizes* the neighbors of the voters influenced in the previous phase to have them vote for their favorite candidates. Clearly, the heuristics fails if it does not find enough voters to influence and stabilize in order to have w the winner of the election.

In [36] it is experimentally shown that their heuristic adds only a limited number of edges. However, their heuristic tends to have a quite large failure rate. The main problem is that the heuristic does not stabilize neighbors of stabilized voters: thus, due to the added edges, some of these voters may become unstable, and this can activate cascading behaviors with severe effects on the outcome of the election. (The problem has been acknowledged also in [36] and the authors propose a fix for it, but, again, the number of new edges added by the heuristics is very high. This causes too many new edges to be added).

Our Contributions. In this work we present a novel algorithm to compute the set of edges to be added to the social network to determine the winner of the election. Our algorithm works under mild condition on the network structure and on the voters' rankings. Moreover, it adds a limited number of edges (comparable to the heuristics in [36]).

As the heuristic in [36], our algorithm works in two phases. In the *influence phase* we look for a voter u that may be influenced to vote for our sponsored candidate w, and we add edges between u and voters that are voting for w or for the candidate that u dislikes the most. These voters are chosen among the ones that have not been influenced yet. This phase is repeated until w obtains the majority of the votes. Thus, if all the non-influenced voters would vote for their favorite candidates (we take care of this hypothesis in the stabilization phase), then w will win the election. Notice that, since we are following the same approach proposed in [36], in this phase we are not adding more edges than their heuristic does.

The *stabilization phase* aims to guarantee that all the non-influenced voters vote for their favorite candidates and it is the crux of our algorithm. We partition the voters to stabilize in three sets: the *superseeds*, the *seeds*, and the remaining voters. Our algorithm uses only 4 edges per node to stabilize a superseed voters and at most 2 edges per node to stabilize all the remaining voters. We prove that it is not possible to stabilize all these voters by adding less edges.

Our algorithm works under a set of mild conditions: the main requirement is that there are sufficiently many voters that do not rank w as the worst candidate (since these voters can be never induced to vote for w), and those have a limited neighborhood (otherwise the available edges are not sufficient to change their minds). There are also other technical requirements, but they concern only a limited number of nodes and they can be easily satisfied whenever the number of voters is large enough.

Finally, in Sect. 5 we run extensive experiments comparing our approach to the one in [36]: they show that both approaches add a number of edges that is more or less of the same order of magnitude, but our algorithm never fails, while the one by Sina et al. [36] fails in about 30% of the simulations.

Related Works. There is a large literature on iterative voting, that allows agents to update several times their vote [23,28,32,33]. These works focus on conditions guaranteeing that strategic voters converge to an equilibrium in an iterative election process: specifically, they consider the issue under different votes' aggregation rules, such as Plurality and Borda rules, or by restricting the set of voters' initial rankings. However, these works do not consider the effect that social influence could have on voters' actions, i.e., in these works every voter has complete knowledge of votes of every other agents.

There is an increasing literature focusing on the election manipulation problem, i.e., on how social media can be used as a powerful tool for subverting the result of an election. One of the first works along this directions analyzed the resistance to bribery of a special aggregation rule based on cp-nets [29]. Moreover, a series of works by Auletta et al. [5,7,8] showed that the in an election setting with only two candidates, and voters influenced by a (weighted) majority of their neighbors, it is always possible for a manipulator to lead a minority (if it is large enough) to become a majority, regardless of the topology of the underlying social relationships. Similarly, in [11] it has been proved that in a similar setting, a manipulator can be able to lead a bare majority to consensus. Interestingly, these results cannot be easily extended to more than two candidates [10]. Other forms of manipulation are considered in [18,21,24]: in particular, [18] considered the case that a manipulator may add edges in the relationship network, just as we do in this paper. Finally, in [37], a more complex voting setting is considered, similar to the one considered in this work, with more than two candidates and a plurality aggregation rule. Note however that in all these works players are not strategic, that is they may change their ranking as effect of the neighbors' influence. In our work the ranking does not change, but the expressed vote may be adapted as effect of a strategic voting behavior.

More in general, there is an intense research on how to model the effects that social pressure may have on people's choices: original models derive from sociological and economical studies [2,16,25]; on top of these, many other models have been proposed [1,6,9,14,15,19,20,35], trying to model more complex aspects, such as the co-evolution of choices and relationships, the presence of both positive and negative influences, and the evolution over the time of the relationships. Some of these models also inspired the one considered in [36] and in this work. However, we stress that no of these papers investigate on whether and how social influence can be used in order to manipulate an election.

2   Model and Definitions

We have a set of *candidates* of size m and a set of *voters* of size n. Voters lie on nodes of a *social network* $G = (V, E)$[1]. We say that the neighborhood of a node u represents the u's *view* of the election. Each voter u has a *preference order*, or ranking, $\succ_u$ over the candidates such that, for any two candidates c, c', we say

---

[1] In the rest of the paper we usually assume that the network is undirected. Indeed, this is the most difficult case for the problem faced in this work. Indeed, when influence are directed is possible to fix the vote of a voter by adding edges without harming the voters from which this influence goes out.

that $c \succ_u c'$ if u prefers c to c'. Moreover, voter u is said to be a *supporter* of the candidate c if u prefers c to every other candidate. For every candidate c, we denote by $\mathsf{Supp}[c]$ the set of the supporters of c. We can also assume that a *poll* is available that makes public the number of supporters for each candidate within a random sample of voters.

The Election Process. The election process works in *rounds*. At round 0 each voter announces to all her neighbors the candidate she supports (i.e., the first candidate in her preference list). At round $i \geq 1$ each voter considers the votes announced by her neighbors in round $i - 1$ and the poll; based on these informations, she strategically chooses to vote a candidate c, possibly different from the candidate that she supports (see below for details about how this choice is done); finally each voter announces to all hes neighbors the candidate she's going to vote.

The *winner* of the election at round i is the candidate that received the majority of votes in that round. A *tie-breaking rule* is adopted to determine the winner when multiple candidates received the same number of votes. Given two candidates c, c', we say that $c > c'$ if c would win the tie-break against c'. The process is repeated until an *equilibrium* is reached, i.e., a round of the election in which no voter changes the vote that she expressed in the previous round. Note that that this dynamics is known to converge under opportune conditions [34]. However, we prove that for all networks in which our manipulation algorithm returns an outcome, the dynamics above will surely converges to an equilibrium.

We are now ready to describe how voters choose who vote at each round. We assume that voters are strategic and at each round they declare a vote that *best-responds* to the votes expressed by their neighbors in the previous round. Thus, a voter changes her vote only if, according to her view, it is crucial to determine the election of a candidate she likes more of the current winner. The following definition describes when a voter u has an incentive to change her vote.

Definition 1. *A voter u is (c_1, c_2)-crucial in round i if c_1 is the candidate that is voted by the majority of neighbors of u at round $i - 1$ (in case of ties, the one that wins the tie-break), and c_2 is a candidate with $c_2 \succ_u c_1$, and one of the following two conditions hold: (i) c_1 and c_2 received the same number of votes among the neighbors of u; (ii) c_2 received one vote less than c_1 and $c_2 > c_1$ (i.e., c_2 wins a tie-break against c_1).*

Clearly, if u is (c_1, c_2)-crucial in round i, then she will decide to vote for c_2 to support an outcome she prefers to the current one. If, instead, u is not crucial, i.e., she cannot influence the outcome of the election in her neighborhood, then she confirms the vote expressed in the previous round.

3   The Manipulation Algorithm

In this section we present our manipulation algorithm. The algorithm takes in input the social network $G = (V, E)$, the list of candidates M, the preference lists of all the voters $\{\succ_u\}_{u \in V}$, and the sponsored candidate w and it returns a set of edges to add to the social network in order to guarantee that w will be the winner of the election. Following the approach presented in [36], our algorithm works in two phases.

Influence Phase. We start by running the first two rounds (round 0 and round 1) of the election on the graph G. Let Aff be the set of voters that voted for w in the round 1, even if they are not supporters of w. Observe that each voter $u \in$ Aff voted for w since this was the best response to what their neighbors announced in round 0. That is, u were (c, w)-crucial in round 1, where $w \succ_u c$.

Even if we assume that all the supporters of w will always vote for this candidate, and that all voters in Aff never change their minds after round 1, it could be the case that w has no sufficient votes to win the election. In this case, we have to induce other voters to vote for w. To this aim we follow the same approach as in [36], and add other edges to the social network according to the following algorithm.

---

1 Let $\mathbf{v} = (v_1, \ldots, v_n)$ be the set of votes at round 1
2 Set Aff $= \{i \colon \mathbf{v}[i] = w\} \setminus$ Supp$[w]$
3 **while** *there is* $c \neq w$ *such that either* $|\{i \colon \mathbf{v}[i] = c\}| > |$Aff $\cup$ Supp$[w]|$ *or*
   $|\{i \colon \mathbf{v}[i] = c\}| = |$Aff $\cup$ Supp$[w]|$ *and* $c > w$ **do**
4   **if** *there is an* affectable *voter* u **then**
5   Let G' be the graph resulting from the corresponding edge addition (see below)
6   Add u to Aff
7   Recompute $\mathbf{v}$
8   **else** stop the influence

Algorithm 1. The Influence Phase

The algorithm looks for *affectable* voters, where a voter u is affectable if $u \notin$ Aff and it satisfies the following conditions: (i) u does not support w; (ii) there is a candidate c such that $w \succ_u c$; (iii) there is a set M_w of w's supporters and a set M_c of non-affected c's supporters that are not adjacent to u and such that if we add links from u to all the nodes in $M_w \cup M_c$ then u in round 1 will be (c, w)-crucial, but not (c, c')-crucial for every $c' \succ_u w$. If such a voter exists, we add new links to the social network between u and the nodes in $M_w \cup M_c$. Let G' be the resulting graph. By running again the first two rounds of the election on graph G', we have that, by hypothesis, u will vote for w. We then add u to Aff and iterate the procedure until we added sufficiently many voters to Aff so that w would be the winner of the election with the votes by her supporters and by voters in Aff.

Let A be the set of links added by Algorithm 1 and let $G' = (V, E \cup A)$ be the resulting graph. We will next formally prove that, when running the election process on G', every voter $u \in$ Aff will vote for w at round 1 and it will confirm her vote in all the successive rounds, as long as all the non-affected voters vote for the candidates they support. Then the following lemma holds.

Lemma 1. *Assume we run the election process on the social network $G' = (V, E \cup A)$ returned by the Influence Phase. If at each round of the election all the voters $v \in V \backslash \mathsf{Aff}$ vote for their favorite candidates, then every voter $u \in \mathsf{Aff}$ votes for w at every round of the election.*

Observe that previous lemma assumes that non-affected voters permanently vote for the candidates they support. However, these voters could decide to change their votes to react to changes in their own view, and this could have destructive cascading effects with respect to our manipulation goal. Consider for example the network in Fig. 1, and assume that voters p, q, r, s have preference $d \succ_p w \succ_p d$, $w \succ_q d \succ_q d$, $c \succ_r w \succ_r d$ and $d \succ_s c \succ_s w$, respectively, whereas voters x_i and z_i support candidates d and w, respectively. Moreover, assume that the tie-breaking rule is $c > d > w$. It is then immediate to see that votes by q, r, s oscillate at each round by passing from w, c, d to d, w, c, respectively.

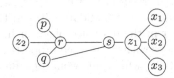

Fig. 1. An instance on which manipulation fails without the stabilization phase

Thus, we have to run a Stabilization Phase in which we add other links to the social network to stabilize non-affected voters and have them voting for the candidates they support.

In the rest of the paper we assume that a non-affected voter is *stable* in round i if she votes for her favorite candidate in this round and she is *unstable* otherwise.

Stabilization Phase. We partition the non-affected voters in three sets, B, Seed and SSeed, defined as follows. Seed is a set of $3m$ non-affected voters containing three supporters for each candidate c, such that if u and v are supporters of the same candidate c in Seed, and w is a neighbor of both u and v, then $w \in \mathsf{Aff} \cup \mathsf{Seed}$, i.e., either w is a voter that has been affected in the influence phase, or it is one of the $3m$ voters selected as seeds. SSeed, instead, is a set of $2m$ non-affected voters that is disjoint from Seed and it contains two supporters for each candidate c that are not adjacent to voters in $\mathsf{Seed} \cup \mathsf{Aff}$. B is the set of all remaining non-affected voters.

The Stabilization Phase works in three rounds: we first stabilize the voters in SSeed, then we stabilize the voters in B, and, finally, we stabilize the voters in Seed.

To stabilize a voter $u \in$ SSeed we connect u to four supporters of the candidate c that is supported by the majority of the neighbors of u (in case of tie, we consider the one that wins the tie-break). These four supporters must be chosen among the voters in B. To stabilize a voter $u \in B$ we connect it to at most two seeds. The selection of these seeds will be done through the Node Stabilization procedure that will be described in the next section. To stabilize a voter $u \in$ Seed we connect u to at most two voters in SSeed, selected through the Node Stabilization procedure.

Let Σ be the set of links added in the Stabilization phase and let $G'' = (V, E \cup A \cup \Sigma)$ be the graph obtained after both Influence and Stabilization Phase have been correctly executed. Then we have the following lemma.

Lemma 2. *If we run en election on the social network $G'' = (V, E \cup A \cup \Sigma)$, at each round every voter $u \notin$ Aff is stable.*

We defer the proof of this lemma to the next section, after we described the node Stabilization procedure.

Observe that Lemmas 1 and 2 prove that whenever our manipulation algorithm is correctly executed, it returns a set of edges to add to the social network that guarantee that the sponsored candidate will win the election. However, it may be the case that either in the influence phase or in the stabilization phase, we are unable to choose nodes with the desired properties. The following theorem describes the conditions under which this would not happen.

Theorem 1. *Our manipulation algorithm returns a network G'' such that the sponsored candidate w is the winner of the election in G'' and the process stops in 2 rounds, as long as we can partition the nodes in G in two sets (L, R) such that:*

- *L contains $\min\left\{\max_c\{\mathsf{Supp}[c]\}, \frac{n}{2}\right\} + 1 - \mathsf{Supp}[w]$ nodes that do not support w;*
- *for every $u \in L$, there are $\max_c \mathsf{Vote}_0[c] - \mathsf{Vote}_0[w] + 2 \leq d_u + 2$ supporters of w that are not in the neighborhood of u, and $\max_c \mathsf{Vote}_0[c] - \mathsf{Vote}_0[\hat{c}] + 2 \leq d_u + 2$ supporters of $\hat{c}$ that are not in L and not in the neighborhood of u, for some $\hat{c}$ such that $w \succ_u \hat{c}$, where, for every c, $\mathsf{Vote}_i[c]$ is the number of neighbors of u that voted for c at round i;*
- *for every candidate c there are in R three distinct subsets S_c, T_c, U_c such that: (i) S_c contains 3 supporters of c with disjoint neighborhood; (ii) T_c contains 2 supporters of c with no neighbors in $S \cup L$; (iii) U_c contains 4 supporters of c with no neighbors in T; where $S = \bigcup_c S_c$ and $T = \bigcup_c T_c$.*

We notice that the number of edges introduced by our manipulation algorithm cannot be larger than the one used by the heuristic proposed in [36]. Indeed, the two influence phases are equivalent (in particular, we can adopt in our algorithm the optimizations introduced in [36]), but our stabilization procedure uses the minimum possible number of edges.

We also highlight that our approach guarantees convergence in the lowest possible number of rounds, namely two, where the first consist in all voters voting for their supported candidate, and the second in strategically adjusting their vote. Theorem 1 then states that no more adjustments are necessary henceforth.

4   Node Stabilization

The Node Stabilization procedure is the core of our stabilization process. It takes in input a voter $u \notin \mathsf{Aff}$ and a subset of voters S containing supporters of all candidates, and returns at most two voters in S such that if u is connected to these voters then u will be stable in each round of the election.

Let us briefly describe the idea behind our approach. Let t be the candidate that u supports and let c_i^* be the candidate that has been voted by the majority of neighbors of u in round i (in case of ties, c_i^* is the one that wins the tie-break). As an example, consider how we can have u to vote for t in round 1. This clearly occurs when u, according to her view, cannot influence the outcome of the election or when u is crucial to make t the winner. Suppose, instead, that there is a candidate $c \neq c_0^*, t$ such that u is (c_0^*, c)-crucial. In this case, u would vote for c instead of t. To avoid this situation, it is sufficient to add a link between u and a supporter of c_0^* in S. Actually, as we will show later, there could be several candidates c, distinct from c_i^*, such that the addition of an edge between u and a supporter of c causes u to vote for her favorite candidate at round i. We will call these candidates *stabilizers* for u in round i and we will denote by St_i the set of these stabilizers.

Thus, by adding an edge between u and a voter in S that is a supporter of a stabilizer in St_0 we have stabilized u for round 1. However, since in round 1 the affected voters changed their vote to w, it may be the case that u, if adjacent to some affected voters, becomes (c_1^*, c)-crucial in round 2, for some $c \neq t$. In this case, u would change her vote in round 2 and vote for c. Thus, we have to stabilize also voters that could change their votes in round 2.

Observe that we cannot use the same approach as above, i.e., to add an edge between u and a supporter of c_1^* in S, since this new edge could make u again unstable in round 1. Indeed, suppose that u is (c_0^*, c)-crucial in round 1 and (c_1^*, c')-crucial in round 2. If $c_1^* = c$ and we add a link between u and supporters of both c_0^* and c_1^*, then u is still (c_0^*, c)-crucial in round 1 and she will remain unstable in this round. However, it is easy to see that we could stabilize u both in round 1 and 2 by simply adding edges between u and two supporters of c_1^*.

In general, we call *blocker* for u a candidate whose supporters cannot be used to stabilize u in round 2 because they would make the voter unstable in round 1. We distinguish two cases: if u is not stable at round 1, then we will denote her set of blockers as Bl_0; otherwise we will denote it as Bl_1. A formal definition of blockers is given later. We also prove that, whereas the addition of a single link between u and a supporter of a candidate $c \in \mathsf{Bl}_i$ is harmful, it is possible to stabilize u both at round 1 and 2 by simply adding edges between u and *two* supporters of a candidate $c \in \mathsf{Bl}_i$.

Our Node Stabilization procedure works as described by Algorithm 2.

Roughly speaking, it distinguishes two cases. Consider first that case that u is not stable in round 1 (i.e., she does not vote for her favorite candidate t). If

1 **if** $|\mathsf{St}_0| > 1$ *and* $t \notin \mathsf{St}_0$ **then**
2   **if** *there is* $c \in \mathsf{St}_0$ *s.t.* u *votes for* t *at round 2 if an edge between* u *and a*
     supporter of c *is added* **then**
3   Add an edge between u and a supporter of c
4   **else if** $c_1^* \notin \mathsf{Bl}_0$ **then**
5   Add edges between u and supporters of c_0^* and c_1^*
6   **else** Add edges between u and two supporters of c_1^*
7 **else if** *there is* $c \in \mathsf{St}_1 \setminus \mathsf{Bl}_1$ **then**
8   Add an edge between u and a supporter of c
9 **else** Add edges between u and two supporters of c_1^*

Algorithm 2. Node Stabilization Procedure

there is a candidate $c \in \mathsf{St}_0$ such that the addition of an edge between u and a supporter of c does not make u unstable in round 2, then we add this edge. if such a candidate does not exist, consider the candidate c_1^* that would win the round 2 of the election in the u's view: if $c_1^* \notin \mathsf{Bl}_0$ we add edges between u and both a supporter of c_0^* and one of c_1^*; if $c_1^* \in \mathsf{Bl}_0$ we add edges between u and two supporters of c_1^*.

If, instead, u is stable in round 1 (i.e., she votes for her favorite candidate t), then either there is $c \in \mathsf{St}_1 \setminus \mathsf{Bl}_1$, and we add an edge between u and a supporter of c; or we add edges between u and two supporters of c_1^*.

In the rest of this section we give formal definitions of the stabilizer and blocker sets, and we prove that the Node Stabilization procedure correctly stabilize voter u adding the *minimum* number of edges.

The Set St_i *of Stabilizers for* u *in Round* i. Let us recall that, given a voter u, we denote by c_i^* the candidate voted by the majority of the neighbors of u at round i (in case of ties, c_i^* is the one that wins the tie-break). For every candidate c, let $\mathsf{Vote}_i[c]$ be the number of neighbors of u that voted for c at round i. The set St_i of stabilizers for u in round i is defined as follows:

Definition 2. *The set* St_i, *for* $i \in \{0,1\}$, *contains all candidates* c *satisfying at least one of the following properties:*

- $c = c_i^*$;
- $\mathsf{Vote}_i[c] = \mathsf{Vote}_i[c_i^*]$ *and for each* c' *with* $\mathsf{Vote}_i[c'] = \mathsf{Vote}_i[c_i^*]$ *it occurs that either* $c > c'$ *or* $c \succ_u c'$;
- $\mathsf{Vote}_i[c] = \mathsf{Vote}_i[c_i^*] - 1$ *and for each* c' *with* $\mathsf{Vote}_i[c'] = \mathsf{Vote}_i[c_i^*]$ *it occurs that* $c > c'$ *and* $c \succ_u c'$, *whereas for each* c' *with* $\mathsf{Vote}_i[c'] = \mathsf{Vote}_i[c_i^*] - 1$ *it occurs that either* $c > c'$ *or* $c \succ_u c'$.

We can prove that if u is unstable in round $i+1$ and there exists a candidate $c \in \mathsf{St}_i$ we can stabilize u for this round by simply adding an edge between u and a supporter of c.

Next lemma states that candidates in St_i are the only nodes whose supporters can "stabilize" u with a single edge. This will be a fundamental insight to prove that our approach to node stabilization is optimal.

Lemma 3. *For $i \in \{0,1\}$, let $u \notin$ Aff be unstable in round $i + 1$. If we add an edge between u and a supporter of a candidate $c \notin$ St$_i$, then u will be still unstable in round $i + 1$.*

The set Bl$_0$ of blockers for a voter u unstable in round 1.

Definition 3. *Let u be a voter unstable in round 1. Candidate $c \in$ Bl$_0$ iff $c \neq c_0^*$ and one of the following properties holds: (i) Vote$_0[c] =$ Vote$_0[c_0^*]$ and $c \succ_u c_0^*$; (ii) Vote$_0[c] =$ Vote$_0[c_0^*] - 1$ and both $c > c_0^*$ and $c \succ_u c_0^*$.*

By Definition 3 it immediately follows that if we add edges between u and a supporter of c_0^* and a supporter of $c \in$ Bl$_0$, it makes u (c_0^*, c)-crucial in round 0. Thus, in round 1 u changes her vote to c. However, by definition of blockers, the addition of edges between u and a supporter of both c_0^* and $c \notin$ Bl$_0$ guarantee that u is stable in round 1.

We notice that to stabilize u in round 1 we can also add edges between u and two supporters of the same candidate $c \in$ Bl$_0$.

The set Bl$_1$ of blockers for a voter u stable in round 1.

Definition 4. *Let u be stable in round 1. Candidate c belongs to Bl$_1$ iff $c \neq c_0^*$ and one of the following properties holds:*

- Vote$_0[c] =$ Vote$_0[t] =$ Vote$_0[c_0^*]$, with $c_0^* \neq t$ and $c > t$, and there is a candidate c' with Vote$_0[c'] =$ Vote$_0[c_0^*]$, $c' > c$, and $c' \succ_u c$;
- Vote$_0[t] =$ Vote$_0[c_0^*] - 1$, with $t > c_0^*$ and c satisfies one of the following conditions:
  - Vote$_0[c] =$ Vote$_0[c_0^*]$, and there exists c' s.t. Vote$_0[c'] =$ Vote$_0[c_0^*]$, $c' > c$, and $c' \succ_u c$;
  - Vote$_0[c] =$ Vote$_0[c_0^*] - 1$, $c > t$, and there is c' s.t. Vote$_0[c'] =$ Vote$_0[c_0^*]$ and $c' \succ_u c$;
  - Vote$_0[c] =$ Vote$_0[c_0^*] - 1$, $c > t$, and there is c' s.t. Vote$_0[c'] =$ Vote$_0[c_0^*] - 1$, $c' > c$ and $c' \succ_u c$;
- St$_0$ contains only c_0^* and c satisfies one of the following conditions:
  - $c \neq c^*$ and Vote$_0[c] =$ Vote$_0[c_0^*]$;
  - Vote$_0[c] =$ Vote$_0[c_0^*] - 1$, $c > c_0^*$ and $c_0^* \succ_u c$;
  - $c \neq t$, Vote$_0[c] =$ Vote$_0[c_0^*] - 1$, $c_0^* > c$ and $c \succ_u c_0^*$;
  - $c \neq t$, Vote$_0[c] =$ Vote$_0[c_0^*] - 2$, $c > c_0^*$ and $c \succ_u c_0^*$.

As above, adding an edge between u and a supporter of $c \in$ Bl$_1$ can be harmful, while adding a link with a supporter of $c \notin$ Bl$_1$ is not. Moreover, adding edges between u and *two* supporters of $c \in$ Bl$_1$ is harmless.

Proof of Lemma 2. Observations above prove that our Node Stabilization procedure correctly stabilizes voter u. Moreover, with a more careful analysis, one can prove that our algorithm uses the minimum number of edges to stabilize u.

We now are ready to prove Lemma 2.

Proof. Let G'' be the graph returned by the Stabilization phase. In order to prove the Lemma we have only to show that in an election on G'' every voter $u \notin \mathsf{Aff}$ will be stable both in rounds 1 and 2. In fact, by Lemma 1 we know that all the affected voters vote for the sponsored candidate w in rounds $i \geq 2$. Hence, in round 3 all the voters confirm votes expressed in the previous round and the election process stops.

We start considering a node $u \in B$. In this case, as indicated above, the claim follows, as long as there are sufficiently many voters in Seed to add the required edges. However, the Stabilization phase requires to add at most two edges between u and voters in Seed supporting of the same candidate that are not neighbors of u. Since Seed includes three supporters for each candidate with no common neighbors, we can always find the supporters required to stabilize u.

Consider now a voter $u \in \mathsf{Seed}$. In this case, to stabilize u we have to add at most two edges between u and two voters in SSeed that are supporters of the same candidate c and are not adjacent to u. Since, by construction, SSeed contains two supporters of each candidate that are not adjacent to seeds, we certainly find the the supporters required to stabilize u.

Finally, consider a voter $u \in \mathsf{SSeed}$. Observe that in the Stabilization phase we add only edges between u and voters in Seed. Since Seed contains 3 supporters of each candidate, then u will have at most 3 new neighbors in G'' voting for each candidate c. Let c_0^* be the candidate that is supported by the majority of neighbors of u. We next show that if we add edges from u to 4 supporters of c_0^* voter u will be stable in round 1. Since u does not have neighbors in Aff, all her neighbors vote in round 1 for their favorite candidate, and thus u does not change her vote in successive rounds.

Consider, indeed, the graph $\tilde{G}$ obtained from G' by adding edges between u and three supporters of each candidate c. Note that the view of u in $\tilde{G}$ is exactly the same as in G'. In particular, c_0^* is still the candidate that is supported by the majority of neighbors of u and the best response for u in $\tilde{G}$ is the same as in G'. Anyway, as stated above we have that it is sufficient to add an edge (the fourth one) between u and a supporter of c_0^*, to stabilize u in round 1. Moreover, this property continues to hold if edges between u and supporters of $c \neq c_0^*$ (that is, if less than 3 seed nodes are connected to u during the seed stabilization phase) are removed or if further edges are added between u and supporters of c_0^* (that is, if more than zero seed nodes supporting c_0^* are connected to u during the stabilization phase). $\qquad\square$

5   Experiments

To validate our algorithm we run extensive experiments and on a real dataset to compare it against the heuristic proposed by [36]. Specifically, we consider the social network dataset "Facebook MHRW" [22], that contains a sample of the Facebook structure taken over about 900,000 nodes. For our tests, we sampled from this network 10 different graphs over 25000 nodes, by running a BFS from 10 different randomly selected nodes. For each of these graphs we assigned the preferences to its nodes according to three different approaches: (i) each voter is assigned a randomly selected preference list; (ii) each voter is assigned a randomly selected single-peaked preference list; (iii) we used a dataset of real preference lists available from PrefLib, that contains the results of surveys about sushi preferences, and assigned to each voter a random preference list among the ones in the dataset. In particular, for each graph we run 30 simulation with *random* preference lists, 10 with random *single-peaked* preference lists, and 10 with *real* preference lists.

For each combination of graph and preference list we consider a setting with 5 candidates, and we select the sponsored candidate w to be the candidate that is ranked as 2nd, 3rd, 4th, and 5th with respect to the number of supporters. Hence, in total we run our simulations on $4 \times 50 \times 10 = 2000$ different settings. For each setting we run both our algorithm, and the code provided by [36].

We observe that our algorithm correct computes a set of edges such that their addition to the original graph, assures that the sponsored candidate w wins the election. We remark that on the same settings, the heuristic of Sina et al. fails in about 30% of the runs, by returning a set of edges that is insufficient to make w the winner of the election.

Next picture shows that this guarantee comes at a limited cost in term of the number of added edges. Indeed, as showed in Fig. 2, the number of edges added by our algorithm is slightly larger but in the same order of magnitude as the one added by [36].

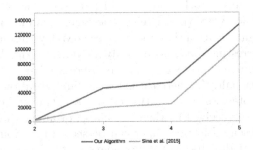

Fig. 2. The number of added edges with respect to the four different choice for the desired candidate w

6   Conclusions

In this paper we presented an algorithm to compute a set of edges to add to a social network in order to manipulate the outcome of an election and have a sponsored candidate to win. We proved that our algorithm adds the minimum number of edges and it works on mild conditions on the structure of the social network and on the preference lists of the voters.

We also run extensive experiments to validate performances of our algorithm. They show that our algorithm adds a number of edges that is similar to their heuristic but it has a 100% success rate. We will also plan to run even more extensive experiments in even more realistic settings.

Our results can be seen as another indication that the control of social media is a great threat to our democracy since the controller has an extraordinary power in determining which information we are exposed to and can use this power to control and influence crucial decisions. This threat was already highlighted by several works in the case that voters are myopic and they are simply influenced by their neighbors (and possibly by their own belief).

In this paper we enforce the message of [36], by showing that manipulation can be often effective even if voters are instead strategic and they can decide to vote for a candidate different from their favourite. Clearly, we acknowledge that neither of these two extremal behaviors fully represents the real world: usually, people's decisions depend on both the influence of their social relationships and by strategic considerations based on their limited view. Hence, it would be interesting to evaluate the extent at which these manipulability results extend to this more realistic environment.

Moreover, most of the works on the election manipulability problem (including this one) make a lot of simplifying assumptions: e.g., voters' knowledge is limited to their own neighborhood; they perfectly know their neighbors' votes; they have a total order of candidates. In a real world setting, some of these assumptions could not hold: e.g., polls can provide an aggregate information about the rest of the network; voters could have only incomplete information about their neighbors' votes (i.e., received messages could be blurry or could be lost in the mess of information that one receives nowadays through social media). It would be an interesting direction to verify at which extent the manipulability results hold when some of these assumptions are relaxed and voters are assumed to have limited rationality[2], where the extent of limited rationality may depend on how much the voters know about the rest of the networks, how confident they are about the signals received by their neighbors, or about their own choices.

The results presented in this paper can be seen a contribution towards the fundamental step of drawing of the boundary of the manipulability of social networks. These results allow not only to establish when an intervention is necessary, but they also suggest some form of intervention, such as constraining the network to be one robust against manipulation. Nevertheless, we highlight that other forms of intervention can be operated, even when it is not possible to work on the network topology: e.g., quarantining particular nodes [4], or including in the network special nodes working as *monitors* [3,39] are among the most effective proposal of intervention that have been recently suggested in literature.

---

[2] Many models are known in literature for dealing with this kind of players: the *mutation* model [26], the *mistake* model [27,38], the *logit* update rule [17] and its corresponding equilibria concepts, quantal response equilibrium [30], and logit equilibrium [12,13].

References

1. Acar, E., Greco, G., Manna, M.: Group reasoning in social environments. In: Proceedings of AAMAS 2017, pp. 1296–1304 (2017)
2. Alon, N., Babaioff, M., Karidi, R., Lavi, R., Tennenholtz, M.: Sequential voting with externalities: herding in social networks. In: Proceedings of EC 2012, p. 36 (2012)
3. Amoruso, M., Anello, D., Auletta, V., Ferraioli, D.: Contrasting the spread of misinformation in online social networks. In: Proceedings of AAMAS 2017, pp. 1323–1331 (2017)
4. Aspnes, J., Chang, K., Yampolskiy, A.: Inoculation strategies for victims of viruses and the sum-of-squares partition problem. J. Comput. Syst. Sci. **72**(6), 1077–1093 (2006)
5. Auletta, V., Caragiannis, I., Ferraioli, D., Galdi, C., Persiano, G.: Minority becomes majority in social networks. In: Markakis, E., Schäfer, G. (eds.) WINE 2015. LNCS, vol. 9470, pp. 74–88. Springer, Heidelberg (2015). https://doi.org/10.1007/978-3-662-48995-6_6
6. Auletta, V., Caragiannis, I., Ferraioli, D., Galdi, C., Persiano, G.: Generalized discrete preference games. In: Proceedings of IJCAI 2016, pp. 53–59 (2016)
7. Auletta, V., Caragiannis, I., Ferraioli, D., Galdi, C., Persiano, G.: Information retention in heterogeneous majority dynamics. In: Devanur, N.R., Lu, P. (eds.) WINE 2017. LNCS, vol. 10660, pp. 30–43. Springer, Cham (2017). https://doi.org/10.1007/978-3-319-71924-5_3
8. Auletta, V., Caragiannis, I., Ferraioli, D., Galdi, C., Persiano, G.: Robustness in discrete preference games. In: Proceedings of AAMAS 2017, pp. 1314–1322 (2017)
9. Auletta, V., Fanelli, A., Ferraioli, D.: Consensus in opinion formation processes in fully evolving environments. In: Proceedings of AAAI 2019 (2019)
10. Auletta, V., Ferraioli, D., Fionda, V., Greco, G.: Maximizing the spread of an opinion when tertium datur est. In: Proceedings of AAMAS 2019 (2019)
11. Auletta, V., Ferraioli, D., Greco, G.: Reasoning about consensus when opinions diffuse through majority dynamics. In: Proceedings of IJCAI 2018, pp. 49–55 (2018)
12. Auletta, V., Ferraioli, D., Pasquale, F., Penna, P., Persiano, G.: Logit dynamics with concurrent updates for local interaction games. In: Bodlaender, H.L., Italiano, G.F. (eds.) ESA 2013. LNCS, vol. 8125, pp. 73–84. Springer, Heidelberg (2013). https://doi.org/10.1007/978-3-642-40450-4_7
13. Auletta, V., Ferraioli, D., Pasquale, F., Penna, P., Persiano, G.: Convergence to equilibrium of logit dynamics for strategic games. Algorithmica **76**(1), 110–142 (2016)
14. Bhawalkar, K., Gollapudi, S., Munagala, K.: Coevolutionary opinion formation games. In: Proceedings of STOC 2013, pp. 41–50 (2013)
15. Bilò, V., Fanelli, A., Moscardelli, L.: Opinion formation games with dynamic social influences. In: Cai, Y., Vetta, A. (eds.) WINE 2016. LNCS, vol. 10123, pp. 444–458. Springer, Heidelberg (2016). https://doi.org/10.1007/978-3-662-54110-4_31
16. Bindel, D., Kleinberg, J.M., Oren, S.: How bad is forming your own opinion? In: Proceedings of FOCS 2011, pp. 57–66 (2011)
17. Blume, L.E.: The statistical mechanics of strategic interaction. Games Econ. Behav. **5**(3), 387–424 (1993)
18. Bredereck, R., Elkind, E.: Manipulating opinion diffusion in social networks. In: Proceedings of IJCAI 2017, pp. 894–900 (2017)

19. Chierichetti, F., Kleinberg, J.M., Oren, S.: On discrete preferences and coordination. In: Proceedings of EC 2013, pp. 233–250 (2013)
20. Ferraioli, D., Goldberg, P.W., Ventre, C.: Decentralized dynamics for finite opinion games. Theoret. Comput. Sci. **648**, 96–115 (2016)
21. Ferraioli, D., Ventre, C.: Social pressure in opinion games. In: Proceedings of IJCAI 2017, pp. 3661–3667 (2017)
22. Gjoka, M., Kurant, M., Butts, C.T., Markopoulou, A.: Walking in Facebook: a case study of unbiased sampling of OSNs. In: Proceedings of INFOCOM 2010, pp. 1–9 (2010)
23. Grandi, U., Loreggia, A., Rossi, F., Venable, K.B., Walsh, T.: Restricted manipulation in iterative voting: condorcet efficiency and borda score. In: Perny, P., Pirlot, M., Tsoukiàs, A. (eds.) ADT 2013. LNCS (LNAI), vol. 8176, pp. 181–192. Springer, Heidelberg (2013). https://doi.org/10.1007/978-3-642-41575-3_14
24. Grandi, U., Turrini, P.: A network-based rating system and its resistance to bribery. In: Proceedings of IJCAI 2016, pp. 301–307 (2016)
25. Hassanzadeh, F.F., Yaakobi, E., Touri, B., Milenkovic, O., Bruck, J.: Building consensus via iterative voting. In: Proceedings of ISIT 2013, pp. 1082–1086 (2013)
26. Kandori, M., Mailath, G.J., Rob, R.: Learning, mutation, and long run equilibria in games. Econ. J. Econ. Soc. **61**(1), 29–56 (1993)
27. Kandori, M., Rob, R.: Evolution of equilibria in the long run: a general theory and applications. J. Econ. Theory **65**(2), 383–414 (1995)
28. Lev, O., Rosenschein, J.S.: Convergence of iterative voting. In: Proceedings of AAMAS 2012, pp. 611–618 (2012)
29. Maran, A., Maudet, N., Pini, M.S., Rossi, F., Venable, K.B.: A framework for aggregating influenced cp-nets and its resistance to bribery. In: Proceedings of AAAI 2013 (2013)
30. McKelvey, R.D., Palfrey, T.R.: Quantal response equilibria for normal form games. Games Econ. Behav. **10**(1), 6–38 (1995)
31. Meir, R.: Iterative voting. In: Trends in Computational Social Choice, pp. 69–86 (2017)
32. Meir, R., Lev, O., Rosenschein, J.S.: A local-dominance theory of voting equilibria. In: Proceedings of EC 2014, pp. 313–330 (2014)
33. Meir, R., Polukarov, M., Rosenschein, J.S., Jennings, N.R.: Convergence to equilibria in plurality voting. In: Proceedings of AAAI 2010, pp. 823–828 (2010)
34. Meir, R., Polukarov, M., Rosenschein, J.S., Jennings, N.R.: Iterative voting and acyclic games. Artif. Intell. **252**, 100–122 (2017)
35. Simon, S., Apt, K.R.: Social network games. J. Log. Comput. **25**(1), 207–242 (2015)
36. Sina, S., Hazon, N., Hassidim, A., Kraus, S.: Adapting the social network to affect elections. In: Proceedings of AAMAS 2015, pp. 705–713 (2015)
37. Wilder, B., Vorobeychik, Y.: Controlling elections through social influence. In: Proceedings of AAMAS 2018, pp. 265–273 (2018)
38. Young, H.P.: The evolution of conventions. Econ. J. Econ. Soc. **61**(1), 57–84 (1993)
39. Zhang, H., Alim, M.A., Thai, M.T., Nguyen, H.T.: Monitor placement to timely detect misinformation in online social networks. In: Proceedings of ICC 2015, pp. 1152–1157 (2015)

Shared-Autonomy Navigation for Mobile Robots Driven by a Door Detection Module

Gloria Beraldo$^{(\boxtimes)}$, Enrico Termine, and Emanuele Menegatti

Intelligent Autonomous System Lab, Department of Information Engineering,
University of Padova, Padua, Italy
{gloria.beraldo,emg}@dei.unipd.it

Abstract. Shared-autonomy approaches are the most appealing for what concerns the control of assistive devices such as wheelchairs and mobile robots, designed to aid disabled and elderly people. In this paper, we propose a shared-autonomy navigation for mobile robots, that combines the user's interaction as well as the robots' perception and the environment knowledge, with the information of important landmarks, namely the doors. In order to facilitate the control of the robot, our system exploits a door detection module, aiming to detect doors and especially to identify their open/close status, making the robot pass through narrow doorways without any user's intervention. We tested the proposed system on a real mobile robot to verify the feasibility.

Keywords: Mobile robots navigation · Robot perception · Human-centered systems

1 Introduction

Assistive robots and wheelchairs represent a change especially for people affected by some diseases or disabilities, giving them the possibility to keep a self-controlled mobility and to maintain relationship with the others [1,3,10,15,29]. In this regards, the shared-autonomy systems appear very appealing solutions referring to the development of "intelligent" robotic devices able to contextualize commands from the human into the representation of the environment coming from their sensory robotic data. Therefore, the agents maintain some degree of autonomy, but, at the same time, they deal with the user's decisions. In the literature, several Shared-Autonomy approaches have been proposed [7,12,21,23]. All are characterized by two key principles: (i) the human's commands define the high-level behavior of the robot; (ii) the robot decides autonomously its low-level behavior accordingly to the surrounding environment information. In this work, we propose a shared-autonomy approach integrating the information of crucial environment landmarks, which are doors [39]. The resulting system enables the robot not only to avoid obstacles and to move according to the user's commands, but also to pass through narrow doorways without any user's intervention, with the aim of reducing the workload required.

© Springer Nature Switzerland AG 2019
M. Alviano et al. (Eds.): AI*IA 2019, LNAI 11946, pp. 511–527, 2019.
https://doi.org/10.1007/978-3-030-35166-3_36

2   Related Works

In the literature, many studies about autonomous and semi-autonomous robots, proposed to identify point of interest such as doors by relying on a priori knowledge of the environment (e.g. topological map) [19,31] and/or fiducial markers [2,37]. These information are then used both for path planning [25,28,33] and to estimate the human's intent [8,35]. In this work, we propose a system that detects the door without specialized sensor setups and that integrates this information in the shared-autonomy navigation of the robot.

As regards the door detection, several studies have proposed methods by using different sensors, features and training methods [5,6,9,11,14,30,41]. One of the most simple approach is based on ultrasonic or laser sensors, that detects the doorway just looking for a hole in the sensor stream and finding the points of interest according to its wide [13,16,33]. The limitation of this approach is that not all gaps necessarily meet this criterion, by generating disagreements between possible targets in the nearby vicinity [22]. To overcome this drawback, some approaches for door detection depend on 3D information including both visual and distance data. For instance, Anguelov et al. [5] combined two 2D laser scanners and a panoramic camera data in input to a probabilistic model, that segments the environment into door and wall objects and learns their properties. Similarly, in [32], sonars are used to confirm the door detection from cameras. In [4,9,30], Hough Transform is used to extract edge lines from images. However, any square-shaped like objects might be treated as a door due to similar edge numbers. Alternatively, in [22], Derry et al. proposed to detect walls as vertical planes in the 3D point cloud by finding gaps in the wall planes. Yuan et al. [36] extend this approach in which wall planes are extracted from the point clouds acquired by a depth camera and the door's opening angle is calculated by analysing the shape of the gap inside the door. In this case, the detection of the location and the orientation of doorways is rapid and robust. These studies support our work in designing the door detection module, however in these cases the authors focused on developing techniques for detecting doors without integrating these information in the shared-autonomy navigation of the robot.

From these point of view, in literature some studies investigated how the robot perception can enhance the shared-autonomy behaviours, especially in the context of assistive wheelchairs, in which assistance is provided to the user who might not possess the fine motor control necessary to handle challenging activities such as doorway traversal [8,22,27,28,35]. An example is NavChair [28,34] that includes the door passage mode: the wheelchair's speed is reduced and the data from a sonar sensors are used to attempt to center the wheelchair within the door as the user drives it through. This approach is very effective when the door is directly ahead. Otherwise, the wheelchair might be driven away from the door in an attempt to center on the door, because the doorway is not actually actively detected. Zeng et al. developed a Collaborative Wheelchair Assistant [27]. In this system a helper can program a path by demonstration and then the user can drive this path controlling the speed. However, there are no sensors to detect collisions and in narrow spaces such as doorways, it relies on the driving skill of the user. In [35] Carlson et al. assign to each target doorway a confidence score based on Euclidean distance to the goal and when it crosses a threshold, the wheelchair is automatically guided through the door. Interesting the idea of designing a local model representing the action moving towards a doorway, nevertheless also in this work the doors are identified with fiducial markers. In [24] the authors demonstrate how the human can be integrated into a semi-autonomous control using Potential Field to generate velocity commands.

Herein, our system considers the attractive/repulsive effects of many components such as the obstacles, the user's input and the doors, by using an approach similar to the Potential Field. However, in contrast to them [20,24,28,40], we merge these information, to determine a position corresponding to the next subgoal the robot has to reach, without affecting its speed. Then, the robot tries to reach the current subgoal avoiding obstacles and updating it continuously according to the user's commands.

3   Methods

In this Section we present our shared-autonomy approach that combines different contributions related to the human input, the obstacle avoidance and the attraction to doors. We describe also our experimental setup and the robot platform we used to test our system.

3.1   Shared-Autonomy Approach for Door Traversal

In our system, the low-level behavior of the robot consists in combining: the information about the laser data, the environment representation, the door detections, as well as the high-level commands from the user, to define a subgoal that has to be reached. Then, once the subgoal is computed, the robot decides the best trajectory to move and it tries to reach it avoiding obstacles. The current subgoal is continuously updated and adjusted according to the human's input, resulting in a smooth navigation. To drive the robot, the human operator can deliver direction commands. Every time the human operator sends a direction command, the system stores three different information (see Fig. 1A):

- **Direction**: the direction angle $\alpha \in [-180°, 180°]$ specified by the human.
- **Robot position**: the (x, y) coordinates of the robot position with respect to the *global* reference system.
- **Robot orientation**: the current rotation angle β of the robot with respect to the *global* reference system.

The previous information are overwritten once the user delivers a new command.

We have modeled the subgoal-setting problem designing an heuristic function h to determine the best direction along which the robot has to move. We consider the attractive/repulsive effect of the following components:

- **Obstacle influence F_o:** the obstacles in the environment generate repulsive forces enabling the robot to avoid the collision with them. In other words, those directions making the robot move too close to obstacles are penalised.
- **User input F_u:** the target direction, chosen by the user, generates an attractive force. In our system, the directions consistent with the user high-level commands are preferred.
- **Direction correction F_c:** it provides an autonomous correction when the current direction, along which the robot is moving, does not correspond to the user command. For instance, it can happen because of the presence of obstacles. Therefore, in order to avoid the robot moving too far, it keeps track of the user commands and, as soon as possible, it adjusts its low-level behavior according to the high-level one chosen by the user.
- **Door attractor F_d:** the doors in the environment become attractors for the robot when the user exhibits his/her intention to pass through them.

By summing the contribution of each component (F_o, F_u, F_c, F_d) multiplied by a certain weight $(\omega_o, \omega_u, \omega_c, \omega_d)$, we obtain the heuristic function h:

$$h = \frac{\omega_o \cdot F_o + \omega_u \cdot F_u + \omega_c \cdot F_c + \omega_d \cdot \sum_{door} F_d}{\omega_o + \omega_u + \omega_c + \omega_d} \tag{1}$$

The corresponding subgoal, the robot has to reach, is found by maximizing the heuristic function h. In addition, the robot exploits a global map of the environment to check the validity of the subgoal (a free cell) and eventually to arrange its coordinates within the neighborhood.

In designing the system, we decided to take advantage of the well known ROS navigation stack[1] for what concerns the robot motion and collision avoidance. We used the 2D SLAM algorithm provided by *Google Cartographer* [38] for the mapping and localization purposes. Furthermore, in our system, the obstacle detection is based on the laser data, according to which each laser ray is associated to a specific direction θ (see Fig. 1B).

In the following paragraphs we describe in details the components of the heuristic function h and the computation of the subgoal.

Obstacle Influence: It deals with the repulsive effect of the obstacles in the environment, thanks to which the robot can move towards safe positions. The influence of the obstacles is measured according to their distance from the robot position. Similarly to [18], we classify the direction along the robot can move into *risky* or *safe* based on the presence of imminent obstacles. For each laser ray, we consider the closest object to the robot in that direction. If the obstacle influence F_o for that object is below a threshold r_{lack}, it means that the corresponding ray laser direction is *risky* for the robot and therefore it is penalised. Otherwise, that direction is *safe* since the robot has enough space to move without colliding with obstacles. In correspondence to the threshold r_{lack}, F_o has a neutral strength.

---

[1] https://github.com/ros-planning/navigation.

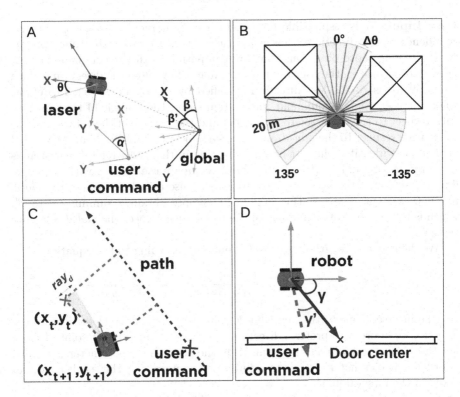

Fig. 1. (A) Schematic representation of the direction command (α) sent by the user with respect to the *global* reference system (blue) and the considered laser direction θ (yellow); (B) Illustrative representation of the obstacle influence computed for each laser ray direction (θ): more green a ray is, more attractive the associated direction is, while red rays correspond to repulsive forces; (C) Descriptive illustration about the direction correction function (F_c): in blue it is represented the ideal linear path computed when the user sends a command (at the blue cross position in the direction according to the dashed line), while ray_d corresponds to the difference between the distance from the current (x_t, y_t) and the predict future (x_{t+1}, y_{t+1}) robot's positions to the ideal path; (D) Illustrative representation of the doors attractor function (F_d): a door is considered only when the angle γ' indicating the direction chosen by the user is less than $60°$. The angle γ relating to the robot reference system (green) is considered in the computation of the function F_d. (Color figure online)

We compute the strength of the obstacle influence $\boldsymbol{F_o}$ as follows:

$$F_o(r_i) = \frac{log(r_i + 1 - r_{lack})}{\max\limits_{r} log(r + 1 - r_{lack})} \tag{2}$$

where r_i is the distance between the robot position and the closest object in the considered laser ray direction (see Fig. 1B). We normalize the computed values with respect to the maximum, in order to obtain values in the interval $[-1, 1]$.

User Input: It is responsible for generating an attractive behavior in correspondence of the directions chosen by the user. In this way, the robot prefers to move along those directions that are compatible with the commands of the user. In other words, the user input F_u evaluates how close the direction of each laser ray (θ) is to the last direction specified by the operator (α). In details, when the user sends a command, the system stores the α angle of the direction with respect to the robot reference system and the β angle of the rotation of the robot with respect to the *global* reference system (see Fig. 1A). Thus, the global angle ϕ that identifies the last human direction in the *global* reference system is given by the sum of α and β. To be able to compare the angle ϕ with the angle θ of a direction of the laser, we have to express also θ with respect to the *global* reference system. The resulting angle θ' is simply obtained summing θ to β', which is the current rotation angle of the robot with respect the *global* reference system.

We define the strength of the user input F_u according to the equation:

$$F_u(\theta) = \epsilon \cdot \frac{1}{\mid (\theta + \beta') - (\alpha + \beta) \mid + \epsilon} = \epsilon \cdot \frac{1}{\mid \theta' - \phi \mid + \epsilon} \tag{3}$$

The inverse is due to the fact that F_u has to be higher the closer θ' is to the direction ϕ, in order to prefer a direction that is, from an angular point of view, not too far from the direction specified by the user. The ϵ parameter is needed in order to avoid that F_u tends to infinity and to normalize the resulting values between the interval $[0, 1]$.

Direction Correction: It creates an additional attractive behavior, to perform an autonomous correction, especially on those directions characterised by similar obstacle influence F_o and user input F_u values. In particular, it is fundamental in the case in which the robot is moving along a different direction from the one chosen by the user, e.g. for the presence of obstacles. Thank to the contribution of the direction correction F_c, the robot is influenced by the attractive effect generated in those directions consistent with the user choice, and therefore it is able to adjust its next movements. In details, when a new command is sent, it computes an ideal linear path (in blue in Fig. 1C), starting from the robot position, at the instant in which the command is received, according to the direction specified by the user (α). For each laser ray direction, we calculate the next position (x_{t+1}, y_{t+1})—with respect to the *global* reference system—along which the robot will move if it is chosen to set the subgoal. To compute the two coordinates of the next position (x_{t+1}, y_{t+1}), we use the angle θ' and the corresponding distance r defined above, in the following way:

$$\begin{cases} x_{t+1} & = x_t + p \cdot \cos \theta' \\ y_{t+1} & = y_t + p \cdot \sin \theta' \end{cases}$$

where x_t and y_t are the current robot coordinates and p is a value in the interval $(0, 1)$. Then, using the basic geometry properties, we computed the difference between the distance from the current robot (x_t, y_t) and the future position (x_{t+1}, y_{t+1}) to the ideal path for each of the possible directions. We have called this difference as *rayleight distance* and we refer to it as ray_d (see Fig. 1C). The strength of the direction correction $\boldsymbol{F_c}$ increases with increasing of ray_d, but it saturates above a certain threshold. Since we want that $\boldsymbol{F_c}$ grows rapidly with ray_d and, at the same time high values of the ray_d must not influence too much the heuristic function h, we design $\boldsymbol{F_c}$ based on a modified version of Rayleigh distribution [26]. In particular, $\boldsymbol{F_c}$ is defined as:

$$F_c(\theta, r) = sign(ray_d) \cdot (1 - e^{-ray_d^2/(2\sigma^2)}) \tag{4}$$

It returns a value in the range $[-1, 1]$. The *sign* multiplication is introduced to assign a strength also to the negative values, for which the Rayleigh distribution is not defined.

Door Attractor: it represents the attractive effect that the doors can have on the robot low-level behavior. In particular, it depends on how the direction chosen by the user fits with the position of the door. In fact, we hypothesize that if the user command corresponds to the direction from the robot position to the centre of the door, there is an high probability the user wants the robot to pass through the door. Every time that a valid door is detected, it is labelled as *influential / not influential*. In details, we consider the angular distance γ' between the user's direction and the angle described by the line connecting the robot position to the door center with respect the *global* reference system (Fig. 1D). If γ' is less than a threshold, it is marked as *influential* and it generates an attractive behavior. Otherwise it is considered as *not influential*. For each *influential* door, we compute the strength of the door attractor $\boldsymbol{F_d}$, defined as the probability density function of a Gaussian distribution with zero mean and 0.05 variance:

$$F_d(\theta, door) = \frac{1}{\sqrt{2\pi \cdot 0.05}} e^{-\frac{(\gamma - \theta)^2}{2 \cdot 0.05}} \tag{5}$$

where the angle γ is achieved by connecting the robot position to the door center with respect to the robot reference system. As reported in the Eq. 1, we sum the $\boldsymbol{F_d}$ contribution of each *influential* door.

3.2 Door Detection and Aperture Estimation Strategy

Our system includes a door detection module, based on the data from a 3D camera sensor, with the aim of detecting the doors and inferring the knowledge about their status (open/close) (see Fig. 2). In other words, it finds the doorway, tracks it during the approach and estimates the detected door's aperture. Although it does not represent the focus of this work.

The doors detections are based on the start-of-the-art *YOLOv3* library[2] [17]. Because of real-time constraints and reduced hardware resources, we decided to

---

[2] https://pjreddie.com/yolo/.

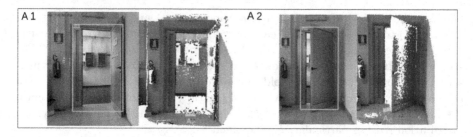

Fig. 2. The RGB frame in which doors are detected and the corresponding point cloud. The computed center of the door's aperture A_C is indicated in green. In this case the aperture of the doors in A1 and A2 are equal to 90° (i.e. completely open) and 45° (i.e. half open). (Color figure online)

use a reduced configuration of *YOLOv3*, structured in 13 convolutional layers. We trained it on a NVIDIA GeForce GT 740M GPU, by giving in input a set of 11'140 door images extracted from the Open Images Dataset v4[3]. The images present different light conditions and resolutions. Furthermore, doors in the images have been taken from different perspectives and include the environmental context (e.g buildings, windows, cars, people and so on). To reduce the number of false positives (e.g. other objects with a rectangular shape) we have implemented a rejection filter for the detected doors, based on the depth image. We filter the detected objects by imposing a constraint only on its estimated height. We average the depth values for those pixels that fall inside the bounding box, obtaining the mean depth value d_{mean}. We have assumed that objects enclosed by the bounding box entirely belong to the plane at distance d_{mean}. Thus, we estimate the object height H_e, using the bounding box width and height with the following formula:

$$H_e = \frac{d_{mean} \times H_p \times H_s}{f \times H_{img}} \tag{6}$$

where H_p is the height of the bounding box in pixels, H_s is the sensor dimension (e.g. we consider the height), f is the camera focal length and H_{img} is the image height in pixels.

Once that a new door is identified, it is stored in a list of doors ($\mathcal{D}$) and it is considered until the ratio between the number of the frames in which it appears and the total one, computed starting from the first detection, become less than a threshold T_D.

The door aperture estimation approach analyzes the point cloud generated by the 3D sensor and uses the detections given by the door detector. We enlarge the size of the bounding box to include also a part of the wall in which the door is placed. Then, we compute the angle δ (see Fig. 3) formed by the line connecting the top-left corner (B_{LC}) of the enlarged bounding box to its center (B_C), approximating it to 30°, 45° or 60°.

---

[3] https://storage.googleapis.com/openimages/web/index.html.

Fig. 3. Graphical representation of the doorway aperture estimation method.

We assume that the point B_{LC} belongs to the wall containing the door, and we use it as reference to set a threshold T_w to define the plane of the door. We store the value of the depth $D_{B_{LC}}$ corresponding to this point. In this way, every other point at a distance in the range $(D_{B_{LC}} - T_w, D_{B_{LC}} + T_w)$ is considered as belonging to the plane of the door. Then, we compute the real coordinates (with respect the 3D sensor) of the points D_J and D_S, identifying respectively the jamb and the shutter of the door (see again Fig. 3). In details, D_J corresponds to the last point with depth belonging to the range $(D_{B_{LC}} - T_w, D_{B_{LC}} + T_w)$, found by searching in the direction of the computed angle δ, starting from the point B_{LC}. While D_S represents the first point with the depth in the same range, obtained by proceeding horizontally from the point D_J. Therefore we estimate the door aperture (A) and the world coordinates of its center (A_C) (see Fig. 2), using the coordinates of the points D_J and D_S:

$$A = \sqrt{(x_{D_S} - x_{D_J})^2 + (z_{D_S} - z_{D_J})^2}$$

$$A_C = \left(\frac{x_{D_J} + x_{D_S}}{2} \quad ; \quad y = 0 \quad ; \quad \frac{z_{D_J} + z_{D_S}}{2}\right)$$

We consider a door closed when it is identified by the detection framework, but the aperture estimation method can not retrieve the D_J point (and then also D_S), since all the points belong to the same plane (i.e. the plane of the door). This means that there is not an open space within the door bounding box.

The doors with a too small estimated aperture are not taken into account in the shared-autonomy algorithm to be sure that the robot can pass through them.

3.3 Computation of the Subgoal

The subgoal given to the robot corresponds to a pose in the environment, that it has to reach:

$$s_g = (x, y, z, qx, qy, qz, qw) \qquad (7)$$

In our algorithm, it is computed from the heuristic function h. In details, among all the considered directions θ (see Fig. 1B), we find the pair (θ_{sg}, r_{sg}) maximizing h, where r_{sg} is the distance between the robot position and the nearest object in the corresponding orientation θ_{sg}. The pose of the subgoal is determined as $s_g = (r_{sg} \cdot cos(\theta_{sg}), r_{sg} \cdot sin(\theta_{sg}), 0, qx_{sg}, qy_{sg}, qz_{sg}, qw_{sg})$, where $(qx_{sg}, qy_{sg}, qz_{sg}, qw_{sg})$ is the quaternion computed from θ_{sg}.

4 Experimental Design

To verify the feasibility of our shared-autonomy algorithm on a mobile robot, we conducted a pilot experiment. It consists in making the robot complete an entire path, passing through a door opened with a 60° angle. We have set respectively a starting and an arrival positions, defining 3 target positions T_1, T_2, T_3 to be reached along the path (see Fig. 4A). The user was sat in a corner of the room, from which he/she could not see directly the robot. He/she received the robot position in the environment map as feedback, which has been updated in real time thanks to Cartographer. The user delivered commands to the robot through a controller connected to a separate computer, that communicated with the robot through a local network. The experiment was performed by four different people (age 24.75 ± 0.96): s_1, s_2, s_3, s_4. Each subject has repeated the experiment three times. Three of these people (s_1, s_2, s_4) did not know the system architecture and its low-level functionalities. For these tests we used the configuration of parameters in Table 1.

Furthermore, we evaluated the importance of shared-autonomy navigation by comparing our approach with a pure manual control. In this case, we asked the user to repeat the experiment controlling the robot with discrete commands sent by the controller but without the assistance of the shared-autonomy navigation and the door detection module.

4.1 Robot Platform

Our telepresence platform consists of a Pioneer P3-AT mobile robot equipped with a Microsoft Kinect RGB-D camera. The 3D camera was mounted at a height of 1.05 m from the floor and it provides RGB-D data with 1920×1080 pixels resolution at 30 frames per second. In our navigation experiments, we acquired color images and depth data at a reduced resolution, namely 960×540 pixels in order to estimate the door aperture faster (Please refer to Sect. 3.2 for further details). For obstacle avoidance, the robot has a 2D LiDAR LMS1000 SICK sensor with an aperture angle of 270° ($\theta \in [-135°, 135°]$) with a constant angle increment of 0.5° and a scanning range of 20 m ($r \in [0, 20]$ m). We integrated our system on an HP laptop equipped with an Intel Core i7 4700MQ 2.4 GHz CPU with an 8 GB RAM and an NVIDIA GeForce GT 740M GPU.

Table 1. The configuration of the shared-autonomy algorithm parameters

h function weights	ω_o	0.5
	ω_u	0.8
	ω_c	0.1
	ω_d	1
Obstacle influence	r_{lack}	0.9
User input	ϵ	0.01
Direction correction	p	0.6
	σ	0.5
Door detection and aperture estimation strategy	T_D	15%
	T_w	60 cm

5   Preliminary Results

All the subjects that performed the experiment[4], independently from the system knowledge, succeeded in all the three trials, making the robot reach all the 3 target positions and the arrival position. We have considered the time taken and the number of commands sent by the user to drive the robot to each target position. The results are shown in Fig. 4C. To verify the contribution of the door attractor on the shared-autonomy navigation system, we carried out an additional qualitative test(See footnote 4). We tested our shared-autonomy navigation algorithm with and without the doors information in the same conditions. By sending the same high-level user command, corresponding to the right direction from the relative position of the robot, the resulting low-level behavior performed by the robot was different. As shown in Fig. 5, when the door detector module was active, the subgoal was positioned along the door direction. In the other case, without considering the door influence (the door attractor contribution F_d equal to zero), it made the system generate a subgoal along the given direction, making the robot turn right but without passing through the door. The importance of the shared-autonomy and the door detection is confirmed in terms of ratio between the number of commands in the two modalities shared-autonomy with door detection module and pure manual control without shared-autonomy and door detection module. In our case we achieved a ration equal to 10.32%. It is possible to notice that the number of commands increased in the pure manual modality. This suggests that without shared-autonomy and door detection module, the user has to send more commands to the robot, increasing the necessary cognitive workload.

To evaluate qualitatively the door aperture estimation, we have tested it on two kinds of doors: a painted wooden door and a metal door. The first is a narrower with a width of only 63 cm; while the second has a width of 85 cm. For each door, we have examining five main angles of aperture, which are 0°

---

[4] An illustrative video is available at https://youtu.be/LuJNzdG143s.

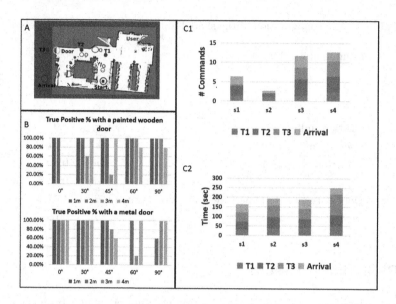

Fig. 4. (A) The experimental environment with the three target positions and the red circles indicating additional mobile obstacles not representing in the global static map; (B) The true positive % related to the detection of the painted wooden and metal doors; (C) Average number of commands and average time in seconds needed to reach each target position for each subject.

(i.e. closed door), 30°, 45°, 60° and 90° (i.e. completely opened door), at four different distances (1, 2, 3 and 4 m). Furthermore, for each pair angle-distance the test has been run 5 times, taking into account the estimated apertures, if the door was detected. The results we achieved are shown in the Fig. 4B in terms of true positive percentages and in the Tables 2 and 3 in terms of the average error made in the door aperture estimation for each pair angle-distance considered. There were few cases that were not able to be well handled by our door detector. The reasons are essentially deficiencies due to the sensor (noise in the Kinect), situation of occlusions and incorrect identification of the wall plane.

Table 2. Painted wooden door aperture estimation error

Distance	Angle				
	0°	30°	45°	60°	90°
1 m	0.0 ± 0.0 cm	1.6 ± 4.8 cm	4 ± 1.3 cm	7.2 ± 5.0 cm	2.5 ± 0.7 cm
2 m	0.0 ± 0.0 cm	13.4 ± 0.9 cm	9.2 ± 1.1 cm	6.1 ± 3.5 cm	2.4 ± 0.4 cm
3 m		3.5 ± 2.2	8.9 ± 0.0 cm	8.8 ± 12 cm	4.3 ± 0.7 cm
4 m		8.7 ± 2.2 cm	7.6 ± 3.3 cm	9.9 ± 1.3 cm	2.9 ± 0.9 cm

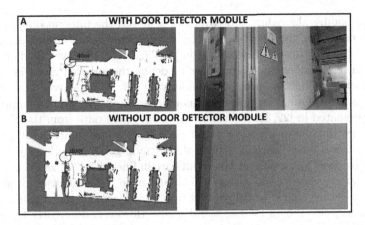

Fig. 5. Comparison of the behaviors performed by the robot when the door detector module was active (A) or disabled (B), by sending the same high-level user command (in the right direction from the relative position of the robot). In A the robot moves correctly through the door, while in B the robot turns in the right direction, but without performing the door passage (it is in front of the wall to the right of the relative position of the robot).

Table 3. Metal door aperture estimation error

Distance	Angle				
	0°	30°	45°	60°	90°
1 m	0.0 ± 0.0 cm	26.8 ± 17.9 cm	1.7 ± 2.7 cm		
2 m	0.0 ± 0.0 cm	10.2 ± 18.3 cm	4 ± 0.5 cm	16.1 ± 5 cm	19.6 ± 0.3 cm
3 m	0.0 ± 0.0 cm	4.3 ± 2.1 cm	3.4 ± 6.4 cm	7.8 ± 0.0 cm	2.8 ± 0.3 cm
4 m	0.0 ± 0.0 cm	11.4 ± 1.7 cm	7.4 ± 8.6 cm	24.9 ± 4.8 cm	7.8 ± 0.3 cm

6   Discussion

The focus of our proposed shared-autonomy navigation system is to transform high-level commands delivered by the user, in terms of preference directions, into effective subgoals that the robot has to reach. In our system we considered the human-robot interaction as well as the fusion between the robot's perception and the environment knowledge. Therefore, this fusion results in the obstacle avoidance and generally in the navigation of the robot, achieved thanks to the combination of the laser data information and representation of the environment. Moreover, in comparison to our previous work [10], we included also an addition level according to which the perception of the robot enables the detection of typical landmarks in the environment, increasing, at the same time, its knowledge about the environment. In this scenario, we have chosen doors as key elements, presenting a full framework, in comparison to [14,30,39], to detect doors and to estimate their aperture in order to understand their open/close status inside a shared-autonomy algorithm. Moreover, we achieved the integration of the door detection module in the shared-autonomy navigation without designing a specific procedure to pass through the door as in [25,28,33]. Simply, we relied on a good estimation of the door aperture center to define the subgoal given in input to the planner, keeping the same logic underlying the obstacle avoidance and the navigation itself. Our door detection module is based to a similar approach to the one presented in [22,36] exploiting the point cloud data from the 3D sensor. However we did not need to search a door by scanning horizontal stripes of the point cloud since we can exploit the bounding box founded by the door detector/tracker. Nevertheless, our results are in line with [22], showing that the doorway aperture estimation is enough robust from different distance and with different aperture angles (average error 5.61 ± 2.24 cm for the painted wooden door and 8.23 cm ± 3.82 for the metal door). However, differently to [22], our method is strong also to closed doors—in all the cases the estimated aperture was exactly 0 m—and in addition it has been tested on a real mobile robot.

Thanks to the door detection module, in our pilot experiments the robot was able to pass through narrow doorways without any user's intervention(See footnote 4). Furthermore, we verified the contribution of the door attractor(See footnote 4), by testing our shared-autonomy navigation algorithm with and without the doors information in the same conditions (see Fig. 5). The qualitative result showed that the robot performed different low-level behavior in correspondence of the same high-level behavior chosen by the user. However, only when the door detection module was active, the robot was able to pass through the door without requiring additional commands to the user. Therefore, this preliminary result might suggest a decrease of number of commands needed to make the robot move through doors, facilitating the user experience and reducing his/her workload.

References

1. Accogli, A., et al.: EMG-based detection of user's intentions for human-machine shared control of an assistive upper-limb exoskeleton. In: González-Vargas, J., Ibáñez, J., Contreras-Vidal, J., van der Kooij, H., Pons, J. (eds.) Wearable Robotics: Challenges and Trends. Biosystems & Biorobotics, vol. 16, pp. 181–185. Springer, Heidelberg (2017). https://doi.org/10.1007/978-3-319-46532-6_30
2. Kim, B.K., Tanaka, H., Sumi, Y.: Robotic wheelchair using a high accuracy visual marker Lentibar and its application to door crossing navigation. In: Proceedings of the 2015 IEEE International Conference on Robotics and Automation (ICRA), pp. 4478–4483. IEEE (2015)
3. Cipriani, C., Zaccone, F., Micera, S., Carrozza, M.C.: On the Shared control of an EMG-controlled prosthetic hand: analysis of user-prosthesis interaction. IEEE Trans. Rob. 24(1), 170–184 (2008)
4. Zheng, C., Green, R.: Feature recognition and obstacle detection for drive assistance in indoor environments. In: Image and Vision Computing New Zealand, IVCNZ 2011 (2011)
5. Anguelov, D., Koller, D., Parker, E., Thrun, S.: Detecting and modeling doors with mobile robots. In: Proceeding of the IEEE International Conference on Robotics and Automation, Proceedings, ICRA 2004, vol. 4, pp. 3777–3784. IEEE (2004)

6. Kim, D., Nevatia, R.: A method for recognition and localization of generic objects for indoor navigation. In: Proceedings of the 1994 IEEE Workshop on Applications of Computer Vision, pp. 280–288. IEEE (1994)
7. Losey, D.P., McDonald, C.G., Battaglia, E., O'Malley, M.K.: A review of intent detection, arbitration, and communication aspects of shared control for physical human-robot interaction. Appl. Mech. Rev. **70**(1), 010804 (2018)
8. Demeester, E., Hüntemann, A., Vanhooydonck, D., Vanacker, G., Van Brussel, H., Nuttin, M.: User-adapted plan recognition and user-adapted shared control: a Bayesian approach to semi-autonomous wheelchair driving. Auton. Robot. **24**(2), 193–211 (2008)
9. Aude, E.P.L., Lopes, E.P., Aguiar, C.S., Martins, M.F.: Door crossing and state identification using robotic vision. IFAC Proc. Vol. **39**(15), 659–664 (2006)
10. Beraldo, G., Antonello, M., Cimolato, A., Menegatti, E., Tonin, L.,: Brain-computer interface meets ROS: a robotic approach to mentally drive telepresence robots. In: Proceedings of the 2018 IEEE International Conference on Robotics and Automation (ICRA), pp. 1–6. IEEE (2018)
11. Cicirelli, G., D'orazio, T., Distante, A.: Target recognition by components for mobile robot navigation. J. Exp. Theor. Artif. Intell. **15**(3), 281–297 (2003)
12. Belaidi, H., Hentout, A., Bentarzi, H.: Human-robot shared control for path generation and execution. Int. J. Soc. Robot. **11**, 1–12 (2019)
13. Budenske, J., Gini, G.: Why is it so difficult for a robot to pass through a doorway using ultrasonic sensors? In: Proceedings of the 1994 IEEE International Conference on Robotics and Automation, pp. 3124–3129. IEEE (1994)
14. Hensler, J., Blaich, M., Bittel, O.: Real-time door detection based on adaboost learning algorithm. In: Gottscheber, A., Obdržálek, D., Schmidt, C. (eds.) EUROBOT 2009. CCIS, vol. 82, pp. 61–73. Springer, Heidelberg (2010). https://doi.org/10.1007/978-3-642-16370-8_6
15. Philips, J., et al.: Adaptive shared control of a brain-actuated simulated wheelchair. In: Proceedings of the 2007 IEEE 10th International Conference on Rehabilitation Robotics, pp. 408–414. IEEE (2007)
16. Hong, J.P., Kwon, O.S., Lee, E.H., Kim, B.S., Hong, S.H.: Shared-control and force-reflection joystick algorithm for the door passing of mobile robot or powered wheelchair. In: Proceedings of the IEEE. IEEE Region 10 Conference. TENCON 1999. Multimedia Technology for Asia-Pacific Information Infrastructure (Cat. No. 99CH37030), vol. 2, pp. 1577–1580. IEEE (1999)
17. Redmon, J., Divvala, S., Girshick, R., Farhadi, A.: You only look once: unified, real-time object detection. In: Proceedings of the IEEE Conference on Computer Vision and Pattern Recognition, pp. 779–788 (2016)
18. Crandall, J.W., Goodrich, M.A.: Characterizing efficiency of human robot interaction: a case study of shared-control teleoperation (2002)
19. Joo, K., Lee, T.-K., Baek, S., Oh, S.Y.: Generating topological map from occupancy grid-map using virtual door detection. In: Proceedings of the IEEE Congress on Evolutionary Computation, pp. 1–6. IEEE (2010)
20. Khatib, O.: Real-time obstacle avoidance for manipulators and mobile robots. In: Cox, I.J., Wilfong, G.T. (eds.) Autonomous Robot Vehicles, pp. 396–404. Springer, New York (1986). https://doi.org/10.1007/978-1-4613-8997-2_29
21. Goodrich, M.A., Crandall, J.W., Stimpson, J.L.: Neglect tolerant teaming: issues and dilemmas. In: Proceedings of the 2003 AAAI Spring Symposium on Human Interaction with Autonomous Systems in Complex Environments, pp. 24–26 (2003)
22. Derry, M., Argall, B.: Automated doorway detection for assistive shared-control wheelchairs, pp. 1254–1259, May 2013

23. Desai, M., Yanco, H.A.: Blending human and robot inputs for sliding scale autonomy. In: Proceedings of the IEEE International Workshop on Robot and Human Interactive Communication, pp. 537–542. IEEE (2005)
24. Aigner, P., McCarragher, B.: Human integration into robot control utilising potential fields. In: Proceedings of the International Conference on Robotics and Automation, vol. 1, pp. 291–296. IEEE (1997)
25. Salaris, P., Vassallo, C., Souères, P., Laumond, J.P.: The geometry of confocal curves for passing through a door. IEEE Trans. Robot. **31**(5), 1180–1193 (2015)
26. Papoulis, A., Saunders, H.: Probability, Random Variables and Stochastic Processes (1989)
27. Zeng, Q., Burdet, E., Rebsamen, B., Teo, C.L.: Evaluation of the collaborative wheelchair assistant system. In: Proceedings of the 2007 IEEE 10th International Conference on Rehabilitation Robotics, pp. 601–608. IEEE (2007)
28. Simpson, R.C., Levine, S.P., Bell, D.A., Jaros, L.A., Koren, Y., Borenstein, J.: NavChair: an assistive wheelchair navigation system with automatic adaptation. In: Mittal, V.O., Yanco, H.A., Aronis, J., Simpson, R. (eds.) Assistive Technology and Artificial Intelligence. LNCS, vol. 1458, pp. 235–255. Springer, Heidelberg (1998). https://doi.org/10.1007/BFb0055982
29. Leeb, R., Tonin, L., Rohm, M., Desideri, L., Carlson, T., Millan, J.D.R.: Towards independence: a BCI telepresence robot for people with severe motor disabilities. Proc. IEEE **103**(6), 969–982 (2015)
30. Munoz-Salinas, R., Aguirre, E., García-Silvente, M., Alex, A.G.: Door-detection using computer vision and fuzzy logic (2004)
31. Barber, R., Salichs, M.A.: Mobile robot navigation based on event maps. In: Proceedings of the Field and Service Robotics, pp. 61–66 (2001)
32. Stoeter, S.A., Le Mauff, F., Papanikolopoulos, N.P.: Real-time door detection in cluttered environments. In: Proceedings of the 2000 IEEE International Symposium on Intelligent Control. Held jointly with the 8th IEEE Mediterranean Conference on Control and Automation (Cat. No. 00CH37147), pp. 187–192. IEEE (2000)
33. Wang, S., Chen, L., Hu, H., McDonald-Maier, K.: Doorway passing of an intelligent wheelchair by dynamically generating Bezier curve trajectory. In: Proceedings of the 2012 IEEE International Conference on Robotics and Biomimetics (ROBIO), pp. 1206–1211. IEEE (2012)
34. Levine, S.P., Bell, D.A., Jaros, L.A., Simpson, R.C., Koren, Y., Borenstein, J.: The NavChair assistive wheelchair navigation system. IEEE Trans. Rehabil. Eng. **7**(4), 443–451 (1999)
35. Carlson, T., Demiris, Y.: Human-wheelchair collaboration through prediction of intention and adaptive assistance. In: Proceedings of the 2008 IEEE International Conference on Robotics and Automation, pp. 3926–3931. IEEE (2008)
36. Yuan, T.H., Hashim, F.H., Zaki, W.M.D.W., Huddin, A.B.: An automated 3D scanning algorithm using depth cameras for door detection. In: Proceedings of the 2015 International Electronics Symposium (IES), pp. 58–61. IEEE (2015)
37. Winiarski, T., Banachowicz, K., Seredyński, D.: Multi-sensory feedback control in door approaching and opening. In: Filev, D., et al. (eds.) Intelligent Systems'2014. AISC, vol. 323, pp. 57–70. Springer, Cham (2015). https://doi.org/10.1007/978-3-319-11310-4_6
38. Hess, W., Kohler, D., Rapp, H., Andor, D.: Real-time loop closure in 2D LIDAR SLAM. In: Proceedings of the 2016 IEEE International Conference on Robotics and Automation (ICRA), pp. 1271–1278. IEEE (2016)

39. Yang, X., Tian, Y.: Robust door detection in unfamiliar environments by combining edge and corner features. In: Proceedings of the 2010 IEEE Computer Society Conference on Computer Vision and Pattern Recognition-Workshops, pp. 57–64. IEEE (2010)
40. Koren, Y., Borenstein, J.: Potential field methods and their inherent limitations for mobile robot navigation. In: Proceedings of the 1991 IEEE International Conference on Robotics and Automation, pp. 1398–1404. IEEE (1991)
41. Chen, Z., Birchfield, S.T.: Visual detection of lintel-occluded doors from a single image. In: Proceedings of the 2008 IEEE Computer Society Conference on Computer Vision and Pattern Recognition Workshops, pp. 1–8. IEEE (2008)

Toward Automated Courseware Production for the ExPLoRAA Learning Environment

Amedeo Cesta[1], Gabriella Cortellessa[1], Riccardo De Benedictis[1(✉)],
Carlo De Medio[2], Francesca Fracasso[1], and Carla Limongelli[2]

[1] ISTC, CNR - Italian National Research Council, Rome, Italy
riccardo.debenedictis@istc.cnr.it
[2] DIA, Roma Tre University, Via della Vasca Navale 79, 00146 Rome, Italy

Abstract. This paper presents a newborn collaboration between heterogeneous AI competences. In particular, it describes current work on the integration of machine learning techniques for the automatic generation of contents for an Intelligent Tutoring System grounded on automated planning techniques. The joint use of these two approaches allows on the one hand to facilitate the task of instructional designers in defining and preparing courses, and on the other hand to dynamically support the use of content according to different users context.

Keywords: AI Technologies Integration · Intelligent learning environments · Authoring tools · Automated planning · Machine learning

1 Introduction

Given the speed of the current societal changes, the need for "continuous education" is really a must. In this regard, the area of Intelligent Tutoring System (ITS) [20, 22] pursues the idea of designing computer systems that, thanks to personalised stimuli sent to the learners, enable situated and meaningful learning, enhancing the effectiveness of the overall experience. Goal of such systems is to radically rethink the learning environment through the application of advanced ICT technology and may represent a valid support to continuous education. Common ITSs aim at replicating the benefits of one-to-one personalized tutoring in contexts where students would have access to one-to-many instruction from a single teacher (e.g., classroom lectures), or no teacher at all (e.g., on-line homework) [21]. Such systems are typically related to classical learning environments, hence neglecting the possibility to act in both *time* (e.g., lifelong) and *space* (e.g., working both at school, in an outdoor environment, during leisure, etc.) and overcoming the classical concept of "lessons". Furthermore, although ITSs have proven to be effective in different domains, they remain intrinsically difficult to build from the authoring perspective, with estimates of 200–300 h of

© Springer Nature Switzerland AG 2019
M. Alviano et al. (Eds.): AI*IA 2019, LNAI 11946, pp. 528–541, 2019.
https://doi.org/10.1007/978-3-030-35166-3_37

development per hour of instruction [1]. While the introduction of ITS development environments encourages instructional designers at defining courseware, indeed, the workload for tutors remains still too steep.

This paper focalises around the two aspects that we consider crucial in modern ITSs (see Fig. 1): (a) the adaptive delivery of lesson that facilitate both personalization and direct experience, (b) the synthesis of facilitators for authoring materials for new learning systems. We have pursued these goals by integrating heterogeneous AI techniques, using Planning for personalizing lessons and

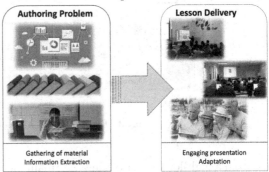

Fig. 1. Authoring and delivering lessons.

Machine Learning (ML) for authoring. This paper describe the current status of the integration by giving some generality of the ExPLoRAA ITS and its current challenges (Sect. 2), presenting the planning part that allows personalization while delivering the lesson (Sect. 3), then the ML approach for supporting the lesson model authoring phase (Sect. 4), and closing with a description of the current status plus an example (Sect. 5).

2   The ExPLoRAA Concept

ExPLoRAA is a Continuous Intelligent Tutoring System, developed in the context of "Città Educante" project[1] (the name means "city that educates" in Italian), which pursues the idea of providing a continuous and dynamic teaching in space and time. This approach evolves from previous works (e.g., [3–5,8]) also based on the idea of dynamically composing lessons through the use of *automated planning* [12]. The key idea beyond the ExPLoRAA system consists in using technology related to automated planning to dynamically compose lessons. Starting from a static representation containing a high-level lesson track, initially stored in a database, the lesson is planned and dynamically adapted and personalized to the involved users. The idea of using automated planning technology relies on the need to create a sufficiently extensive didactic experience to reproduce a large number of different situations which are, at the same time, characterized by a high variability of stimuli, aimed at increasing the involvement level of users. Automated planning, indeed, favors the generation of different lessons that would be too complicated to obtain with a simple pre-compilation of stories. The timeline-based approach to automated planning [19], in particular, represents the unifying element of the various modules by ensuring the dynamic adaptability of plans by promoting experiential learning.

---

[1] http://www.cittaeducante.it.

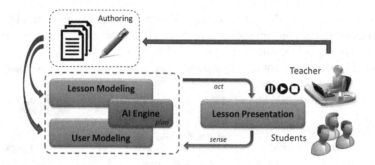

Fig. 2. The ExPLoRAA general idea.

From a high-level point of view, the main modules of the system are described in Fig. 2. In particular, it is possible to distinguish between two kinds of involved **users**: the *students*, i.e., a group of people, potentially, of any age, interested in using the learning services offered by the ExPLoRAA environment, and the *teachers*, i.e., users with special privileges who have the opportunity to observe students, monitor and control the progress of the lessons and of the overall learning environment. Once the lesson authoring phase is finished, a timeline-based planner takes care of keeping the model of the involved users consistent with the lesson model, resulting in a planned lesson which is customized to the involved students. The arising plan will then be executed, bringing to the dispatching of stimuli to a lesson presentation module which presents them to the users in an appealing way. The module is also responsible for collecting information from users (customization parameters) aimed at dynamically modifying the user's model and, consequently, the lesson presented. According to the needs of the specific lesson, indeed, this information can include physiological parameters of the users, collected through Bluetooth bracelets, or geographical coordinates, collected through mobile devices, thus allowing the interpretation of the concept of learning with a wider attention, breaking down the barriers of time and space within which the classical lessons are confined (for a more detailed description of the applicationt of ExPLoRAA to cultural visits, for example, refer to [3]). In Sect. 3 we describe the concepts underlying the timeline-based planning and how it was used to keep the representation of users and lessons consistent. The three concepts of *timeline, token* and *rule* constitute the basis of this kind of reasoning. The latter, in particular, must in some way be defined by the domain experts (i.e., the teachers) during the authoring phase (see again Fig. 2). For this reason, in this work, we focus on the automatic extraction of rules from digital materials, so as to relieve application designers as much as possible from handcrafting them.

2.1   The Challenge: Supporting Content Definition

The task performed by the teacher during the lesson design phase is both critical and complex. Specifically, the teacher must take into account *all* the feasible evolutions of the lesson, considering *all* the possible stimuli for the students, their relationships and how these are related to the state of the users. In particular, these possible evolutions are defined, ultimately, by defining the planning rules which, although allow the problem to be easily broken down into subproblems and, therefore, help designing the lesson, are currently handwritten on a text file, without the support of any editor specifically built to take account of the application context. The use of authoring tools such as, for example, the Cognitive Tutor Authoring Tools (CTAT), would certainly be able to reduce the workload assigned to course designers [1]. Nevertheless, this paper describes how we have tackled the problem by using ML techniques, so as to be able to automate and, therefore, to facilitate as much as possible the task of designing the lessons, while maintaining the dynamic adaptation characteristics offered by the tutoring systems relying on timeline-based planning.

Our goal is to achieve a system that, starting from a high-level topic (e.g., the "Trevi Fountain" topic) automatically generates the planning rules (e.g., in order to better understand "Trevi Fountain", you must have information on "Nicola Salvi", "Roman Holiday", "Trevi (rione of Rome)", etc.) for the ExPLoRAA system. The planning subsystem will reason on these rules by autonomously generating a lesson over time and dynamically adapting it according to the specific evolution of the context (e.g., sending at proper time information about "Nicola Salvi" to those interested in architecture, about "Roman Holiday" to those interested in cinema, about "Trevi (rione of Rome)" to those interested in city planning, etc.).

3   Timeline-Based Planning for Dynamic Lesson Synthesis

Since most of the components of the ExPLoRAA system strongly depend on temporal aspects, we have chosen to rely on a specific automated planning technique, called timeline-based, which allows to explicitly reason on time. Timeline-based planning, indeed, allows to reason about events in time and, hence, represents a valid tool for meeting our pedagogical needs. Planning a lesson, in particular, requires dispatching information at proper time. Additionally, reacting to users' interactions requires plan adaptation capabilities which can more hardly be achieved through other automatic planning techniques. Furthermore, the dynamic adaptation of the user profiles, which can take place on the different features that represent the user's model, can also be achieved through timelines.

The main data structure, for timeline-based planning, is the *timeline* which, in generic terms, is a function of time over a finite domain. Values on the timelines are extracted from a set of temporally scoped predicates (i.e., predicates endowed with extra arguments belonging to the Time domain $\mathbb{T}$, either real or discrete), with their parameters, called tokens. Formally, a *token* is an expression of the form $n(x_0, \ldots, x_i) @ [s, e, \tau]$, where n is a predicate name, $x_0, \ldots, x_i$ are the predicate's parameters (i.e., constants, numeric variables or object variables), s and e are temporal parameters belonging to $\mathbb{T}$ such that $s \leq e$ and τ is a parameter (i.e., a constant or an object variable) representing the timeline on

which the token apply. The overall idea pursued in ExPLoRAA consists in
using such tokens for representing both the model of the users and the planned
stimuli. Compared to the general formalization above, however, we can afford
some simplifications. Specifically, since the stimuli have no duration, the s and
e variables of each token would always be equal. We address this by removing
one of the two variables, e.g., the e variable. As an example, the expression
st_0 () @$[10:00, l_0]$ would represent a stimulus st_0 (for instance, a text message)
which is planned to be dispatched at time 10:00 for the lesson l_0.

It is worth noticing that the tokens' parameters, including the temporal ones,
are constituted, in general, by the variables of a constraint network [10, 15]. In
order to reduce the allowed values for such parameters, bringing the system to
a desired behavior, it is possible to impose constraints among them (and/or
between the parameters and other possible variables). Such constraints include
temporal constraints, usually expressed by means of interval relations [2], binding constraints between object variables as well as linear constraints among
numerical, including the temporal one, variables. In particular, the set of tokens
and constraints is used to describe the main data structure that will be used
to represent the "nodes" of the timeline-based search space: the token network.
Specifically, a *token network* is a tuple $\pi = (\mathcal{T}, \mathcal{C})$, where $\mathcal{T} = \{t_0, \ldots, t_j\}$ is
a set of tokens and $\mathcal{C}$ is a set of constraints, required to be consistent, on the
variables of the tokens in $\mathcal{T}$.

Additionally, tokens can be partitioned into two groups: *facts* and *goals*.
While facts are, by definition, inherently true, goals have to be achieved. Specifically, causality, in the timeline-based approach, is defined by means of a set o
rules indicating how to achieve goals. Formally,

Definition 1. *A rule is an expression of the form*

$$n(x_0, \ldots, x_k) @ [s, e, \tau] \leftarrow r$$

where:

- $n(x_0, \ldots, x_k) @ [s, e, \tau]$ *is the* head *of the rule, i.e., an expression in which n
  is a predicate name, $x_0, \ldots, x_k$ are numeric variables or object variables, s
  and e are temporal variables belonging to $\mathbb{T}$ such that $s \leq e$ and τ is an object
  variable representing the timeline on which the token apply.*
- r *is the* body *of the rule (or the* requirement*), i.e., either a slave token, a
  constraint among tokens (possibly including the $x_0 \ldots x_k$ variables), a conjunction of requirements or a disjunction of requirements.*

Rules define causal relations that must be complied to in order for a given goal
to be achieved. For *each* goal having the "form" of the head of a rule, the
body of the rule must also be present in the token network. As an example, the
expression $\{st_0 () @[s, l] \leftarrow \{st_1 () @[s_1, l] \land 10 \leq s - s_1 \leq 20\}\}$ represents a rule
asserting that, for each stimulus st_0 there must exist, from 10 to 20 s before,
a stimulus st_1. It is worth noting that, in this case, the body of the rule is a
logical conjunction of a token and a constraint. More generally, however, it is

also possible to have disjunctions. In the latter case the solver will choose among the various disjuncts.

We have now all the ingredients to define a timeline-based planning problem. In particular, the definition can rely on the above concept of requirement. Specifically, a timeline-based *planning problem* is a triple $\mathcal{P} = (\mathbf{T}, \mathcal{R}, \mathbf{r})$, where $\mathbf{T}$ is a set of timelines, $\mathcal{R}$ is a set of rules and $\mathbf{r}$ is a requirement, i.e., either a (fact or goal) token, a constraint among tokens, a conjunction of requirements or a disjunction of requirements.

Roughly speaking, the role of a timeline-based solver consists in, starting from a token network described by the problem's requirement, applying the proper rules, so that each goal has its corresponding rule applied, incrementally refining the current token network by adding new tokens and new constraints according to the rules' bodies. It is worth noticing, indeed, that, in general, the application of the rules might result in the introduction of further goals into the token network. Such goals, also called sub-goals, require to be achieved as well. The process ends up when, for all the goals of the token network, either the body of its corresponding rule is present in the token network or it is recognized as semantically equivalent to another token (in this case we talk about *unification* of the tokens). Additionally, in case the bodies of the rules contain disjunctions, the solver will choose among the available disjuncts. Finally, the solver will assign a value to all the tokens' parameters such that all the constraints of the token network are satisfied (possibly, backtracking to another available disjunct whenever the constraints cannot be made consistent). Notice that, despite the simplicity of the above solving procedure, the combination of disjunctions and constraints in the rules make the resolution process, in generally, extremely challenging from a computational point of view. For this reason, indeed, heuristics are often used to make the resolution process more efficient (see, for example, [6,7]).

3.1   Modeling Students and Lessons Through Timelines

As already mentioned, the ExPLoRAA system is composed of different functional blocks. In particular, the user modeling module aims at creating and dynamically maintaining an updated model of the users which is used as a starting point for the personalization of the lessons. By pursuing the overall objective of enhancing the learning experience, indeed, it is necessary to keep a user model up-to-date in order to consider how their emotional, psychological, physiological and geographical parameters can influence the learning process. Specifically, the student modeling has three main objectives: (i) to model and monitor relevant factors through which the lesson can be customized; (ii) to develop a model that can represent the user's profile; and (iii) to provide a high level guidance for customizing learning objectives.

The parameters that are relevant for personalization are, in general, dependent on the type of lesson. Basically, the system keeps up to date a number of parameters that can be chosen according to the domain and context of learning (lesson at the university, support to cultural visits, etc.). For instance they can be related to the personal/psychological and emotional aspect such as: the personal interests, the level of engagement, the current performance assessment and the fatigue (in case of a cultural visit around a historical city). This type of parameters can be measured by using questionnaires dynamically dispatched to the students or by making use of physiological devices like the Bluetooth bracelets (e.g., the Empatica E4[2]), through which it is possible to extract physiological values such as peripheral skin temperature, skin conductance, heart rate and heart variability to derive the emotional state of the users. Additionally, through the use of mobile devices, it is possible to leverage on geo-localization services to get a good estimate of the users' position in time, so as to contextualise the planned stimuli according to their geographical position. Finally, the profile of a student can also be updated exploiting the interactions of the users with the system asking them, for example, to answer to sporadic questions. As an example, the users' *engagement* is measured through a five levels Likert-type scale which is administered to the users at regular intervals. Finally, particular emphasis is given to the students' *performance* which is monitored and observed through the administration of questions and the interpretation of the provided answers. By processing the above information, the system generates a user model that is constantly updated to perceive and represent significant changes in the emotional state (note that parameters can generally change over time).

The modeling of the lessons is the key feature of the ExPLoRAA system since it creates and manages the *network of stimuli* that guides the entire learning session. Nodes on this network are tokens and are intended to represent temporally annotated stimuli (e.g., videos, text messages, questions, etc.) to be sent, at appropriate time, to the users while edges represent causal and temporal relations among such stimuli introduced either in the planning problem definition or through the application of the rules. Additionally, tokens are endowed with additional information including a set of covered topics (e.g., "art", "architecture", "religion", etc.) and some content dependent on the nature of the stimulus (e.g., a text for textual stimulus or a URL for a video stimulus).

It is worth noting that although the above network is initialized in order to represent an abstract blueprint of a lesson, it is afterwards customized and dynamically adapted to the profile of the involved user. Personalization, indeed, takes place both in terms of users' interest in some topics, as explained earlier, as well as in terms of the type (and the number) of tokens in the token network. Specifically, adaptations to the network are made thanks to the application of a set of rules (introduced in Definition 1) associated to each lesson, which define how to "react" to the users' profile, to their updates and to their actions (e.g., moving to a specific location or answering to a question). Such rules, in particular, are intended to create the "conditions", in terms of events and their relations within the network, for other events to be present. An example of rule can be "in order to stimulate the cognitive activity of the group, either propose a simple crosswords and the group's performance is low, or propose a complex crosswords and the group's performance is high". Notice that by taking advantage of the possibility of defining disjunctions within the rules and being able to combine

---

[2] https://www.empatica.com/research/e4.

such rules sequentially, it is possible to obtain a great wealth of possible lessons' evolutions. Finally, since some of these rules may contain conditions which concern the user model, not all of them are applicable (e.g., in the above example, in case the group's current performance is low, only the simple crosswords is proposed), resulting in an overall network which is always compatible with the current users' profiles. It is worth noting, however, that establishing which and how personalization parameters affect the adaptation of the lesson constitutes, ultimately, an additional load on the shoulders of the teacher during the authoring phase, which will have to worry about defining the rules that will allow the planner to achieve dynamic adaptation.

4 Courseware Production Through Machine Learning

The contribution of ML has the purpose of automatizing the phases that involve tutor intervention. Specifically, the most difficult and time-consuming task for the teacher regards the formulation of the lesson model, through the definition of the planning rules, during the authoring phase (see Fig. 1).

Wiki Course Builder (WCB) system generates short educational courses, entirely based on Wikipedia pages, starting from a query of the system. The teacher queries the system with the didactic goal, and the related context. WCB explores Wikipedia recommending some pages related to the query. The teacher selects the interesting pages and the system automatically sequences them according to the prerequisite relations between them. This approach allows a fast generation of didactic paths, and the reliability of its contents is guaranteed by an in-depth study that compared Wikipedia with the British encyclopedia, showing the same accuracy percentage [13]. The fact that each article is virtually subject to constant verification make it a good candidate for the extraction of truthful information. With more than 5.9 millions of articles and an average 577 new articles per day[3], Wikipedia provides a rich knowledge base for teachers and instructional designers, and can be a great help in the activity of course creation. As said, Wikipedia is an excellent knowledge base, but the approach can be generalized to all linked open data such as DBPedia or Wikidata.

The two main characteristics of WCB, the recommender and the sequencing engine, are respectively presented in [9, 11].

4.1 The Recommender Engine

Here, the recommendation is based on the preference of the users in the platform Grasha Teaching Styles (TS) Model [14] which models the registered teachers and Wikipedia pages in a way that the teachers are guided by the system towards material chosen by similar teachers. In detail, the teacher is first modeled by means of a questionnaire at the signup step: the Grasha-Riechmann TS survey. Secondly, every time a Wikipedia page is inserted in a course, the page is labeled

---

[3] https://en.wikipedia.org/wiki/Wikipedia:Statistics (visited September, 12 2019).

with the TS of the teacher that selected it. If other teachers choose the same page, the TS of that page are updated according to the averages for each of the five categories of Grasha-Reichmann. In this way, it is possible to define a metric of similarity between the teacher who performs the search and the pages with a similar subject, chosen by other teachers. This step suffers from the cold-start problem that is solved by equipping the engine with other content-based metrics such as Tf-Idf, Information Gain, and Latent Semantic Index, thus allowing reliable results.

4.2   The Sequencing Engine

The approach evaluates a set of hypotheses for understating the feasibility of exploiting the Wikipedia content in order to automatically define prerequisite relationships between learning objects. We follow a traditional ML approach [18] applied to a dataset of LOs by performing a comparative analysis of several features of the LOs. We define the features according with peculiar aspects of the representative topics such as content length, generality, or specialization. So then, the topics are analyzed and the related LOs features computed. Finally, the dependency relation between two LOs is inferred taking their features under consideration: this computation is obtained by feeding the features into a ML-based classifier.

4.3   Feature Extraction and Machine Learning Approach

Initially, a traditional approach was applied to the classification problem, applying the calculation of Tf-Idf as described in [16]. The first experiments based on a model build on six hypothesis, gave accuracy values of 60% not considered acceptable. From the six hypotheses with a feature selection process we identified 15 features characterizing the problem. Below is the description of the methodology applied for the configuration of a neural network based on multilayer perceptron whose validation is published in [11].

After Wikipedia pages detection, we perform feature extraction on pairs of pages, so to construct instances vector for the prerequisite classifier based on multilayer perceptron. Then a supervised learning paradigm takes the vector and carries on the classification task, deciding whether a prerequisite relationship does exist between the pages. Under the assumption that an ML approach can learn to obtain accurate predictions based on a small number of training instances, the automatic prerequisite detection (and the consequent translation into rules) reduces the effort required to human experts that, otherwise, have to establish the prerequisites manually.

In our model, knowledge representation is multilayered. As sketched in Fig. 3, each layer identifies a set of features. The full set of features is shown in [11]. In the first layer from the bottom (I), we perform a lexical analysis on the pages text, which is tokenized into a sequence of tokens. The length of the term sequence is represented by $f_l^{(lo)}$. A part-of-speech (POS) tagger extracts the term sequence and recognize term, namely, noun, verb, article, adjective, preposition and pronoun. Since we are more interested in terms that represent people, places, things, or classes of these elements, we look in particular to the nouns of the pages. The second layer (II), provides Wikipedia features related to the page structure. In particular, the length of the page $f_l^{(c)}$ and its internal links $f_L^{(c)}$, that is, references between articles and other analysis. Complex entities that have several references to other pages may refer to concept that should be discussed later in a learning process, whereas, by contrast, longer discussions may describe introductory topics that should be learn before others. The top layer (III) analyzes the categories that Wikipedia makes available to the users for recognize pages on similar subjects. The categories can be normally found at the end of each Wikipedia page. Each page may be assigned to one or more categories. Exploiting the results from the Information Gain algorithm, we asses that the features that belong to this layer are the most important in the classification process. The accuracy of this approach is validated by means of experimental evaluations as shown in [11].

5   The Integrated Prototype

The integrated version of the prototype provides first automatic support for the rules definition process. In particular, the use of WCB prevents the teacher from writing all the rules by hand and allows to quickly create lesson models for each type of domain. Specifically, starting from a goal identified by the teacher, WCB processes the query representing the goal and returns a list of Wikipedia pages which are considered as the prerequisites of the goal. These pages are translated into the slave tokens of the body of a rule whose head is the original goal of the query. Additionally, temporal constraints, generated from the features of the preconditions, are introduced so as to allow the students a sufficient amount time for the assimilation of the stimuli. In particular, the ratio between the number of concepts and the length of the page, defined as the *semantic density* of the page [17], has been used to temporally outdistance stimuli over time. The role of the teacher, during the lesson authoring process, remains still active, maintaining the possibility to select the interesting prerequisites from which, iteratively, WCB extracts further prerequisites. In general, given the i-th Wikipedia page found at level k, p_k^i, WCB extracts a list of n pages prerequisite of p_k^i: $[p_{k.1}^{i+1}, \ldots, p_{k.n}^{i+1}]$. The teacher selects one or more pages from this list and WCB iterates the prerequisite search on the selected pages. At the end of the authoring phase, there will be a list of rules that can be fed to the planner to allow the construction of the personalized lesson.

5.1   The System at Work

A teacher wants to compose a lesson about Fontana di Trevi. S(he) starts to query WCB with "Fontana di Trevi" using, for example, the word "Rome" for disambiguation. The system scans all the outgoing link to the page to build

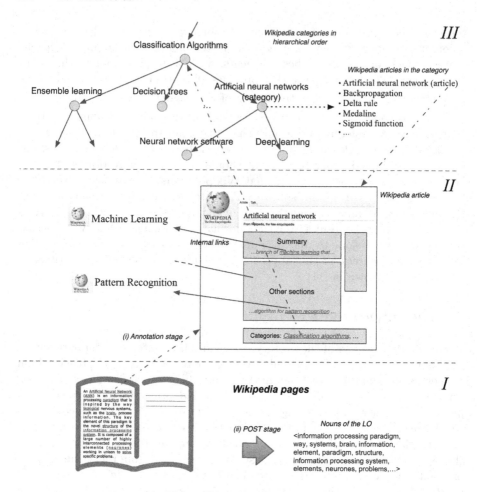

Fig. 3. Extraction schema.

a knowledge graph. In this graph, nodes represent entities in Wikipedia while arcs are the links between pages. The system extracts the concepts closest to the query using three, appropriately weighted, metrics (TfxIdf, IG and LSI) and creates a list of outgoing links to possible prerequisites of the concept. From this list, the system extracts instances for the binary classifier (one for each element of the list) and, from these results, the analysis of prerequisites starts. In the *Trevi Fountain* example, among the most likely prerequisite pages there are the entities associated with the pages *Acqua vergine* and *Palazzo Poli*, identified by the system. Starting from this prerequisite analysis, an example of generated rule for the ExPLoRAA system is, therefore, represented by $\{tf\,()\,@[s,l] \leftarrow \{av\,()\,@[s_1,l] \land sd_{av} \leq s - s_1 \land pp\,()\,@[s_2,l] \land sd_{pp} \leq s - s_2 \land \dots\}\}$ asserting that, for each stimulus tf (representing a pointer to the *Trevi Fountain* page) there must exist, at least sd_{av} seconds before, a stimulus av (representing a pointer to the *Acqua vergine* page), and at least sd_{pp} seconds before, a stimulus pp (representing a pointer to the *Palazzo Poli* page). The constants sd_{av} and sd_{pp} represent, respectively, the semantic density of the *Acqua vergine* and the *Palazzo Poli* pages. Proceeding in this way, looking at the prerequisites starting from the new root *Acqua vergine*, we can create further rules.

Unfortunately the prerequisite recognizer is trained to work on sets of Wikipedia pages associated with subjects, as described in the previous chapter. However, we are still able to recognize the most obvious relationships. The first problems are the lack of all the features described in the previous chapter, and specifically the relationships that the study of the Information Gain turned out to be more significant for evaluation have gone from being real numbers to simple binary relationships; in the classification process the analysis of the links between the pages are used to recognizing if a page points to the second one (considering also that we look for them in the Wikipedia graph often the relation is worth 1 for all the analyzed pages); moreover it is not possible to calculate the number and the average lengths of the topics associated to the concept.

Furthermore, the exploit of Wikipedia in Italian is limited by the number of entities that are present online. Wikipedia (EN) is composed of 5,700,000 pages with an average words count of 640 Average Word Count (AWC) while Wikipedia (IT) by 1,500,000 pages much less characterized than those in the original language. In future, for a better comparison between Wikipedia pages, a different training model starting from datasets manually generated by experts of the domain will be inquired.

6   Conclusions

This paper describes work done to integrate heterogeneous AI techniques to serve an example of intelligent learning environment. In particular, we have addressed a known bottleneck of "knowledge intensive" AI systems (well exemplified by ITSs) that stay in the huge effort required to handcraft knowledge for the actual functioning of the system. We strongly believe that the goal of integrating AI systems generated by different cultural tradition is a key aspect in the AI debate for the immediate future.

This paper results can be read as a feasibility study for the integration of a ML approach in a plan-based ITS. The current results demonstrate that such direction is worth being pursued. At present, we are investigating the idea of a complete automation of the authoring process in order to identify potential limitation of the approach. Nevertheless, it is worth noting that also an intermediate approach that opens to the possibility of a user-refinement after or in combination with the ML phase would be really acceptable given the criticality of the authoring phase. The full exploration of possible alternative approaches to authoring is one of the directions for future work.

References

1. Aleven, V., McLaren, B.M., Sewall, J., Koedinger, K.R.: The cognitive tutor authoring tools (CTAT): preliminary evaluation of efficiency gains. In: Ikeda, M., Ashley, K.D., Chan, T.-W. (eds.) ITS 2006. LNCS, vol. 4053, pp. 61–70. Springer, Heidelberg (2006). https://doi.org/10.1007/11774303_7
2. Allen, J.F.: Maintaining knowledge about temporal intervals. Commun. ACM **26**(11), 832–843 (1983)
3. Cesta, A., Cortellessa, G., Benedictis, R.D., Fracasso, F.: ExPLoRAA: an intelligent tutoring system for active ageing in (flexible) time and space. In: Proceedings of the 4th Italian Workshop on Artificial Intelligence for Ambient Assisted Living 2018, pp. 92–109 (2018)
4. Cesta, A., Cortellessa, G., De Benedictis, R.: Training for crisis decision making - an approach based on plan adaptation. Knowl.-Based Syst. **58**, 98–112 (2014)
5. Cesta, A., Cortellessa, G., De Benedictis, R., Fracasso, F.: Active aging by continuous learning: a training environment for cultural visits. In: Leone, A., Caroppo, A., Rescio, G., Diraco, G., Siciliano, P. (eds.) ForItAAL 2018. LNEE, vol. 544, pp. 521–533. Springer, Cham (2019). https://doi.org/10.1007/978-3-030-05921-7_42
6. De Benedictis, R., Cesta, A.: Integrating logic and constraint reasoning in a timeline-based planner. In: Gavanelli, M., Lamma, E., Riguzzi, F. (eds.) AI*IA 2015. LNCS (LNAI), vol. 9336, pp. 424–437. Springer, Cham (2015). https://doi.org/10.1007/978-3-319-24309-2_32
7. De Benedictis, R., Cesta, A.: Investigating domain independent heuristics in a timeline-based planner. Intell. Artif. **10**, 129–145 (2016)
8. De Benedictis, R., Cortellessa, G., Fracasso, F., Cesta, A.: Technology-enhanced learning to support active ageing (in Italian). Form@re - Open J. per la Form. Rete **19**(1), 301–311 (2019)
9. De Medio, C., Gasparetti, F., Limongelli, C., Sciarrone, F.: Modeling teachers and learning materials: a comparison among similarity metrics. In: Information Visualisation - Biomedical Visualization, Visualisation on Built and Rural Environments and Geometric Modelling and Imaging, IV 2018, pp. 536–541 (2018)
10. Dechter, R.: Constraint Processing. Elsevier Morgan Kaufmann, Burlington (2003)
11. Gasparetti, F., De Medio, C., Limongelli, C., Sciarrone, F., Temperini, M.: Prerequisites between learning objects: automatic extraction based on a machine learning approach. Telematics Inform. **35**(3), 595–610 (2018)
12. Ghallab, M., Nau, D., Traverso, P.: Automated Planning: Theory and Practice. Morgan Kaufmann Publishers Inc., Burlington (2004)
13. Giles, J.: Special report internet encyclopaedias go head to head. Nature **438**, 900–901 (2005)
14. Grasha, A.: Teaching with Style: A Practical Guide to Enhancing Learning by Understanding Teaching and Learning Styles. Alliance Publishers, Pittsburgh (1996)
15. Lecoutre, C.: Constraint Networks: Techniques and Algorithms. Wiley-IEEE Press, Hoboken (2009)
16. Liang, C., Wu, Z., Huang, W., Giles, C.L.: Measuring prerequisite relations among concepts. In: Proceedings of the 2015 Conference on Empirical Methods in Natural Language Processing, pp. 1668–1674. Association for Computational Linguistics, Lisbon, Portugal, September 2015
17. Limongelli, C., Lombardi, M., Marani, A.: Towards the recommendation of resources in coursera. In: Micarell, A., et al. (eds.) ITS 2016, vol. 9684, p. 461. Springer, Cham (2016)

18. Mitchell, T.M.: Machine Learning, 1st edn. McGraw-Hill Inc., New York (1997)
19. Muscettola, N.: HSTS: integrating planning and scheduling. In: Zweben, M., Fox, M.S. (eds.) Intelligent Scheduling. Morgan Kauffmann (1994)
20. Ohlsson, S.: Some principles of intelligent tutoring. Instr. Sci. **14**(3), 293–326 (1986)
21. VanLehn, K.: The relative effectiveness of human tutoring, intelligent tutoring systems, and other tutoring systems. Educ. Psychol. **46**(4), 197–221 (2011)
22. Wenger, E.: Artificial Intelligence and Tutoring Systems: Computational and Cognitive Approaches to the Communication of Knowledge. Morgan Kaufmann Publishers Inc., San Francisco (1987)

Artificial Intelligence for Dramatic Performance

Rossana Damiano[1,3(✉)], Vincenzo Lombardo[1,3], Giulia Monticone[1], and Antonio Pizzo[2,3]

[1] Dipartimento di Informatica, Università di Torino, Turin, Italy
{rossana.damiano,vincenzo.lombardo}@unito.it,
giulia.monticone276@edu.unito.it
[2] Dipartimento di Studi Umanistici, Università di Torino, Turin, Italy
antonio.pizzo@unito.it
[3] CIRMA Interdepartmental Center of Research on Multimedia and Audiovisual,
Turin, Italy
http://www.cirma.unito.it

Abstract. In the last years, digital media have challenged traditional narrative models with an increasing request for interaction with the user, leading to novel paradigms of storytelling and performance. While most research in interactive storytelling and drama has addressed the role of automation in the story generation process, in this paper we present a framework that relies on Artificial Intelligence techniques to augment the performer–audience interaction in a storytelling setting. Step after step, the emotional response of the audience is automatically detected, the performer decides about her/his attitude towards the audience, and the story is composed and delivered to the audience by the joint system-performer initiative on an augmented stage. Initially designed as training tool for interactive story editing, the system has been deployed to create a public performance in February 2019.

Keywords: Interactive drama · Emotion recognition · Computational models of narrative

1 Introduction

For more than two decades, digital storytelling has been developing models and techniques for creating interactive narratives, in response to an increasing request for interactivity by digital media [16,21]. In parallel with this trend, innovation in performance has led to the integration of digital devices into the stage, resulting in groundbreaking changes in the relation between the performer and the public, as reviewed by [19]. Although the advent of digital media in dramatic performance has been described as "mediaturgy" by drama scholars [17], so as to stress the impact of computational schemes in traditional dramaturgy, most work in digital performance has addressed the physical enactment of drama on stage.

© Springer Nature Switzerland AG 2019
M. Alviano et al. (Eds.): AI*IA 2019, LNAI 11946, pp. 542–557, 2019.
https://doi.org/10.1007/978-3-030-35166-3_38

Fig. 1. A moment of the performance with DoPPioGioco (Turin, February 8th 2019). Notice in foreground the tablet employed by the performer to control the story continuation.

In this work, we describe a computational platform to support the performer role on an augmented stage, called DoPPioGioco ("Double Play"), which relies on Artificial Intelligence techniques in two main ways: on the one side, the factorization of the story into units that are composed on the fly based on the response of the audience, following an established paradigm in computer-based, interactive storytelling; on the other side, the deployment of affect detection techniques to capture the emotions expressed by the audience through facial expressions, and their use to inform the choices of the performer. Thus, DoPPio-Gioco fills a gap in the landscape of digital techniques for dramatic performance by leveraging computational models of narrative and affect to address the core of the performance, namely the performer-audience interaction in an innovative way [9]. DoPPioGioco intervenes in the performer-audience relationship as an "intelligent prompt" which suggests the performer the next story chunk, taking into account both the emotional response of the audience and the performer's decisions. In practice, after the performer has delivered a story chunk, the system detects the audience's emotional response and allows the performer to choose whether to please or to oppose that response, choosing also the level of intensity. Once the performer has made a choice, the system prompts the next suitable story chunk to be delivered, and so on through the story end. At the core of this model of interactivity lays an emotional system that is employed for tagging the story chunks and a real-time engine that prompts the story chunk to be delivered. Initially designed as training tool for interactive story editing and testing, in February 2019 DoPPioGioco was deployed to create a public performance (Fig. 1).[1]

This paper is organized as follows: in the next section, we provide the theoretical background behind the design of DoPPioGioco. In Sect. 3, we illustrate the detection of emotions and their mapping to story continuations within the paradigm of emergent narrative. Section 4 describes the architecture and implementation of the system; the deployment of DoPPioGioco in the public performance of February 2019 is presented and discussed in Sect. 5. Conclusion ends the paper.

2   Background and Motivations

Designed with the goal of supporting the performers' ability to interpret the script in response to the emotional response of the audience [1], the conception of DoPPioGioco and its design acknowledge the traditional distinction between author and performer in story design and delivery. The narrative component is handled offline by the author at the story editing time, by representing the story as a graph of storylines annotated with emotion tags. Online, the system computes the available continuations based on the emotional response of the audience, leaving the performer the final decision about which attitude to take towards the audience. Moving the focus from the design of the emotional response at the story level to the continuous, adjustable level of story delivery, DoppioGioco puts equal emphasis on the performer and on the audience, respectively, transforming the interactive delivery of the story into a tight interplay of emotional responses by the audience and counter-responses by the performer.

This approach partly relies on the paradigm of improvisational theatre, traditionally exploited in interactive digital storytelling to manage the complexity of emergent storytelling [2,27]. As observed by [27], the paradigm of improvisational theater increases the sense of dramatic presence and the engagement of the users. The dynamics of improvisational theater has been described by [6] in the perspective of interactive storytelling, using the Decision Cycle from Newell's Unified Theory of Cognition (*receive* new inputs, *elaborate* new knowledge, *propose* actions to take, *select* one of those actions, *execute* the action) as a conceptual framework for analyzing the way each improviser takes advantage of the scene advancing moves of the others.

While most research in interactive story generation tends to focus on the consistency of the plot in terms of characters' goals and actions (see for example [21]), DoPPioGioco departs from this approach to exploit the emotions of the audience as the pivotal element of the story construction. In interactive drama, the dominant approach to audience emotions consists in optimizing the engagement of the audience during the performance according to some predefined design patterns. In Mateas' pioneering work [18], Façade, the generation of the interactive drama was driven by a function that kept the emotional engagement of

---

[1]   http://www.cirma.unito.it/portfolio_page/doppiogioco/.

the user close to a target curve; in the Distributed Dramatic Management of the Emergent Narrative [30], predetermined emotional trajectories were employed as a metric for dramatic impact in the process of the character's action-selection. On the contrary, drawing inspiration from the notion of "subversive player" [28], developed in game studies to describe the user's attempts at breaking the boundaries of the interactivity allowed for by games, in DoPPioGioco the emotional response becomes a propellant of the performer-audience interaction, where the performer is free to manage the response of the audience following her/his inspiration within the space of possible story continuations.

3   Modelling the Emotional Response of the Audience

In the last decade, audience emotions have been explored in performance and audience studies, both as way to study the aesthetic experience of the individuals and as a way to assess the impact of cultural experience on society [12,14,25,29]. For example, the Sense-Making Methodology (SMM) [12] includes questions about the participant's feelings and emotions as part of the in-depth, surface-breaking questionnaire delivered to audience members of performing arts with the goal of assessing the quality of their experience. The investigation of aesthetic experience has been conducted also by measuring physiological cues of engagement, such as heart rate, skin conductance or eye movements [26,29]. However, since these measurements have raised further questions about the relation between engagement and the cognitive and cultural levels of audience response, some scholars have resorted to self-reported emotions to investigate this relation [14,25] in a more explicit way: their studies have pointed out that the range of audience emotions includes also emotion types that are intrinsically related with social and moral values, such as anger or embarrassment, and that a correlation with physiological cues of engagement can be found [14]. In addition to this trend, scholars in Computer Human Interaction have stressed the role of negative emotions in the fruition of art and entertainment, proposing negative emotions as an inescapable and intrinsic component of user experience, which can be planned and manipulated by computer-based systems [7,8].

Given the relevance and articulation of the emotional component in audience and user experience, the use of a formal model of emotions is crucial to the implementation of the story engine, since it guarantees that the story can be manipulated by the performer in predictable ways in spite of the emotional response of the audience. Different computational models of emotions have been proposed in the last two decades, for purposes that range from the annotation of emotions in media to the generation of emotions in synthetic characters. The former systems typically rely on dimensional models, such as Russell's circumflex model of affect [23] or Plutchik's wheel of emotions [20], which lend themselves to the general description of the affective content of media, while the latter systems tend to draw inspiration from cognitive models of emotions [24], easily integrated in goal-directed characters [3,5].

In DoPPioGioco, emotions are accounted for through the GEMEP model [4], a dimensional model of emotions originally devised to annotate a corpus of clips displaying the perfomance of emotions by human actors, known as the GEneva Multimodal Emotion Portrayals. Thanks to its syncretic and methodologically robust design, geared on performance and informed upon an extensive survey of emotion theories and models, GEMEP is especially suitable to annotate the affective content of performance. In GEMEP, emotions are grouped along two axes: *polarity* (positive/negative) and *intensity* (high/low). The combination of these two axes provides four emotion families, each including three emotion types; within each family, the emotion types are mainly characterized by different arousal levels:

- **Positive, high intensity**: amusement, pride, joy;
- **Positive, low intensity**: relief, interest, pleasure;
- **Negative, high intensity**: hot anger, panic fear, despair;
- **Negative, low intensity**: irritation, anxiety, sadness.

In DoPPioGioco, GEMEP model plays a twofold role: at story editing time, the emotion families are employed to tag the story chunks; during the performance, the rules that implement the performer's reaction in favour or against the audience rely on the four dimensions of GEMEP. GEMEP provides the core model of emotions of the system: when a specific emotion detection systems is plugged into the platform within a specific production, its output must mapped onto the GEMEP emotion families and types, leaving the core of the engine unchanged.

4   System Architecture

In DoPPioGioco, the story is formally structured as a directed graph [15], as exemplified by the visualization in Fig. 2. The interaction with the audience determines the transition to the next node: after the emotional response of the audience has been detected, the transitions that are not compatible with the audience emotions are filtered out, and the performer is prompted to decide whether to play in favour or against the audience, then the continuation is selected and delivered on stage by the system. This approach requires that the story units are annotated offline, by encoding not only their position in the story graph, but also the affective information brought by the unit.[2] So, each unit is labeled with a set of emotion tags, which represent the emotions that the author expects the audience to feel when the unit is delivered. Also, each unit is associated with a text and an audiovisual clip which accompanies the performance. A detailed description of the platform and of the annotation tool can be found in [11].

As anticipated in the previous section, the polarity–based account on emotions of GEMEP is suitable to deal with the polarity of the performer's attitude

---

[2] The GEMEP model also encompasses 5 extra emotion types that don't fit in the dimensional classification (Admiration, Tenderness, Disgust, Contempt, Surprise) and have been omitted from DoPPioGioco.

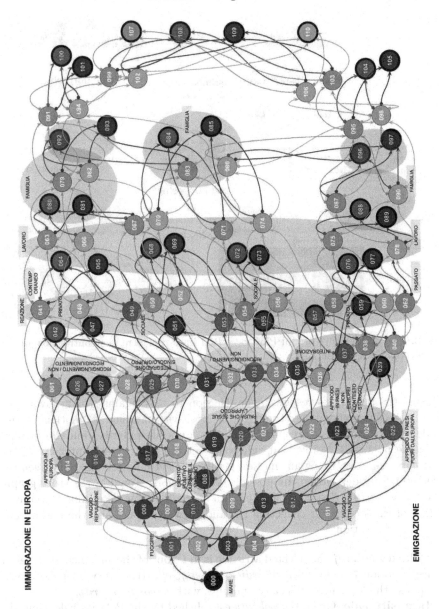

Fig. 2. The visualization of the story plot. Negative emotions are marked in blue (dark blue for the high intensity family and light blue for the low intensity family); positive emotions are marked in red (bright red for the high intensity family and light red for the low intensity family). Green circles represent the emergence of specific topics within the plot, manually annotated on the graph by the authors (in Italian). (Color figure online)

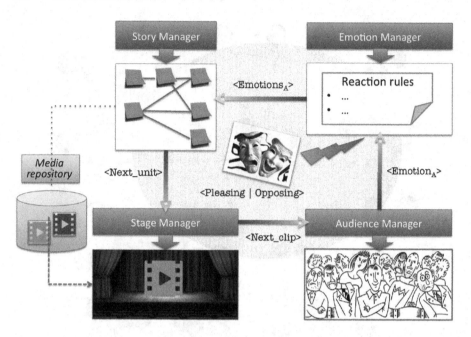

Fig. 3. The architecture of DoPPioGioco. Red lines represent the control flow of the system. (Color figure online)

towards the audience's response: the decision to play against (or in favour of) the audience is mapped onto the negative/positive dimension of emotions in this model, with "against" corresponding to the "opposite polarity" and "in favour" to "same polarity". Notice that rules only set the polarity and intensity of the next clip, thus identifying an emotion family: the actual available units given the selected family depend on the possible continuations stored in the story graph. The following *Reaction rules*, applied in a cascading flow, determine the continuation of the story after collecting the audience's response and the performer's subsequent reaction:

– **Polarity rule**: *If* the selected attitude is in favour of the audience, *then* select the emotion families with the *same polarity*; *else* (the storyteller decides to oppose the audience), select the families with *opposite polarity*.
– **Intensity rule**: Given the *polarity* established by the Polarity rule, tune the intensity level of the reaction to the selected *intensity* (low or high).

The architecture of the system encompasses four main modules (see Fig. 3): the Story Manager, the Stage Manager, the Emotion Manager, and the Audience Manager. The knowledge about the story and the media assets, created and uploaded offline through the annotation interface of the platform, are embedded, respectively, into the Story Manager and into the Stage Manager (where they are stored in the Media Repository). The system loop orchestrates the interaction of the four modules in the following way:

1. The **Audience Manager** accounts for the reaction of the audience. For training purposes, an audience simulation module can be plugged into the system, as described in [11]. When the platform is employed to support live performance, an emotion detection module is employed (see Sect. 5). Provided that it can be mapped onto the polarity/intensity dimensions in GEMEP, different emotion detection modules can be plugged into the system depending on the characteristics and the artistic goals of the single production.
2. The **Emotion Manager** takes as input the audience's response and the attitude (in favour or against) selected by the performer in reaction, and applies the Reaction Rules to compute the candidate emotion family, which becomes the input to the Story Manager.
3. The **Story Manager** retrieves the next candidate units from the story graph given the emotion family selected by the Emotion Manager. In order to emphasize the elements of arbitrariness that characterize a live performance, and to introduce differences over the performances, the system randomly selects the next unit among the available ones, so that the performer does not have complete control on the selection.
4. The **Stage Manager** takes as input the unit selected by the Story Manager and sends the related media (text, videoclip, sound, etc.) to the player, thus providing the properly called intelligent prompt to the performer on stage.

Each module of the system is implemented as a web service, so as to allow the portability of the system across different devices and media. The services are written in PHP and rely on a mySql database. The current interfaces have been developed as web pages and rely on the Ajax technology to support a fluid interaction with the user during both the real time and the annotation phases. In order to favour the portability of the system and its adaptation to different settings and productions, the system is deployed using the Docker container management system.[3] All the services composing the platform, from the database server to the playback and face recognition services, are orchestrated through Docker, with advantages for scalability and real time execution.

5 Going Live

On February 8th 2019, DoPPioGioco was exploited to create a public performance at the Studium Lab at the University of Turin. Studium Lab is an open lab equipped with a technological infrastructure (cameras, lighting, projection system), multimedia stations for editing and pre-visualization, and a configurable space that can accommodate up to 50 persons. Figure 1 shows a moment of the performance (see also Fig. 4).

---

[3] https://github.com/docker.

Fig. 4. The augmented stage during the location setup. Notice the projection of the recognized emotion type on the floor ("contempt") on a light grey background. (Color figure online)

5.1   Production and Setting

The production of the performance was carried out at the lab from 4th to 8th February 2019 and the performance took place on February 8th 2019 with 4 sessions of about 25' in the afternoon. The production was based on the story designed and edited by a team of graduate students of the school of Arts and Media under the guidance of an expert writer and drama theorist as part of the Interactive Storytelling Lab. Intended as a training activity in interactive media editing, the story editing was accomplished in 4 weeks from November 2018 to January 2019 by using the web based version of DoPPioGioco described in [10].

The assignment given to the students concerned the subject of migrations: given the story graph created during the lab, the production phase consisted in pruning and refining the graph to obtain a set of storylines with a duration included in the target range of 10'–20' (roughly equivalent to 4–8 story units), organized so as to develop a set of relevant topics revolving around migrations, as depicted in Fig. 2. The final story graph consisted of 110 units. Audiovisual clips were produced from the annotations attached to the units in the previous editing phase by composing existing public domain material on migrations. In addition to the audiovisual clip, each unit was accompanied by a script of proportional

Fig. 5. Pre-visualization of the performance setting.

length which was performed by a professional actress. A sound clip was produced for each emotion family by a sound designer. By using the web based platform for the editing and annotation tasks, the units, their metadata and accompanying media were subsequently smoothly exported to the production version of DoPPioGioco.

The stage was equipped with a large projection screen for the playback of the clips located behind the performer and a second projector oriented towards the stage floor, where emotional feedback collected from the audience was given to audience and performer. The text of the the unit being played was displayed to the performer on two displays posited on the stage, not visible to the audience. A camera oriented to the audience recorded the audience during the performance; the location could sit up to 12 people. The stage layout and equipment can be seen in the visualization shown in Fig. 5, created during the production design phase to arrange the stage and the sitting area.

In parallel with the production of the units and the system deployment, rehearsal took place so as to allow the performer to acquire familiarity with the technical apparatus and become expert in the use of the system. The available storylines were rehearsed several times to tune their length to the target duration, making minor modifications when needed. Extensive rehearsing was required also to adapt the performance to the narrative content and emotional tags of the units. Sessions were regulated by the following protocol: after selecting the first unit, the performer started the system trough a tablet she used to control the system. The script associated to the unit was enacted by the performer in the style of narrative theatre, while the clip was streamed on the projection screen. 10 seconds before the end of the clip, the system started recording the audience, sending frames to the emotion detection service for analysis. When the clip ended, the resulting emotion was revealed to the audience and performer through the floor projection system; the name of the emotion type and a matching color were appeared on the floor of the stage. Based on the emotional response of the audience, the performed decided whether to play against or in favour of the audience by selecting the desired option through the tablet, thus triggering the start of the subsequent unit.

5.2   Emotion Recognition at Work

The production platform was deployed with Docker using the local network of the lab; the face expression detection system was provided by the Face API of the Cognitive Services suite by Microsoft Azur, which returns a values for each emotion type (happiness, surprise, neutral, anger, disgust, fear, contempt and sadness) for each detected face in the frame.[4]

In order to ensure a timely interpretation of the emotional response of the audience, we decided to sample frames in the incoming stream from the audience camera at fixed intervals of 2'', so as to reduce the transmission and response time, and synchronously calling the Face APIs to collect face analysis results in the right sequence. Figure 6 illustrates the process of collecting the emotional response of the audience and mapping it onto the tagging system of DoPPio-Gioco. The emotion analysis pipeline, aimed at accounting for the activation of emotions along all the recording time, consists of the following steps:

1. The video streaming is sampled and selected frames are captured and sent to the Face API for analysis (5 frames are sent to the API in the current implementation);
2. Results returned by the face analysis service (in JSON format) are stored by system; the JSON file contains a feature–value list of all emotions types for each detected face. Values below a given threshold are discarded so as to avoid obtaining a significant overall value for frequent emotions with a low activation level, and to promote emotional peaks;
3. Finally, for each emotion type, the final value is computed by summing its values through all faces and collected frames, and the emotion type with the highest final value is returned.

After computing the most relevant emotion, the emotion type was mapped onto the emotion tagging system of DoPPioGioco, which is informed on the GEMEP emotion model as described in Sect. 3. Given the two dimensions acknowledged by the model (polarity and intensity), and the analysis of the emotion types in the literature, the 8 emotion types returned by the Face API were mapped on the emotion families in DoPPioGioco as follows:

---

[4] https://azure.microsoft.com/id-id/services/cognitive-services/face/.

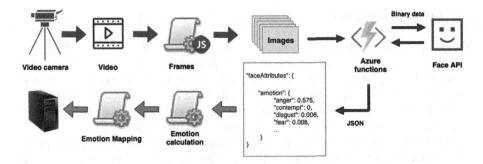

Fig. 6. Audience emotion analysis

- Positive, high intensity: happiness, surprise
- Positive, low intensity: neutral
- Negative, high intensity: anger, disgust, fear
- Negative, low intensity: contempt, sadness

5.3 Audience Reception

The public performance consisted in 4 sessions of about 25' in the afternoon of February 8th 2019. In each session, an audience of 12 people attended two subsequent performances; however, thanks to the variability of the performer's choices, the differences in the audience's emotional responses and the random elements in DoPPioGioco, all sessions were significantly different, each time following a different narrative and emotional trajectory across the story graph. The average length of each performance consisted of 4,3 units, with a minimum of 3 and a maximum of 7 units; duration ranged from 8' to 24' with an average of 15,5'.

Although the data collected during the sessions are far from significance due to the size of the sample, they show that, for all runs, audience emotions were consistent with the tagging of the units when the intensity was high, for both polarities. 27 times out of 35 the emotional response of the audience matched the polarity of the emotion tags attached to the units concerning (77%). If we consider not only the polarity but also the intensity (high or low), the exact match was obtained for 14 units (40% of responses and 52% of the matches on the polarity dimension). A closer examination of the cases in which the emotional response of the audience did not match the annotation reveals that in 4 cases out 7 the recognized emotion was "surprise", that is often considered neutral in the literature with respect to the positive/negative distinction [22]; in the remaining 3 cases, the audience responded with a positive emotion to a unit annotated with a negative emotion. Finally, the performer's attitude did not seem to affect the emotional response of the audience: the performer decided to oppose the audience in 13 cases out of 27, but no correlation can be found between her attitude and the response of the audience.

6 Lesson Learned

Facing a real production and a real audience was a challenge for the design of DoPPioGioco, with an added value in terms of awareness about the assumptions underlying the platform. Although the production turned out to be a valuable experience for both the story editing team and the performer and a novel experience for the audience, some issues emerged that were partly accounted for by adjusting the design of the sessions and of the platform itself.

First of all, due to environmental conditions, capturing the face expressions of the audience was harder than expected, notwithstanding the moderate lighting on the sitting area. Also, although the audience were aware of the interactive nature of the performance, the initiative was still mostly in the hands of the performer, so participants were less active than expected, since the test sessions. In order to compensate for these factors, we decided to increase the awareness of the audience by inserting an explicit signal that emotion recording was in progress (a progress bar and the recording symbol), so as to stimulate the audience to assume an active attitude in the emotional response. Similarly, in [13] the explicit emotional feedback of the audience is employed to direct a music performance. In addition, we decided to change the protocol by inserting an initial training phase in which participants were encouraged to try individually the Face API. A dedicated installation was posited outside the theatre with an application that prompted the user to fake facial expressions for fun, with the goal of acquiring familiarity with the face expression detection service.

A more subtle issue was given by the partial mismatch between the emotion model of DoPPioGioco and the actual emotion types returned by the face expression recognition software. Since the poetics of the story was built on the emotion model embedded in the system, by asking the team of authors to tag units with the available emotion tags, a mismatch could be observed during the sessions. For example, the face expression expressing strong sadness triggered by the vision of some clips displaying war refugees and children in war episodes were interpreted as contempt by the Face APIs instead of the intended sadness and anxiety. So, despite the assumed universality of face expressions, this mismatch reveals that emotion tags and types must be carefully selected in artistic projects.

Finally, in order to enhance the involvement of the audience, we decide to provide a final reward at the end of the session by printing on screen the intensity of their overall emotional feedback. This integration was also intended as a way to adjust the balance of power in favour of the audience. In DoPPioGioco, the performer's freedom to encourage or discourage the emotional response of the audience creates a space where audience and performer negotiate their interaction in an overt way: thanks to the adjustments brought about in the redesign phase, the opportunity for the performer to frustrate the expectations of the audience, a modality listed by [7] as a major source of discomfort, is rebalanced by the opportunity given to the audience to repay her/him in the same way with unexpected responses, and receive at the same time a reward for getting in the game.

7   Conclusion and Future Work

In this paper, we described the deployment and consequent adaptation e redesign of DoPPioGioco for a real performance. DoPPioGioco, an intelligent prompt system that allows the performer to adapt the story continuation to the emotional response of the audience, was employed in the production of a dramatic performance in a interactive multimedia setting.

The Artificial Intelligence techniques embedded in the system, namely the factorization and online composition of the story and the modelling and recognition of the audience emotions, proved to be functional to the artistic goals of the writer and performer roles, thus effectively providing novel and valuable experience to both performer and audience. However, the testing of the platform on the field suggests that the overall interaction design must be conducted very carefully to ensure proper engagement and that the emotion model must be tuned to the emotional range of the specific production.

As future work, we intend to test different modalities for collecting the emotional response of the audience, including large-scale and continuous detection systems, more suitable to explore the temporal dynamics of the emotional response to the performance in progress. Also, the adoption of a purely dimensional model of emotions will be explored as a replacement for the current mixed dimensional and categorial model, so as to support a larger range of interactive performance formats and settings.

References

1. Alrutz, M., Listengarten, J., Wood, M.V.D.: Playing with Theory in Theatre Practice. Palgrave Macmillan, London (2011)
2. Aylett, R., Louchart, S.: I contain multitudes: creativity and emergent narrative. In: Proceedings of the 9th ACM Conference on Creativity & Cognition, pp. 337–340. ACM (2013)
3. Aylett, R.S., Louchart, S., Dias, J., Paiva, A., Vala, M.: FearNot! – an experiment in emergent narrative. In: Panayiotopoulos, T., Gratch, J., Aylett, R., Ballin, D., Olivier, P., Rist, T. (eds.) IVA 2005. LNCS (LNAI), vol. 3661, pp. 305–316. Springer, Heidelberg (2005). https://doi.org/10.1007/11550617_26
4. Bänziger, T., Scherer, K.R.: Introducing the Geneva multimodal emotion portrayal (gemep) corpus. In: Blueprint for Affective Computing, pp. 271–294 (2010)
5. Battaglino, C., Damiano, R., Lesmo, L.: Emotional range in value-sensitive deliberation. In: AAMAS International Conference on Autonomous Agents and Multiagent Systems, IFAAMAS, vol. 2, pp. 769–776 (2013)
6. Baumer, A., Magerko, B.: Narrative development in improvisational theatre. In: Iurgel, I.A., Zagalo, N., Petta, P. (eds.) ICIDS 2009. LNCS, vol. 5915, pp. 140–151. Springer, Heidelberg (2009). https://doi.org/10.1007/978-3-642-10643-9_19
7. Benford, S., Greenhalgh, C., Giannachi, G., Walker, B., Marshall, J., Rodden, T.: Uncomfortable interactions. In: Proceedings of the SIGCHI Conference on Human Factors in Computing Systems, pp. 2005–2014. ACM (2012)
8. Benford, S., et al.: Discomfort—the dark side of fun. In: Blythe, M., Monk, A. (eds.) Funology 2. HIS, pp. 209–224. Springer, Cham (2018). https://doi.org/10.1007/978-3-319-68213-6_13

9. Borowski, M., Sugiera, M.: Worlds in Words: Storytelling in Contemporary Theatre and Playwriting. Cambridge Scholars Publishing, Cambridge (2010)
10. Damiano, R., Lombardo, V., Pizzo, A.: DoppioGioco. Playing with the audience in an interactive storytelling platform. In: Barolli, L., Terzo, O. (eds.) CISIS 2017. AISC, vol. 611, pp. 287–298. Springer, Cham (2018). https://doi.org/10.1007/978-3-319-61566-0_27
11. Damiano, R., Lombardo, V., Pizzo, A.: Thinning the fourth wall with intelligent prompt. In: Nunes, N., Oakley, I., Nisi, V. (eds.) ICIDS 2017. LNCS, vol. 10690, pp. 206–218. Springer, Cham (2017). https://doi.org/10.1007/978-3-319-71027-3_17
12. Foreman-Wernet, L., Dervin, B.: In the context of their lives: how audience members make sense of performing arts experiences. In: The Audience Experience: A Critical Analysis of Audiences in The Performing Arts, pp. 67–82. Chicago: Intellect (2013)
13. Giardina, M., et al.: Conveying audience emotions through humanoid robot gestures to an orchestra during a live musical exhibition. In: Barolli, L., Terzo, O. (eds.) CISIS 2017. AISC, vol. 611, pp. 249–261. Springer, Cham (2018). https://doi.org/10.1007/978-3-319-61566-0_24
14. Latulipe, C., Carroll, E.A., Lottridge, D.: Love, hate, arousal and engagement: exploring audience responses to performing arts. In: Proceedings of the SIGCHI Conference on Human Factors in Computing Systems, pp. 1845–1854. ACM (2011)
15. Li, B., Lee-Urban, S., Johnston, G., Riedl, M.: Story generation with crowdsourced plot graphs. In: AAAI (2013)
16. Louchart, S., Truesdale, J., Suttie, N., Aylett, R.: Emergent narrative: past, present and future of an interactive storytelling approach. In: Interactive Digital Narrative. History, Theory and Practice, pp. 185–199. Routledge (2015)
17. Marranca, B.: Performance as design: the mediaturgy of john jesurun's firefall. PAJ: J. Perform. Art 32(3), 16–24 (2010)
18. Mateas, M., Stern, A.: Façade: an experiment in building a fully-realized interactive drama. In: Game Developers Conference, vol. 2 (2003)
19. Pizzo, A., Lombardo, V., Damiano, R.: Algorithms and interoperability between drama and artificial intelligence. Drama Rev. 63(4), 14–32 (2019)
20. Plutchik, R.: Emotion: A psychoevolutionary synthesis. Harpercollins College Division (1980)
21. Riedl, M.O., Young, R.M.: Narrative planning: balancing plot and character. J. Artif. Intell. Res. 39(1), 217–268 (2010)
22. Roseman, I.J.: Appraisal in the emotion system: coherence in strategies for coping. Emot. Rev. 5(2), 141–149 (2013)
23. Russell, J.A.: Core affect and the psychological construction of emotion. Psychol. Rev. 110(1), 145 (2003)
24. Scherer, K.R.: Appraisal Theory. Handbook of Cognition and Emotion, pp. 637–663 (1999)
25. Silvia, P.J.: Looking past pleasure: anger, confusion, disgust, pride, surprise, and other unusual aesthetic emotions. Psychol. Aesthet. Creat. Arts 3(1), 48 (2009)
26. Stevens, C., Glass, R., Schubert, E., Chen, J., Winskel, H.: Methods for measuring audience reactions. In: Proceedings of the Inaugural International Conference on Music Communication Science, p. 155. HCSNet (2007)
27. Swartjes, I., Theune, M.: An experiment in improvised interactive drama. In: Nijholt, A., Reidsma, D., Hondorp, H. (eds.) INTETAIN 2009. LNICST, vol. 9, pp. 234–239. Springer, Heidelberg (2009). https://doi.org/10.1007/978-3-642-02315-6_25

28. Tanenbaum, J.: How i learned to stop worrying and love the gamer: reframing subversive play in story-based games. In: Proceedings of DiGRA (2013)
29. Tschacher, W., Greenwood, S., Kirchberg, V., Wintzerith, S., van den Berg, K., Tröndle, M.: Physiological correlates of aesthetic perception of artworks in a museum. Psychol. Aesthet. Creat. Arts **6**(1), 96 (2012)
30. Weallans, A., Louchart, S., Aylett, R.: Distributed drama management: beyond double appraisal in emergent narrative. In: Interactive Storytelling, pp. 132–143 (2012)

Periodicity Detection of Emotional Communities in Microblogging

Corrado Loglisci[1,2]([⊠]) and Donato Malerba[1,2]

[1] Department of Computer Science, Universita' degli Studi di Bari "Aldo Moro",
Bari, Italy
{corrado.loglisci,donato.malerba}@uniba.it
[2] CINI - Consorzio Interuniversitario Nazionale per l'Informatica, Rome, Italy

Abstract. Social media allow users convey emotions, which are often related to real-world events, social relationships or personal experiences. Indeed, emotions can determine the propension of the users to socialize or attend events. Similarly, interactions with people can influence the personality and feelings of the individuals. Therefore, studying emotional content generated by the users can reveal information on the behavior of users or collectives of users. However, such an information is related only to a specific moment when the emotions are sporadic or episodic, therefore they could have little usefulness. On the contrary, it can have greater significance tracing emotions over time and understanding whether they may appear with regularity or whether they are associated to behaviors already observed in past and could recur.

In this paper, we focus on the periodicity with which emotional words appear in the micro-blogs as indication of a collective emotional behavior expressed with regularity. We propose a computational solution that builds a cyberspace based on the emotional content produced by the users and determines communities of users who express with periodicity similar emotional behaviors. We show the viability of the method on the data of the social media platform Twitter and provide a quantitative evaluation and qualitative considerations.

1 Introduction

The widespread of social media has been one the main contributors to stimulate the formation of new forms of collectives. Individuals overcome the diffidence to establish face-to-face relationships with new modalities of interaction based on online boards, forums and chats. The communication language becomes essentially textual, but this does not obstacle the individuals to convey typical verbal expressions, feelings and emotions. Interactions and emotions are therefore interrelated and inherently variable. The emotional status of an individual can change because of the interaction with others, as well as personal sensations and experiences can limit the use of social media platforms and can even change the relationships with users with whom there is already interaction. Relationships and emotions can be also co-active [9], in the sense that, at the same time,

M. Alviano et al. (Eds.): AI*IA 2019, LNAI 11946, pp. 558–571, 2019.
https://doi.org/10.1007/978-3-030-35166-3_39

individuals can have affinity with someone and aversion with some others, an individual can express joy when observed in a group of users and, on the contrary, to be angry when observed in another group. Thus, it emerges that the study of the emotions and interactions can play a relevant role in the dynamics of the social communities, especially because emotional affinities can guide the individuals in the choice of the users with whom they socialize and communities to follow. To conduct this kind of study, we should consider the content that individuals (users) generate when they use online boards, forums and chats and we cannot directly adopt classical techniques of community detection why they rely on the relationships based on social ties, which would constraint the analysis to the inter-connected users, with the risk to introduce bias in the variety and dynamics of emotional status.

However, the complexity of the psychological processes makes difficult, even with information technologies, studying what triggers the manifestation of an emotion. Indeed, emotions are often unpredictable, why perhaps related to unexpected behaviors or to events that occur sporadically. Other times instead, they could not be unexpected, why related to behaviors already expressed in past and thus likely to repeat. Thus, what is worth of being investigated is the occurrence and repeatability of the emotions rather than their raising. Indeed, emotions which occur over time with a certain regularity or that are manifested at regular periods can provide information on the predictability of emotions, behaviors and interactions with other individuals.

Extracting emotions from social media and tracing their repetitions is a challenging new research topic because social media has become widespread only in the past decade and the studies on the occurrence and repeatability of the emotional status we register are really few and come from border disciplines of the Artificial Intelligence and Natural Language Processing [5, 21]. In this paper, we are interested in tracking groups of users with homogeneous emotional status, *emotional communities*, over time by identifying those *periodic*, that is, those repeated at regular periods of time. To do that, we could group users which have similar emotions in each time point, but this would disregard possible emotions stimulated by interactions and would consider the punctual information while neglecting the durable aspect of the emotional status. To this end, we focus on the simplest form of interaction, that is, a pair of users, and extract pairs which convey similar emotional content over time. The resulting emotional communities are groups of pairs which convey the homogeneous emotional status at regular time-periods.

The computational solution relies on a cyberspace that quantifies the categorical information of the emotional words used in the microblogs in English. The dimensions of the cyberspace depict the axis along which emotions are represented, so the points of the cyberspace mirror emotional content conveyed by pairs of users. Then, we consider dense groups of points (groups of pairwise users having similar emotional content) and search for equi-distanced occurrences of those groups.

In the Sect. 2 we provide notions fundamental behind the cyberspace and concepts necessary for the detection of periodic ECs. The computational solution is illustrated in Sect. 3, while a preliminary empirical evaluation on the microblogs (in English) produced on Twitter is presented in Sect. 4. A discussion on the related work (Sect. 5) and conclusions (Sect. 6) complete this work.

2   Basics

The cyberspace is structured in two levels, termed as *content-space* and *feature-space*, respectively. The definition of the content-space relies on theoretical models proposed in the literature of Psychology on the human behavior, according to which the emotions can be distinguished in distinct and well-identifiable classes. Without loss of generality, we will refer to the pioneering model of Ekman [3] formulated on seven basic categories of emotions, namely *joy, fear, anger, sadness, disgust, shame, guilt*, which, in this work, stand for the dimensions of the content-space. One more dimension is introduced to represent the discrete time axis, composed of equally spaced time-instants. Thus, an 7-dimensional point of the content-space depicts the emotional content expressed in the messages associated to a user. We denote as $p(u) : \langle (p_1, \tau_1), (p_2, \tau_2), \ldots, (p_m, \tau_m) \rangle$ the sequence of points associated to user u, where $p_i \in [0, 1]^7$ is the point at the time-instant τ_i for the user u).

However, in the current form, the content-space is able to only arrange punctual information, whilst we are interested in representing interactions and time-aware emotional status. To this aim, we introduce a new class of features, termed as *Emotional Discrepancy (ED)*, in order to capture the difference between two users in the use of emotional words of an emotion category. So, when there is no difference, it means that the two users convey the same emotional content, that is, the way a user expresses an emotion in the social media over time is similar to the one of the other user.

ED is determined for each emotion category and is computed as the difference between the two angles formed by the straight lines (each drawn on the two points of a user) and reference axis over the time-instants $\langle \tau_i, \tau_{i+1} \rangle$ (Fig. 1). ED has values in the range $[-90, 90]$ and returns 0 when the quantity expressed by two users respectively remains unchanged, while returns $90°$ (or $-90°$) when the quantities have opposite variations, one goes from 0 to 1, the other one goes from 1 to 0 (or viceversa). For instance, in Fig. 1, the emotional discrepancy for joy is θ_r-θ_s. Intuitively, the larger the difference, the greater the discrepancy in expressing the emotion. It should be noted that the emotional discrepancy equals zero even when the two straight lines are parallel but not coincident, that is, when the quantities remain constant although with different values.

By considering the new class of features ED, we can build seven new features upon the emotion categories of the content-space. The feature-space is completed with a dimension (the eighth one) corresponding to the time interval-based axis, built on the discrete time axis. So, a new feature ED maps the points of two users u_r and u_s, drawn at the consecutive time instants $\langle \tau_i, \tau_{i+1} \rangle$ of the content-space

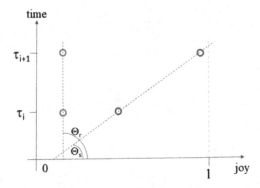

Fig. 1. Representation of the feature-space with the feature ED built on the emotion *joy* and discrete time axis).

for the emotion category c, into a numeric value over the time-interval $\langle \tau_i, \tau_{i+1} \rangle$ (we use the notation $ED_c|_{\langle \tau_i, \tau_{i+1} \rangle}(p(u_r), p(u_s)))$).

The notions introduced above are fundamental for the concepts reported in the following:

A *Pair Set* $\mathcal{G} = \{(u_r, \mathcal{R}) \mid u_r \notin \mathcal{R}\}$ is a set of paired users that have one user in common (that is, u_r).

Definition 1 [*Emotional Community*]. *Let $\mathcal{G}$ be a pair set, ED_c be the feature ED for the emotion category c: $\mathcal{G}$ is an emotional community iff there exists a finite sequence of time-intervals T : $\{\langle \tau_i, \tau_{i+1} \rangle, \ldots, \langle \tau_n, \tau_{n+1} \rangle\}$ s.t. $\forall (u_r, u_s) \in \mathcal{G}, (ED_c|_{\langle \tau_j, \tau_{j+1} \rangle}(p(u_r), p(u_s))) \leq \epsilon, \forall \langle \tau_j, \tau_{j+1} \rangle \in T.$*

An emotional community (EC) is centered on one user (u_r) and includes users whose emotional content is similar to the one of the user u_r, which hence turns out to be a reference individual. Intuitively, an EC collects users who conform to similar emotional content over time, not necessarily continuous. Clearly, we expect that the sequences T of different ECs are well-distinct, without overlapping time-intervals, that is, a pair of users should not appear at the same times in different ECs.

To capture emotional behaviors which are regularly repeated over time, we have to search for ECs with equi-spaced time-intervals. Thus, not all the ECs are of interest, but only those for which the sequence T has *(i)* at least a minimum number of repetitions ρ (time-intervals), and *(ii)* all the time-interval δ-separated, that is, $\forall \langle \tau_i, \tau_{i+1} \rangle, \langle \tau_j, \tau_{j+1} \rangle \in T, \delta - 1 \leq j - i \leq \delta + 1$ and there are no time-intervals $(\tau_h, \tau_{h+1}), i < h < j$, s.t. $\delta - 1 \leq j - h \leq \delta + 1, \delta - 1 \leq h - i \leq \delta + 1$.

The term δ stands for the periodicity with which the emotional content of EC is exhibited over time and establishes the maximum distance and minimum distance between two consecutive repetitions. This does not guarantee the identical distance between two consecutive repetitions, but, on the other hand, allows us to capture also ECs with some disturbances between the repetitions, which is a particular periodicity known in the literature as *asynchronous* [6].

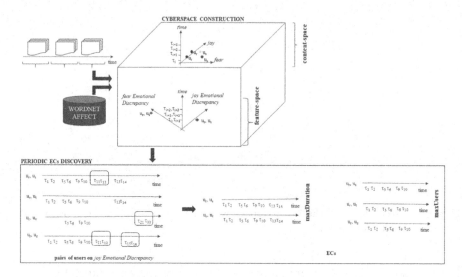

Fig. 2. The block diagram of the computational solution to detect periodic ECs. The first module is in charge of processing of user-generated content and projecting messages into the cyberspace. The second module is in charge of building valid ECs from the periodicities on the pairs of users.

3   The Computational Solution

The computational solution to discover ECs consists of two main modules (Fig. 2). The module CYBERSPACE CONSTRUCTION processes user-generated content and projects messages into the cyberspace. The module PERIODIC ECs DISCOVERY finds out periodic repetitions of similar emotional status on the pairs of users and then combines them together to build valid ECs.

3.1   Projection of Message Content into Cyberspace

To project message content into the cyber-space we need to build the two levels, content-space and feature-space. The content level provides a numeric representation of the emotional content of the messages. To implement it, we should recognize mentions or references of the emotions of the Ekman's model within the messages and build a quantification. This can be basically done with two approaches [18], *(i)* language processing approach and *(ii)* machine learning. The first approach relies on lexical resources, while the second approach asks for more. Indeed, machine learning algorithms require the creation of annotated message corpus and resolution of annotation discrepancies to train accurate classification/regression models. The use of classification algorithms, in particular, introduces another downside for the problem at the hand, that is, the constraint to use only the categorical information of the emotion-labels, while overlooking some peculiarities of the social messages, for instance, the presence of multiple emotions and the use of different words to emphasize an emotional status. This could result in making the quantification of the emotions which have not really been expressed in the text.

These are the reasons why we adopt a language processing approach and use the lexical resources of the database WordnetAffect [22], which straightforwardly arranges the emotions of the Ekman's model. However, this choice does not exclude the possibility of using any other lexicon supporting the same psychological model [19]. In WordnetAffect, the emotions are termed as *affective labels*, to which sets of synonyms (synsets) are assigned. The categories of the Ekman's model are identified with the labels *joy, negative-fear, anger, sadness, disgust, shame, guilt*. This way, to detect mentions or references of the emotions, we spot the key-words of the *synsets* associated to the seven categories. The quantification is obtained by computing the relative frequency of the emotions for a user. It is the number of the occurrences of the key-words out of the number of messages posted by the user in a time-interval and has values in the range [0,1]. In the case a message has more emotional key-words, we count it as many times.

Procedurally, for each word of the message that has part-of-speech tag as noun, verb, adverb or adjective, we first search for the synset in which that word occurs (by using its lemmatized form and pos-tagging annotation), then, we take the emotion category associated to the synset. In the case the word occurs in more synsets, we consider the most frequent synset, according to the ordering established in WordNet [17]. This way, the values of the relative frequency of the several emotions determine the collocation of the user over the seven dimensions of the content-space. For instance, the frequencies computed on the messages posted in the time spans [Sept_9th_2012,Sept_11th_2012] and [Sept_12th_2012,Sept_14th_2012] determine the points at the two consecutive time-instants τ_i and τ_{i+1}.

Once the relative frequencies for all the users have been determined and projected into the content-space, we compute the values of the class of features ED for each emotion category by using the formulation reported in Sect. 2. As a result, we have eight-dimensional feature vectors (points of the second level of the cyber-space) which represent the discrepancy of the emotional content computed for each pair of users u_r and u_s over the time-interval $\langle \tau_i, \tau_{i+1} \rangle$.

3.2 Detection of Periodic Emotional Collectives

To detect periodic ECs, an approach is building pair sets and then searching for the repetitions of similar emotional content for each pair set. It asks for the preliminary identification of admissible pair sets and requires that the repetitions of all the pairs of users (of a pair set) are always coincident (identical time-intervals $\langle \tau_j, \tau_{j+1} \rangle$). However, this could lead to miss ECs which are smaller (in the sense of number of users) but which have longer sequences of repetitions. Thus, we prefer a *generate-and-test* strategy that searches for the sequences T of repetitions for each pair of user and builds the sequence T for a pair set by considering the repetitions which are in common to the paired user (member of the pair set).

As preliminary operation, we remove the pairs of users (resulting from the first module, Fig. 2) whose time-intervals are less than the threshold ρ (Sect. 2). Then, we start with the first time-intervals (according to the temporal order) of the pair of users currently considered and incrementally evaluate the current time-intervals $\langle \tau_j, \tau_{j+1} \rangle$ with the latest time-intervals $\langle \tau_i, \tau_{i+1} \rangle$ inserted into the set T. So, if they are δ-separated, then the $\langle \tau_j, \tau_{j+1} \rangle$ is inserted into the set T, otherwise it will be considered to start the construction of the set T of a new candidate EC by using the previous pair of users, but different repetitions. Finally, the sequences T which have less than ρ are filtered out.

Once the candidate pairs of sets have been selected, we group them by pair sets (user u_r in common) and detect the respective periodicities by generating the sequence T with the repetitions which are in common to the users of the pair set. This can be done by adapting the technique of computation of the intersections between sequences, each possibly discontinued, proposed in [11]. Our adaptation first matches a primary sequence against those remaining and then evaluates the intersection between the time-intervals of the primary sequence and time-intervals of the other sequences by means of two binary search operations. These operations work on two sorted lists of time-intervals, one is composed of the first time-instants τ_i of the time-intervals $\langle \tau_i, \tau_{i+1} \rangle$, the other is composed of the second time-instants τ_{i+1}. The intersecting time-instants are thus sorted by temporal order and combined to form the candidates. Finally, we select the sequence that satisfies a user preference criterion, which, implicitly, chooses also the pair set of the EC. There are two alternative preference criteria, the first one (*maxDuration*) chooses the pair set having the longest sequence, while the second one (*maxUsers*) chooses the pair set with more users. This criterion is also used for the initial selection of the primary sequence. Indeed, the option *maxDuration* picks the longest sequence present in the pair sets, while the option *maxUsers* picks the shortest sequence. Finally, the sequences T which do not exceed the threshold ρ are discarded.

An example is reported in Fig. 2 (module PERIODIC ECs DISCOVERY), which we comment in the following. We have four pairs of users $\{(u_r, u_s), (u_r, u_t), (u_r, u_v), (u_r, u_z)\}$. Supposing $\delta = 4$, we remove the time-intervals $\langle \tau_{11}, \tau_{12} \rangle$, $\langle \tau_{21}, \tau_{22} \rangle$, and $\langle \tau_{11}, \tau_{12} \rangle$ and $\langle \tau_{15}, \tau_{16} \rangle$, for the pairs (u_r, u_s), (u_r, u_v) and (u_r, u_z) respectively. Then, supposing $\rho = 3$, the sequence of the pair (u_r, u_v) can be excluded for further computation. Finally, the criterion *maxDuration* will identify the EC composed of the pair set $\{(u_r, u_s), (u_r, u_t)\}$ with sequence T : $\{\langle \tau_1, \tau_2 \rangle, \langle \tau_5, \tau_6 \rangle, \langle \tau_9, \tau_{10} \rangle, \langle \tau_{13}, \tau_{14} \rangle\}$, while the criterion *maxUsers* will identify the EC composed of the pair set $\{(u_r, u_s), (u_r, u_t)\}, (u_r, u_z)\}$ with sequence T : $\{\langle \tau_1, \tau_2 \rangle, \langle \tau_5, \tau_6 \rangle, \langle \tau_9, \tau_{10} \rangle\}$.

4   Experimental Evaluation

The proposed computational solution has been applied to microblogging posts of the Twitter platform. The original dataset concerns the 2012 U.S. Presidential Election and collects tweets posted between August 1, 2012 and November 6,

2012 that mention the words "Obama" and/or "Romney" [1]. We considered an excerpt that covers the period November 1, 2012 – November 5, 2012. For each tweet, we took the text of the tweet, time-stamp when the message was written and nickname of the author, then we removed URLs, emoticons and hash-tags, discarded messages that had only social tagging and no textual content. Finally, we kept the tweets that were longer than 35 chars. The initial dataset has a daily average of almost 47000 tweets (including re-tweets and replies), standard deviation equal to 48461, comprises almost 236.000 tweets and almost 117.000 users, but, to identify ECs spanning a relatively long time, we considered the posts of the first 1000 users with higher number of tweets. The final corpus has around 69.000 tweets with a daily peak of 28 per single user.

Evaluation setup and Comparisons. As to the evaluation, we quantified the ability of the method (hereafter, *PEREC*) to discovering ECs of high quality, that is, ECs in which sequences T and pair sets are well-distinct, which corresponds to when a pair of users has similar emotional content in the sequence T' of an EC' and cannot do the same in the sequence T'' of another EC". To measure this, we resorted to the Silhouette index [20] (an internal clustering validation schema), which is based on the concept of separation between points we revised to determine the dissimilarity (separation) between two pairs of users p_1 and p_2 of different ECs:

$$separation(p_1, p_2) = \frac{1}{|T'| \times |T''|} \sum_{\tau_i \in T'} \sum_{\tau_j \in T''} separation(\tau_i, \tau_j), \qquad (1)$$

$$separation(\tau_i, \tau_j) = \begin{cases} 1 & \text{if } \langle \tau_i, \tau_{i+1} \rangle \cap \langle \tau_j, \tau_{j+1} \rangle == \oslash \\ 1 & \text{if } \langle \tau_i, \tau_{i+1} \rangle \cap \langle \tau_j, \tau_{j+1} \rangle \neq \oslash, p_1 \neq p_2 \\ 0 & \text{otherwise} \end{cases} \qquad (2)$$

The separation has values in $[0,1]$ and approaches to 0 if the two pairs appear in the two ECs at the same time-intervals, therefore, the Silhouette index has values in $[-1,1]$.

Empirical comparisons were conducted with two different algorithms. The first algorithm (afterward *ECbas*) corresponds to a baseline designed to handle only two emotion categories, that is, positive and negative, which are the most general classes than those used to design our proposal, according to the categorization reported in [22]. The main difference is that the cyber-space of ECbas has a smaller set of features. The Silhouette index is computed as for PEREC. The second algorithm (afterward *Swarm*) uses a clustering technique to group points based on the notion of closeness in a metric space [13]. We adapted Swarm to work on the content-space. In this comparative study, Swarm has been used to find out and track clusters of users (swarms) repeated over time, by using only the content-space, that is, the frequency values of the emotional words. To

---

[1] The corpora was downloaded on January 2018 from the link https://old.datahub.io/dataset/twitter-2012-presidential-election/resource/9bb14d78-9519-459a-9fad-e630e3e9a0a1.

compute the Silhouette index, we could not consider the feature values of paired users, but took the frequency values (within the content-space) of the individual users as clusterized by Swarm.

Experiments were performed at *(i)* different configurations of the cyber-space and *(ii)* different values of the threshold δ. The several configurations of cyber-space were obtained with different time granularities of the time-intervals, more precisely we defined the time-instants by aggregating posts at 60, 120, 240, 480, 960 min.

Results. For space limitations, we present the results of the emotion with highest quality and emotion with lowest quality for perEC and Swarm. In Table 1, we report the average values of Silhouette index computed on all the ECs detected at the different time-granularities of the cyber-space. All the algorithms were required to discover ECs of at least five users, periodicity threshold $\delta = \{3, 4, 5\}$ and number of repetitions $\rho = 5$, that is, the repetitions have to be at least 5 and have to be distanced by 3, 4, 5 time-instants. So, for instance, when the time-granularity is 60 and $\delta = 3$, the distance between two consecutive repetitions is greater than 180 min ($\delta - 1$) and less than 240 min ($\delta + 1$).

By inspecting Table 1, we observe that the emotion categories expressed with larger regularity and homogeneity are *anger* and *joy*, while the emotional words associated to *shame* and *disgust* are those used without particular regularity. The result is confirmed by the experiments on PEREC and Swarm, indeed the two algorithms agree on the emotion for each time-granularity configuration, although with different values of the Silhouette index. This is mainly due to the difference in terms of algorithmic choices, in fact Swarm requires the closeness among all the users, while PEREC searches for similar values of the feature ED per pairs of users. We observe also that the relatively smaller time-granularities facilitate the formation of periodic ECs around to *anger* (60 and 120 min), while, for the largest time-granularities, *joy* is the emotion more repeated. This can indicate that the users, when posting Tweets with political content, utilize emotional words related to *anger* for shorter time-spans and likely for discussions which are very brief, while the emotional words related to *joy* are used less on shorter time-spans but have an homogenous presence among the users over longer time-spans. In all the time-granularities, PEREC does better than ECbas, meaning that aggregating the content of several emotions, even referred to the same category, is not beneficial whether we aim at interpreting the way the microblogs are used to express emotions.

In Table 2, we report the average values of Silhouette index computed on all the ECs detected at the different values of periodicity δ. All the algorithms were required to work on a time-granularity of 30 min (in one time-instant they gather the tweets posted in 30 min) and discover ECs of at least five users, number of repetitions $\rho = 4$, that is, the repetitions have to be at least 4.

By inspecting Table 2, we see that, for the algorithms PEREC and Swarm, there is large homogeneity in the use of emotional words related to *anger* and *joy*, and this behavior is replicated with a basis of at most 3 h for *anger* (30 min multiplied by $\delta = 6$), while, in the case of *joy* is repeated every 4 h. On the

Table 1. Silhouette index computed at different time-granularities of the cyber-space. The emotion showing highest quality and lowest quality are reported in the brackets.

	Highest perEC	Lowest perEC	Highest ECbas	Lowest ECbas	Highest swarm	Lowest swarm
60	(anger)0.34	(shame)−0.1	Negative(0.1)	(positive)−0.1	(anger)0.22	(shame)0.07
120	(anger)0.41	(shame)−0.1	Negative(0.19)	(positive)−0.14	(anger)0.17	(shame)0.04
240	(joy)0.42	(shame)−0.1	Negative(0.22)	(positive)−0.14	(joy)0.22	(shame)−0.13
480	(joy)0.28	(disgust)−0.18	Positive(0.1)	(negative)−0.08	(joy)0.14	(disgust)−0.1
960	(joy)0.22	(disgust)−0.18	Positive(0.1)	(negative)−0.08	(joy)0.12	(disgust)−0.2

contrary, the lowest quality of *shame* and *fear* mirror the low tendency of the users to post tweets containing *shame* and *fear*. We observe also that, generally, the Silhouette index tends to decrease as the periodicity grows up, which can reveal homogeneity in the manifestation of the emotions at the beginning and a blurred similarity when times getting longer. Also in this case, ECbas does not provide a clear response neither in terms of emotion nor in terms of quality values.

Table 2. Silhouette index computed at different thresholds of periodicity.

	Highest perEC	Lowest perEC	Highest ECbas	Lowest ECbas	Highest swarm	Lowest swarm
4	(anger)0.38	(shame)−0.1	Negative(0.18)	(positive)−0.1	(anger)0.39	(shame)0.1
5	(anger)0.33	(shame)−0.1	Negative(0.19)	(positive)−0.13	(anger)0.28	(shame)0.08
6	(anger)0.29	(sadness)−0.3	Negative(0.22)	(positive)−0.14	(joy)0.22	(fear)−0.07
7	(joy)0.25	(fear)−0.1	Positive(0.1)	(negative)−0.08	(joy)0.24	(fear)−0.1
8	(joy)0.22	(fear)−0.1	Positive(0.1)	(negative)−0.08	(joy)0.12	(fear)−0.2

In Table 3, we report the values of the Silhouette index computed on the ECs distinguished by emotion. The ECs have been detected at the different values of periodicity δ by the algorithm PEREC. The algorithm is required to work on a time-granularity of 30 min (in one time-instant they gather the tweets posted in 30 min) and discover ECs of at least five users $\rho = 4$, that is, the repetitions have to be at least 4. We observe that groups of "emotionally" homogeneous users can be basically detected on *anger* and *joy*, which can be evidence of the

Table 3. Silhouette index computed on the ECs distinguished by emotion.

	Joy	Fear	Anger	Sadness	Disgust	Shame
4	0.29	−0.01	0.38	0.04	0.03	−0.1
5	0.23	−0.01	0.33	0.1	−0.01	−0.1
6	0.27	−0.08	0.29	−0.3	0.04	0.01
7	0.25	−0.1	0.19	0.1	−0.08	0.07
8	0.22	−0.1	0.2	0.1	−0.08	0.08

uniformity with which the users express these two emotions on the microblogs. On the contrary, there is no a clear indication on how the users express the remaining emotions, considered that there are not values lower than -0.1.

5   Related Works

The studies on the periodicity of the emotions find space especially in the Sociology and Psychology, while very few attempts can be listed in Computer Science. In [5], quantitative indicators have been defined to measure circadian rhythms of positive and negative moods on Twitter. More recently, in [21], the author study the cyclicity of the emotions expressed by individual users on blogs. They propose a representation built on time series of the frequency of the emotional words expressed by the users. The cyclicity on weekly and monthly basis is analyzed through auto-correlation and power spectral density.

A larger interest attracts instead the temporal-based analysis of the emotions. The work proposed in [2] uses descriptive statistics for a time-sensitive analysis aiming at quantifying the intensity of the basic emotions and recognizing different types of users. The study proposed in [4] investigates the reactivity of the users of instant messaging in comparison to persistent communication, in order to capture the real-time interactions between users. They provide an agent-based model of emotional interaction which works on the power-law distribution of the communication activity of the users. The agent recovers patterns based on user activity and emotions in chat rooms. However, this does not guarantee the identification of users with similar emotions, which is one of the purposes of the current work. In [23] the method explores the correlation between emotion subjectivity and topics discussed in the posts. They first extract subjective corpora and then track the evolution of the emotions with respect to sub-topics. A similar problem is investigated in [24] through a time-aware topic modeling method. They combine two probabilistic models, one to represent the evolutions of the topics and the other one to represent the evolutions of the emotions in a state space. In [12], the authors use socialization measures to estimate the quantify the emotions expressed in the tweets posted from a geographic area, social connections and demographics. In [10] it is presented an analysis of the evolution of the stance in political tweets of user communities over four fixed and pre-defined temporal phases. The communities are built with a classic network-based algorithm working on Twitter linkage and the evolution consists of the differences (manually spotted) on communities statistics. The notion of emotional communities have been presented in [8], but without temporal connotation. The authors inject the emotional state detected on the tweets and social activity in an algorithm of community detection based on the social network structures to identify groups of users particularly influential. Clustering tasks on emotional texts have been mostly addressed for community detection algorithms which exploit the social ties in social networks. Jin and Zafarani [7] performs a multi-level analysis which starts with user information and ends at the whole network information. Finally, in a previous research [14], we investigate how grouping users on the basis of similar emotional changes, without necessarily considering social ties. In that paper, we did not yet account for the temporal information offered by the periodicity, which is what concerns the current work.

6   Conclusions

In this paper, we have investigated the novel problem to trace the periodicity of "emotionally" homogeneous groups of users, that is, users which convey similar emotional content. The problem becomes crucial and relevant when designing technologies and tools for online communities platforms, cyber-bullying monitoring systems and social media campaigns services. We have proposed a method which sees emotions as collectors of individuals, whose emotional status can recur, even with regularity. The emotional collectives are not the representation of effective interactions happened in the social media, but indicate the presence of homogenous behaviors in conveying emotions. The proposed method first exploits a representational mechanism to quantify emotions from social media texts and then searches for the repetitions of collectives of individuals with similar use of the emotional words. The application to the Twitter posts reveals that two specific emotion, anger and joy, can be considered as particular aggregators of homogenous behaviors.

As future work, we plan to upgrade the research in three directions: *(i)* change analysis of the emotional state of network-based communities [16] (rather than individual users), *(ii)* quantification of the emotional content through regression-based techniques to estimate the emotional intensity at the level of single message [15], *(iii)* informativeness-based mechanisms in order to rank periodic ECs [1].

Acknowledgments. This work fulfills the objectives the project "Computer-mediated collaboration in creative projects" (8GPS5R0) collocated in "Intervento cofinanziato dal Fondo di Sviluppo e Coesione 2007-2013 – APQ Ricerca Regione Puglia - Programma regionale a sostegno della specializzazione intelligente e della sostenibilita' sociale ed ambientale - FutureInResearch".

References

1. Ceci, M., Loglisci, C., Macchia, L.: Ranking sentences for keyphrase extraction: a relational data mining approach. In: Agosti, M., Catarci, T., Esposito, F. (eds.) Pushing the Boundaries of the Digital Libraries Field - 10th Italian Research Conference on Digital Libraries, IRCDL 2014, Padua, Italy, 30–31 January 2014. Procedia Computer Science, vol. 38, pp. 52–59. Elsevier (2014). https://doi.org/10.1016/j.procs.2014.10.011

2. Chen, X., Sykora, M.D., Jackson, T.W., Elayan, S.: What about mood swings: identifying depression on twitter with temporal measures of emotions. In: Companion Proceedings of the The Web Conference 2018, WWW 2018, International World Wide Web Conferences Steering Committee, pp. 1653–1660 (2018). https://doi.org/10.1145/3184558.3191624

3. Ekman, P.: Facial expression and emotion. Am. psychol. **48**, 384–92 (1993)

4. Garas, A., Garcia, D., Skowron, M., Schweitzer, F.: Emotional persistence in online chatting communities. Sci. Rep. **2**, 402 (2012). https://doi.org/10.1038/srep00402
5. Golder, S., Macy, M.: Diurnal and seasonal mood vary with work, sleep, and daylength across diverse cultures. Science **333**(6051), 1878–1881 (2011). https://doi.org/10.1126/science.1202775
6. Huang, K., Chang, C.: SMCA: a general model for mining asynchronous periodic patterns in temporal databases. IEEE Trans. Knowl. Data Eng. **17**(6), 774–785 (2005). https://doi.org/10.1109/TKDE.2005.98
7. Jin, S., Zafarani, R.: Emotions in social networks: distributions, patterns, and models. In: Proceedings of the 2017 ACM on Conference on Information and Knowledge Management, CIKM 2017, pp. 1907–1916 (2017). https://doi.org/10.1145/3132847.3132932
8. Kanavos, A., Perikos, I.: Towards detecting emotional communities in twitter. In: 9th IEEE International Conference on Research Challenges in Information Science, RCIS 2015, Athens, Greece, 13–15 May 2015, pp. 524–525 (2015). https://doi.org/10.1109/RCIS.2015.7128919
9. Keene, J.R., Lang, A.: Dynamic motivated processing of emotional trajectories in public service announcements. Commun. Monogr. **83**(4), 468–485 (2016). https://doi.org/10.1080/03637751.2016.1198040
10. Lai, M., Patti, V., Ruffo, G., Rosso, P.: Stance evolution and twitter interactions in an Italian political debate. In: Silberztein, M., Atigui, F., Kornyshova, E., Métais, E., Meziane, F. (eds.) NLDB 2018. LNCS, vol. 10859, pp. 15–27. Springer, Cham (2018). https://doi.org/10.1007/978-3-319-91947-8_2
11. Layer, R.M., Skadron, K., Robins, G., Hall, I.M., Quinlan, A.R.: Binary interval search: a scalable algorithm for counting interval intersections. Bioinformatics **29**(1), 1–7 (2013). https://doi.org/10.1093/bioinformatics/bts652
12. Lerman, K., Arora, M., Gallegos, L., Kumaraguru, P., Garcia, D.: Emotions, demographics and sociability in twitter interactions. In: Tenth International Conference on Web and Social Media, Cologne, Germany, vol. 2016, pp. 201–210 (2016)
13. Li, Z., Ding, B., Han, J., Kays, R.: Swarm: mining relaxed temporal moving object clusters. PVLDB **3**(1), 723–734 (2010). https://doi.org/10.14778/1920841.1920934
14. Loglisci, C., Andresini, G., Impedovo, A., Malerba, D.: Analyzing microblogging posts for tracking collective emotional trajectories. In: Ghidini, C., Magnini, B., Passerini, A., Traverso, P. (eds.) AI*IA 2018. LNCS (LNAI), vol. 11298, pp. 123–135. Springer, Cham (2018). https://doi.org/10.1007/978-3-030-03840-3_10
15. Loglisci, C., Appice, A., Malerba, D.: Collective regression for handling autocorrelation of network data in a transductive setting. J. Intell. Inf. Syst. **46**(3), 447–472 (2016). https://doi.org/10.1007/s10844-015-0361-8
16. Loglisci, C., Ceci, M., Malerba, D.: Discovering evolution chains in dynamic networks. In: Appice, A., Ceci, M., Loglisci, C., Manco, G., Masciari, E., Ras, Z.W. (eds.) NFMCP 2012. LNCS (LNAI), vol. 7765, pp. 185–199. Springer, Heidelberg (2013). https://doi.org/10.1007/978-3-642-37382-4_13
17. Miller, G.A.: Wordnet: a lexical database for English. Commun. ACM **38**(11), 39–41 (1995). https://doi.org/10.1145/219717.219748
18. Mohammad, S., Bravo-Marquez, F., Salameh, M., Kiritchenko, S.: Semeval-2018 task 1: affect in tweets. In: Proceedings of The 12th International Workshop on Semantic Evaluation, SemEval@NAACL-HLT 2018, New Orleans, Louisiana, USA, 5–6 June 2018, pp. 1–17 (2018)
19. Nissim, M., Patti, V.: Semantic Aspects in Sentiment Analysis. Morgan Kaufmann, Burlington (2016). https://doi.org/10.1016/B978-0-12-804412-4.00003-6

20. Rousseeuw, P.J.: Silhouettes: a graphical aid to the interpretation and validation of cluster analysis. J. Comput. Appl. Math. **20**, 53–65 (1987). https://doi.org/10.1016/0377-0427(87)90125-7

21. Sano, Y., Takayasu, H., Havlin, S., Takayasu, M.: Identifying long-term periodic cycles and memories of collective emotion in online social media. PLoS ONE **14**(3), e0213843 (2019). https://doi.org/10.1371/journal.pone.0213843

22. Strapparava, C., Valitutti, A.: Wordnet affect: an affective extension of wordnet. In: Proceedings of the Fourth International Conference on Language Resources and Evaluation, LREC 2004, Lisbon, Portugal, 26–28 May 2004. European Language Resources Association (2004)

23. Zhou, Q., Zhang, C.: Emotion evolutions of sub-topics about popular events on microblogs. Electron. Lib. **35**(4), 770–782 (2017). https://doi.org/10.1108/EL-09-2016-0184

24. Zhu, C., Zhu, H., Ge, Y., Chen, E., Liu, Q.: Tracking the evolution of social emotions: a time-aware topic modeling perspective. In: 2014 IEEE International Conference on Data Mining, ICDM 2014, Shenzhen, China, 14–17 December 2014, pp. 697–706 (2014). https://doi.org/10.1109/ICDM.2014.121

Mapping Lexical Knowledge to Distributed Models for Ontology Concept Invention

Manuel Vimercati, Federico Bianchi$^{(\boxtimes)}$, Mauricio Soto, and Matteo Palmonari

University of Milan-Bicocca, Viale Sarca 336, Milan, Italy
m.vimercati15@campus.unimib.it,
{federico.bianchi,mauricio.sotogomez,matteo.palmonari}@unimib.it

Abstract. Ontologies are largely used but the abstraction process required to create them is a complex task that leads to incompleteness. Concept invention offers a valid solution to extending ontologies by creating novel and meaningful concepts starting from previous knowledge. The use of distributed vector representations to encode knowledge has become a popular method in both NLP and Knowledge Representation. In this paper, we show how concept invention can be complemented with distributed representation models to perform ontology completion tasks starting from lexical knowledge. We propose a first approach based on a deep neural network trained over distributed representations of words and ontological concept. With this model, we devise a method to generate distributed representations for novel and unseen concepts and we introduce a methodology to evaluate these representations. Experiments show that, despite some limitations, our model provides a promising method for concept invention.

1 Introduction

Ontologies define the terminology adopted to represent structured knowledge in a variety of application domains. *Knowledge Graphs* (KGs) are prominent examples of structured knowledge bases used today in the industry and science, which represent entities, their properties and binary relations between them. *Ontology concepts* specify which types of entities are described in KGs. Their meaning is usually defined by axioms from formal languages like Description Logics [1], which can specify relations between concepts (e.g., subclass of, disjoint with) and constrain their usage with properties (e.g., by domain and range restrictions over properties).

Large KGs require to cover entities that are instance of many different concepts and their ontologies are often incomplete. This issue has different origins like the complex abstraction processes required to model a domain, the selection of a subset of important concepts to be represented, and the intrinsic dynamic nature of KGs and ontologies. For example, the DBpedia ontology includes concepts such as *'Guitarist'* and *'Singer'* but does not include concepts such

© Springer Nature Switzerland AG 2019
M. Alviano et al. (Eds.): AI*IA 2019, LNAI 11946, pp. 572–587, 2019.
https://doi.org/10.1007/978-3-030-35166-3_40

as *'Pianist'* and *'DJ'*, despite entities that are pianists and DJs are described therein.

The task of adding more concepts to a given ontology can be viewed as an ontology completion problem. Ontology completion can be interpreted under different perspectives [10]. For instance, completion can be understood as adding *subclass of* relations between concepts that already exist. Another possible completion mechanism is concept invention, where a new concept is created in the ontology. This can be achieved by concept blending or concept induction [10]. In concept blending, new concepts are obtained by combining existing concepts from the ontology, leveraging schema-level evidence and, in particular, their logical specifications. In concept induction, new concepts deemed to be relevant are generated using evidence about instances in the ontology or knowledge graphs. A large body of work in concept invention has been developed in the context of logic-based approaches to define the semantics of concepts, and many of them are based on Description Logics [10]. These languages provide the foundations for languages like RDFS and OWL, which are widely used to model real-world ontologies of large knowledge graphs. In this work, we want to study a concept invention problem, and, in particular concept induction, for ontologies represented using *Distributed Models* (DMs).

DMs have been recently introduced as complementary approaches to represent the semantics of KG elements, including ontology concepts, after their uptake in computational linguistics. In this field, some model implementations like Word2vec [27] and ELMo [31] have become standard techniques for downstream NLP applications [31], and many scientists have argued for their cognitive groundedness [24]. Those models provide lexical knowledge starting from natural language texts and are based on Distributional Semantics, whose main hypotheses are that words' meaning is based on their usage and that words that appear in similar contexts are similar. For example, the representations of *'Guitarist'* and *'Pianist'* will be similar because those words are used in similar contexts. Although many approaches have proposed models for learning distributed representations entities and properties [5], few of them learn distributed representations of ontology concepts. For example, Type2Vec [2,3] proposes concept representations based on distributional semantics that encode similarity and/or relatedness between the concepts. Other approaches have been proposed to encode the *subclass of* relation and concept hierarchies [23,29,33] by using hyperbolic geometries that are better suited to capture tree-like structures [22].

Distributed models are vector-based representations of entities or properties or concepts that are generated from data through machine learning approaches by optimizing one or more functions. Even if the individual components of the generated vectors are hard to interpret, geometric relations between the vectors encode semantic relations between the represented elements, like similarity or the subclass of relation.

In this work, we aim to show how DMs can provide a natural and suitable framework to support novel ontology completion tasks that require concept invention. The key intuition behind the use of DMs for concept creation tasks is the following: each one of the infinite set of vectors in a vector space representing concepts encodes some semantics; vectors that are not associated with a known concept may, in fact, be potential new concepts in the ontology; relevant new concepts can be identified by finding some *hot spots* in the space, based on some evidence. For example, we expect to assign a suitable position for the unseen concept *'Pianist'*, by using available evidence.

We propose, to the best of our knowledge, one of the first approaches towards supporting concept induction in DMs using lexical knowledge as a source of evidence. In particular, we use a neural network to learn an alignment function that generates distributed concept representations from distributed word representations. As a source of the alignment, we use distributed representations based on the ELMo model [31], where each word is associated to several vectors reflecting the different meanings that the word assumes in different contexts. As target of the alignment, we consider two different distributed concept spaces: a hyperbolic space, which represents the hierarchical relations between concepts, and a Euclidean space, which is built with Type2Vec, encoding the distributional semantics. This twofold representation allows us to capture simultaneously the semantic similarity derived from the use of the concepts in the data and the dependencies between concepts obtained from an ontology. Intuitively, the function learns how to map concept labels to concept representations, and, more importantly, entity names to the representations of their respective concepts. For example, we learn to generate the representation of the concept *'Guitarist'* by mapping guitarists' names to the representation of this concept in the two concept spaces. As a consequence, we can then feed several names of pianists to the network, to generate the representation of the concept *'Pianist'* in the two spaces.

The main contributions of this paper are: (i) we illustrate how distributed models can be used to represent concepts; (ii) we provide a model which can be used to obtain data set without bias; (iii) we show how new concept representations can be generated using the semantics inside distributed models; (iv) we propose an evaluation method and discuss about its limitations; (v) we provide a first example of implementation and discuss the results obtained with our models.

The paper is structured as follows: we establish terminology and notation in Sect. 2 and discuss related work in the concept invention and ontology completion fields in Sect. 3; after explaining our method in Sect. 4, we discuss the methodology proposed to evaluate the invention process and our experimental results in Sect. 5. Conclusions and future work end the paper.

2   Preliminaries

For this work, we can define a Knowledge Graph (KG) as a tuple $<C, E, \subseteq, \in >$, where:

- C is a set of concepts (often also referred to as classes), e.g., *Pianist*;

- E is a set of entities that represent domain objects, e.g., *Elton_John*;
- $\subseteq$ is a *subclassOf* relation that holds between pairs of concepts in C; we assume that the relation is transitive, reflexive and anti-symmetric and defines a partial order over the set of concepts, e.g., *Pianist* $\subseteq$ *MusicalArtist*;
- $\in$ is the *instance-of* relation that holds between an instance and a concept, e.g., *Elton_John* $\in$ *Pianist*

We use a minimal definition of KG, where we only assume that a partial order over the concepts is defined and entities are associated with concepts. This makes our approach very general and applicable to ontologies defined using expressive logical languages as well as to ontologies defined as simple schemas of KGs.

Distributed Models (DMs), frequently named embeddings, are vector-based models which are used to represent different knowledge resources, such as word meanings and ontology concepts. A distributed model is a vector space $\mathbb{R}^n$ which uses vectors in the space to represent the objects. The semantics of the represented objects is captured by geometrical or mathematical relations between labelled vectors in the space. Distributed models are often generated by training a model with a data set. For example, word embeddings are built using a text corpus. Vector spaces used in distributed models contain, by definition, an infinite set of vectors, even though only a few of them are explicitly associated with an element after training, usually, the vectors that correspond to some element in the training data, e.g., words in the corpus. We will refer to these vectors as labelled vectors, because they are explicitly associated with a label, e.g., the word they are associated with, and to all the other vectors as unlabelled vectors. The dimension of the space is a parameter that depend on the method used to create the DM. Moreover, DM can be built to encode different kinds of semantics, in this paper we consider two main kinds of semantics as detailed below.

- **Distributional semantics (DS):** [19] is a semantic principle according to which the distribution of words in a corpus, i.e., their usage, determines their meaning. Different count-based [11,14,17,30] or predictive [12,27,31] approaches can be used to generate distributed models inspired by the DS principle. All these approaches return distributed models such that we can expect that vectors of similar words will appear close in the vector space. In fact, DS encodes relatedness among words, where the relatedness can be computed using cosine similarity or Euclidean distance. DS has been used to account for word meaning extensively in a number of models such as Word2Vec [27], Glove [30] and BERT [12]. In particular, we will use ELMo [31] as input word space in our approach. However recent work has also proposed to use DS as a principle to provide distributed representations of entities and concepts of knowledge graph. Type2Vec [3] provides a way to embed DBpedia types in the vector space by considering type to type co-occurrence over a text corpus: the corpus is firstly annotated with entities (using entity linking techniques) and then entities are replaced with their most specific type thus generating a document containing ordered sequences of types.

- **Hierarchical Semantics (HS):** Hyperbolic metric spaces have proved to be useful when representing hierarchical relations [22]. The most common use of this type of embedding is graph representation, namely to assign to each node in the graph a point in a low dimensional hyperbolic space in such a way that neighbours are placed close. The quality of the embedding is usually measured by the capacity of reconstruct the original graph starting from the representation; or by the link prediction task [29] which aims to predict edges previously removed from the input graph before the embedding phase.

  Since Taxonomies represent hierarchical relations, recent methods [23, 29, 33] use Hyperbolic Geometry Models to create a high quality representation on low dimensional hyperbolic spaces. Following this line of work, we use HS to express hierarchical relations between *concepts* from a given ontology.

The most common Hyperbolic models used to create graph embedding are Lorentz Model (which is the upper sheet S^+ of the Hyperboloid model) and Poincaré Disk Model (Fig. 1), which is the choice in our model. The Poincaré Disk Model is a two-dimensional disk of radius r endowed with its natural hyperbolic metri (Eq. 1). In this model, distance between points scales exponentially when we move from the origin toward the border circumference. This property makes this model particularly suitable to represent tree-like structures, in which the number of elements usually grows exponential with depth. In fact, all trees can be isometrically embedded using this model [18].

$$d(x, y) = arccosh\left(1 + \frac{2*r^2*\|x-y\|^2}{(r^2-\|x\|^2)*(r^2-\|y\|^2)}\right) \tag{1}$$

Slightly abusing the terminology, from now on we will refer to distributional models (or representations), to refer to distributed models (representations) inspired by DS. Based on this distinction we define here the three distributed representation spaces that we will use in our approach: a distributional representation space of words, a hyperbolic representation space of ontology concepts, and a distributional representation space of concepts.

A Distributional representation space of words V_W (Fig. 2) can be built over a tuple $<T, W>$. V_W is a distributed model which is built by applying the DS over a generic corpus T. A corpus T is a collection of sentences, a sentence is an ordered set of words $w \in W$ and word phrases (like *'New York Times'*) $wp \in W$. Depending on the applied model, a labelled vector $v_w \in V_W$ exists for each word $w \in W$ (Word2Vec [27] or GLOVE [30]) or for each occurrence of each word $w \in W$ (ELMo [31] and BERT [12]).

A Hierarchical representation space of concepts H_C is built over a tuple $<C, \subseteq>$. H_C is a distributed model of the concepts C in the POSet structure of a KG. For example, in [33] for each $c \in C$ a labelled vector $h_c \in H_C$ is created with the Poincaré disk model.

A Distributional representation space of concepts D_C (Fig. 3) can be built over a tuple $<C, \varepsilon, \in, T_C, \lambda, KG>$. D_C is a distributed model built applying the DS over a corpus T_C. T_C is obtained by replacing each entity ε in a generic corpus with $\lambda(\varepsilon)$, λ is a function which represents an *Entity Linker* which map each entity ε into c if in KG the relation $\varepsilon \in c$ is true; otherwise, in the case that ε is not in the KG then nothing is returned. So T_C is a collection of sentences composed by ordered $c \in C$. To obtain D_C a *DS based* method is applied over T_C.

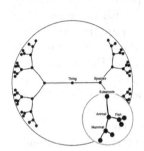

Fig. 1. Example of tree embedding in a Poincaré disk model

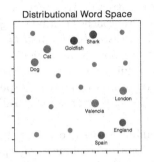

Fig. 2. Example of distributional representation of words

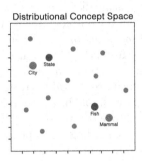

Fig. 3. Example of distributional representations of concepts

3 Related Work

Inspired by the Computational Creativity research field [9,37], we divide concept invention into four tasks [39]:

- *Concept Extraction* is the task of extracting a conceptual representation from an existing but different representation of the same idea after an adequate transformation; this research field is related to the information extraction methods, for example, Hearts patterns [20] which are able to extract hyponym/hypernym relations between words from text corpora.
- *Concept Induction* is based on *instances of concepts* from which a concept or concepts are learned; this can be supervised (Concept Learning) or unsupervised (Concept Discovery). An example of concept learning is the task of automatic taxonomy construction from NLP resources like the approaches surveyed in [36,38] which use text corpora to learn concepts organized into hierarchies. In Concept Discovery concepts are obtained by applying unsupervised techniques like clustering or LDA [4].
- *Concept Recycling* is the creative re-use of existing concepts. The most remarkable approaches of this kind are those based on concept blending [15,16]. However, studies about semantic shift in temporal word embeddings [13] and novel word sense detection [21] are also somehow relevant to the (post hoc) study of concept recycling.
- *Concept Space Exploration* takes as input a search space of possible new concept and locates interesting concepts in it.

The ontology completion task can be faced with two strategies: by finding new triples or by extending the set of concepts and defining new *subclassOf* relations. The former can be tackled with the use of KG embeddings which encode entities as vectors and properties as spatial transformations to predict new triples [5,28], recent methods combine *rule templates* with DR created using gaussian distributions [6]; the latter derives new concepts and rules starting from the ontology itself. These approaches can be designed with *Inductive Logic Programming* [7] or even with *Statistical Relational Learning* approaches [34,35]

Recently [23] has used text corpora to infer hierarchical concepts. This work is based on an hyperbolic embedding and a revisited version of Hearst patterns, which are lexical patterns used to find Hyponym/Hypernym relations in a text. (for example in the sentence *'DJ and other artists'* 'DJ' can be recognized as an instance of 'Artist').

Regarding conceptual combination some recent approaches tried to define a framework to face the creation of combined concepts starting from already known concepts. For example, [25] uses conceptual spaces and a combination of prototype theory and random set theory which can capture both typicality and semantic uncertainty. On the other hand, [10] shows how the description logic EL+ can be used to support conceptual combination and introduces a novel operator which can be helpful for this task. [26] Proposes a framework based on description logic in which combine DL are combined with probabilities and other heuristics to support concept combination. Our work applies the Concept Induction definition to generate the representations for new concepts.

4   Ontology Concept Induction with Lexical Knowledge Mapping

We begin by providing an overview of the proposed approach. In the following we will discuss each of its components in detail.

4.1   Approach Overview

We define the concept invention process as a mapping function $\Pi : \mathbb{R}^n \to \mathbb{R}^m \times \mathbb{R}^q$ from the word vector space into two different concept vector spaces: a distributional type space and hierarchical type space respectively. We implement Π as a Neural Network which is trained in a Multi-Task learning (MTL [8]) setup (but any other machine learning model can be also applied). Figure 4 depicts a high level representation of the neural architecture.

Starting from a set of concepts C, we create $C_T \subset C$ and $C_I \subset C$, with $C_T \cap C_I = \emptyset$. C_T represents the set of concepts that will be used during the training phase to learn the mapping function Π, while C_I is the set of concepts that we the model will invent: their representation will be created using Π. Since we will test on the C_I set the network will have to predict the representation of unknown concepts.

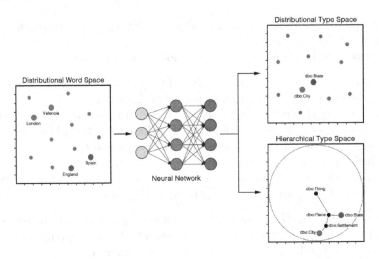

Fig. 4. Multi-task learning for concept invention schema

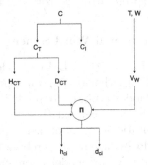

Fig. 5. Schema of resource usage

To reduce bias in our experimentation, we build the distributed representations without using concepts which will be invented. Thus, we create an hierarchical representation space H_{C_T} and a distributional representation space D_{C_T} using resources which contain **only** concept $c \in C_T$. A corpus T is used to create a distributional space V_W of words W. A schema that illustrates this procedure is showed in Fig. 5.

In our work, we want to perform concept invention starting from words. This can be seen as a *Concept Induction* task. To learn a mapping function which can project words to their respective concepts we need a data set composed of examples of $<word, concept>$ alignment.

This kind of dataset is *model and vector independent*, because is an alignment between symbols who represent *words* and *concepts* (e.g., $<Elton\_Jhon, Pianist>$). Since we are using DMs we need to retrieve vectors to compose the training tuples. Thus, once we have the pairs of words

and concept we can create training examples with the representation vectors:
$<w_{word}, d_{concept}, h_{concept}>$

Therefore, we build our dataset in the following way:

1. For each $c \in C_T$ retrieve from the KG all the entities ε for which the relation $\varepsilon \in c$ is defined in the KG, this step creates the E_c set.
2. For each $\varepsilon_c \in E_c$ find the word $w_{\varepsilon_c} \in W$ which represents ε_c (for instance, the word phrase 'Elton Jhon' for the DBpedia entity dbr:Elton_Jhon), and create the couple $<w_{\varepsilon_c}, c>$; if the representation of an ε_c cannot be found in W, discharge that ε_c.
3. For each pair $<w_\varepsilon, c>$, we retrieve all vectors $v_w \in V_W$, for each v_w create a tuple $<v_w, d_c, h_c>$ with $d_c \in D_{C_T}$ and $h_c \in H_{C_T}$

Once the function Π is learned, we are able to generate concept representations. Thus, starting from our test set of concept C_I and applying (1) and (2) we can retrieve words in W which belong to concepts in C_I.

Π can be used to predict $h_{c_i} \in H_{C_T}$ and $d_{c_i} \in D_{C_T}$ and performing a concept invention. The quality evaluation of this vectors will be discussed in Sect. 6.

4.2 The Source: Distributional Word Space

The V_W is obtained using ELMo [31]. ELMo is a deep learning model which creates a language model during the training on a prediction task. ELMo uses a Bidirectional Language Model (BiLM) to predict a word based on its left context (forward model) or its right context (backward model). Once the BiLM is trained, ELMo's representations are obtained through a fine-tuning on the target task which lets ELMo learn how to combine the representations which come from the forward and backward models to maximize the performances in the fine-tuning task (which can be another prediction task or other NLP tasks).

The *pre-training* of our ELMo model is performed on the *Billion Word Corpus*[1]. The model is then *fine-tuned* obtain a proper representation of DBpedia Abstract Corpus[2] language model, and reflect the distributional word's meaning in this corpus. In V_W each word occurrence representation is based on his sentence context in the *DBpedia abstract corpus* and on all contexts of all occurrences of that word in the *Billion Word Corpus*.

ELMo model produces three vectors for each occurrence of each word in the fine-tuning corpus, we use the vectors at *layer 1* because these vectors embody the contextual representation of the word. Due to the ELMo's hyperparameters, the dimension of a contextual word representation is 1024.

4.3 The Target: Distributed Concept Spaces

Distributional Concept Space. D_{C_T} is obtained using DBpedia's Types as concepts and is generated with Type2Vec [3], a Word2Vec [27] model applied

---

[1]   https://opensource.google.com/projects/lm-benchmark.
[2]   http://downloads.dbpedia.org/2016-10/core-i18n/en/long_abstracts_en.tql.bz2.

over a processed corpus: starting from the *DBpedia abstract corpus* an *entity linking algorithm* is used to obtain the DBpedia entities contained in the corpus, unlinked words are eliminated and subsequently each entity is replaced with its most specific *Type* in *DBpedia ontology tree*[3]. The dimension of the a representation is 100 due to Type2Vec's hyperparameter.

Hierarchical Concept Space. H_{C_T} is created with HyperE [33], an algorithm that embeds a graph in a Poincaré Disk Model. The obtained embedding has a *low distortion*, meaning that node distances in the graph are preserved. In particular we obtain H_{C_T} by applying the HyperE approach to the DBpedia ontology tree. The vectors are 2-dimensional and they embody the hierarchical structure of the ontology tree. Each labelled vector $h_c \in H_C$ (h_{Thing} excluded) has $Norm(h_t) \sim 1$, this is a consequence of the HyperE approach and it is a property that has to be treated in the learning phase since these vectors are very close to the boundary of the Poincaré Disk and then could be mapped out of the domain.

4.4 Multi-task Learning for Concept Invention

We model the invention problem as a Multi-Task Learning (MTL) problem, this choice is motivated mainly for two reasons: (i) D_C and H_C capture different semantic properties: a combined loss which receives the feedback from both spaces using back-propagation can use the information from one space to improve the performance on the other; (ii) as noticed in many cases, in MTL each task works as a regularization function w.r.t. to other tasks, thus avoid overfitting [32], since the training process generates intermediate representations which take into account the different objective tasks. Figure 6 shows the architecture of the network. The multiobjective loss function optimized by the MTL network is $L = \lambda L_D + (1 - \lambda)L_H$ which is a convex combination of two loss functions that encode the distance in the respective spaces:

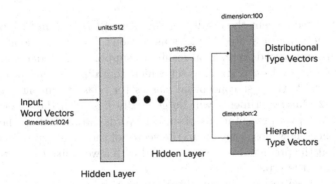

Fig. 6. Architecture of the multi-task feedforward network

---

[3] http://mappings.dbpedia.org/server/ontology/classes/.

- L_D is the mean cosine similarity (Eq. 2) between the predictions and the real vectors for each example e in the training set TS. Minimizing this generates vectors which are *distributionally similar* to the real ones because of share a very similar angle w.r.t. the origin.

$$L_D = \frac{\sum_{e \in TS} cossim(pred, true)}{|TS|} \qquad (2)$$

- L_H (Eq. 3) is the mean hyperbolic distance between the predictions and the real vectors for each example e in the training set TS with a penalization term. By minimize this value, we force the prediction to be closer to the real vectors, the concept of closeness is based on the Poincaré Disk Model topology.

$$L_H = \frac{\sum_{e \in TS} d_H(pred, true)}{|TS|},$$

$$d_H(p, t) = \phi(p) arccosh \left(1 + 2 \frac{\|p - t\|^2}{max(K, 1 - \|p\|^2)(1 - \|t\|^2)} \right) \qquad (3)$$

$$\phi(p) = \begin{cases} 1 & \text{if } R < \|v\| < 1 \\ P & \text{otherwise} \end{cases}$$

In Equation (3) K is a penalization parameter forcing the predicted vectors to be in the disk of radius 1, while P is a penalization parameter that amplifies the distance if the predicted vector is inside the radius R disk ($R < 1$). The former penalization is imposed to force the predicted vectors to be placed in the Poincaré disk model domain (inside the unit disk); conversely, the latter penalization forces the vectors to be near from the edge of the disk, which is the region where the predictions are placed in our dataset.

5   Evaluation: Preliminary Results and Discussion

In this section, we present the results for the *Concept Invention* task performed by the MTL network presented in previous sections. We present some examples of predictions and provide numerical results to support our model. The training of the model is based on a training set which contains 15 conceptual classes, showed in Table 1; the test conceptual classes (or 'class to invent') are shown in the Table 2 Our experiments will be generally based on the following task: generating concept representations of unseen words (words not in the training set) and to check how close they are to the vector of their real type. For example, we expect that the predicted vector associated with a word like *beaver* to be close to the vector of the type *Mammal*.

Note that these results are not obtained from unbiased spaces: in fact, the sets H_{C_T} and D_{C_T} correspond to the entire set of concepts C, thus we have H_C and D_C. While this might impact our results, we believe that this setting can be used to provide a first feedback over the validity of our assumptions, showing that we can indeed construct representations of unseen concept that are close to the real ones.

For each class $c \in C_I$ we have multiple predicted vectors so h_c and d_c are to be imputed. We think that generating predictions from multiple word vectors V_w of words w which belong to the concept c is a good process: a generalization of concept *'Fish'* has a better quality when it is based on different instances of fish. All our data, experimental procedures and complete architectures of the neural networks are available online for replication[4].

Table 1. Composition of the training dataset

DB. type	Uniq. words	# vectors
Arch.Structure	480	5077
Award	113	2335
Bird	203	1435
Colour	47	6938
Company	1536	36647
EthnicGroup	556	6411
Fic.Character	1127	8026
Insect	189	953
Language	385	20566
Mammal	331	9510
Planet	64	2140
Plant	901	13465
Sport	198	4459
SportsTeam	129	828
Weapon	64	2043

Table 2. Composition of the invention dataset

Class	Uniq. words	# Vectors
Amphibian	23	78
Crustacean	43	140
Currency	8	298
EducationalInstitution	10	49
Fish	185	737
GovernmentAgency	37	1954
Game	64	991
Mollusca	56	360
Reptile	56	414
SportsLeague	11	41

5.1 Qualitative Analysis

To evaluate the quality of the concept invention process we selected words which belong to entities that in DBpedia2016 were defined as instances of the OWL concept *Thing*, that is, the top of the concepts' partial order. We choose these words because we want to show that our model can be used to assign a more expressive type to these entities. We recorded the similarities between the centroid of the predicted vectors and the labelled vectors in the concept spaces. Table 3 shows some examples of predictions.

---

[4] https://github.com/NooneBug/Multi_task_concept_invention.

Table 3. Qualitative results on word of unseen concepts

Word	Ranking in D_C	Ranking in H_C
Algae	Plant	Thing
	Conifer	Species
	Fern	ChemicalSubstance
	Insect	Polyhedron
Beaver	Mammal	Species
	Bird	ChemicalSubstance
	Reptile	Thing
	Fish	Polyhedron
JPEG	Company	Agent
	Bank	Award
	Automobile	Thing
	Software	PublicService

5.2   Quantitative Analysis

Measures. For the evaluation, we use similarity ranking between the predicted vectors and the labelled vectors. For a given predicted vector we compute its neighbourhood and obtain the position of its true type label. Relying on these ranks we compute (and report) the mean rank of the true type label inside the ranking list (Avg). We also report the mean position of the true type label in the neighbourhood of a centroid for each semantic class ($Cent$). Both methods are computed over the distributional D and hyperbolic H space.

Settings. We consider two different settings: (i) $Cent$ and Avg of predictions about unseen words which belong to concepts used during training and (ii) $Cent$ and Avg of predictions about unseen words which belong to unseen concepts. The former will evaluate the invention task as standard in machine learning, we test the generalization ability on trained concepts. The latter is performed to explore how similarity between word representations can be used to infer different concepts, thus being a task closer to real concept invention. We consider one baseline model and propose two neural networks.

- Random Forest (**RF**), a random forest regressor model trained to predict the concept vector in the hyperbolic space or in the distributional type space based on the word vector.
- Feed Forward Neural Network with Single Output (**SO**), a neural network which takes in input the word vector and returns a vector in one concept space, performing a regression task.
- Multi-Task Neural Network with Double Output (**DO**), a neural network which takes in input the word vector and returns two vectors: one in the hyperbolic type space and one in the distributional type space. This network

uses the loss function $L = \lambda L_D + (1 - \lambda)L_H$ showed above (we use $\lambda = 0.91$, experimentally computed).

5.3 Results

Table 4 shows that the neural model can correctly project a centroid into the distributional concept space and, on average, the projected vectors into the hierarchical concept space have a correct position. The quantitative results show that the distributional projection is probably noisy, show also that the hyperbolic centroid procedure is highly affected by 'wrong' predictions. Results suggest that while the performance of the models is still far from one of a perfect predictor, the approach is promising; moreover the qualitative predictions (Table 3) seem to support this mapping methodology. The neural models seem to be better suited for this task then the baseline, but still DO suffers from some limitations that might be due to the optimization process; nevertheless, its ability to learn from two different spaces and aggregate the information is important for novel tasks related to concept invention; results are heavily influenced by the hyperparameters of the MTL model (e.g., λ). These considerations are valid for both setups (Tables 4 and 5) with different sensibility when the model has to predict the position of an unseen concept.

Table 4. Predictions ranks on unseen words but with known concepts

Model	Avg D	Cent D	Avg H	Cent H
RF	108	64	**16**	234
SO	**85**	4	17	208
DO	115	5	18	**206**

Table 5. Prediction ranks with unseen words and concepts

Model	Avg D	Cent D	Avg H	Cent H
RF	181	107	**18**	372
SO	**175**	82	35	**330**
DO	183	82	31	333

6 Conclusions and Future Work

In this paper, we have proposed a first approach to tackle concept invention combining information coming from distributed representations. The results obtained with a preliminary implementation and evaluation of the approach suggest that the approach is promising for supporting concept invention tasks, in particular to generate representations in the hyperbolic space that capture a generalization relations between the concepts.

Nevertheless, the proposed approach has some limitation that we aim to solve in future work. First, in the training process, we aim to find a way to associate words to concepts that makes the learning more robust; for example, we might want to avoid introducing words that are too ambiguous. Second, we would like to investigate methods to evaluate more systematically the performance of the approach with words that currently do not have a specific type in existing KGs (e.g., Pianist in DBpedia). Third, we would like to improve the method used to generate the final representation of the vectors after the application of the network to a set of words: operations in high-dimensional spaces require careful considerations.

References

1. Baader, F., Calvanese, D., McGuinness, D.L., Nardi, D., Patel-Schneider, P.F. (eds.): The Description Logic Handbook: Theory, Implementation, and Applications. Cambridge University Press, New York (2003)
2. Bianchi, F., Palmonari, M., Nozza, D.: Towards encoding time in text-based entity embeddings. In: International Semantic Web Conference (2018)
3. Bianchi, F., Soto, M., Palmonari, M., Cutrona, V.: Type vector representations from text: an empirical analysis. In: DL4KGS@ESWC (2018)
4. Blei, D.M., Ng, A.Y., Jordan, M.I.: Latent dirichlet allocation. In: NIPS, pp. 601–608 (2001)
5. Bordes, A., Usunier, N., García-Durán, A., Weston, J., Yakhnenko, O.: Translating embeddings for modeling multi-relational data. In: NIPS, pp. 2787–2795 (2013)
6. Bouraoui, Z., Schockaert, S.: Automated rule base completion as Bayesian concept induction. In: AAAI (2019)
7. Bühmann, L., Lehmann, J., Westphal, P.: DL-Learner: a framework for inductive learning on the semantic web. J. Web Semant. **39**, 15–24 (2016)
8. Caruana, R.: Multitask learning: a knowledge-based source of inductive bias. In: ICML, pp. 41–48. Morgan Kaufmann (1993)
9. Colton, S., Wiggins, G.A.: Computational creativity: the final frontier? In: ECAI, pp. 21–26 (2012)
10. Confalonieri, A., et al.: Concept invention: Foundations, Implementation, Social aspects and Applications. Springer, Heidelberg (2018). https://doi.org/10.1007/978-3-319-65602-1
11. Deerwester, S.C., Dumais, S.T., Landauer, T.K., Furnas, G.W., Harshman, R.A.: Indexing by latent semantic analysis. JASIS **41**(6), 391–407 (1990)
12. Devlin, J., Chang, M.W., Lee, K., Toutanova, K.: BERT: pre-training of deep bidirectional transformers for language understanding. arXiv preprint arXiv:1810.04805 (2018)
13. Di Carlo, V., Bianchi, F., Palmonari, M.: Training temporal word embeddings with a compass. In: Proceedings of the AAAI Conference on Artificial Intelligence (2019)
14. Dumais, S.T.: Latent semantic analysis. Ann. Rev. Inf. Sci. Technol. **38**(1), 188–230 (2004)
15. Eppe, M., et al.: A computational framework for conceptual blending. Artif. Intell. **256**, 105–129 (2018)
16. Fauconnier, G., Turner, M.: Conceptual integration networks. Cogn. Sci. **22**(2), 133–187 (1998)
17. Golub, G.H., Reinsch, C.: Singular value decomposition and least squares solutions. In: Bauer, F.L. (ed.) Linear Algebra, vol. 2, pp. 134–151. Springer, Heidelberg (1971). https://doi.org/10.1007/978-3-662-39778-7_10
18. Gromov, M.: Metric Structures for Riemannian and Non-Riemannian Spaces. Birkhäuser Basel, Basel (2007)

19. Harris, Z.S.: Distributional structure. Word **10**(2–3), 146–162 (1954)
20. Hearst, M.A.: Automatic acquisition of hyponyms from large text corpora. In: ACL, pp. 539–545. Association for Computational Linguistics (1992)
21. Jana, A., Mukherjee, A., Goyal, P.: Detecting reliable novel word senses: A network-centric approach. In: SAC, pp. 976–983. ACM, New York (2019)
22. Krioukov, D., Papadopoulos, F., Kitsak, M., Vahdat, A., Boguñá, M.: Hyperbolic geometry of complex networks. Phys. Rev. E **82**, 036106 (2010)
23. Le, M., Roller, S., Papaxanthos, L., Kiela, D., Nickel, M.: Inferring concept hierarchies from text corpora via hyperbolic embeddings. arXiv preprint arXiv:1902.00913 (2019)
24. Lenci, A.: Distributional semantics in linguistic and cognitive research. Ital. J. Linguist. **20**(1), 1–31 (2008)
25. Lewis, M., Lawry, J.: Hierarchical conceptual spaces for concept combination. Artif. Intell. **237**, 204–227 (2016)
26. Lieto, A., Pozzato, G.L.: A description logic of typicality for conceptual combination. In: Ceci, M., Japkowicz, N., Liu, J., Papadopoulos, G.A., Raś, Z.W. (eds.) ISMIS 2018. LNCS (LNAI), vol. 11177, pp. 189–199. Springer, Cham (2018). https://doi.org/10.1007/978-3-030-01851-1_19
27. Mikolov, T., Sutskever, I., Chen, K., Corrado, G.S., Dean, J.: Distributed representations of words and phrases and their compositionality. In: NIPS, pp. 3111–3119 (2013)
28. Nguyen, D.Q., Sirts, K., Qu, L., Johnson, M.: STransE: a novel embedding model of entities and relationships in knowledge bases. In: NAACL, pp. 460–466. The Association for Computational Linguistics (2016)
29. Nickel, M., Kiela, D.: Poincaré embeddings for learning hierarchical representations. In: NIPS, pp. 6341–6350 (2017)
30. Pennington, J., Socher, R., Manning, C.D.: Glove: global vectors for word representation. In: EMNLP, pp. 1532–1543. ACL (2014)
31. Peters, M.E., et al.: Deep contextualized word representations. In: NAACL, pp. 2227–2237. ACL (2018)
32. Ruder, S.: An overview of multi-task learning in deep neural networks. arXiv preprint arXiv:1706.05098 (2017)
33. Sala, F., Sa, C.D., Gu, A., Ré, C.: Representation tradeoffs for hyperbolic embeddings. ICML **80**, 4457–4466 (2018)
34. Šourek, G., Manandhar, S., Železný, F., Schockaert, S., Kuželka, O.: Learning predictive categories using lifted relational neural networks. In: Cussens, J., Russo, A. (eds.) ILP 2016. LNCS (LNAI), vol. 10326, pp. 108–119. Springer, Cham (2017). https://doi.org/10.1007/978-3-319-63342-8_9
35. Völker, J., Niepert, M.: Statistical schema induction. In: Antoniou, G., Grobelnik, M., Simperl, E., Parsia, B., Plexousakis, D., De Leenheer, P., Pan, J. (eds.) ESWC 2011. LNCS, vol. 6643, pp. 124–138. Springer, Heidelberg (2011). https://doi.org/10.1007/978-3-642-21034-1_9
36. Wang, C., He, X., Zhou, A.: A short survey on taxonomy learning from text corpora: issues, resources and recent advances. In: EMNLP, pp. 1190–1203. Association for Computational Linguistics (2017)
37. Wiggins, G.A.: Searching for computational creativity. New Gener. Comput. **24**(3), 209–222 (2006)
38. Wong, W., Liu, W., Bennamoun, M.: Ontology learning from text: a look back and into the future. ACM Comput. Surv. **44**(4), 20:1–20:36 (2012)
39. Xiao, P., et al.: Conceptual representations for computational concept creation. ACM Comput. Surv. (CSUR) **52**(1), 9 (2019)

A New Measure of Polarization in the Annotation of Hate Speech

Sohail Akhtar, Valerio Basile$^{(\boxtimes)}$, and Viviana Patti

Dipartimento di Informatica, University of Turin, Turin, Italy
sohail.akhtar@edu.unito.it, {basile,patti}@di.unito.it

Abstract. The number of social media users is ever-increasing. Unfortunately, this has also resulted in the massive rise of uncensored online hate against vulnerable communities such as immigrants, LGBT and women. Current work on the automatic detection of various forms of hate speech (HS) typically employs supervised learning, requiring manually annotated data. The highly polarizing nature of the topics involved raises concerns about the quality of annotations these systems rely on, because not all the annotators are equally sensitive to different kinds of hate speech. We propose an approach to leverage the fine-grained knowledge expressed by individual annotators, before their subjectivity is averaged out by the gold standard creation process. This helps us to refine the quality of training sets for hate speech detection. We introduce a measure of polarization at the level of single instances in the data to manipulate the training set and reduce the impact of most polarizing text on the learning process.

We test our approach on three datasets, in English and Italian, annotated by experts and workers hired on a crowdsourcing platform. We classify instances of sexist, racist, and homophobic hate speech in tweets and show how our approach improves the prediction performance of a supervised classifier. Moreover, the proposed polarization measure helps towards the manual exploration of the individual instances of tweets in our datasets.

Keywords: Hate speech detection · Linguistic annotation · Inter-rater agreement · Data augmentation

1 Introduction

Hate speech (HS) is a form of abusive language directed at specific targets and inciting hatred and violent actions. *Online hate speech* (or *cyber-hate*) takes different forms and its rapid growth raises concerns that it may be a catalyst for harmful behavior [16]. The issue needs considerable attention from researchers and policy makers in order to protect the disadvantaged social groups. While some countries define some expressions of hate speech as illegal in their laws and regulations [1], a culturally shared definition of what constitutes hate speech is still under debate. Hate speech is quite subjective in nature.

© Springer Nature Switzerland AG 2019
M. Alviano et al. (Eds.): AI*IA 2019, LNAI 11946, pp. 588–603, 2019.
https://doi.org/10.1007/978-3-030-35166-3_41

From a natural language processing perspective, hate speech detection is often approached with similar techniques to sentiment analysis i.e., the task of identifying the opinions expressed in subjective utterances, from product and service reviews to comments to political events. However, online hate can be characterized by incitement to hate and to violent acts [24], rather than just a display of emotion.

A supervised learning approach typically relies on manual human annotation in order to create reference data to train models. The annotation is done either by experts or paid contributors on crowdsourcing platforms. In supervised learning, during the process of annotating data, the cultural background of annotators is usually ignored [25]. Judging the quality of gold standard data on subjective phenomena has been investigated recently, e.g., by [5], where expert and crowdsourced annotation of sentiment polarity and irony is compared. As a consequence of inter-annotator agreement issues, the benchmarks based on datasets created with traditional methods may be inadequate, leading to unstable results.

The main contributions of this paper are two: (1) to improve the quality of hate speech detection corpora, and consequently models trained on them, by considering the impact of different opinions of annotators and how they differ on individual messages; (2) a mean to manually explore the data and understand the topics and issues with polarizing nature.

Our working hypothesis is that diverging opinions expressed by annotator groups are valuable source of information rather than noise in gold standard data. This information can help to create better quality data to train machine learning models for the prediction of highly subjective phenomena such as cyber-hate. In particular, we focus on inter-annotator agreement computed for subdivisions of the annotator set, and on the level of polarization of the human judgments. We test our hypothesis empirically on three different datasets, in English and Italian, to further gain insight in a multilingual setting.

We introduce a novel measure of polarization of opinions in Sect. 3, along with a pilot study to verify its effectiveness. In Sect. 5, we present the result of an experimental evaluation on several datasets of hate speech in social media (described in Sect. 4). We present a discussion and qualitative analysis in Sect. 6, and draw conclusions in Sect. 7.

2   Related Work

Hate speech usually refers to disparaging individuals or groups because of their ethnicity, gender, race, color, sexual orientation, nationality, religion, or other similar characteristics – see for instance the U.S. constitution [21]. People from different backgrounds may have different opinions when asked about a particular event or topic and the opinions expressed are also influenced by various factors including the knowledge of a domain. The increase in social media usage, where users often express personal opinions, resulted in new opportunities to collect and analyze rich datasets on online harassment and abuse, often targeting women and minority groups based on race, ethnicity and gender [11,30], and similarly highly controversial topics. Controversiality is not a new concept in the study of social media. Usually, the controversial topics are identified and user responses or opinions are detected on those topics or issues [3,6]. Therefore, the literature mostly focuses on the controversiality of a message or other aspects of the content rather than on the polarization among annotator opinions during the development of gold standard corpora for hate speech detection, which is the focus of this work. Controversy in text stems from events, topics or social issues with varying responses from online users [23]. High controversiality can impact the manual annotation of such phenomena in terms of agreement between human judges because it can lead to polarized judgments.

Literature on hate speech detection in NLP has been recently surveyed by [14]. Scholars addressing the task utilized various surface level features such as bags of uni-grams and n-grams [10,32], syntax, lexical semantics, and combinations thereof [20,27–29,31]. The work in [7] focused not only on detecting HS but also finding the counter measures based on certain social or political events that actually triggered HS among the general public. Targeted hate is also the main topic of recent evaluation campaigns in several languages [4,8,12,13]. An interesting by-product of such initiatives is the creation of publicly available gold standard datasets, annotated by experts or by crowdsourcing. Inter-annotator agreement measures such as Fleiss' Kappa and Krippendorff's Alpha [2] are typically used to assess annotation quality. [9] highlights the shortcomings of such inter-annotator agreement measures in the crowdsourcing scenario, and proposes an improved measure to solve them. Similarly, [15] notes how the reliability of the crowd contributors may be inconsistent compared to the traditional expert annotation scenario, and proposes the MACE method to create gold standard datasets accounting for the annotators' reliability. [26] proposed a method to leverage the disagreement of annotators as a source of knowledge rather than treating it as noise in the data. In the present work, disagreement is leveraged too, however with a focus on its interpretation as a measure of divergence of opinion between groups.

3   Method

We propose a method aiming at creating higher quality benchmarks for supervised learning of subjective phenomena by introducing a new index that measures how polarized a message is, when annotated by two different groups. Our approach exploits the fine granularity of single annotations, e.g., resulting from crowdsourcing. We analyze the inter-annotator agreement in a setting where the annotators do not form one homogeneous group. We split the annotators in two groups with the highest divergence of opinions by performing an exhaustive search, and define a quantitative index of opinion polarization based on such split. Finally, we use such measure to automatically manipulate the training set of a supervised algorithm for hate speech detection.

3.1 Polarization Index

We provide a novel method to measure polarization in opinions about individual tweets. We aim at understanding the role of factors like ethnicity and social background of the annotators and how it is reflected in their judgment. In a sense, we are testing a *homophily* hypothesis [18] with respect to opinions, and on a larger (even global) scale: just as homophily in social groups strongly shape their social network, we postulate that the common background of some annotators shapes their opinions as well, leading to polarized judgments on certain kinds of messages. While polarization of opinions stems from the high subjectivity of some phenomena (e.g., hate speech), it differs from inter-annotator agreement, as the latter is influenced by factors such as text comprehension and interpretation, e.g., of ironic content. Our goal is instead to capture the influence of personal background of the annotators at a macro-level. Note that high polarization does not necessarily equates to low agreement: we consider the set of judgments on an utterance to be highly polarized if different groups show high agreement on different opinions. On the contrary, if the agreement is low overall, including among members of the same group, then there is no polarization, according to our definition.

We measure the level of polarization in a message given a set of annotations provided by two groups of annotators. Given a set of messages N and a set of annotators M, $g_{i,j}$ denotes the annotation of an annotator j on the message i. For each message $i \in N$, we can split the set of its annotations $G_i = \{g_{i,1}, \ldots g_{i,m}\}$ into k subsets $G_i^1, \ldots, G_i^k$. As a measure of agreement of the annotations on a single message, we use the normalized χ^2 statistics, that is, a test of independence of the distribution of the annotations against a uniform distribution. The rationale for this choice is that we consider a uniform distribution of annotations as total disagreement. For instance, if three out of six annotators decide for a label in a binary classification setting, and the other three assign the other label, the distribution (3, 3) is uniform, and therefore the disagreement is maximum. Normalizing the χ^2 by dividing the statistic by the number of annotation, we obtain a value between 0 (total disagreement) and 1 (perfect agreement):

$$a(G_i) = 1 - \frac{\chi^2(G_i)}{|M|} \tag{1}$$

We compute the *polarization* index (P-index) of a message i as:

$$P(i) = \frac{1}{k} \sum_{1 \leq w \leq k} a(G_i^w)(1 - a(G_i)) \tag{2}$$

P is a number between 0 and 1, where 0 indicates no polarization and 1 indicates maximum polarization. It is designed to take a higher value when at the same time, the agreement between members of same group is high and the agreement between the members of different groups is low. To give a few examples with $k = 2$, if $G_i^1 = \{1, 1, 0\}$ and $G_i^2 = \{1, 1, 1\}$, then $a(G_i^1) \approx 0.11$ (low intra-group agreement), $a(G_i^2) = 1$ (high intra-group agreement), $a(G_i) \approx 0.44$, thus

$P(i) \approx 0.31$. If instead $G_i^1 = \{0, 0, 0\}$ and $G_i^2 = \{1, 1, 1\}$, that is, each group is in total agreement but on different labels, then $a(G_i^1) = 1, a(G_i^2) = 1, a(G_i) = 0$, thus $P(i) = 1$.

3.2 Pilot Study

In order to validate the metric, we created a small, manually annotated dataset of English tweets on Brexit gathered from the corpus developed by [17], where around 5 million tweets were collected by querying Twitter with the hashtag *#Brexit* between the June 22nd and 30th, 2016. This dataset was initially annotated and used for stance detection. We filtered the dataset to only retrieve the tweets containing keywords related to immigrants and Muslims that reflect our work on HS detection: *Immigration, migration, immigrant, migrant, foreign, foreigners, terrorism, terrorist, Muslim, Islam, jihad, Quran, illegals, deport, anti-immigrant, rapefugee, rapugee, paki, pakis, nigger.* The keywords used are selected based on a study by [19].

We manually labelled 119 randomly selected tweets by following the scheme and guidelines proposed in [22,24] with 4 dimensions: *hate speech, aggressiveness, offensiveness,* and *stereotype*. We asked three volunteers with specific demographic features, i.e. first- or second-generation migrants and students from the developing countries to Europe and the UK, of Muslim background, to annotate the dataset. The other three volunteers were researchers with western background with experience in linguistic annotation. The two groups annotated exactly the same data with the same guidelines. The final data set is therefore annotated by six people divided into two groups, which we refer to as *target* (T) and *control* (C).

For current work, we only focus on the main class, i.e., hate speech. We measured the inter-annotator agreement between all annotators by using Fleiss' Kappa obtaining a value of 0.35. We hypothesize that the high subjectivity of the task is one of the reasons for the low Kappa value. Interestingly, the agreement on hate speech classification is higher than the other labels included in the schema: aggressiveness (0.21), offensiveness (0.30), and stereotype (0.20). Since the groups are formed by people having different ethnic background and culture, we expect a higher level of polarization than what we could measure by splitting the groups randomly. The mean P-index for the original split is 0.18, while the average mean P-index for the 9 other possible splits is 0.09. This result indicates that the P-index successfully picks up the divergence of opinions coming from different communities and ethnic backgrounds.

In the presence of a given split of the annotator groups, in addition to the overall agreement (*inter-group* agreement), we can also calculate the *intra-group* agreement for each group. On the Brexit data, we computed an intra-group agreement of 0.54 for both groups. By computing pair-wise agreement, we induce a network of fine-grained agreements between the annotators. The topology of such network provides an insight on the relationships between the opinions of single annotators and their groups. On the Brexit dataset, the pair-wise agreement between the couples of annotators from the same group is rather high, between 0.52 and 0.56 in the control group and between 0.46 and 0.60 in the target group. However, the pair-wise agreement between pairs where the two annotators are from different groups drops significantly, between 0.16 and 0.36 with a median of 0.24 and standard deviation of 0.06.

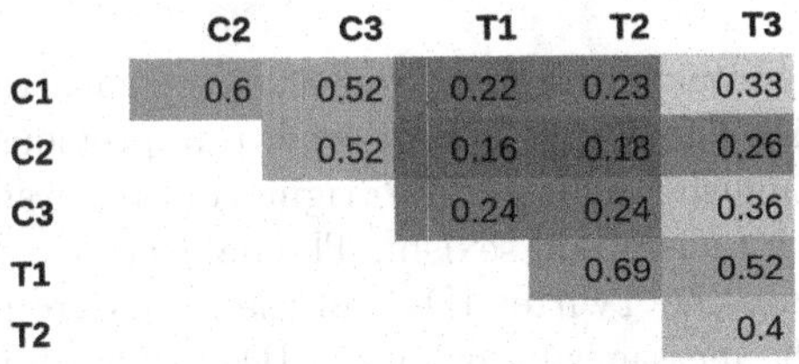

	C2	C3	T1	T2	T3
C1	0.6	0.52	0.22	0.23	0.33
C2		0.52	0.16	0.18	0.26
C3			0.24	0.24	0.36
T1				0.69	0.52
T2					0.4

Fig. 1. Pairwise agreement on the Brexit dataset annotation, between the target group (T) and control group (C).

The pair-wise agreement measured on the Brexit dataset is shown in Fig. 1. It is clear from the picture that the two groups of annotators show a much higher intra-groups agreement (top-left and bottom-right area of the figure) than their inter-group agreement (top-right area).

3.3 Enhancing the Training Data

The polarization index introduced in Sect. 3.1 provides useful information on the annotation of highly subjective messages. Here, we propose a method employing this metric to improve gold standard data and therefore improve classification performance. In a supervised learning fashion, a training set is needed, made by manually annotated instances of the text paired with the judgments of a set of annotators. Supposing that complete information about the annotation is available, i.e., not only the aggregated values but each single annotation, then we can compute the P-index of each instance in the dataset. It is important to note that even when the complete annotation is available, in general, we do not have background information about the annotators. However, based on the result of the pilot study presented in Sect. 3.2, we assume that it is reasonable to split the annotators in two groups in a way that maximizes the total polarization.

We compute the P-index for each instance in the training set and then replicate the instances based on its value. The intuition is that if the P-index of an instance is low, a classifier can learn more than if the instance is more polarizing. Therefore, we replicate the instances in the training set a number of times inversely proportional to their P-index. Instances with a P-index of 1 are removed from the training set. In order to verify that our approach works, we experimented with different strategies. First, we only remove instances with a maximum P-index value and do not replicate the rest of the instances. Alternatively, we do not remove the tweets with a maximum value of P but only replicate the instances. Finally, we combine the two approaches. Our method only modifies the training set in a fully automated supervised learning approach, while no change is made to the test set.

4   Data

In order to test the approach introduced in Sect. 3, we gathered a dataset of hate speech in social media. The corpus is borrowed from previous studies by [30] on HS detection in the English language. The original dataset was composed of 6,909 tweets annotated with racism and sexism. The dataset is available on a Github repository[1], where only the Twitter IDs and the labels are provided. Querying Twitter to retrieve the messages by using the IDs resulted in the collection of a smaller dataset consisting of 6,361 tweets, due to the perishability of the data on the online platform.

Experts (feminist and anti-racism activists) annotated the data. These experts were allowed to skip any instances that they were unsure of. The annotations from experts were aggregated into a single label. Non-experts were hired via a crowdsourcing platform[2] and they worked on the same tweets annotated by experts, following the guidelines developed by [31]. Each tweet was annotated by at least four annotators. The total number of annotators was not disclosed for privacy reasons. The gold labels are computed by majority vote, and ties are broken by giving preference to the judgment of expert annotators. For current work, we treat all annotators (experts and non-experts) equally.

We also employ an additional set of tweets in Italian, to test the application of our method in a multilingual perspective. The Italian dataset comprises 1,859 tweets on topics related to the LGBT community. The homophobia dataset was annotated by volunteers. The details of our datasets and the distributions of labels are shown in Table 1.

Table 1. Datasets used in the experiments with distribution of the labels.

Dataset	Positive class	Negative class	Total
Sexism	810	5,551	6,361
Racism	100	6,261	6,361
Homophobia	224	1,635	1,859

4.1   Sexism

The dataset from [30] contains tweets annotated according to four categories: *sexism, racism, both,* and *neither,* in a multi-label fashion. We isolated the sexism

---

[1] https://github.com/ZeerakW/hatespeech.

[2] https://www.figure-eight.com/.

and racism classes to focus on them individually with two binary classification tasks. In other words, we converted the labels *sexism* and *both* to *sexist*, and the labels *racism* and *neither* to *non-sexist*. In the resulting Sexism dataset, 810 tweets out of 6,361 (12.7%) are marked as *sexist*.

The overall agreement (Fleiss' Kappa) between the four annotators in Sexism dataset is 0.58, indicating a moderate agreement. Following the methodology of the pilot study conducted on the Brexit data (see Sect. 3.2), we compute the P-index of all the tweets in the dataset for all possible splits of four annotators, and select the combination that maximizes the average P-index, in order to create two annotator groups. We measured the intra-group agreement for two groups, resulting in 0.53 and 0.64 respectively. Figure 2 shows examples from the Sexism dataset with their P-index values. Notice that the two examples with P-index = 1 are polarized in opposite directions with each group having different annotation for a single tweet.

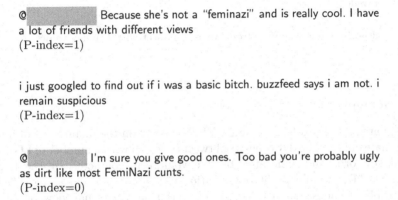

@▒▒▒▒▒▒ Because she's not a "feminazi" and is really cool. I have a lot of friends with different views
(P-index=1)

i just googled to find out if i was a basic bitch. buzzfeed says i am not. i remain suspicious
(P-index=1)

@▒▒▒▒▒ I'm sure you give good ones. Too bad you're probably ugly as dirt like most FemiNazi cunts.
(P-index=0)

Fig. 2. Three examples from Sexism dataset with P-index values.

4.2 Racism

We extracted a binary labeled Racism dataset from the data of [30] following the same procedure we applied to derive the Sexism dataset (Sect. 4.1). The annotation scheme remains the same as with the original dataset explained in Sect. 4. The only difference is the mapping of the original labels: *racism* and *both* are mapped to *racist*, while *sexism* and *neither* are mapped to *non-racist*. In the resulting Racism dataset, 100 tweets out of 6,361 (1.57%) are marked *racist*. The overall agreement (Fleiss' Kappa) between all annotators in the Racism dataset is 0.23, indicating relatively high disagreement between the annotators. We divide the annotators into two groups by selecting the split that maximizes the average P-index, and measure an intra-group agreement of 0.22 and 0.25. Figure 3 shows examples from the Racism dataset with their computed P-index values. Each tweet in the first two examples is oppositely polarized, with each group having different annotation for the tweet.

Headed out #coon #hunting with some friends on the back of the #farm.
This is his first time. Kinda https://t.co/vDofdeemhY
(P-index=1)

jumping in the #BlameOneNotAll tag.I expect to find all kinds of bigoted
fucktards telling me how I'm the problem http://t.co/MwgmqJXPiR
(P-index=1)

Why do #Blacks #Coon on television or the movies?
http://t.co/je4HUxhMEt If they don't...they won't work they won't
make money...
(P-index=0)

Fig. 3. Three examples from Racism dataset with P-index values.

4.3   Homophobia

We exploited a dataset from the ACCEPT project[3] on the monitoring of homophobic hate online. The data consist of tweets selected with a number of LGBT+-related keywords and annotated by five volunteers contacted by the largest Italian LGBT+ non-for-profit organization (Arcigay)[4] selected along different demographic dimensions such as age, education and personal view on LGBT stances. The original dataset is labeled in a multi-class fashion according to four categories: *homophobic, not homophobic, doubtful* or *neutral*. We map *not-homophobic, doubtful* and *neutral* to *not homophobic* and leave the label *homophobic* unchanged, to restrict the problem definition to a binary classification task.

The agreement between the five annotators (Fleiss' Kappa) is 0.35 (moderately low). Similarly to the Sexism and Racism datasets, we split the annotators into two groups, by computing the average P-index for all the possible combinations of 3 + 2 groups, and selecting the split that maximizes the average P-index. The intra-group agreement for the two groups is 0.40 and 0.39. Figure 4 shows examples from the Homophobia data set with their English translations and their computed P-index values. The tweets with high P-index are oppositely polarized, i.e., one group detected HS whereas the other group did not.

---

[3] http://accept.arcigay.it/.
[4] https://www.arcigay.it/en/.

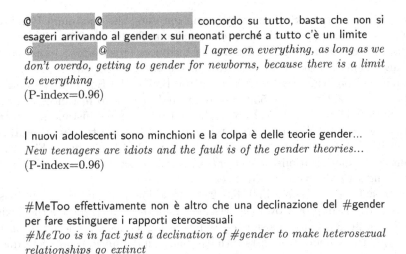

I nuovi adolescenti sono minchioni e la colpa è delle teorie gender...
New teenagers are idiots and the fault is of the gender theories...
(P-index=0.96)

#MeToo effettivamente non è altro che una declinazione del #gender
per fare estinguere i rapporti eterosessuali
*#MeToo is in fact just a declination of #gender to make heterosexual
relationships go extinct*
(P-index=0)

Fig. 4. Three examples from Homophobia dataset with P-index values.

5 Evaluation

We evaluate the method introduced in Sect. 3 with cross-validation experiments on the datasets described in Sect. 4. At each fold, we randomly split the dataset into a training set (80%) and a test set (20%). We refer to the "positive" and "negative" classes as a generalization over the actual labels, which are different (but comparable) for each dataset. All the datasets are highly unbalanced. We did not balance the data artificially, in order to obtain realistic results.

We employ a straightforward supervised learning approach, keeping the test set fixed and only modifying the training set prior to giving it as input to the classifier. We employ a basic classifier, to focus on the impact of the modified training sets rather than the effect of hyper-parameters of more sophisticated models. The classifier is based on a Support Vector Machine model (SVM) with Bag of Word features and TF-IDF weighting. Specifically, we implemented the classifier with the *Scikit-learn* Python library with default parameters, and the *TfIdfVectorizer* function. The only parameter we optimize for the different datasets is the number of features (unigrams) in the vectorized representations of the tweets.

The performance is measured in terms of overall Accuracy, Precision, Recall and F1-score on the positive class, averaged over five folds. The baseline results are given by the classifier trained on the original, unmodified training sets.

We train the classifier on a training set modified according to the polarization of its textual instances. We compute the P-index for all the tweets in the training set, and replicate them according to their value. The first modification to the training set consists in the removal of instances with the maximum P-index value

(*P-max filter*). For the Sexism and Racism datasets, the maximum P-index is 1, whereas for Homophobia dataset, the maximum P-index is 0.96^5. The second modification consists in the replication of instances (*replication*) based on the following scheme: for the Sexism and Racism datasets, tweets with $0 \leq P < 0.375$ are replicated one time (two instances in total). For the Homophobia dataset, tweets with $0.3552 \leq P < 0.5328$ are replicated once (two instances in total), tweets with $0.32 \leq P < 0.3552$ are replicated twice (three instances in total), tweets with $0.0528 \leq P < 0.32$ are replicated twice (four instances in total) and tweets with $0 \leq P < 0.0528$ are replicated to a total of five copies.[6] Finally, we combine both modifications (*P-max filter+replication*). These changes concern the training set only, while the test set is unchanged.

The results are presented in Tables 2, 3 and 4. The performance of the classification generally improves over the baseline on all three datasets. On the Sexism dataset, the performance boost is caused by a higher recall. The recall on the Racism and Homophobia datasets with baseline result is substantially low, due to the datasets being highly skewed. However, both precision and recall improve on these datasets. Interestingly, the recall improves in every experiment, including when some training data is removed (P-max filter). This indicates that indeed highly polarizing instances tend to generate confusion for the classifier.

Table 2. Results of the prediction on Sexism dataset (1700 features).

Classifier	Accuracy	Precision	Recall	F1
SVM	95.11	**87.60**	71.60	78.74
SVM+P-max filter	95.13	86.40	73.01	79.11
SVM+replication	**95.27**	87.01	73.40	79.67
SVM+P-max filter+replication	**95.27**	86.60	**74.01**	**79.83**

Table 3. Results of the prediction on Racism dataset (1700 features).

Classifier	Accuracy	Precision	Recall	F1
SVM	98.55	55.40	11.01	18.40
SVM+P-max filter	98.58	59.01	12.01	19.88
SVM+replication	**98.61**	**70.01**	19.60	29.49
SVM+P-max filter+replication	**98.61**	69.80	**19.80**	**29.74**

---

[5] This difference is due to having five annotators in total, therefore uneven group sizes.
[6] The threshold values come from the observation of actual P-index values in the data.

Table 4. Results of the prediction on Homophobia dataset (3500 features).

Classifier	Accuracy	Precision	Recall	F1
SVM	**88.81**	61.01	11.40	19.02
SVM+P-max filter	**88.81**	**63.60**	13.60	22.30
SVM+replication	86.55	50.40	18.40	26.83
SVM+P-max filter+replication	87.63	47.90	**26.20**	**33.67**

6 Discussion

The impact of our method on the classification of sexism is reflected in a higher recall, at the cost of lower precision. This indicates that ignoring the disagreement between annotators is likely to generate greater confusion on borderline sexist messages, that in turn produces a higher number of false negatives. The results on the Racism data show a different pattern, where the precision in particular improves by a large margin by applying agreement-based training set manipulation. This suggests that injecting knowledge about polarization in the model helps us in disambiguation of potential false positives. A similar pattern is observed on the Homophobia dataset, but with the P-max filter providing a higher precision boost, as opposed to the replication strategy, which was giving the best precision performance on the Racism dataset.

It is worth noting that the measure of polarization introduced in this article is useful to support manual exploration of the data, besides providing a tool for supervised text classification. By ranking the instances of a dataset by P-index, the most polarizing tweets emerge naturally at the top of the list. In the Sexism dataset, the vast majority of the tweets with $P = 1$ contain race-related remarks along with misogyny, as in the following example:

> @▇▇▇▇▇▇ uh... did you watch the video? one of the women talked about how it's assumed she's angry because she's latina.

Similarly, we found several instances of sexism among the most polarizing tweets in the Racism set. Humour (albeit black) also seems to play a role in generating confusion and polarization among the annotators, as we found several instances of (often inappropriate) jokes at the top of the racism P-index ranking, e.g.:

> Another #Arab car #terror attack in #Jerusalem #Israel. Will #Obama call it random traffic infringement? http://t.co/XrxajfBXKF

Finally, by manually inspecting the Homophobia dataset ranked by P-index, we found that the most polarized tweets mention a restricted number of topics (gender theories and their education in school, family values) very consistently, while such topics are otherwise distributed in the corpus equally among other topics such as news, law, gossip, politics and homophobia. In fact, the relative frequency of the word $gender$[7] is about seven times higher among the tweets with $P = 0.96$ than those with $P = 0$. Tweets about homophobia are generally not controversial or polarized, with the relative frequency of the word $homophobic$ (and its variations) being almost three times higher among the tweets with $P = 0$ than those with $P = 0.96$.

7   Conclusion and Future Work

In this paper, we presented a method that leverages different opinions emerging from groups of annotators to improve the automatic classification of highly subjective phenomena such as hate speech. We tested our approach in a cross-validation experiment on datasets containing sexism, racism and homophobia in social media. The experimental results show a consistent improvement of the prediction performance due to the pre-processing induced by our method, even using simple models and features (bags of words).

Our results suggest that consensus-based methods to create gold standard data are not necessarily the best choice when dealing with highly subjective phenomena, and the knowledge coming from the disagreement and the polarization of opinions is indeed highly informative. Finally, we show how the P-index can effectively be employed as a tool to manually explore the data, ranking the instances to identify messages that are more likely to generate confusion and polarization among the annotators.

The future work aims at exploring more dimensions of the background of annotators, including native language, demographic factors, and how they interplay with the measured polarization of their annotations in a group. Moreover, we believe that involving the victims of hate speech in the process of annotating the data in hate related detection tasks can provide new insights and improve the quality of the data. On the other hand, the information about the background of annotators is often not available in publicly distributed datasets. Moreover, the set of annotations could be sparse, e.g., in a crowdsourcing context. Therefore, we propose to extend our method to effectively cluster larger annotator sets based on their annotation (e.g., with a K-nearest neighbors approach) and more than two groups in order to make diverging opinions emerge on polarizing topics. Finally, let us emphasize that this first work on polarization of annotators' opinions is rooted in the somewhat strong assumption that there exists a latent background divide in the annotator population. Even stronger is the assumption that the number of groups is fixed. Although the experimental results confirm the existence of the polarization phenomenon, it will be interesting to investigate how the method can be refined by relaxing the division constraints and aiming for a more flexible, perhaps clustering-based procedure.

Acknowledgments. The work of Valerio Basile and Viviana Patti is partially funded by Progetto di Ateneo/CSP 2016 (S1618_L2_BOSC_01, *Immigrants, Hate and Prejudice in Social Media*).

---

[7] In Italian, the English word $gender$ is used as a borrowing only to refer to the modern gender theories.

References

1. Abbondante, F.: Il ruolo dei social network nella lotta all'hate speech: un'analisi comparata fra l'esperienza statunitense e quella europea. Informatica e diritto **26**(1–2), 41–68 (2017)
2. Artstein, R., Poesio, M.: Inter-coder agreement for computational linguistics. Comput. Linguist. **34**(4), 555–596 (2008). https://doi.org/10.1162/coli.07-034-R2
3. Basile, A., Caselli, T., Nissim, M.: Predicting controversial news using Facebook reactions. In: Proceedings of the Fourth Italian Conference on Computational Linguistics (CLiC-it 2017), Rome, Italy, 11–13 December 2017 (2017)
4. Basile, V., et al.: SemEval-2019 task 5: multilingual detection of hate speech against immigrants and women in Twitter. In: Proceedings of the 13th International Workshop on Semantic Evaluation (SemEval-2019). Association for Computational Linguistics (2019)
5. Basile, V., Novielli, N., Croce, D., Barbieri, F., Nissim, M., Patti, V.: Sentiment polarity classification at EVALITA: lessons learned and open challenges. IEEE Trans. Affect. Comput. (2018)
6. Beelen, K., Kanoulas, E., van de Velde, B.: Detecting controversies in online news media. In: Proceedings of the 40th International ACM SIGIR Conference on Research and Development in Information Retrieval, SIGIR 2017, pp. 1069–1072. ACM, New York (2017). https://doi.org/10.1145/3077136.3080723
7. Benesch, S., Ruths, D., Dillon, K.P., Saleem, H.M., Wright, L.: Counterspeech on Twitter: a field study. In: A Report for Public Safety Canada under the Kanishka Project (2016)
8. Bosco, C., Dell'Orletta, F., Poletto, F., Sanguinetti, M., Tesconi, M.: Overview of the EVALITA 2018 hate speech detection task. In: Proceedings of the Sixth Evaluation Campaign of Natural Language Processing and Speech Tools for Italian. Final Workshop (EVALITA 2018) co-located with the Fifth Italian Conference on Computational Linguistics (CLiC-it 2018), Turin, Italy, 12–13 December 2018. CEUR Workshop Proceedings, vol. 2263. CEUR-WS.org (2018)
9. Checco, A., Roitero, K., Maddalena, E., Mizzaro, S., Demartini, G.: Let's agree to disagree: fixing agreement measures for crowdsourcing. In: Proceedings of the Fifth AAAI Conference on Human Computation and Crowdsourcing, HCOMP 2017, Québec City, Québec, Canada, 23–26 October 2017, pp. 11–20. AAAI Press (2017)
10. Chen, Y., Zhou, Y., Zhu, S., Xu, H.: Detecting offensive language in social media to protect adolescent online safety. In: Proceedings of the 2012 ASE/IEEE International Conference on Social Computing and 2012 ASE/IEEE International Conference on Privacy, Security, Risk and Trust, SOCIALCOM-PASSAT 2012, pp. 71–80. IEEE Computer Society, Washington, DC, USA (2012). https://doi.org/10.1109/SocialCom-PASSAT.2012.55
11. Duggan, M.: Online harassment 2017. Technical report, Pew Research Center (2017)
12. Fersini, E., Nozza, D., Rosso, P.: Overview of the EVALITA 2018 task on automatic misogyny identification (AMI). In: Proceedings of the Sixth Evaluation Campaign of Natural Language Processing and Speech Tools for Italian, Final Workshop (EVALITA 2018) co-located with the Fifth Italian Conference on Computational Linguistics (CLiC-it 2018), Turin, Italy, 12–13 December 2018. CEUR Workshop Proceedings, vol. 2263. CEUR-WS.org (2018)

13. Fersini, E., Rosso, P., Anzovino, M.: Overview of the task on automatic misogyny identification at IberEval 2018. In: IberEval@SEPLN (2018)

14. Fortuna, P., Nunes, S.: A survey on automatic detection of hate speech in text. ACM Comput. Surv. **51**(4), 85:1–85:30 (2018)

15. Hovy, D., Berg-Kirkpatrick, T., Vaswani, A., Hovy, E.: Learning whom to trust with MACE. In: Proceedings of the 2013 Conference of the North American Chapter of the Association for Computational Linguistics: Human Language Technologies, pp. 1120–1130. Association for Computational Linguistics, Atlanta, June 2013. https://www.aclweb.org/anthology/N13-1132

16. Izsák-Ndiaye, R.: Report of the special rapporteur on minority issues, Rita Iizsák: Comprehensive study of the human rights situation of Roma worldwide, with a particular focus on the phenomenon of anti-Gypsyism. Technical report, UN, Geneva, 11 May 2015. http://digitallibrary.un.org/record/797194. Submitted pursuant to Human Rights Council resolution 26/4

17. Lai, M., Tambuscio, M., Patti, V., Ruffo, G., Rosso, P.: Extracting graph topological information and users' opinion. In: Jones, G., et al. (eds.) CLEF 2017. LNCS, vol. 10456, pp. 112–118. Springer, Cham (2017). https://doi.org/10.1007/978-3-319-65813-1_10

18. Mcpherson, M., Smith-Lovin, L., Cook, J.: Birds of a feather: homophily in social networks. Annu. Rev. Sociol. **27**, 415–444 (2001). https://doi.org/10.3410/f.725356294.793504070

19. Miller, C., et al.: From brussels to Brexit: islamophobia, xenophobia, racism and reports of hateful incidents on twitter. DEMOS (2016). https://www.demos.co.uk/wp-content/uploads/2016/07/From-Brussels-to-Brexit_-Islamophobia-Xenophobia-Racism-and-Reports-of-Hateful-Incidents-on-Twitter-Research-Prepared-for-Channel-4-Dispatches-%E2%80%98Racist-Britain%E2%80%99-.pdf

20. Nobata, C., Tetreault, J., Thomas, A., Mehdad, Y., Chang, Y.: Abusive language detection in online user content. In: Proceedings of the 25th International Conference on World Wide Web, WWW 2016, pp. 145–153. International World Wide Web Conferences Steering Committee, Republic and Canton of Geneva, Switzerland (2016). https://doi.org/10.1145/2872427.2883062

21. Nockleby, J, T.: Hate speech. In: Encyclopedia of the American Constitution, vol. 3, pp. 1277–1279. Macmillan (2000)

22. Poletto, F., Stranisci, M., Sanguinetti, M., Patti, V., Bosco, C.: Hate speech annotation: analysis of an Italian Twitter corpus. In: Proceedings of the Fourth Italian Conference on Computational Linguistics (CLiC-it 2017), Rome, Italy, 11–13 December 2017. CEUR Workshop Proceedings, vol. 2006. CEUR-WS.org (2017)

23. Popescu, A.M., Pennacchiotti, M.: Detecting controversial events from Twitter. In: Proceedings of the 19th ACM International Conference on Information and Knowledge Management, CIKM 2010, pp. 1873–1876. ACM, New York (2010). https://doi.org/10.1145/1871437.1871751

24. Sanguinetti, M., Poletto, F., Bosco, C., Patti, V., Stranisci, M.: An Italian Twitter corpus of hate speech against immigrants. In: Proceedings of the Eleventh International Conference on Language Resources and Evaluation (LREC-2018). European Language Resource Association (2018). http://aclweb.org/anthology/L18-1443

25. Sheerman-Chase, T., Ong, E.J., Bowden, R.: Cultural factors in the regression of non-verbal communication perception, pp. 1242–1249, November 2011. https://doi.org/10.1109/ICCVW.2011.6130393

26. Soberón, G., Aroyo, L., Welty, C., Inel, O., Lin, H., Overmeen, M.: Measuring crowd truth: disagreement metrics combined with worker behavior filters. In: Proceedings of the 1st International Conference on Crowdsourcing the Semantic Web, CrowdSem 2013, vol. 1030, pp. 45–58. CEUR-WS.org, Aachen (2013). http://dl.acm.org/citation.cfm?id=2874376.2874381

27. Sood, S., Antin, J., Churchill, E.: Profanity use in online communities. In: Proceedings of the SIGCHI Conference on Human Factors in Computing Systems, CHI 2012, pp. 1481–1490. ACM, New York (2012). https://doi.org/10.1145/2207676.2208610

28. Van Hee, C., et al.: Detection and fine-grained classification of cyberbullying events. In: Proceedings of the 10th Recent Advances in Natural Language Processing (RANLP 2015), Hissar, Bulgaria, October 2015

29. Warner, W., Hirschberg, J.: Detecting hate speech on the world wide web. In: Proceedings of the Second Workshop on Language in Social Media, LSM 2012, pp. 19–26. Association for Computational Linguistics, Stroudsburg (2012). http://dl.acm.org/citation.cfm?id=2390374.2390377

30. Waseem, Z.: Are you a racist or am i seeing things? Annotator influence on hate speech detection on Twitter. In: Proceedings of the First Workshop on NLP and Computational Social Science, pp. 138–142 (2016)

31. Waseem, Z., Hovy, D.: Hateful symbols or hateful people? Predictive features for hate speech detection on Twitter. In: Proceedings of the NAACL Student Research Workshop, pp. 88–93. Association for Computational Linguistics (2016). https://doi.org/10.18653/v1/N16-2013. http://aclweb.org/anthology/N16-2013

32. Xu, J.M., Jun, K.S., Zhu, X., Bellmore, A.: Learning from bullying traces in social media. In: Proceedings of the 2012 Conference of the North American Chapter of the Association for Computational Linguistics: Human Language Technologies, NAACL HLT 2012, pp. 656–666. Association for Computational Linguistics, Stroudsburg (2012). http://dl.acm.org/citation.cfm?id=2382029.2382139

Author Index